Teen Friendship Networks, Development, and Risky Behavior

Teen Friendship Networks, Development, and Risky Behavior

EDITED BY MARK E. FEINBERG
AND D. WAYNE OSGOOD

OXFORD
UNIVERSITY PRESS

Oxford University Press is a department of the University of Oxford. It furthers
the University's objective of excellence in research, scholarship, and education
by publishing worldwide. Oxford is a registered trade mark of Oxford University
Press in the UK and certain other countries.

Published in the United States of America by Oxford University Press
198 Madison Avenue, New York, NY 10016, United States of America.

© Mark E. Feinberg and D. Wayne Osgood 2024

All rights reserved. No part of this publication may be reproduced, stored in
a retrieval system, or transmitted, in any form or by any means, without the
prior permission in writing of Oxford University Press, or as expressly permitted
by law, by license, or under terms agreed with the appropriate reproduction
rights organization. Inquiries concerning reproduction outside the scope of the
above should be sent to the Rights Department, Oxford University Press, at the
address above.

You must not circulate this work in any other form
and you must impose this same condition on any acquirer.

Library of Congress Cataloging-in-Publication Data
Names: Feinberg, Mark E., editor. | Osgood, D. Wayne, editor.
Title: Teen friendship networks, development, and risky behavior /
edited by Mark E. Feinberg and D. Wayne Osgood.
Description: New York, NY : Oxford University Press, [2024] |
Includes bibliographical references and index.
Identifiers: LCCN 2023011422 (print) | LCCN 2023011423 (ebook) |
ISBN 9780197602317 (hardback) | ISBN 9780197602331 (epub) |
ISBN 9780197602348
Subjects: LCSH: Friendship in adolescence. | Teenagers—Social networks. |
Risk-taking (Psychology) in adolescence. | Adolescence.
Classification: LCC BF724.3.F64 T44 2024 (print) | LCC BF724.3.F64 (ebook) |
DDC 158.2/5—dc23/eng/20230623
LC record available at https://lccn.loc.gov/2023011422
LC ebook record available at https://lccn.loc.gov/2023011423

DOI: 10.1093/oso/9780197602317.001.0001

Printed by Integrated Books International, United States of America

Mark E. Feinberg:
To my favorite teens and young adults, Talia, Noam, and Shira—who have their own dynamic peer network.

D. Wayne Osgood:
To all my PhD students and collaborators, who have made the journey so much more rewarding.

CONTENTS

List of Figures ix
List of Tables xiii
List of Contributors xv

SECTION I: Setting the stage

1. Friendships and peer groups in the teen years—our perspective 3
   D. Wayne Osgood

2. Overview of the PROSPER prevention trial's rationale, methods, and findings: The context for the friendship network study 34
   Richard Spoth, Lisa M. Schainker, Mark Greenberg, and Janet Welsh

3. Network methods: Explanations and issues 66
   James Moody and D. Wayne Osgood

4. A descriptive overview of social networks and behavior among PROSPER youth 88
   Erin Tinney

SECTION II: Risky behaviors, relationships, and development

5. Teen friendships, networks, and substance use 113
   Daniel T. Ragan and D. Wayne Osgood

6. Does criminal justice contact alter friendship ties? 146
   Wade C. Jacobsen and Erin Tinney

7. Depression, self-harm, and network position 171
   Molly Copeland and Sonja E. Siennick

8. The role of parenting in shaping the friendship context of adolescent substance use 190
   Kelly L. Rulison, Avery Chahl, and Evelien M. Hoeben

9. Dating, sexuality, and adolescent friendship networks 218
   Nayan G. Ramirez, Rose Wesche, and Derek A. Kreager

10. Variation in network processes across community and school district contexts 247
    Cassie McMillan, Daniel T. Ragan, and Alana Colindres

11. Peer networks and the diffusion of intervention outcomes 264
    Kelly L. Rulison and Mark E. Feinberg

12. Genetic susceptibility to peers 293
    Gabriel L. Schlomer, Amanda M. Griffin, H. Harrington Cleveland, and David J. Vandenbergh

SECTION III: Conclusions

13. Future directions for research on networks and adolescent health 315
    Thomas W. Valente

14. The growth of longitudinal social network analysis: A review of the key data sets and topics in research on child and adolescent development 326
    René Veenstra, Teresa Bertogna, and Lydia Laninga-Wijnen

15. Social capital and adolescent development: Concluding thoughts 353
    Mark E. Feinberg

Appendix 361
    Part 1: Publications of the PROSPER Peers project 361
    Part 2: PROSPER Peers project personnel 367
Index 369

FIGURES

1.1 An example network 14
1.2 Peer influence implied by network 15
1.3 Varieties of peer influence 16
1.4 Types of selection 18
1.5 Two versions of a PROSPER network, colored for delinquency and gender 19
1.6 Negative ego selection and positive alter selection for smoking 20
1.7 Levels of analysis and the interplay of network concepts and nonnetwork variables in PROSPER Peers 22
2.1 PROSPER intervention outcome model: partnership-based EBI pathways of effects across developmental phases 40
2.2 In-school survey and young adult follow-up assessment: total participation by wave 44
2.3 Organizational structure for PROSPER partnership-based delivery system 47
2.4 Marijuana new user rates by condition and risk status 53
2.5 Narcotic new user rates by condition and risk status 53
3.1 A small network and its adjacency matrix 70
4.1 Percentage of total eligible students who completed surveys by grade and cohort 90
4.2 Percentage of eligible students who completed surveys by race and sex 91
4.3 Average number of friendship ties by wave 95
4.4 Average number of friend nominations by race and sex 96
4.5 Average number of nominations received by race and sex 96
4.6 Percentage of friendships reciprocated by sex 98
4.7 Stability: percentage of friendships retained from prior wave by sex 98
4.8 Percentage of friendships with youth of same sex 99
4.9 Percentage of friendships with youth of same race (i.e., white vs. nonwhite) 100
4.10 Percentage of youth categorized as a member of a group by sex 101

4.11	Percentage of youth categorized as a core group member by race	101
4.12	Percentage of youth categorized as a core group member by free/reduced lunch (FRL) status	102
4.13	Unstructured socializing by friend nomination rank	104
4.14	Correlation between network characteristics and selected attitudes and behaviors	105
4.15	Average delinquency by race and sex	106
4.16	Average delinquency by free/reduced-price lunch (FRL) status	106
4.17	Correlations between network characteristics and risky behaviors	107
5.1	Rates of past month substance use, by gender, 6th through 12th grade	117
5.2	Percentage of respondents reporting that they ever used various substances by spring of 12th grade for PROSPER and the Monitoring the Future national probability sample, 2009	118
5.3	Influence and selection results from Osgood et al., 2015	122
5.4	Group positions and substance use, logistic coefficients for differences from core members	128
5.5	Standardized associations between mean group behavior and group structure	133
5.6	Developmental change in the correlation between friends for substance use	137
5.7	Development change in the strength of homophilic selection and peer influence toward similarity	139
6.1	PROSPER youth against backdrop of national trends in justice involvement	147
6.2	Cumulative prevalence of arrest	156
6.3	Gender differences in association between arrest and friendship ties	162
8.1	How each parenting variable affects friendship selection and influence	200
8.1A	Effects of parental discipline on friendship selection	200
8.1B	Effects of unsupervised time with friends on friendship selection	200
8.1C	Effects of parental discipline on influence from friends	200
8.1D	Effects of parental knowledge on influence from friends	200
8.2A	Link between parental knowledge and alcohol use	204
8.2B	Link between inconsistent discipline and alcohol use	204
9.1	Number of same-sex friendship ties across time by sexual minority status and sex	235
11.1	Figure shows the program effect for the relationship between each centrality measure and a composite measure of problem behavior, delinquency, substance use attitudes, and substance use	271
11.2	Partial correlation between each of the traditional analytic measures and substance use diffusion	275
11.3	Partial correlation between each of the social network analytic measures and diffusion scores	276

Figures

12.1 Interaction forms for diathesis stress and differential susceptibility 298
14.1 The number of longitudinal social network papers per 4-year period 328
14.2 The number of longitudinal social network papers for the most used data sets 328
14.3 The time window of the most used social network data sets 334

TABLES

2.1 Key constructs, measures, and indicators for high school and post–high school assessments 46
6.1 Random-effects linear regression coefficients showing associations between arrest and friendship ties 158
6.2 Random-effects linear regression coefficients (standard errors) showing associations between arrest and friendship ties, including race and gender interactions with arrest 161
7.1 Descriptive statistics for study variables 180
7.2 Multilevel regression coefficients predicting depression and self-harm from lagged network characteristics and controls 182
7.3 Multilevel regression coefficients predicting network outcomes from lagged depression and self-harm 183
8.1 Summary of three PROSPER Peers studies that tested how parents and peers interact to shape substance use 197
9.1 Differences in network outcomes by sexual minority status and sex 234
10.1 Variability of network selection and influence processes 256
10.2 Coefficients for community- and school-level variation in network selection and influence processes 258
11.1 Description and summary of key results for each of the network-based selection strategies 281
13.1 Potential interactions between network- and individual-level metrics 321
14.1 Characteristics of the most used social network data sets 331

CONTRIBUTORS

Teresa Bertogna
Master of Science Candidate in Behavioral and Social Sciences
University of Groningen
Groningen, The Netherlands

Avery Chahl
Graduate Student, Department of Human Development and Family Studies
The Pennsylvania State University
University Park, PA, USA

H. Harrington Cleveland
Professor of Human Development and Family Studies
The Pennsylvania State University
University Park, PA, USA

Alana Colindres
Graduate Student, School of Criminology & Criminal Justice
Northeastern University
Boston, MA, USA

Molly Copeland
Assistant Professor, Department of Sociology
Michigan State University
East Lansing, MI, USA

Mark E. Feinberg
Research Professor, Prevention Research Center
The Pennsylvania State University
University Park, PA, USA

Mark Greenberg
Emeritus Professor, Human Development and Family Studies
The Pennsylvania State University
University Park, PA, USA

Amanda M. Griffin
Researcher, Chapin Hall
University of Chicago
Chicago, IL, USA

Evelien M. Hoeben
Researcher
Netherlands Institute for the Study of Crime and Law Enforcement (NSCR)
Amsterdam, The Netherlands

Wade C. Jacobsen
Associate Professor, Department of Criminology and Criminal Justice
University of Maryland
College Park, MD, USA

Derek A. Kreager
Liberal Arts Professor of Sociology and Criminology
The Pennsylvania State University
University Park, PA, USA

Lydia Laninga-Wijnen
Senior Research Fellow, INVEST Flagship - Developmental Psychology
University of Turku
Turku, Finland

Cassie McMillan
Assistant Professor of Sociology and Criminology
Northeastern University
Boston, MA, USA

James Moody
Professor of Sociology and Director of the Duke Network Analysis Center
Duke University
Durham, NC, USA

D. Wayne Osgood
Professor Emeritus of Criminology and Sociology
The Pennsylvania State University
University Park, PA, USA

Daniel T. Ragan
Associate Professor, Department of Sociology
University of New Mexico
Albuquerque, NM, USA

Nayan G. Ramirez
Associate Professor of Criminology and Justice Studies
California State University, Northridge
Northridge, CA, USA

Kelly L. Rulison
Associate Professor, Human Development and Family Studies
The Pennsylvania State University
University Park, PA, USA

Lisa M. Schainker
Extension Assistant Professor, Home & Community Department
Utah State University
Logan, UT, USA

Gabriel L. Schlomer
Associate Professor, Division of Educational Psychology and Methodology
University at Albany, SUNY
Albany, NY, USA

Sonja E. Siennick
Professor, College of Criminology and Criminal Justice
Florida State University
Tallahassee, FL, USA

Richard Spoth
F. Wendell Miller Senior Prevention Scientist
Partnerships in Prevention Science Institute
Human Development and Family Studies
Iowa State University
Ames, IA, USA

Erin Tinney
Doctoral Candidate, Criminology and Criminal Justice Studies
University of Maryland
College Park, MD, USA

Thomas W. Valente
Professor, Population and Public Health Sciences, Keck School of Medicine
University of Southern California
Los Angeles, CA, USA

David J. Vandenbergh
Professor of Biobehavioral Health, Department of Biobehavioral Health
The Pennsylvania State University
University Park, PA, USA

René Veenstra
Professor of Sociology
University of Groningen
Groningen, The Netherlands

Janet Welsh
Research Professor of Health and Human Development
The Pennsylvania State University
University Park, PA, USA

Rose Wesche, PhD
Assistant Professor of Child and Adolescent Development,
Department of Human Development and Family Science
Virginia Polytechnic Institute and State University
Blacksburg, VA, USA

SECTION I

Setting the stage

1

Friendships and peer groups in the teen years—our perspective

D. WAYNE OSGOOD ■

INTRODUCTION

This volume presents research from the PROSPER (P̲romoting S̲chool-community-university P̲artnerships to E̲nhance R̲esilience) Peers project, which for over a decade has sought to illuminate how adolescent friendship networks channel and facilitate the spread of developmental outcomes such as substance use, other risky behaviors, mental health problems, and educational success. In addition, we have probed the role of friendship networks in extending the impact of school and family-based prevention programs aimed at reducing substance misuse and improving adolescents' futures. The chapters presented here bring together results from PROSPER Peers' more than 50 publications along with new analyses and findings. All of this work was made possible by tracking the friendship networks and behaviors of thousands of students in 27 Iowa and Pennsylvania communities across middle and high schools.

This first chapter lays out the nature and aims of the PROSPER Peers study and presents our overarching conceptual perspective. The introductory section of the book also provides background and context for the empirical work through a chapter that describes the PROSPER prevention trial that made PROSPER Peers possible, a chapter that explains methods of social network analysis used throughout the book, and a chapter that describes the world of friendships among the rural and small-town youth we studied. The heart of the book is eight empirical chapters presenting findings from PROSPER Peers that address topical areas ranging from substance use and delinquency to prevention programs and behavioral genetics. The final section of the book ends with concluding thoughts from this volume's lead editor, Mark Feinberg, which are preceded by two commentaries

D. Wayne Osgood, *Friendships and peer groups in the teen years—our perspective*. In: *Teen Friendship Networks, Development, and Risky Behavior*. Edited by: Mark E. Feinberg and D. Wayne Osgood, Oxford University Press.
© Mark E. Feinberg and D. Wayne Osgood 2024. DOI: 10.1093/oso/9780197602317.003.0001

on PROSPER Peers' body of work by leading scholars: Tom Valente, who specializes in peer networks and public health, and René Veenstra and Lydia Laninga-Wijnen, who study a wealth of topics about adolescents' social networks.

PROSPER PEERS

The opportunity. The PROSPER Peers project owes its existence to a single, simple decision. The lead investigators of the PROSPER prevention trial decided to use the last page of their questionnaire to ask students to list the names of their closest friends at school. The rest of the questionnaire had covered the essential topics for the study's primary mission of evaluating a community-partnership-based dissemination system for delivering evidence-based prevention programs. Dick Spoth and Cleve Redmond of Iowa State University and Mark Greenberg, Karen Bierman, and Mark Feinberg of Pennsylvania State University knew that the evaluation's funding could not support processing and analyzing these friendship data. They added the peer network question anyway because they realized that, for negligible additional cost, they could collect immensely valuable data on a topic of great interest. The result has been one of the premiere adolescent peer network data sets in the world to date, combining a large sample, longitudinal data collection, a randomized intervention, and rich measures of adolescents' attitudes, behaviors, family relationships, and competencies. With these data in hand, I led a large team of investigators and students in applying for further funding to put the friendship data to good use. Our work was made possible by joint funding from the W. T. Grant Foundation (for 3 years) and the National Institute on Drug Abuse (NIDA) (ultimately extending to 9 years).

Like scholars throughout the social and behavioral sciences, prevention scientists have long been concerned about how adolescents' friendships affect the paths their lives take (Gest et al., 2011; Veenstra & Laninga-Wijnen, 2022). Indeed, helping adolescents avoid negative peer influence is a major theme of prevention programs. Having the PROSPER students name their friends enabled especially convincing research by making it possible to link students' questionnaire responses with their friends' responses. In most studies of peer influence, researchers must ask students both to report on their own behaviors and to describe their friends' behaviors. Relying on one person to report on both sides of the equation yields data that say too much about the respondents and too little about the friends (Bauman & Ennett, 1994; Jussim & Osgood, 1989; Kandel, 1996; Wilcox & Udry, 1986).

The PROSPER respondents' reports of their friendships also make full-scale social network analysis possible. The beginning of PROSPER's data collection in fall 2002 coincided with growing prominence of the study of networks, social and otherwise. The first major publications using the landmark social network data from the Add Health study had just been published (Alexander et al., 2001; Haynie, 2001; Moody, 2001), and influential popular press books on the emerging field of network science would soon appear (Barabási, 2003; Watts, 2003). Social science research on networks already had a long but sporadic history (see Moody et al., 2010), with highlights such as Moreno's creation of the sociogram (1953), Cartwright and Harary's (1956) network formulation of Heider's (1958) balance theory, Coleman's (1960) use of networks to reveal the social structures of high schools, and Cairns and colleagues' (1988; Cairns & Cairns, 1995) insights into the peer structure of elementary classrooms. Yet, social network analysis had remained a limited domain of specialists working with small-scale data. Recent examples like the new articles based on Add Health and the systematic application of a network perspective to substance use by Bauman and Ennett (1994, 1996; Ennett & Bauman, 1993, 1994) were at last showing that larger scale social network research was feasible and held great potential. Advances in research methods and computing power had come together to make this possible if only the appropriate data were available. The PROSPER friendship data presented the opportunity to be part of a new wave of studies that soon followed their lead, such as the School Project of the Netherlands Institute for the Study of Crime and Law Enforcement (NSCR) in Amsterdam (Weerman, 2011; Weerman & Smeenk, 2005); the Tracking Adolescents' Individual Lives Survey (TRAILS) and Social Network Analyses of Risk behavior in Early adolescence (SNARE) studies of the University of Groningen, Netherlands (Dijkstra et al., 2015; Veenstra et al., 2007); the University of California–Los Angeles (UCLA) Middle School and High School Diversity Project (Echols & Graham, 2020; Graham et al., 2014); and Kerr and Stattin's longitudinal study of the entire student population of a small town in Sweden (Burk et al., 2012; Kerr et al., 2007).

The research design of the PROSPER evaluation meant that its simple question about students' friendships could be the basis for an especially strong study of peer networks and risky behavior. In Chapter 2, Dick Spoth provides a well-rounded overview of PROSPER, but I touch on a few especially relevant features here. First, because PROSPER's preventive interventions targeted all the students in the same grade at an intervention school (school districts were randomized to intervention and control conditions), the target samples for the student questionnaires were also the full grade cohorts. Thus, PROSPER obtained data from both the respondents and their friends in the same grade and school. Further, these friendship linkages for entire grade cohorts provide a strong basis for full network analysis of well-defined, interacting populations. Second, the prospects were quite favorable for successfully matching respondents with their friends and thus for a good representation of the full networks. Response rates were high due to PROSPER's excellent relationships with the communities, administration of annual student surveys in school, and the use of opt-out rather than opt-in parental permission procedures (approved by the institutional review boards, based on to school and community support for the prevention efforts). Third, PROSPER included 28 entire small school districts (each with one high school). The study therefore included not only a very large sample of individual students, but also a meaningfully large sample of separate networks of students. One district did not provide friendship data, so there were 54 separate peer networks (27 districts × 2 cohorts). This combination provides both the statistical power for unusually precise findings and the capacity to test the consistency of findings across communities, rather than assessing students in one community and generalizing findings under the assumption that peer cultures are uniform from place to place. Fourth, PROSPER ultimately gathered eight waves of data from sixth through twelfth grade, thus spanning almost all of adolescence. Gathering longitudinal data like this is far more expensive and time consuming than short-term studies, but it is essential for tracing the evolution of peer relations and outcomes and for addressing critical methodological issues.

Previous studies that could match responses from adolescents and their friends had been few and far between, but they were often influential. Although some of those studies were fairly large and some had longitudinal data, none came close to matching PROSPER's combination of size and longitudinal duration (e.g., Cairns et al., 1988; Ennett & Bauman, 1994; Kandel, 1978; Reiss & Rhodes, 1964). For instance, Add Health set a new standard by gathering cross-sectional network data for a nationally representative sample of 90,000 students, but its longitudinal network data were limited to three waves and a few thousand students, most of them at two schools (Alexander et al., 2001; Haynie, 2001). And unlike any of the previous studies, the PROSPER prevention trial had randomly assigned entire school districts to either receive preventive interventions or serve as controls, thereby providing a unique experimental framework to test an intervention's effects on school-wide peer processes. Of the newer studies being launched, only the UCLA Middle School and High School Diversity Project matched the scope of PROSPER for size and duration. Our two studies provide an excellent opportunity for comparison and replication because they follow comparably large samples from sixth through twelfth grade. Furthermore, in contrast to PROSPER's focus on risky behavior in a largely white and rural or small-town sample, the UCLA project's emphasis is on the role of race and ethnicity in peer relations among an urban and highly diverse sample (Echols & Graham, 2020; Graham et al., 2014).

The PROSPER Peers team. Realizing the great potential of the PROSPER friendship data depended on forming a strong research team that committed itself to the project and obtained funding. With backing from Penn State University's Social Science Research Institute (SSRI), about a dozen researchers from many fields gathered monthly during the 2002–2003 academic year to talk about their interests in adolescence, peers, risky behavior, and networks and about how best to use the PROSPER friendship data.

The core group that emerged to launch PROSPER Peers was Karen Bierman, Mark Feinberg, Scott Gest, Jim Moody, and myself. All were at Penn State except Jim (then at Ohio State), who was recruited to the team. He had presented to the group about his work with Add Health, which showed how much we needed his network analytic expertise and what a good partner he would be. I volunteered to head up the effort because I was at a good point in my career to take on a new large project, and an upcoming sabbatical was well timed for leading the initial proposals for funding.

The research team represented several disciplines and research traditions relevant to the intersection of peers, adolescence, networks, and risky behavior. The list includes developmental psychology, sociology, social networks, child clinical psychology, social psychology, prevention science, criminology, and substance use. This diversity of perspectives has proven invaluable for expanding our perspectives and enriching our work.

Finding funding for PROSPER Peers was essential. The peer study was a tremendous bargain because the prevention trial had covered the cost of data collection. Yet, it was far from free. The heart of the peer study is connecting data from respondents with data from their friends, and the eight waves of questionnaires ultimately included over 360,000 handwritten names of friends. Matching those names to questionnaire identification numbers via student rosters required thousands of hours of typing, database management, coders' judgments, and data file manipulation. Penn State's SSRI provided seed funding for a trial run of a computer-assisted coding process, which enabled us to demonstrate to potential funders that this cost-efficient approach yielded high quality data for analysis.

Gaining funding was a long, slow road, and it often appeared that we would not succeed. Ultimately, we had the good fortune that the first phase of our work was jointly funded by the W. T. Grant Foundation and NIDA, beginning August 2007. Both were excellent partners who helped improve our work in many ways. In addition to the initial phase, which covered the processing and analysis of the friendship data for sixth through ninth grades, NIDA provided renewal funding, beginning September 2013, which extended our analyses through the twelfth-grade friendship networks.

We began PROSPER Peers convinced that the PROSPER friendship data could be the basis for a body of valuable research on many topics, and the project has succeeded beyond our hopes. We could not have anticipated that it would be the source of more than 50 publications, with the large majority appearing in highly ranked journals and quite a few already widely cited. Notably, the range of topics covered by these articles and book chapters (listed in the appendix to this volume) goes well beyond what we envisioned as we planned the study and wrote proposals for funding. An essential source of our success is the variety of interests and backgrounds of the many collaborators who joined our team, bringing excellent ideas as they further expanded our interdisciplinary range. Our rich data also have proved a fruitful basis for former graduate assistants to stay involved as they became faculty members and developed their own programs of research. Indeed, most of the authors of the empirical chapters of this volume were once graduate assistants for the project.

We list the people who have been a significant part of PROSPER Peers in the appendix, but here I mention three who have been part of the core team since the project was first funded. Sonja Siennick's involvement began when she led the friendship-matching process for the first five waves of data as an advanced graduate student. Sonja saved the day when this task turned out to be even more complex than we had thought. Since then, Sonja has headed up our work on the connection of peers with depression and internalizing symptoms, which became a major focus with the renewal funding. Kelly Rulison wrote the first doctoral dissertation that took advantage of our data, and early on she handled essential and difficult computing tasks, especially the gargantuan file management challenge and use of cluster computers required for applying the rSIENA program to our data. Kelly has become a leader of our research on friendship networks and effects of prevention programs. As the project was about to begin, Derek Kreager came to Penn State as a new assistant professor, already doing excellent research on peers, adolescence, delinquency, and romantic relationships. We invited him to join our team, and he quickly became a key member. He has led our work on the intersection of peers and romantic relationships, which was also a focus of the renewal funding.

WHY STUDY FRIENDSHIP NETWORKS AND RISKY BEHAVIOR IN ADOLESCENCE?

Risky behavior in adolescence. Adults have worried about the misbehavior of adolescents since ancient times, all too often claiming "kids nowadays are worse than ever" (Bernard & Kurlychek, 2010). Although this sense of decline compared to the good old days is usually baseless, there is still reason to focus on problematic behavior and mental health problems during adolescence. It is a period of emergence and rapid growth for problems such as substance use (Miech et al., 2021); illegal behavior (Hirschi & Gottfredson, 1983); precocious sexuality (Zimmer-Gembeck & Helfand, 2008); and depression (Lewinsohn et al., 1994). All of these are rare before about age 12, but approach adult levels by age 18–20. Though many of these behaviors are legal and widespread among adults, they are generally not acceptable for minors and go by labels such as risky behavior, problem behavior, and deviance (Elliott et al., 1989; Gibbs, 1981; Jessor & Jessor, 1977). Most importantly, all of these problems carry both short-term and long-term risks for health, well-being, and successful adjustment (Laub & Sampson, 2003; Osgood, Foster, et al., 2005; Robins, 1966).

Peers and adolescence. Peers play an enormous role in the lives of children and adolescents. Not only are peers central in daily experience, but also they contribute to development in domains ranging from language and basic cognitive skills to physical well-being and sexuality (Rubin et al., 2015). As children enter adolescence, many changes converge to heighten the importance of friendships and peer relations (Bukowski et al., 1996). For instance, they experience greater need for personal validation through interpersonal intimacy (Buhrmester, 1990), and they gain the skills to maintain friendships in the face of conflict (Berndt et al., 1986; Laursen et al.1996).

In industrialized Western cultures like the United States, adolescence also coincides with changes in parenting and school organization that create a less constrained social ecology for peer relations (Osgood et al., 2022). Schools shift from small, self-contained elementary classrooms to large, heterogeneous middle schools and then high schools, where classroom composition shifts throughout the day, and students mix in a growing variety of extracurricular activities (Blyth et al., 1983; Wigfield et al., 2015). Meanwhile, parents grant adolescents increasing autonomy, such as allowing them to spend longer periods away from adult supervision and to be farther from home (Osgood, Anderson, & Shaffer, 2005). With this increased independence, adolescents spend less time with their families and more with peers (Felson & Gottfredson, 1984; Larson et al., 1996). Thus, peers become increasingly important to adolescents' personal and social development, while parents have a diminishing role in their offspring's friendship choices and social activities. A long and rich tradition of research spanning fields of psychology, sociology, education, and anthropology documents the resulting social world of adolescents, including topics of teen culture, youth groups and gangs, and adolescent society (e.g., Brown, 1990; Coleman, 1961; Crosnoe, 2011; Eckert, 1989; Short & Strodtbeck, 1965; Thrasher, 1927).

Peers and risky behavior. Social or interpersonal influence is the idea that people's behavior, values, and attitudes are shaped by their connections to other individuals and groups, and it is one of the most prominent themes in social and behavioral science. This idea is at the heart of social learning theory (Bandura, 1977); symbolic interaction theory (Mead, 1934); and reference group theory (Merton & Kitt, 1950; Sherif, 1948). Though these theories differ as to whether processes of reinforcement, perspective taking, or identification underly interpersonal influence, all agree that influence is fundamental to social life. Theories of risky behavior have placed great emphasis on interpersonal influence. It is the primary focus of Sutherland's differential association theory (1939); Burgess and Akers's (1966) and Patterson's (1986) social learning theories; Jessor and Jessor's problem behavior theory (1977); and Oetting and Beauvais's peer cluster theory (1986). Further, many explanations of risky behavior that emphasize other causal factors give a prominent role to interpersonal influence as well. For instance, although life-course offenders are the main focus of Moffitt's typological theory, she argued that most adolescent delinquency arises from the influence of life-course offenders on their peers during that period. Early social disorganization theory (Shaw & McKay, 1942); strain theory (Cloward & Ohlin, 1960; Cohen, 1955); and labeling theory (Tannenbaum, 1938) all focused on explaining why youth joined deviant groups and then relied on peer influence to explain the ultimate outcomes.

Given the emergence of risky behavior in adolescence, research has focused on peers as a source of influence. Empirical studies have revealed several connections between peers and risky behavior, which provides support for the theoretical attention. First, risky behaviors tend to happen with friends: It has long been known that adolescents are far more likely to engage in delinquency and substance use when they are with companions rather than alone (Bernasco et al., 2013; Erickson & Jensen, 1977). Further, the more time adolescents spend "hanging out" with friends (i.e., socializing in an unstructured way, often without adult supervision), the more often they engage in a wide variety of risky behaviors (Hoeben et al., 2016; Osgood et al., 1996). Who one's friends are also matters. For instance, delinquent activities increase sharply when adolescents join gangs and decrease again after leaving them (Thornberry et al., 1993). More broadly, one of the most robust findings in the study of risky behavior is that the more that someone's friends engage in any risky behavior, the more likely they are to do so themselves (Elliott et al., 1989; Ennett & Bauman, 1994; Jessor & Jessor, 1977; Kandel, 1978). In fact, some authors consider friends' risky behavior to be the single strongest predictor of an individual's own behavior (Elliott et al., 1989; Warr, 2002). Though I am on record as being skeptical that peer influence has such singular importance (due to measurement issues discussed below; Haynie & Osgood, 2005), peer influence is definitely among the most consistent and robust correlates of risky behavior.

Learning more about the contribution of peers to risky behaviors is important because it has implications for ways to reduce and prevent them. A primary goal of the PROSPER Peers project is to add to the knowledge base for refining those efforts. In line with theory and research, most well-known programs for preventing risky behavior do place considerable emphasis on combating peer influence, but the empirical basis for the specifics of the programs tends to be thin (Henneberger et al., 2019; Veenstra & Langinga-Wijnen, 2022). For instance, programs typically feature lessons on "resistance skills," which are meant to empower youth to withstand invitations to use substances. There is little evidence, however, that invitations to reluctant participants play much role in substance use initiation. We believe that a social network perspective on adolescents' peer relations is an especially promising approach that is already pointing to useful avenues for strengthening interventions. For instance, some prevention programs use peers as coleaders who work alongside teachers or adults to deliver lessons, with the expectation that youth may be more receptive to messages delivered by opinion-leading peers than by adults (Perry et al., 1996). Valente and colleagues have used social network theory and methods to refine the selection of groups and leaders to enhance the effectiveness of this approach (Valente et al., 2003; Valente & Pumpuang, 2007).

A NETWORK-BASED CONCEPTUAL FRAMEWORK FOR PROSPER PEERS

Selection and influence

Traditionally, selection versus influence has been the central issue concerning peers and risky behavior. Is peer influence the reason that friends are similar to one another and that risky behavior tends to occur in groups? Or do those patterns arise merely because people choose friends who are similar to themselves? On one side are the many theoretical perspectives that emphasize social influence. On the other side, some well-known scholars have argued against a meaningful contribution of peer influence, instead portraying risky behaviors as resulting from individual pathology or personality traits (Glueck & Glueck, 1950; Gottfredson & Hirschi, 1990) or from inadequate connections to social institutions like family, school, and community (Hirschi, 1969). In their views, the connection of peers to risky behavior reflects some combination of problematic youth being rejected by others and preferring the company of associates like themselves (i.e., selection).

We, too, were focused on the question of selection versus influence as we began PROSPER Peers. It has major implications for the utility of having programs address influence (like resistance skill training), and we were excited that we had such strong data for taking on the methodological challenges the topic entails. This section lays out those methodological issues, showing how a network approach helps clarify them and noting the value of the PROSPER friendship data for addressing them.

Taking a network perspective on similarity of friends' behaviors also led us away from that starting point of viewing selection of friends versus influence from friends as separate, competing processes. Much research on peer similarity and influence has attempted to determine the relative strengths of these processes and identify the predominant factor. However, as I explain in this section, the two are intertwined in a fundamental way, and recognizing this led us to a richer set of research questions and to realizing some important policy implications.

Measuring friends' behavior. The first methodological challenge for determining whether friends influence each other's risky behavior is to measure the behavior of a respondent's friends in a way that is not biased by the respondent's own attitudes and behavior. Most studies have asked respondents to report about their friends, typically using questions like "How many of your friends smoke marijuana?" Many researchers interested in peer influence have argued against this approach based on consistent findings that these perceptions about one's friends are insufficiently correlated with the friends' reports of their own behavior and too highly correlated with the respondent's behavior (Bauman & Ennett, 1994; Jussim & Osgood, 1989; Kandel, 1996; Wilcox & Udry, 1986). That pattern matches a well-established bias of projection or assumed similarity, in which people describe their friends as more like themselves than is actually the case (Byrne & Blaylock, 1963; Newcomb, 1961). A potential conceptual strength of the perceptual measure is that people might be more directly influenced by what they think their friends do than by what the friends actually do (Jussim & Osgood, 1989), but it is clear that a perceptual measure alone is not adequate. Projection bias, rather than either subjective influence or selection, accounted for much of the association between respondent behavior and perceptions about friends in the two studies that examined both processes (Jussim & Osgood, 1989; Young et al., 2014). Further, based on their study of delinquency using the Add Health study's network data, Haynie and Osgood (2005) concluded that, due to projection bias that enlarges the correlation between friends, perceptual measures systematically inflate the importance of peer influence relative to other explanatory factors.

Avoiding the bias inherent in respondents' perceptions about their friends requires a measure of their behavior that is independent from the respondent. There are several plausible sources of independent data, such as direct observations, administrative records, and asking other informed parties like parents or teachers. Nevertheless, the most efficient and common solution, at least for adolescents, is to study full schools or grade cohorts and ask respondents both to describe their own behaviors and to name their friends. The friendship choices provide the linkages to the friends, who have completed the questionnaire as well. This is the research design used in PROSPER, Add Health, and almost all other studies with independent data about friends (e.g., Ennett & Bauman, 1994; Kandel, 1978).

I first became excited about PROSPER Peers because it provided independent measures of friends' behavior. In the 1980s, I directed a study of peer influence among incarcerated adolescents, and our findings had convinced me that this measurement approach was essential for meaningful work on peer influence (Gold & Osgood, 1992; Jussim & Osgood, 1989). I still believe that, but my experience with PROSPER Peers has led me to understand that this research design is even more valuable because of the richness of the data it yields. The other approach of studying peers by asking respondents to report about their friends is quite limited by comparison. That approach assesses only one friend variable at a time, it doesn't differentiate among the friends, and it is uninformative about anything respondents don't reliably know about their friends. In contrast, linking respondent and friend data yields a full set of measures for both parties, it allows researchers to combine data across friends however they wish (e.g., to determine the number of same-sex and opposite-sex friends who do and don't smoke), and it opens up topics beyond respondents' knowledge, like the friends' relationships with their parents and who the friends' friends are (which we sometimes refer to as indirect friendships). As I had originally hoped, being able to link questionnaires for respondents and friends has helped us do strong work on peer influence. Even better, it has opened the door to studying lots of new and interesting topics that go far beyond our original plans.

Taking selection into account. Controlling for selection is essential for a study of peer influence to be convincing. Interestingly, the term *selection* applies in two different senses that happen to come together in this particular case. The first is selection as social science's generic alternative to a causal influence. Here some selection process, rather than the cause of interest, creates a spurious link between the outcome and explanatory variable. For instance, when evaluating an intervention program, a problem of selection arises if the people who chose to be in the program were already on the path to better outcomes (perhaps being more motivated to succeed), compared to people who chose not to be in the program. For peer influence, the alternative explanation is that people who choose delinquent friends are already inclined to delinquency, regardless of who they choose as friends. The challenge is to obtain an estimate of peer influence that adequately takes that selection process into account.

How to rule out selection in the absence of random assignment is a matter of considerable debate, and standards vary among the social and behavioral sciences. The most basic approaches are to statistically control for important variables that could influence respondents' behavior and whether they select risky peers. Longitudinal studies that measure the outcome on multiple occasions are valuable for this purpose because prior behavior typically is the best predictor of future behavior and thus the single most useful control variable. PROSPER's eight waves of questionnaires spanning sixth through twelfth grade are valuable for this purpose (even if insufficient to meet the strictest standards for claims of causality; Morgan & Winship, 2015).

This first meaning of selection corresponds to the standard focus on influence versus selection in research on peer influence. Selection is a competing hypothesis, something to rule out so we can find out what we really want to know. In this view, selection is of no interest in its own right, and if we could simply eliminate it by randomly assigning some adolescents to risky friends and others to nonrisky friends, so much the better.

The second sense in which the term *selection* applies here is not so generic, but rather it is part of the specific meaning of the focal explanatory variable for peer influence. That variable, friends' behavior, is defined by, first, who respondents select as their friends and, second, those friends' risky behavior. What influence people receive, whether toward or away from risky behavior, is totally dependent on their own friendship selections.

In light of this, framing this topic as selection *versus* influence is misguided because, instead, selection *defines* the influence. People's friendship choices create the set of potential influences they receive. Yes, it is important to take friendship selection processes into account to obtain valid estimates of peer influence. Yet, those selection processes are very much of interest in their own right because they define the direction of the influence. Indeed, this dynamic is implicit in the theories of risky behavior that focus on processes that lead some youth to have deviant peers (Cloward & Ohlin, 1960; Moffitt, 1993). Recognition of this role for selection processes has led to useful studies about factors associated with affiliating with deviant peers (Chapple, 2005; Warr, 2005), and it has become a central aspect of the research of the PROSPER Peers project. Next, we turn to the way that social network analysis characterizes the interplay of selection and influence processes.

Peer influence from a network perspective

The remainder of this chapter introduces the primary themes of research from PROSPER Peers in terms of social network concepts, pointing out examples of our work that make use of them. Chapter 3 describes corresponding methods for social network analysis. Further chapters, which are organized by topical area, more fully describe the PROSPER Peers network studies and results. Some good sources to learn more about social networks and how to study them are books by Borgatti et al. (2018), Kadushin (2012), and Knoke and Yang (2019).

First, what is a network? Networks have two types of elements: nodes and links. The nodes are whatever sort of entity is of interest, the links are connections or relationships between pairs of nodes, and the set of links among a population of nodes defines a network. In PROSPER Peers, the nodes are adolescents, the links are friendships, and a network is all the friendship choices among the students who make up a grade cohort of a school. To illustrate, Figure 1.1 shows a simple network of four individuals (A, B, C, and D), and the lines and arrowheads indicate who has chosen whom as a friend. A chose B and C as friends, but not D. A was chosen by B and D, but not C. The friendships between A and B and between C and D are reciprocal, while A's choice of C and D's choice of A are unreciprocated.

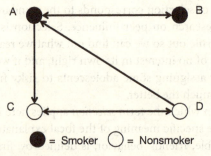

Figure 1.1 An example network.

We are usually interested in how the pattern of connections in a network relates to attributes of the individuals, and the figure uses the different shading of the nodes to indicate an attribute of interest. In this case, the shading reflects whether or not an adolescent smokes cigarettes with dark circles for smokers (A and B) and light circles for nonsmokers (C and D).

The research of the PROSPER Peers project focuses on friendship networks, as is typical in the study of peers in adolescence. Network concepts apply to any type of connection, however, and others types of relationship deserve attention as well. The PROSPER Peers team has also investigated romantic relationships and their interplay with friendships (see Chapter 9). Other groups of scholars have published valuable research about bully/victim relationships (Felmlee & Faris, 2016; Veenstra et al., 2007) and disliking or rejection (Fujimoto et al., 2017; Huitsing et al., 2014).

The network perspective is well matched to the idea of social influence, which entails someone who is the source of the influence and a recipient who may be affected by it, constituting a pair of linked nodes. These linkages combine to form a network that represents the paths through which influence may spread through the population. Accordingly, social influence is a core topic of social network theory and analysis, where it is often discussed in terms of the diffusion of attitudes and behavior (Coleman et al., 1966; Friedkin, 1998; Valente, 2010).

Considering influence in terms of a network graph reveals aspects that are less evident when it is conceived as simply the effect of one variable (friends' behavior) on another (the respondents' behavior). Figure 1.2 shows the paths of influence that arise from the network of Figure 1.1. The straight links show the same friendship choices as before, and the additional curved lines indicate the implied influences on Person A, based on the typical assumption that people are influenced by the friends they choose. Because Person A chooses B and C as friends, A will directly receive influence from both of them, which is represented by the solid curved lines in the opposite direction of the friendship choice. Consistent with this, both B and C would be included in a measure of "friends' behavior" for A. Yet such a measure does not include additional paths of indirect influence that stem from other people's friendship choices. Person A will also be subject to indirect influences from the people who B and C chose, represented here by the

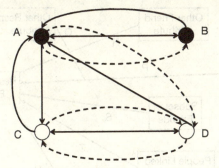

Figure 1.2 Peer influence implied by network.

dashed curved lines. Person D has an indirect influence on A by influencing C, and A experiences circular forms of indirect influence on him- or herself through the reciprocal relationship with B and indirectly by influencing D, who influences C. In addition to a direct influence on A, C is a source of indirect influence going from C to D, back to C, and on to A. All this complexity arises with only three potential influencers for one target individual; the possibilities escalate exponentially as network size increases. Any network of friendship choices implies distinct sets of influence paths for every individual that depend on both their own friendship choices and those of everyone else to whom they are directly or indirectly connected.

These additional complexities of influence create methodological issues because standard statistical methods do not take them into account. For instance, failing to allow for reciprocal influence will tend to bias results toward overestimating the strength of influence by, in effect, counting the combined influence in both directions. Furthermore, network data are quite prone to violate the standard statistical assumption of independence. That assumption requires that there be no systematic patterns among cases for the residuals of an analysis, which would only happen in the unlikely event that a model captured all the potential sources of similarity between linked individuals. As a result, conventional analyses will tend to overestimate the precision of estimates and provide unduly optimistic significance tests. To address these concerns, social network methodologists have developed specialized network analytic methods that explicitly recognize these features of the influence process (e.g., Friedkin, 1998; Snijders, 2001; Steglich et al., 2010).

Research on peer influence by PROSPER Peers. In addition to these methodological concerns, a network perspective on influence has substantive implications because it opens the door to a wealth of valuable topics to investigate, as shown in Figure 1.3. Studies of peer influence have been a major portion of the PROSPER Peers research portfolio, and we have taken advantage of the flexibility of network data to investigate many forms of influence. Almost all research on peer influence has concerned the form of influence illustrated by Path P of Figure 1.3. In this case, the attribute of the friends is the same variable as the outcome, which in our research has most often been alcohol use, smoking cigarettes, or delinquency (see

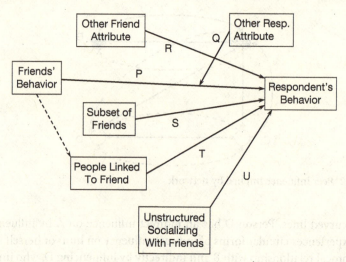

Figure 1.3 Varieties of peer influence. Resp = respondent.

especially Chapters 5, 8, and 10). This form of influence increases similarity between friends on the behavior of interest.

A simple and useful elaboration of this type of peer influence is to examine whether the strength of this basic form of influence (Path P) varies, depending on some attribute or experience of the respondent, which is represented as Path Q in Figure 1.3. Because the respondent attribute is affecting (or moderating) a relationship, Path Q is drawn as the effect of a variable on another effect (the influence Path P, from peer behavior to respondent behavior). For instance, influence might be stronger for extroverted adolescents than for introverted adolescents. Examples of PROSPER Peers research about this type of moderation in the influence process includes studies of whether peer influence for substance use varies in relation to internalizing symptoms (see Chapter 7), a specific genetic variation (Chapter 12), gender (McMillan et al., 2018), parenting practices, unstructured time with peers, and attitudes about substance use (see Chapter 8).

The next variation of assessing peer influence, shown as Path R, is to study other attributes of the friends as sources of influence, rather than being limited to the friends' status on the outcome measure. An example would be whether having more cross-gender friends is an influence toward risky behavior. Our ability to link respondents to their friends' questionnaires opens the door to addressing research questions about a wide range of friends' characteristics as potential sources of peer influence. We have taken advantage of this option to investigate the influence of friends' beliefs versus their behavior (Ragan, 2014; see Chapter 5), the influence of friends' general deviance versus a specific type of substance use (Widdowson et al., 2020), attitudes toward substance use (see Chapter 9), and the influence of friends' participation in a treatment program (see Chapter 11).

These studies of multiple sources of peer influence also enable investigators to explore direct and indirect effects among sources of influence and multiple outcomes. For instance, Rulison, Feinberg, and colleagues (2015) established that having friends whose families participated in PROSPER's family-focused program led to reduced substance use, and that one part of that effect was direct, but another part was mediated by the friends' changed attitudes about substance use (see Chapter 11).

Some PROSPER Peers investigators have used the flexibility of network data to study the influence of particular types of friends, rather than all friends (Path S in Figure 1.3). Widdowson and his colleagues (2020) tested Moffitt's (1993) social mimicry hypothesis by first identifying friends who were persistently delinquent (based on five waves of data) and then focusing on their influence. To investigate whether the effects of unstructured socializing with friends depended on whether the friends engaged in different types of risky behavior, Hoeben and her colleagues (2021) used a similar strategy, forming a series of measures of time use for each respondent that differed according to the type of friends.

Another way in which friends can be part of the influence process is represented by Path T, in which the respondent's friendships with others serve as a bridge to influence from additional people to whom the friends are connected. This type of influence is of interest because, as Figure 1.2 illustrates, being connected to someone makes us indirectly subject to the influence they receive through their connections. In addition, having a friendship means that we sometimes directly interact with the friends' friends and hear about those indirect friends' activities and opinions (Payne & Cornwell, 2007). Two streams of PROSPER Peers research concern this type of bridged influence. The first (Cleveland et al., 2012; Ragan et al., 2014) examines the influence of friends' parents on respondents, studied through the friends' reports about the parenting they receive (see Chapter 8). In that work, friends serve as a bridge to influence on adolescents from adults beyond their own families. The second stream of work (Kreager, Haynie, et al., 2016) investigates romantic partnerships as a bridge to influence from an additional peer group (see Chapter 9). This work capitalizes on a PROSPER question asking respondents to name their romantic partners. Those responses provide not only a direct link to the romantic partner, but also an indirect link to the partners' friends, who tend not to have been the respondent's friends.

An additional form of peer influence: Unstructured socializing. In addition to these forms of influence that stem from attributes of friends, our work includes a situational form of influence tied to activities with friends (Warr, 2002), specifically unstructured socializing away from adult supervision (Path U in Figure 1.3). My colleagues and I (Osgood et al., 1996) have argued that spending time this way increases the chances of risky behaviors because the presence of friends makes risky behavior easier and more rewarding, the absence of adults reduces the chances of detection and consequences, and the lack of an agenda leaves time available. Many studies have documented the association between unstructured socializing and a wide variety of risky behaviors (Hoeben et al., 2016), and there is good evidence that delinquent incidents and substance use are especially likely to occur during unstructured socializing (Bernasco et al., 2013). Because the PROSPER friendship questions asked respondents how frequently they spent time this way with each friend they named, we are able to apply a network approach to the topic.

Unstructured socializing has been a component of several different types of studies in PROSPER Peers. Siennick and Osgood (2012) took advantage PROSPER's friend-specific data to study with which friends adolescents more often spent time in unstructured socializing. Hoeben and her colleagues (2021) traced linkages between the amount of unstructured socializing respondents did with different types of friends and whether they were more likely to specialize in delinquency or substance use. Wesche and her colleagues (2015) also extended previous work on the influence of romantic partners and the partners' friends by examining unstructured socializing with them as an additional form of influence (see Chapter 9).

Friendship selection from a network perspective

From our social network perspective, selection concerns who chooses whom as a friend and thus which linkages are present in the network. This topic is fundamental in network research because the links define the network. Social network analysis differentiates four primary types of selection, which are represented in Figure 1.4. For selection processes, the outcome of interest is whether or not a link exists, corresponding to the dashed link from the respondent (also referred to as ego) to a potential friend (referred to as alter).

Selection for similarity. The first type of selection is based on similarity, and it also is known as homophilic selection. Similarity-based selection occurs when people tend to choose friends who are like themselves on some attribute, rather than people who are different. The tendency to have friendships with people similar to oneself is ubiquitous, having been found across almost all attributes studied, including race, religion, education, and delinquency (McPherson et al., 2001; Warr, 2002).

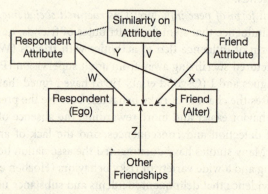

Figure 1.4 Types of selection.

Figure 1.4 represents selection for similarity by Path V from similarity on an attribute to the friendship. The dotted lines from similarity to attributes of the respondent and friend are in recognition that, together, they define similarity. The network in Figure 1.1 illustrates selection for similarity on smoking. Due to the reciprocal friendships between Smokers A and B and between Nonsmokers C and D, all four possible ties between similar adolescents are present (two ties for each pair). In contrast, of the eight possible cases of students choosing friends unlike themselves, only two occur.

As discussed above, controlling for prior similarity with friends is essential for obtaining appropriate estimates of peer influence. Yet, we are also interested in knowing whether adolescents systematically select similar friends because that choice shapes the influence they receive. If there is strong selection toward similarity, any peer influence that occurs will be in the direction of maintaining and expanding previous variation on the outcome. For most outcomes we have studied, we have found evidence of both a selection preference for similar friends and of peer influence toward similarity with friends (e.g., see Chapters 5 and 8).

Selection for similarity is also of interest as part of the overall organization of a network. The stronger the selection for similarity on an attribute, the more it will serve as a basis of clustering among similar individuals and of separation and division between those who differ. For instance, consider Figure 1.5, which shows two versions of the friendship network of one of the PROSPER schools in the sixth grade. They differ only for the attribute represented by the shading of the nodes. In the version on the left, the dark nodes are students in the top 25% for delinquency versus light shading for the other 75%. There is some indication of selection for similarity on delinquency because almost all of the more delinquent youth are on the right side of the graph, and there are quite a few connections

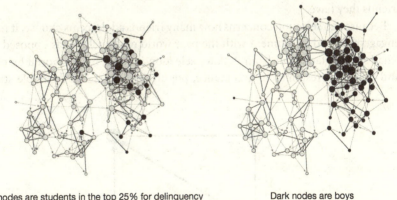

Dark nodes are students in the top 25% for delinquency   Dark nodes are boys
Light nodes are the remaining 75% of students   Light nodes are girls

Figure 1.5 Two versions of a PROSPER network, colored for delinquency (left) and gender (right). The size of nodes reflects the number of friendship connections. Darker lines are reciprocated friendships, and lighter lines are unreciprocated friendships, with arrowheads indicating who chose whom.

among them. The selection for similarity is not very strong, however, and most delinquent youth also have plenty of friendships with nondelinquent youth. In the second version of this network on the right, the dark nodes are boys and the light nodes are girls. Selection for gender similarity is far more potent, with almost all girls on one side and boys on the other. Only a very small percentage of friendships bridge the two sides, and most of the students only have friendships with their own gender. Such strong clustering for gender is typical, especially in early adolescence, and these data are from the fall term of sixth grade. Another PROSPER Peers study (Osgood et al., 2022), focuses on this aspect of the organization of friendship networks by examining levels of similarity for 12 attributes, tracing their evolution from sixth through eleventh grade (Chapters 4 and 5).

Ego and alter selection. Ego selection concerns whether an attribute is associated with sending out more links to others, such as girls naming more friends than boys or extraverts naming more friends than introverts. This is an impact of a respondent attribute on likelihood of a friendship link, which corresponds to Path W in Figure 1.4. Alter selection is comparable, but is based on whether an attribute is associated with receiving more versus fewer links, as in Path X. For instance, adolescents might tend to choose older students or good athletes as friends more often than they choose younger students or poor athletes.

Figure 1.6 illustrates these two types of selection through a network graph. There is negative ego selection for smoking because smokers chose fewer friends in this example. The two smokers, E and F, each chose only one friend (each other), while Nonsmoker G chose all three of the other people, and H chose two of them. In contrast, alter selection for smoking is positive because the smokers are more often chosen as friends (two times for E and three for F) than the nonsmokers (one time each). Note that full network data are necessary to study alter selection because it requires knowing how many other people choose each target person. In contrast, ego selection can be studied by simply asking respondents how many friends they have.

Because ego selection concerns how many friends adolescents choose, it reflects engagement and attachment with the peer world of the school, as opposed to alienation or detachment from it. Alter selection is about being chosen by others, and thus it corresponds to acceptance, popularity, and status. A simple strategy

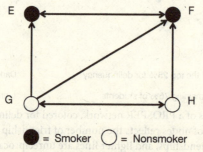

Figure 1.6 Negative ego selection and positive alter selection for smoking.

for investigating these two types of selection is to treat the count of friendship nominations given (known as out-degree) or of nominations received (known as in-degree) as outcome variables. For example, Kreager, Staff, and colleagues (2016) examined the consequences of sexual behavior for peer acceptance by using in-degree as their outcome measure (see Chapter 9).

Alter selection is especially relevant to peer influence because being chosen by many other people means being a potential source of influence on many people and playing a bigger role in the influence process (Osgood, Ragan, et al., 2013). For instance, if a small set of wealthy students is named as friends by most other students, their influence extends well beyond their numbers. If the wealthy students also are heavy drinkers, then their combined peer influence tends to raise the overall rate of drinking. Alter selection is therefore of special interest for studies of peer influence. Indeed, it has been a major focus of our joint studies of influence and selection (see Chapters 5, 8, and 10), and the primary theme of Chapter 6, on arrests and peer connections. In this vein, Rulison and her colleagues (2014) used in-degree as an outcome measure in order to test Moffitt's hypothesis that persistent delinquents gain influence over many other youth during adolescence.

Studies from PROSPER Peers have pursued this topic further by testing whether various respondent attributes are associated with choosing friends who engage in risky behavior. In terms of network concepts, this corresponds to Path Y in Figure 1.4, which is the effect of a respondent attribute on alter selection and thus an interaction between the two. For instance, Siennick and her colleagues (2016) investigated whether students who reported more internalizing (depressive and anxiety) symptoms were also more likely to choose friends who used cigarettes, alcohol, and marijuana (see Chapter 7). Other research linking respondent attributes and experiences to choosing particular types of friends appears in Chapter 5 on substance use; Chapter 6 on delinquent behavior, arrests, and school suspensions; Chapter 8 on family relationships; and Chapter 12 on genetics.

Structural selection. The fourth type of selection is structural, which is the influence of surrounding network connections on whether a specific link occurs. Structural selection processes do not involve attributes of the individuals, but rather their connections. Figure 1.4 represents structural selection as an effect from other friendships on the friendship of interest (Path Z). Two examples of structural selection processes are if people are (1) more likely to reciprocate a friendship from someone who chose them or (2) less likely to become friends with someone with whom they share no connections than they are to choose the friend of a friend. Social psychologists and microsociologists have long been interested in how such forms of interdependence affect the patterning of relationships. These ideas trace back to early theoretical work by Simmel about ease of communication and potential for conflict (1950) and by Heider about preference for cognitive consistency (1958). Many common structural patterns also are consistent with a simple process of propinquity (physical and social proximity) because we are likely to become aware of and to encounter people who have connections with our current friends, which then creates the opportunity for them to become our friends as well (Echols & Graham, 2020; Festinger et al., 1950).

Our studies of peer influence that use dynamic network analysis (Steglich et al., 2010) routinely take into account prominent forms of structural selection, but we do so primarily for statistical control, rather than for substantive interests. One PROSPER Peers study with a substantive focus on structural selection shows how interesting the topic can be, however. Kreager and his colleagues (2016) examined the formation of dating relationships in relation to existing patterns of friendship (see Chapter 9). They found that partner choices were less likely to grow out of previous direct or indirect friendships than to stem from having similar levels of prominence or status in the network.

Individuals' positions in network

Figure 1.7 provides an overarching view of the interplay of network concepts and nonnetwork variables across levels of analysis in studies by the PROSPER Peers team. Like the processes of peer influence and friend selection, individual-level network indices are tools for understanding the role of friendship networks in individual adolescents' lives. These indices characterize people's positions in networks (Borgatti et al., 2018), and they are useful for investigating factors that influence both how adolescents are situated in their peer communities and the ways that those positions affect individual outcomes.

Centrality indices capture various aspects of actors' prominence in the network, and they make up a large share of the many indicators of individuals'

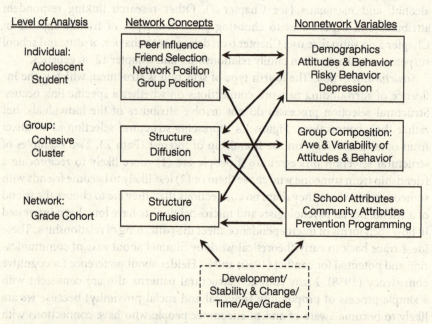

Figure 1.7 Levels of analysis and the interplay of network concepts and nonnetwork variables in PROSPER Peers. Ave = average.

network positions. The simplest are out-degree and in-degree, discussed above under ego and alter selection. More complex examples are Bonacich centrality, which reflects both the number of friends a person has and how many friends those friends have, and betweenness centrality, which indicates an actor's prominence for linking other people in the network. Other indices of individuals' network positions reflect the nature of the connections within an individual's set of immediate friends. These include, for instance, the proportion of the individual's friendships that are reciprocal and the connectedness of these friends with one another, expressed through indices such as transitivity and closeness.

Several studies from PROSPER Peers have addressed research questions about individual-level networks, beginning with those mentioned above that used in-degree as an outcome reflecting status and popularity. In their study of the effect of the transition from middle school to high school, Felmlee and her colleagues (2018) extended this focus by adding isolation (the absence of friendships) as an outcome capturing a lack of engagement and popularity. Chapter 9 compares the network positions of sexual minority and nonminority youth across a variety of these indices. Studies that focused on individual-level network indices as explanatory variables include work on adolescent popularity and young adult sexual behavior (see Chapter 9); isolation and substance use (see Chapter 7); self-harm and young adult depression (see Chapter 7); and adolescent trajectories of popularity predicting substance use (Moody et al., 2011). In addition, Siennick and her colleagues (2017) treated in-degree, isolation, and betweenness centrality as both outcomes and predictors in their investigation of the connection between peer relations and whether students transfer in and out of schools.

Groups within networks

In social network analysis, groups serve as an intermediate level of aggregation between individuals and the full network population (see Figure 1.7). The groups are cohesive clusters of people identified empirically through algorithms that sort individuals into groups by maximizing the number of connections among members of a group compared to their connections with nonmembers (see Chapter 3). The groups provide a means to ask research questions about small communities of friends, including topics such as their social organization, individuals' positions in the groups, and the attributes of their members.

PROSPER Peers' studies have made use of these cohesive groupings in a variety of ways. One set of studies used the groups as a vehicle for studying how the organization of groups varied according to the differing types of members in the group (i.e., the group-level arrow in Figure 1.7, here specifically the association between group structure and group composition). These studies have compared groups with differing levels of delinquency and alcohol use (see Chapter 6), gender composition (Molloy et al., 2014), and depression and anxiety (see Chapter 7). These studies examined how the groups differed in size and in network attributes such as density of connections, reciprocity, and transitivity. They also examined other attributes of the members to see if they might account for those findings. For instance, Kreager and his colleagues (2011) concluded that the somewhat weaker organization of more delinquent groups was likely due to other attributes of the members that predict delinquency, rather than to delinquency itself (see Chapter 5). Also, to address the interesting question of why some adolescents join mixed-gender peer groups and others do not, Molloy and her colleagues (2014) examined which individual attributes predicted future group membership.

Two of our studies investigated friendship groups as a source of influence on their members. The first (Cleveland et al., 2012) examined adolescents' friendship groups as a bridge to indirect influence from other adults, specifically parents of other group members (see Chapter 8). The average of the group members' reports about the parenting they received served as the explanatory variable, comparable to the average of an adolescent's friends in most individual-level studies of peer influence. This approach shifted the focus from influence as a strictly dyadic process between pairs of people to a process impinging on the group as a whole. The second study, by Fisher (2018), investigated variation in the strength of the within-group influence process by analyzing which aspects of group structure predicted levels of group consensus, after controlling for selection into the groups.

An additional topic of interest about cohesive friendship groups is members' positions in their groups and nonmembers' relationships to groups. In Figure 1.7, this topic is shown as one of the individual-level network concepts, and it is analogous to individual positions in the overall network. Among group members, this topic involves structural positions in the group, including how strongly versus weakly they are connected to their groups. Nonmembers also vary in their relationships to groups. Some nonmembers lack connection to any group, while other nonmembers have connections that bridge multiple groups, potentially serving as liaisons between them. We (Osgood et al., 2014) investigated the relationship of these network positions to substance use (see Chapter 5), improving on prior studies of the topic through the strengths of our data set, methodological advances in defining these roles, and strategically using control variables to clarify the meaning of the findings.

Network-level concepts

Our most highly aggregated level of analysis is the full friendship network for the grade cohort of a school (the bottom row of Figure 1.7). The PROSPER research design includes eight waves of full network data for two grade cohorts in each of 27 small school districts, which provides a sizable sample of network and a strong basis for systematic analyses at this level. Social network analysis provides many network-level indices for characterizing the organization of full networks (see Chapter 3), and they cover several general themes: The overall level of connectedness can be dense or sparse; the connections can be widely dispersed and diffuse versus tightly clustered; connections may be highly concentrated on relatively few people (centralized) or more equally distributed. Temkin and her colleagues

(2018) used such indices to determine how transitions between levels of schooling (elementary to middle school to high school) affect friendship networks. In the study of evolving similarity between friends mentioned previously (Osgood et al., 2022; see Chapters 4 and 5), correlations between friends served as a network-level outcome variable. The analyses examined grade cohort size and attribute variability as mediators of trends across grades in similarity.

Network analytic tools also enable researchers to formulate custom indices to suit specific research questions, and our work has made good use of these with regard to diffusion processes. For instance, to examine the effect of the PROSPER prevention program on friendship networks we (Osgood, Feinberg, et al., 2013) developed indices of each network's potential for peer influence toward risky behavior that reflect the association between network centrality and risky behavior (see Chapter 11). Also in this vein, Rulison, Gest, and Osgood (2015) designed a set of indices for the potential of beneficial program effects to diffuse throughout a school friendship network, and they tested them for the PROSPER schools (see Chapter 11). These indices take into account a network's organization and the network locations of students who did and did not participate in the program.

An especially interesting example of network-level analysis of diffusion is McMillan and Schaefer's (2021) use of empirically grounded simulations to study the likely effects of alternative targeting strategies for programs to prevent adolescent alcohol use (see Chapter 11). They based their simulations on PROSPER's observed friendship networks and empirical estimates of selection and influence processes. By conducting simulations of unfolding selection and influence processes to represent diffusion, they estimated how much program impact would result from targeting students in different network positions and in the context of different network conditions.

Development and change

The theme of development and change overlays PROSPER Peers' foundation of network concepts. The PROSPER network data span sixth through twelfth grades to cover almost the full range of adolescence. During our respondents' progression from the end of middle childhood to the threshold of emerging adulthood, rates of problem behavior progress from low (delinquency, alcohol use) or even rare (marijuana use, sexual intercourse) to relatively common. Change and development are necessarily prominent themes for all the topical areas of PROSPER Peers.

This theme appears in our work in a variety of ways. For instance, the Jacobsen study (2020; and see Chapter 6) examines the effects of school sanctions in terms of stability versus change in adolescents' friendships. Some of our studies address developmental change in the standard form of describing and explaining changing levels across ages or grades, for instance for similarity between friends (Osgood et al., 2022; see Chapters 4 and 5) and for the strength of friendship selection and peer influence processes (Ragan, 2020, see Chapter 5). Rulison and her colleagues (2014) elaborated this approach by examining differential trends in popularity across ages for adolescents in the three categories of Moffitt's (1993) delinquency typology. At the community level, a pair of studies has examined how the local timing of school transitions altered age trends in friendships, one at the network level (Temkin et al., 2018) and the other at the individual level (Felmlee et al., 2018). Molloy and her colleagues (2014) studied development as the evolving interplay of individuals and cohesive friendship groups as they probed the growing prominence of mixed-gender groups across adolescence. Moody and his colleagues (2011) took a particularly interesting approach by focusing on changing popularity as a potential influence on substance use, and they summarized individuals' progressions of popularity as trajectories.

CONCLUSION

This introductory chapter provides background information that will help readers understand and appreciate the rest of volume. It has covered the history of the PROSPER Peers project's growth out of a unique opportunity created by the PROSPER prevention trial. I have stressed the special value of the combination of having adolescents name their friends and PROSPER's unique research design. The chapter emphasizes themes from the study of peer influence, which is the background I brought to the project. The bulk of the chapter laid out our conceptual framework, which uses major concepts from social network analysis to organize the range of research questions addressed across the empirical work of PROSPER Peers, presented in Chapters 5 through 12. Next, Chapter 2 provides an overview of the goals, methods, and results of the PROSPER prevention trial. Chapter 3 discusses major aspects of our research methods, including greater detail about network concepts and their measurement, and Chapter 4 provides a descriptive picture of the peer networks in the PROSPER schools.

I hope you find this volume rewarding and useful. It has been a privilege to be part of this research team along with so many talented, thoughtful, committed, and collegial scholars, young and old. I am proud of what we have contributed to the growing wave of network-based research on adolescents' social worlds.

REFERENCES

Alexander, C., Piazza, M., Mekos, D., & Valente, T. (2001). Peers, schools, and adolescent cigarette smoking. *Journal of Adolescent Health, 29*(1), 22–30.
Bandura, A. (1977). *Social learning theory*. Prentice Hall.
Barabási, A.-L. (2003). *Linked: How everything is connected to everything else and what it means for business, science, and everyday life*. Plume.
Bauman, K. E., & Ennett, S. T. (1994). Peer influence on adolescent drug use. *American Psychologist, 49*, 820–882.

Bauman, K. E., & Ennett, S. T. (1996). On the importance of peer influence for adolescent drug use: Commonly neglected considerations. *Addiction, 91*, 185–198.

Bernard, T. J., & Kurlychek, M. C. (2010). *The cycle of juvenile justice*. Oxford University Press.

Bernasco, W., Ruiter, S., Bruinsma, G. J., Pauwels, L. J., & Weerman, F. M. (2013). Situational causes of offending: A fixed-effects analysis of space–time budget data. *Criminology, 51*(4), 895–926.

Berndt, T. J., Hawkins, J. A., & Hoyle, S. G. (1986). Changes in friendship during a school year: Effects on children's and adolescents' impressions of friendship and sharing with friends. *Child Development, 57*(5), 1284–1297.

Blyth, D. A., Simmons, R. G., & Carlton-Ford, S. (1983). The adjustment of early adolescents to school transitions. *The Journal of Early Adolescence, 3*(1–2), 105–120.

Borgatti, S. P., Everett, M. G., & Johnson, J. C. (2018). *Analyzing social networks*. Sage.

Brown, B. B. (1990). *Peer groups and peer cultures*. Harvard University Press.

Buhrmester, D. (1990). Intimacy of friendship, interpersonal competence, and adjustment during preadolescence and adolescence. *Child Development, 61*, 1101–1111.

Bukowski, W. M., Newcomb, A. J., & Hartup, W. W. (Eds.) (1996). *The company they keep: Friendship during childhood and adolescence*. Cambridge University Press.

Burgess, R., & Akers, R. (1966). A differential association-reinforcement theory of criminal behavior. *Social Problems, 14*, 128–147.

Burk, W. J., Van Der Vorst, H., Kerr, M., & Stattin, H. (2012). Alcohol use and friendship dynamics: Selection and socialization in early-, middle-, and late-adolescent peer networks. *Journal of Studies on Alcohol and Drugs, 73*(1), 89–98.

Byrne, D., & Blaylock, B. (1963). Similarity and assumed similarity of attitudes between husbands and wives. *Journal of Abnormal and Social Psychology, 67*, 636–640.

Cairns, R. B., & Cairns, B. D. (1995). *Lifelines and risks*. Cambridge.

Cairns, R. B., Cairns, B. D., Neckerman, H. J., Gest, S. D., & Gariepy, J.-L. (1988). Social networks and aggressive behavior: Peer support or peer rejection? *Developmental Psychology, 24*, 815–823.

Cartwright, D., & Harary, F. (1956). Structural balance: A generalization of Heider's theory. *Psychological Review, 63*(5), 277.

Chapple, C. L. (2005). Self-control, peer relations, and delinquency. *Justice Quarterly, 22*(1), 89–106.

Cleveland, M. J., Feinberg, M. E., Osgood, D. W., & Moody, J. (2012). Do peers' parents matter? A new link between positive parenting and adolescent substance use. *Journal of Studies on Alcohol and Drugs, 73*(3), 423–433.

Cloward, R. A., & Ohlin, L. E. (1960). *Delinquency and opportunity: A theory of delinquent gangs*. Free Press.

Cohen, A. (1955). *Delinquent boys*. Free Press.

Coleman, J. S. (1961). *The adolescent society*. Free Press.

Coleman, J. S., Katz, E., & Menzel, H. (1966). *Medical innovation: A diffusion study*. Bobbs-Merrill Company.

Crosnoe, R. (2011). *Fitting in, standing out: Navigating the social challenges of high school to get an education*. Cambridge University Press.

Dijkstra, J. K., Kretschmer, T., Pattiselanno, K., Franken, A., Harakeh, Z., Vollebergh, W., & Veenstra, R. (2015). Explaining adolescents' delinquency and substance use: A test of the maturity gap: The SNARE study. *Journal of Research in Crime and Delinquency, 52*(5), 747–767.

Echols, L., & Graham, S. (2020). Meeting in the middle: The role of mutual biracial friends in cross-race friendships. *Child Development, 91*(2), 401–416.

Eckert, P. (1989). *Jocks and burnouts: Social categories and identity in the high school.* Teachers College Press.

Elliott, D. S., Huizinga, D., & Menard, S. (1989). *Multiple problem youth: Delinquency, substance use, and mental health problems.* Springer-Verlag.

Ennett, S. T., & Bauman, K. E. (1993). Peer group structure and adolescent cigarette smoking: A social network analysis. *Journal of Health and Social Behavior, 34*, 226–236.

Ennett, S. T., & Bauman, K. E. (1994). The contribution of influence and selection to adolescent peer group homogeneity: The case of adolescent cigarette smoking. *Journal of Personality and Social Psychology, 67*, 653–663.

Erickson, M. L., & Jensen, G. F. (1977). Delinquency is still group behavior!: Toward revitalizing the group premise in the sociology of deviance. *Journal of Criminal Law and Criminology, 68*, 262–273.

Felmlee, D., & Faris, R. (2016). Toxic ties: Networks of friendship, dating, and cyber victimization. *Social Psychology Quarterly, 79*(3), 243–262.

Felmlee, D., McMillan, C., Inara Rodis, P., & Osgood, D. W. (2018). Falling behind: Lingering costs of the high school transition for youth friendships and grades. *Sociology of Education, 91*(2), 159–182.

Felson, M., & Gottfredson, M. (1984). Social indicators of adolescent activities near peers and parents. *Journal of Marriage and the Family, 46*(3), 709–714.

Festinger, L., Schachter, S., & Back, K. (1950). The Spatial Ecology of Group Formation. In L. Festinger, S. Schachter, & K. Back (Eds.), *Social pressure in informal groups* (pp. 141–161). Chapter 4.

Fisher, J. C. (2018). Exit, cohesion, and consensus: Social psychological moderators of consensus among adolescent peer groups. *Social Currents, 5*(1), 49–66.

Friedkin, N. E. (1998). *A structural theory of social influence.* Cambridge University Press.

Fujimoto, K., Snijders, T. A., & Valente, T. W. (2017). Popularity breeds contempt: The evolution of reputational dislike relations and friendships in high school. *Social Networks, 48*, 100–109.

Gest, S. D., Osgood, D. W., Feinberg, M., Bierman, K. L., & Moody, J. (2011). Strengthening prevention program theories and evaluations: Contributions from social network analysis. *Prevention Science, 12*(4), 349–360.

Glueck, S., & Glueck, E. (1950). *Unraveling juvenile delinquency.* Harvard University Press.

Gibbs, J. P. (1981). *Norms, deviance, and social control: Conceptual matters.* Elsevier Science Limited.

Gold, M., & Osgood, D. W. (1992). *Personality and peer influence in juvenile corrections.* Greenwood Press.

Gottfredson, M. R., & Hirschi, T. (1990). *A general theory of crime.* Stanford University Press.

Graham, S., Munniksma, A., & Juvonen, J. (2014). Psychosocial benefits of cross-ethnic friendships in urban middle schools. *Child Development, 85*(2), 469–483.

Haynie, D. L. (2001). Delinquent peers revisited: Does network structure matter? *American Journal of Sociology, 106*, 1013–1057.

Haynie, D. L., & Osgood, D. W. (2005). Reconsidering peers and delinquency: How do peers matter? *Social Forces, 84*(2), 1109–1130.

Heider, F. (1958). *The psychology of interpersonal relations*. Psychology Press.

Henneberger, A. K., Gest, S. D., & Zadzora, K. M. (2019). Preventing adolescent substance use: A content analysis of peer processes targeted within universal school-based programs. *The Journal of Primary Prevention, 40*(2), 213–230.

Hirschi, T. (1969). *Causes of delinquency*. University of California Press.

Hirschi, T., & Gottfredson, M. (1983). Age and the explanation of crime. *American Journal of Sociology, 89*(3), 552–584.

Hoeben, E. M., Meldrum, R. C., Walker, D. A., & Young, J. T. (2016). The role of peer delinquency and unstructured socializing in explaining delinquency and substance use: A state-of-the-art review. *Journal of Criminal Justice, 47*, 108–122.

Hoeben, E. M., Osgood, D. W., Siennick, S. E., & Weerman, F. M. (2021). Hanging out with the wrong crowd? The role of unstructured socializing in adolescents' specialization in delinquency and substance use. *Journal of Quantitative Criminology, 37*(1), 141–177.

Huitsing, G., Snijders, T. A. B., Van Duijn, M. A. J., & Veenstra, R. (2014). Victims, bullies, and their defenders: A longitudinal study of the co-evolution of positive and negative networks. *Development and Psychopathology, 26*, 645–659.

Jacobsen, W. C. (2020). School punishment and interpersonal exclusion: Rejection, withdrawal, and separation from friends. *Criminology, 58*(1), 35–69.

Jessor, R., & Jessor, S. L. (1977). *Problem behavior and psychosocial development: A longitudinal study of youth*. Academic Press.

Jussim, L., & Osgood, D. W. (1989). Influence and similarity among friends: An integrative model applied to incarcerated adolescents. *Social Psychology Quarterly, 52*, 98–112.

Kadushin, C. (2012). *Understanding social networks: Theories, concepts, and findings*. Oxford University Press.

Kandel, D. B. (1978). Homophily, selection and socialization in adolescent friendships. *American Journal of Sociology, 84*, 427–436.

Kandel, D. B. (1996). The parental and peer contexts of adolescent deviance: An algebra of interpersonal influences. *Journal of Drug Issues, 26*, 289–315.

Kerr, M., Stattin, H., & Kiesner, J. (2007). Peers and problem behavior: Have we missed something? In R. C. M. E. Engels, M. Kerr, & H. Stattin (Eds.), Friends, lovers, and groups: Key relationships in adolescence (pp. 125–153). John Wiley & Sons Ltd.

Knoke, D., & Yang, S. (2019). *Social network analysis*. Sage Publications.

Kreager, D. A., Haynie, D. L., & Hopfer, S. (2013). Dating and substance use in adolescent peer networks: A replication and extension. *Addiction, 108*(3), 638–647.

Kreager, D. A., Molloy, L. E., Moody, J., & Feinberg, M. E. (2016). Friends first? The peer network origins of adolescent dating. *Journal of Research on Adolescence, 26*(2), 257–269.

Kreager, D. A., Rulison, K., & Moody, J. (2011). Delinquency and the structure of adolescent peer groups. *Criminology, 49*(1), 95–127.

Kreager, D. A., Staff, J., Gauthier, R., Lefkowitz, E. S., & Feinberg, M. E. (2016). The double standard at sexual debut: Gender, sexual behavior and adolescent peer acceptance. *Sex Roles, 75*(7), 377–392.

Larson, R. W., Richards, M. H., Moneta, G., Holmbeck, G., & Duckett, E. (1996). Changes in adolescents' daily interactions with their families from ages 10 to 18: Disengagement and transformation. *Developmental Psychology, 32*(4), 744–754.

Laub, J. H., & Sampson, R. J. (2003). *Shared beginnings, divergent lives: Delinquent boys to age 70.* Harvard University Press.

Laursen, B., Hartup, W. W., & Koplas, A. L. (1996). Towards understanding peer conflict. *Merrill-Palmer Quarterly, 42*(1), 76–102.

Lewinsohn, P. M., Clarke, G. N., Seeley, J. R., & Rohde, P. (1994). Major depression in community adolescents: Age at onset, episode duration, and time to recurrence. *Journal of the American Academy of Child & Adolescent Psychiatry, 33*(6), 809–818.

McMillan, C., Felmlee, D., & Osgood, D. W. (2018). Peer influence, friend selection, and gender: How network processes shape adolescent smoking, drinking, and delinquency. *Social Networks, 55,* 86–96.

McMillan, C., & Schaefer, D. R. (2021). Comparing targeting strategies for network-based adolescent drinking interventions: A simulation approach. *Social Science & Medicine, 282,* 114136.

McPherson, M., Smith-Lovin, L., & Cook, J. M. (2001). Birds of a feather: Homophily in social networks. *Annual Review of Sociology, 27*(1), 415–444.

Mead, G. H. (1934). *Mind, self and society.* University of Chicago Press.

Merton, R. K., & Kitt, A. S. (1950). Contributions to the theory of reference-group behavior. In G. E. Swanson, T. M. Newcomb, & E. L. Hartley (Eds.), *Readings in Social Psychology* (2nd ed., pp. 430–444). Hold, Rinehart, and Winston.

Miech, R. A., Johnston, L. D., O'Malley, P. M., Bachman, J. G., Schulenberg, J. E., & Patrick, M. E. (2021). *Monitoring the future national survey results on drug use, 1975–2020: Volume I, Secondary school students.* Institute for Social Research, the University of Michigan.

Moffitt, T. E. (1993). Adolescence-limited and life-course-persistent antisocial behavior: A developmental taxonomy. *Psychological Review, 100*(4), 674.

Molloy, L. E., Gest, S. D., Feinberg, M. E., & Osgood, D. W. (2014). Emergence of mixed-sex friendship groups during adolescence: Developmental associations with substance use and delinquency. *Developmental Psychology, 50*(11), 2449.

Moody, J. (2001). Race, school integration, and friendship segregation in America. *American Journal of Sociology, 107*(3), 679–716.

Moody, J., Brynildsen, W. D., Osgood, D. W., Feinberg, M. E., & Gest, S. (2011). Popularity trajectories and substance use in early adolescence. *Social Networks, 33*(2), 101–112.

Moody, J., Feinberg, M. E., Osgood, D. W., & Gest, S. D. (2010). Mining the network: Peers and adolescent health. *Journal of Adolescent Health, 47*(4), 324–326.

Moreno, J. L. (1953). *Who shall survive?* Beacon House Press.

Morgan, S. L., & Winship, C. (2015). *Counterfactuals and causal inference.* Cambridge University Press.

Newcomb, T. M. (1961). *The acquaintance process.* Holt, Rinehart, and Winston.

Oetting, E. R., & Beauvais, F. (1986). Peer cluster theory: Drugs and the adolescent. *Journal of Counseling and Development, 65,* 17–22.

Osgood, D. W., Anderson, A. L., & Shaffer, J. N. (2005). Unstructured leisure in the after-school hours. In J. L. Mahoney, R. W. Larson, & J. S. Eccles (Eds.), *Organized activities as contexts of development* (pp. 57–76). Psychology Press.

Osgood, D. W., Feinberg, M. E., Gest, S. D., Moody, J., Ragan, D. T., Spoth, R., Greenberg, M., & Redmond, C. (2013). Effects of PROSPER on the influence potential of prosocial versus antisocial youth in adolescent friendship networks. *Journal of Adolescent Health, 53*(2), 174–179.

Osgood, D. W., Feinberg, M. E., Wallace, L. N., & Moody, J. (2014). Friendship group position and substance use. *Addictive Behaviors, 39*(5), 923–933.

Osgood, D. W., Foster, E. M., Flanagan, C., & Ruth, G. R. (2005). *On your own without a net: The transition to adulthood for vulnerable populations.* University of Chicago Press.

Osgood, D. W., Ragan, D. T., Dole, J. L., & D. A. Kreager. (2022). Similarity of friends versus nonfriends in adolescence: Developmental patterns and ecological influences. *Developmental Psychology, 58*(7), 1386–1401.

Osgood, D. W., Ragan, D. T., Wallace, L., Gest, S. D., Feinberg, M. E., & Moody, J. (2013). Peers and the emergence of alcohol use: Influence and selection processes in adolescent friendship networks. *Journal of Research on Adolescence, 23*(3), 500–512.

Osgood, D. W., Wilson, J. K., O'Malley, P. M., Bachman, J. G., & Johnston, L. D. (1996). Routine activities and individual deviant behavior. *American Sociological Review, 61*(4), 635–655.

Patterson, G. R. (1986). Performance models for antisocial boys. *American Psychologist, 41*, 432–444.

Payne, D. C., & Cornwell, B. (2007). Reconsidering peer influences on delinquency: Do less proximate contacts matter? *Journal of Quantitative Criminology, 23*(2), 127–149.

Perry, C. L., Williams, C. L., Veblen-Mortenson, S., & Toomey, T. L. (1996). Project Northland: Outcomes of a community wide alcohol use prevention program during early adolescence. *American Journal of Public Health, 86*, 956–965.

Ragan, D. T. (2014). Revisiting "what they think": Adolescent drinking and the importance of peer beliefs. *Criminology, 52*(3), 488–513.

Ragan, D. T. (2020). Similarity between deviant peers: Developmental trends in influence and selection. *Criminology, 58*(2), 336–369.

Ragan, D. T., Osgood, D. W., & Feinberg, M. E. (2014). Friends as a bridge to parental influence: Implications for adolescent alcohol use. *Social Forces, 92*(3), 1061–1085.

Reiss, A. J., Jr., & Rhodes, A. L. (1964). An empirical test of differential association theory. *Journal of Research in Crime and Delinquency, 1*, 5–18.

Robins, L. N. (1966). *Deviant children grown up: A sociological and psychiatric study of sociopathic personality.* Williams and Wilkins.

Rubin, K. H., Bukowski, W. M., & Bowker, J. C. (2015). Children in peer groups. In M. H. Bornstein, T. Leventhal, & R. M. Lerner (Eds.), *Handbook of child psychology and developmental science: Ecological settings and processes* (pp. 175–222). John Wiley & Sons Inc.

Rulison, K. L., Feinberg, M., Gest, S. D., & Osgood, D. W. (2015). Diffusion of intervention effects: The impact of a family-based substance use prevention program on friends of participants. *Journal of Adolescent Health, 57*(4), 433–440.

Rulison, K. L., Gest, S. D., & Osgood, D. W. (2015). Adolescent peer networks and the potential for the diffusion of intervention effects. *Prevention Science, 16*(1), 133–144.

Rulison, K. L., Kreager, D. A., & Osgood, D. W. (2014). Delinquency and peer acceptance in adolescence: A within-person test of Moffitt's hypotheses. *Developmental Psychology, 50*(11), 2437.

Shaw, C. R., & McKay, H. D. (1942). *Juvenile delinquency and urban areas.* University of Chicago Press.

Sherif, M. (1948). *An outline of social psychology.* Harper and Row.

Siennick, S. E., & Osgood, D. W. (2012). Hanging out with which friends? Friendship-level predictors of unstructured and unsupervised socializing in adolescence. *Journal of Research on Adolescence*, 22(4), 646–661.

Siennick, S. E., Widdowson, A. O., & Ragan, D. T. (2017). New students' peer integration and exposure to deviant peers: Spurious effects of school moves? *The Journal of Early Adolescence*, 37(9), 1254–1279.

Siennick, S. E., Widdowson, A. O., Woessner, M., & Feinberg, M. E. (2016). Internalizing symptoms, peer substance use, and substance use initiation. *Journal of Research on Adolescence*, 26(4), 645–657.

Simmel, G. (1950). The triad. In Kurt Wolff (Ed.), *The sociology of Georg Simmel* (pp. 145–169). Simon and Schuster.

Short, J. F., and F. L. Strodtbeck. (1965). *Group process and gang delinquency*. Chicago: University of Chicago Press.

Snijders, T. A. (2001). The statistical evaluation of social network dynamics. *Sociological Methodology*, 31(1), 361–395.

Steglich, C., Snijders, T. A., & Pearson, M. (2010). Dynamic networks and behavior: Separating selection from influence. *Sociological Methodology*, 40(1), 329–393.

Sutherland, E. H. (1939). *Principles of criminology* (4th ed.). J. P. Lippincott.

Tannenbaum, F. (1938). *Crime and the community*. Columbia University Press.

Temkin, D. A., Gest, S. D., Osgood, D. W., Feinberg, M., & Moody, J. (2018). Social network implications of normative school transitions in non-urban school districts. *Youth & Society*, 50(4), 462–484.

Thornberry, T. P., Krohn, M. D., Lizotte, A. J., & Chard-Wierschem, D. (1993). The role of juvenile gangs in facilitating delinquent behavior. *Journal of Research in Crime and Delinquency*, 30(1), 55–87.

Thrasher, F. M. (1927). *The gang: A study of 1,313 gangs in Chicago*. University of Chicago Press.

Valente, T. W. (2010). *Social networks and health: Models, methods, and applications*. Oxford University Press.

Valente, T. W., Hoffman, B. R., Ritt-Olson, A., Lichtman, K., & Johnson, C. A. (2003). Effects of a social-network method for group assignment strategies on peer-led tobacco prevention programs in schools. *American Journal of Public Health*, 93(11), 1837–1843.

Valente, T. W., & Pumpuang, P. (2007). Identifying opinion leaders to promote behavior change. *Health Education & Behavior*, 34(6), 881–896.

Veenstra, R., & Laninga-Wijnen, L. (2022). Peer network studies and interventions in adolescence. *Current Opinion in Psychology*, 44, 157–163.

Veenstra, R., Lindenberg, S., Zijlstra, B. J., De Winter, A. F., Verhulst, F. C., & Ormel, J. (2007). The dyadic nature of bullying and victimization: Testing a dual-perspective theory. *Child Development*, 78(6), 1843–1854.

Warr, M. (2002). *Companions in crime: The social aspects of criminal conduct*. Cambridge University Press.

Warr, M. (2005). Making delinquent friends: Adult supervision and children's affiliations. *Criminology*, 43(1), 77–106.

Watts, D. J. (2003). *Six degrees: The science of a connected age*. Norton.

Weerman, F. M. (2011). Delinquent peers in context: A longitudinal network analysis of selection and influence effects. *Criminology*, 49(1), 253–286.

Weerman, F. M., & Smeenk, W. H. (2005). Peer similarity in delinquency for different types of friends: A comparison using two measurement methods. *Criminology, 43*(2), 499-524.

Wesche, R., Kreager, D. A., & Lefkowitz, E. S. (2019). Sources of social influence on adolescents' alcohol use. *Journal of Research on Adolescence, 29*(4), 984-1000.

Widdowson, A. O., Ranson, J. A., Siennick, S. E., Rulison, K. L., & Osgood, D. W. (2020). Exposure to persistently delinquent peers and substance use onset: A test of Moffitt's social mimicry hypothesis. *Crime & Delinquency, 66*(3), 420-445.

Wigfield, A., Eccles, J. S., Fredricks, J. A., Simpkins, S., Roeser, R. W., & Schiefele, U. (2015). Development of achievement motivation and engagement. In M. E. Lamb & R. M. Lerner (Eds.), *Handbook of child psychology and developmental science: Socioemotional processes* (pp. 657-700). John Wiley & Sons Inc.

Wilcox, S., & Udry, J. R. (1986). Autism and accuracy in adolescent perceptions of friends' sexual attitudes and behaviors. *Journal of Applied Social Psychology, 16*, 361-374.

Young, J. T., Rebellon, C. J., Barnes, J. C., & Weerman, F. M. (2014). Unpacking the black box of peer similarity in deviance: Understanding the mechanisms linking personal behavior, peer behavior, and perceptions. *Criminology, 52*(1), 60-86.

Zimmer-Gembeck, M. J., & Helfand, M. (2008). Ten years of longitudinal research on U.S. adolescent sexual behavior: Developmental correlates of sexual intercourse, and the importance of age, gender and ethnic background. *Developmental Review, 28*(2), 153-224.

2

Overview of the PROSPER prevention trial's rationale, methods, and findings

The context for the friendship network study

RICHARD SPOTH, LISA M. SCHAINKER, MARK GREENBERG, AND JANET WELSH ■

INTRODUCTION

Achieving a public health impact through reduction of adolescent substance misuse and associated problem behaviors has been greatly impeded by the lack of infrastructures supporting effective evidence-based intervention (EBI) delivery mechanisms, and, as a result, these programs don't reach a large share of U.S. communities (U.S. Department of Health and Human Services & Office of the Surgeon General, 2016). Emerging literature in the 1990s highlighted the need to rigorously test the effectiveness of EBIs delivered by community-based coalitions and partnerships. Our research team applied lessons learned from earlier randomized controlled prevention trials evaluating youth and family-focused EBIs during the 1990s, in which program implementation was assisted by the Cooperative Extension System (CES; also abbreviated "Extension") at land grant universities (see Spoth, 2007, for a summary).

Stated briefly, our primary focus has been to refine and test a partnership-based delivery system for sustained, high-quality implementation of youth and family EBIs designed to reduce youth substance misuse and associated problem behaviors; the delivery system is called PROSPER (Promoting School-community-university Partnerships to Enhance Resilience). PROSPER was

Richard Spoth, Lisa M. Schainker, Mark Greenberg, and Janet Welsh, *Overview of the PROSPER prevention trial's rationale, methods, and findings*. In: *Teen Friendship Networks, Development, and Risky Behavior*. Edited by: Mark E. Feinberg and D. Wayne Osgood, Oxford University Press. © Mark E. Feinberg and D. Wayne Osgood 2024.
DOI: 10.1093/oso/9780197602317.003.0002

designed to be integrated within a state's CES, which is the land grant university system for outreach and knowledge transfer that has reach into all counties in every state. The CES offers a wide variety of programming for youth, adults, and families. Utilizing the reach of the CES linked with public schools and community service organizations, PROSPER facilitates ongoing technical assistance (TA) to organize and support community-based prevention coalitions (known as local PROSPER teams) focused on partnership development, EBI implementation, and sustainability. The implementation quality and outcomes-related evidence from the randomized controlled study of 28 rural communities indicates the delivery system worked as designed. Moreover, a family of PROSPER studies, including the original trial and multiple spinoff studies, has contributed over 125 published articles to the science of prevention. One of the most productive lines of research involves friendship networks, as is described in detail in this volume.

To provide the research context for this volume, this chapter describes (1) the knowledge gaps addressed by the PROSPER prevention trial; (2) the conceptual underpinnings of PROSPER's intervention model and posited pathways of developmental change; (3) the PROSPER trial's design, samples, and study procedures; (4) PROSPER's intervention and implementation models; (5) and findings to date from the PROSPER trial and from spinoff studies, other than the friendship network investigations covered elsewhere in this volume.

The goals of the PROSPER prevention trial focused on evaluating the longitudinal effects of a partnership-delivered, multicomponent intervention on substance misuse and other problem behaviors, along with the processes producing those effects. To accomplish these aims, the PROSPER trial spanned the developmental phases of early adolescence, adolescence, and emerging adulthood. Essentially, results from the PROSPER trial indicate effectiveness across a number of key domains central to PROSPER's purpose: effective mobilization and functioning of community teams; relatively high participation in EBIs; long-term, high-quality EBI implementation; sustainability of teams and EBIs; increases in community social capital; and economic analyses indicating that delivery of EBIs through PROSPER is more cost-efficient than typical implementation of those EBIs. Most importantly, the findings include an array of long-term, positive outcomes for participating youth.

In sum, this chapter presents the rationale, research aims, design, and outcomes of the PROSPER trial in order to provide background information and research context for the friendship network studies presented in the following chapters.

SUMMARY OF SIGNIFICANCE AND GAPS ADDRESSED

Overview

Overall, the significance of the PROSPER trial is best conveyed by its unique combination of salient features. It is an effectiveness trial conducted in "real-world" conditions, grounded in the land grant university CES, which has been characterized as the world's largest informal education and dissemination system. This rigorous trial used a cohort sequential, randomized controlled design, with a large sample of school districts and student participants. It applied a multimethod, multi-informant measurement approach, including peer nominations and genetic data collection. Importantly, data collection occurred across three developmental stages to examine a wide range of substance misuse outcomes, along with youth skills and behaviors that were expected to mediate those outcomes. This evaluation design allowed for close examination of hypothesized primary outcomes, moderating or mediating variables possibly affecting the outcomes, and intervention crossover effects (effects on nontargeted outcomes). In addition, it addressed translation science questions concerning the quality of intervention implementation and sustainability under real-world conditions. Finally, it addressed a number of critically important gaps in the research literature.

Need for family- and youth-focused EBIs

Epidemiological data over the last three decades have underscored a critical need for the diffusion of family- and youth-focused EBIs designed to reduce risk for adolescent substance misuse and other problem behaviors that carry risks into adulthood, *particularly in underserved rural areas* (Spoth, 2007). The literature (e.g., see reviews in Carnegie Council on Adolescent Development, 1995; U.S. Department of Health and Human Services & Office of the Surgeon General, 2016) highlights how prevalence rates of youth substance misuse, conduct problem behaviors, and related concerns like academic failure are unacceptably high, with problematic health, social, and economic consequences. The literature also documents that early adolescence is associated with substance experimentation, which predicts long-term use patterns, as well as increases in conduct problem behaviors and early sexual activity. Early adolescence also is an important period for bolstering protective factors, including youth competencies and coping skills. Universal school-based EBIs that promote competencies in all students (e.g., peer refusal, problem-solving skills) have been effective in reducing youth problem behaviors, while universal family-focused EBIs address powerful risk and protective factors that originate in the family (Dishion et al., 1991; Spoth, Kavanagh, & Dishion, 2002; Spoth & Redmond, 2002). Notably, foundational research prior to the PROSPER trial indicated that combining universal family-focused and school-based interventions can positively influence these two primary socializing environments of youth in a complementary fashion, thereby building youth competencies and reducing adolescent substance misuse, along with associated conduct problem behaviors (Spoth et al., 2005).

CES and public schools: Underutilized EBI delivery infrastructures

The literature over the past two decades makes a compelling case for more rigorous study of the role of community coalitions in the diffusion of EBIs, reflecting the difficulty of evaluating community partnerships (Kreuter et al., 2000; Roussos & Fawcett, 2000; U.S. Department of Health and Human Services & Office of the Surgeon General, 2016). Yet, most school and community-level prevention efforts lacked systematic evaluation or evidence of effectiveness (e.g., Rohrbach et al., 1996). There have been few randomized controlled trials evaluating the effectiveness of prevention partnerships and even fewer longitudinal studies of their life cycle and context (Flanagan et al., 2018).

There have been especially clear gaps in the study of effective family- and youth-focused EBI *delivery systems*. Although there has been an increasing number of prevention initiatives that link school-based and family-focused EBIs (U.S. Department of Health and Human Services & Office of the Surgeon General, 2016), these studies have not adequately studied the effects of EBIs in schools and communities when managed by community teams led by representatives of the CES and public schools. PROSPER was intended to be an innovation that would take better advantage of CES and public school infrastructures that have been underutilized for promotion and dissemination of EBIs (Grumbach & Mold, 2009; Rohrbach et al., 1996; Spoth & Greenberg, 2011). Further, around the time the PROSPER trial began, EBIs had not been widely adopted in school and community settings (Gottfredson, Wilson, & Najaka, 2003; Hallfors et al., 2002). Even when schools and communities utilized EBIs, it was difficult for them to access sufficient TA and other resources needed for high-quality implementation and sustainability (Adelman & Taylor, 2003), partially because of challenges in working with scientists to evaluate programs (Spoth & Greenberg, 2005).

The PROSPER trial had the bold goal of applying a rigorous research design to the evaluation of an innovative but complex, multicomponent intervention focusing on universal EBIs delivered via linked CES and public school systems. The CES historically has been very successful with translating science into practice in the United States, especially in rural communities (Grumbach & Mold, 2009). It has a set of TA systems for county-based agents, including university-supported regional coordinators, program directors, and CES faculty/state specialists in multiple content domains (Halpert & Sharp, 1991). To take advantage of these resources, the PROSPER project provided CES personnel with training and experience in EBI implementation and other aspects of prevention science (e.g., evaluation and sustainability). Schools, on the other hand, often lack the expertise, personnel, and other resources needed to provide effective, high-quality prevention programs and may have particular difficulty with family outreach (Adelman & Taylor, 2003). The PROSPER project provided support in these areas to schools.

Gaps in knowledge of what mediates and moderates intervention effects on outcomes

The PROSPER trial also was designed to advance understanding of ways by which EBIs produce youth and family outcomes, including mechanisms and pathways of intervention effects. Although there were some controlled efficacy studies before the PROSPER trial that had examined mediating factors of EBIs, pathways of intervention effects on proximal outcomes (e.g., peer influences) and on more distal outcomes (e.g., use of marijuana in high school) had not been replicated under "real-world" implementation conditions. Research of this kind remains relatively rare (e.g., U.S. Department of Health and Human Services & Office of the Surgeon General, 2016).

PROSPER also focused on understanding broad public health impact potential by examining whether universal preventive interventions can produce positive effects across levels of individual youth risk. Examination of "risk-related moderation" helps to determine whether lower and higher risk subgroups benefit equally well from an intervention. This issue is important because the public health value of the universal delivery system would be greatest if both higher and lower risk participants exhibited benefits, even if these effects were not entirely equal.

When the PROSPER trial began, there was limited research on risk moderation of school-based interventions (e.g., C. H. Brown & Liao, 1999; Stoolmiller et al., 2000), indicating compensatory effects in some cases—showing greater benefit for higher risk subgroups. Less work had examined risk moderation of family-focused interventions for general populations. Most studies of universal family-focused EBIs have found no risk moderation of outcomes; however, when found, they suggest greater effects for higher risk youth (Spoth & Redmond, 2002; Spoth et al., 1998, 2006). It was unclear, however, if such results would persist when recruitment and implementation quality were managed and sustained by local teams (vs. by researchers); the PROSPER prevention trial was well poised to address that question.

CONCEPTUAL UNDERPINNINGS: INTERVENTION AND DEVELOPMENTAL CHANGE MODELS

Here, we summarize basic conceptual underpinnings for (1) our intervention model leveraging the CES as infrastructure for supporting a prevention delivery system, based on theoretical work concerning diffusion of innovation, and (2) our model of intervention-related pathways of developmental change.

EBI diffusion based in education systems

The PROSPER model of a partnership-based EBI delivery system is grounded in Rogers's diffusion of innovation theory (Rogers, 1995), particularly his treatment of diffusion networks and organizational-level diffusion processes. Rogers discussed both the CES and public school educational networks as models for organization-level diffusion of innovation, based on the seminal work of Walker (e.g., Walker, 1977).

In the context of presenting the CES and public schools as models for diffusion, Rogers noted how the U.S. public school network can facilitate diffusion of innovative educational methods or resources. The PROSPER partnership-based intervention model aimed to take advantage of that facilitative aspect of the public school system in conjunction with a research-driven information dissemination approach often utilized in the CES. This approach is one whereby extension agents/educators communicate or disseminate information about research-based innovations to prospective clients and thereby serve a "linking" function between innovation providers and potential innovation users. Basically, Rogers (1995) describes this linking function as creating organizational change by connecting "resource systems" (resource providers like the CES or those partnering with the CES) with "clients" (i.e., students in public schools) in organizations that have *internal capacity agents*.

As applied through the PROSPER intervention, an internal capacity agent in a public school is one who can build, coordinate, and sustain resources for the "clients" of EBIs (i.e., both students and their family members). PROSPER's intervention design was intended to bolster such capacity building through linkages between what Rogers described as *external resource agents* in the CES and school-based, capacity-building agents. Generally, external resource agents are those from agencies "outside" of local public schools, either from the state-level public education system—the state university, state department of education, curriculum providers, and regional education agencies—or from the local community (e.g., human service providers). In other words, applying Rogers's organization change model entailed an approach that linked internal capacity builders (e.g., teachers, curriculum directors, or counselors) who wished to promote an innovative program for students with external linking agents outside of the local school system (e.g., county-based CES staff) who could provide resources to implement and evaluate the program.

As implemented through the PROSPER intervention model, essential to this type of organization change are collaborating agents operating through two different types of linkages. That is, one type of linkage is a *horizontal* linkage (local school-based agents collaborating with the local CES-based agents); the other type is a *vertical* linkage (e.g., local school-based and CES collaboration linked with and supported by TA from regional or state-level staff in the CES and land grant university). Both types of linkages were intended to facilitate quality and sustained implementation of evidence-based program innovations.

The diffusion-oriented PROSPER intervention model entailed a partnership-based EBI delivery system that grew out of our prior work with CES partnership-assisted research projects (e.g., Spoth, 2007; Spoth & Molgaard, 1999) and then expanded in Iowa and Pennsylvania as part of the PROSPER trial. Notably, we strengthened features of organizational-level diffusion networks, especially partnerships to implement family and youth EBIs through each state's CES and its linkages with public schools. As anticipated, PROSPER delivery systems in Iowa and Pennsylvania then served as models that other states adopted, thus creating a state-level diffusion process similar to that described by Rogers (1995). This state-level diffusion of PROSPER has been summarized by Spoth, Greenberg, et al. (2004) and by Spoth and Greenberg (2011, 2015). The organizational structure for the partnership-based delivery system is described in more detail below.

Model for pathways of developmental change

The PROSPER model of developmental change posits that interventions across systems (school and family) can set in motion changes in participants that can be described as a series of positive developmental cascades. In this context, developmental cascades refer to the intervention-generated spread of positive effects through interactive pathways of influences over time. Positive effects at one time point support further positive effects later in development (Dodge et al., 2009). Our heuristic model for developmental change was grounded in etiological theories (e.g., Dishion et al., 1991) that have informed our intervention outcome research, as summarized in earlier publications (Spoth et al., 1996, 1998; Spoth, Trudeau, et al., 2009) and frameworks for developmental cascades (e.g., Masten & Cicchetti, 2010). The model in Figure 2.1 shows the developmental progression from proximal youth and family outcomes to more distal outcomes, illustrating hypothesized mechanisms and pathways of intervention effects.

Consistent with earlier research (Dishion et al., 1991), the model in Figure 2.1 illustrates a mediational process starting with young adolescents in middle school, continuing with adolescents in high school, and extending to emerging adults after high school. In each of these developmental phases, sets of key factors operate together to compose pathways of influences leading to the distal emerging adult outcomes. That is, the model illustrates pathways of effects, beginning with EBI implementation influencing proximal youth and family competency outcomes. Pathways continue with the influence of these proximal outcomes on more distal adolescent problem behavior outcomes (e.g., adolescent substance misuse). Finally, adolescent problem behavior outcomes influence even more distal, long-term outcomes in emerging and young adulthood (e.g., more severe types of

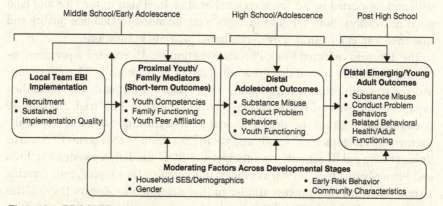

Figure 2.1 PROSPER intervention outcome model: partnership-based EBI pathways of effects across developmental phases. SES = socioeconomic status.

substance misuse), functioning in domains of school or work, relationships, and physical/sexual health. Throughout this process, relevant individual, family, and school/community contextual factors are expected to both directly and indirectly influence outcomes and, in some instances, moderate EBI effects on proximal and distal outcomes.

This model was informed by earlier prevention trials for which intervention effects on emerging adult substance misuse were hypothesized to be primarily indirect, particularly via effects on adolescent substance misuse, and thus a further result of the positive developmental cascade portrayed by the model. Through our previous prevention trials, we demonstrated and replicated findings that the effects of universal family-focused interventions on emerging adult outcomes were achieved by delaying initiation of use and decreasing the average level of use in the middle and high school years (Spoth, Trudeau, et al., 2009, 2014). As a result, we expected that PROSPER intervention effects on more serious types of substance use (e.g., high-frequency use of illicit substances) among emerging adults would be mediated through already-observed effects on substance misuse observed through high school.

Not only do adolescent problem behaviors affect the corresponding behaviors in emerging adulthood, but also they predict broader detrimental effects on adult functioning, including lower educational and occupational attainment, poorer quality relationships, or negative sexual and other health outcomes (e.g., Mason et al., 2010; Newcomb & Bentler, 1988; Riggs & Pentz, 2009). Our prevention trials preceding PROSPER also provided evidence suggesting that another key factor in intervention effectiveness is reduction in opportunities for youth to use substances (Blozis et al., 2007; Spoth, Guyll, & Shin, 2009), which supports the relationship between intervention effects on adolescents and emerging adult outcomes indicated in the developmental change model.

PROSPER TRIAL DESIGN, SAMPLES, PROCEDURES, AND PRIMARY HYPOTHESES

The PROSPER study entailed a cohort sequential design with 14 public school districts from both Iowa and Pennsylvania, for a total of 28 school districts, with half of the 14 districts from each state randomly assigned to intervention (implementation of PROSPER) and half to control groups. The study involved two cohorts of sixth-grade youth (designated Cohort 1 and Cohort 2). Districts/communities agreed to participation prior to randomization. Districts were blocked on state, then matched on size (there were six "medium" and eight "small" districts identified in each state; see description below) and geographic region to form seven pairs of districts/communities per state for randomization. One of the randomly assigned intervention sites in Iowa and one in Pennsylvania withdrew and were replaced prior to intervention implementation.

The PROSPER trial consisted of three phases funded by the original grant and two competing continuation grants. The individuals participating in the third phase (emerging adult) were a subset of the original adolescent sample (6th–12th graders), so we describe them separately.

As noted above, reports from two longitudinal prevention trials that preceded the PROSPER trial laid its groundwork (see Spoth, 2007), informing its intervention design (described in detail below) and providing a rationale for the hypotheses tested in the trial. Most importantly, the earlier longitudinal trials demonstrated that a community-university partnership approach to universal EBI implementation in rural areas resulted in an encouraging pattern of significant intervention effects. These effects slowly emerged from middle school (starting about 1 year following the intervention) and were detectable through the 12th grade, up to 6 years following baseline (Spoth & Redmond, 2002; Spoth, Redmond, et al., 2002, 2004; Spoth et al., 1999, 2000, 2005). These studies also showed benefits extending to symptoms of diagnosable disorders in the young adulthood stage (Mason et al., 2007; Spoth et al., 2005). In addition, these earlier studies suggested that it would be viable to address the intervention-related knowledge gaps summarized above. That is, they demonstrated that small community teams could assume responsibility for implementing family-focused and school-based EBIs in a quality, sustained way when provided with proactive TA guided by prevention scientists at the land grant university. Based on these prior findings, we hypothesized that PROSPER intervention effects on adolescent substance use would initially be observed 1 year following the family-focused intervention, and 1½ years following baseline (seventh grade). We also hypothesized that these outcomes would be followed by gradually increasing effects into high school, with enduring effects into emerging adulthood.

Study samples

School district selection. School district eligibility criteria for inclusion included (1) no previous or current involvement in an Iowa State or Penn State University intervention evaluation study; (2) a school district size falling into "small" (1,301 to 2,600 students) or "medium" (2,601 to 5,200 students) categories; (3) a location in a nonmetropolitan area (to facilitate the building of local community-based teams); (4) a school district not being in a community affiliated with a university; and (5) a location where at least 15% of district families were eligible for free or reduced-cost school lunches (ensuring the inclusion of families under economic stress and at significant risk). Districts were located in communities in which the local CES, the schools, as well as key community partners, demonstrated willingness to abide by the randomization procedures and to participate fully in the intervention.

During the young adolescent and adolescent stages (6th through 12th grades), primary data for the PROSPER outcome evaluation were collected from the two cohorts of students in the intervention and control school districts. The data were collected through questionnaires administered in schools. More in-depth data collection was conducted with a randomly selected subsample of families of Cohort 2 students in the in-home family assessments, including parent/child interviews, questionnaire completion and videotaped recordings of parent-child interactions, along with teacher assessments.

School and in-home assessment samples. Cohort 1 students were enrolled in the sixth grade during the 2002–2003 school year; Cohort 2 students were enrolled in the sixth grade the following year. Data were collected from each cohort in the fall of sixth grade prior to intervention exposure and each spring thereafter through 12th grade. We sought to include all currently enrolled students on each occasion, whether or not they had been enrolled previously. Student surveys were paper and pencil and machine-scored; they required one class session in length to complete. Procedures approved by the university review board included passive parental consent with student assent. A total of 5,515 intervention condition and 5,334 control condition sixth graders completed the Wave 1 (pretest) in-school assessment. On average, 85% of all eligible students completed the in-school assessment at each data collection point up to Grade 12 (Wave 8).

For the in-depth, in-home assessment, 2,267 families of Cohort 2 students were recruited through mail, telephone, and in-person visits; of those recruited, 980 (43%) participated. These assessments also were conducted on the same schedule as the in-school surveys. Written questionnaires were completed independently by adolescents, mothers, and fathers (whichever caregivers were present in the household), and parent-child interactions were recorded for subsequent coding. During the ninth-grade data collection, parents also were asked to consent to adolescent DNA collection, and 537 (73%) consented. DNA was collected by buccal swabs. Initial in-home assessment retention rates were 83%, 82%, and 80% during the spring of sixth through eighth grades, respectively.

To test for selection bias, youth in the in-home sample were compared to youth in the total sample population using a number of key demographic and behavioral measures. Youth in the in-home sample were not different from the total sample population at Wave 1 on sociodemographic variables or substance use initiation, although they did have lower rates of delinquent behavior and perceived fewer benefits from using substances (Lippold et al., 2011).

Emerging adult samples. A randomly selected and stratified subsample of 1,985 youth was recruited for continued follow-up beyond 12th grade. Selection for the emerging adult follow-up was stratified by school district, gender, and risk status. Risk status was determined by participant reports at baseline on the following five risk factors: lifetime gateway substance use (any use of alcohol, cigarettes, or marijuana vs. no use); conduct problem behaviors (at least 2 of 12 possible behaviors during the past year); eligibility for the free and reduced-cost school lunch program; lower family cohesion (dichotomized); and living with one or no biological parents (vs. two biological parents). Students were classified as higher risk if they reported (1) any three or more of the five risk factors or (2) both gateway substance use and conduct problems. Higher risk participants were oversampled and comprised 37.4% of the emerging adult subsample versus 29.2% of the eligible sample. We collected data at ages 19, 23 and 25 years using either online or telephone surveys, based on respondent preference (about 90% were online; see Figure 2.2).

Figure 2.2 In-school survey and young adult follow-up assessment: total participation by wave.

Intervention process assessment samples. The study sample for the intervention process monitoring assessments included 150 local team members in the 14 intervention communities during spring 2002. These Wave 1 process interviews also were conducted with 63 individuals serving in roles comparable to those of the local team members in the 14 control communities. In addition, interviews with directors or administrators of agencies or organizations with which team members were affiliated were completed in the 14 intervention communities; corresponding directors or administrators were interviewed in the 14 control communities ($N = 80$). Four follow-up waves of process interviews occurred with local team members, agency directors, and parallel control community representatives.

Key outcome constructs and measures

Assessments during the adolescent stage primarily addressed youth competency and family functioning variables, other youth risk and protective factors, problem behaviors, internalizing symptoms, and service utilization. Key individual constructs and their empirical indicators across school-based and in-home assessments are summarized in Table 2.1.

PROSPER PARTNERSHIP-BASED DELIVERY SYSTEM MODEL AND IMPLEMENTATION

Overview of PROSPER's five core components

The PROSPER partnership-based EBI delivery system has five core components: (1) small, strategic teams of community stakeholders; (2) a three-tiered, state-level partnership model with the CES as the link between local implementers and prevention science experts; (3) evidence-based, family-focused, and school-based interventions from a menu of programs; (4) a multiphase developmental process focused on sustainability; and (5) evaluation, including a set of standardized tools for monitoring implementation quality. Considering space constraints, this section focuses on the first four core components, starting with the partnership model structure that was applied in the original PROSPER trial.

The PROSPER partnership-based delivery system structure

As illustrated in Figure 2.3, the PROSPER three-tiered state partnership structure consisted of multiple county or community (local) teams, a team of prevention coordinators/TA providers, and a state management team (see Spoth, Redmond, et al., 2004, for a summary of the partnership model as originally conceived and graphically represented).

Table 2.1 KEY CONSTRUCTS, MEASURES, AND INDICATORS FOR HIGH SCHOOL AND POST–HIGH SCHOOL ASSESSMENTS

Construct	Empirical indicator(s) (source)
Substance use (Alcohol, tobacco, marijuana, & other drugs)	Lifetime use, past month use, annual use (Botvin et al., 1995; NSDDU) [a,b] Rutgers alcohol problem index [b]
Conduct problem behaviors	Conduct problems index (selected items—Elliot et al., 1983; NSDDU) [a,b]
Substance abuse & dependence	DIS [b]
Conduct-related disorders	DIS [b]
Anxiety, depressive symptoms	Internalizing behavior scales (PFS) [a] Adult self report (Achenbach, 2005) [b]
Sexual risk behaviors	SSDP & NSHS Items [b]
Substance-related skills	Assertiveness (Gambrill & Richey, 1975), stress management (Wills, 1985) [a,b] Peer resistance (PFS), goal setting (PFS), decision-making (Wills, 1985) [a,b]
Substance use-related knowledge & attitudes	Substance use knowledge (Botvin et al., 1995) [a,b] Substance use attitudes (SSDP) [a,b] Intention to use substances (Botvin et al., 1995) [a,b]
Normative beliefs	Estimated peer & adult substance use (Botvin et al., 1995; SSDP) [a,b]
Affiliation with antisocial peers	Antisocial peer affiliation (PPS) [a,b]
Parent-child affective quality	Parent-child affective quality (short version—PFS) [a]
Effective child management	General child management (short version—PFS) [a]
Child involvement in family activities	Child involvement (short version—PFS) [a]
SES	Economic stress (PFS) [a,b]
Mental health service utilization	(Horwitz et al., 2001) [a,b]
Parent substance use & adjustment	Adapted from DIS [b]
Stressful life events	Project family life events inventory (PFS) [a,b]
Psychological characteristics	Self-efficacy (Paulhus, 1990) [a,b] Social anxiety (Richardson & Tasto, 1976) [a,b]

Note. Reference to parent(s) includes stepparents or other guardians. DIS = Diagnostic Interview Schedule; NSDDU = National Survey of Delinquency and Drug Use; NSHS = National Stress and health Study; PFS = Project Family Scales; PPS = PROSPER Scales; SSDP = Seattle Social Development Project.

[a]Measures used in the in-school survey.
[b]Measures used in the post–high school assessments.

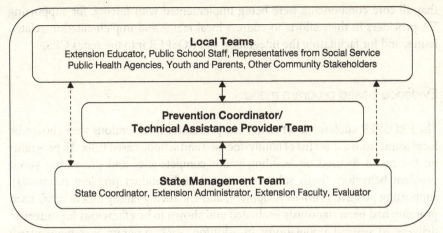

Figure 2.3 Organizational structure for PROSPER partnership-based delivery system.

Represented by the top tier in Figure 2.3, *PROSPER local teams* were the core action units that were responsible for prevention program selection and implementation, as well as the long-term sustainability of the effort. These small, strategic teams started with 8–10 members from key stakeholder groups, such as human service and public health agencies, law enforcement, juvenile justice, the faith-based community, and parent and youth representatives. Local teams were led by CES educators, who generally had a background in youth development/ 4-H or family and consumer sciences. These CES educators served the linking change agent roles central to the EBI diffusion process, linking public schools with beneficial resources outside of their system. A school district representative frequently functioned in a coleadership capacity for the local team, serving in an "internal capacity-building" role by keeping the school engaged with the PROSPER effort, ensuring quality implementation of the school-based program, and supporting delivery of the family-focused program.

The middle tier in Figure 2.3 represents the *prevention coordinator or TA provider team*. Individuals in this role included prevention, program implementation, and/or community development specialists, who provided proactive, ongoing TA to local teams and served as the liaisons between their assigned local team(s) and the state management team. They attended local team meetings and maintained regular contact with local team leaders in order to support them through all aspects of program adoption, implementation, and sustainability. They also met regularly with the state management team to share successes and concerns regarding team processes and progress toward developmental benchmarks.

The *state management team* (bottom tier in Figure 2.3) comprised university researchers, faculty-level professionals, and CES administrators. This team provided oversight for PROSPER implementation in the state, was responsible for coordinating with state-level agencies (e.g., public health, education), and sought funding sources to sustain the effort since initial grant funding for implementation typically decreases over time. This team also was responsible for ensuring that all core components were being implemented with fidelity, for supporting TA providers in their efforts to address local team- and implementation-related issues, and for facilitating the integration of PROSPER into the state's CES.

Evidence-based program menu

The PROSPER adolescent substance use preventive interventions were chosen by local teams from a short list of family-focused and school-based EBIs. All programs on the menu focused on building youth competencies and preventing youth problem behaviors (both substance-related and conduct problem behaviors), supporting positive youth development, and enhancing family functioning. Each program had been rigorously evaluated and shown to be efficacious for universal delivery to general populations; in addition, each program was manualized; trainers and technical assistants were available to support implementation. Each local team was responsible for selecting one of the family-focused programs to implement with sixth graders and their families and one of the school-based programs to implement in seventh grade.

Family-focused programs. In the original PROSPER prevention trial, the three family-focused programs available to local teams were the *Adolescent Transitions Program* (ATP; Dishion et al., 1996); *Preparing for the Drug Free Years* (now called *Guiding Good Choices*; Haggerty et al., 1999), and the *Strengthening Families Program: For Parents and Youth 10–14* (SFP 10-14; Molgaard & Spoth, 2001; Molgaard et al., 1997). All 14 local teams selected the SFP 10-14 as their family-focused program. The SFP 10-14 includes seven weekly 2-hour sessions. For the first hour, parents and youth meet with facilitators separately; they then come back together as a family for the second hour. Parent content focuses on providing support while setting appropriate limits and monitoring youth behaviors, as well as clearly articulating beliefs and expectations related to alcohol and drug use. Youth content focuses on goals and dreams for the future, appreciating parents, dealing with stress and emotions, and building skills to deal with peer pressure. Family segments include opportunities for parents and youth to practice communicating, problem-solving, identifying family values and strengths, and learning how to have family meetings.

School-based programs. In the PROSPER trial, the three evidence-based school programs on the menu included *All Stars* (Hansen, 1996); *LifeSkills Training* (Botvin, 2000; Botvin et al., 1995); and *Project Alert* (Ellickson et al., 1988). These programs were designed to be taught as part of the seventh-grade curriculum by a regular classroom teacher. All Stars is a 13-session program designed to increase the accuracy of students' beliefs about peer norms regarding substance use and violence, to help students make a personal commitment to avoid substance use and violent behavior, and to strengthen students' bonding to school. LifeSkills Training is a 15-session program designed to promote the development of peer resistance, self-management, assertiveness, and other social skills, as well as to provide students with information about how various substances affect the body.

Project Alert is an 11-session program designed to change students' beliefs about substance use norms and about the consequences of using substances, to help students identify and resist pro-substance use pressures, and to build resistance self-efficacy. Each school-based program was delivered in a class normally taken by all seventh-grade students, generally by a trained classroom teacher (Spoth, Redmond, et al., 2007).

PROSPER program implementation supports

The PROSPER multicomponent intervention was designed so that information, related resources, and tailored TA were provided proactively to local teams as they moved through each phase of program implementation (e.g., program selection, planning and logistics, initial delivery, ongoing implementation). In addition, the state management team worked with the TA providers to ensure that local teams received the supports needed to facilitate their progress through the multiphase developmental process toward sustainability (see the description of our sustainability model in Spoth & Greenberg, 2011).

A variety of training and learning opportunities were offered in each of PROSPER's developmental phases. For example, local team leaders participated in quarterly learning communities that prepared them for implementation tasks and allowed them to learn from each other's successes and challenges. All local team members were invited to annual trainings that addressed topics such as prevention science, team development, selection and quality implementation of the programs, and resource generation strategies to support sustainability. In addition, standardized resources such as PowerPoint presentations, handouts, and data reports were provided for local teams to use with a variety of audiences.

PROSPER also included ongoing TA and implementation monitoring processes to support local teams. Implementation quality monitoring in the form of family and school program observations assessed whether programs were delivered as designed, while surveys conducted with local team members measured their perceptions of team functioning and progress.

Program implementation challenges and solutions

Local teams typically faced four key challenges: difficulty recruiting and retaining families for multisession programs, maintaining high levels of program implementation quality, sustaining a well-functioning team (especially with ongoing active involvement of local school districts), and sustaining the implementation of the family-focused and school-based programs year after year. PROSPER implementation addressed these common issues through training and proactive TA to local teams and through networking opportunities for team leaders and members. Central to the proactive TA was a "benchmarking system" entailing ongoing implementation quality monitoring that focused on PROSPER's five core components. In addition, implementation data were routinely shared with all stakeholders (local team leaders, TA providers, and prevention scientists) to help identify areas for improvement, in terms of both program implementation and the team's functioning. Taken together, these features set local teams up for long-term sustainability and for creating a community-level, public health impact.

PROSPER FINDINGS

Process evaluation: Recruitment, team functioning, sustained implementation quality

Recruitment and team functioning. Local teams were responsible for recruiting the families of sixth graders to participate in the SFP 10-14. Local teams achieved relatively high recruitment rates for an in-person, multisession, universal family-focused EBI (Spoth, Clair, et al., 2007). Across two cohorts, on average 21% of all eligible sixth-grade families signed up, and over 17% attended at least one session (among the families that attended one session, 91.6% regularly attended other sessions). Over 2,650 family members across the two cohorts participated in the intervention. Other studies on recruitment suggested that the levels observed were at the high end of the range of rates for recruitment into multisession, universal interventions for families conducted by research staff (Spoth et al., 2005). Attrition was predicted by risk factors such as low family income and youth having deviant peer associations, while youth report of school bonding was associated with program attendance (LoBraico et al., 2021). As expected, indicators of effective team functioning were associated with recruitment rates. The ratings of the effectiveness of teams' collaborations with TA providers showed the strongest associations. We infer that the PROSPER partnership structure shown in Figure 2.3, with its state-level support for technical assistants providing ongoing, proactive TA to local teams, played an important role in facilitating recruitment success.

Level of implementation quality. One of the most salient barriers to effective diffusion of EBIs is low-quality intervention implementation, which diminishes outcomes (Backer, 2003; Fixsen et al., 2005). PROSPER's ongoing, proactive TA was intended to address this issue and to evaluate whether high-quality implementation was actually being accomplished by the local teams. Each local team conducted independent observations, which showed consistently high implementation quality for both the family (adherence, group participation, and facilitator quality) and the school EBIs (adherence and student engagement), with greater than 90% overall adherence in both cohorts (Spoth, Guyll, et al., 2011). These adherence rates are higher than investigations of similar interventions at the time, which have reported adherence ranging from 42% to 86% (Fagan & Mihalic, 2003; Gottfredson & Gottfredson, 2001).

Sustained quality EBI implementation. With ongoing TA, each of the 14 PROSPER local teams initiated implementation of the family-focused EBI with sixth graders in their communities in 2002. Their goal was to sustain quality implementation past the period of grant support. Most (80%) of the PROSPER local teams successfully delivered and sustained their selected programs for at least 12 years, with nearly half remaining active beyond 16 years. Local teams sustained themselves through a wide variety of state and local funding sources (Greenberg et al., 2015).

Proximal outcomes: Family functioning and adolescent competencies

The sample analyzed for this study of outcomes comprised those completing at least the fall sixth-grade assessment and a follow-up assessment in the spring of seventh grade (9,871). Starting in middle school, the in-school surveys assessed substance misuse attitudes, behaviors, and beliefs, along with related risk and protective factors, such as conduct problems, family cohesion, school bonding, and parent-child communication (Redmond et al., 2009). Analyses confirmed pretest equivalence of the experimental conditions and showed no evidence of differential attrition. Multilevel, intent-to-treat analyses of covariance were conducted. These controlled for study design effects (state, cohort, and block), pretest levels of the outcome variables, and presence of two biological parents; they also accounted for the nested structure of the study design (random assignment to experimental condition at the school district level). In this context, it is worth noting that even though PROSPER is a universal type of intervention through which intervention components are offered to general population youth and families, not all students and families participated in the family-focused program, as noted in the section on recruitment above. In addition, some students typically are absent for some of the school-based program sessions. With intent-to treat analyses, data from all assessed students are used, regardless of the "dose" of intervention they received.

Results regarding changes in parenting behaviors showed that youth in intervention communities reported significantly better child management practices by parents and improved parent-child affective quality and family environment. Targeted adolescent competencies also showed significant effects; adolescents in intervention communities reported higher substance-related peer refusal efficacy, greater intention to avoid substance use, and improved problem-solving skills (Redmond et al., 2009).

Distal outcomes: Adolescent problem behavior

Analyses of the problem behavior outcome data at the *seventh-grade follow-up* supported our hypothesized outcomes for that time point. Results showed significant intervention effects on substance initiation (reductions in new user rates that control for use prior to baseline) for marijuana, methamphetamine, ecstasy, and inhalants, as well as lower rates on two substance initiation indices: gateway substance initiation (lifetime use of alcohol, cigarettes, and marijuana) and illicit substance initiation (lifetime use of marijuana, methamphetamine, ecstasy, and nonprescription use of prescription drugs). In addition, there were significant reductions in past year use of marijuana and inhalants. Reductions in new user rates of cigarettes and lifetime drunkenness approached significance, as did reductions in past year drunkenness. Individual- and community-level effect sizes were both in the small-to-medium range, with community-level effect sizes primarily in the medium range (see Spoth et al., 2019).

As noted, the original PROSPER proposal hypothesized that initial intervention effects on substance misuse would be observed at the seventh-grade assessment, followed by gradually increasing effects into high school. Consistent with this hypothesis, analyses of *10th-grade* substance misuse outcomes showed stronger results 4.5 years following baseline (Spoth, Redmond, et al., 2011). Subsequently, analyses examined substance misuse outcomes *at the 11th and 12th grades* (Spoth, Redmond, et al., 2013). Analyses of data from each of the 11th- and 12th-grade data collection points showed positive results across multiple lifetime substance use measures, dichotomous current (past month/past year) substance use measures (scored 0 [*no current use*] or 1 [*use*]), and frequency of current substance use measures. Consistent with the developmental stage of participants, findings showed a pattern of stronger effects for more serious substance misuse at the 12th-grade follow-up, whereas effects on lifetime use of gateway substances, which were in evidence at the 7th- and 10th-grade follow-ups, were no longer statistically significant.

Consistent with the research aim to help clarify the longitudinal pattern of findings across middle and high school, a subsequent analysis examined substance misuse growth across the *6th to 12th grades*. The tested model included modeling factors for state, cohort, condition, block, and risk status, with corresponding higher level interaction effects, consistent with earlier published findings (Spoth, Redmond, et al., 2011). Results of the longitudinal growth analysis illustrated a pattern of diverging intervention-control substance misuse trajectories, as well as risk-related moderation; there were stronger effects for higher risk adolescents across the middle and high school years. Results for marijuana and narcotic misuse are illustrated in Figures 2.4 and 2.5, respectively.

The pattern of limited significant effects on alcohol initiation measures warrants discussion. Consistent with the literature, our earlier studies have taught us that the timing of intervention is important in the level of effects observed on alcohol initiation. That is, effects on alcohol initiation are observed only when the intervention is implemented sufficiently early in the phase during which young adolescents initiate experimentation. Unfortunately, in the PROSPER trial, the base rates of alcohol initiation in sixth grade were much higher than observed at similar ages in earlier studies and appear to have suppressed the intervention effect on that outcome. Initiation effects were found for substances with lower base rates (e.g., marijuana, ecstasy, methamphetamines). Notably, on the one alcohol outcome with a lower base rate (drunkenness) positive results approached statistical significance (based on classroom surveys), while another

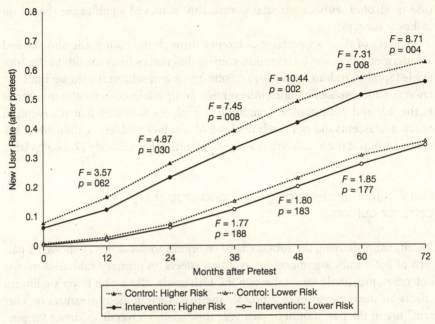

Figure 2.4 Marijuana new user rates by condition and risk status.

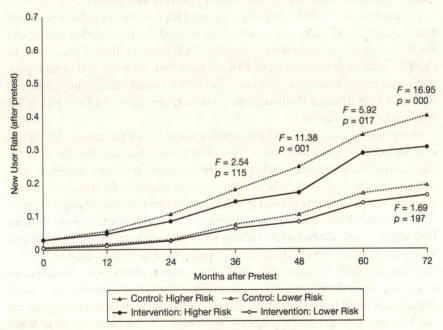

Figure 2.5 Narcotic new user rates by condition and risk status.

(use of alcohol without parental permission) achieved significance (based on in-home surveys).

Analyses of conduct problem outcomes through the 10th grade also showed a pattern of increasing intervention-control differences from the 6th to the 10th grade (Spoth, Trudeau, et al., 2015). Point-in-time results indicated significantly fewer conduct problems among intervention group adolescents relative to controls at the 9th and 10th grades. Longitudinal analyses indicated that intervention group adolescents did not reach the level of conduct problems exhibited by the control group at the eighth-grade assessment until approximately 17 months later.

Distal outcomes: Emerging adulthood problem behavior outcomes

Results from studying the subsample of emerging adults *at age 19* showed a pattern of statistically significant intervention effects on primary substance misuse outcomes, previously found through the 12th grade, albeit with fewer significant effects on some measures of substance use (e.g., dichotomous measures of "current" use in the past month or past year time frame). Overall, evidence for positive intervention effects was most pronounced for the lifetime misuse of illicit substances and nonprescribed narcotics, drug use problems, and non-alcohol-related frequency of use over past month or past year time frames.

The reasons for the lack of significant results for current use outcomes are not entirely clear; in all cases, the mean scores favored the intervention group, and the relative reduction rates were in the 10%–20% range in three of four cases. To clarify, a relative reduction rate of 20% suggests that, for every 100 general population emerging adults (i.e., from non-PROSPER communities/school districts) who have ever misused the particular substance, only about 80 from PROSPER sites would have misused it.

In the case of marijuana use, intervention effect tests were statistically significant for both lifetime and frequency of current use, suggesting that the dichotomous, current use measures might have been less sensitive to intervention-control differences. There also might have been different patterns of current use among subgroups of participants defined by college enrollment or other changes in physical and social environments (e.g., change to a nonrural residence). As in the later high school years, alcohol-related effects were nonsignificant at age 19. Although significant intervention effects for conduct problem behaviors were found through high school (Spoth, Trudeau, et al., 2015), intervention effects were nonsignificant at age 19, when developmental trends indicate that these behaviors in general populations begin to decline (Sameroff et al., 2004). In contrast to findings during the 11th and 12th grades (Spoth, Redmond, et al., 2011), there also were fewer positive risk moderation results at age 19. In part, this may be due to the smaller sample selected for the emerging adult follow-up. Nonetheless, the pattern showed intervention-control differences that were generally stronger for the higher risk intervention subgroup on most outcome variables.

These findings provide support for the utility of the PROSPER delivery system to provide enduring preventive or behavioral health benefits into emerging adulthood. It is noteworthy that despite the changes occurring in participants' social environments following high school, evidence of positive intervention impact endured for some outcomes. As an indication of the practical significance of the findings, relative reduction rates for the dichotomous outcomes ranged from 9.4% to 41.0%.

A manuscript reporting the findings from the *age 23 and 25 follow-ups* was recently published (Spoth et al., 2022). The intervention impacts persisting into adulthood were primarily in the domain of illicit drug use and, to some extent, misuse of prescribed medications. In general, the most positive results were observed in growth analyses for lifetime use measures; most point-in-time current use outcomes were null. More specifically, intervention effects on lifetime illicit drugs (e.g., ecstasy, cocaine, methamphetamine, LSD and other hallucinogens) and nonprescribed narcotics were the most robust findings, consistent with the age 19 results, but mostly in evidence in the emerging adult growth analyses. There were no age 23 or 25 effects on alcohol use or marijuana use; this may be in part because the use of alcohol becomes more normative with increasing age, and the legalization of marijuana use in many states during the period of the PROSPER trial, in one form or another, may have contributed to more widespread use by young adults in both the intervention and the control groups.

Growth analyses using 10 outcome measures available across all waves of data collected over 14 years showed the strongest intervention effects. Overall, intervention condition participants demonstrated lower levels of use on 8 of 10 outcomes, including lifetime use of illicit substances and prescription narcotics, along with lifetime drunkenness and cigarette use. Results were relatively weaker for marijuana use and for lifetime alcohol use across all waves of data collection, only approaching significance.

Concerning the overall pattern of outcomes summarized above, from early adolescence through emerging adulthood, the longitudinal results from nearly 15 years of PROSPER outcome research suggest that intervention impacts vary, depending on stages of development and, perhaps, their corresponding life challenges. Brain development in early adolescence—accompanied by evolving academic and social-emotional skills that set the stage for later adult functioning—can be negatively impacted by substance initiation and use. PROSPER's reduction in gateway drug initiation during this critical period might have enabled youth to better manage substance use at later ages when regular use becomes more normative and less developmentally problematic (e.g., Feinstein et al., 2012). In emerging adulthood, however, observed substance misuse effects appear to shift away from legal substance use and toward illicit substances that can be uniquely threatening to successful adult functioning; effects on current substance use largely disappeared. Considered altogether, the pattern of findings highlight an important process of positive, cascading effects that build from adolescence into young adulthood, as further suggested by observed crossover effects during emerging adulthood.

Distal outcomes: Crossover effects

Our team also has examined crossover effects, defined as outcomes that are beneficial but not specifically targeted by the intervention. One report examined crossover effects of adolescent substance misuse preventive interventions on academic success in college (Spoth et al., 2016). At age 19, study participants ($N = 1,488$) enrolled in 4-year and community colleges reported on college grades. We found significant indirect effects of the intervention observed on college grades, with this effect partially occurring through pathways, including high school levels of school engagement, problem-solving skills, and substance misuse. Interestingly, the magnitude of the direct intervention effect was larger than the total indirect effects, suggesting that there are ways beyond the specific indirect effects tested by which the interventions delivered during middle school convey their effects into college.

Recently completed studies of PROSPER long-term effects also have shown additional crossover effects on young adult educational attainment and financial well-being (McCauley et al., 2021, unpublished manuscript); on enhanced romantic relationship quality (LoBraico et al., 2022); and, in the early months of the COVID-19 pandemic, on life satisfaction and parental warmth among a subsample of youth participants who had become parents (Feinberg et al., 2022).

Economic outcomes: Cost-efficiency and cost-effectiveness

An extensive cost analysis produced realistic cost estimates for states and communities considering PROSPER implementation (https://www.blueprintsprograms.org/). Findings from the cost analysis indicated that "day-of-implementation" costs in the PROSPER partnership context are substantially lower than those previously calculated for the same programs when delivered as a "stand-alone" program, without PROSPER (Crowley et al., 2012). Analyses have also indicated that PROSPER is cost-effective in reducing youth prescription drug misuse (Crowley et al., 2014), and that PROSPER reduces Medicaid-supported service utilization among emerging adults (Crowley et al., 2022, unpublished manuscript).

Additional areas of outcome study: Ongoing PROSPER trial spin-off studies

In addition to the peer network studies that are the subject of this volume, there are several other programs of research using PROSPER-related data sets to investigate topics beyond those of the original PROSPER trial.

Studies of gene-moderated effects. As noted, genetic data were collected during adolescence and emerging adulthood, with the goal of exploring possible intervention effect differences by varying genetic profiles, including genes for alcohol misuse and aggression. These data have yielded findings on genetic factors associated with substance misuse and moderation of PROSPER effects by specific genes (e.g., Cleveland et al., 2018; see Chapter 12). For example, one study examined the potential moderating role of the *DRD4* gene on aggression. As hypothesized, there was a significant maternal hostility by intervention interaction, suggesting that the intervention reduced the negative impact of maternal hostility on aggressive behavior problems during the adolescent stage. That is, control group adolescents with the gene and with hostile mothers showed increasing aggressive behavior problems. In contrast, in the intervention group, aggression decreased for adolescents with the gene and with similarly hostile mothers.

Study of second-generation effects. Another current, spin-off study underway examines the potential multigenerational impacts of PROSPER through follow-up with the original participants as they transitioned to parenthood. Hypotheses being tested through this study include focus on how the quality of parenting experienced in adolescence is directly related to the quality of parenting provided to offspring.

Study of PROSPER plus a screening-referral process. Yet another spin-off study with a new sample of school districts in Iowa examines the effect of implementing an adaptation of PROSPER, including a screening, brief intervention, and referral to treatment (SBIRT) component. This PROSPER intervention model is grounded in a "continuum-of-intervention" approach (National Research Council and Institute of Medicine, 2009). In this case, along with universal preventive interventions, all middle school students are screened for problem behavior risk; those at higher risk and their families are provided with the opportunity for additional brief intervention (e.g., visits with school counselors, parenting instruction) and referral to treatment outside of the school setting, as indicated.

Further study of parenting received during adolescence. Another series of investigations entails examination of the effects of parent characteristics (e.g., lability in parental warmth and hostility) or other parenting processes (interparental conflict, nurturant-involved parenting) and their relations with adolescent problem behaviors and well-being. One investigation, for example, examines competing hypotheses, based in a cognitive-contextual framework, regarding how interparental conflict may impact adolescent substance misuse (Fosco & Feinberg, 2018). Findings support adolescents' family threat appraisals as a direct risk factor for escalating cigarette use, while interparental conflict is a direct predictor of increased alcohol use over time. Another study evaluated mediational processes in nurturant-involved parenting, suggesting that suboptimal nurturant-involved parenting by fathers is associated with higher levels of substance misuse via increases in adolescent social anxiety symptoms and subsequent decreases in substance refusal efficacy (Weymouth et al., 2019).

SUMMARY, FUTURE DIRECTIONS, AND CONCLUSIONS

The PROSPER trial of a community-university, partnership-based EBI delivery system is the largest, longest study of its kind. When it began, the investigator team could not find any rigorous longitudinal studies of university-supported community partnership models for the prevention of substance misuse combining evidence-based family and school interventions for sustained, healthy family functioning and youth resilience. Measures at multiple time points (10 assessments) conducted across 14 years have shown that effects on substance misuse are robust through the adolescent period, and that effects on other outcomes have emerged during young adulthood.

Importantly, fidelity of EBI delivery assessments have demonstrated high levels of sustained implementation quality for both the family-focused and school-based interventions (Spoth, Guyll, et al., 2011). Active local teams also have been self-sustaining (Greenberg et al., 2015); as noted, 80% of the teams sustained themselves for at least 12 years. The majority of the original PROSPER local teams now have reached the end of their active life cycles; new teams have been organized in Iowa, Pennsylvania, and additional states that also utilize the PROSPER approach. The focus of these teams continues to be effective delivery of preventive EBIs using a CES-led community coalition, provision of ongoing TA, attention to implementation quality, and the use of evaluation data to enhance delivery.

Future directions for PROSPER-related research include addressing its generalizability to larger and more diverse communities. While PROSPER has emerged as a successful model for delivering universal, preventive EBIs in small, mostly rural communities, its viability in larger and more diverse communities is less clear. In particular, future research will evaluate the degree to which risk and protective factors more prominent in those communities (i.e., racial discrimination, acculturation, and so on) influence PROSPER intervention impacts.

Research also will continue on ways to improve TA to community coalitions implementing EBIs, with a particular emphasis on efficiency and cost-effectiveness. A large-scale randomized controlled trial is currently underway examining the effects of the Coalition Check-Up, a TA model for prevention coalitions (L. D. Brown et al., 2021). Findings from this research could have significant implications for broad scale-up of PROSPER, including addressing issues with engagement of participants in in-person programs.

In conclusion, it is noteworthy that positive outcomes of the PROSPER delivery system have been underscored by independent, systematic reviews of the literature (Flanagan et al., 2018). Along with demonstrated cost-effectiveness and cost-efficiency, these positive outcomes highlight how it is responsive to recommendations in the most recent surgeon general report (U.S. Department of Health and Human Services & Office of the Surgeon General, 2016) on addiction in America. That report emphasizes the practical benefits of community-based prevention delivery systems for EBIs, particularly those embedded in national delivery systems and/or those supporting practitioner-scientist partnerships (Grumbach & Mold, 2009; Spoth & Greenberg, 2005, 2011).

The PROSPER trial findings have clear public health implications. To begin, its benefits apply as much or more to those at higher risk for addictions and other serious problems. Long-term outcome evaluations are showing important crossover effects on nontargeted outcomes like academic performance or attainment, financial well-being, and quality of intimate relationships. Overall, the follow-up evaluations of the PROSPER partnership-based delivery system have supported its potential for public health impact, both because it has been shown to effectively support implementation of EBIs and because it has been shown to produce enduring, long-term outcomes in a practical, cost-effective way. In other words, PROSPER has potential to facilitate effective and efficient translation of proven universal preventive or behavioral health interventions into community practice.

Among the most noteworthy findings bearing on PROSPER's public health potential are friendship network effects described in this volume. In a nutshell, the patterns of findings from the friendship network studies suggest that population-level effects of PROSPER may well be enhanced by diffusion through friendship network effects, promising a substantial benefit of scaling up its implementation. There is a clear argument for more of this type of friendship network research and a public policy approach that could support such work (e.g., interdepartmental funding and coordination), along with programs of research on universal prevention delivery systems.

REFERENCES

Achenbach (2005). *Manual for the adult self-report and adult behavior checklist.* University of Vermont. Department of Psychiatry.

Adelman, H. S., & Taylor, L. (2003). Creating school and community partnerships for substance abuse prevention programs. *Journal of Primary Prevention, 23*(3), 329–369.

Backer, T. E. (2003). *Evaluating community collaborations.* Springer.

Blozis, S. A., Feldman, B., & Conger, R. D. (2007). Adolescent alcohol use and adult alcohol disorders: A two-part random-effects model with diagnostic outcomes. *Drug and Alcohol Dependence, 88,* S85–S96.

Botvin, G. J. (2000). *Life skills training: Promoting health and personal development.* Princeton Health Press.

Botvin, G. J., Baker, E., Dusenbury, L., Botvin, E. M., & Diaz, T. (1995). Long-term follow-up results of a randomized drug abuse prevention trial in a white middle-class population. *Journal of the American Medical Association, 273,* 1106–1112.

Brown, C. H., & Liao, J. (1999). Principles for designing randomized preventive trials in mental health: An emerging developmental epidemiology paradigm. *American Journal of Community Psychology, 27*(5), 673–710.

Brown, L. D., Chilenski, S. M., Wells, R., Jones, E. C., Welsh, J. A., Gayles, J. G., Fernandez, M. E., Jones, D. E., Mallett, K. A., & Feinberg, M. E. (2021). Protocol for a hybrid type 3 cluster randomized trial of a technical assistance system supporting coalitions and evidence-based drug prevention programs. *Implementation Science, 16*(1), 64. https://doi.org/10.1186/s13012-021-01133-z

Carnegie Council on Adolescent Development. (1995). *Great transitions: Preparing adolescents for a new century.* Carnegie Corporation.

Cleveland, H. H., Griffin, A. M., Wolf, P. S., Wiebe, R. P., Schlomer, G. L., Feinberg, M. E., Greenberg, M. T., Spoth, R. L., Redmond, C., & Vandenbergh, D. J. (2018).

Transactions between substance use intervention, the oxytocin receptor (OXTR) gene, and peer substance use predicting youth alcohol use. *Prevention Science, 19*(1), 15–26.

Crowley, D. M., Jones, D. E., Coffman, D. L., & Greenberg, M. T. (2014). Can we build an efficient response to the prescription drug abuse epidemic? Assessing the cost effectiveness of universal prevention in the PROSPER trial. *Preventive Medicine, 62,* 71–77.

Crowley, D. M., Jones, D. E., Greenberg, M. T., Feinberg, M. E., & Spoth, R. L. (2012). Resource consumption of a diffusion model for prevention programs: The PROSPER delivery system. *Journal of Adolescent Health, 50*(3), 256–263.

Crowley, D. M., Jones, D. E., & Meyer Chilenski, S. (2022). Investing in Prevention Infrastructure: Economic Evaluation of the PROSPER System. Unpublished manuscript.

Dishion, T. J., Andrews, D. W., Kavanagh, K., & Soberman, L. H. (1996). Preventive interventions for high-risk youth: The adolescent transitions program. In R. D. Peters & R. J. McMahon (Eds.). *Preventing childhood disorders, substance abuse, and delinquency* (pp. 184–214). Sage.

Dishion, T. J., Patterson, G. R., Stoolmiller, M., & Skinner, M. L. (1991). Family, school, and behavioral antecedents to early adolescent involvement with antisocial peers. *Developmental Psychology, 27*(1), 172.

Dodge, K. A., Malone, P. S., Lansford, J. E., Miller, S., Pettit, G. S., & Bates, J. E. (2009). A dynamic cascade model of the development of substance-use onset. *Monographs of the Society for Research in Child Development, 74*(3), vii–119.

Ellickson, P. L., Bell, R. M., Thomas, M. A., Robyn, A., & Zellman, G. L. (1988). *Designing and implementing project ALERT*. Rand Corporation.

Elliott, D. S., Ageton, S. S., Huizinga, D., Knowles, B. A., & Canter, R. J. (1983). *The prevalence and incidence of delinquent behavior: 1976–1980*. Boulder, CO: Behavioral Research Institute.

Fagan, A. A., & Mihalic, S. (2003). Strategies for enhancing the adoption of school-based prevention programs: Lessons learned from the Blueprints for Violence Prevention replications of the Life Skills Training program. *Journal of Community Psychology, 31*(3), 235–253.

Feinberg, M., Fang, S., Fosco, G., Carlie Sloan, C., Mogle, J., & Spoth, R. (2022). Long-term effects of adolescent substance use prevention on participants, partners, and their children: Resiliency and outcomes 15 years later during the COVID-19 pandemic. *Prevention Science, 23*(3), 1264–1275.

Feinstein, E. D., Richter, L., & Foster, S. E. (2012). Addressing the critical health problem of adolescent substance use through health care, research, and public policy. *Journal of Adolescent Health, 50,* 431–436.

Fixsen, D., Naoom, S., Blasé, K., Friedman, R., & Wallace, F. (2005). *Implementation research: A synthesis of the literature*. National Implementation Research Network, Louis de la Parte Florida Mental Health Institute.

Flanagan, S. K., Varga, S. M., Zaff, J. F., Margolius, M., & Lin, E. S. (2018). *Comprehensive community initiatives: The impact on population-level children, youth, and family outcomes, A systematic review*. Weiss Institute.

Fosco, G. M., & Feinberg, M. E. (2018). Interparental conflict and long-term adolescent substance use trajectories: The role of adolescent threat appraisals. *Journal of Family Psychology, 32*(2), 175.

Gambrill, E. D., & Richey, C. A. (1975). An Assertion Inventory for use in assessment and research. *Behavior Therapy, 6,* 550–561.

Gottfredson, D. C., Wilson, D. B., & Najaka, S. S. (2003). School-based crime prevention. In *Evidence-based crime prevention* (pp. 56–164). Routledge.

Gottfredson, G. D., & Gottfredson, D. C. (2001). What schools do to prevent problem behavior and promote safe environments. *Journal of Educational and Psychological Consultation, 12*(4), 313–344.

Greenberg, M. T., Feinberg, M. E., Johnson, L. E., Perkins, D. F., Welsh, J. A., & Spoth, R. L. (2015). Factors that predict financial sustainability of community coalitions: Five years of findings from the PROSPER partnership project. *Prevention Science, 16*(1), 158–167.

Grumbach, K., & Mold, J. W. (2009). A health care cooperative extension service: Transforming primary care and community health. *Journal of the American Medical Association, 301*(24), 2589–2591.

Haggerty, K., Kosterman, R., Catalano, R. F., & Hawkins, J. D. (1999). *Preparing for the drug free years* (OJJDP Juvenile Justice Bulletin NCJ 173408). U.S. Department of Justice, Office of Juvenile Justice and Delinquency Prevention.

Hallfors, D., Cho, H., Livet, D., Kadushin, C. (2002). Fighting back against substance abuse: Are community coalitions winning? *American Journal of Preventive Medicine, 23*(4), 237–245.

Halpert, B. P., & Sharp, T. S. (1991). Utilizing Cooperative Extension services to meet rural health needs. *The Journal of Rural Health, 7*(1), 23–29.

Hansen, W. B. (1996). Pilot test results comparing the All Stars program with seventh grade D.A.R.E. program integrity and mediating variable analysis. *Substance Use and Misuse, 31,* 1359–1377.

Horwitz, S. M., Hoagwood, K., Stiffman, A. R., Summerfeld, T., Weisz, J. R., Costello, E. J., et al. (2001). Reliability of the services assessment for children and adolescents. *Psychiatr Serv, 52,* 1088–1094. Available: http://www.ncbi.nlm.nih.gov/pubmed/11474056

Kreuter, M. W., Lezin, N. A., & Young, L. A. (2000). Evaluating community-based collaborative mechanisms: Implications for practitioners. *Health Promotion Practice, 1*(1), 49–63.

Lippold, M. A., Greenberg, M. T., & Feinberg, M. E. (2011). A dyadic approach to understanding the relationship of maternal knowledge of youths' activities to youths' problem behavior among rural adolescents. *Journal of Youth and Adolescence, 40,* 1178–1191.

LoBraico, E. J., Fosco, G. M., Fang, S., Spoth, R. L., Redmond, C., & Feinberg, M. E. (2022). Collateral benefits of evidence-based substance use prevention programming during middle-school on young adult romantic relationship functioning. *Prevention Science, 23*(4), 618–629.

LoBraico, E. J., Fosco, G. M., Feinberg, M. E., Spoth, R. L., Redmond, C., & Bray, B. C. (2021). Predictors of attendance patterns in a universal family-based preventive intervention program. *The Journal of Primary Prevention, 42*(5), 409–424.

Mason, A., Hitch, J. E., Kosterman, R., McCarty, C. A., Herrenkohl, T. I., & David Hawkins, J. (2010). Growth in adolescent delinquency and alcohol use in relation to young adult crime, alcohol use disorders, and risky sex: A comparison of youth from low-versus middle-income backgrounds. *Journal of Child Psychology and Psychiatry, 51*(12), 1377–1385.

Mason, W. A., Kosterman, R., Haggerty, K., Hawkins, J. D., Spoth, R., & Redmond, C. (2007). Influence of a family-focused substance use preventive intervention on growth in adolescent depressive symptoms. *Journal of Research on Adolescence, 17*(3), 541–564.

Masten, A., & Cicchetti, D. (2010). Developmental cascades. *Development and Psychopathology, 22*, 491–495.

McCauley, D. M., Fang, S., LoBraico, E. J., Feinberg, M., Redmond, C., Spoth, R., & Fosco, G. M. (2021). PROSPER intervention effects on adolescents' school engagement: Implications for young adult educational attainment and financial well-being. Unpublished Manuscript.

Molgaard, V. M., Kumpfer, K. L., & Fleming, E. (1997). *Strengthening Families Program for Parents and Youth 10–14: A video-based curriculum*. Institute for Social and Behavioral Research.

Molgaard, V. M., & Spoth, R. L. (2001). Strengthening Families Program for young adolescents: Overview and outcomes. In S. I. Pfeiffer & L. A. Reddy (Eds.), *Innovative mental health programs for children: Programs that work* (pp. 15–29). Haworth Press.

National Research Council (US) and Institute of Medicine (US) Committee on the Prevention of Mental Disorders and Substance Abuse Among Children, Youth, and Young Adults: Research Advances and Promising Interventions; O'Connell ME, Boat T, Warner KE, editors. Preventing Mental, Emotional, and Behavioral Disorders Among Young People: Progress and Possibilities. Washington (DC): National Academies Press (US); 2009. Available from: https://www.ncbi.nlm.nih.gov/books/NBK32775/.doi:10.17226/12480

Newcomb, M. D., & Bentler, P. M. (1988). *Consequences of adolescent drug use: Impact on the lives of young adults*. Sage.

Paulhus, D. L., & Van Selst, M. (1990). The spheres of control scale: 10 yr of research. *Personality and Individual Differences, 11*(10), 1029–1036.

Redmond, C., Spoth, R., Shin, C., Schainker, L., & Greenberg, M. (2009). Proximal outcomes of an evidence-based universal family-focused intervention implemented byteams. 2006. *Journal of Primary Prevention, 30*, 513–530.

Richardson, F. C., & Tasto, D. L. (1976). Development and factor analysis of a social anxiety inventory. *Behavior Therapy, 7*(4), 453–462.

Riggs, N. R., & Pentz, M. A. (2009). Long-term effects of adolescent marijuana use prevention on adult mental health services utilization: The Midwestern Prevention Project. *Substance Use & Misuse, 44*(5), 616–631.

Rogers, E. M. (1995). *Diffusion of innovations* (4th ed.). ACM the Free Press, pp. 15–23.

Rohrbach, L. A., D'Onofrio, C. N., Backer, T. E., & Montgomery, S. B. (1996). Diffusion of school-based substance abuse prevention programs. *American Behavioral Scientist, 39*(7), 919–934.

Roussos, S. T., & Fawcett, S. B. (2000). A review of collaborative partnerships as a strategy for improving community health. *Annual Review of Public Health, 21*(1), 369–402.

Sameroff, A. J., Peck, S. C., & Eccles, J. S. (2004). Changing ecological determinants of conduct problems from early adolescence to early adulthood. *Development and Psychopathology, 16*(4), 873–896.

Spoth, R. (2007). Opportunities to meet challenges in rural prevention research: Findings from an evolving community-university partnership model. *The Journal of Rural Health, 23*, 42–54.

Spoth, R., & Greenberg, M. T. (2005). Toward a comprehensive strategy for effective practitioner–scientist partnerships and larger-scale community health and well-being. *American Journal of Community Psychology, 35*(3–4), 107–126.

Spoth, R., & Greenberg, M. (2011). Impact challenges in community science-with-practice: Lessons from PROSPER on transformative practitioner-scientist partnerships and prevention infrastructure development. *American Journal of Community Psychology, 48*(1), 106–119.

Spoth, R., & Molgaard, V. (1999). Project Family: A partnership integrating research with the practice of promoting family and youth competencies. In *Serving children and families through community-university partnerships* (pp. 127–137). Springer.

Spoth, R., & Redmond, C. (2002). Project Family prevention trials based in community-university partnerships: Toward scaled-up preventive interventions. *Prevention Science, 3*(3), 203–221.

Spoth, R., Clair, S., Greenberg, M., Redmond, C., & Shin, C. (2007). Toward dissemination of evidence-based family interventions: Maintenance of community-based partnership recruitment results and associated factors. *Journal of Family Psychology, 21*(2), 137.

Spoth, R., Greenberg, M., & Bierman, K. (2000). Public education/extension prevention partnerships: Proposed diffusion research. Invited presentation to the U.S. Department of Education Safe and Drug Free Schools Program, Washington, DC.

Spoth, R., Greenberg, M., Bierman, K., & Redmond, C. (2004). PROSPER community-university partnership model for public education systems: Capacity-building for evidence-based, competence-building prevention. *Prevention Science, 5*(1), 31–39.

Spoth, R., Guyll, M., Redmond, C., Greenberg, M., & Feinberg, M. (2011). Six-year sustainability of evidence-based intervention implementation quality by community-university partnerships: The PROSPER study. *American Journal of Community Psychology, 48*(3–4), 412–425.

Spoth, R., Guyll, M., & Shin, C. (2009). Universal intervention as a protective shield against exposure to substance use: Long-term outcomes and public health significance. *American Journal of Public Health, 99*(11), 2026–2033.

Spoth, R., Kavanagh, K. A., & Dishion, T. J. (2002). Family-centered preventive intervention science: Toward benefits to larger populations of children, youth, and families. *Prevention Science, 3*(3), 145–152.

Spoth, R., Randall, G. K., Shin, C., & Redmond, C. (2005). Randomized study of combined universal family and school preventive interventions: Patterns of long-term effects on initiation, regular use, and weekly drunkenness. *Psychology of Addictive Behaviors, 19*(4), 372.

Spoth, R., Redmond, C., Clair, S., Shin, C., Greenberg, M., & Feinberg, M. (2011). Preventing substance misuse through community–university partnerships: Randomized controlled trial outcomes 4½ years past baseline. *American Journal of Preventive Medicine, 40*(4), 440–447.

Spoth, R., Redmond, C., & Shin, C. (1998). Direct and indirect latent-variable parenting outcomes of two universal family-focused preventive interventions: Extending a public health-oriented research base. *Journal of Consulting and Clinical Psychology, 66*(2), 385.

Spoth, R., Redmond, C., Shin, C., & Azevedo, K. (2004). Brief family intervention effects on adolescent substance initiation: School-level growth curve analyses 6 years following baseline. *Journal of Consulting and Clinical Psychology, 72*(3), 535.

Spoth, R., Redmond, C., Shin, C., Greenberg, M., Clair, S., & Feinberg, M. (2007). Substance-use outcomes at 18 months past baseline: The PROSPER community–university partnership trial. *American Journal of Preventive Medicine*, 32(5), 395–402.

Spoth, R., Redmond, C., Shin, C., & Huck, S. (1999). A protective process model of parent-child affective quality and child mastery effects on oppositional behaviors: A test and replication. *Journal of School Psychology*, 37(1), 49–71.

Spoth, R., Redmond, C., Shin, C., Greenberg, M., Feinberg, M., & Schainker, L. (2013). PROSPER community–university partnership delivery system effects on substance misuse through 6 1/2 years past baseline from a cluster randomized controlled intervention trial. *Preventive Medicine*, 56(3–4), 190–196.

Spoth, R., Redmond, C., Shin, C., Greenberg, M. T., Feinberg, M. E., & Trudeau, L. (2017). PROSPER delivery of universal preventive interventions with young adolescents: Long-term effects on emerging adult substance misuse and associated risk behaviors. *Psychological Medicine*, 47(13), 2246–2259.

Spoth, R., Redmond, C., Shin, C., Trudeau, L., Greenberg, M. T., Feinberg, M. E., & Welsh, J. (2022). Applying the PROSPER prevention delivery system with middle schools: Emerging adulthood effects on substance misuse and conduct problem behaviors through 14 years past baseline. *Child Development*, 93(4), 925–940.

Spoth, R., Redmond, C., Trudeau, L., & Shin, C. (2002). Longitudinal substance initiation outcomes for a universal preventive intervention combining family and school programs. *Psychology of Addictive Behaviors*, 16(2), 129.

Spoth, R., Shin, C., Guyll, M., Redmond, C., & Azevedo, K. (2006). Universality of effects: An examination of the comparability of long-term family intervention effects on substance use across risk-related subgroups. *Prevention Science*, 7(2), 209–224.

Spoth, R., Trudeau, L., Guyll, M., Shin, C., & Redmond, C. (2009). Universal intervention effects on substance use among young adults mediated by delayed adolescent substance initiation. *Journal of Consulting and Clinical Psychology*, 77(4), 620.

Spoth, R., Trudeau, L., Redmond, C., & Shin, C. (2014). Replication RCT of early universal prevention effects on young adult substance misuse. *Journal of Consulting Clinical Psychology*, 82(6), 949–963.

Spoth, R., Trudeau, L., Redmond, C., & Shin, C. (2016). Replicating and extending a model of effects of universal preventive intervention during early adolescence on young adult substance misuse. *Journal of Consulting and Clinical Psychology*, 84(10), 913.

Spoth, R., Trudeau, L., Redmond, C., Shin, C., Greenberg, M., Feinberg, M., & Hyun, G. (2015). PROSPER partnership delivery system: Effects on conduct problem behavior outcomes through 6.5 years past baseline. *Journal of Adolescence*, 45, 44–55.

Spoth, R., Trudeau, L., Shin, C., Ralston, E., Redmond, C., Greenberg, M., & Feinberg, M. (2013). Longitudinal effects of universal preventive intervention on prescription drug misuse: Three randomized controlled trials with late adolescents and young adults. *American Journal of Public Health*, 103(4), 665–672.

Spoth, R., Trudeau, L., Redmond, C., Shin, C., Feinberg, M. E., & Greenberg, M. T. (2019). Brief report on PROSPER academic outcomes: Extended model of crossover effects on young adult college success. *Child Development*, 90(6), 1847–1855.

Spoth, R., Yoo, S., Kahn, J. H., & Redmond, C. (1996). A model of the effects of protective parent and peer factors on young adolescent alcohol refusal skills. *Journal of Primary Prevention*, 16(4), 373–394.

Trudeau, L.T., Spoth, R. L., Mason, W. A., Randall, G. K., Redmond, C., & Schainker, L. (2016). Effects of an adolescent universal substance misuse preventive intervention on young adult depression symptoms: Mediational model. *Journal of Abnormal Child Psychology, 44*(2), 257–268.

US, M. H. S. A., & Office of the Surgeon General (US). (2016). Early intervention, treatment, and management of substance use disorders. In *Facing Addiction in America: The Surgeon General's Report on Alcohol, Drugs, and Health [Internet]*. US Department of Health and Human Services.

Stoolmiller, M., Eddy, J. M., & Reid, J. B. (2000). Detecting and describing preventive intervention effects in a universal school-based randomized trial targeting delinquent and violent behavior. *Journal of Consulting and Clinical psychology, 68*(2), 296.

U.S. Department of Health and Human Services & Office of the Surgeon General. (2016). Facing addiction in America: The surgeon general's report on alcohol, drugs, and health. https://www.ncbi.nlm.nih.gov/books/NBK424859/

Walker, J. L. (1977). Setting the agenda in the U.S. Senate: A theory of problem selection. *British Journal of Political Science, 7,* 423–445.

Weymouth, B. B., Fosco, G. M., & Feinberg, M. E. (2019). Nurturant-involved parenting and adolescent substance use: Examining an internalizing pathway through adolescent social anxiety symptoms and substance refusal efficacy. *Development and Psychopathology, 31*(1), 247–260.

Wills, T. A. (1985). Stress, coping, and tobacco and alcohol use in early adolescence. In S. Shiffman & T. A. Wills (Eds.), *Coping and substance use* (pp. 67–94). New York: Academic.

Network methods

Explanations and issues

JAMES MOODY AND D. WAYNE OSGOOD ■

INTRODUCTION

Network models for youth behavior have been a mainstay of social research since Moreno's discussions of runaway youth in the 1930s argued poetically that relations influence conduct just as surely as gravity rules the behavior of stars and planets (*New York Times*, 1933). The promise of network analysis has always been to make invisible social forces visible and liberate researchers from the unrealistic, but convenient and mathematically tractable, assumptions of statistical independence that govern traditional approaches (Gest et al., 2011). This theoretical promise comes at a high methodological cost, but thankfully these methods have become computationally tractable over the last 30 years, making projects like PROSPER Peers possible. The work necessary to build the models reported in this volume, while never trivial, rests on a much wider foundation of prior work and methodological insight than was available when we embarked on this project all these years ago. And, we expect that these data will contribute to the development of more sophisticated models in the future.

The PROSPER Peers project fits within a long tradition of studying school social networks, with the modern sociometric approach tracing back to at least Coleman's *Adolescent Society* (1961). Substantive work has been broad, focusing on patterns and dynamics of interpersonal relations (Eder & Hallinan, 1978; Hallinan, 1974); adolescent transitions from childhood to adulthood (Dunphy, 1963); and a host of papers attempting to understand how peers affect health (Billy et al., 1984; Kandel, 1978), education (Cohen, 1977, 1983; Cosaro & Eder, 1990), and/or risky behavior (Hagan, 1991; Haynie & Osgood, 2005).

Studying these topics requires a set of tools and techniques that go beyond the standard methods for social and health sciences. Here we briefly introduce two aspects of our work that thread throughout the book. First, we discuss the basic methodological challenges of capturing social interdependence by introducing social network analysis data and methods. Second, we note how the interdependencies in these data and having multiple school settings create challenges for standard statistical modeling techniques that require using network dynamics models and multilevel modeling. For more detailed reviews and deeper methodological treatments on networks, see Light and Moody (2020). For a more detailed description of dynamic network models, see Duxbury (2022), and for multilevel modeling, see Raudenbush and Bryk (2002).

THEORY: CONNECTIONS VERSUS POSITIONS

Social networks are all around us—from our peers at work to neighbors, friends, and kin. Intuitively, we all sense that our networks matter: These are the people we discuss important social life events with, who help us when we are in need, or who inform us when we are confused. These are the people whose opinions we have in mind when we worry about our reputations and whom we wish to impress. A focus on our relationships, and thus social networks, has deep roots in sociological theory, with Durkheim's insights into how social integration and exchange shape social cohesion (Durkheim, 1893/1997) and Simmel's attention to microsocial structures (Simmel, 1950) being perhaps the clearest early examples. Structural anthropology (Nadel, 1957/2013), particularly the rich work on kinship and family exchange networks, featured the most mathematically rigorous early explorations, demonstrating regularities in patterns of kinship ties across cultures (Bearman, 1997).

Modern network theory traces its roots to sociometry, a term coined by Moreno (1934) to describe inquiry into connections, alliances, and subgroups. From this beginning, two main social network traditions developed into sophisticated methodological and theoretical approaches that crystallized in the second half of the twentieth century (see Freeman, 2004, for history). One line of work emanated from scholars at Harvard University and the University of Chicago—including Harrison White and James Coleman. This branch focused on large-scale patterns and regularities in social networks, and people's positions within these structures, to emphasize how patterns of relations defined status hierarchies, social roles ("leader," "follower," "partner") and norms (White, 1965; White et al., 1976). The second line of work emerged from a group of mathematical sociologists and graph theorists centered at Stanford University and the University of California Irvine, who focused on formalizing microinteraction (i.e., dyadic and triadic) patterns identified and proposed by social psychologists. This branch includes substantial work generalizing Heider's notion of balance, which is a tendency of triadic and small-group relations to move toward consistency among social ties and shared attitudes and behavior (Davis, 1963, 1970; Davis & Leinhardt, 1972; Hallinan & Kubitschek, 1990). This work focused primarily on the ways that networks were conduits for the flow of resources and formalized notions of social prominence via measurement of network centrality—identifying who was most likely to act as the pivotal point(s) in a system of exchanges (Freeman, 1978; Friedkin, 1991)— and developed mathematical models of peer influence on attitudes and behavior (Friedkin, 1998). The discipline of social network analysis crystalized organizationally around the International Network for Social Network Analysis (INSNA) and the "sunbelt" meetings founded in the 1970s, led by Linton Freeman and Barry Wellman. A comprehensive, capstone text by Wasserman and Faust (1994) demonstrated the field's growing rigor and sophistication.

Networks matter for many reasons, and we find it generally useful to distinguish two broad classes of network effects that roughly follow the historical West Coast (Freeman, Friedkin) and East Coast (White, Coleman) divide. (See Light & Moody, 2020, and Rawlings et al. 2023, for more details.) The West Coast model focuses on how resources (potentially positive and negative) flow through networks, which we refer to as *connectionist* approaches, whereas the East Coast scholars focus on individuals' roles and status within the larger network, which we term *positional* approaches.

Connectionist approaches to networks treat our social relations as conduits for the flow of something. The obvious example here is disease networks: One catches COVID-19 by having had contact with another person, who passed the infection to you. Similarly, gossip travels through a network because people who know some bit of reputationally relevant information tell it to their friends. Children learn what behaviors are acceptable by observing peers. In this conception of networks, people are effectively pools of resources, and relations are pipes through which the contents of these pools flow. A common example of work within the connectionist paradigm is modeling peer influence. In the basic peer influence model, people who are connected to each other share ideas, beliefs, and behaviors with each other, leading each other to adjust their own, and then the process repeats (Friedkin, 1998). Modeling peer influence has been a mainstay of research on adolescent peer relations, focusing on how friends affect outcomes such as smoking, drinking, school performance, criminal activity, or victimization.

Social and behavioral diffusion is hard to estimate due to the inherent mutual dependence of peer influence with the selection processes that lead to those social connections in the first place (as also discussed in Chapter 1). The general observation that linked individuals are similar—that they exhibit *homophily*, in the jargon of social network analysis—is a necessary but not sufficient condition for inferring social diffusion. In other words, social influence leads to greater similarity between friends than nonfriends. However, the presence of similarity does not necessarily imply influence because similarity also can cause friendship formation. This "selection-or-influence" problem permeates much of the literature on peer effects (Aral & Nicolaides, 2017; Ennett & Bauman, 1994; Kandel, 1978; Shalizi & Thomas, 2011), and managing this problem puts heavy requirements on both the data collected and the statistical methodology (see below). As we point out in Chapter 1, however, this mutual dependence also means that selection determines the influence an individual receives, so understanding selection is essential for understanding influence.

Despite the methodological handwringing over the problem, careful analyses almost always find that observed similarity is due to both factors (as do our results presented throughout the book). Much like classic "nature-or-nurture" debates, contention over selection *or* influence is simpleminded and undertheorized: Kids, like all people, move in a world where they reciprocally shape the world around them while dynamically adjusting their responses (Giddens, 1977).

In contrast to connectionist models, positional models focus on how being embedded in a pattern of network ties shapes one's social role and thus behavior. The focus here is not so much on information or resources that flow through the network, but rather on how the world looks different (and influences one differently) depending on one's location in the overall pattern of network connections or ties. For example, school is likely a more pleasant place for students with many school friends who all get along with each other than for students who are socially isolated or have few reciprocated friendships. And students with strong positive reputations in school—popular kids liked by many others—may feel the pressure of being watched by many others and thus be more sensitive to how their behaviors are seen by others. A positional approach thus takes the individual's location in a particular pattern of relationships as the source for their attitudes and behavior—rather than the resources that flow through each connection. Positional approaches consequently often take the form of social-relational models of status and popularity, linking back to early ideas from Coleman (1961), White (1963), or Nadel (1957/2013). The archetypical method for positional models is the relational block model (White et al., 1976), where one identifies sets of people who have similar types of ties to similar people (all "uncles" are somebody's parent's brother; all "cousins" are somebody's parent's sibling's child). For adolescents, "nerds" are stereotypically kids who have few positive ties to popular rich kids, have strong positive ties with teachers and intellectual adults, and suffer ridicule from "in" kids. Importantly, such kids need not be friends with other similarly situated students; they might be, but it's not necessary for the role. Generalizations of the archetypical approach use single indices of position within a network to capture one's social situation. Common examples include social isolation, popularity, or being a bridge between peer groups.

Statistical complications of nonindependent data

In both approaches, the causal logic of network influence is that people's behavior depends on the behavior of others in the network—either as direct contagion (connectionist) or as signaling appropriate behavior (role/position). To model the effects of these processes, we need to know how people are connected to each other and how their behaviors are related. In traditional social science, statistics are based on the fundamental assumption that individuals in a study sample are independently selected from the population of interest, and calculation of probabilities depends on the independence of data points. However, in social networks, the core focus on how people and their behaviors are connected means that our data points are not independent. The sampling of individuals depends in part on their relations. In technical terms, for any given actor, the error term in any model of their behavior is likely correlated with the error term(s) of their peers, leading to bias and inefficiency in model estimation. (If the only problem is pure network autocorrelation, then like all autocorrelation, the effect is to bias error estimation but not coefficient estimation. In most cases, however, the concern is simultaneously autocorrelated error and unobserved heterogeneity/selection effects, which can lead to bias in both effect and error estimates.) While there is no single magic bullet that solves the problem of nonindependent data—particularly for those who take a hard-line position about the problem of unobserved prior selection effects (Shalizi & Thomas, 2011)—having dynamic, multiwave network data and rich sets of covariates (measures of characteristics associated with network features and behaviors) allows one to do a reasonably good job of parsing likely sources of network selection from the network processes of interest, particularly if one uses tools designed specifically for this purpose (as discussed below).

POINTS AND LINES: BASIC NETWORK METHODS

To understand network effects, it is useful to first outline how network data differ from more standard social and behavioral data and the sorts of metrics commonly calculated from these sources.

Data structure

Network analysis requires somewhat unique data structures; a minimal representation of a network requires one data structure for the relations and one for the actor attributes. We provide an informal summary of these here; for more rigorous treatment, see Wasserman and Faust (1994).

Figure 3.1 illustrates the nature of network data by representing hypothetical relations among seven adolescents in a small setting. The graphical

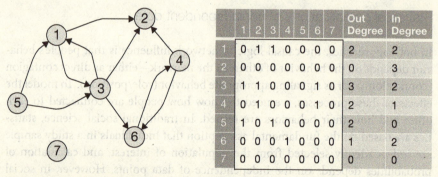

Figure 3.1 A small network and its adjacency matrix.

representation—a sociogram—is given on the left, while the "adjacency matrix" representation is given on the right. For illustration, the two additional columns on the right contain network indices measured for the individuals.

Graphically, a relation between two nodes is represented by an arrow from the respondent to the friend he or she nominated. Here, we see that person 1 nominates persons 2 and 3 as friends. In the adjacency matrix, each person is represented as both a row (horizontal) and a column (vertical), and a nomination is recorded by placing a "1" in the row of the respondent who "sent" the nomination and the column of the nominee. So, the two friends of Person 5 are in the (5, 1) and (5, 3) cells of the matrix. This network is *directed*, meaning that a nomination from one person to another does not necessitate a nomination in return. In this example, the nomination from Person 1 to Person 3 is reciprocated (3 and 1 nominate each other), but the nomination from Person 1 to Person 2 is not reciprocated.

In this example, the relation is *binary*, indicating "friend" or "not friend," but the network data might take a range of values instead. For instance, the relationship data could be ratings of how close people feel to each other on a 7-point scale. Similarly, a researcher can layer multiple types of relations on the same set of nodes to produce a "multiplex" network. In the PROSPER data, for example, we ask for "best friends," "other close friends," and "romantic partners." The answers to each of these questions can be represented as a separate adjacency matrix—and these separate matrices can be combined in a three-dimensional representation. In that case, the ties between Persons 5 and 1, for example, can exist in any or all of the layers.

Levels of analysis

Networks are complex data structures that enable multiple levels of analysis. At the most microlevel we might only be interested in the characteristics of each connected dyad. In that case, the unit of analysis is the dyad, and there are 10 connected dyads in Figure 3.1. Alternatively, we could focus on just the relations around a focal person—an "ego"—in which case the network yields seven observations (treating each individual as ego in turn), and we would ask questions about the number of ties for each individual or the mean behavior for each individual's local context (i.e., set of friends). Membership in the ego networks varies, depending on which type of relation is of interest. For example, Person 1's *send* ego network consists of Persons 2 and 3 (the people Person 1 chooses); Person 4's *receive* ego network consists of Person 6 (the people who choose Person 4); Person 3's total network includes Nodes 1, 2, 5, and 6 (either). Node 7 has a null or empty ego network of all three types.

Between the level of ego network and whole networks are "cohesive groups"—subsets of the population who have more ties with each other than with anyone else in the network. The literature on methods for identifying cohesive groups or "communities" in network data is vast (see Fortunato, 2010; Moody & Coleman,

2015; Shai et al., 2020, for reviews). For intuitive purposes, these methods are means for identifying sets of individuals who are socially most relevant to each other, corresponding to "cliques" or "crowds" that one might recognize visiting the lunchroom or that kids would point out as who typically hangs out with whom. Applying a community detection algorithm to Figure 3.1 (which would be odd given its small size) might indicate that individuals 1, 2, 3, and 5 are in one group, individuals 4 and 6 in another, and person 7 in a "group" alone.

The final level of analysis is the network as a whole, in which case Figure 3.1 represents a single observation. Most network studies are also case studies, in that they concern a single network, such as one school, workplace, or club. This has traditionally been one of the major weaknesses of network analysis since despite having a population of cases in any setting, each setting is still a single case. PROSPER Peers joins a small number of hallmark studies that break with that limitation by providing data for a meaningful larger sample of networks in the same type of setting. Specifically, PROSPER Peers collected network data for two grade cohorts in 27 small school districts on eight occasions from sixth through twelfth grades.

Indices

For many sorts of analyses, the question of interest involves asking how a feature of the network is related to adolescent behavior. To do so, we must define a set of indices that summarize relevant dimensions of the network. In general, we are interested in five sorts of network indices: volume, composition, connectivity, position, and community. Each of these cross-cut units of analysis. So, for example, we can have a volume measure like density at the ego-network, community or whole-network level.

Volume: How much connection? The simplest network measures are of volume and capture how often actors relate to each other in sundry ways. The most common volume measure is degree: the count of the number of nodes each node is connected to. In directed networks we distinguish number of ties sent—*out-degree*—from number of ties received—*in-degree*. In Figure 3.1, the two columns to the right of the adjacency matrix provide the out-degree and in-degree for each node. For positive social relations such as PROSPER's friendship nominations, out-degree is a good measure of sociality or social gregariousness—reflecting how engaged each person is with others. In-degree is a good measure of sociometric popularity—capturing how often people want to be friends with someone. (There is a rich literature on the meaning of asymmetric relations [see Hallinan, 1974; Johnsen, 1985; Kitts & Diego, 2021]. Intuitively, we might expect that "friendship" would be symmetric: If A is a "friend" of B, then B should be a friend with A. Empirically, we do see greater reciprocity than one would expect by chance, but the majority of observed social relations are not reciprocated. Some of this nonreciprocation is an artifact induced by limited nomination ability.) At the full network level, volume measures capture one dimension of cohesiveness or integration of the entire setting. The traditional measure is density, which is the number of ties as a proportion of the number possible. For the network in Figure 3.1, 10 of 42 possible ties are present, yielding a density of 0.24. When comparing across networks of different sizes, differences in density become confused with differences in size (since its denominator grows with the square of setting size), and then average degree provides a more useful comparison across settings.

Composition: Who is connected to whom? While volume measures capture the amount of connection, composition metrics capture the types of nodes linked together. At the individual ego network level, we are often interested in characterizing the local friendship context for each adolescent by scores such as the proportion of their peers who are regular smokers or the proportion who are the same race or sex as the respondent. As Chapter 1 discusses, these measures about respondents' friends are central to the study of peer influence. While there are numerous composition metrics one can employ, we generally focus on two types: measures that capture a central tendency and measures that capture dispersion. The most common central tendency measure is just the average across an individual's friends for beliefs or behaviors. For example, we might capture the normative context for smoking by the average of each person's friends' ratings for how acceptable smoking is or the importance of school performance by the average grade point average (GPA) of peers. For categorical features like race, we typically use the Blau heterogeneity index, which captures the probability that any two randomly chosen members of the set are different.

Composition measures are useful for studying the observed level of similarity or homophily at some level of the network. As with most network features, we can examine composition at multiple scales, ranging from dyads (same vs. different), friends in an ego network (proportion same as ego, means, heterogeneity), peer groups (overall mean levels of x), and entire networks (odds of same-race ties in a school, pairwise correlations of attribute values).

Two complications should be considered when using composition measures. The first is the composition relative to the risk set, and the second is score-limiting features imposed by network size. Observing an ego network with low attribute heterogeneity (e.g., a group limited to nonsmokers) might be seen as an indicator of homophily. Yet, if the baseline behavior is very rare, then finding that most people share the nonactivity is substantively less interesting than in the setting where the behavior is more common (a school with very few smokers versus one where half of the students smoke). As such, it is often advisable to normalize composition measures by chance expectations for the setting as a whole. Second, dispersion measures will be highly truncated in small local networks. People who have only one friend, for example, must have an ego network heterogeneity score of 0. Those with two friends can have a score of 0 or 0.5. As such, it is almost always recommended to examine dispersion or heterogeneity net of volume.

Network components. Volume and composition measures are summaries of how often people are connected or the types of people that are generally connected to each other. Volume and composition measures are to networks what atomic weight is to chemistry: It describes what atoms are, but not how they are arranged. But carbon is still carbon whether it is graphite or diamond; what distinguishes a gemstone from a lubricant is how the atoms are arranged. So, too, with networks: To capture the character of a social system, we need to move past simple composition measures and characterize the pattern of ties directly, which requires understanding indirect connectivity. Intuitively, a network is "held together" well if the pattern of relations in the network is such that anyone in the network can reach anyone else easily (through friends and friends of a friend, etc.). In a cohesive or well-connected network, it would require many changes to break the network up and prevent individuals from reaching others. The extent to which this intuitive notion is true depends on the indirect connections between nodes, known as paths. A path in a network is a nonrepeating sequence of connections between nodes. In Figure 3.1, for example, the sequence starting at Node 1: {1 → 3 → 6 → 4} is a three-step path from 1 to 4. The largest set of nodes in a network that can be linked by at least one path is a *component*. A component is the minimal requirement for defining a cohesive network. If paths respect directionality, then we distinguish *strong components*, where each person can reach every other person, from *weak components*, where at least one member of each pair could reach the other. As the number of unique paths in the network increases, the network becomes increasingly cohesive (Moody & White, 2003). In Figure 3.1, Nodes 1 through 6 are in a single weakly connected component. The connectivity structure governs where information flows in a network and thus who can likely influence whom indirectly. We sometimes construct metrics that take the number of steps in a path ("path distance") into account. For example, we could define a measure that is the number of smokers within three steps of ego as a way to characterize the local smoking context for each person.

Positions in the network. The third type of metric captures a node's position within the overall network, which we typically measure via some version of a centrality score (though alternative group models are possible). Centrality scoring is a deep and highly nuanced topic (see Borgatti & Everett, 2020, for review). Informally, the main idea is to array people between the "center" and "periphery" of a network, but the meaning of those terms depends entirely on which underlying feature of the network one is emphasizing. The four most common types of centrality scores are based on volume (degree centrality, discussed above); path distance ("closeness centrality"); bridging ("betweenness centrality"); and "power" or "status"—captured by the extent to which central people interact with other central people ("Bonacich power centrality" or other eigenvector-based measures).

Closeness centrality counts the average number of steps from each respondent to every other respondent (their "distance" to all others) and then inverts it to get closeness. In Figure 3.1, Node 3 would have the highest closeness centrality (as it is one step from most of the others and within two steps from all but Node 7). As discussed above, degree centrality is generally useful as an indicator of local engagement (for out-degree) or popularity (in-degree). Closeness centrality, in contrast, is best suited for theoretical problems that turn on generalized diffusion in the network. We would expect that nodes with high closeness centrality typically can get their points of view out to the wider network quickly and are more likely to be aware of the attitudes and beliefs of many people in the network. Betweenness centrality is most useful in situations where bridging disparate groups is important: Students who hang out with both school-oriented cliques and deviant cliques, for example, might have high betweenness centrality. Power centrality is a good indicator of generalized status—particularly when calculated on incoming nominations. In that case, it captures the set of students who are popular among other popular kids.

At the individual level, there is a set of special positional metrics that capture social isolation. Pure social isolates neither send nor receive friendship nominations from any other student in their grade. On the one hand, pure isolates are not embedded in the peer network and as such are not likely to see the school as a welcoming, positive place. On the other hand, they are also not exposed to school deviants and thus may be less likely to take on oppositional points of view. Beyond the pure isolate case, there are kids who are in-isolates (receive no nominations), out-isolates (send no nominations), and "disconnected"—kids who have one or two friends, but as a collective they cannot reach anyone else in the school (see Copeland et al., 2018, for a more detailed discussion; also discussed in Chapter 7).

While individual scores are useful for characterizing people's positions within each setting, the distribution of centrality scores captures an important aspect of the overall network shape. Theoretically, one can imagine interpolating between a purely centralized system where one node dominates the network, to a purely equal system where everyone has the exact same centrality score. This notion defines *centralization* and captures the relational equality in each network setting.

Block models. Centrality scores define position along a single metric dimension; block models, in contrast, allow one to identify sets of students who have similar relational patterns overall. There is a long theoretical literature on block models (Bearman, 1997; Burt, 1990; White et al., 1976), though their use in empirical work generally and health work in particular is less common.

Block models capture position in the network through *network equivalence*. Two nodes are said to be *structurally equivalent* if they have the same type of ties to the same people (White et al., 1976). Two perfectly structurally equivalent nodes could not be distinguished by their connections, but only by their node ID. Theoretically, the "to the same people" restriction of structural equivalence is generally too strict as we are interested in sets of nodes with the same sort of relational pattern. For this, we use *regular equivalence*: Two nodes are regularly equivalent if they have similar types of ties to similar alters. In practice, this means that regularly equivalent nodes have similar summary scores across a wide range of metrics. For example, a "leading crowd" might include nodes with high in-degree, high-(in)power centrality, strong transitivity, high out-reciprocity and low out-degree. In PROSPER peers, we follow Burt (1990) and use the triad census to capture how nodes are related to every other pair of nodes in the network and add centrality scores to capture relational status beyond direct ties. We then use hierarchical clustering to identify sets of nodes with similar patterns.

Cohesive groups in networks. The final class of metrics we calculate is within-network community members. Adolescent research has focused on the close set of peers as a core socialization concept since at least Coleman's *Adolescent Society* (1961). The main notion here is that kids act in groups: sets of kids that hang out together, take on similar beliefs and attitudes, and are friends with each other. As a general rule, we expect that behaviors are much more homogeneous within a closely connected peer group than between peer groups.

Identifying cohesive peer groups is challenging methodologically as the number of possible ways to sort kids into groups is much larger than one can possibly search. As such, there is a vast literature on "community detection" that attempts to refine various heuristic models for peer group membership. Most of these models have as their main goal the maximization of relative in-group density. It ought to be the case that kids who are members of a cohesive group have more ties with that group than with anyone else. Increasingly, this has been operationalized via the network's modularity score (Girvan & Newman, 2002), which captures the extent to which ties fall within communities beyond chance levels:

$$Q = \sum_{ij} \frac{1}{2m}\left(A_{ij} - \gamma \frac{K_i K_j}{2m}\right)\delta(C_i C_j) \quad (3.1)$$

where i and j index all pairs in the network, m is the number of edges, k is each node's degree, A is the adjacency matrix, δ is an indicator for whether nodes i and j are in the same subgroup or not, and γ is a "resolution parameter" that identifies the scale at which clustering is observed (Fortunato & Barthelemy, 2007; Reichardt & Bornholdt, 2006). Substantively, $[K_i K_j / 2m]$ represents the null model—the expected likelihood of contact between two nodes—here simply dependent on the degrees of the pair, so $(A_{ij} - [\gamma \frac{K_i K_j}{2m}])$ is the connectivity above random expectation, normalized by the total volume of ties in the network, and $\delta(C_i C_j)$ is an indicator for the nodes being in the same community. An alternative metric that might be more intuitive for social scientists is the freeman segregation index, which captures the simple difference between the number of cross-group ties observed in the network and the number expected by chance, following a chi-square or contingency table logic. See Moody and Coleman (2015) for a review of some of these alternatives.

Regardless of the metric chosen to evaluate the clustering solution, one needs a heuristic to search through the set of possible group assignments to find a close-to-optimal solution. Our model builds from Moody (2001) to find groups that have the highest likelihood of being a source for peer influence. We augmented this approach in two ways. First, we seed our search with groups defined by a factor analysis of the adjacency matrix following precedent from work in developmental psychology (Cairns & Cairns, 1994; Gest et al., 2003). This gives us a good first pass that helps initialize the search. We then use the iterative pseudo–peer influence process to create similarity scores and cluster these two sources of similarity to get our initial groupings. Finally, we do an iterative node-level pass to ensure that each node is contributing to the overall group-specific modularity score. If a group would have a higher score if a node were switched to a different group, and that switch improved the score of the target group, we switched their membership. If, removing the node improves the fit if the initial group, but there was no other group that would benefit by having the node, this indicates a "bridge" or "joint" membership, and such nodes were placed in their own class. We discuss the characteristics of these groups in Chapters 4 and 7.

Analyzing friendship selection and peer influence processes with SIENA

The Simulation Investigation for Empirical Network Analysis (SIENA) network analysis method has been PROSPER Peers's primary tool for addressing research questions about friendship selection and peer influence (Osgood, Ragan, et al., 2013; Osgood, Feinberg, et al., 2015; Ragan, 2014). SIENA provides a flexible analytic framework for studying these processes, and it resolves difficult statistical problems inherent in the task (Snijders, 2001; Snijders et al., 2010; Steglich et al., 2010). This section briefly describes the purposes and nature of SIENA and how we have implemented it in our work. To learn more about the method, see Snijders and colleagues (2010) helpful introduction, and the SIENA manual contains a wealth of additional information (Ripley et al., 2021).

Many of our research questions have not required a specialized network analytic method like SIENA. Often, the relevant social network information can be summarized with indices of the sort described in previous sections of this chapter (e.g., in-degree, centrality, density, correlation between friends), and those indices can then serve as outcome or explanatory variables in analyses not specially designed for network data.

Specialized network analytic methods such as SIENA are necessitated by three types of complexity that often arise when analyzing selection and influence processes. The first is that these processes often are inherently endogenous, or self-influencing, due to patterns of mutual or circular influence among cases and processes. For instance, the tendency to reciprocate friendships means that the presence of one friendship raises the probability the return friendship will occur. This pattern creates endogenous dependence among both network ties in friendship selection processes and individuals in peer influence processes (see Chapter 1, Figure 1.2). The second complexity is that a statistical analysis will also need to allow for the correlations among individuals and friendships produced by these patterns of dependence, which will otherwise distort significance tests and standard errors. The third reason for specialized network analytic approaches is that they provide means for specifying network processes that are not readily translated to variables that can be added to conventional analyses. This arises because the processes concern patterns involving multiple nodes and links. For instance, transitivity, which is being the friend of a friend's friend, entails a minimum of three individuals and three potential friendships, and any individual or link can be part of numerous transitive triads. Programs for network analysis include facilities for extracting the relevant information and incorporating it in a statistical model.

SIENA is designed for analyzing a change in data for full networks measured on multiple occasions, which is a good match to PROSPER's research design. SIENA estimates two models simultaneously, a network model for the friendship selection processes and a behavior model for the influence processes. The network model translates the selection processes to probabilities for the presence versus absence of each of the ties that make up the network matrix. Similarly, the behavior model translates the peer influence processes to probabilities for higher and lower values on the individual-level attribute that serves as its outcome variable. Thus, the conceptual core of SIENA is the correspondence between the processes of interest and which friendships and behaviors have higher and lower probabilities. For instance, a preference for reciprocated friendships is a selection process that would be associated with a higher probability of forming new friendships that are reciprocated than for those that are not reciprocated and a lower probability of dropping a current reciprocated friendship than for dropping one that is not reciprocated.

Both the selection and behavior models take the form of discrete choice models, meaning that they concern the relative probability of making each of the choices out of a set of alternatives. For the network model, the choice is which (if any) tie to change, by either adding a new friendship or dropping a current one. For the behavior model, the choice is between increasing one level on the behavior (e.g., going from smoking once a week to smoking more than once a week), decreasing one level, or not changing. The researcher chooses which selection and influence processes to include in the model based on the research questions of interest. For each process, the results include a logistic regression coefficient that indicates the direction and strength of its impact on the probabilities of the alternative choices.

For interested readers, Equations 3.2 through 3.5 (from Steglich et al., 2010) show the mathematical form of these models. The discrete choice model for the network links is

$$P(\Delta_{x_{ij}}) = \frac{exp(f(\Delta_{x_{ij}}))}{\sum_{m=1}^{M} exp(f(\Delta_{x_{im}}))} \quad (3.2)$$

$P(\Delta_{x_{ij}})$ is the probability of person i changing the friendship tie with person j, $f(\Delta_{x_{ij}})$ is the log odds of this choice versus other choices, and the summation is across M actors, corresponding to the possible changes in the network (with $j = i$ representing no change). Equation 3.3 elaborates the log odds for each potential friendship choice as a linear equation, expressed as a summation across the k network processes the researcher chooses to include in the model:

$$f(\Delta_{x_{ij}}) = \sum_{k=0}^{K}\left[\beta_k NS_k\left(X\mid\Delta_{x_{ij}}, a_i, b_j, c_{ij}\right)\right] \tag{3.3}$$

In this equation, β_k is the logistic coefficient expressing the strength of process k, and NS_k is a network statistic that corresponds to that process. The remainder of the equation indicates the information that may contribute to the network statistic, which includes the state of the network if this tie is changed ($X\mid\Delta_{x_{ij}}$) as well as attributes of the actor (a_i), the alter (b_j), and their relationship (c_{ij}). The SIENA manual includes the formulas for the network statistics of the many processes that can be modeled (Ripley et al., 2021). A simple example is that the network statistic for the tendency to reciprocate ties is the count of reciprocated ties for actor i, so β_k indicates how much higher the log odds are for adding a friendship that is reciprocated (thus raising this count) versus adding an unreciprocated friendship.

Equation 3.4 shows the discrete choice model for behavior, which requires the outcome measure to be coded as ordered categories:

$$P(y_i = l) = \frac{\exp(g(y_i = l))}{\sum_{m=L-1}^{L+1}\exp(g(y_i = m))} \tag{3.4}$$

Here $P(y_i = l)$ is the probability of person i changing behavior y to level l, $g(y_i = l)$ is the log odds of person i choosing level l, L is the current level of behavior, and the summation is from one below the current level to one above. Equation 3.5 is a linear equation for the log odds of the behavior choices, comparable to Equation 3.1:

$$g(y_i = l) = \sum_{k=0}^{K}\left[\gamma_k BS_k\left(y\mid y_i = l, X, a_i, b_j, c_{ij}\right)\right] \tag{3.5}$$

In this case, γ_k is the logistic coefficient for behavior process k. The behavior statistic BS_k varies across the levels of the outcome, and it may incorporate the same sources of information as the network statistics. For instance, a behavior statistic to reflect peer influence can be formed by using the information in the network matrix X to identify person i's friends and compute their average on the behavior of interest (treating the measure of behavior as a b_j variable). The network statistics of Equation 3.3 may be affected by the behavior model because y can serve as one of the a_i variables, and the behavior statistics of Equation 3.5 may be affected by the network model because X is an input. Thus, the two models are endogenous to one another and interdependent.

SIENA takes the unusual and creative approach of deriving estimates for the coefficients from the data through a simulation process. These simulations take the data at Time 1 as a starting point and then use the network and behavior models to simulate the evolution of the network and the behavioral outcome between Time 1 and Time 2. The simulations proceed through a series of microsteps in which a randomly chosen individual has the opportunity for changing either a network tie or a behavioral change. The simulated choices are probabilistically determined by applying the network selection or behavior influence model of Equations 3.2 to 3.5 to the current state of the network and behaviors (which have evolved due to previous microsteps), using preliminary estimates of the coefficients for the processes. At the end of the simulation, the simulated data at Time 2 are compared to the actual data for features relevant to the processes. For instance, if the number of reciprocated friendships resulting in the simulation is higher or lower than in the actual Time 2 data (regardless of which specific friendships are reciprocated), the preliminary estimate of the coefficient for reciprocity is adjusted accordingly. The process of simulation and adjustment continues until the simulations reliably match the data on the features relevant to the processes in the two models. The resulting estimates inherently take into account the interdependence among all the processes because they are jointly influencing the evolution of the simulated networks. SIENA produces separate estimates for each network in the data set (i.e., each grade cohort in a school district). In PROSPER, SIENA produces selection and influence (and many other) estimates for up to 54 networks (2 grade cohorts × 27 schools), which are then combined through a meta-analysis.

SIENA is particularly well suited to PROSPER Peers's research design, with its many waves of full network data and large number of networks. The scale of the PROSPER data also means that using SIENA is a challenging task. With so many grade-cohort networks, running SIENA requires creating many hundreds of data files in very specific formats. We invested considerable effort in developing, and later refining, a base selection model that provides a suitable fit to all of our networks in terms of distributions of in-degree, out-degree, and triads (Ripley et al., 2021). Incorporating this base model in all of our substantive models reduces the risk that findings of interest will be distorted by failing to fit extraneous aspects of the data. Our current base model can be seen in articles by Ragan (2020) and Hoeben and colleagues (2021). In addition, SIENA is computationally intensive, with a single analysis on a moderate-size network typically requiring several hours of high-speed computing. Estimating a single model for our entire data set requires many days of computing on Penn State's high-speed cluster computing facilities (which are excellent, thanks to the university's major programs in fields such as meteorology and astrophysics).

Lessons learned: Implications beyond SIENA. SIENA has proved an invaluable tool for our work, and we make heavy use of it. Our experiences and findings carry some lessons with broader implications for studying adolescents' friendships and risky behavior. The first is that PROSPER's large scale brings a high level of precision and statistical power that is extremely useful; many studies lack such precision as they are based on small samples from one or only a few schools. This point applies to all of our work, but our experience with SIENA has made it most apparent. A recent meta-analysis of SIENA studies of peer influence and selection for similarity on delinquency illustrates this well (Gallupe et al., 2019). It showed that a large share of studies yielded results so imprecise that confidence intervals ranged from very small or negative effects to large ones, and thus they were of little value until combined in the meta-analysis. In contrast, the estimates from PROSPER Peers closely matched the overall results of the meta-analysis in definitively showing moderate levels of both selection and influence, with narrow confidence intervals (Osgood, Feinberg, et al., 2015). Furthermore, having data from many communities has been helpful to determine how much the processes we studied vary from place to place and across cohorts of adolescents (see Chapter 10). Our multilevel meta-analyses of SIENA results from our sample of networks have consistently found that, though estimates vary widely across our networks, in most cases that variation is largely due to imprecision (reflected in their standard errors) rather than to meaningful differences between communities (Osgood, Ragan, et al., 2013; Osgood, Feinberg, et al., 2015; Ragan et al., 2022).

A second lesson we have taken from our experience with SIENA is that estimates of peer influence on risky behavior from more conventional analyses appear less problematic than we might have assumed. Several authors had suggested that conventional analyses would overestimate peer influence because they do not address the endogeneity of influence in networks or control for complex forms of selection (Friemel, 2012; Knecht et al., 2011; Veenstra et al., 2013). Yet, many studies cannot meet SIENA's requirements, which include not only repeated waves of full network data, but also a minimum density of links and a moderate level of stability for both links and behavior. For instance, our own data for romantic ties are too sparse for SIENA analysis. We were curious to see how badly conventional analyses would overestimate influence compared to SIENA. To find out, we conducted a series of comparable analyses using both SIENA and more conventional regression analyses (Ragan et al., 2022). To our surprise, we found little tendency toward overestimation. This is hardly a guarantee that either SIENA or non-SIENA analyses are accurate, but given this limited evidence of bias, we believe that careful non-SIENA analyses should be taken seriously rather than routinely dismissed.

Multilevel models

Multilevel regression models feature prominently in data analyses for PROSPER Peers, and this section provides a brief, nontechnical overview of our use of them. Also known as hierarchical linear models, multilevel models are designed for studies in which sets of cases are nested within groups, such as sets of residents from many neighborhoods or repeated observations about each individual in a sample. Groupings like these tend to produce violations of the standard statistical assumption of independence because cases in the same group are more similar to one another than can be accounted for by the explanatory variables (so their residuals are correlated). Failing to take this dependence into account leads to overly optimistic significance tests and underestimating standard errors. To address this problem, multilevel models capture the unexplained correlation or dependence among cases in the same group through additional residual variance terms at the more aggregate level (also known as random effects). For instance, a multilevel model of residents within neighborhoods not only would include the usual individual level residual variance, but also add a separate residual variance term for unexplained mean differences between neighborhoods (Raudenbush & Bryk, 2002).

The nesting or grouping structure of the PROSPER research design is complex. The highest level of aggregation is the 27 small school districts (or communities) that participated in the study and provided network data. Within the districts, students are grouped both within their grade cohorts and within the schools they progress through across grades (i.e., middle schools or junior high and high schools). The most fine-grained level of analysis is waves of data collection (i.e., Wave 1 in fall of Grade 6, Wave 2 in spring of Grade 6, Wave 3 in spring of Grade 7, etc.). Analyses of the friendships are also subject to dependence in the form of extra similarity between individuals linked by friendship, as we discuss elsewhere in this chapter and in Chapter 1. This form of dependence is addressed by network methods such as SIENA, rather than by multilevel models.

Our most elaborate multilevel model has four levels, with waves of data as Level 1, nested within individuals as Level 2, nested within schools as Level 3, which are in turn nested within school districts (or communities) as Level 4. Accordingly, the model has residual variance terms that allow for unexplained mean differences on the outcome at each level (also called random intercepts). The model does not treat cohorts as a level because schools and cohorts are crossed, meaning that neither is nested within the other. Instead, the model allows for mean differences between cohorts within school districts through a random coefficient for cohort (represented by a dummy variable). The random coefficients for cohort provide an alternative means of allowing for any unexplained mean differences between the two grade cohorts in each school district.

None of the published PROSPER Peers studies have required all of these elements. The two most complex multilevel models used network indices as their outcomes (Osgood, Feinberg, et al., 2013, Osgood et al., 2022), so they did not have an individual student level of analysis, but included all of the other elements. Our most common strategy has been to combine information about school district, grade cohort, and school into 54 combinations of school district and grade cohort. These combinations capture almost all of the total variance from those three levels, which is far less than variance at the individual and wave levels. The school district and grade cohort combinations also correspond to the networks that we follow across all eight waves of data collection. This approach yields a three-level model (waves within individuals within district-cohort combinations) with random intercepts at each level.

We have also used multilevel models for meta-analyses for our studies in which the outcome variable was a statistic computed for a network. This arose when outcomes were regression coefficients (Osgood, Feinberg, et al., 2013), correlations (Osgood et al., 2022), and SIENA estimates (e.g., Ragan, 2020). In these cases, the outcome variable contains more error for some networks than others, depending on the network's sample size and perhaps on other features such as collinearity. Meta-analytic models take this varying error into account and place more weight on the networks with smaller standard errors. Multilevel models accomplish this through an additional residual variance term equal to the squared standard error of the statistic for each network. Our SIENA analyses produce separate estimates for each combination of grade cohort and school district, and they combine information across schools and waves. We combine the estimates across networks through multilevel meta-analyses that treat cohorts as nested within school districts and base the meta-analytic error variance on SIENA's standard errors.

SUMMARY AND CONCLUSION

Network analysis is a deep and rapidly growing field and this introduction to the methodological issues has just scratched the surface (see Light & Moody, 2020, and Rawlings et al., 2023, for deeper methods reviews). The power of network analysis stems from taking seriously the ways in which our social relations form a personalized context that shapes how we experience the world around us. As Simmel noted long ago (1908/2009, 1955), what makes people unique is that they sit at the intersection of multiple social circles, uniquely occupying positions that define their social self. Network contexts combine issues that standard social science methods have traditionally treated as separate: We have long-standing models for neighborhood contexts (Raudenbush & Bryk, 2002), for measuring network features (Wasserman & Faust, 1994), and for understanding complex causal systems (Bollen, 1989; Perl, 2009), for example. But because teens actively adjust their relations in response to the activities of others in their orbit, youth networks are necessarily endogenous systems that generally confound each of these approaches. This has necessitated new methods for disentangling these effects (Snijders, 2001), which we have availed ourselves to here; we are among the first teams to integrate these models across multiple contexts (see also Lomi et al., 2016; McFarland et al., 2014). There is, of course, much more work to be done with such models both methodologically and substantively, and we hope that this chapter has made clear that the difficulties associated with estimation and design are not only real, but also tractable, and that others continue to take up the challenge to explore the network contexts that shape adolescent lives.

REFERENCES

Aral, S., & Nicolaides, C. (2017). Exercise contagion in a global social network. *Nature Communications, 8*(1), 1–8.

Bearman, P. S. (1997). Generalized exchange. *American Journal of Sociology, 102*(5), 1383–1415.

Billy, J. O., Rodgers, J. L., & Udry, J. R. (1984). Adolescent sexual behavior and friendship choice. *Social Forces, 62*, 653–678.

Bollen, K. 1989. *Structural equations with latent variables.* Wiley.

Borgatti, S. P., & Everett, M. G. (2020). Three perspectives on centrality. In L. Ryan & J. Moody (Eds.), *Oxford handbook of social networks.* Oxford University Press.

Burt, R. S. (1990). Detecting role equivalence. *Social Networks, 12*, 83–97.

Cairns, R. B., & Cairns, B. D. (1994). *Lifelines and risks: pathways of youth in our time.* Cambridge University Press.

Cohen, J. M. (1977). Sources of peer group homogeneity. *Sociology of Education, 50*, 227–241.

Cohen, J. M. (1983). Peer influence on college aspirations. *American Sociological Review, 48*, 728–734.

Coleman, J. S. (1961). *The adolescent society.* Free Press of Glencoe.

Copeland, M., Fisher, J. C., Moody, J., & Feinberg, M. E. (2018). Different kinds of lonely: Dimensions of isolation and substance use in adolescence. *Journal of Youth and Adolescence, 47*(8), 1755–1770.

Corsaro, W. A., & Eder, D. (1990). Children's peer cultures. *Annual Review of Sociology, 16*, 197–220.

Davis, J. A. (1963). Structural balance, mechanical solidarity, and interpersonal relations. *American Journal of Sociology, 68*, 444–462.

Davis, J. A. (1970). Clustering and hierarchy in interpersonal relations: Testing two graph theoretical models on 742 sociomatrices. *American Sociological Review, 35*, 843–851.

Davis, J. A., & Leinhardt, S. (1972). The structure of positive relations in small groups. In J. Berger, M. Zelditch, & B. Anderson (Eds.), *Sociological theories in progress* (Vol. 2, pp. 218–251). Houghton Mifflin.

Dunphy, D. C. (1963). The social structure of urban adolescent peer groups. *Sociometry, 26*, 230–246.

Durkheim, E. (1997). *The division of labour in society* (Trans. W. D. Halls, intro. Lewis A. Coser). Free Press. (Original work published 1893)

Duxbury, S. W. (2022). *Longitudinal network models.* Sage.

Eder, D., & Hallinan, M. (1978). Sex differences in children's friendships. *American Sociological Review, 43*, 237–250.

Ennett, S., & Bauman, K. (1994). The contribution of influence and selection to adolescent peer group homogeneity: The case of adolescent cigarette smoking. *Journal of Personality and Social Psychology, 67*(4), 653–663.

Fortunato, S. (2010). Community detection in graphs. *Physics Reports, 486*, 75–174. https://doi.org/10.1016/j.physrep.2009.11.002

Fortunato, S., & Barthelemy, M. (2007). Resolution limit in community detection. *PNAS: Proceedings of the National Academy of Science, 104*(1), 36–41. https://doi.org/10.1073/pnas.0605965104

Freeman, L. (1978). Centrality in social networks: Conceptual clarification. *Social Networks, 1*, 215–239.
Freeman, L. (2004). *The development of social network analysis*. Empirical Press.
Friedkin, N. E. (1991). Theoretical foundations for centrality measures. *American Journal of Sociology, 96*, 1478–1504.
Friedkin, N. E. (1998). *A structural theory of social influence*. Cambridge University Press. https://doi.org/10.1017/CBO9780511527524
Friemel, T. N. (2012). Network dynamics of television use in school classes. *Social Networks, 34*(3), 346–358.
Gallupe, O., McLevey, J., & Brown, S. (2019). Selection and influence: A meta-analysis of the association between peer and personal offending. *Journal of Quantitative Criminology, 35*(2), 313–335.
Gest, S. D., Farmer, T. W., Cairns, B. D., & Xie, H. (2003). Identifying children's peer social networks in school classrooms: Links between peer reports and observed interactions. *Social Development, 12*, 513–529. https://doi.org/10.1111/1467-9507.00246
Gest, S. D., Osgood, D. W., Feinberg, M., Bierman, K. L., & Moody, J. (2011). Strengthening prevention program theories and evaluations: Contributions from social network analysis. *Prevention Science, 12*, 349–360.
Giddens, A. (1977). *New rules of sociological method: A positive critique of interpretative sociologies*. Basic Books.
Girvan, M., & Newman, M. E. J. (2002). Community structure in networks. *Proceedings of the National Academies of Science of the United States of America, 99*, 7821–7826.
Hagan, J. (1991). Destiny and drift: Subcultural preferences, status attainments, and the risks and rewards of youth. *American Sociological Review, 56*(5), 567–582.
Hallinan, M. T. (1974). A structural model of sentiment relations. *American Journal of Sociology, 80*(2), 364–378.
Hallinan, M. T., & Kubitschek, W. N. (1990). The formation of intransitive friendships. *Social Forces, 69*(2), 505–519.
Haynie, D. L., & Osgood, D. W. (2005). Reconsidering peers and delinquency: How do peers matter? *Social Forces, 84*(2), 1109–1130. http://www.jstor.org/stable/3598492
Hoeben, E. M., Rulison, K. L., Ragan, D. T., & Feinberg, M. E. (2021). Moderators of friend selection and influence in relation to adolescent alcohol use. *Prevention Science, 22*(5), 567–578.
Johnsen, E. C. (1985). Network macrostructure models for the Davis-Leinhardt set of empirical sociomatrices. *Social Networks, 7*, 203–224.
Kandel, D. B. (1978). Homophily, selection and socialization in adolescent friendships. *American Journal of Sociology, 84*, 427–436.
Kitts, J. A., & Diego, L. (2021). What isn't a friend: Dimensions of the friendship concept among adolescents. Social Networks, 66, 161–170.
Knecht, A. B., Burk, W. J., Weesie, J., & Steglich, C. (2011). Friendship and alcohol use in early adolescence: A multilevel social network approach. *Journal of Research on Adolescence, 21*(2), 475–487.
Light, R., & Moody, J. (2020). *The Oxford handbook of social networks*. Oxford University Press.
Lomi, A., Robins, G., & Tranmer, M. (2016). Introduction to multilevel social networks. *Social Networks, 44*, 266–268.

McFarland, D. A., Moody, J., Smith, J., Diehl, D., & Thomas, R. J. (2014). Adolescent societies—Their form, evolution, and variation. *American Sociological Review, 79,* 1088–1121.

Moody, J. (2001). Peer influence groups: Identifying dense clusters in large networks. *Social Networks, 23,* 261–283.

Moody, J., & Coleman, J. (2015). Clustering and cohesion in networks: Concepts and measures. In: J. D. Wright (Ed. in Chief), *International encyclopedia of the social & behavioral sciences* (2nd ed., Vol 3, pp. 906–912). Elsevier.

Moody, J., & White, D. R. (2003). Structural cohesion and embeddedness: A hierarchical conception of Social Groups. *American Sociological Review, 68,* 103–127.

Moreno, J. L. (1934). *Who shall survive?: A new approach to the problem of human interrelations.* Nervous and Mental Disease Publishing. https://doi.org/10.1037/10648-000

Nadel, S. F. (2013). *The theory of social structure.* Routledge. (Original work published 1957)

Emotions Mapped by New Geography. *New York Times,* (1933, April 3), 17.

Osgood, D. W., Feinberg, M. E., Gest, S. D., Moody, J., Ragan, D. T., Spoth, R., Greenberg, M., & Redmond, C. (2013). Effects of PROSPER on the influence potential of prosocial versus antisocial youth in adolescent friendship networks. *Journal of Adolescent Health, 53*(2), 174–179.

Osgood, D. W., Feinberg, M. E., & Ragan, D. T. (2015). Social networks and the diffusion of adolescent problem behavior: Reliable estimates of selection and influence from sixth through ninth grades. *Prevention Science, 16*(6), 832–843.

Osgood, D. W., Ragan, D. T., Dole, J. L., & Kreager, D. A. (2022). Similarity of friends versus nonfriends in adolescence: Developmental patterns and ecological influences. *Developmental Psychology, 58*(7), 1386–1401.

Osgood, D. W., Ragan, D. T., Wallace, L., Gest, S. D., Feinberg, M. E., & Moody, J. (2013). Peers and the emergence of alcohol use: Influence and selection processes in adolescent friendship networks. *Journal of Research on Adolescence, 23*(3), 500–512.

Perl, J. (2009). *Causality: Models, reasoning and inference* (2nd ed.). Cambridge University Press.

Ragan, D. T. (2014). Revisiting what they think: Adolescent drinking and the importance of peer beliefs. *Criminology, 52*(3), 488–513.

Ragan, D. T. (2020). Similarity between deviant peers: Developmental trends in influence and selection. *Criminology, 58*(2), 336–369.

Ragan, D. T., Osgood, D. W., Ramirez, N. G., Moody, J., & Gest, S. D. (2022). A comparison of peer influence estimates from SIENA stochastic actor-based models and from conventional regression approaches. *Sociological Methods & Research, 51*(1), 357–395.

Raudenbush, S. W., & Bryk, A. S. (2002). *Hierarchical linear models: Applications and data analysis methods.* Sage.

Rawlings, C. M., Smith, J. A., Moody, J., & McFarland, D. A. (2023). *Network analysis.* Cambridge University Press.

Reichardt, J., & Stefan, B. (2006). Statistical mechanics of community detection. *Physical Review E, 74,* 016110.

Ripley, R. M., Snijders, T. A., Boda, Z., Vörös, A., & Preciado, P. (2021). *Manual for RSIENA.* University of Oxford, Department of Statistics, Nuffield College.

Shai, S., Stanley, N., Granell, C., Taylor, D., & Mucha, P. J. (2020). Case studies in network community detection. In R. Light & J. Moody (Eds.), *The Oxford handbook of social networks* (pp. 310–333). Oxford Academic. https://doi.org/10.1093/oxfordhb/9780190251765.013.16

Shalizi, C. R., & Thomas, A. (2011). Homophily and contagion are generically confounded in observational social network studies. *Sociological Methods and Research*, 40(2), 211–239.

Simmel, G. (1950). The dyad and the triad. In Kurt Wolff (Ed.), *Sociology of Georg Simmel* (pp. 118–169). Free Press.

Simmel, G. (1955). *Conflict and the web of group-affiliations*. Free Press.

Simmel, G. (2009). *Sociology*. Koninklijke Brill. (Original work published 1908)

Snijders, T. A. B. (2001). The statistical evaluation of social network dynamics. *Sociological Methodology*, 31(1), 361–395.

Snijders, T. A. B., van de Bunt, G. G., & Steglich, C. E. G. (2010). Introduction to stochastic actor-based models for network dynamics. *Social Networks*, 32(1), 44–60.

Steglich, C., Snijders, T. A., & Pearson, M. (2010). Dynamic networks and behavior: Separating selection from influence. *Sociological Methodology*, 40(1), 329–393.

Veenstra, R., Dijkstra, J. K., Steglich, C., & Van Zalk, M. H. (2013). Network–behavior dynamics. *Journal of Research on Adolescence*, 23(3), 399–412.

Wasserman, S., & Faust, K. (1994). *Social network analysis*. Cambridge University Press.

White, H. C. (1963). *An anatomy of kinship: Mathematical models for structures of cumulated roles*. Prentice-Hall.

White, H. C. (1965). Notes on the constituents of social structure [Unpublished manuscript]. Social Relations Department, Harvard University.

White, H. C., Boorman, S. A., & Breiger, R. L. (1976). Social structure from multiple networks I. *American Journal of Sociology*, 81, 730–780.

4

A descriptive overview of social networks and behavior among PROSPER youth

ERIN TINNEY

INTRODUCTION

A major emphasis of the research regarding the PROSPER (Promoting School-community-university Partnerships to Enhance Resilience) youth project is the importance of peer relationships for adolescents' behavior. As such, youth were asked about their friendships in the annual questionnaires administered in school, yielding the data from which the research in this volume originate. Several of the chapters in this volume highlight the importance of peers in the development and prevalence of adolescent substance use and risky behavior. The purpose of this chapter is to provide additional context for the reader to understand the findings presented in further chapters.

First, I begin with a discussion of the settings—the school districts that participated in PROSPER. Whereas Chapter 2 provides a discussion of the district selection process, my purpose here is to contextualize student experiences through descriptive statistics about the districts. Second, I discuss the friend nomination measure and provide an overview of the patterns of relationships that we see among the PROSPER youth. Third, I provide additional descriptive information for the friendship networks in terms of structural characteristics presented in Chapter 3. Finally, I present some descriptive statistics regarding the composition of the networks, focusing on how characteristics such as a variety of risk-related attitudes and behaviors correspond to peer relationships.

Erin Tinney, *A descriptive overview of social networks and behavior among PROSPER youth*. In: Teen Friendship Networks, Development, and Risky Behavior. Edited by: Mark E. Feinberg and D. Wayne Osgood, Oxford University Press.
© Mark E. Feinberg and D. Wayne Osgood 2024. DOI: 10.1093/oso/9780197602317.003.0004

Sample sizes, completion rates, and demographic data

Peer networks do not exist in a vacuum; rather, they are shaped by their environment. In this case, the settings are the individual schools and the surrounding overall community. Characteristics of school districts influence how youth relate to one another and shape individual behavior. Recall from Chapter 2 that 28 school districts were selected from rural and semirural regions of Iowa and Pennsylvania to participate in the study. Fourteen of these school districts were randomly assigned (7 from each state) to the intervention condition (the PROSPER program). Administrators of one school district decided not to permit the friendship questions, so network data are available for 27 of the 28 PROSPER communities. The study began in the adolescents' 6th grade (with two sequential cohorts), and the data collection continued through the adolescents' 12th-grade year. Within a given year, each adolescent attended a single school (middle or high school), which sat within a certain participating school district. For many school districts, youth from multiple middle schools funneled into the same high school (Freelee et al., 2023). Thus, established elementary school peer networks often received shocks of new individuals in the 9th or 10th grades. Network composition also shifted over time as youth transferred into and out of each of the school districts. An important aspect of the friendship nomination process (described below) was that the friendships studied throughout this volume were limited to individuals in the same grade at the same school.

Demographic characteristics. One's friendships may be impacted by demographic characteristics such as race, sex, and socioeconomic status. The school districts involved in the PROSPER Peers study all had majority white student populations. Averaged across all waves, in only two districts did fewer than 70% of students identify as white, with most districts having over 88% of their students identify as white. The distribution of nonwhite students was as follows: 44% were Hispanic, 21% were Black, 4% were Indigenous, 8% were Asian, and 24% reported multiple or other racial identities. As explained in Chapter 2, the school districts were selected for having relatively high rates of youth who qualified for free or reduced-price lunch (FRL; a measure of low socioeconomic status). In schools that were over 90% white, 26% of students were eligible for FRL, whereas in schools that were less than 90% white, 28% of students were eligible for FRL. In the two districts with fewer than 70% of the students identifying as white, 31% of students qualified for FRL. In sum, the PROSPER schools had majority white student bodies who varied in socioeconomic status, and there was a modest association between the percentage of white students in a school district and socioeconomic status.

Sample size and completion rates. Despite the relative similarity in student demographic composition across schools, student body population size and study completion rates varied by district. The smallest school district had 178 student participants (both cohorts combined, at Wave 1), and the largest had 866 students. Some students completed all eight waves of the study (fall of 6th grade to spring of 12th grade), but attrition did occur. The number of students who finished the

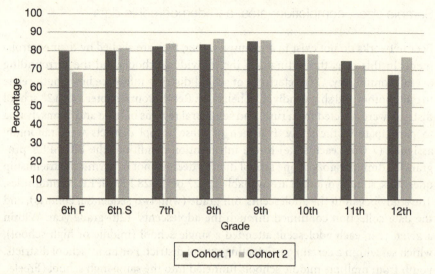

Figure 4.1 Percentage of total eligible students who completed surveys by grade and cohort. 6th F and 6th S refer to the fall and spring semesters of the 6th grade, respectively.

surveys completely each year varied by school district and wave. For our purposes, completing a survey is defined as the individual reaching the end of the survey, where the friendship nomination section was located. The percentage of student surveys that were completed varied from year to year. On average, the percentage of all eligible students who completed surveys was 81%; this peaked during the ninth grade at 86% (Figure 4.1).

The percentage of surveys that were fully completed declined after the ninth grade. The lower rate of survey completion among the oldest students is important to note. There are a few possible reasons for the decline in the number of surveys completed in the 12th grade. First, youth may have dropped out of school by this time. For reference, rural youth tend to have similar dropout rates to their counterparts in urban areas (Jordan et al., 2012). Alternatively, youth may have transferred to a school not involved in the PROSPER project. Last, youth may have still been enrolled at the school but were absent the day the survey was administered, were involved in more off-grounds activities than in earlier grades (e.g., internship, volunteering, work), or were less inclined to complete the survey.

The percentage of surveys completed also varied by demographic characteristics. Figure 4.2 shows survey completion by sex and race. As is shown in this figure, white girls had the highest percentage of survey completion. This is followed by white boys, then nonwhite girls and nonwhite boys. Thus, girls consistently completed surveys more than boys, but white youth overall had higher completion rates. The relative order of these groups stayed consistent over time, and all four groups generally followed the same trend in terms of percentage of surveys completed (i.e., completion peaked in the ninth grade and declined afterward).

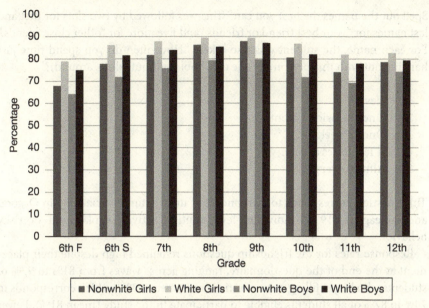

Figure 4.2 Percentage of eligible students who completed surveys by race and sex.

There was a wider gap in survey completion between students who did and did not qualify for FRL in early waves, but this difference decreased over time. Youth who qualified for FRL were consistently less likely to complete surveys in their entirety than their peers. Changes in survey completion from youth of low socioeconomic status may be due to school dropout among poorer students (Rumberger, 2006) or because older students were less likely to report their FRL status.

THE PROSPER FRIENDSHIP NETWORK DATA

Friendship nomination questions

This section describes the friendship data gathered as part of the PROSPER prevention trial, which is the basis for our network analyses and, indeed, the entire PROSPER Peers project and this volume. Chapter 2 provides information about the data collection method and other measures. For our focus on friendship networks, it is worth noting that all currently enrolled students in two consecutive cohorts in the 28 school districts were eligible to participate in each wave, whether or not they were enrolled at earlier waves. The targeted sample included all of the students within the entire school; thus it potentially captured all within-grade friendship networks at all waves of data collection. The friendship questions were the final section of the questionnaire for PROSPER's in-school data collection. The students were asked: "Who are your best and closest friends in your grade?

Spell out the names the best you can." This was followed by two slots for first and last names for "your best friend or friends" and five more for "other close friends." For each name, the student was also asked: "How often do you spend time just hanging out with this person outside of school (without adults around)?"

1. = Never
2. = Once or twice a month
3. = Once a week
4. = A few times a week
5. = Almost every day

This question corresponds to the concept of unstructured socializing in Osgood and colleagues (1996) individual-level routine activity explanation of risky behavior.

Response rates for the friendship questions remained high despite their placement at the end of the questionnaire, ranging across waves from 81% to 97% of students who began filling out a questionnaire (mean 93%), which corresponds to 74% to 87% of all students eligible to participate in the study (mean 81%). Fewer students reached the end of the questionnaire during the first wave of data collection in the fall of sixth grade (81% completion vs. at least 91% for other waves), likely because students were least familiar with the questionnaire, questionnaire administration was less efficient during this first implementation, and reading comprehension improved with age.

Time constraints meant that it was not feasible to allow more than seven friendship choices. Although unlimited choices are often recommended for social network research (Neal, 2020), constraining the number of nominations has the advantage of maintaining a focus on closer rather than more peripheral relationships. Further, allowing up to seven friends compares favorably with many other studies of adolescent friendship networks that have been limited to three or fewer friends per respondent (e.g., Burk et al., 2012; Ennett & Bauman, 1993; Kandel, 1978).

The friendship question tells respondents to name only friends in the same grade, but it does not specify that the friends should be in the same school. Our research can only include friends at the same school, however, because outside friends were not on school rosters and did not complete questionnaires and thus could not be matched to nominations. This approach results in somewhat fewer friendships for analysis, but it ensures that nominated friends included are among the respondents' closest friends. To gain perspective on the named friends versus their other friendships, beginning in the fourth wave (eighth grade), the questionnaire included the following pair of questions:

How many friends do you have in other grades in your school who are AS CLOSE or CLOSER to you than the friends you listed above?

How many friends do you have who go to other schools who are AS CLOSE or CLOSER to you than the friends you listed above?

Coding the friendship nominations

For each wave of data collection, an average of 9,139 students completed the questionnaire through the friendship section, including respondents who choose not to list any friends. They named an average of 5.0 friends, for a total of 362,371 handwritten names to be matched to student rosters. The staff of the PROSPER prevention trial entered the names and respondent identification numbers in computer files as part of questionnaire data entry. Sonja Siennick developed the name-matching procedures and software and managed the name-matching process for the first five waves of data. Nayan Ramirez managed the name-matching process for the last three waves of data, with assistance from Wade Jacobsen. The name matching in PROSPER began with a lengthy data-cleaning process to correct inconsistencies among study identification numbers for individual, school, school district, and cohort in the files for rosters of students, names of friends written by respondents, and questionnaires.

Friends' names were matched to study ID numbers through a multistage, computer-assisted process. The first stage compared the names written by respondents to names on class rosters, using routines that took into account common spelling errors and variations. This step identified potential matches and rated the level of uncertainty, ranging from exact and unique matches to modest similarity with multiple possible matches. The next stage was computer-assisted matching by coders, who reviewed the nonexact matches and searched for matches not identified by the automated routines. Two coders reviewed each name, and the matching program displayed the full roster of names for searching and considering matches. The two coders agreed for 98% of the friendship nominations. A third coder resolved disagreements, such as about whether to accept a computer-suggested match, deciding between two coder-suggested matches, or whether to accept a match suggested by one coder that the other coder either did not find or did not consider acceptable.

To ensure confidentiality, coders saw only the names of the nominated friends and the class rosters. They did not have access to the name of the nominating respondent, any identification numbers, or any questionnaire respondents. Additionally, coders did not review names for any community in which any of their acquaintances or family members resided.

Match rates. This process succeeded in matching 79% of the friends' names to the rosters for the grade cohorts of the respondents. We regard this as a high rate of success considering that the question asking respondents to name their friends did not restrict them to the same school. This matching rate ranged from a high of 85% for the seventh grade to a low of 73% in the eleventh grade, with a generally decreasing trend across grades. We suspect this decline reflects an increasing tendency to have close friendships outside of their grade or school as students grew older. The lowest reported match rate in one district in one wave was 57%, and the highest was 98%.

The bulk of the unmatched friendships (18%) were names that could not be found on the grade cohort roster, 2% were plausibly matched multiple names on the roster, and 1% were inappropriate responses, such as celebrities or fictional characters. Coders reported that almost all the unmatched names were unambiguously poor matches to any name on the roster, rather than responses that were difficult to match due to ambiguous or insufficient information.

We have no specific test for the validity of the name matching, but we have clear evidence that the resulting friendship networks are internally consistent and coherently structured. For instance, our data strongly demonstrate the tendency toward reciprocation that is ubiquitous in social networks (Rivera et al., 2010). Of our students' friendships, 48% were reciprocated, and this rose to 76% for the first-named friend and 66% for the second-named friend. By chance alone, the rate of reciprocation would be well under 5% (given 3.9 matched friendships per respondent and a mean of over 150 students per school grade cohort). More broadly, our friendship network data produce findings consistent with the broader research literature for features like similarity between friends (Osgood et al., 2022); triad census (Moody et al., 2011); structural selection processes (Osgood, Ragan, et al., 2013); and stability (Jacobsen, 2020).

NETWORK STRUCTURE

The previous chapter outlined key network concepts and metrics for characterizing schools' social networks. For PROSPER Peers, youth in the same grade and school form one network, which is measured at each wave of data collection. Networks consist of nodes (individual people) and ties (the connections between them); in this section I provide a variety of descriptive information about the networks. I begin with the number of ties (volume) and then turn to the nature of the ties. Specifically, ties can be reciprocated or unreciprocated. Reciprocity refers to whether two youth nominate one another as friends in the same year (irrespective of the classification of "best" and "close" friend). Stability is also of interest, reflecting how much friendships between the same youth shift over the years as new nodes come into and leave the network, and friendship ties are broken or formed. Next, this section considers individuals' connections with cohesive friendship groups, which are identified by methods described in the previous chapter. The final topic of the section is whether the overall organizations of the networks tend to reflect a systematic hierarchy of popularity or relative equality.

Number of friendships: In-degree and out-degree

One of the most basic characteristics of social networks is the number of ties sent and received by individuals. The ties that an individual receives (friends who nominate them) are referred to as their *in-degree*. The number of ties that an individual sends (who they nominate) are referred to as their *out-degree*. Thus, the in-degree refers to how many people consider an individual as their friend, and the out-degree refers to how many people an individual considers to be their friend.

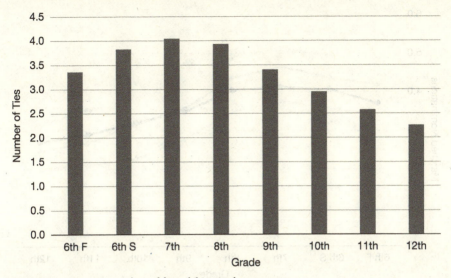

Figure 4.3 Average number of friendship ties by wave.

Youth can have up to $N-1$ number of in-degree ties (with N representing the number of students in their school and grade). However, students can only have an out-degree of up to seven in 1 year.

For an entire network, mean in-degree and mean out-degree are necessarily the same: the total number of friendships divided by the number of students. Figure 4.3 shows that this average number of ties received and given peaks in the seventh and eighth grades and steadily declines.

As is shown by Figure 4.4, out-degree, the number of friends named, tended to peak in Wave 4 (eighth grade) and steadily declined throughout high school. In general, white youth nominated more friends than nonwhite youth, and female students named more friends than male students. Figure 4.5 highlights the intersection of race and sex, with nonwhite boys naming the fewest friends and white girls naming the most. The discrepancies between youth in the number of friendships one had at school may have occurred because students who are nonwhite, male, or of low socioeconomic status may have had social networks that existed outside of their schools, been less likely to have friends at school, or been more reluctant to name their friends compared with white, female, or higher socioeconomic status students.

Youth who did not qualify for FRL generally named more friends than youth who did qualify for FRL. At the match peak in Wave 4, youth without FRL named about 4.5 friends, and youth with FRL named a little more than 3. This relative difference between these two groups in number of friends remained consistent over time despite changes in the number of friendship matches made in each wave.

Figure 4.5 shows the in-degree (received nominations) ties for youth over all study waves broken down by race and sex. On average over an entire network, out-degree and in-degree nominations are the same number when looking at the

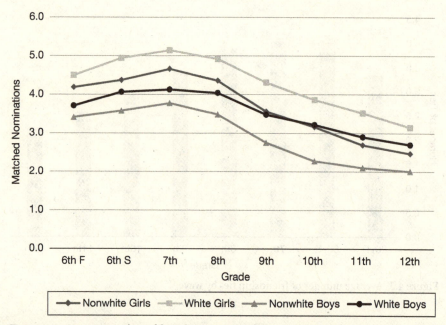

Figure 4.4 Average number of friend nominations by race and sex.

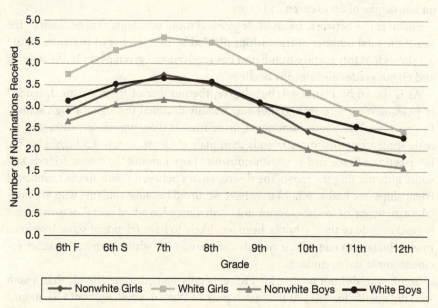

Figure 4.5 Average number of nominations received by race and sex.

average number of friendships and only matched friendships. The two can differ for subgroups, however, because how many friends a subgroup names may diverge from how many friends they attract. Also, in-degree is necessarily limited to matched friendships because the chosen friend must be identified to receive credit. Accordingly, the means for in-degree in Figure 4.5 are lower than those for out-degree in Figure 4.5. Youth received the most friendship nominations on average in the seventh grade, and this number steadily declined over the next five waves. White girls consistently received the most friendship nominations, while nonwhite boys consistently received the least. White boys and nonwhite girls received similar numbers of friendship ties over time. This is the same relative ranking that occurred with out-degree nominations, suggesting that white girls both received and sent the most ties, while nonwhite boys both received and sent the fewest ties.

Reciprocity

To what extent are the PROSPER students' friendships mutual, with both parties reciprocating the friendship choice of the other, versus one-sided? Reciprocity in friendship nominations both confirms the existence of a friendship (vs. one student nominating another from an aspirational basis) and indicates a higher quality of relationship than a one-sided nomination. On average, 48% of ties were reciprocated, although as mentioned previously, best friends had a much higher reciprocation rate. The proportion of all friendships that were reciprocal did not shift considerably over time, as is shown in Figure 4.6. Nominations from female youth were reciprocated at a higher level than male youth. The reciprocity for ties from female youth peaked at about 60%, while the reciprocity for ties from male youth peaked at about 40%. This is consistent with other friendship measures in that female students tended to have more ties with other students in the network.

Stability of friendship ties

Another informative marker of the character of PROSPER friendships is the stability of ties over time. What proportion of friendship choices are consistent over time, indicating that relationships are an ongoing part of respondents' lives over an extended period, versus being more transitory? The stability of friendship ties refers to whether a friendship tie was maintained in the next wave (regardless of whether an individual's "rank" in their friend's nomination list changed). Figure 4.7 shows the general trend of friendship stability across waves. From Waves 2 to 3 (sixth to seventh grade), there was a large drop in the percentage of friendships that were retained. The percentage of these remaining friendships that were maintained over time steadily increased throughout middle and high school, but never exceeded 50% after the spring of sixth grade. The percentage of

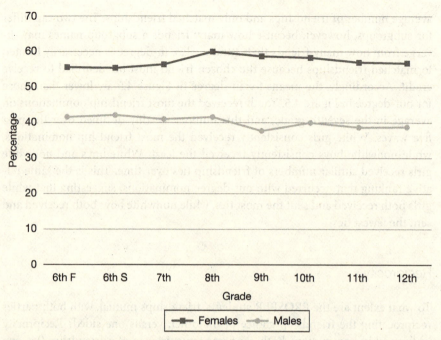

Figure 4.6 Percentage of friendships reciprocated by sex.

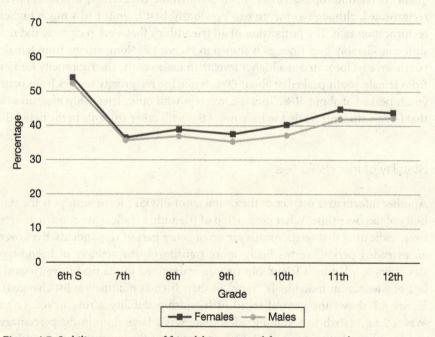

Figure 4.7 Stability: percentage of friendships retained from prior wave by sex.

friendships retained and the general trend of friendship retention over time did not vary greatly by sex. It is important to note that Waves 1 and 2 occurred in the fall and spring of the same year. Thus, the stability in friendship ties from Waves 1 to 2 was higher over this 6-month period than in the 12-month periods between subsequent waves.

Homophily

To what extent do youth share characteristics with their friends? Homophily is an important aspect of the study of friendship ties, particularly in studies on peer selection and influence (McMillan et al., 2018; Chapter 1 of this volume). Youth may either form friendships with peers who are similar to them in characteristics or behavior (selection) or may adjust their behavior to be more similar to their friends (influence). Regardless of whether selection, influence, or both shape homophily within friendships, youth tended to be similar to their friends in many aspects.

Figure 4.8 shows homophily for all ties (sent and received) by sex, and Figure 4.9 shows homophily for all ties by race. Youth tended to have friendships with those of the same sex, although the proportion of one's friends who were the same sex as oneself tended to decrease slightly over time. White youth consistently had friendships with other white youth, while nonwhite youth had fewer than 50% of their friendships with other nonwhite youth. This may be due to the small proportion of students who were nonwhite in these school districts, so they had fewer choices of youth with whom to form same-race friendships. Similarity by race, as

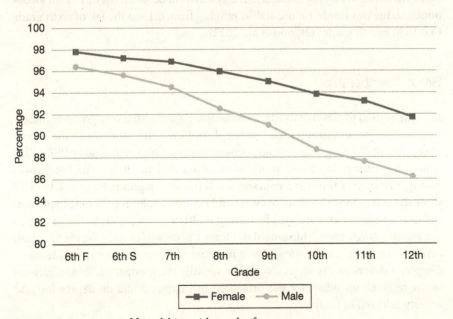

Figure 4.8 Percentage of friendships with youth of same sex.

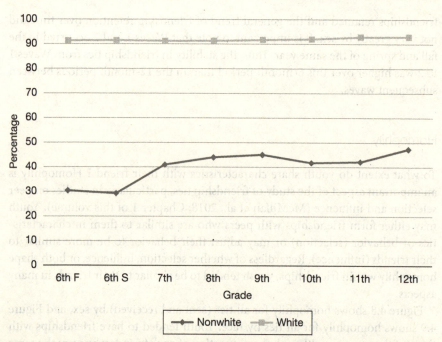

Figure 4.9 Percentage of friendships with youth of same race (i.e., white vs. nonwhite).

reflected in the correlation between friends (Moran's *I*), ranged from 0.09 in the fall of sixth grade to 0.18 in the ninth grade. Homophily by sex was far higher, with the correlation in friendships ranging from 0.73 to 0.89 (the lower end of the range occurred in late high school). The correlation between friends in socioeconomic status was low but more stable, ranging from 0.13 in the fall of sixth grade to 0.16 in eighth grade (Osgood et al., 2022).

Group membership

Moving beyond the level of dyadic friendships, Figure 4.10 shows group membership by sex. Rates of group membership show how many students in the school were a member of a group. Group membership was common among PROSPER youth, suggesting that most youth were connected to their school networks during a given year through a cohesive small friendship group. Figures 4.11–4.12 show the extent to which students were embedded in cohesive friendship groups. Being a core member is defined by having multiple connections to the group, so the loss of a single friendship would not leave the person outside the group. Thus, being in the "core" can be viewed as a measure of integration or embeddedness. Chapter 3 describes the methods used to identify the groups, which are featured in the research on substance use presented in Chapter 5 and on depression and anxiety featured in Chapter 7.

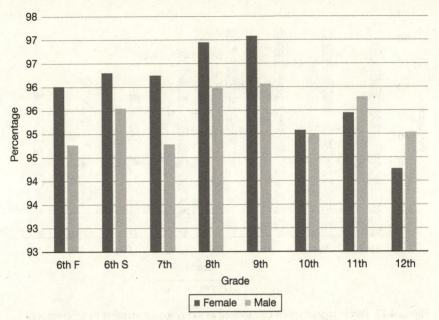

Figure 4.10 Percentage of youth categorized as a member of a group by sex.

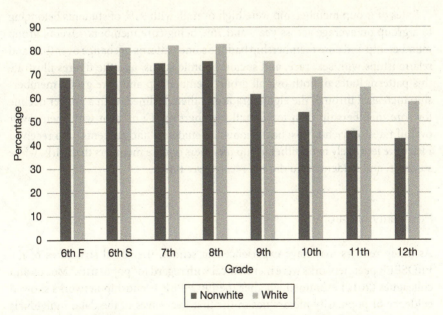

Figure 4.11 Percentage of youth categorized as a core group member by race.

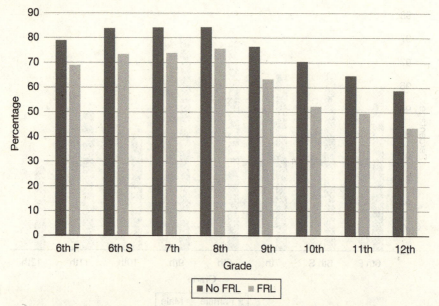

Figure 4.12 Percentage of youth categorized as a core group member by free/reduced lunch (FRL) status.

Rates of group membership were high overall, with 91% of students belonging to a group on average across years and 75% being core members. Overall group membership and core membership had the same patterns of change over time and relationships with sex, race, and socioeconomic status, and the figures illustrate this pattern. Rates of both overall group membership and core group membership increased through the eighth grade and then declined, with a greater decline for core membership than for overall membership. Consistent with their lower overall rates of friendships, boys, nonwhite students, and students who received FRL were less likely to be either group members or core members than girls, white students, and students who did not receive free lunch.

Popularity hierarchy

As many readers may have experienced in school, the social structures of the PROSPER peer networks were hierarchical with regard to "popularity." Moody and colleagues (2011) examined whether the PROSPER friendship networks showed evidence of popularity hierarchies in the first five waves of the data. Individuals who had more ties and were in the center of their networks are considered to have been "popular" students. Popular students received the most friendship nominations from others (in-degree ties) compared to other students. Popularity tended to be unstable, as many adolescents experienced high and low popularity at different points throughout the study period, which Moody and colleagues referred to as "popularity mobility." The majority of youth experienced either high popularity or very low popularity at some point during the study period. About 50% of students had at least 1 year in which they were in the top quintile of popularity compared to their peers, and 57% of students were never in the lowest quintile. Based on the relative prevalence of all possible patterns of connection among triads (sets of three students), the authors concluded that the networks of PROSPER youth tended to follow more of a hierarchical than a clustered (egalitarian) structure. In addition, girls were more likely to be popular than boys because they received more friendship ties (Moody et al., 2011). Whole networks may exist as one overall hierarchy with almost every node connected or in separate, less connected cliques that had their own hierarchal structures.

ADOLESCENT BEHAVIOR AND NETWORKS

The final section of the chapter provides an overview of ways that some key attitudes and behaviors were embedded in the organization of adolescents' friendships. The empirical chapters in the remainder of this volume elaborate on such relationships in greater depth in the course of addressing a wide variety of topics. This section focuses on four aspects of friendships, three of which were also considered in the previous section but are here considered in relation to risky behaviors. Out-degree is the number of friends a respondent named, and it reflects a respondent's engagement in this friendship network. In-degree corresponds to the number of times other students named this individual as a friend, and thus it indicates attractiveness or popularity. Similarity (homophily) is the correlation between friends for an attribute or behavior, indicating how strongly friendships were clustered or grouped on this basis. The fourth aspect, which we start with, is unstructured socializing.

Unstructured socializing

As youth age, they spend more time with their peers and less time with their parents and other authority figures (Warr, 1993), which allows them more freedom in their behavior. As described in Chapter 1, unstructured socializing occurs when peer groups spend time together without opportunities for structured activities or authority figures present (Osgood et al., 1996). The PROSPER Peers research team was interested in unstructured socializing because this creates an environment that facilitates substance use and other risky behaviors (Hoeben et al., 2020). Figure 4.13 shows the average amount of time in unstructured socializing with each named friend, comparing all youth to those who nominated seven friends. (See the description of the PROSPER friendship network data above for our measure of unstructured socializing with each named friend.)

On average, youth spent the most time in unstructured socializing with those who were listed as their best friends, suggesting that unstructured socializing was associated with subjective reported "closeness" with one's friends.

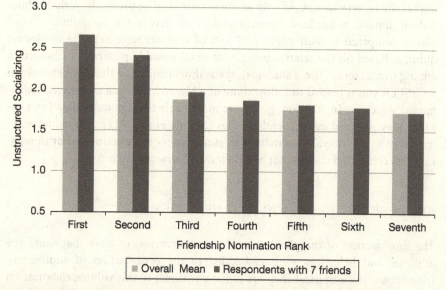

Note: Unstructured socializing is measured for each friend on a scale from 0-4. A score of 0 means "Never," and a score of 4 means "Every day."

Figure 4.13 Unstructured socializing by friend nomination rank.

Associations of network variables with attitudes and behaviors

Figure 4.14 reveals that various attitudes and behaviors have quite different associations with the four network variables. School grades, bonding with school, and frequent religious attendance were all positively correlated with both choosing more friends (out-degree) and being chosen more often (in-degree). In contrast, strong family relations and higher risk and sensation seeking were associated with choosing fewer friends and were not related to being chosen by others. Friends demonstrated similarity across all five of these attitudes and behavior, but that similarity was considerably stronger for school grades and bonding and quite weak for family relations. Finally, students who were higher on risk and sensation seeking spent considerably more time in unstructured socializing with their friends, while those who were more engaged in school (as indicated by grades and school bonding) spent less.

Risky behavior. One major focus of the PROSPER Peers study and the PROSPER intervention team was adolescent participation in risky behaviors, which consist of both substance use and other forms of delinquency. The measures of substance use inquired about use in the past month; Chapter 5 describes them in greater detail and provides descriptive statistics. Delinquency is measured as a variety score of 12 illicit behaviors (including police contact and excluding substance use). Delinquency, police contact, and friendship are discussed in Chapter 6.

Figures 4.15 and 4.16 display the prevalence of delinquency by sex, race, and socioeconomic status over all waves. As in the general population, reports of

Social Networks and Behavior in PROSPER

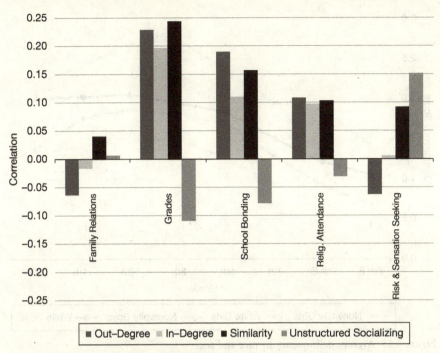

Notes: Variables are averaged across eight waves. Unstructured socializing is measured for one's first nominated friend (best friend).

Figure 4.14 Correlation between network characteristics and selected attitudes and behaviors.

PROSPER youth indicated that their level of delinquency tended to increase over time. However, delinquency dropped off slightly toward the 12th grade, possibly because more youth engaged in delinquency dropped out of school, were absent on the day of the survey, or declined to complete the measure. Male youth were involved in more delinquent behaviors on average than female youth, although the trend over time in participation for both sexes was similar. Nonwhite students participated in more delinquency and tended to have a slightly higher peak in participation than white students. When comparing across race and sex, nonwhite boys reported the greatest participation in delinquency, with a sharper peak compared to the other three demographic groups. Delinquency among nonwhite girls tended to decrease to match delinquency participation among white girls by the 12th grade. Students who qualified for FRL also participated in more delinquency than students who did not qualify for FRL.

Figure 4.17 shows the correlation between risky behaviors and certain patterns of friendship ties. Youth who were engaged in risky behaviors generally sent and received fewer ties than their peers. Drinking alcohol, however, was associated with receiving more ties. This aligns with prior research suggesting that drinking alcohol among the PROSPER youth was a predictor of popularity (Osgood, Ragan, et al., 2013; see Chapter 5). This pattern held for getting drunk as well as

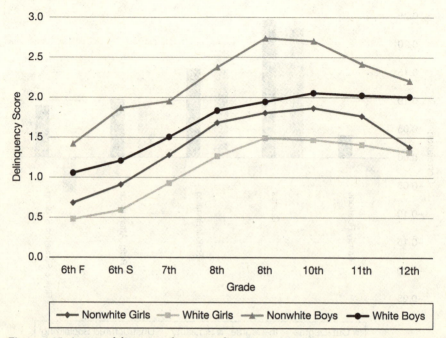

Figure 4.15 Average delinquency by race and sex.

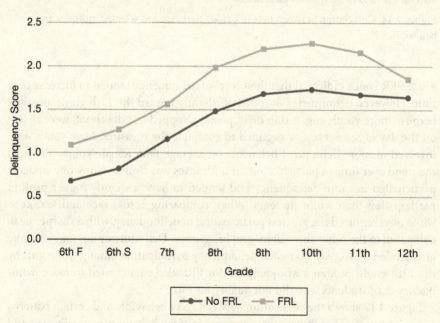

Figure 4.16 Average delinquency by free/reduced-price lunch (FRL) status.

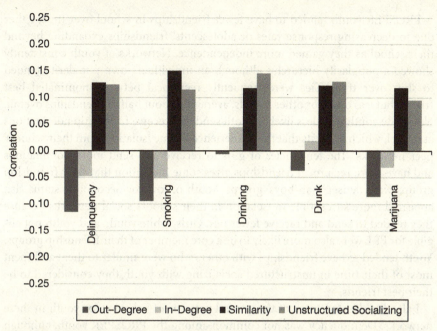

Notes: Variables are averaged across eight waves. Unstructured socializing is measured for one's first nominated friend (best friend).

Figure 4.17 Correlations between network characteristics and risky behaviors.

for drinking at all. However, risky behavior was consistently negatively associated with friendship nominations sent by an individual.

The correlation between all the risky behaviors and network characteristics was positive for the time spent with one's best friend and for similarity. Across waves, spending more time with one's best friend was associated with more risky behavior, and youth tended to have friends who were similar to them in their risky behaviors. As discussed in Chapter 5, similarity between friends for substance use increased markedly across grades. Similarity for delinquency was mostly stable over time, although somewhat higher during late middle school and early high school than before or after.

CONCLUSION

In this chapter, I summarized the patterns of friendship ties and individual outcomes for youth in the PROSPER Peers study. Social networks and friendship ties not only impacted how youth navigated their social environments but also shaped their individual behavior. I have shown in this chapter that characteristics of social networks differed between schools and that participation in a network was impacted by demographic characteristics and behavior.

PROSPER youth tended to have fewer friendships in school over time, either due to decreasing response rates or adolescents' friendships expanding beyond their school as they gained more independence. Networks of youth consistently showed a popularity hierarchy, although an individual's own popularity tended to shift over time. Ties were frequently reciprocal between nominated best friends but less often for other friends, averaging about half of friendships overall. Nonwhite youth were less likely to both send and receive friendship nominations at school, which suggests that they experienced some isolation from their schools' peer networks. The tendencies of girls to receive and send more nominations and have more reciprocal friendships gives some indication that their friendship groups were denser than boys' groups. Youth of low socioeconomic status also appeared more susceptible to isolation in their school's social networks because they tended to send and receive fewer ties. Girls, white youth, and youth not eligible for FRL were also more likely to be a core member of their friendship groups. Youth tended to have friendships with others who were similar to them and spent most of their time in unstructured socializing with youth they considered to be their best friends.

I also highlighted some of the general patterns of behavior for youth in these networks. Delinquency was not common among the PROSPER youth, although participation generally increased over time and varied by demographic characteristics, with nonwhite boys showing the highest prevalence of delinquency. Risky behavior was generally associated with similarity (homophily) in one's friendships, and drinking behaviors were associated with being more popular. Those engaged in other forms of risky behavior, however, tended to be more isolated from their peers. The relationship between friends' risky behavior and one's own shifted over time depending on the type of behavior. Similarity between friends also varied by levels of school and family bonding, religiosity, and risk seeking. Friends tended to be similar with regard to risky behavior, and time spent with friends was positively associated with risky behavior, suggesting that risky behavior played a role in shaping friendship patterns and/or was shaped by them, and that friendships may have provided opportunities for risky behavior.

I conclude with two considerations regarding friendships and behavior among the PROSPER youth drawn from these descriptive data. First, the friendship patterns and behaviors of the PROSPER youth were highly connected to one another. Second, friendships frequently changed, which may have affected how PROSPER youth behaved and interacted with one another—the implications of which are explored throughout the remainder of the volume.

REFERENCES

Burk, W. J., Van Der Vorst, H., Kerr, M., & Stattin, H. (2012). Alcohol use and friendship dynamics: Selection and socialization in early-, middle-, and late-adolescent peer networks. *Journal of Studies on Alcohol and Drugs, 73*(1), 89–98.

Ennett, S. T., & Bauman, K. E. (1993). Peer group structure and adolescent cigarette smoking: A social network analysis. *Journal of Health and Social Behavior*, 34, 226–236.

Freelin, B. N., McMillan, C., Felmlee, D., & Osgood, D. W. (2023). Changing contexts: A quasi-experiment examining adolescent delinquency and the transition to high school. *Criminology*, 61(1), 40–73.

Hoeben, E. M., Osgood, D. W., Siennick, S. E., & Weerman, F. M. (2020). Hanging out with the wrong crowd? The role of unstructured socializing in adolescents' specialization in delinquency and substance use. *Journal of Quantitative Criminology*, 37, 141–177.

Jacobsen, W. C. (2020). School punishment and interpersonal exclusion: Rejection, withdrawal, and separation from friends. *Criminology*, 58(1), 35–69.

Jordan, L., Kostandini, G., & Mykerezi, E. (2012). Rural and urban high school dropout rates: Are they different? *Journal of Research in Rural Education*, 27(12), 1.

Kandel, D. B. (1978). Homophily, selection and socialization in adolescent friendships. *American Journal of Sociology*, 84, 427–436.

McMillan, C., Felmlee, D., & Osgood, D. W. (2018). Peer influence, friend selection, and gender: How network processes shape adolescent smoking, drinking, and delinquency. *Social Networks*, 55, 86–96.

Moody, J., Brynildsen, W. D., Osgood, D. W., Feinberg, M. E., & Gest, S. (2011). Popularity trajectories and substance use in early adolescence. *Social Networks*, 33(2), 101–112.

Neal, J. W. (2020). A systematic review of social network methods in high impact developmental psychology journals. *Social Development*, 29(4), 923–944.

Osgood, D. W., Feinberg, M. E., Gest, S. D., Moody, J., Ragan, D. T., Spoth, R., Greenberg, M., & Redmond, C. (2013). Effects of PROSPER on the influence potential of prosocial versus antisocial youth in adolescent friendship networks. *Journal of Adolescent Health*, 53(2), 174–179.

Osgood, D. W., Ragan, D. T., Dole, J. L., & Kreager, D. A. (2022). Similarity of friends versus nonfriends in adolescence: Developmental patterns and ecological influences. *Developmental Psychology*, 58(7), 1386–1401.

Osgood, D. W., Ragan, D. T., Wallace, L., Gest, S. D., Feinberg, M. E., & Moody, J. (2013). Peers and the emergence of alcohol use: Influence and selection processes in adolescent friendship networks. *Journal of Research on Adolescence*, 23(3), 500–512.

Osgood, D. W., Wilson, J. K., O'malley, P. M., Bachman, J. G., & Johnston, L. D. (1996). Routine activities and individual deviant behavior. *American Sociological Review*, 61(4), 635–655.

Rivera, M. T., Soderstrom, S. B., & Uzzi, B. (2010). Dynamics of dyads in social networks: Assortative, relational, and proximity mechanisms. *Annual Review of Sociology*, 36, 91–115.

Rumberger, R. W. (2006). Tenth grade dropout rates by native language, race/ethnicity, and socioeconomic status. UC Berkeley: University of California Linguistic Minority Research Institute. https://escholarship.org/uc/item/2903c3p3

Warr, M. (1993). Age, peers, and delinquency. *Criminology*, 31(1), 17–40.

SECTION II

Risky behaviors, relationships, and development

5

Teen friendships, networks, and substance use

DANIEL T. RAGAN AND D. WAYNE OSGOOD ■

INTRODUCTION

Alcohol, tobacco, and marijuana use are the behaviors that have received the most attention in PROSPER (PRomoting School-community-university Partnerships to Enhance Resilience) Peer's program of research, as is evident throughout this volume. The current chapter presents our main research specifically devoted to understanding the relationships between peers and adolescent substance use, while other chapters investigate connections of both to additional topics such as internalizing symptoms (Chapter 7), relations with parents (Chapter 8), romantic involvement (Chapter 9), and prevention programming (Chapter 11). It is not surprising that substance use has been at the forefront of the PROSPER Peers research agenda. The primary mission of the PROSPER prevention trial was to evaluate a dissemination system based on a community-partnership for delivering evidence-based substance use prevention programs (see Chapter 2). An important element of the evaluation involved collecting data about not only students' substance use, but also a variety of factors believed to impact these behaviors, including measures related to the family, school, and community. These data, combined with the exceptional friendship network data that were also collected as a part of the PROSPER evaluation, created a unique opportunity to advance the literature on what is known about the links between peers and substance use.

In the current chapter, we review our body of work on substance use in three areas: (1) how adolescent substance use is shaped by friendships and the ways that the use of those substances contributes to the formation of friendships; (2) the network positions occupied by adolescents who use substances and the network structure of groups whose members use the substances; and (3) whether peer

Daniel T. Ragan and D. Wayne Osgood, *Teen friendships, networks, and substance use*. In: *Teen Friendship Networks, Development, and Risky Behavior*. Edited by: Mark E. Feinberg and D. Wayne Osgood, Oxford University Press.
© Mark E. Feinberg and D. Wayne Osgood 2024. DOI: 10.1093/oso/9780197602317.003.0005

network processes related to substance use change during adolescence. Taken together, our conclusions from this research highlight how a network approach is invaluable for understanding the development of adolescent substance use, while unanswered questions from this work highlight the need for continued research and avenues of future research that may be especially useful. These studies in turn set the context for the work in further chapters that connects peers and substance use to additional topics.

The use of alcohol and other drugs by adolescents is linked to many undesirable outcomes. Underage drinking and teen marijuana use, for example, both are associated with traffic accidents and fatalities, high risk of addiction or dependence in adulthood, and a variety of adult health and mortality risks (Volkow et al., 2014; Windle et al., 1996). Cigarette smoking in adolescence also brings a high risk of long-term adult cigarette use, with its well-established catastrophic consequences for health and mortality (Chassin et al., 1990).

Despite the clear risks associated with alcohol and other drugs, the use of these substances has been and remains an enduring part of adolescent life. In the year that the PROSPER evaluation data collection began, 48% of high school seniors nationwide reported drinking alcohol in the past month, 24% reported smoking cigarettes, and 21% reported using marijuana (Johnston et al., 2021). Further, the reported past-month use among eighth-grade students during this time—20% for alcohol, 10% for cigarettes, and 8% for marijuana—indicated this behavior emerges far earlier, and certainly before students enter high school. Consequently, understanding the etiology of substance use must necessarily capture the decisions to engage in (or not engage in) these behaviors during early adolescence as well as during mid- and late adolescence.

There is some evidence that substance use among adolescents has decreased since the beginning of the PROSPER evaluation program. According to the annual estimates from the nationally-representative Monitoring the Future survey, for example, under 30% of high school seniors reported any past-month alcohol use (with a comparable decline for being drunk in the past month), and fewer than 6% of these students reported past-month cigarette use in 2019, figures that are well below those reported in the early 2000s (Johnston et al., 2021). Even with these decreases, however, the number of students across the country who use substances remains substantial due to the sheer number of high school students in the United States. Predicting the future of this behavior is further complicated by a number of recent developments with impacts that are as of yet unclear. In stark contrast to the consistent decrease in cigarette smoking over a period of nearly 20 years, for instance, the proportion of high school seniors who reported vaping nicotine in the past month rose from 11% in 2017 to over 25% in 2019 (Johnston et al., 2021). The legal status of marijuana has also undergone change over the past decade, as a number of states have passed laws allowing for the legal use of marijuana for medical or recreational purposes. Though notable differences in the use and perceived availability of marijuana among high school students have not been observed to date, the proportion of high school seniors who reported that they believed there to be "great risk" associated with smoking marijuana regularly declined to nearly 30% in 2019. This figure is both the lowest since the Monitoring the Future survey began and less than half of what was reported by high school seniors from the early 1980s through mid-1990s. These observations illustrate several of the reasons why adolescent substance use remains a focus of many prevention efforts: Even when rates of use decline, a considerable number of students continue to report engaging in such behaviors, and reversals in declining use may emerge quickly due to technological, legal, and cultural changes.

Three areas of research on peers and substance use

Given that the use of alcohol and other drugs often emerges during adolescence and is associated with undesirable outcomes, it is unsurprising that there exists a deep literature devoted to understanding the development of these behaviors. This research has identified peers and friendships as especially important for understanding adolescent substance use. In this chapter, we present studies from PROSPER Peers that sought to advance our understanding of this topic, and they encompass three areas of research on peers and substance use.

The first area of research involves both how adolescent substance use is shaped by friendships and the ways that the use of those substances contributes to the formation of the friendships. In terms of the network conceptual framework of this volume, shown in Figure 1.7 of Chapter 1, this work concerns peer influence and friend selection at the individual level. A long line of research has examined the reasons for a high degree of similarity between friends for substance use. Many studies have seen such similarity in use as evidence of social influence, while friendship selection processes, and particularly homophilic selection (choosing friends similar to oneself), have been offered as an alternative explanation. Our work builds on a more recent understanding of these selection and influence processes, specifically that they are complementary rather than competing processes. That is, peer selection processes determine which adolescents have the opportunity to exert social influence, and that in turn implies understanding selection is necessary for understanding social influence. Further, our work goes beyond the traditional focus on homophilic selection to consider additional types of selection. Specifically, we investigate the role of substance use in tendencies for adolescents to have more (or fewer) friends, both through the process of naming more friends and through more often being chosen by others.

Our second area of research concerns the nature of the links between substance use and the organization of adolescent friendship networks. This involves two lines of inquiry. The first involves examining the friendship group position of those who use substances, which is the topic of group position, at the individual level of analysis. That is, do individuals who use these substances occupy different locations within the social structure of the network (e.g., whether they are linked to many other individuals or are peripheral members of their desired friendship groups) compared to nonusers? The second involves examining the peer group structure of those who are engaged in substance use, which is the topic of group structure, at the group level of analysis. This line of inquiry includes examining whether friendship groups with adolescents who use substances have different characteristics, such as whether the groups are larger or more interconnected, than friendship groups of students who do not use substances.

The third and final area of research that we explore in this chapter addresses whether network-related peer processes for substance use change during adolescence. We begin by addressing whether, across adolescence, adolescents come to have friends who are more similar to themselves in regard to substance use. In terms of the larger PROSPER Peer conceptual framework (Figure 1.7 in Chapter 1), this topic takes the form of a connection between development/change and network-level structure. We then turn to examine whether there is development or change across grades in the individual-level processes of peer influence toward substance use or selection based on more similar substance use.

Rates of substance use

The research we present in this chapter focuses on three forms of substance use that are common during adolescence: alcohol, tobacco, and marijuana use. These three are sufficiently prevalent in a general population (rather than high-risk) sample such as ours to potentially play a large role in the general peer culture and to support detailed statistical analysis. Our primary measures were items asking about use in the past 30 days. Our specific version of the questions was taken from the work of Botvin and colleagues (1997), but this type of measure has been widely used for decades in research on adolescent substance use (Johnston et al., 2021). We have typically dichotomized these as "no use" versus "any use," though our analysis of selection and influence that rely on the Simulation Investigation for Empirical Network Analysis (SIENA) program have used the ordinal distinction of "none," "once," and "two or more times."

Figure 5.1 illustrates the dramatic growth of substance use in the PROSPER sample, from relatively rare in the fall of sixth grade to common by the spring of twelfth grade. Over this period, the percentage of students who reported drinking alcohol in the past month rose from 7% for girls and 10% for boys to 48% and 50%, respectively. Similarly, past month cigarette smoking grew, respectively, from 4% for girls and boys in the sixth grade to 27% and 30% in the twelfth grade, and marijuana use increased from 0.4% for girls and 1% for boys to 17% and 24%. Thus, the PROSPER sample appears well suited for investigating the emergence of substance use.

Although boys engage in some risky behavior, such as delinquency, far more than girls (e.g., Elliott et al., 1989), gender differences in adolescent substance use are generally small (e.g., Johnston et al., 2021). As Figure 5.1 shows, gender differences in rates of substance use for PROSPER were, indeed, small and inconsistent, with girls' rates of any drinking and smoking cigarettes exceeding boys' about as often as not. For marijuana, boys' use more consistently exceeded girls' use.

To gain additional perspective on substance use by the PROSPER sample, Figure 5.2 provides comparisons to a national sample. The PROSPER sample

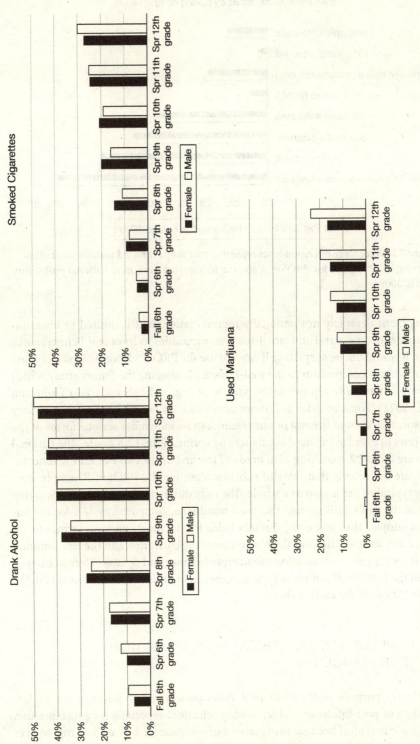

Figure 5.1 Rates of past month substance use, by gender, 6th through 12th grade. Spr = spring.

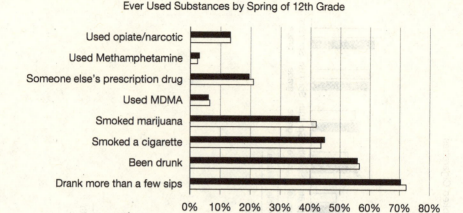

Figure 5.2 Percentage of respondents reporting that they ever used various substances by spring of 12th grade for PROSPER and the Monitoring the Future national probability sample, 2009.

is large, but definitely not nationally representative, as it is limited to lower-to-moderate income, rural and small-town communities in Iowa and Pennsylvania. Thus, it would not be surprising if rates of use for PROSPER were atypical. Figure 5.2 provides a comparison to the well-known Monitoring the Future study, which surveys a nationally representative sample of high schools each year (Johnston et al., 2021). For a broader and more sensitive view, we go beyond the primary measures we used in the rest of our research to include more serious forms of use and rates of ever having used substances by spring of the 12th grade. The national rates are for 2009, matching 12th grade of the first of the two PROSPER cohorts.

Figure 5.2 reveals that rates of substance use for the PROSPER sample were quite typical of the nation as a whole. The only difference larger than 2% was that 36% of the PROSPER sample had used marijuana, compared to 42% for the national sample. The close comparability holds for the most common forms of substance use, such as drinking alcohol and smoking cigarettes, and the less common and most serious, such as using methamphetamines and opiates. Thus, substance use in the PROSPER sample is typical, rather than unusual, for adolescents in the United States in the early 2000s.

PEER INFLUENCE AND FRIENDSHIP SELECTION FOR SUBSTANCE USE

A primary purpose of the PROSPER Peers project was to advance our understanding of peer influence and friendship selection, especially for substance use. This topic is critical because explanations of substance use give a key role to peer influence (e.g., Elliott et al., 1989; Jessor & Jessor, 1977; Oetting & Beauvais, 1986), and addressing the role of peers is central to programs for reducing substance use (Botvin & Griffin, 2004; Hansen & Dusenbury, 2004; Henneberger et al., 2019). Our team has investigated many aspects of this subject, and the current section summarizes findings from several of our main studies.

The essence of the concept of peer influence is that people's attitudes and behavior are changed by those of the other people with whom they have relationships or spend time. Chapter 1 points out that this theme is not limited to explanations of substance use and risky behavior, but rather is prominent in general theories of social behavior (e.g., social learning, Bandura, 1977; symbolic interaction, Mead, 1934). Widespread evidence of similarity between friends for many important outcomes is often interpreted as evidence for peer influence. Yet skeptics have argued that the similarity arises instead from selection processes because people prefer friends who are similar to themselves (Glueck & Glueck, 1950; Hirschi, 1969).

As Chapter 1 stresses in presenting the network-based conceptual framework for PROSPER Peers, it is essential to study selection and influence jointly. Both a preference for having friends like oneself and being influenced by one's friends will make friends more similar to each other. Therefore, methodologically, it is important to control for one when studying the other. Yet a key point of our network-based conceptual framework is that treating peer influence and friendship selection merely as alternative hypotheses is a serious mistake that misses their inherent interdependence. Rather than functioning in opposition to one another, they inherently operate in combination because the peer influence that adolescents receive comes from whichever friends they choose. An adolescent who chooses substance-using friends will receive influence toward use, in contrast to an adolescent who chooses friends who oppose substance use. In this essential sense, selection determines what influence is received, and influence helps determine later selection—so the two processes must be studied together and the results interpreted jointly.

PROSPER's methodological advantages for studying selection and influence

As noted in Chapter 1, the PROSPER Peers study offers several advantages related to the study of peer friendship networks and adolescent substance use. Here, we briefly review several characteristics that are particularly relevant.

First, the social network data from PROSPER allow for direct, rather than perceptual, measures of peer attributes. A long line of research about adolescent substance use has positioned peer use as among the strongest predictors of this behavior (Warr, 2002). Much of this research, however, relied on perceptual measures. That is, peer attributes were measured by asking individuals to report on the characteristics of their friends. We now know that measures of peer attributes created this way are biased, as adolescents tend to report that their friends' attitudes and behaviors are more similar than do independent measures (Bauman

& Ennett, 1994; Kandel, 1996). The use of social network data alleviates this measurement issue, as adolescents are only asked to report who their friends are, rather than ascertain the attitudes and behaviors of those friends.

Second, the PROSPER Peers study allows for the creation of sociocentric, rather than egocentric, social network data. That is, the social network data for the PROSPER Peers study covers all the individuals in the population (the students who are enrolled in the same school and grade) rather than network data derived from asking independently sampled individuals about their social connections, with no basis for identifying whether the corresponding individuals are connected to each other. When studying selection and influence, having full sociocentric network data allows us to use sophisticated data analytic methods that take into account the full complexity of these processes. As Chapter 1 details, this includes indirect, reciprocal, and circular patterns of influence, as well as structural aspects of selection, none of which can be investigated with egocentric data. The sociocentric data also are essential for addressing the second major topic of the present chapter, friendship groups and substance use.

Third, the PROSPER Peers study followed adolescents from the sixth through the twelfth grade. This duration covers most of adolescence and offers a unique opportunity to study social network properties and mechanisms during a time when substance use is emerging. At the sixth grade, few adolescents had experimented with substance use in our sample, let alone used these substances with any regularity. Yet by the end of the study, the adolescents in our sample are entering adulthood, and substance use is relatively common.

Finally, the PROSPER Peers study is notable because data were collected from 27 different school districts, representing distinct communities in two states, and they include a very large number of students: at least 9,000 at every wave of data collection and over 15,000 different students over time. Although the PROSPER study is certainly not the only source of data that employs direct peer measures, sociocentric network data, or longitudinal data collection, PROSPER's exceptional sample size is advantageous. These data allow for more precise estimates of complex network processes that may be difficult to disentangle in smaller, more limited, data sets (Ragan et al., 2022). Further, the availability of multiple grade and school networks provides an opportunity to determine whether the results of any network are observed elsewhere or are idiosyncratic, a topic explored in Chapter 10, on community context.

The strength of peer influence and friendship selection

We begin with a review of Osgood et al. (2015), our study of the overall influence and selection processes for alcohol use and cigarette smoking. (This study also investigated peer influence and selection for delinquency, yielding very similar results.) This article applied the PROSPER network data to address the traditional core question in the study of peer influence, namely, the strengths of peer influence toward similarity and of homophilic selection of similar friends. Unlike most studies, however, we interpreted these processes as complementary rather than opposed. Further, this study implemented the broader perspective on selection found in social network analysis, and it thereby examined aspects of adolescents' friendship choices that go beyond preferences for similarity.

Previous studies presented an inconsistent picture of the strength and even existence of both peer influence and homophilic selection. Several recent studies had taken advantage of key methodological advances by using network data to assess friends' behavior and new network analytic methods to assess selection and influence (e.g., Hall & Valente, 2007; Knecht et al., 2011; Mercken et al., 2009; Popp et al., 2008). Their implications were unclear, however, because their findings about the strength and statistical significance of these processes varied. The goal of our study was to capitalize on strengths of the PROSPER data to resolve this uncertainty. Not only would the PROSPER data enable us to use the same strong research methods, but also our much larger sample would yield more precise results.

The analyses of peer influence and friendship selection that we report throughout this chapter used the SIENA framework and software (Snijders, 2001; Steglich et al., 2010). This approach takes advantage of longitudinal network data such as PROSPER's to jointly analyze a wide variety of selection and influence processes. Importantly, SIENA allowed for the complex interdependence that is inherent to them, as discussed in the introduction and methods chapters of this volume (Chapters 1 and 3). Here we limit our description of SIENA to aspects with specific substantive relevance, and we refer readers to Chapter 3 for more general information about the approach.

These analyses used the first five waves of data from PROSPER, which covered fall of sixth grade through spring of ninth grade, as did our other studies of selection and influence we discuss in this section of the chapter. The grade cohorts of each community (or school district) defined the networks for the analyses, and analyses were successfully completed for 49 networks for alcohol use and for 41 networks for smoking cigarettes.

Although the structural aspects of friendship selection, which were introduced in Chapter 1, were not themselves a focus of this study, we briefly describe them here because they are an important component of SIENA analyses. These processes are ways that the pattern of existing friendships influence which new friendships arise and which old friendships continue. Structural patterns tend to be quite strong, so taking them into account is valuable for accurately determining the contribution of other selection and peer influence processes. For instance, in this study, the odds of maintaining an old friendship or starting a new one were seven times greater if the friendship was reciprocated than if it was not. Among the other structural selection processes included in the analysis were tendencies toward friendships with friends of one's current friends (labeled transitive triplets in SIENA), hierarchies in groups of friends (negative three cycles), and stable individual differences in attracting friendships (in-degree popularity).

Findings. Social network analysis distinguishes three selection processes associated with an individual-level attribute or behavior, such as substance use (see Chapter 1). For ego selection, an attribute (e.g., substance use) is associated with the respondent (ego) choosing more friends, while for alter selection it is associated with more often being chosen by others. The third type of selection, homophilic selection, is a tendency toward choosing friends similar to oneself in terms of substance use. In addition to assessing all three processes in relation to substance use, the analyses also control for all three types of selection based on gender and race. The preference for friends of the same gender was especially strong, with matching gender between two students doubling the chance of starting or maintaining a friendship compared to a male-female dyad.

Figure 5.3 shows the primary results from this study. For both alcohol use and smoking cigarettes, analyses revealed a strong tendency for students to choose friends who were more similar to themselves over students who were different. For instance, the odds that a student would form a new friendship were 55% higher if that student matched their smoking behavior (i.e., both smoking more than once in the past month compared to one student doing so and the other not smoking at all). Further, students who drank alcohol or smoked cigarettes tended to attract more friendships from other students (positive alter selection), but substance use was, at most, only weakly related to whether students chose more friends themselves (ego selection).

The study also found strong evidence for peer influence on both drinking and smoking. Students whose friends drank or smoked much more (or less) than they did were very likely to change their behavior to be more like their friends. This pattern of findings held even though the analysis of change in behavior also controlled for past substance use behavior, demographic factors, school bonding, family relations, and sensation seeking.

Overall, the study yielded reliable evidence of peer influence, selection for similarity, and a general tendency to choose friends who used alcohol and smoke

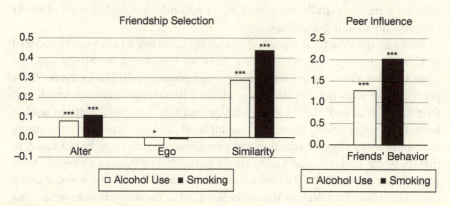

Siena parameter estimates.
* $p < .05$
*** $p < .001$

Figure 5.3 Influence and selection results from Osgood et al., 2015; logistic coefficients from SIENA. *$p < 0.05$.

cigarettes (positive alter selection). In combination, these findings show that, not only are adolescents influenced by the behavior of their friends for both these types of substance use, but also there is a systematic pattern to the influence they will receive. Selection for similarity means that the most influence will be in the direction of maintaining or enlarging previous differences between youth in substance use. Yet, the alter selection finding means that this general pattern is overlaid with greater influence by substance-using youth because they attract more friends. Their greater influence will tend to promote overall increases in rates of substance use.

How else do peers contribute to the emergence of alcohol use?

The next study we discuss, Osgood et al. (2013), explored additional aspects of peer influence and selection processes in the emergence of alcohol use that could provide useful guidance for shaping programs to address this problem. First, because adolescent alcohol use tends to occur in very social settings, we investigated the possibility that simply having more friends would be an additional peer influence on drinking. Second, we wanted to learn more about what factors predicted which adolescents chose drinking versus nondrinking friends, thereby exposing themselves to being influenced toward drinking. In conjunction, we explored whether the peer processes surrounding the emergence of alcohol use were specific to whether or not friends actually drank versus being a byproduct of the profile of risk factors associated with drinking.

This study used the same research methods as our study discussed in the preceding section (Osgood et al., 2015), taking the form of a SIENA analysis of the five waves of PROSPER data from fall of grade six through spring of grade nine. The statistical model included all the selection and influence processes from that study and yielded consistent results about them. Here, we focus on the additional elements, which build on those shared findings.

Is having more friends a risk factor for drinking? Based on our work with routine activity theory (Osgood et al., 1996), we hypothesized that attracting a lot of friends would itself contribute to more drinking, above and beyond the influence of the friends' alcohol use. The theory argues that problem behavior increases when youth have more exposure to appealing opportunities to engage in it. For drinking, opportunities are concentrated in parties and social gatherings (Bachman et al., 2011, pp. 56–58), and we reasoned that having many friends could mean being included in more of those events.

Our analyses tested for this possibility and found that, indeed, being named as a friend more frequently was associated with increases in drinking. Each additional friend added 5% to the odds of initiating or increasing drinking. For someone named as a friend by eight peers, the 5% increases would compound to 55% higher odds of initiating or increasing drinking, compared to someone named by none. Notably this finding controls for the influence of friends' alcohol use and for a student's own individual-level risk factors (e.g., composite risk, sex, race).

Choosing friends who drink. What factors contribute to whether adolescents have friends who drink and thereby become exposed to peer influence toward drinking? Osgood and colleagues (2015) study showed that drinkers generally attract more friendships than nondrinkers, and here we tested whether the strength of the attraction was any stronger or weaker in relation to the basic demographic factors of gender, race/ethnicity, and socioeconomic status (as indicated by receiving free or reduced-price school lunch). In addition, we considered the role of students' general risk for alcohol use, as reflected in a composite (i.e., an average) of several key measures in our data set that are consistently associated with risky behaviors. These included negative attitudes toward school, low self-reported grades, negative family relationships, little religious participation, and high levels of sensation seeking. Across these five waves of data, the correlation of this risk measure with alcohol use was 0.37.

Beyond the tendency to select friends who are similar, the sole direct predictor of a tendency to choose friends who drink was a weak effect for socioeconomic status. (In the SIENA friendship selection model, these effects take the form of interactions between ego attributes and alter drinking. The similarity selection effect for drinking corresponds to an interaction between ego drinking and alter drinking.) Students who received free or reduced-price school lunch were slightly more likely to choose drinkers as friends. Thus, the general preference for friends who drink was fairly consistent across students, modified by little other than the preference for friends who are similar on drinking status we discussed above.

Although the composite risk measure did not directly contribute to choosing drinkers as friends, it still plays an indirect role. There was a tendency toward selecting friends who were similar on this composite risk measure, with the strength comparable to the tendency toward choosing friends similar for alcohol use. Given the sizable correlation between the risk measure and alcohol use, these tendencies combined toward considerable clustering of friends on a nexus of alcohol use and its associated risk factors. Overall, we interpreted the study's findings as suggesting that, among early adolescents, drinking is an attractive, high-status activity, and that deeper immersion in the larger world of friendships exposes adolescents to the risk of drinking through enhanced opportunities to do so.

Influence from what friends think or what they do

A pair of our studies has examined the contributions of beliefs to network selection and peer influence processes for drug use, revisiting the important question of whether the importance of friends is a consequence of "what they think or what they do" (Warr & Stafford, 1991). These studies, one concerning adolescent drinking (Ragan, 2014) and the other smoking (Ragan, 2016), pursued long-standing questions about the interplay of influences between beliefs and behavior. Whether attitudes influence behavior has been a classic issue for social psychology (Fishbein & Ajzen, 1975), and prominent criminological theories have treated peer influences on beliefs as central to the explanation of crime (Akers, 1985; Sutherland, 1939). Although early research had concluded that beliefs did not play an important role in the influence process for risky behaviors (Warr & Stafford, 1991), that work relied on respondents' perceptions about their friends and would not meet current standards for studying peer influence.

We investigated the importance of two types of beliefs that would appear especially relevant for substance use. The first is *moral approval* of the behavior, measured by asking students "how wrong" they believed it was for someone their age to drink or smoke. The second type of belief was *positive social expectations* that the students associated with the behavior. The measure related to smoking asked the students how much they agreed with statements that "teens who smoke have more friends," "smoking cigarettes makes you look cool," and "smoking cigarettes lets you have more fun." The measure for alcohol use was created from similar items referring to drinking, plus two additional items: "drinking alcohol is a good way of dealing with your problems" and "drinking helps you get along with other people."

Like the other studies discussed in this section, we addressed these research questions through SIENA analyses of the first five waves of the PROSPER data. The models examined the roles of measures of both types of beliefs in the friendship selection process, and they also considered them as sources of peer influence and as outcomes subject to peer influence.

These two studies produced evidence that beliefs about drinking and smoking contributed to both friendship selection and peer influence processes. Not surprisingly, adolescents who viewed drinking and smoking as "less wrong" and believed substances conferred social benefits were more likely to use the substances themselves. But the results from these studies suggested that students' beliefs were not independent of their friends. Rather, adolescents tended to change their beliefs to match those of their friends. Thus, when adolescents were connected to friends who were more approving of alcohol and cigarette use and expected more positive consequences from these behaviors, they tended to become more approving and have higher expectations for themselves. These results are evidence of indirect effects of peer beliefs on adolescent drinking and smoking: friends' beliefs about these behaviors influence individual beliefs, which in turn predict the individual's own behavior. We discovered direct associations between peer beliefs and individual behavior as well, although the association differed between the two types of substance use. For drinking, the association between friends' moral approval and individuals' drinking remained statistically significant even when controlling for friends' expectations and both types of individual beliefs. For smoking, it was friends' expectations for cigarette use that continued to influence individuals' smoking in the full analysis with both types of belief for both friends and oneself included in the model.

We also found beliefs about both drinking and smoking to be consequential in the friendship selection process. Selecting friends with beliefs similar to one's own beliefs was observed for both moral approval and positive expectations about drinking and smoking. Additionally, adolescents who reported having more positive expectations for smoking tended to receive more friendship nominations, and there was some evidence that adolescents who are more approving of alcohol and cigarette use were named as friends at a higher rate than peers who were less approving.

The results from these studies about the network connections of beliefs with adolescent drinking and smoking carry several implications for our understanding of these behaviors. Much of the extant research that examines how peers contribute to adolescent substance use focuses on the roles that friends' behaviors play. Our work on beliefs illustrates how other attributes of the friends may be consequential for understanding the development of these behaviors. Additionally, these beliefs may be particularly important in early adolescence. During this period adolescents begin reporting beliefs that are more open and accepting of drinking and smoking, before they actually engage in the behaviors. This provides an opportunity for prevention programs to target attributes relevant to the development of drinking and smoking before the behaviors become prevalent.

SUBSTANCE USE AND FRIENDSHIP GROUPS

To this point, we have been discussing peer influence and selection processes related to substance use, which illustrates the connectionist tradition in the study of social networks. Next, we shift our attention to two PROSPER Peers studies that are examples of the positional tradition. As explained in Chapter 3, the connectionist approach attends to flows through networks (e.g., information, opinion, influence), while the positional tradition concerns people's varying patterns of connection with others. The positional tradition provides a rich set of conceptual and methodological tools for examining the organization of networks and positions of individuals and groups within them.

These two positional studies focused on adolescents' involvement in groups, an important aspect of social life, especially during adolescence (as discussed in Chapters 1 and 3). Not only are friendship groups important to adolescents' daily experience and well-being, but also they are a source of reputations (Brown, 1990; Cairns et al., 1985). The tendencies for friendships to be reciprocal and for friends to have other friends in common (transitivity) are not strong enough to yield strictly bounded groups whose members are friends only with one another. Rather, they yield looser aggregations in which friendships with one another predominate over outside connections. Chapter 3 discusses how network clustering algorithms use these patterns to identify groups and describes the specific methods used in PROSPER Peers.

Friendship group position and substance use

Although most adolescents are members of cohesive friendship groups, many are not. This section discusses an article by the PROSPER Peers team (Osgood et al., 2014) that addressed whether adolescents' rates of substance use differed depending on whether and how they were connected to a friendship group.

The notion that being connected to groups would help prevent harmful behaviors like substance use is found in in the traditions of social control theory and strain theory, and it traces back to Durkheim's writing about social integration and suicide (1897/1993). According to social control theory (Hirschi, 1969; Jessor & Jessor, 1977), belonging to a group constitutes a social bond that helps prevent norm-violating behaviors, such as substance use. From both the perspective of strain theory (Agnew, 1992; Merton, 1938) and the conception of substance use as self-medication (Khantzian, 1997), not being part of a group constitutes a frustration or stressor that a person might seek to alleviate through substance use. In an early notable study on this topic, Ennett and Bauman (1993) found high rates of smoking among isolates not connected to any group.

Prior studies of group position and substance use distinguished two types of nonmembers, arguing that one should be more problematic than the other. For some adolescents, not being a group member is part of a general pattern of isolation and absence of social connection (Cusick, 1973; Eder, 1985; see also Chapter 7 of this volume), so the theories predict a high risk of substance use. Liaisons are also nonmembers, but instead of lacking connections, they have friends in two or more groups, without clearly belonging to any one of them (Ennett & Bauman, 1993). Liaisons thus show some degree of social integration, but it is debatable whether their connections to multiple groups show a healthy flexibility or carry added stress from competing friendship demands (Osgood et al., 2014).

In addition to these comparisons to nonmembers seen in earlier studies, our study also explored the possibility that any preventive effects of group membership would depend on how strongly members were integrated into their group. We reasoned that peripheral members, who have only one or two friends in a group, would benefit less than core members, who have more extensive connections.

The analyses used the first five waves of the PROSPER friendship data, covering sixth through ninth grades for two grade cohorts in the 27 school districts that provided friendship data, with a total of approximately 9,500 respondents per wave. The group identification algorithm identified from 818 to 914 groups per wave of data, with average sizes of 9.72 to 11.43 members.

Our analytic strategy went beyond previous studies in two respects. First, to avoid confounding findings about group positions with effects of peer influence, our analyses controlled for the substance use of respondents' friends, unlike most previous studies of the topic. Second, we strategically used control variables to help clarify the meaning of our results. As a baseline analysis, we limited our attention to relationships between group position and substance use that were not explained by demographic factors (gender, race/ethnicity, age, family structure, low income, state, grade cohort) or effects of the PROSPER intervention program.

We then tested how much of those baseline associations could be accounted for by controlling for our respondents' adjustment in other life domains. Specifically, we controlled for school grades, attitudes about school, relationships with their families, and religious involvement.

Findings. The methodological strengths of the PROSPER friendship data provide further improvements over prior work (Ennett & Bauman, 1993; Fang et al., 2003; Henry & Kobus, 2007; Kobus & Henry, 2010; Pearson & Michell, 2000; Pearson et al., 2006). Previous studies analyzed much smaller samples from few networks, covered brief age spans, and restricted friendships in ways ill-suited to identifying cohesive groups in networks by allowing only three or fewer friendships or including only reciprocal friendships.

The grouping algorithm assigned 92.9% of students to groups, with 77.5% as core members and 15.4% as peripheral members, who could be disconnected from the group by removing a single friendship. Of the total sample, 2.7% qualified as liaisons (nonmembers with friends in multiple groups), 3.5% as isolates (no friends or one who has no other friends), and 0.8% as "other nonmembers" (varied idiosyncratic patterns).

Results are from multilevel logistic regression analyses with waves of data collection as Level 1, nested within individual students as Level 2, nested within school districts' grade cohorts as Level 3 (see Chapter 3). Figure 5.4 summarizes the main results reported by Osgood and colleagues (2014). The core group members (the largest category) served as the reference group for comparisons to the other three

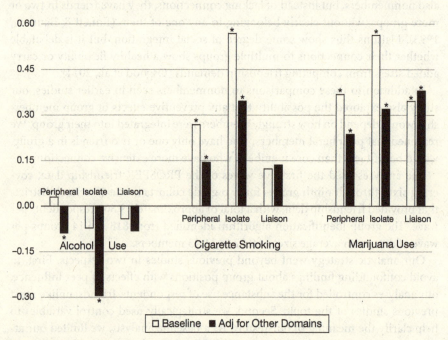

Figure 5.4 Group positions and substance use, logistic coefficients for differences from core members. *$p < 0.05$.
Adapted from Osgood et al., 2014.

groups, and the bars in the chart show how much higher or lower each of those group's rate of use was in terms of log odds of substance use.

Turning to the main findings, the overall trend for cigarette smoking and marijuana use was consistent with the predictions of social control and strain theories for peripheral members and isolates to use more than core members, though the picture is mixed for liaisons. When the analysis also controlled for other aspects of adjustment (shown by the black bars), those differences diminished by about 40% but remained statistically significant and relatively large in most cases. Liaisons also used marijuana more often than core members, and in this case respondents' adjustment in the other domains did not account for that difference (reflecting that the liaisons differed little from core members on those measures).

For alcohol use, differences between group positions were not evident in the baseline model, but after controlling for adjustment in the other domains, use was higher among core members than peripheral members and isolates. This pattern of findings resulted from the combination that, first, poorer adjustment in those domains is associated with higher rates of all three types of substance use, and, second, core members had considerably better adjustment than peripheral members and isolates. Consequently, core members used alcohol at about the same level as peripheral members and isolates, but their use was higher than expected given their adjustment in other ways.

Putting the results together, we see that adolescents' positions relative to cohesive friendship groups were related to substance use in a complex way, with each position carrying greater risk of at least one substance, but not others. The findings for greater cigarette smoking and marijuana use by isolates were a clear match to social control and strain theories' prediction that a lack of social integration will bring greater use. That is also true for peripheral group members, but less strongly so because both their substance use and their integration into friendship groups fell between the core members and isolates. Liaisons stand out only for a high level of marijuana use, despite their favorable adjustment in other domains. Thus, their marijuana use appears to be a function of the unique connection to multiple friendship groups. Finally, compared to peripheral members and isolates, core members' higher rates of alcohol use (after controlling for their adjustment) shows that engagement in adolescent peer culture promotes alcohol use in a way that simply did not apply to the other substances and was inconsistent with control and strain theories.

Substance use and the structure of friendship groups

In one of the first articles from PROSPER Peers, Kreager and colleagues (2011) investigated the relationship between the structure of friendship groups and group members' average levels of delinquency and alcohol use. This study revived a tradition of research on groups and gangs that dated to the early 1900s (Thrasher, 1927) and remained dominant through the 1960s (Cloward & Ohlin, 1960; Short & Strodtbeck, 1965). Attention to groups had receded by the mid-1970s, as individual-level theory and random sample surveys became dominant. Kreager and colleagues showed that a network-based study of groups such as PROSPER can yield unique insights. In this section, we present their study and a new version of their analyses that added cigarette smoking and marijuana use to original risky behaviors of delinquency and alcohol use.

The structure of groups has special importance for explanations of risky behavior. Theories that emphasize peer influence (Burgess & Akers, 1966; Oetting & Beauvais, 1986; Sutherland, 1939) argue that risky behaviors arise from the same social influence processes as conventional behaviors, implicitly assuming that delinquent and substance-using groups have sufficient cohesion and stability to enable that influence. In contrast, control theories (Gottfredson & Hirschi, 1990; Hirschi, 1969) argue that traits like impulsiveness and risk seeking or an absence of social bonds lead to risky behavior. These theories take the position that deviant groups lack sufficient cohesion and warmth to convey peer influence, and any similarity among group members in risky behavior is a spurious result of shared risk factors.

Hagan (1991) offered an alternative view that risky behavior is embedded in two different adolescent subcultures: a "party" subculture of drinking and early dating and a delinquent subculture of violence and serious property crime. Hagan saw the party culture as a tacitly valued aspect of adolescence (Matza & Sykes, 1961), with participation bolstering members' social capital through more extensive network ties and heightened peer status. In contrast, the delinquent subculture is less accepted by most youth. The problematic behavior of delinquent group members, combined with lack of success in school and lower socioeconomic standing, will give these groups lower status and less cohesion.

Kreager and colleagues (2011) took advantage of the PROSPER research design to make important advances relative to prior work. First, an important shortcoming of early research on gangs and groups was studying only groups selected for their risky behavior without comparing them to other groups. These studies often were limited to urban, poor, and minority populations, thereby conflating risky behavior with differences due to key demographic factors, a shortcoming resolved by the high level of participation (e.g., > 90%) of students in PROSPER's public school districts.

Second, this network-based examination of group structure built on studies of friendship quality and risky behavior from the 1980s forward. Individual-level studies using self-report data on friendships (Giordano et al., 1986) and peer nominations (Baerveldt et al., 2004; Houtzager and Baerveldt, 1999) reported the friendships of delinquent youth to be as close and stable as those of other youth. Kreager and colleagues (2011) applied insights from these studies of individual-level self-report to a study of actual groups.

Similar to the study of group positions in the previous section, the study of group structure and risky behavior used different sets of control variables to help clarify the meaning of those relationships. In this case, the analyses began with a baseline model examining the link between group members' risky behaviors and the group structure, which controlled only for the groups' rates of the other risky behaviors. The next model controlled for the groups' demographic compositions, and the third model controlled for attitude and behavior measures in the domains of family, school, and religious involvement as well.

This study focused specifically on the PROSPER data collected in the spring of ninth grade, which corresponds to students' average age of about 15 years. By this age, substance use and delinquency are common enough to play a meaningful role in adolescents' peer relations, but the respondents are still young enough that alcohol consumption and cigarette smoking are not normatively acceptable. The cohesive group identification methods described in Chapter 3 yielded 897 groups, whose 9,385 members comprised 91% of the total sample and corresponded to an average group size of 10.5 members.

The explanatory variables of primary interest were group means for self-reported delinquency (based on item response theory scores [Osgood et al., 2002] for a 12-item measure) and dichotomous measures of past-month use of alcohol, tobacco, and marijuana. Four measures of group structure and two measures of status served as the outcome measures. The first measure of group structure was *reciprocity*, the proportion of within-group friendships that were mutual. *Transitivity* reflected the strength of the tendency for "friends of friends" to also be friends with one another (calculated within the group). The group's *structural cohesion* concerned the number of independent paths that connected members to one another. *Group stability* was based on the consistency of a group's membership since the previous year (i.e., how many pairs of members shared a group the previous year). The first measure of status was *popularity*, captured by the average number of friendship nominations members received, converted to a percentile rank within the school. The second was the group's *centrality* in terms of the number of friendships it receives from and sends to other groups, weighted by the popularity of the groups sending them (Bonacich, 1987).

The demographic measures used as control variables were proportions of group members receiving free or reduced-price school lunch and living with both biological parents, and dummy variables were for being a predominantly (at least 90%) male group or female group (versus mixed gender) and for being a predominantly white group (versus mixed race/ethnicity). Along with the demographic variables, we also controlled for whether the school district received the PROSPER preventive intervention and average group attitudes and behaviors (school grades, attitudes about school, respondents' relationships with their families, and religious involvement). In addition, this final model controlled for group size and the group members' average number of out-of-school friends.

Findings. The results we present here are from a reanalysis that extended Kreager and colleagues' findings by including group means for cigarette smoking and marijuana use as additional explanatory variables. This addition had negligible impact on the findings for the group levels of delinquency and alcohol use, and the findings we report for their relationships with group structure were fully consistent with those reported by Kreager and colleagues, 2011.

The analyses took the form of multilevel regression models with cohesive friendship groups as Level 1, nested within-school grade cohorts as Level 2. Figure 5.5 reports results as standardized coefficients.

The results for delinquency provide a context for the findings for substance use, which is our primary focus. The baseline model (white bars in the figure) captured the overall association of groups' average delinquency with their structure, controlling for substance use, but no other factors. Delinquent groups had weaker structure by all measures, including diminished connectedness (reciprocation, transitivity, and structural cohesion), less stability, and lower status (popularity and centrality). Those associations appeared largely attributable to the demographic makeup of the groups because only the lower levels of structural cohesion and popularity remained statistically significant in the second model (gray bars in the figure). Further, the negative associations of delinquency with group structure were either fully eliminated or reversed by taking into account attitudinal and behavioral risk factors in the next model (the black bars in the figure). Indeed, associations became significantly positive for transitivity and popularity, indicating that delinquent groups fared better than expected in these regards after controlling for demographic, attitudinal, and behavioral characteristics.

The results for alcohol use were in sharp contrast to delinquency, with the baseline associations of alcohol use all in the direction of stronger structure, significantly so for the measures of connectedness and status (but not stability).

Demographic factors accounted for much of the association between groups' alcohol use and their stronger structural features (30%–65%). This occurred because groups with higher rates of alcohol use tended to have female and white members, and both are associated with stronger structure. Yet, substantial positive associations of drinking with group structure remained even controlling for demographic factors, and these associations were not further reduced by controlling for the attitudinal and behavioral risk factors. Thus, consistent with Hagan's (1991) portrayal of a party subculture, drinking groups carried high social status (popularity and centrality) and had strong social connections (reciprocity, transitivity, and structural cohesion).

Similar to delinquency, groups with higher rates of cigarette smoking had weaker group structure in the baseline model, significantly so for transitivity, structural cohesion, popularity, and centrality. Controlling for demographic factors reduced these associations somewhat, but much less than for delinquency (5%–33% vs. 48%–100%, respectively). Adding the controls for attitudinal and behavior factors was more consequential, however, further reducing each of the significant relationships by roughly half.

Groups' structural characteristics were less associated with their rates of marijuana use than with the other risky behaviors in all three models, with statistically

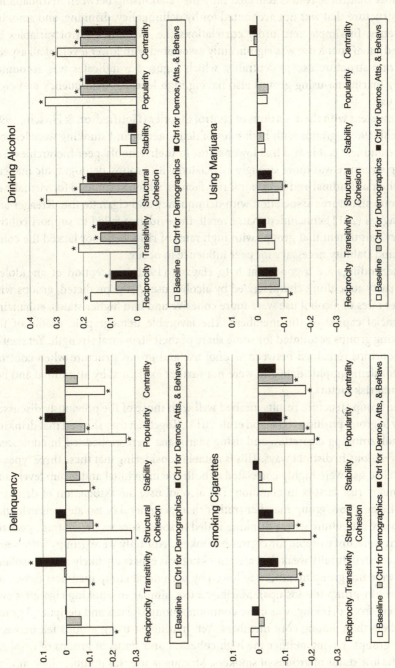

Figure 5.5 Standardized associations between mean group behavior and group structure. *$p < 0.05$.

significant associations only for less reciprocity in the baseline model and less structural cohesion controlling for demographic factors. It is important to remember that these results reflected only the relationship between marijuana use and structure that was not accounted for by delinquency, drinking, and smoking cigarettes. In simple zero-order correlations (i.e., without control variables included), marijuana use was significantly associated with lower levels of all aspects of group structure except centrality, which Figure 5.5 indicates was accounted for by marijuana-using groups also having high levels of delinquency and cigarette use.

Consistent with the assertions of control theories (Gottfredson & Hirschi, 1990; Hirschi, 1969), groups with high rates of delinquency and smoking were less cohesive and less stable and had lower status in their schools' peer hierarchies. Yet, group structure was more strongly associated with groups' demographic makeup and their attitudinal and behavioral risk factors, which accounted for virtually all of group structure's association with delinquency and cigarette use. Kreager and colleagues (2011) concluded that, overall, the evidence failed to support control theory's argument that groups with high rates of risky behavior lacked the cohesion and stability necessary for peer influence to occur.

The findings are a good match to Hagan's (1991) conception of an adolescent party subculture characterized by alcohol use. As he predicted, groups with higher rates of alcohol use were more cohesive and had higher status, enhancing the social capital of the members. The favorable demographic profile of the drinking groups accounted for some share of their structural strength. Yet sizable relationships remained between alcohol use and group structure when controlling for demographic data and were not further explained by attitudinal and behavioral risk factors.

The group structure results meshed well with those of the previously discussed study of group positions (Osgood et al., 2014). Together, they showed that drinking alcohol, smoking cigarettes, and using marijuana were embedded in adolescent peer relations in distinct ways. This is notable considering that these three types of substance use were highly correlated at both the individual and group levels and had many risk factors in common. For alcohol use, the association of drinking with being a core group member (rather than peripheral or isolate) was evidence of a party subculture where drinking is tied to social success. In contrast, peer relations were unfavorable for cigarette smokers. Not only were groups with many smokers structurally weak, but also smoking was especially likely among isolates who were not group members, followed by peripheral group members (who had few within-group friendships). Marijuana use, similar to smoking cigarettes and different from drinking, was more common among isolates and peripheral group members than among core members. Yet, marijuana-using groups fell between these groups, having neither the high cohesion and status of groups of drinkers nor the low status of groups of smokers. Marijuana use was uniquely high among liaisons who had ample social connections with multiple groups, rather than being integrated in any single one.

CHANGE ACROSS ADOLESCENCE IN THE CONNECTION BETWEEN PEERS AND SUBSTANCE USE

A final topic we address in this chapter is how network processes related to substance use change during adolescence. Adolescence is the period of emergence and rapid increase for substance use, as it is for several other risky behaviors. Previously in this chapter we demonstrated that this dramatic increase in substance use clearly occurs in the PROSPER sample as well (see Figure 5.2). Because the risky behaviors first become notable problems in adolescence, research heavily emphasizes this period (Sampson & Laub, 1992), yet far fewer studies focus on the dramatic developmental changes occurring then, which should be key for understanding why problem behaviors emerge so dramatically (Ragan, 2020). Developmental change has been an important topic of our work on substance use and peers, and this section is devoted to those studies.

Developmental change in the similarity of friends

We begin this section with our study of change across adolescence in the similarity of friends (Osgood et al., 2022). The tendency for friends to be more similar than nonfriends, known as homophily, is one of the most consistent findings in the study of social relationships at any age (McPherson et al., 2001). So far in this chapter, we have approached similarity of friends from an interest in the processes that create it, notably selection preferences and peer influence. This next study, in contrast, investigated similarity in its own right as an indicator of the organization of the friendships in a community of adolescents. The tendency toward being friends with similar people, captured by the strength of the correlation between friends on a demographic, attitudinal, or behavioral measure, is of special interest because it reflects how much an attribute serves as a basis for clustering among friends and division from nonfriends. Friendship patterns like this shape adolescents' daily experience of who they spend time with and the variety of influences to which they are exposed. Note that this study's focus was at the network level of analysis because it concerned the organization of the friendships within a population of adolescents. For the purposes of the current chapter, we are interested in the study's findings about similarity for substance use and about how that similarity changes across adolescence. The study also investigated nine other attributes, and we briefly comment on differences among them to place substance use in this broader context.

A key reference point for homophily in adolescence is that gender has dominated friendship choices in the preceding years. Friendship groups are almost totally divided by gender through the elementary school years (Maccoby, 1998), but mixed-gender groups emerge and become common by late adolescence (Poulin & Pedersen, 2007; Shrum et al., 1988). We hypothesized that this decline in gender homophily would be accompanied by increases in homophily for most other attributes, including substance use. We reasoned that, at least in industrialized Western cultures like the United States, entering adolescence brings reduced adult supervision and increased time with peers versus family (Larson et al., 1996; Osgood et al., 2005). These changes provide opportunities for more wide-ranging friendship choices, allowing friendships to form based on many different attributes, whether through preferences, peer influence, situational influences, or the propinquity of meeting others while pursuing shared interests.

As our index of homophily, we computed correlations between friends on each attribute, calculated across all friendship pairs in a network. The specific correlation coefficient was Moran's *I*, which is designed to capture network or spatial autocorrelation (and its formula is very similar to the usual Pearson product-moment correlation). For alcohol use, this correlation was calculated for all seven waves of data through the 11th grade. The correlations for cigarette and marijuana use were examined from 7th through 11th grade, omitting 6th grade because in many networks none of the students reported use, and correlations were undefined. We omitted the 12th grade data because the sample changed quite a bit due to school dropout, early graduation, and general nonresponse, making the comparisons to earlier grades less meaningful.

Findings. Across all 12 attributes we studied, correlations between friends were consistently positive and statistically significant. As simple averages over waves and networks, the mean correlations for substance use were 0.12 for alcohol use, 0.19 for smoking cigarettes, and 0.14 for marijuana use. Consistent with findings going back to early work by Kandel (1978), these were in the moderate range among the larger set of attributes.

These values, however, obscure dramatic increases in homophily for substance use across adolescence, shown in Figure 5.6. Correlations between friends for alcohol use grew from only 0.03 in the fall of sixth grade to 0.21 by the spring of 11th grade. Similarly, the correlation for cigarette use increased from 0.12 in the spring of seventh grade to 0.22 in the spring of 11th grade, and the correlation for marijuana use increased from 0.07 to 0.19 over this same period. All of these adjusted mean correlations (from a three-level meta-analytic model, controlling for state, grade cohort, and treatment program status) were statistically significant ($p < 0.005$ for fall sixth-grade alcohol use, all others $p < 0.001$). Although the magnitude of these correlations remains only moderate even toward the end of high school, the marked increase indicates growing importance of substance use in the organization of peer relationships.

Our mediation analyses determined that growing variation among individuals in whether or not they used substances accounted for most of this increase in correlations between friends. Our interest in variability as a mediator was based on the logic that low variation would tend to limit correlations. The lower the variability on an attribute, the stronger and more fine-grained distinctions among potential friends would have to be in order to yield the same level of correlation. Further, low rates of substance use in the early waves corresponded to limited variability in the form of small standard deviations, and variability increased considerably across grade levels as rates of use increased. Because network standard

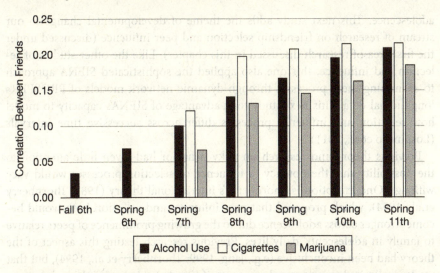

Note: The correlation coefficient is Moran's *I*, corrected for a small negative bias that is inversely proportional to network size. *N*s are 449 networks for alcohol use, 292 for smoking cigarettes, and 285 for marijuana use. Each network is a distinct combination of time point, grade cohort, and school. Figure based on results reported by Osgood et al., 2022.

Figure 5.6 Developmental change in the correlation between friends for substance use.

deviations for substance use also strongly predicted correlations between friends, variability was a source of strong indirect effects of grade level on homophily for substance use.

The larger context for this trend of increasing correlations for substance use was that, as expected, homophily for gender declined from an extraordinary correlation of 0.89 in fall of 6th grade to 0.73 in spring of 11th grade. Although homophily for gender remained far greater than for any other attribute, the decline left room for significant increases to emerge, as predicted, for 10 of the 11 other attributes (the sole exception being receiving free or reduced-price school lunch). Yet, the increases were especially large for the three substance use measures, matched only by that for school grades (from a correlation of 0.19 in fall of 6th grade to 0.31 in spring of 11th grade). Thus, by mid-to-late adolescence, the singular dominance of gender had loosened, and friendships became moderately clustered for many different attributes. As drinking alcohol, smoking cigarettes, and using marijuana had become more common over the span of adolescence, they also joined the list of attributes that organize adolescents' friendships.

Developmental change in peer influence and friendship selection

Next, we turn to a PROSPER Peers study (Ragan, 2020) that explored some of the mechanisms that contribute to this change in similarity between friends across adolescence. This next study adds the theme of developmental change to our stream of research on friendship selection and peer influence (discussed under the first area of research discussed in this chapter). Like the other studies of selection and influence, this one also applied the sophisticated SIENA approach to examining these processes through dynamic network models of PROSPER's longitudinal data. This next study took advantage of SIENA's capacity to model how selection and influence processes differ across successive time intervals (Lospinoso et al., 2011).

Previous theory and research on risky behavior had given little attention to the possibility that the potency of influence or selection processes would vary with age. One exception is Thornberry's interactional theory (1987; Thornberry et al., 1994), which proposed that peer influence and selection both would become stronger across adolescence due to the growing prominence of peers relative to family in adolescents' daily lives. Previous research testing this aspect of the theory had been inconclusive (e.g., Jang, 1999; Thornberry et al., 1994), but that work was limited to perceptual measures of peer behavior, and it lacked the network data needed for a thorough analysis of selection processes.

Our study (Ragan, 2020) considered change from early to mid-adolescence in two of the processes of greatest interest as sources of similarity between friends: the tendency to select friends similar to oneself (homophilic selection) and peer influence. Within the SIENA framework, we operationalized peer influence as the tendency of individuals to change their behavior to become more similar to the mean of their friends. We examined two forms of substance use, drinking alcohol and cigarette smoking, and we estimated models for the PROSPER data collected from students in sixth through ninth grade.

The starting point for the study was the models of selection and influence from the study by Osgood and colleagues (2015), similar to those we presented previously. In line with our previous findings, the new estimates for the overall processes of homophilic selection and peer influence were both positive and statistically significant, indicating that each process contributed to similarity between friends. These initial estimates represent average levels for each process across all time periods. We then re-estimated each of the behavior-specific models two times, first allowing the estimates for the homophilic selection parameter to vary over time, and then a second time allowing the estimates for the social influence parameter to vary. The estimates from these models, which appear in Figure 5.7, demonstrate clear and consistent patterns: For both drinking and smoking, homophilic selection became greater in magnitude as students progressed from the sixth through the ninth grade, while the estimates of social influence for each behavior decreased during this same time period.

The findings about change in selection and influence are especially interesting when considered alongside those regarding similarity, which we just discussed. We see that the *increasing similarity between peers for substance use* during adolescence, at least for alcohol and cigarette use, is a consequence of a *stronger tendency to select friends similar to oneself*. In contrast, the *tendency to change these behaviors to match friends is decreasing* during this time.

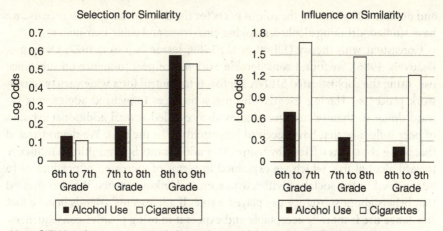

Note: SIENA estimates, meta-analytic results combining estimates from 46 grade cohort-school district networks for alcohol use and 32 for smoking cigarettes. Figure based on results reported by Ragan, 2020.

Figure 5.7 Development change in the strength of homophilic selection and peer influence toward similarity.

We are continuing to pursue this topic, and our additional analyses extend these findings in two ways (Ragan, 2018). First, we extended the analyses of alcohol use to include the additional waves of data collected through the end of high school. Preliminary analysis of this longer time period revealed that the trend of increasing homophilic selection persisted through the 12th grade.

In addition, this new work took advantage of SIENA's additional capacity to separately model the selection processes contributing to forming new friendships (i.e., whether or not any current nonfriend becomes a friend) versus the selection processes for maintaining current friendships (vs. dropping them). These analyses suggested that the increased homophilic selection was entirely for the formation of new friendships and not at all for which old friendships continued. Thus, alcohol contributes to the choices of new friends in a way that it does not for whether or not adolescents continue their ongoing friendships.

CONCLUSIONS

As we noted in this chapter, theorists and program designers have considered peers and friendships to be central to the etiology and prevention of adolescent substance use (e.g., Botvin & Griffin, 2004; Elliott et al., 1989). The PROSER Peers research presented in this chapter provides strong support for this view. Important connections between peers and substance use were evident in all three research areas: peer influence and friendship selection, peer group structure and membership, and developmental change in friendship network organization and peer processes. These studies also have identified both important commonalities and notable differences in the role of peers for the three forms of substance use we have studied: drinking alcohol, smoking cigarettes, and using marijuana.

Consistent with theory (Elliott et al., 1989; Jessor & Jessor, 1977; Oetting & Beauvais, 1986), we found considerable evidence of peer influence on substance use, using the sophisticated SIENA approach to control for a wide variety of network processes. Having friends who use substances influenced adolescents toward doing so themselves. Our studies also revealed several additional avenues of peer influence that have received less attention in the past. We demonstrated that being chosen as a friend by many other adolescents is an additional influence toward alcohol use, which we explained in terms of increased opportunities to be involved in the social activities where most drinking occurs. We also showed that beliefs about substance use played a role. If adolescents' friends believe that substance use is morally acceptable and expect it to bring positive consequences, their views moved in that direction as well, which in turn promoted their own use.

We view friendship selection processes as a critical aspect of peer influence because they determine the direction of the influence individuals will receive. Our results demonstrated that adolescents tend to choose friends similar to themselves in several respects relevant to substance use, including not only substance use itself, but also beliefs about substance use and a composite measure of risk factors for use. This pattern will tend to maintain and potentially accentuate previous differences in substance use. In addition to selection for similarity, we were interested in whether substance users tended to attract more or fewer friendships than nonusers (alter selection), which is especially relevant to the spread of substance use. We found that substance users did attract more friendship choices than nonusers, placing them in a position to exert disproportionate influence on their peers.

Our work about substance use and adolescents' memberships in cohesive peer groups revealed that different types of substance use are embedded in adolescent peer culture in different ways. Involvement in the peer culture appeared to promote rather than deter alcohol use. Drinking was especially likely among core group members rather than peripheral members and isolates, and groups with high rates of alcohol use tended to be more strongly integrated and to hold higher status in the overall school network. In contrast, smoking was highest among isolates, followed by peripheral group members. Further, smoker's groups were less integrated and had lower status. The place of marijuana use in the peer culture was more similar to smoking than to drinking, but with some differences as well. Marijuana use was higher not only among peripheral members and isolates, but also among liaisons, who had plenty of friendships and were reasonably well adjusted in terms of family relationships, school performance and bonding, and religious participation. In addition, groups with high rates of marijuana use had moderate levels of cohesiveness and status.

Our third area of research addressed change across adolescence in the connection between peers and substance use. We found that substance use played an increasing role in the organization of friendships over the span of the study, with correlations between friends growing markedly. This rise could largely be explained by greater variability in substance use (due to rising rates), making it a more readily available basis for distinction. These correlations remained only moderate, however, and substance use was only one of many factors on which adolescents tend to be similar to their friends. Our investigation of change across grades in influence and selection processes for alcohol and tobacco use indicated that peer influence on use diminished over time, while the tendency to prefer similar friends increased. Thus, the increasing correlations between friends appeared to be more a function of friendship choice—in part due to growing variability among adolescents—than of influence.

We hope that the work presented here will prove useful for substance use researchers by demonstrating the breadth of insights that can be gained from a network approach to studying the contributions of peers. With network data, the study of peer influence is readily expanded beyond the usual direct influence of peer behavior to encompass additional avenues of influence, such as other attributes of friends (e.g., beliefs), friends' relationships with others (see Chapter 8 on parents and Chapter 9 on romantic partners), as well as indirect effects (as for peer beliefs) and interactions between attributes of respondents and of their friends (see moderators of influence in Chapter 8). As we have shown, selection processes also can be a rich source of substantive research questions, rather than merely the alternative hypothesis to be considered in estimating peer influence. Our work showed it is especially useful to combine insights about influence and selection (representing the connectionist tradition of social network research) with an examination of ways that substance use is associated with patterns of connections throughout networks (representing the positional tradition, see Chapter 3). Although we identified important changes across adolescence in the organization of friendship and in selection and influence processes, we suspect we have only scratched the surface. We encourage other researchers to devote more attention to ways that the emergence of risky behaviors during adolescence is rooted in the dramatic developmental changes of the period (Ragan, 2020).

We finish with a few brief comments about policy implications, leaving more substantial coverage to Chapter 11, which presents our work on prevention programing. The findings in this chapter demonstrated that peers are, indeed, an appropriate focus for interventions addressing substance use. Further, the many and varied connections between peers and substance use made clear that much more could be done to affect the initiation and intensification of substance use during adolescence than the typical approach of teaching refusal skills. We strongly support Henneberger and colleagues (2019) call for balancing that emphasis with attention to the contribution of selecting friends who do or do not use substances. Our findings also suggested that different intervention approaches may be required for different substances. Interventions to address alcohol use must confront the challenge that drinking is associated with having more friends (the cool kids *are* doing it), while programs addressing smoking would need to deal with smoking being most likely for relatively isolated and less integrated adolescents.

REFERENCES

Agnew, R. (1992). Foundation for a general strain theory of crime and delinquency. *Criminology, 30*, 47–88.

Akers, R. L. (1985). *Deviant behavior: A social learning approach* (3rd ed.). Wadsworth.

Bachman, J. G., Johnston, L. D., & O'Malley, P. M. (2011). *Monitoring the future: Questionnaire responses from the nation's high school seniors, 2010*. Institute for Social Research.

Baerveldt, C., Van Rossem, R., Vermande, M., & Weerman, F. (2004). Students' delinquency and correlates with strong and weaker ties: A study of students' networks in Dutch high schools. *Connections, 26*, 11–28.

Bandura, A. (1977). *Social learning theory*. Prentice Hall.

Bauman, K. E., & Ennett, S. T. (1994). Peer influence on adolescent drug use. *American Psychologist, 49*, 820–882.

Bonacich, P. (1987). Power and centrality: A family of measures. *American Journal of Sociology, 92*(5), 1170–1182.

Botvin, G. J., Epstein, J. A., Baker, E., Diaz, T., & Ifill-Williams, M. (1997). School-based drug abuse prevention with inner-city minority youth. *Journal of Child and Adolescent Substance Abuse, 6*(1), 5–19.

Botvin, G. J., & Griffin, K. W. (2004). Life skills training: Empirical findings and future directions. *Journal of Primary Prevention, 25*(2), 211–232.

Brown, B. B. (1990). Peer groups and peer cultures. In S. S. Feldman & G. R. Elliott (Eds.), *At the threshold: The developing adolescent* (pp. 171–196). Harvard University Press.

Burgess, R., & Akers, R. (1966). A differential association-reinforcement theory of criminal behavior. *Social Problems, 14*, 128–147.

Cairns, R. B., Perrin, J. E., and Cairns, B. D. (1985). Social structure and social cognition in early adolescence: Affiliative patterns. *Journal of Early Adolescence, 5*, 339–355.

Chassin, L., Presson, C. C., Sherman, S. J., & Edwards, D. A. (1990). The natural history of cigarette smoking: Predicting young-adult smoking outcomes from adolescent smoking patterns. *Health Psychology, 9*(6), 701–716.

Cloward, R. A., & Ohlin, L. E. (1960). *Delinquency and opportunity: A theory of delinquent gangs*. Free Press.

Cusick, P. (1973). *Inside high school*. Holt, Rinehart and Winston.

Durkheim, E. (1993). In G. Simpson (Ed.), *Suicide: A study in sociology*. Free Press. (Original work published 1897)

Eder, D. (1985). The cycle of popularity: Interpersonal relations among female adolescents. *Sociology of Education, 58*, 154–165.

Elliott, D. S., Huizinga, D., & Menard, S. (1989). *Multiple problem youth: Delinquency, substance use, and mental health problems*. Springer-Verlag.

Ennett, S. T., & Bauman, K. E. (1993). Peer group structure and adolescent cigarette smoking: A social network analysis. *Journal of Health and Social Behavior, 34*, 226–236.

Fang, X., Li, X., Stanton, B., & Dong, Q. (2003). Social network positions and smoking experimentation among Chinese adolescents. *American Journal of Health Behavior, 27*, 257–267.

Fishbein, M., & Ajzen, I. (1975). *Belief, attitude, intention and behavior: An introduction to theory and research*. Addison-Wesley.

Giordano, P. C., Cernkovich, S. A., & Pugh, M. D. (1986). Friendships and delinquency. *American Journal of Sociology, 91*, 1170–1202.

Glueck, S., & Glueck, E. (1950). *Unraveling juvenile delinquency.* Harvard University Press.

Gottfredson, M. R., & Hirschi, T. (1990). *A general theory of crime.* Stanford University Press.

Hagan, J. (1991). Destiny and drift: Subcultural preferences, status attainments, and the risks and rewards of youth. *American Sociological Review, 56*, 567–582.

Hall, J. A., & Valente, T. W. (2007). Adolescent smoking networks: The effects of influence and selection on future smoking. *Addictive Behaviors, 32*, 3054–3059.

Hansen, W. B., & Dusenbury, L. (2004). All stars plus: A competence and motivation enhancement approach to prevention. *Health Education, 104*(6), 371–381.

Henneberger, A. K., Gest, S. D., & Zadzora, K. M. (2019). Preventing adolescent substance use: A content analysis of peer processes targeted within universal school-based programs. *The Journal of Primary Prevention, 40*(2), 213–230.

Henry, D. B., & Kobus, K. (2007). Early adolescent social networks and substance use. *The Journal of Early Adolescence, 27*, 346–362.

Hirschi, Travis (1969). *Causes of delinquency.* University of California Press.

Houtzager, B., & Baerveldt, C. (1999). Just like normal: A social network study of the relation between petty crime and the intimacy of adolescent friendships. *Social Behavior and Personality, 27*, 177–192.

Jang, S. J. (1999). Age-varying effects of family, school, and peers on delinquency: A multilevel modeling test of interactional theory. *Criminology, 37*, 643–686.

Jessor, R., & Jessor, S. L. (1977). *Problem behavior and psychosocial development: A longitudinal study of youth.* Academic Press.

Johnston, L. D., Miech, R. A., O'Malley, P. M., Bachman, J. G., Schulenberg, J. E., & Patrick, M. E. (2021). *Monitoring the future national survey results on drug use 1975–2020: Overview, key findings on adolescent drug use.* Institute for Social Research, University of Michigan.

Kandel, D. B. (1996). The parental and peer contexts of adolescent deviance: An algebra of interpersonal influences. *Journal of Drug Issues, 26*, 289–315.

Kandel, D. B. (1978). Similarity in real-life adolescent friendship pairs. *Journal of Personality and Social Psychology, 36*(3), 306.

Khantzian, E. J. (1997). The self-medication hypothesis of substance use disorders: A reconsideration and recent applications. *Harvard Review of Psychiatry, 4*, 231–244.

Knecht, A. B., Burk, W. J., Weesie, J., & Steglich, C. (2011). Friendship and alcohol use in early adolescence: A multilevel social network approach. *Journal of Research on Adolescence, 21*, 475–487.

Kobus, K., & Henry, D. B. (2010). Interplay of network position and peer substance use in early adolescent cigarette, alcohol, and marijuana use. *The Journal of Early Adolescence, 30*, 225–245.

Kreager, D. A., Rulison, K., & Moody, J. (2011). Delinquency and the structure of adolescent peer groups. *Criminology, 49*(1), 61–94.

Larson, R. W., Richards, M. H., Moneta, G., Holmbeck, G., & Duckett, E. (1996). Changes in adolescents' daily interactions with their families from ages 10 to 18: Disengagement and transformation. *Developmental Psychology, 32*(4), 744–754.

Lospinoso, J. A., Schweinberger, M., Snijders, T. A. B., & Ripley, R. M. (2011). Advancing and accounting for time heterogeneity in stochastic actor oriented modes. *Advances in Data Analysis and Classification, 5*, 147–176.

Maccoby, E. E. (1998). *The two sexes: Growing up apart, coming together.* Belknap Press of Harvard University Press.

Matza, D., & Sykes, G. M. (1961). Juvenile delinquency and subterranean values. *American Sociological Review, 26*(5), 712–719.

McPherson, M., Smith-Lovin, L., & Cook, J. M. (2001). Birds of a feather: Homophily in social networks. *Annual Review of Sociology, 27*(1), 415–444.

Mead, G. H. (1934). *Mind, self and society.* University of Chicago Press.

Mercken, L., Snijders, T. A. B., Steglich, C., & de Vries, H. (2009). Dynamics of adolescent friendship networks and smoking behavior: Social network analyses in six European countries. *Social Science & Medicine, 69*, 1506–1514.

Merton, R. K. (1938). Social structure and anomie. *American Sociological Review, 3*, 672–682.

Oetting, E. R., & Beauvais, F. (1986). Peer cluster theory: Drugs and the adolescent. *Journal of Counseling and Development, 65*, 17–22.

Osgood, D. W., Anderson, A. L., & Shaffer, J. N. (2005). Unstructured leisure in the after-school hours. In J. L. Mahoney, R. W. Larson, & J. S. Eccles (Eds.), *Organized activities as contexts of development: Extracurricular activities, after-school and community programs* (pp. 45–64). Lawrence Erlbaum.

Osgood, D. W., Feinberg, M. E., & Ragan, D. T. (2015). Social networks and the diffusion of adolescent behavior: Reliable estimates of selection and influence from sixth through ninth grades. *Prevention Science, 16*(6), 832–843.

Osgood, D. W., Feinberg, M. E., Wallace, L. N., & Moody, J. (2014). Friendship group position and substance use. *Addictive Behaviors, 39*, 923–933.

Osgood, D. W., McMorris, B. J., & Potenza, M. T. (2002). Analyzing multiple-item measures of crime and deviance I: Item response theory scaling. *Journal of Quantitative Criminology, 18*(3), 267–296.

Osgood, D. W., Ragan, D. T., Dole, J. L., & Kreager, D. A. (2022). Similarity of friends versus nonfriends in adolescence: Developmental patterns and ecological influences. *Developmental Psychology, 58*(7), 1386–1401.

Osgood, D. W., Ragan, D. T., Wallace, L., Gest, S. D., Feinberg, M. E., & Moody, J. (2013). Peers and the emergence of alcohol use: Influence and selection processes in adolescent friendship networks. *Journal of Research on Adolescence, 23*, 500–512.

Osgood, D. W., Wilson, J. K., O'Malley, P. M., Bachman, J. G., & Johnston, L. D. (1996). Routine activities and individual deviant behavior. *American Sociological Review, 61*(4), 635–655.

Pearson, M., & Michell, L. (2000). Smoke rings: Social network analysis of friendship groups, smoking and drug-taking. *Drugs: Education, Prevention, and Policy, 7*, 21–37.

Pearson, M., Sweeting, H., West, P., Young, R., Gordon, J., & Turner, K. (2006). Adolescent substance use in different social and peer contexts: A social network analysis. *Drugs: Education, Prevention, and Policy, 13*, 519–536.

Popp, D., Laursen, B., Kerr, M., Stattin, H., & Burk, W. K. (2008). Modeling homophily over time with an actor–partner interdependence model. *Developmental Psychology, 44*, 1028–1039.

Poulin, F., & Pedersen, S. (2007). Developmental changes in gender composition of friendship networks in adolescent girls and boys. *Developmental Psychology, 43*(6), 1484–1496.

Ragan, D. T. (2018, November). Peer selection and delinquency: Theory, evidence, and future directions [Conference presentation]. Presented at the Annual Meeting of the American Society of Criminology, Atlanta, GA.

Ragan, D. T. (2020). Similarity between deviant peers: Developmental trends in influence and selection. *Criminology, 58*(2), 336–359.

Ragan, D. T. (2014). Revisiting what they think: Adolescent drinking and the importance of peer beliefs. *Criminology, 52*(3), 488–513.

Ragan, D. T. (2016). Peer beliefs and smoking in adolescence: A longitudinal social network analysis. *American Journal of Drug and Alcohol Abuse, 42*(2), 222–230.

Ragan, D. T., Osgood, D. W., Ramirez, N. G., Moody, J., & Gest, S. D. (2022). A comparison of peer influence estimates from SIENA stochastic actor-based models and from conventional regression approaches. *Sociological Methods & Research, 51*(1), 357–395.

Sampson, R. J., & Laub, J. H. (1992). Crime and deviance in the life course. *Annual Review of Sociology, 18*, 63–84.

Short, J. F., & F. L. Strodtbeck. (1965). *Group process and gang delinquency*. University of Chicago Press.

Shrum, W., Cheek Jr., N. H., & Hunter, S. M. (1988). Friendship in school: Gender and racial homophily. *Sociology of Education, 61*(4), 227–239.

Snijders, T. A. (2001). The statistical evaluation of social network dynamics. *Sociological Methodology, 31*(1), 361–395.

Steglich, C., Snijders, T. A., & Pearson, M. (2010). Dynamic networks and behavior: Separating selection from influence. *Sociological Methodology, 40*(1), 329–393.

Sutherland, E. H. (1939). *Principles of criminology* (4th ed.). Lippincott.

Thornberry, T. P. (1987). Toward an interactional theory of delinquency. *Criminology, 25*, 863–891.

Thornberry, T. P., Lizotte, A. J., Krohn, M. D., Farnworth, M., & Jang, S. J. (1994). Delinquent peers, beliefs, and delinquent behavior: A longitudinal test of interactional theory. *Criminology, 32*, 47–83.

Thrasher, F. M. (1927). *The gang: A study of 1,313 gangs in Chicago*. University of Chicago Press.

Volkow, N. D., Baler, R. D., Compton, W. M., & Weiss, S. R. (2014). Adverse health effects of marijuana use. *New England Journal of Medicine, 370*(23), 2219–2227.

Warr, M. (2002). *Companions in crime: The social aspects of criminal conduct*. Cambridge University Press.

Warr, M., & Stafford, M. (1991). The influence of delinquent peers: What they think or what they do? *Criminology, 29*, 851–866.

Windle, M., Shope, J. T., & Bukstein, O. (1996). Alcohol use. In Ralph J. DiClemente, William B. Hansen, & Lynn E. Ponton (Eds.), *Handbook of adolescent health risk behavior* (pp. 115–159). Springer.

6

Does criminal justice contact alter friendship ties?

WADE C. JACOBSEN AND ERIN TINNEY ■

INTRODUCTION

In the early 1980s, political and media attention to drug use and violence pushed the nation into a "tough-on-crime" era in which an increasingly large share of the population, including youth, would experience involvement with the justice system (Travis et al., 2014). PROSPER (Promoting School-community-university Partnerships to Enhance Resilience) youth were born in the early 1990s, in the midst of this era (Figure 6.1). In 2002, when the baseline survey was administered to the first cohort, there were 13.8 million arrests in the United States (4,734 per 100,000; 1.5 times the rate today), and 16% of these were of children and youth (Bureau of Justice Statistics, 2022; Office of Juvenile Justice and Delinquency Prevention 2022). Further, the share of the nation's population under correctional supervision (i.e., parole, probation, incarceration) reached its peak at 2.4% (7.3 million) in 2007 when PROSPER youth were in their freshman and sophomore years of high school. Thus, these data were collected during a time of historically high prevalence of justice involvement and at a stage of child development in which risky behaviors increase the likelihood of contact with police (Farrington, 1986; Moffitt, 1993). This chapter focuses on the prevalence of justice system involvement among PROSPER youth and the ways in which contact with the legal system may affect relationships with peers. In particular, we focus on arrest, which an estimated 18% of U.S. youth experience (Brame et al., 2012) and which is associated with poor mental health, dropping out of high school, and greater justice system involvement (e.g., Kirk & Sampson, 2013; Liberman et al. 2014; Sugie & Turney 2017).

In considering the potential impacts of an arrest on an adolescent's ties to peers, we rely on theory in social psychology about stigma and interpersonal

Wade C. Jacobsen and Erin Tinney, *Does criminal justice contact alter friendship ties?* In: *Teen Friendship Networks, Development, and Risky Behavior.* Edited by: Mark E. Feinberg and D. Wayne Osgood, Oxford University Press.
© Mark E. Feinberg and D. Wayne Osgood 2024. DOI: 10.1093/oso/9780197602317.003.0006

Criminal Justice Contact and Friendship Ties   147

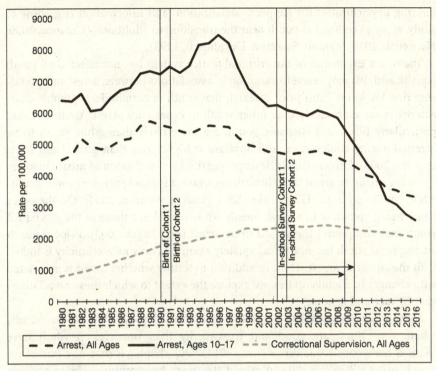

Figure 6.1 PROSPER youth against backdrop of national trends in justice involvement. Sources: Bureau of Justice Statistics (https://www.bjs.gov/index.cfm?ty=kfdetail&iid= 493); Office of Juvenile Justice and Delinquency Prevention (https://www.ojjdp.gov/ojsta tbb/crime/ucr_trend.asp?table_in=1&selOffenses=1&rdoGroups=1&rdoDataType=3).

relationships. In particular, Goffman (1963, p. 3) argued that stigma emerges when a characteristic is perceptible (i.e., peers know about it) and "deeply discrediting" (i.e., harms a person's reputation among their peers). In the rural context of PROSPER schools, an arrest meets these criteria. It becomes perceptible to peers if it takes place on school grounds (Na & Gottfredson, 2013; Theriot, 2009), in the presence of other youth, or is heard about through small-town gossip. An arrest is discrediting because conventional stereotypes portray people who are involved in the justice system as being dangerous or dishonest (Hirschfield & Piquero, 2010). These stereotypes permeate mainstream culture, making it harder for people who have experienced contact with the justice system to access employment or higher education (Stewart & Uggen, 2020; Uggen et al., 2014). As youth develop conceptions of justice involvement that are based on these stereotypes, an arrest may trigger reactions among their peers. In this study, we focus on two such reactions: rejection and withdrawal (Jacobsen 2020; Jacobsen et al., 2022). Rejection occurs when youth avoid, in response to the arrest, friendships with peers who have been arrested. Withdrawal occurs when arrested youth react to their own arrest by avoiding relationships with their peers. These processes, which we discuss in detail below, constrain a youth's friendship networks, thereby limiting opportunities for support, socialization, and information (e.g., how to study, apply to college) as youth near the transition to adulthood (Crosnoe, 2000; Narr et al., 2019; Stanton-Salazar & Dornbusch, 1995).

The broad expansion of the criminal justice system has not affected all youth equally, and this may result in variation in associations between arrest and friendship ties. We know from prior research that youth of certain demographic characteristics are more likely than other youth to experience arrest. Youth of color, particularly Black and Hispanic youth, are more likely than white youth to be arrested during adolescence, and boys are at higher risk than girls (Laub 2014; Piquero, 2008). On one hand, the disproportionate distribution of justice involvement may make an arrest less stigmatizing where it is more prevalent: among nonwhite youth and boys (Hirschfield, 2008; Pettit & Western, 2004). On the other hand, being nonwhite in a rural, mostly white school like those of the PROSPER youth may compound the stigma of an arrest (e.g., Pager, 2003). Prior research among rural youth has not yet adequately examined how race/ethnicity is linked with the effects of arrest. Thus, in addition to testing whether arrest is associated with changes in friendship ties, we explore the extent to which these associations vary by race and gender.

Some prior research has suggested that arrested youth have fewer friends whom they think are good and trustworthy than nonarrested youth have (Kirk & Sampson, 2013; Wiley et al., 2013). Our chapter is part of a line of research using PROSPER data to extend this work by examining the impacts of stigmatizing sanctions, by not only the criminal justice system, but also schools, on an adolescent's friendship networks. In particular, Tinney (2023) found that PROSPER youth whose friends had been picked up by the police were more likely to experience their own police contact, adjusting for delinquency and other potential confounders. In addition, Jacobsen (2020) found that PROSPER youth who experienced a school suspension were less likely to maintain the relationships they had with school peers in the previous year. We build on this earlier work here with three main objectives. First, before examining outcomes of arrest, we examine its prevalence among the PROSPER youth. In doing so, we focus on the cumulative prevalence of arrest (i.e., the proportion of youth ever arrested, which increases with age) among white and nonwhite girls and boys. Second, we test associations between arrest and friendship using data from whole networks of school peers. This allows us to distinguish changes in the preferences of peers toward arrested youth (rejection) from those of arrested youth toward their peers (withdrawal). If an arrest is stigmatizing, then youth who are arrested should experience declines in friendship ties from one time point to the next, holding constant the youth's behaviors and other characteristics that may also affect any changes in friendship ties. Third, we assess the extent to which associations between arrest and friendship ties vary across white and nonwhite youth and across girls and boys. Our study advances an understanding of the consequences of justice involvement for adolescent development and informs policies about the policing of youth in rural communities and schools like those in the PROSPER study.

ARREST IN ADOLESCENCE

Prevalence and disproportionality

Administrative records from criminal justice agencies capture arrest rates for the national context in the years that the PROSPER data were collected. U.S. juvenile arrest rates were high for much of the participants' adolescence and then declined as they neared young adulthood (Figure 6.1). However, this picture captures annual snapshots of the prevalence of arrest rather than the prevalence of having ever been arrested as it accumulates with age. For example, one prior study estimated the cumulative prevalence of arrest using the National Longitudinal Survey of Youth 1997 (NLSY97), a cohort in which most had already reached young adulthood by the time the PROSPER youth were starting sixth grade. Findings from that study suggested that about 18% of youth had experienced at least one arrest by age 18 (Brame et al., 2012). Similarly, we can examine the cumulative prevalence of arrest for PROSPER youth as they moved from grade to grade. Importantly, this ever-arrested group represents the share of youth whom we expect to experience consequences of arrest, which we propose includes declines in friendship ties.

Another important aspect of the national context in which the PROSPER data were collected is that justice system contact was disproportionately concentrated among youth of color, and this has not changed despite steep declines in annual arrest rates. In particular, when data collection began in 2002, racial minority youth in the United States were arrested at 1.5 times the rate of white youth, and today they are arrested at 1.8 times the rate of white youth (Office of Juvenile Justice and Delinquency Prevention, 2022). Disproportionality by race and gender is also reflected in cumulative prevalence estimates of prior research. Findings from the NLSY97 suggest that 30% of Black boys and 12% of Black girls were arrested by age 18 compared to 22% of white boys and 12% of white girls (Brame et al., 2014). If such disparities exist among PROSPER youth, we would expect that the negative consequences of arrest for friendship were also concentrated among nonwhite youth and boys.

PROSPER offers an alternative to the national focus of the NLSY97 and other large-scale surveys, and this is important for advancing an understanding of the prevalence of justice contact among adolescents. Although 8.2 million U.S. youth (Grades 6 to 12) attend public school outside a city or suburb (based on our analysis of urban-centric locale information from the National Center for Education Statistics, 2022), most prior research on youth contact with police has drawn from large-scale national or disadvantaged urban samples rather than rural or small-town populations (e.g., Geller, 2021; Kirk & Sampson, 2013). As arrest rates have declined in recent decades, some research suggests this decline has been slower in rural areas (Rad et al., 2020), and that racial inequality in rural justice involvement may be similar to that of urban areas (Eason et al., 2017). However, researchers have not yet adequately examined the prevalence and disproportionality of justice contact among rural youth. Therefore, we extend beyond prior research by examining the cumulative prevalence of arrest and its distribution by race (white/nonwhite) and gender among PROSPER youth, who attended school in rural contexts.

Effects on friendship ties

Among PROSPER youth, arrest may be associated with subsequent declines in friendship ties among school peers. To understand the associations between arrest and peer relationships, we drew from Goffman's (1963) work on social stigma. Characteristics and events are stigmatizing in contexts where they are discrediting and easily perceived by others. Indeed, Goffman specifically cited arrest as an example (p. 47). In the rural context of PROSPER schools, there were two primary reasons why arrest may be stigmatizing among peers. First, rural communities are characterized by small populations and often dense social ties (Crockett et al., 2000; Freudenburg, 1986; Osgood & Chambers, 2000), making it likely that youth will know about a peer's arrest because they witnessed it firsthand or learned of it through small-town gossip (Haugen & Villa, 2006). Second, rural areas are often culturally homogeneous and provide rewards for adherence to culturally acceptable norms of behavior and censure norm violation (Sherman, 2006). For example, some research found that political conservatism, which is common in rural areas, is associated with negative attitudes toward people who have been involved in the justice system (Hirschfield & Piquero, 2010). As community norms are transmitted intergenerationally from adults to youth and imported into schools by teachers and administrators, they may shape friendship preferences among school peers.

For examining the impacts of arrest on friendship ties, it is useful to apply a broader definition of arrest than has been used in prior research. Most prior research on criminal justice stigma has relied on official criminal records or used self-reports of criminal history, such as in an application for employment or higher education (e.g., Hjalmarsson, 2008; Stewart & Uggen, 2020; Uggen et al., 2014). However, not all arrests are formally recorded by the police, and there is wide variation in the conditions of arrests that are officially recorded (Kirk, 2006; Miller, 2014; Sherman & Glick, 1984). It is common for police to apprehend youth without formally recording the incident as an arrest, perhaps especially in rural areas (Schulenberg, 2010; Weisheit et al., 1994). In our focus on consequences for peer relationships, whether or not an arrest was officially recorded is less important than the extent to which peers know that a youth was apprehended by police. The rural setting of PROSPER and our focus on friendship make it appropriate that we included not only officially recorded arrests but also "unofficial arrests," or police apprehensions not formally recorded. Thus in this study, we defined arrest as self-reports of being picked up by police for suspected law violation, and we make no distinction between official and unofficial arrests.

The stigma from an arrest could affect a youth's relationship with peers through two reactive processes: rejection and withdrawal. Rejection refers to reactions of peers toward arrested youth. As stereotypes of arrested youth call into question their trustworthiness or morality, adolescents may avoid relationships with such youth (whether of their own accord or prompted by parents) to escape the negative influence of bad friends. Additionally, youth may avoid friendships with arrested peers in order to escape being perceived as guilty of the same supposed behaviors that prompted the arrest (Goffman, 1963; see also Tinney, 2023, and Zhang, 1994). These reactions would be manifested by a decline in an adolescent's number of incoming friendship nominations (i.e., peers who report in a survey that they prefer a certain adolescent as a close friend) following an arrest. Withdrawal refers to the reactions of arrested youth toward their peers. The same stereotypes that affect how youth perceive their arrested peers may also take on personal significance when an adolescent experiences his or her own arrest. Withdrawal thus involves defensively avoiding relationships with peers out of a fear or in anticipation of being rejected by them (Link & Phelan, 2001). It would be manifested by a decline in an adolescent's number of outgoing friendship nominations (i.e., peers whom an adolescent prefers as a close friend). Rejection and withdrawal are important because they result in fewer normative friendships—close ties to friends who are involved in conventional activities and avoid most risky behaviors—and thus limit an adolescent's access to a key source of social capital (i.e., resources accessible through friendship ties and social networks; Coleman, 1988; Crosnoe, 2000). Therefore, we examined the association of arrest with declines in friendship nominations received (rejection) and friendship nominations made (withdrawal).

Differences in effects by race and gender

Given the uneven distribution of justice involvement in the United States and what we think will be a similarly disproportionate distribution among PROSPER youth, we expect that associations between arrest and friendship ties will vary by gender and race. This is because the extent to which a given characteristic is stigmatizing depends in part on its prevalence in a given context. Among demographic groups that experience high rates of police contact and legal system involvement, arrests may be seen as a normative event in a person's life rather than a particularly discrediting one (Pettit & Western, 2004; Western, 2006). For example, Hirschfield (2008) found that juvenile arrests carried little stigma in disadvantaged racial minority communities of Chicago, where justice involvement is common (although still harmful; e.g., Kirk & Sampson, 2013). Even in the mostly white communities of PROSPER, youth of color may be more likely than white youth to experience police contact, making arrest seem like a normative experience for youth of color, thus "watering down" any stigmatizing effects on friendship ties.

Alternatively, the opposite may be true in rural schools. The stigma of arrest may be amplified for youth of color because in racially homogeneous white communities, being Black or Latino makes an arrest more perceptible (i.e., more likely to be known about) among school peers and may reaffirm racial stereotypes and biases against racial minority peers. Indeed, youth of color in these schools already have fewer friends than their white peers (e.g., Felmlee et al., 2018), and an arrest may exacerbate this marginalization. Prior research on the extent to which the effects of justice system involvement on individual outcomes vary by race has produced mixed results (e.g., Chiricos et al., 2007; Massoglia, 2008); however, some research suggests stigma may be amplified for youth of color. For example, among young adults, the effect of a criminal record on the likelihood that a job applicant will be called back for an interview is larger for Black applicants than it is for white applicants (Pager, 2003). Thus, we build on prior research by focusing on adolescence and testing whether associations between arrest and friendship ties are weaker or stronger for youth of color relative to their white peers.

Regarding gender differences, there are two reasons why the stigma of arrest among adolescent peers may be less salient for boys than it is for girls. First, boys are more likely than girls are to experience police contact and to engage in behaviors that would lead to an arrest (Fagan, 2002). This difference in prevalence may give peers the impression that arrest is normative for boys. Related to this point is the fact that boys are more likely to have friendship ties with other boys (especially at younger ages; Shrum et al., 1988), so these peers may be more forgiving of an arrested youth if they have experienced an arrest themselves or have friends who have experienced it. Second, gender norms often justify antisocial or delinquent behavior among boys while condemning it for girls. Conventional norms reinforce stereotypes that "boys will be boys" but that girls should be "ladylike" (Dennis, 2012; Steffensmeier & Allan, 1996). Thus, for girls, an arrest may be a signal to peers of a violation of conventional gender norms, and they may face stronger exclusionary reactions as a result. For example, some criminal justice research found more perceived stigma and stronger labeling effects for women and girls than for men and boys (Chiricos et al., 2007; McGrath, 2014). Thus, we expect to see greater declines in friendship ties (rejection and withdrawal) among arrested girls than we see among arrested boys.

Study contributions

In examining associations between arrest and friendship ties among PROSPER youth, we expected that an arrest will be associated with fewer friendship nominations received (rejection) and fewer friends nominated (withdrawal), and that these associations will vary by race (white/nonwhite) and be stronger for girls than for boys. In testing these hypotheses, we built on prior research regarding the consequences of justice involvement for youth and several studies on the effects of arrest on friendship ties in particular. Two studies found that arrested youth had fewer prosocial friends (i.e., friends that were perceived as honest, good students, respectful, etc.) than matched samples of nonarrested youth had (Kirk & Sampson, 2013; Wiley et al., 2013). Another study found that justice contact was associated with a subsequent increase in involvement with peers who engage in delinquency (Bernburg et al., 2006).

These prior studies offered an important starting point for understanding associations between justice involvement and friendship selection, and we built on them in three ways. First, rather than using a static approach of examining associations between police contact at one point in time with subsequent friendship support (i.e., between-person comparisons), we focused on *changes* in friendship ties experienced by a single adolescent from one point in time to another (i.e., within-person comparisons). This more accurately captures rejection and withdrawal, which we have defined as changes in friendship preferences that are associated with arrest. This approach also improves causal inference because it ensures that we are controlling for all time-stable characteristics and traits, observed or unobserved, that may distinguish youth at risk of arrest from youth who are not at risk of arrest. Second, rather than relying only on adolescents' perceptions of their friendships (e.g., "tell us about your friends"), we also examined the friendship preferences of peers toward the respondents. This allowed us to distinguish between rejection (changes in preferences of peers) and withdrawal (changes in preferences of respondent). Third, we also moved beyond the question of whether these associations were present to assess the extent to which the associations varied by race and gender, which few prior studies have examined. Fourth, we departed from the urban or national focus in prior studies to rely on a population of rural youth, about whom prior research has produced little knowledge about the prevalence, disproportionality, or outcomes of arrest.

In addition to building on prior research on arrest and other forms of justice involvement, our study also extended a line of PROSPER research that examined the impacts of institutional sanctions on an adolescent's friendship networks. First, Tinney (2023) examined the impacts of a friend's arrest on one's own likelihood of arrest. She found that PROSPER youth whose friends had been picked up by the police were more likely to experience their own police contact the next year, adjusting for delinquency and other potential confounders. Moreover, this association remained even if the friendship with the arrested youth ended. These findings suggest that the stigma of arrest, as manifested by police surveillance instead of friendship preferences, may stay with an adolescent despite their attempts to avoid it. Second, Jacobsen (2020) used the in-home subsample of PROSPER to examine associations between school suspension (i.e., temporary removal from school for disciplinary reasons) and discontinuity in friendship ties from one grade to the next. He found that suspended youth were less likely to be nominated by their friends from the previous year and were also less likely to nominate the friends they nominated in the previous year. These findings are consistent with our predictions regarding rejection and withdrawal for arrest but rather than focus on discontinuity only (dissolution of existing friendship tie), we broadened our scope by focusing on changes in the number of any friendship ties. We also turned our attention from sanctions administered in schools to interventions by the police that may happen in school or elsewhere in the broader community. Therefore, our analyses speak to a growing body of research on the unintended consequences of justice involvement for those who experience it and help to inform efforts to improve behavioral interventions for youth.

METHODS AND RESULTS

Methods

Our analyses proceeded in three stages, consistent with our three main objectives. First, we examined descriptively the cumulative prevalence of arrest at each grade among PROSPER youth who participated in the baseline survey (fall of sixth grade). We limited this stage of our analysis to participants who responded to the baseline questionnaire to avoid issues with unknown arrest histories of students who entered the study school district late or left early. Students who entered the school districts after the fall of sixth grade (baseline questionnaire) were excluded at this stage so that we could retain a consistent number of students as the denominator of the proportion arrested across waves of data collection. Thus, the denominator is the number of baseline-questionnaire participants, and the numerator is the number of participants who had ever reported an arrest by a given wave. Whereas missing data on arrest due to item nonresponse or refusal to participate was low at each wave, some loss of information occurred when baseline questionnaire participants left the school district. For this, we followed Brame and colleagues (2012) by assuming that unknown values of arrest are unknown at random, and we present these estimates within upper and lower bounds based on assumptions about the arrest history of students who have exited or not participated. The upper bound takes the assumption that all students with an unknown arrest history at a given wave were arrested, and the lower bound assumes that none of these students was arrested.

Second, we tested the association between arrest and friendship ties. For this stage of our analyses, which was drawn from Jacobsen and colleagues (2022), we included not only participants of the baseline questionnaire but also students who entered the study after the baseline questionnaire. This includes data from 47 peer networks and six waves of data collection. Data from the baseline questionnaire were excluded to ensure the appropriate temporal ordering of our variables (some survey items at Wave 2 asked about the past year, which overlapped with the time period referred to in the baseline survey). Data from Wave 8 were also excluded to avoid issues with low response rates in some school districts at that wave. Friendship ties were measured in two ways, consistent with our definitions of rejection and withdrawal. The first was the number of friendship nominations the respondent received from peers in the same grade and school (in-degree). Finding a past arrest associated with fewer current incoming ties, controlling for observed confounders, would be consistent with our hypotheses for rejection. The second measure was the number of friendship nominations the respondent made to peers in the same grade and school (out-degree). Finding arrest associated with fewer outgoing ties, adjusting for the effects of observed covariates, would be consistent with our hypotheses for withdrawal. Arrest in the context of PROSPER was measured as being "picked up by police for breaking a law." For this analysis, we used a measure of whether or not a student ever reported having been arrested by a given wave of data collection. This measure corresponded with our focus on stigma, which was assumed to remain with a person over time. Arrest was given a value of 1 at the wave an arrest was first reported and at each subsequent wave; youth who never reported an arrest always had a value of 0. Arrests prior to the baseline wave of data collection were assumed to be 0 for all participants, and we feel this was a safe assumption because arrests at early ages are rare (less than 1% of juvenile arrests are of youth younger under age 10; Federal Bureau of Investigation, 2020).

To test hypotheses about the relationship between arrest and friendship ties, we used a series of random-effects models in which the main explanatory variable, whether the student was ever arrested by a given wave, was centered within students (see online Appendix of Jacobsen & colleagues, 2022). Thus, our arrest variable represents the wave-specific deviations from the student-level means of arrest. We used this variable to capture the within-person association between arrest and friendship (i.e., comparing a person's friendship ties before they were arrested to their friendship ties after their arrest). The student-level means were also included as a control. We used this to assess the between-person association (i.e., comparing friendship ties of arrested youth with those of nonarrested youth). This random-effects hybrid model or between-within approach (Allison, 2009) was ideal for our research questions because it allows for the examination of within-individual associations between arrest and friendship ties (i.e., associations between arrest and friendship ties for students who experienced arrest). It also preserves statistical power that would be lost through the alternative approach of regression modeling with individual fixed effects (Firebaugh et al., 2013). Like other forms of statistical regression, our between-within approach may suffer from bias due to time-varying characteristics that were not observed in PROSPER, but causal inference is improved because, like fixed-effects regression, it controls for all time-stable differences between arrested and nonarrested youth, whether observed or unobserved. Another limitation of this approach is that it does not account for the interdependency of students within the same networks as stochastic actor-based (SAB) models can (but see Ragan et al., 2022), but Jacobsen and colleagues (2022) relied on this SAB approach and found results to be consistent across methods in terms of direction and statistical significance. Control variables for their regression models included school district and cohort, student demographic characteristics, school absences, school attachment, family relations, delinquency in the past year, marijuana and alcohol in the past month, risk-seeking behaviors, free or reduced-price lunch (as an indicator of socioeconomic status), and wave (grade) to capture the increasing risk of arrest with age.

Our third stage of the analyses, which are reported for the first time in this chapter, assessed the extent to which associations between arrest and friendship ties varied by race and gender by adding a set of interaction terms to our between-within regression models. For this, we multiplied the person-centered arrest variable by the gender variable and included this new interaction variable in the model (Jaccard & Turrisi, 2003). We then followed a similar pattern for race. This allowed us to examine whether associations between arrest and friendship ties differed between girls and boys or between whites and nonwhites. Our time-stable variables for gender and race were based on self-reports. Males were coded 1, and females were coded 0. Similarly, whites were coded 1, and nonwhites were coded 0.

Results: Prevalence and disproportionality

Figure 6.2 presents cumulative prevalence estimates of arrest for 8,484 baseline participants of all 27 school districts. This excludes 128 observations of students of the first cohort who were retained a grade and thus entered the second cohort.

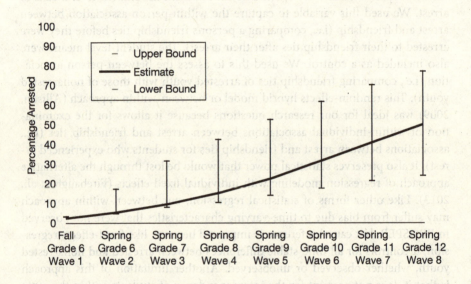

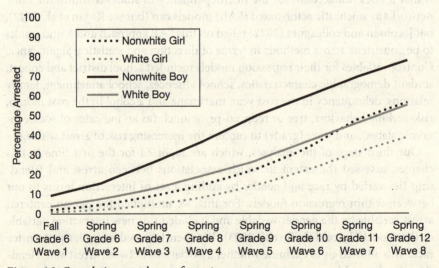

Figure 6.2 Cumulative prevalence of arrest.

Baseline participants from both cohorts were combined and followed across the eight waves, so that the denominator of the percentage arrested was consistent across waves. By Wave 8, 34% of baseline participants were no longer in a PROSPER school district, and another 16% were on the school rosters but had missing data due to absence, refusal, or incomplete information. To account for these unknown arrest histories, we placed bounds (lower, upper) around our prevalence estimates to indicate the range of possibilities given the number of unknown trajectories. The top panel shows the estimated cumulative prevalence of arrest over time. The solid line is based on the assumption that arrest histories are unknown at random. The upper bound holds the assumption that students with unknown arrest histories have all been arrested, and the lower bound assumes that none has been arrested.

In the fall of sixth grade, 3% of students had already been picked up by the police for breaking the law. By spring of their senior year, this increased to an estimated 52% (25%, 77%) of baseline participants. This figure is higher than the estimate of 18% (16% to 27%) in the NLSY97 (Brame et al., 2012), but that study asked about being "arrested or taken into custody for an illegal or delinquent offense" and excluded "arrests for minor traffic violations." Thus, the NLSY97 may be less likely to capture unofficial arrests (apprehensions that were not officially recorded as arrests), and it excludes any arrests (recorded or not) for minor traffic violations. Therefore, the differences in estimates between PROSPER and NLSY97 are likely due to differences in question wording, with our measure of arrest capturing a wider variety of police apprehensions for suspected law violation. The bottom panel of Figure 6.2 shows prevalence estimates for white and nonwhite boys and girls. The most striking thing here is that for nonwhite boys, the risk of arrest started early (9% at baseline, compared to 4% of white boys) and remained high throughout adolescence. By their senior year, 79% of nonwhite boys had been arrested at least once, compared to 57% of nonwhite girls, 57% of white boys, and 41% of white girls.

Results: Arrest and friendship ties

Table 6.1 presents the results of our regression models by Jacobsen and colleagues (2022), which examined the association between arrest and friendship ties. The table shows two sets of models. Models 1 and 2 present results for the association between arrest and out-degree. Models 3 and 4 show results for in-degree. Our main interest was in the coefficients for the within-person association between arrest and friendship ties because they provide estimates of this relationship for youth who experienced arrest (i.e., change in number of friends from before to after their arrest). We also accounted for the between-person associations to adjust for preexisting differences in friendship ties between arrested and nonarrested youth.

Beginning with Model 1, results showed that arrested youth named an average of 1.192 fewer friends in years after they were arrested than they named before their first-reported arrest ($p < 0.001$). This estimate accounted for the

Table 6.1 RANDOM-EFFECTS LINEAR REGRESSION COEFFICIENTS SHOWING ASSOCIATIONS BETWEEN ARREST AND FRIENDSHIP TIES

Explanatory variable	Nominations made (Out-degree) Model 1 Arrest	Nominations made (Out-degree) Model 2 Add controls	Nominations received (In-degree) Model 3 Arrest	Nominations received (In-degree) Model 4 Add controls
Ever reported arrest (between)	−0.810 (0.057)***	−0.328 (0.048)***	−0.386 (0.067)***	0.086 (0.060)
Ever reported arrest (within)	−1.192 (0.045)***	−0.205 (0.045)***	−1.258 (0.051)***	−0.324 (0.053)***
Selected control variables				
Marijuana use, past month		−0.318 (0.036)***		−0.135 (0.044)**
Drinking, past month		0.029 (0.023)		0.158 (0.028)***
Delinquency, past year		−0.016 (0.005)**		0.015 (0.006)*
Sensation seeking		0.003 (0.011)		0.121 (0.013)***
Male		−0.678 (0.026)***		−0.451 (0.034)***
White		0.288 (0.038)***		0.152 (0.049)**
Constant	4.567 (0.172)***	2.371 (0.153)***	4.116 (0.201)***	2.466 (0.196)***

Notes. PROSPER Waves 2 to 7. N observations = 43,788; N students = 11,946. Of 48,747 completed survey observations, we dropped 86 cases in which students were retained and another 4,873 with missing data. Control variables that were included in Models 2 and 4 but not shown in the table include school absence, school attachment, family relations, free or reduced-price lunch, and wave (grade). In addition, Model 2 controlled for in-degree and whether the youth nominated an arrested peer. Model 4 controlled for out-degree and whether the youth nominated an arrested peer.

***$p < 0.001$; **$p < 0.01$; *$p < 0.05$ (two tail).

between-person association, which is that arrested youth nominated 0.810 fewer friends overall than nonarrested youth did ($p < .001$). Results in Model 2 revealed that much of the within-person association (82%) was explained by our control variables, but a negative association between arrest and friendship ties remained after accounting for these controls. In years after they were arrested, arrested youth named 0.205 fewer friends than they named in years before their first-reported arrest ($p < 0.001$). This accounted for a between-person difference of 0.328 fewer friends for arrested relative to nonarrested youth ($p < 0.001$).

Turning to results for in-degree, Model 3 indicated that arrested youth received 1.258 fewer friendship nominations from their school peers in years after they were arrested than they received in years before their first-reported arrest ($p < 0.001$). This accounts for a between-person difference of 0.386 fewer friendship nominations for arrested compared to nonarrested youth ($p < 0.001$). Results in Model 4 indicated that nearly all of this between-person association between arrest and friendship ties was explained by the control variables; in this model, the coefficient was reduced to nearly zero ($b = 0.086$) and was no longer statistically significant. In other words, differences between arrested and nonarrested youth in friendship nominations received appeared to be due to differences in characteristics that were captured by our control variables. However, a significant within-person association remained that was consistent with our hypotheses. In years after they were arrested, arrested youth received 0.324 fewer friendship nominations from their school peers than they received in years before their first-reported arrest ($p < 0.001$).

Considered together, these findings suggested that arrested youth chose fewer friends (decline of about one fifth of a friend) and were less often chosen as a friend (decline of about one third of a friend) after their arrest. These results were not trivial given that youth only have between three and four close friends on average, and those at greater risk of arrest (males and nonwhites) already had relatively fewer friends.

Several control variables also predicted change in the number of friendship nominations. Youth who used marijuana at least once in the past month named 0.318 fewer friends and received 0.135 fewer nominations than youth who did not use marijuana. There was no significant association of drinking alcohol in the past month with the naming of friends, but those who drank received 0.158 more friendship nominations than those who did not drink. This result aligns with prior research on popularity and drinking in adolescence (Osgood, Ragan, et al., 2013; see Chapter 5). Delinquency, measured as the sum of different types of delinquent behaviors in the past year, was associated with a small decrease in the number of friends nominated ($b = 0.016$) and increase in nominations received ($b = 0.015$), suggesting a slight popularizing effect. Similarly, sensation-seeking behaviors were not associated with change in outgoing ties but were associated with an increase in incoming ties of 0.121 friends. Male students named 0.678 fewer friends and received 0.451 fewer nominations than female youth, and white youth named 0.288 more friends and received 0.152 more nominations than nonwhite youth.

Results: Differences in effects by race and gender

The results of Table 6.2 extend beyond those of our earlier paper (Jacobsen et al. 2022, online appendix), which were presented in Table 6.1, to show tests for interactions of arrest with race and gender. The models in Table 6.2 are identical to those of Table 6.1, with the exception that these included interaction terms. To avoid issues with collinearity, we centered our variables for race, gender, and arrest on their grand means before centering our arrest variable on the person-level means and prior to constructing our interaction terms. Models 1 and 2 focused on out-degree, and Models 3 and 4 address in-degree. We first discuss Models 1 and 3, which focused on the interaction between arrest and race, and then Models 2 and 4, which focused on gender.

Results in Model 1 revealed a small positive coefficient for the interaction between race and arrest (b = 0.039) predicting friendship ties that were not statistically significant when all the controls were included in the model. In models not shown, we also examined whether the interaction term reached statistical significance prior to the inclusion of the control variables, and it did (b = 0.265, $p < 0.05$). These findings indicated that the negative association between arrest and friendship nominations was weaker for white youth, but this difference may be accounted for by other variables in the model. In particular, supplementary analyses suggested that this association was driven primarily by the inclusion of in-degree as a control variable (as nonwhite youth received fewer friendship nominations on average than white youth in these networks). Results of Model 3 are similar to those of Model 1 in that the coefficient for the interaction term (b = 0.123) was not statistically significant, but supplementary analyses suggested this was the case even without the inclusion of control variables in the model.

Turning to gender, results in Model 2 indicate a positive, statistically significant coefficient for the interaction between arrest and gender (b = 0.266, $p < 0.01$), even with the inclusion of the control variables. For ease of interpretation, we present these findings graphically in Figure 6.3. Results indicated that the association between arrest and friendship nominations made was stronger for girls than it was for boys. In other words, the loss of friends that youth chose was greater for arrested girls than it was for arrested boys. Model 4 reveals a similar pattern for in-degree. The coefficient for the interaction between arrest and gender (b = 0.259, $p < 0.01$) was positive and statistically significant, suggesting that the negative association between arrest and friendship ties received was stronger for girls than it was for boys. This means that the loss of nominations received after an arrest was greater for girls relative to boys. Taken together, the tendency to lose friends after being arrested was concentrated among girls rather than boys, as made especially evident in Figure 6.3. This holds for both how many friends they chose and how many chose them. Thus, if arrest is stigmatizing among peers as we have assumed, then our results suggested that this stigma was gendered, such that it was present for girls more than boys.

Table 6.2 RANDOM-EFFECTS LINEAR REGRESSION COEFFICIENTS (STANDARD ERRORS) SHOWING ASSOCIATIONS BETWEEN ARREST AND FRIENDSHIP TIES, INCLUDING RACE AND GENDER INTERACTIONS WITH ARREST

Explanatory variable	Nominations made (Out-degree)		Nominations received (In-degree)	
	Model 1 Race	Model 2 Gender	Model 3 Race	Model 4 Gender
Ever reported arrest (between)	−0.328 (0.048)***	−0.327 (0.048)	0.086 (0.061)	0.087 (0.061)
Ever reported arrest (within)	−0.205 (0.045)***	−0.224 (0.045)***	−0.324 (0.053)***	−0.342 (0.054)***
White	0.288 (0.038)***		0.152 (0.049)**	
Ever reported arrest (within) × white	0.039 (0.120)		0.123 (0.142)	
Male		−0.678 (0.026)***		−0.451 (0.034)***
Ever reported arrest (within) × male		0.266 (0.083)**		0.259 (0.098)**
Constant	2.581 (0.149)***	2.009 (0.152)***	2.611 (0.191)***	2.266 (0.194)***
N observations	43,788	43,788	43,788	43,788
N students	11,946	11,946	11,946	11,946

Notes. PROSPER Waves 2 to 7. Of 48,747 completed survey observations, we dropped 86 cases with missing data on any variable. All models include dummy variables for 47 networks, and control variables: marijuana use, drinking, delinquency, risk-seeking behaviors, school absence, school attachment, family relations, free or reduced-price lunch, wave (grade), and whether youth nominated an arrested peer. Models 1 and 2 control for in-degree; Models 3 and 4 control for out-degree.

*** $p < 0.001$; ** $p < 0.01$; * $p < 0.05$ (two tail).

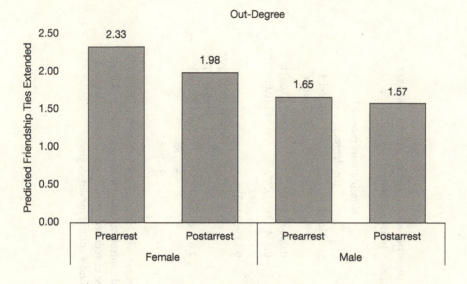

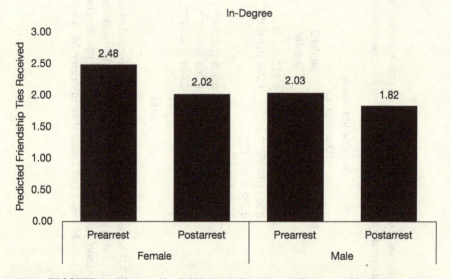

Notes: PROSPER participants, N = 8,484. Arrest based on self-reports of having ever been picked up by the police for breaking the law. Results from between-within random-effects regression models with interactions between gender and within-person change in arrest. Control variables include marijuana use, drinking, delinquency, risk-seeking behaviors, school absence, school attachment, family relations, free or reduced-price lunch, wave (grade), and nominations.

Figure 6.3 Gender differences in association between arrest and friendship ties.

CONCLUSION

Adolescence marks a time of increased police contact, and this is especially salient for the historical context in which the PROSPER youth were growing up. Being picked up for breaking the law is a common experience in the lives of these youth with potentially harmful consequences. In this study, we had three objectives regarding the prevalence and outcomes of arrest. First, we examined the cumulative prevalence and disproportionality of arrest among PROSPER youth. Second, we tested the association between arrest and friendship nominations made and between arrest and friendship nominations received. Third, we assessed the extent to which these associations varied by race and gender. Here, we discuss each of our key findings and their implications for research and policy.

Prevalence and disproportionality

In terms of the cumulative prevalence of arrest, our findings suggested that this form of justice contact was much more common than has been suggested by prior research relying on more conservative definitions (e.g., Brame et al., 2012, 2014). We estimated that about half (between 25% and 77%) of the PROSPER youth who participated in the baseline questionnaire were picked up by the police for suspected law violation by their senior year of high school.

Furthermore, arrests were unevenly distributed across youth of different race and gender categories and most heavily concentrated among nonwhite boys. By the time they finished high school, more than three quarters of nonwhite boys who participated at baseline had been arrested at least once, compared to a slight majority of nonwhite girls and white boys, and more than one third of white girls. Thus, among white and nonwhite youth alike, being picked up by the police for suspected law violation was a common experience in these rural communities. But arrest was most prevalent among nonwhite youth and especially boys. Prior research on national samples has suggested that criminal justice involvement has become so common among disadvantaged Black males that it may be considered a normative life course experience for this group (Pettit & Western, 2004). Our findings were consistent with this prior work and suggested that for nonwhite boys, even in these rural, mostly white communities, getting apprehended by the police was an expected part of growing up. Any outcomes of arrest were also likely to be concentrated among this group, thus perpetuating patterns of racial inequality in rural areas.

Arrest and friendship ties

Regarding the relationship between arrest and friendship ties, findings suggested that among PROSPER youth, an apprehension by police was associated with modest declines in friendship ties to school peers. Holding other observed characteristics constant, arrested youth experienced reductions in the number of peers who preferred them as a friend (decline of about one third of a friend, comparing the years before to after a student's first-reported arrest) and the number of peers they considered to be close friends (decline of about one fifth of a friend, again comparing their prearrest and postarrest years). From our theoretical perspective

(Goffman, 1963), we assumed that these declines were driven by the stigma of criminal justice involvement because arrests (whether officially recorded or not) were both perceptible to peers and discrediting. Such stigma may be driven by stereotypes about people involved in the justice system (Hirschfield & Piquero, 2010), as well as the dense social ties and cultural homogeneity that are often characteristic of rural communities (Osgood & Chambers, 2000; Sherman, 2006).

The socialization of youth to cultural stereotypes may foster reactions to justice involvement among school peers. Youth who are arrested may lose friends because they are rejected by their peers or withdraw from them out of fear of rejection (Goffman, 1963; Link & Phelan, 2001). We have not measured these rejection and withdrawal processes directly. For this, future research should collect data on not only youth self-reports of arrest but also their perceptions of the arrest histories of their peers and attitudinal measures for capturing stigma directly (e.g., Moore & Tangney, 2017; Zhang, 1994). Nevertheless, the findings of this study are consistent with prior research, which has suggested that arrested youth have fewer friends with prosocial attributes (e.g., honest, good students) (Kirk & Sampson, 2013; Wiley et al., 2013). Our results also add to prior PROSPER research on the impacts of institutional sanctions on adolescent peer networks. They are consistent with findings by Jacobsen (2020), who found that youth who are suspended are more likely to lose friends over time. Indeed, our findings suggest that a similar pattern holds for criminal justice contact, implying that stigmatizing forms of institutional sanctions weaken adolescent networks to school peers. Our findings also extend those of Tinney (2023), who found that the likelihood of arrest increases after one's friends have been arrested. Considering those findings alongside our results for the impacts of arrest on friendship, it seems possible that peers avoid arrested youth in order to avoid guilt by association (Goffman, 1963) and to minimize their own risk of criminal justice involvement. Given the importance of close friendships for youth development and well-being (Crosnoe, 2000; Cuadros & Berger, 2016; Narr et al., 2019; Stanton-Salazar & Dornbusch, 1995), the loss of friends among school peers is an outcome of police contact that may be harmful for adolescent development.

Differences in effects by race and gender

We were especially interested in the extent to which the relationship between arrest and friendship ties varied by race and gender. Our findings suggested that the negative associations of arrest with incoming and outgoing ties were stronger for girls than for boys, but we found little evidence of differences in the association between white and nonwhite youth. In examining differences between boys and girls, we found that the negative associations of arrest with friendship ties were more heavily concentrated among girls. This finding is consistent with prior research that has found stronger perceived stigma and larger labeling effects among females than males (Chiricos et al., 2007; McGrath, 2014). From our theoretical perspective, this may be because arrests are more common among boys and therefore seen as more normative, leading to lower stigma. Furthermore, boys are more likely to have friendship ties with other boys (Shrum et al., 1988), and these friends may be more forgiving of an arrested youth if they are more likely to have experienced an arrest (or to have participated in the same delinquent behavior) themselves. Common gender stereotypes may justify deviant behavior among boys while condemning it for girls (Dennis, 2012; Steffensmeier & Allan, 1996; see Kreager et al., 2016, and Chapter 9 on the sexual double standard for girls in PROSPER). Thus, the stigma of an arrest in these rural schools may be gendered, such that girls faced stronger exclusionary reactions than boys did.

In examining differences between white and nonwhite youth, we found little variation in the association between arrest and friendship ties when adjusting for our control variables. This was contrary to each of our competing hypotheses. The first hypothesis was that the association would be weaker for nonwhite youth because they were at greater risk of experiencing arrest (Hirschfield, 2008; Western, 2006), making the arrest of a nonwhite youth appear more normal to school peers. The second hypothesis was that the association would be stronger for nonwhite youth, similar to what has been found in the relationship between criminal history and getting called back about a job application (Pager, 2003). This is because being a racial minority in these racially homogeneous schools increases the perceptibility of arrest among peers and reaffirms the student's otherness. It may be that our interaction term for race was rendered null by the balance of these two opposing forces. Alternatively, it is possible that the associations between arrest and friendship ties varied across specific racial categories (e.g., Black, Latino, white, Asian) rather than by our broad white-nonwhite classifications. However, there were too few students of any one of these specific categories in our data to make meaningful comparisons. Even though we found little variation between white and nonwhite youth in the association between arrest and friendship ties, the larger prevalence of arrest among nonwhite youth relative to white youth suggests that arrest-related declines in friendship were more commonly experienced by nonwhite youth, who already had fewer friendship ties than their white peers (e.g., Felmlee et al., 2018). Therefore, a heavy reliance on police intervention (formal or informal) may be one way that the criminal justice system contributes to racial inequality in rural communities (Eason et al., 2017).

Limitations and implications

Before concluding, a few limitations of our study should be reiterated. First, our measure of arrest did not distinguish between "official" and "unofficial" (i.e., not formally recorded) arrests. While informal police apprehensions are common among youth, and perhaps especially in rural areas (Schulenberg, 2010), it is possible that formally recorded arrests are more stigmatizing because they involve more serious offenses or stay with a person longer (e.g., when applying for a job or college). Second, we lack data on the outcome of the arrest (e.g., probation, incarceration). Thus, there may be heterogeneity in effects across different criminal justice experiences. However, our reliance on school-based survey data means that youth who are incarcerated, or otherwise miss school because of their criminal justice involvement, are not likely to be included in our data. Finally, given the disproportionate concentration of criminal justice involvement among youth of color and especially Black youth in the United States (e.g., Brame et al., 2014), an important limitation of our study is that there were too few racial minorities to make comparisons across specific racial categories. Future research in this area should draw from racial minority populations in rural areas (Lichter et al., 2007) in order to more adequately examine racial differences in the outcomes of arrest for friendship ties.

Taken together, our results were consistent with our theoretical framework regarding the social psychological effects of stigma (Goffman, 1963). Whereas prior research has proposed that criminal justice involvement may interfere with opportunities for employment, education, and stable adult relationships (Kirk & Sampson, 2013; Stewart & Uggen, 2020; Sweeten 2006; Turney & Wildeman, 2013), our findings suggested that even though many adolescents in these rural schools experienced arrest, getting arrested may interfere with having normative friendships at school. Future research should investigate the extent to which our findings are generalizable to other rural areas and to urban and suburban areas as well. However, given the importance of close peer relationships for all youth, for academic success and normative development (Crosnoe, 2000; Narr et al., 2019), our findings imply that police intervention among adolescents in these rural communities should be minimized. We also argue, given the findings in other chapters regarding the PROSPER intervention, that efforts to address adolescent behavior problems may be most effective when combined with evidence-based, peer-related interventions (Osgood, Feinberg, et al., 2013). Furthermore, our findings suggest that the consequences of arrest for friendship appear to be primarily concentrated among girls. Thus, intervention programs for helping youth who have been involved in the justice system (e.g., Siennick et al., 2020) should consider efforts to minimize the stigma that arrested youth may face among school peers and should be gender informed, focusing especially on the experiences of girls relative to boys (National Resource Center on Justice Involved Women, 2016). An example is the promotion of person-centered language by school personnel (e.g., using the phrase "students who have been arrested" rather than "delinquents" or "violent offenders") in order to minimize the process of labeling, similar to efforts that have been implemented by the U.S. Department of Justice and other organizations (Denver et al., 2017).

REFERENCES

Allison, P. D. (2009). *Fixed effects regression models*. Sage.

Bernburg, J. G., Krohn, M. D., & Rivera, C. J. (2006). Official labeling, criminal embeddedness, and subsequent delinquency: A longitudinal test of labeling theory. *Journal of Research in Crime and Delinquency*, 43(1), 67–88.

Brame, R., Bushway, S. D., Paternoster, R., & Turner, M. G. (2014). Demographic patterns of cumulative arrest prevalence by ages 18 and 23. *Crime & Delinquency*, *60*(3), 471–486.

Brame, R., Turner, M. G., Paternoster, R., & Bushway, S. D. (2012). Cumulative prevalence of arrest from ages 8 to 23 in a national sample. *Pediatrics*, *129*(1), 21–27.

Bureau of Justice Statistics. (2022). Arrest Data Analysis Tool. https://www.bjs.gov/index.cfm?ty=datool&surl=/arrests/index.cfm

Chiricos, T., Barrick, K., Bales, W., & Bontrager, S. (2007). The labeling of convicted felons and its consequences for recidivism. *Criminology*, *45*(3), 547–581.

Coleman, J. S. (1988). Social capital in the creation of human capital. *American Journal of Sociology*, *94*(Supp.), 95–120.

Crockett, L. J., Shanahan, M. J., & Jackson-Newsom, J. (2000). Rural youth: Ecological and life course perspectives. *Adolescent Diversity in Ethnic, Economic, and Cultural Contexts*, *10*, 43–74.

Crosnoe, R. (2000). Friendships in childhood and adolescence: The life course and new directions. *Social Psychology Quarterly*, *63*(4), 377–391.

Cuadros, O., & Berger, C. (2016). The protective role of friendship quality on the wellbeing of adolescents victimized by peers. *Journal of Youth and Adolescence*, *45*(9), 1877–1888.

Dennis, J. P. (2012). Girls will be girls: Childhood gender polarization and delinquency. *Feminist Criminology*, *7*(3), 220–233.

Denver, M., Pickett, J. T., & Bushway, S. D. (2017). The language of stigmatization and the mark of violence: Experimental evidence on the social construction and use of criminal record stigma. *Criminology*, *55*(3), 664–690.

Eason, J. M., Zucker, D., & Wildeman, C. (2017). Mass imprisonment across the rural-urban interface. *The Annals of the American Academy of Political and Social Science*, *672*(1), 202–216.

Fagan, A. A. (2002). *Gender*. Sage.

Farrington, D. P. (1986). Age and crime. *Crime and Justice*, *7*, 189–250.

Federal Bureau of Investigation. (2020). Crime in the United States 2018. https://ucr.fbi.gov/crime-in-the-u.s/2018/crime-in-the-u.s.-2018/topic-pages/persons-arrested

Felmlee, D. H., McMillan, C., Rodis, P. I., & Osgood, D. W. (2018). The evolution of youth friendship networks from 6th to 12th grade: School transitions, popularity and centrality. In D. F. Alwin, D. H. Felmlee, & D. A. Kreager (Eds.), *Social Networks and the Life Course* (pp. 161–184). Springer.

Firebaugh, G., Warner, C., & Massoglia, M. (2013). Fixed effects, random effects, and hybrid models for causal analysis. In S. L. Morgan (Ed.), *Handbook of causal analysis for social research* (pp. 113–132). Springer.

Freudenburg, W. R. (1986). The density of acquaintanceship: An overlooked variable in community research? *American Journal of Sociology*, *92*(1), 27–63.

Geller, A. (2021). Youth-police contact: Burdens and inequities in an adverse childhood experience, 2014-2017. *American Journal of Public Health*, *111*(7), 1300–1308.

Goffman, E. (1963). *Stigma: Notes on the management of spoiled identity*. Simon and Schuster.

Haugen, M. S., & Villa, M. (2006). Big Brother in rural societies: Youths' discourses on gossip. *Norsk Geografisk Tidsskrift-Norwegian Journal of Geography*, *60*(3), 209–216.

Hirschfield, P. J. (2008). The declining significance of delinquent labels in disadvantaged urban communities 1. *Sociological Forum*, *23*(3), 575–601.

Hirschfield, P. J., & Piquero, A. R. (2010). Normalization and legitimation: Modeling stigmatizing attitudes toward ex-offenders. *Criminology*, 48(1), 27–55.

Hjalmarsson, R. (2008). Criminal justice involvement and high school completion. *Journal of Urban Economics*, 63(2), 613–630.

Jaccard, J., & Turrisi, R. (2003). *Interaction effects in multiple regression*. Sage. https://books.google.com/books?hl=en&lr=&id=n0pIZTQqvmIC&oi=fnd&pg=PP7&dq=jaccard+2003&ots=Lf-0VnuvWO&sig=V9nvWoRGX48B5WC2WW8bsLYj6NM#v=onepage&q=jaccard%202003&f=false

Jacobsen, W. C. (2020). School punishment and interpersonal exclusion: Rejection, withdrawal, and separation from friends. *Criminology*, 58(1), 35–69.

Jacobsen, W. C., Ragan, D. T., Yang, M., Nadel, E. L., & Feinberg, M. E. (2022). Arrested friendships? Justice involvement and interpersonal exclusion in rural schools. *Journal of Research in Crime and Delinquency*, 59(3), 365–409.

Kirk, D. S. (2006). Examining the divergence across self-report and official data sources on inferences about the adolescent life-course of crime. *Journal of Quantitative Criminology*, 22(2), 107–129.

Kirk, D. S., & Sampson, R. J. (2013). Juvenile arrest and collateral educational damage in the transition to adulthood. *Sociology of Education*, 86(1), 36–62.

Kreager, D. A., Staff, J., Gauthier, R., Lefkowitz, E. S., & Feinberg, M. E. (2016). The double standard at sexual debut: Gender, sexual behavior, and adolescent peer acceptance. *Sex Roles*, 75, 377–392.

Laub, J. H. (2014). Understanding inequality and the justice system response: Charting a new way forward. https://wtgrantfoundation.org/wp-content/uploads/2015/09/Inequality-and-the-Justice-System-Response-Charting-a-New-Way-Forward.pdf

Liberman, A. M., Kirk, D. S., & Kim, K. (2014). Labeling effects of first juvenile arrests: Secondary deviance and secondary sanctioning. *Criminology*, 52(3), 345–370.

Lichter, D. T., Parisi, D. P., Grice, S. M., & Taquino, M. C. (2007). National estimates of racial segregation in rural and small-town America. *Demography*, 44(3), 563–581.

Link, B. G., & Phelan, J. C. (2001). Conceptualizing stigma. *Annual Review of Sociology*, 27(1), 363–385.

Massoglia, M. (2008). Incarceration, health, and racial disparities in health. *Law & Society Review*, 42(2), 275–306.

McGrath, A. J. (2014). The subjective impact of contact with the criminal justice system: The role of gender and stigmatization. *Crime & Delinquency*, 60(6), 884–908.

Miller, E. J. (2014). Challenging police discretion. *Howard Law Journal*, 58, 521.

Moffitt, T. E. (1993). Adolescence-limited and life-course-persistent antisocial behavior: A developmental taxonomy. *Psychological Review*, 100(4), 674–701.

Moore, K. E. T., & Tangney, J. P. (2017). Managing the concealable stigma of criminal justice system involvement: A longitudinal examination of anticipated stigma, social withdrawal, and post-release adjustment. *Journal of Social Issues*, 73(2), 322–340.

Na, C. G., & Gottfredson, D. C. (2013). Police officers in schools: Effects on school crime and the processing of offending behaviors. *Justice Quarterly*, 30(4), 619–650.

Narr, R. K., Allen, J. P., Tan, J. S., & Loeb, E. L. (2019). Close friendship strength and broader peer group desirability as differential predictors of adult mental health. *Child Development*, 90(1), 298–313.

National Center for Education Statistics. (2022). ELSI Table Generator. https://nces.ed.gov/ccd/elsi/tablegenerator.aspx

National Resource Center on Justice Involved Women. (2016). Fact sheet on justice involved women in 2016. https://cjinvolvedwomen.org/wp-content/uploads/2016/06/Fact-Sheet.pdf

Office of Juvenile Justice and Delinquency Prevention. (2022). Estimated number of arrests by offense and race, 2002. https://www.ojjdp.gov/ojstatbb/crime/ucr.asp?table_in=2&selYrs=2002&rdoGroups=1&rdoData=c. Released on July 8th, 2022.

Office of Juvenile Justice and Delinquency Prevention. (2022). Juvenile arrest rate trends. https://www.ojjdp.gov/ojstatbb/crime/JAR_Display.asp?ID=qa05279&text=yes&print=yes. Released on July 8th, 2022.

Osgood, D. W., & Chambers, J. M. (2000). Social disorganization outside the metropolis: An analysis of rural youth violence. *Criminology, 38*(1), 81–116.

Osgood, D. W., Feinberg, M. E., Gest, S. D., Moody, J., Ragan, D. T., Spoth, R. S., Greenberg, M., & Redmond, C. (2013). Effects of PROSPER on the influence potential of prosocial versus antisocial youth in adolescent friendship networks. *Journal of Adolescent Health, 53*(2), 174–179. https://www.sciencedirect.com/science/article/pii/S1054139X13001080

Osgood, D. W., Ragan, D. T., Wallace, L., Gest, S. D., Feinberg, M. E., & Moody, J. (2013). Peers and the emergence of alcohol use: Influence and selection processes in adolescent friendship networks. *Journal of Research on Adolescence, 23*(3), 500–512. https://onlinelibrary.wiley.com/doi/full/10.1111/jora.12059

Pager, D. (2003). The mark of a criminal record. *American Journal of Sociology, 108*(5), 937–975.

Pettit, B., & Western, B. (2004). Mass imprisonment and the life course: Race and class inequality in US incarceration. *American Sociological Review, 69*(2), 151–169.

Piquero, A. R. (2008). Disproportionate minority contact. The future of children, 59–79.

Rad, A., Yang, W., & Wunschel, F. (2020). The arrest-jail admission gap. https://www.vera.org/blog/the-arrest-jail-admission-gap-jail-admission-rates-surpass-arrest-rates-in-small-and-rural-counties

Ragan, D., Osgood W., Ramirez, N., Moody, J., & Gest, S. D. (2022). A comparison of peer influence estimates from SIENA stochastic actor-based models and from conventional regression approaches. *Sociological Methods and Research, 51*(1), 357–395.

Schulenberg, J. L. (2010). Patterns in police decision-making with youth: An application of Black's theory of law. *Crime, Law and Social Change, 53*(2), 109–129.

Sherman, J. (2006). Coping with rural poverty: Economic survival and moral capital in rural America. *Social Forces, 85*(2), 891–913.

Sherman, L. W., & Glick, B. D. (1984). The quality of police arrest statistics. https://www.policefoundation.org/wp-content/uploads/2015/07/Sherman-et-al.-1984-The-Quality-of-Police-Arrest-Statistics.pdf

Shrum, W., Cheek, N. H., Jr., & MacD, S. (1988). Friendship in school: Gender and racial homophily. *Sociology of Education, 61*(4), 227–239.

Siennick, S. E. B., Samantha, J., Mears, D. P., Pesta, G. B., Montes, A. N., & Collier, N, L. (2020). School-based services for youth with prior police contact: A randomized control trial. *Journal of Experimental Criminology, 16*, 207–226.

Stanton-Salazar, R. D., & Dornbusch, S. M. (1995). Social capital and the reproduction of inequality: Information networks among Mexican-origin high school students. *Sociology of Education, 68*(2), 116–135.

Steffensmeier, D., & Allan, E. (1996). Gender and crime: Toward a gendered theory of female offending. *Annual Review of Sociology*, 22(1), 459–487.

Stewart, R., & Uggen, C. (2020). Criminal records and college admissions: A modified experimental audit. *Criminology*, 58(1), 156–188.

Sugie, N. F., & Turney, K. (2017). Beyond incarceration: Criminal justice contact and mental health. *American Sociological Review*, 82(4), 719–743.

Sweeten, G. (2006). Who will graduate? Disruption of high school education by arrest and court involvement. *Justice Quarterly*, 23(4), 462–480.

Theriot, M. T. (2009). School resource officers and the criminalization of student behavior. *Journal of Criminal Justice*, 37(3), 280–287.

Tinney, E. (2023). Investigating the "STICKINESS" of stigma following a friend's police contact. *Criminology*, 61(2), 354–383.

Travis, J., Western, B., & Redburn, F. S. (2014). *The Growth of Incarceration in the United States: Exploring Causes and Consequences*. National Academies Press.

Turney, K. W., & Wildeman, C. (2013). Redefining relationships: Explaining the coutervailing consequences of paternal incarceration for parenting. *American Sociological Review*, 78(6), 949–979.

Uggen, C., Vuolo, M., Lageson, S., Ruhland, E., & K. Whitam, H. (2014). The edge of stigma: An experimental audit of the effects of low-level criminal records on employment. *Criminology*, 52(4), 627–654.

Weisheit, R. A., Wells, L. E., & Falcone, D. N. (1994). Community policing in small town and rural America. *Crime & Delinquency*, 40(4), 549–567.

Western, B. (2006). *Punishment and inequality in America*. Russell Sage Foundation.

Wiley, S. A., Slocum, L. A., & Esbensen, F. A. (2013). The unintended consequences of being stopped or arrested: An exploration of the labeling mechanisms through which police contact leads to subsequent delinquency. *Criminology*, 51(4), 927–966.

Zhang, L. (1994). Peers' rejection as a possible consequence of official reaction to delinquency in Chinese society. *Criminal Justice and Behavior*, 21(4), 387–402.

7

Depression, self-harm, and network position

MOLLY COPELAND AND SONJA E. SIENNICK ∎

INTRODUCTION

Poor mental health presents a critical risk to well-being in adolescence (Clayborne et al., 2019; Lu, 2019). Symptoms of mental distress, including depressive symptoms and self-harm, often first arise in adolescence (Hankin, 2006; Nock, 2010), with rates increasing in recent years (Mojtabai et al., 2016; Nock, 2010). Experiencing adolescent depressive symptoms predicts a host of long-term risks to well-being, including lower educational attainment, unemployment, and recurrent psychological disorder (Clayborne et al. 2019). Even mild-to-moderate levels of depressive symptoms can have long-term consequences (Allen et al., 2014). During adolescence, depressive symptoms also often co-occur with other risky or unhealthy behaviors, such as substance use (Siennick et al., 2015) and delinquency (Capaldi & Kim, 2014).

Similarly, self-harm, or deliberate self-inflicted damage to one's body, also presents a significant risk to youth, and current estimates suggest that over 17% of adolescents outside of clinical treatment settings have self-harmed (Swannell et al., 2014). Self-harm often co-occurs with other indicators of mental distress, such as depressive symptoms (Marshall et al., 2013) and harmful behaviors like substance use or disordered eating (Nock, 2010). Self-harm also is associated with risks to long-term well-being, including subsequent suicidal behavior (Swannell et al., 2014).

Although depressive symptoms and self-harm are important indicators of mental distress relevant to peer relationships, there are some key ways in which they may differ. For example, self-harm is potentially more visible than internalized depressive symptoms (Burke et al., 2019). Self-harm can manifest on the body, so that an individual must then choose to conceal or reveal signs of self-harm

Molly Copeland and Sonja E. Siennick, *Depression, self-harm, and network position*. In: *Teen Friendship Networks, Development, and Risky Behavior*. Edited by: Mark E. Feinberg and D. Wayne Osgood, Oxford University Press.
© Mark E. Feinberg and D. Wayne Osgood 2024. DOI: 10.1093/oso/9780197602317.003.0007

(Chandler, 2018). Research also indicated that while self-harm and depressive symptoms often co-occur, self-harm is associated with peer networks net of any depressive symptoms (Copeland et al., 2019). As such, studying both self-harm and depressive symptoms clarifies our understanding of the broader scope of how peers matter for teens' mental health and allows for potential distinctions between these different manifestations of mental distress in relation to peer networks.

Here, we review work that used PROSPER (Promoting School-community-university Partnerships to Enhance Resilience) Peers data to examine how psychological distress is associated with peer networks in adolescence. While both depressive symptoms and self-harm indicate risks to well-being with immediate and long-term consequences for youth, both also have distinctly social dimensions in adolescence (Bentley et al., 2014; Prinstein & Giletta, 2016). However, questions persist regarding the conditions under which the number or features of peer friendships relate to better or worse mental health and whether such relations are general or specific to certain symptoms of distress or certain features of networks.

The existing research indicates that different facets of teens' positions among peers in the web of social connections in a school affect depressive symptoms and self-harm (Copeland et al., 2019; Falci & McNeely, 2009). However, friendship ties should not be assumed to be uniformly beneficial for mental health. Connections with peers may provide benefits that support mental health, or they may induce depressive symptoms and self-harm. The idea that peer relations or positions among peers can induce mental distress is often called the interpersonal risk model (Kochel et al., 2012).

As described in Chapter 1 of this volume, teens' individual positions in the network structure indicate how adolescents relate to one another and fit into the social world of peer relations in the school setting. Many different facets of individuals' network positions relate to multiple aspects of mental health, including depressive symptoms, anxiety, and self-harm (Copeland et al., 2019; Siennick & Picon, 2019). Examining many aspects of how network positions predict depressive symptoms and self-harm can help us to understand how peer connections generally contribute to overall adolescent mental health and well-being in ways that are not limited to a specific symptom or network characteristic.

One key feature discussed in this chapter is that just as peer networks can affect mental health, mental distress can also affect peer networks. The latter is often called the symptoms-driven model (Kochel et al., 2012). For example, peer groups with higher depressive symptoms are less tight-knit compared to less depressive groups (Siennick & Picon, 2019), and teens experiencing depressive symptoms are more likely to withdraw from peers (Schaefer et al., 2011) or be excluded by peers (Cheadle & Goosby, 2012). Understanding the complex interplay between peer networks affecting teens' distress and distress affecting social networks requires careful analysis of depressive symptoms and self-harm, both predicting and predicted by, peer networks.

We build on our team's prior research by providing new analyses examining how depressive symptoms and self-harm predict cohesion among close friends, popularity, and Bonacich centrality in the overall network. We then examine how these network features in turn predict depressive symptoms and self-harm. In doing so, we contribute to our understanding of the complex relationship between depressive symptoms, self-harm, and peer networks in adolescence.

PEERS AND MENTAL HEALTH IN ADOLESCENCE

Both depressive symptoms and self-harm have distinctly social dimensions in adolescence that relate these facets of mental health to teens' relationships with friends and positions in the wider web of connections in the peer environment (Falci & McNeely, 2009; Nock, 2010). Prior research provides some intuition for how peer relations might affect mental health, as well as for how mental health can affect peer networks.

Peers benefit mental health

First, greater connections in the peer network generally benefit mental health. Social integration is often considered a key resource for mental well-being, and social ties can support mental health in multiple ways (Kawachi & Berkman, 2001). For example, peer networks may benefit mental health if peers provide socioemotional support that buffers against distress or if popularity provides a boost in social status (Kornienko & Santos, 2014; Ueno, 2005). The opposite side of this coin is that lacking these connections may predict relatively worse mental health. Being a social isolate who lacks ties with school peers, or occupying a relatively disconnected, low-status position among peers can predict worse mental health for youth (Hall-Lande et al., 2007; Kochel et al., 2012).

Peers harm mental health

Although disconnection may predict poor mental health, it is also possible that certain types of peer network integration may be detrimental, rather than beneficial, for mental health. The interpersonal risk model suggests that having poor peer relations can induce depressive symptoms for teens (Kochel et al., 2012). Similarly, having too many connections with peers may induce stress, feelings of scrutiny, or overregulation of behavior (Abrutyn & Mueller, 2016; Falci & McNeely, 2009), or occupying a high-status position among peers may generate harmful pressure to maintain status (Kornienko & Santos, 2014; Mayeux et al., 2008; Moody et al., 2011). Teens who are connected to only a few other peers, or those who bridge different peer groups, may face particular social stressors associated with their peripheral positions (Kobus & Henry, 2010). Thus, teens' connections with peers should not be assumed to always benefit mental health.

Mental health affects peer networks

A third way that peer networks may be relevant for mental health is through teens' depressive symptoms and self-harm affecting their position in the peer network. This pattern represents the symptoms-driven model and is relatively understudied compared to the interpersonal risk model where peers affect mental health (Kochel et al., 2012). However, there are many ways that depressive symptoms may disrupt connections with peers (Allen et al., 2014). For example, teens experiencing depressive symptoms may demand excessive social support from friends (Prinstein & Giletta, 2016), or distressed teens may coruminate with friends, fixating on negative emotions and events in ways that exacerbate friends' own depressive feelings (Schwartz-Mette & Smith, 2016). Stigma against poor mental health may also make distressed teens less popular among peers (Burke et al., 2019; Schaefer et al., 2011). As depression in youth is particularly associated with irritability, teens with depression may create conflict in peer relations (Kochel et al., 2012) or be viewed as less desirable friends by peers. Furthermore, depressive symptoms may reduce similarity or compatibility among friends, undermining friendship stability (Laursen & Veenstra, 2021; Siennick & Picon, 2019). As a result, teens with elevated depressive symptoms may be excluded from the network over time (Cheadle & Goosby, 2012). Finally, a key symptom of depression is social withdrawal, and thus teens with depressive symptoms may withdraw from peers (Schaefer et al., 2011).

Again, it is worth noting that self-harm is particularly understudied compared to depressive symptoms or other indicators of mental health in relation to peer networks. Research on self-harm suggests that it may increase stress or conflict in friendships, or alternatively that it may increase intimacy among close friends (Walsh, 2006). The potential visibility and the nonnormative nature of self-harm may make it more highly stigmatized among peers compared to more internal experiences of mental distress, like depressive symptoms (Burke et al., 2019). General theories of self-harm indicate social dimensions of the behavior associated with peer relations (Nock, 2010), and studies considering peer network structure and self-harm suggest that self-harm is indeed associated with structural network positions (You et al., 2016). Moreover, peer relations, depressive symptoms, and self-harm are often linked in dynamic processes, such as friends' depressive symptoms spurring teens' engagement in self-harm (Giletta et al., 2013). Consequently, it is worth further examining the effect of networks on self-harm and complementary effects of self-harm on peer networks.

Network structure and mental health

A complex web of relationships connects individuals with close friends, friends of friends, and distant peers across the breadth of the network of social ties. As discussed in Chapters 1 and 3, many different aspects of peer network structure can be relevant for teens' well-being and behaviors, and this is equally true for teens' mental health. We can consider how individuals' network positions have features related to connections with close friends and in the overall network, both of which may relate to mental health.

First, both the individual's direct connections with friends and patterns of ties among those friends can be relevant to distress. The presence or absence of certain relationship dynamics may affect mental health, including support, conflict, and corumination (Prinstein & Giletta, 2016; Schwartz-Mette & Smith, 2016). Mental health can also relate to the cohesion of a teen's friend group, such as whether or not one's friends are also friends with each other. Cohesively or densely connected friends may enhance the ability of that friend group to provide social support, foster trust, or enforce conformity with in-group norms (Falci & McNeely, 2009; McGloin et al., 2014).

Second, it is not just connections with or among close friends that matter for teens: the positions teens occupy in the broader network can be important for distress (Copeland, 2021; Guan & Kamo, 2016). For example, being popular among other highly popular peers may convey beneficial social status or detrimental social pressure (Kornienko & Santos, 2014; Mayeux et al., 2008). Such facets of individuals' positions can be examined with measures defined by information from the structure of the whole network, such as Bonacich centrality, which indicates not only a teen's own popularity, but also the successive popularity of that teen's friends, then friends' friends, and so on. In this way, considering patterns of ties both among close friends and as a function of the overall network is important for fully understanding the potential of peer networks associated with adolescent depressive symptoms and self-harm.

MENTAL HEALTH AND NETWORKS IN PROSPER

Due to three key advantages, the PROSPER data provide a critical opportunity to examine peer networks and mental health in adolescence. First, the PROSPER survey collected mental health data across 4 years of high school, providing several consecutive years of network and mental health data over time with measures of depressive symptoms and self-harm for Grades 9–12 for the entire in-school sample. PROSPER is also one of the few studies that collected self-harm data and also assessed whole networks.

Second, the whole network data in PROSPER also provide a much richer view of the peer context than the ways that networks typically are examined in relation to mental health. For example, many studies consider how teens' distress is associated with victimization, where peer relations indicate bullying or aggressive interactions rather than friendships (Kochel et al., 2012). Many studies examine dyadic friendships, such as best friends, but do not provide a broader picture of teens' social standing in the wider peer environment (Schwartz-Mette & Smith, 2016). Other research considers perceptual measures of who is well liked or perceived as popular (Mayeux et al., 2008), or measures of relationship quality, such as perceived social support from peers (Oppenheimer & Hankin,

2011). While these aspects of peer networks are all valuable in their own right, the whole-network measures in the PROSPER survey provide an important opportunity to examine adolescents' places or positions in the larger peer context. Examining peer networks in this way, versus via self-reports of perceived popularity or likability, for example, is also particularly important when considering mental health because experiencing mental distress may skew individuals' perceptions of social acceptance, social competence, and relationships with peers (Allen et al., 2014; McGrath & Repetti, 2002). With PROSPER, researchers can investigate structural features of friendship connections beyond relationship qualities, specific behaviors like bullying, or perceptions that may be skewed by mental distress.

Third, another important methodological advantage of whole-network information is in measuring attributes of the friends to whom respondents are connected. Mental health depends on both *how* teens are connected to each other (peer network structure) and characteristics of *who* is connected (Copeland, 2021; Reynolds & Crea, 2015). For example, we (Siennick et al., 2015) found that teens experiencing depressive symptoms were less likely to begin smoking as a result of friends' smoking behavior, indicating that adolescent health depends on complex, intertwined aspects of connections with peers, friends' behavior, and mental health status. As noted in Chapter 1, perceptual measures that rely on teens' reports of friends' behaviors are often biased, and such measures may be even less reliable for reporting friends' internal states, such as depressive symptoms, or behaviors that are highly stigmatized, such as self-harm (Chandler, 2018). The PROSPER design enables linking surveys across friendships (as described in Chapter 1), so that we can examine peer behavior for potentially stigmatized characteristics like depressive symptoms and self-harm. In this way, capturing network position through a combination of network structure and individuals' self-reports of their own behaviors and mental health can provide insight into these processes in a different way from perceptual information about peer behavior or positions among peers.

PROSPER Peers research on depressive symptoms and self-harm

Our program of research on depressive symptoms and self-harm using the PROSPER data has yielded important insights regarding the role of peer networks in shaping teen mental health. Our work has identified ways depressive symptoms and self-harm predict peer relations, as well as how the interplay between peer relations and mental health affects other health behaviors. Our research in this area has expanded the understanding of how multiple dimensions of mental distress relate to networks by examining data on self-harm in PROSPER. Our work also contributes to the understanding of the generality of peer network dimensions in relation to mental health by examining many different aspects of network positions.

First, our published studies indicate how depressive symptoms can shape relations between peer behaviors and an adolescents' own behaviors over time. For example, we found that mental distress altered the impact of friends' behaviors on teen's own behavior, with depressive symptoms weakening the effects of friends' smoking on the likelihood of smoking initiation among teens experiencing depressive symptoms (Siennick et al., 2015). Depressive symptoms also moderated some of the effects of the PROSPER substance use preventive intervention over time (details of which are discussed in Chapter 2). Specifically, among youth in the control condition, higher levels of depressive symptoms were associated with a belief that substance use has social benefits and is prevalent among peers, as well as with having more friends who used substances. In contrast, these associations were reduced in intervention school districts (Siennick et al., 2016), indicating that the intervention may buffer more depressed teens from factors associated with substance use.

Prior work also documented how peer network position was linked to mental health, consistent with the interpersonal risk model. For example, one study longitudinally examined how depressive symptoms were associated with structural embeddedness—a measure of how difficult it is to disconnect an individual from the overall network by breaking one or several ties. Increased embeddedness predicted decreased depressive symptoms in general, but for girls with more depressive friends, being more structurally embedded in the network was more detrimental to mental health (Copeland, 2023). However, increased cohesion among close friends (i.e., greater density of ties among one's close friends) mitigated the risks of more depressive friends for girls. In this way, connections with close peers and one's position in the overall network are both associated with depressive symptoms, but in different ways for girls with more depressive friends (Copeland, 2023).

Our research also suggested that associations between peer networks and depressive symptoms can extend beyond adolescence into young adulthood. For teens who experience higher depressive symptoms, popularity predicted fewer depressive symptoms in young adulthood. However, very high prestige (i.e., being popular among other highly popular youth) predicted greater depressive symptoms later, in young adulthood (Copeland, 2021). Being part of more cohesive groups of depressive friends as a teen also predicted greater depressive symptoms in young adulthood (Copeland, 2021). This work indicated the developmental importance of peers in adolescence, where peer network structures experienced as a teen are associated with mental health years later.

A third branch of our team's research has demonstrated that levels of depressive symptoms among members of a friendship group were associated with the network features of that group, consistent with the symptoms-driven model. For example, friendship groups with higher average levels of depressive symptoms tended to be smaller in size and less cohesive (i.e., to have lower density and reciprocity between dyads within the group) compared to groups with lower levels of average depressive symptoms (Siennick & Picon, 2019). This work also highlighted the importance of considering multiple facets of distress in relation to peer network structure: We found that higher average anxiety symptoms in a peer group predicted higher rates of reciprocity within a group, whereas higher average depressive symptoms predicted lower rates of reciprocity within a group (Siennick & Picon, 2019). Greater variation in depressive and anxiety symptoms within groups also related to lower group density, with variation in anxiety symptoms also related to larger group size and greater group transitivity of and variability in anxiety and depression symptoms within the groups, as well as how different aspects of mental health can relate to peer networks differently.

Finally, prior PROSPER studies have documented an association between self-harm and multiple aspects of peer network structure over time. Connections that bridge friends were associated with higher self-harm among teens, while the number of sent friendship nominations predicted lower self-harm for boys only (Copeland et al., 2019). These associations persisted after controlling for depressive symptoms, suggesting that findings were specific to self-harm rather than generalized distress. This work indicated that self-harm was related to peer processes that were at least somewhat distinct from the ways that depressive symptoms were linked to peer processes. Future work using the PROSPER data can further identify the direction of these associations over time to consider how self-harming behaviors may affect teens' positions in peer networks.

Together, these studies suggested that depressive symptoms played an important role connecting peer networks with other health behaviors (Siennick et al., 2015, 2016), and that they were shaped by peer network positions (Copeland, 2021, 2023), as was self-harm (Copeland et al., 2019). In addition, the studies suggested a potential reciprocal association between depressive symptoms and mental health-related outcomes, such that symptoms and self-harm may also influence peer network characteristics (Siennick & Picon, 2019). Overall, this work indicates the complex ways that structures of connections among peers relate to adolescent mental well-being.

New analyses on network position, depressive symptoms, and self-harm

Here, we extend our previously published body of work on peer networks and mental health with new analyses examining bidirectionality between teens' social network positions and both depressive symptoms and self-harm. As such, we provide a test of both the interpersonal risk and symptoms-driven models. In this new work, we built on prior findings by considering multiple network dimensions, including close friend cohesion, popularity, and Bonacich centrality in the overall network. We also considered these associations net of friends' levels of depressive symptoms and self-harm. The resulting four broad research questions explored characteristics of network position associated with mental distress:

1. How do depressive symptoms predict peer network position?
2. How does self-harm predict peer network position?

3. How do peer network positions predict depressive symptoms?
4. How do peer network positions predict self-harm?

METHODS

Data

The new analyses that we present next drew on the last four waves of the PROSPER in-school data collection (i.e., the surveys administered in 9th through 12th grade). We used observations with complete information on all study variables (i.e., listwise deletion), and we lagged time-varying predictors by one wave in our analyses (meaning that all adolescents in our sample participated in at least two waves of data collection). Our analytical sample size was 17,072 observations on 8,430 adolescents. For these analyses, comparable to the total PROSPER sample, the adolescents in our analytical sample were 46% male and 87% white; 80% lived in two-parent families; and 18% received free or reduced-price school lunch.

Measures

Depressive symptoms. The time-varying measure of depressive symptoms was the average of eight ordinal items assessing feelings and behaviors, such as loneliness, crying, and feeling sad over the 6 months prior to the survey. Higher scores indicated higher levels of depressive symptoms. The scale had good reliability. This measure captured symptoms, not clinical diagnoses, meaning that results do not necessarily generalize to adolescents diagnosed with depression.

Self-harm. The time-varying measure of self-harm was a dichotomous indicator of whether the adolescent had deliberately hurt him- or herself in the 6 months prior to the survey.

Peer network position. We included three time-varying measures of network position. The first, *cohesion*, was measured as ego-network density, or the proportion of pairs of friends within the adolescent's set of friends who were friends with each other. The second, *Bonacich centrality*, was an index of the adolescent's "connectedness" or prominence in the school. This version of centrality is a function of the respondent's number of friends weighted by his or her friends' own centrality. High Bonacich centrality scores indicate teens who are popular among other popular youth. The third measure of network position, *popularity*, was a count of the number of friendship nominations that the adolescent received, or in-degree, at that wave. See Chapter 4 in this volume, Wasserman and Faust (1994), and Valente (2010) for additional discussion of measures of network volume and connectivity.

Covariates. To account for homophily, our models included time-varying controls for adolescents' *friends' average depression* scores on the scale described above and for the *proportion of adolescents' friends who engaged in self-harm*. We

Table 7.1 DESCRIPTIVE STATISTICS FOR STUDY VARIABLES ($N = 17,072$ OBSERVATIONS ON 8,430 ADOLESCENTS)

Variable	Mean	SD	Minimum	Maximum
Depression	0.36	0.45	0	2
Self-harm	0.08	—	0	1
Cohesion	0.23	0.21	0	1
Bonacich centrality	0.90	0.60	0	4.44
Popularity	3.60	2.44	0	18
Friends' average depression	0.37	0.27	0	2
Proportion of friends who engage in self-harm	0.09	0.16	0	1
Wave	5.87	0.81	5	8
Male	0.46	—	0	1
White	0.87	—	0	1
Two-parent family	0.80	—	0	1
Free or reduced-price lunch recipient	0.18	—	0	1
Treatment condition (1 = intervention)	0.48	—	0	1

also controlled for *wave* of data collection, *male* gender, *white* race/ethnicity, whether the adolescent lived in a *two-parent family*, whether he or she was a *free or reduced-price lunch recipient*, and whether he or she lived in a *treatment community* in the PROSPER experimental design. Descriptive statistics for our sample are shown in Table 7.1.

Analytical strategy

Our analyses were multilevel random effects pooled regression models predicting first, depression and self-harm from peer network position, and then, the peer network measures from depression and self-harm. The results of these models showed whether adolescents who were more or less integrated into their school social networks later had higher or lower levels of depression and self-harm, and whether adolescents with higher or lower depression and self-harm later had greater or lower network integration.

The regression models had several notable features. First, observations were clustered within adolescents who themselves were clustered within community/cohort combinations, violating the independence assumption of regression analysis. Our use of three-level regression models adjusted our standard errors for this clustering through the inclusion of variance components for adolescent and for community/cohort (Raudenbush & Bryk, 2002; see Chapter 4 section on multilevel modeling). Second, we used linear models for most outcomes, but used logistic models for the dichotomous self-harm outcome. Third, to preserve temporal ordering, we predicted the outcomes from lagged versions of the focal predictor measures; for example, we predicted depression at time t from cohesion, Bonacich centrality, and popularity at time $t - 1$.

RESULTS

Predicting depression and self-harm from peer network position

Table 7.2 shows longitudinal associations between network position and later depressive symptoms and self-harm. Models 1 through 3 present results for the depression outcome. Cohesion at one wave did not predict depressive symptoms at the following wave, but Bonacich centrality and popularity did. Adolescents who were more central in their networks and those who received more friendship nominations went on to have lower depressive symptoms scores. Standardizing these coefficients by multiplying them by the ratio of the standard deviations of the predictor and the outcome revealed that these associations were modest. Specifically, an increase of one standard deviation in Bonacich centrality and an increase of one standard deviation in popularity were respectively associated with decreases of 0.05 and 0.02 standard deviations in later depressive symptoms.

Models 4 through 6 of Table 7.2 present results for the self-harm outcome. Cohesion and popularity did not significantly predict later self-harm, but Bonacich centrality did. Adolescents who had higher centrality scores went on to have lower log-odds of engaging in self-harm. Exponentiating that coefficient revealed that a one-unit increase in Bonacich centrality—approximately one fourth of that measure's total range—was associated with a 23% decrease in the odds of self-harm. Taken together, these six models revealed modest-to-moderate associations of some aspects of network position with later internalizing problems. Notably, these associations remained net of adolescents' friends' own depressive symptoms scores and self-harm and, in the self-harm models, net of adolescents' depressive symptoms as well.

Predicting peer network position from depression and self-harm

The next set of models used depressive symptoms and self-harm at a given wave to predict indicators of network position at the following wave. Table 7.3 shows the results. The leftmost model shows that both depressive symptoms and self-harm negatively predicted later friend cohesion. That is, adolescents with higher depressive symptoms scores and teens who engaged in self-harm went on to have less cohesive ego networks than adolescents with lower levels of these internalizing problems. These associations were modest, with standardized coefficients indicating that a one standard deviation increase in depressive symptoms and moving from no self-harm to any self-harm, respectively, predicted decreases of 0.02 and 0.07 standard deviations in later cohesion. While these associations were relatively small in magnitude, the effects could accumulate over time to have a greater cumulative impact over the years of adolescence.

We found similar results in predicting Bonacich centrality and popularity from depressive symptoms and self-harm. Net of each other, each predictor was

Table 7.2 MULTILEVEL REGRESSION COEFFICIENTS PREDICTING DEPRESSION AND SELF-HARM FROM LAGGED NETWORK CHARACTERISTICS AND CONTROLS (N = 17,072 OBSERVATIONS ON 8,430 ADOLESCENTS)

	Outcome: Depression						Outcome: Self-harm			
	Model 1		Model 2		Model 3		Model 4		Model 5		Model 6
Predictor	b (SE)	b (SE)	b (SE)	b (SE)	b (SE)	b (SE)
Cohesion	0.00 (0.01)	—	—	−0.11 (0.18)	—	—
Bonacich centrality	—	−0.03 (0.01)***	—	—	−0.26 (0.07)***	—
Popularity	—	—	−0.003 (0.00)*	—	—	−0.01 (0.02)
Wave	−0.02 (0.00)***	−0.02 (0.00)***	−0.02 (0.00)***	−0.26 (0.04)***	−0.27 (0.05)***	−0.26 (0.05)***
Male	−0.17 (0.01)***	−0.17 (0.01)***	−0.17 (0.01)***	0.08 (0.08)	0.06 (0.08)	0.08 (0.08)
White	−0.01 (0.01)	0.00 (0.01)	−0.01 (0.01)	−0.36 (0.11)**	−0.33 (0.11)**	−0.36 (0.11)**
Two-parent family	−0.04 (0.01)***	−0.04 (0.01)***	−0.04 (0.01)***	−0.10 (0.09)	−0.08 (0.09)	−0.10 (0.09)
Free/reduced lunch	0.03 (0.01)**	0.02 (0.01)*	0.03 (0.01)**	0.35 (0.09)***	0.31 (0.09)***	0.35 (0.09)***
Treatment community	0.01 (0.01)	0.01 (0.01)	0.01 (0.01)	−0.08 (0.11)	−0.09 (0.11)	−0.08 (0.11)
Depression	—	—	—	1.85 (0.07)***	1.83 (0.07)***	1.85 (0.07)***
Friends' average on outcome	0.13 (0.01)***	0.12 (0.01)***	0.13 (0.01)***	0.98 (0.20)***	0.89 (0.20)***	0.97 (0.20)***
Constant	0.55 (0.03)***	0.59 (0.03)***	0.57 (0.03)***	−2.44 (0.31)***	−2.20 (0.31)***	−2.43 (0.32)***

Note. Linear coefficients shown for depression models; logistic coefficients shown for self-harm models. * $p < 0.05$, ** $p < 0.01$, *** $p < 0.001$.

Table 7.3 MULTILEVEL REGRESSION COEFFICIENTS PREDICTING NETWORK OUTCOMES FROM LAGGED DEPRESSION AND SELF-HARM ($N = 17,072$ OBSERVATIONS ON 8,430 ADOLESCENTS)

Predictor	Cohesion b	SE	Bonacich centrality b	SE	Popularity b	SE
Depression	−0.01	(0.00)*	−0.08	(0.01)***	−0.17	(0.04)***
Self-harm	−0.02	(0.01)*	−0.05	(0.02)***	−0.15	(0.06)*
Wave	0.00	(0.00)	−0.06	(0.00)***	−0.43	(0.02)***
Male	−0.05	(0.00)***	−0.07	(0.01)***	−0.43	(0.04)***
White	0.02	(0.01)***	0.15	(0.02)***	0.41	(0.06)***
Two-parent family	0.02	(0.00)***	0.09	(0.01)***	0.27	(0.05)***
Free or reduced-price lunch recipient	−0.02	(0.00)***	−0.15	(0.01)***	−0.52	(0.05)***
Treatment community	0.01	(0.01)	0.00	(0.01)	0.19	(0.11)
Friends' average on depression	−0.01	(0.01)	−0.14	(0.02)***	−0.28	(0.08)***
Proportion of friends who engage in self-harm	−0.05	(0.01)***	−0.10	(0.03)***	−0.25	(0.11)*
Constant	0.26	(0.02)***	1.07	(0.04)***	5.36	(0.15)***

Note. Linear coefficients shown. * $p < 0.05$, ** $p < 0.01$, *** $p < 0.001$.

negatively associated with both network outcomes. Standardizing the coefficients revealed that a one standard deviation increase in depressive symptoms was associated with a 0.06 standard deviation decrease in later network Bonacich centrality and engaging in self-harm with a 0.09 standard deviation decrease in later Bonacich centrality. Similarly, a one standard deviation increase in depressive symptoms was associated with a 0.03 standard deviation decrease in later popularity; the analogous decrease in popularity associated with self-harm was 0.06. As with the results presented above, these associations also remained net of adolescents' friends' depressive symptoms and self-harm.

CONCLUSION

Several decades of research have shown that adolescents' mental health is intertwined with their social relationships (Falci & McNeely, 2009; Nock, 2010). Yet questions remain about the direction of mental health problems preceding or following from peer factors, the generality versus specificity of associations, and the positive or negative nature of associations between connections with peers and teen mental distress. Research from PROSPER Peers has demonstrated that both depressive symptoms and self-harm were associated with a variety of social network indices, and these works suggested that internalizing problems and network position may longitudinally predict each other (Copeland, 2021; Siennick

& Picon, 2019). This chapter extended our work by examining potential bidirectional associations between depressive symptoms, self-harm, and three indices of social network position.

The new results suggested that there may be some bidirectionality and some generality in the examined associations. Results supported bidirectional associations in that select network indicators—namely, Bonacich centrality and popularity—were negatively associated with depressive symptoms and self-harm 1 year later, and in turn depressive symptoms and self-harm were negatively associated with future network integration. There was also some generality here, as multiple network measures examined here related to both facets of mental health: Bonacich centrality was negatively associated with both later depressive symptoms and later self-harm, popularity was also negatively associated with later depressive symptoms, and both depressive symptoms and self-harm were negatively associated with later scores on three measures of peer network integration. These results suggested that patterns observed here represent general associations that were not limited to one specific aspect of teen mental health or connections with peers. Yet cohesion did not predict later depressive symptoms or self-harm, and popularity did not predict later self-harm. Thus, measures of internalizing problems were more consistently associated with measures of later network position than the reverse.

In this way, this work also highlighted the importance of considering distinct types of social network integration for adolescent mental health. For example, cohesion among close friends did not predict subsequent mental distress, but being popular among popular friends was negatively associated with later distress, as indexed by both depressive symptoms and self-harm. This result suggested that popularity among other high-status teens may have a protective effect during adolescence, conveying greater social status or indicating social skills that provide returns to subsequent mental health. This pattern may indicate that it may not be the simple presence of peer ties that protects later mental health, but rather the overall pattern of peer ties may convey status and prestige that yield greater returns to mental well-being. Such a pattern also suggested a difference in processes relating distress to peer ties at the ego-network level versus the whole-network level. Examining perceived popularity, dyads, or even a simple count of friends can mask informative distinctions between different aspects of how teens are connected to peers. Future work should continue to disentangle how and why distinct aspects of peer network integration affect mental distress, as well as how distress predicts different facets of connections with peers.

These findings provide evidence for the symptoms-driven model, or the idea that depression, self-harm, and other mental health problems undermine adolescents' positions in their peer networks (Kochel et al., 2012). Internalizing symptoms and behaviors may be highly stigmatized or may be linked to conduct that peers find aversive and, through these mechanisms, may reduce affected adolescents' peer status (Burke et al., 2019; Kochel et al., 2012; Prinstein & Giletta, 2016; Schaefer et al., 2011). Such a process would explain why depressive symptoms and self-harm negatively predicted network integration 1 year later.

Yet, our findings also provided partial support for a peers-driven perspective of internalizing problems, as select features of adolescents' social standings predicted later depressive symptoms and self-harm. Bonacich centrality and popularity negatively predicting later distress also aligns with expectations of benefits, rather than potential harm, from greater integration among peers. This pattern is consistent with the idea that peers offer resources, such as support and status, that can benefit mental health (Kornienko & Santos, 2014; Ueno, 2005).

The evidence for both models in our results indicated that a transactional model may best describe the internalizing-networks association (Sameroff & Mackenzie, 2003). That is, depression and self-harm may elicit negative peer reactions, which in turn may reinforce depressive symptoms and self-harm. Further research is needed to examine the interplay between network position and mental distress in a transactional perspective.

Importantly, our analyses did not isolate causal effects of internalizing problems and network positions on each other. Rather, our study was correlational, identifying characteristics of adolescents that indicated risk for mental distress and peer outcomes in the near future. On the basis of our models, we know only which predicted which, but that does not prove causality. We cannot tell whether, for example, depressive symptoms themselves reduced popularity, or whether adolescents who were depression-prone tended to be less popular for other reasons we were unable to take into account. However, the associations found here indicated that these follow-up questions of causality are worth pursuing, ideally through experimental or quasi-experimental studies.

In addition to further specifying the causal direction of these patterns, future research should also consider how facets of mental health like depressive symptoms and self-harm affect other peer-linked facets of well-being for youth over time, including other health-related behaviors, such as substance use or physical health, and long-term outcomes for both mental health and social relationships over the life course. For example, the symptoms-driven, interpersonal risk, and transactional models have been investigated with respect to the associations between internalizing problems and peer victimization (Krygsman & Vaillancourt, 2017; Sentse et al., 2017); school performance and problem drinking (Davis et al., 2018); and specific functions of peer relationships, such as support and conflict (Yang et al., 2020). We also note that the association between self-harm and peer network structure is one particular area where much more research is needed to clarify further correlates, timing, and mechanisms of how peer networks are associated with self-harm.

Broadly, our work showed the importance of peer connections for adolescent mental health in ways that might be relevant to policymakers, school personnel, and parents. For instance, policies and programs that consider how peer relationships affect health behaviors like substance use could be enhanced by also considering how peer relationships affect more psychological factors, such as mental health. In addition, socially integrated youth could be effective peer leaders in interventions aimed at reducing self-harm and internalizing symptoms if they personally enjoy better mental health (Veenstra & Laninga-Wijnen, 2022). In converse, parents, teachers, or those working with youth can consider how experiencing mental distress may have the less obvious cost of subsequent decreases in friendships, peer integration, and social capital, which may lead to further spillover of negative consequences of distress. Similarly, schools and parents can consider lacking integration as an indicator of potential risk to mental health, for example, if teens who lack friendship nominations generally aren't viewed as part of the peer social context by others and then face heightened risks for depressive symptoms. Moreover, experiencing even subclinical levels of depressive symptoms as a teen can lead to long-term challenges, such as poor academic performance (Chow et al., 2015) and loneliness and isolation in adulthood (Allen et al., 2014). Consequently, understanding how integration in peer networks can be leveraged to reduce psychological distress can have cumulative and long-term benefits for youth.

In sum, studies using the PROSPER data provide insight into the relationship between teen mental health and peer networks in ways that indicate the importance of peer relationships for healthy adolescent development. The distinct aspects of peer relations captured by PROSPER's network data reveal that internalizing problems are linked to teens' social standing among peers. These measures go beyond individual adolescents' perceptions of their social integration or dyadic friendships, and they permit the study of depression and self-harm in more comprehensive peer contexts. Schools are a key aspect of adolescent social life, and school-based network studies like ours are an invaluable addition to the study of adolescent friendships and mental health.

REFERENCES

Abrutyn, S., & Mueller, A. S. (2016). When too much integration and regulation hurts: Reenvisioning Durkheim's altruistic suicide. *Society and Mental Health*, 6(1), 56–71. https://doi.org/10.1177/2156869315604346

Allen, J. P., Chango, J., Szwedo, D. & Schad, M. (2014). Long-term sequelae of subclinical depressive symptoms in early adolescence. *Development and Psychopathology*, 26(01), 171–180. https://doi.org/doi:10.1017/S095457941300093X

Bentley, K. H., Nock, M. K., & Barlow, D. H. (2014). The four-function model of nonsuicidal self-injury: Key directions for future research. *Clinical Psychological Science*, 2(5), 638–656. https://doi.org/10.1177/2167702613514563

Burke, T. A., Piccirillo, M. L., Moore-Berg, S. L., Alloy, L. B., & Heimberg, R. G. (2019). The stigmatization of nonsuicidal self-injury. *Journal of Clinical Psychology*, 75(3), 481–498. https://doi.org/10.1002/jclp.22713

Capaldi, D. M., & Kim, H. K. (2014). Comorbidity of depression and conduct disorder. In C. S. Richards & M. W. O'Hara, *The Oxford handbook of depression and comorbidity* (pp. 186–199). Oxford University Press.

Chandler, A. (2018). Seeking secrecy: A qualitative study of younger adolescents' accounts of self-harm. *Young*, 26(4), 313–331. https://doi.org/10.1177/1103308817717367

Cheadle, J. E., & Goosby, B. J. (2012). The small-school friendship dynamics of adolescent depressive symptoms. *Society and Mental Health*, 2(2), 99–119. https://doi.org/10.1177/2156869312445211

Chow, C. M., Tan, C. C., & Buhrmester, D. (2015). Interdependence of depressive symptoms, school involvement, and academic performance between adolescent friends: A dyadic analysis. *British Journal of Educational Psychology*, 85(3), 316–331. https://doi.org/10.1111/bjep.12075

Clayborne, Z. M., Varin, M., & Colman, I. (2019). Systematic review and meta-analysis: Adolescent depression and long-term psychosocial outcomes. *Journal of the American Academy of Child and Adolescent Psychiatry*, 58(1), 72–79. https://doi.org/10.1016/j.jaac.2018.07.896

Copeland, M. (2021). The long shadow of peers: Adolescent networks and young adult mental health. *Social Sciences*, 10(6), 231.

Copeland, M. (2023). Embedded distress: Social integration, gender, and adolescent depression. *Social Forces*, 101(3), 1396–1421. https://doi.org/10.1093/sf/soac034

Copeland, M., Siennick, S. E., Feinberg, M. E., Moody, J., & Ragan, D. T. (2019). Social ties cut both ways: Self-harm and adolescent peer networks. *Journal of Youth and Adolescence*, 48(8), 1506–1518. https://doi.org/10.1007/s10964-019-01011-4

Davis, J. P., Dumas, T. M., Merrin, G. J., Espelage, D. L., Tan, K., Madden, D., & Hon, J. S. (2018). Examining the pathways between bully victimization, depression, academic achievement, and problematic drinking in adolescence. *Psychology of Addictive Behaviors*, 32(6), 605–616.

Falci, C., & McNeely, C. (2009). Too many friends: Social integration, network cohesion and adolescent depressive symptoms. *Social Forces*, 87(4), 2031–2062.

Giletta, M., Burk, W. J., Scholte, R. H. J., Engels, R. C. M. E., & Prinstein, M. J. (2013). Direct and indirect peer socialization of adolescent nonsuicidal self-injury. *Journal of Research on Adolescence*, 23(3), 450–463. https://doi.org/10.1111/jora.12036

Guan, W., & Kamo, Y. (2016). Contextualizing depressive contagion: A multilevel network approach. *Society and Mental Health*, 6(2), 129–145. https://doi.org/10.1177/2156869315619657

Hall-Lande, J., Eisenberg, M., Christenson, S. L., & Neumark-Sztainer, D. (2007). Social isolation, psychological health, and protective factors in adolescence. *Adolescence*, 42(166), 265–286.

Hankin, B. L. (2006). Adolescent depression: Description, causes, and interventions. *Epilepsy and Behavior*, 8(1), 102–114. https://doi.org/10.1016/j.yebeh.2005.10.012

Kawachi, I., & Berkman, L. F. (2001). Social ties and mental health. *Journal of Urban Health: Bulletin of the New York Academy of Medicine*, 78(3), 458–467. https://doi.org/10.1093/jurban/78.3.458

Kobus, K., & Henry, D. B. (2010). Interplay of network position and peer substance use in early adolescent cigarette, alcohol, and marijuana use. *The Journal of Early Adolescence*, 30(2), 225–245. https://doi.org/10.1177/0272431609333300

Kochel, K. P., Ladd, G. W., & Rudolph, K. D. (2012). Longitudinal associations among youth depressive symptoms, peer victimization, and low peer acceptance: An interpersonal process perspective. *Child Development*, 83(2), 637–650. https://doi.org/10.1111/j.1467-8624.2011.01722.x

Kornienko, O., & Santos, C. E. (2014). The effects of friendship network popularity on depressive symptoms during early adolescence: Moderation by fear of negative evaluation and gender. *Journal of Youth and Adolescence, 43*(4), 541–553. https://doi.org/10.1007/s10964-013-9979-4

Krygsman, A., & Vaillancourt, T. (2017). Longitudinal associations between depression symptoms and peer experiences: Evidence of symptoms-driven pathways. *Journal of Applied Developmental Psychology, 51,* 20–34.

Laursen, B., & Veenstra, R. (2021). Toward understanding the functions of peer influence: A summary and synthesis of recent empirical research. *Journal of Research on Adolescence, 31,* 889–907. https://doi.org/10.1111/jora.12606

Lu, W. (2019). Adolescent depression: National trends, risk factors, and healthcare disparities. *American Journal of Health Behavior, 43*(1), 181–194.

Marshall, S. K., Tilton-Weaver, L. C., & Stattin, H. (2013). Non-suicidal self-injury and depressive symptoms during middle adolescence: A longitudinal analysis. *Journal of Youth and Adolescence, 42*(8), 1234–1242. https://doi.org/10.1007/s10964-013-9919-3

Mayeux, L., Sandstrom, M. J., & Cillessen, A. H. N. (2008). Is being popular a risky proposition? *Journal of Research on Adolescence, 18*(1), 49–74. https://doi.org/10.1111/j.1532-7795.2008.00550.x

McGloin, J. M., Sullivan, C. J., & Thomas, K. J. (2014). Peer influence and context: The interdependence of friendship groups, schoolmates and network density in predicting substance use. *Journal of Youth and Adolescence, 43,* 1436–1452. https://doi.org/10.1007/s10964-014-0126-7

McGrath, E. P., & Repetti, R. L. (2002). A longitudinal study of children's depressive symptoms, self-perceptions, and cognitive distortions about the self. *Journal of Abnormal Psychology, 111*(1), 77–87. https://doi.org/10.1037/0021-843X.111.1.77

Mojtabai, R., Olfson, M., & Han, B. (2016). National trends in the prevalence and treatment of depression in adolescents and young adults. *Pediatrics, 138*(6), e20161878. https://doi.org/10.1542/peds.2016-1878

Moody, J., Brynildsen, W. D., Osgood, D. W., Feinberg, M., & Gest, S. (2011). Popularity trajectories and substance use in early adolescence. *Social Networks, 33*(2), 101–112. https://doi.org/10.1016/j.socnet.2010.10.001

Nock, M. K. (2010). Self-injury. *Annual Review of Clinical Psychology, 6,* 339–363. https://doi.org/10.1146/annurev.clinpsy.121208.131258

Oppenheimer, C. W., & Hankin, B. L. (2011). Relationship quality and depressive symptoms among adolescents: A short-term multiwave investigation of longitudinal, reciprocal associations. *Journal of Clinical Child and Adolescent Psychology, 40*(3), 486–493. https://doi.org/10.1080/15374416.2011.563462

Prinstein, M. J., & Giletta, M. (2016). Peer relations and developmental psychopathology. In D. Ciccetti (Ed.), *Developmental psychopathology* (3rd ed., vol. *1*, pp. 527–579). Wiley.

Raudenbush, S. W., & Bryk, A. S. (2002). *Hierarchical linear models: Applications and data analysis methods. Advanced quantitative techniques in the social sciences* (Vol. 2).

Reynolds, A. D., & Crea, T. M. (2015). Peer influence processes for youth delinquency and depression. *Journal of Adolescence, 43,* 83–95. https://doi.org/10.1016/j.adolescence.2015.05.013

Sameroff, A. J., & Mackenzie, M. J. (2003). Research strategies for capturing transactional models of development: The limits of the possible. *Development and Psychopathology, 15*(3), 613–640. https://doi.org/10.1017/S0954579403000312

Schaefer, D. R., Kornienko, O., & Fox, A. M. (2011). Misery does not love company: Network selection mechanisms and depression homophily. *American Sociological Review, 76*(5), 764–785. https://doi.org/10.1177/0003122411420813

Schwartz-Mette, R. A., & Smith, R. L. (2016). When does co-rumination facilitate depression contagion in adolescent friendships? Investigating intrapersonal and interpersonal factors. *Journal of Clinical Child & Adolescent Psychology, 47*(6), 912–913. https://doi.org/10.1080/15374416.2016.1197837

Sentse, M., Prinzie, P., & Salmivalli, C. (2017). Testing the direction of longitudinal paths between victimization, peer rejection, and different types of internalizing problems in adolescence. *Journal of Abnormal Child Psychology, 45*(5), 1013–1023. https://doi.org/10.1007/s10802-016-0216-y

Siennick, S. E., & Picon, M. (2019). Adolescent internalizing symptoms and the "tightknittedness" of friendship groups. *Journal of Research on Adolescence, 30*(52), 391–402. https://doi.org/10.1111/jora.12484

Siennick, S. E., Widdowson, A. O., Woessner, M., & Feinberg, M. E. (2015). Internalizing symptoms, peer substance use, and substance use initiation. *Journal of Research on Adolescence, 26*(4), 645–657. https://doi.org/10.1111/jora.12215

Siennick, S. E., Widdowson, A. O., Woessner, M. K., Feinberg, M. E., & Spoth, R. L. (2016). Risk factors for substance misuse and adolescents' symptoms of depression. *Journal of Adolescent Health, 60*(1), 50–56. https://doi.org/10.1016/j.jadohealth.2016.08.010

Swannell, S. V., Martin, G. E., Page, A., Hasking, P., & St. John, N. J. (2014). Prevalence of nonsuicidal self-injury in nonclinical samples: Systematic review, meta-analysis and meta-regression. *Suicide and Life-Threatening Behavior, 44*(3), 273–303. https://doi.org/10.1111/sltb.12070

Ueno, K. (2005). The effects of friendship networks on adolescent depressive symptoms. *Social Science Research, 34*(3), 484–510. https://doi.org/10.1016/j.ssresearch.2004.03.002

Valente, T. W. (2010). *Social networks and health*. Oxford Press.

Veenstra, R., & Laninga-Wijnen, L. (2022). Peer network studies and interventions in adolescence. *Current Opinion in Psychology, 44*, 157–163. https://doi.org/10.1016/j.copsyc.2021.09.015

Walsh, B. W. (2006). *Treating self injury: A practical guide*. Guilford Press.

Wasserman, S. S., & Faust, K. (1994). *Social network analysis: Methods and applications* (vol. 8). Cambridge University Press.

Yang, Y., Chen, L. Zhang, L., Ji, L., & Zhang, W. (2020). Developmental changes in associations between depressive symptoms and peer relationships: A four-year follow-up of Chinese adolescents. *Journal of Youth and Adolescence, 49*(9), 1913–1927. https://doi.org/10.1007/s10964-020-01236-8

You, J., Zheng, C., Lin, M. P., & Leung, F. (2016). Peer group impulsivity moderated the individual-level relationship between depressive symptoms and adolescent nonsuicidal self-injury. *Journal of Adolescence, 47*, 90–99. https://doi.org/10.1016/j.adolescence.2015.12.008

8

The role of parenting in shaping the friendship context of adolescent substance use

KELLY L. RULISON, AVERY CHAHL, AND EVELIEN M. HOEBEN ■

INTRODUCTION

Parents and peers are arguably the two most important social contexts in adolescents' lives (Hawkins et al., 1992; Kandel, 1996; Trucco, 2020; Warr, 1993). For example, multiple parenting factors, such as favorable attitudes toward substance use, a lack of parental monitoring, and problematic parent-child relationships, are strongly linked to substance use and delinquency in adolescence (Hoeve et al., 2009; Pinquart, 2017; Steinberg, 2001; Yap et al., 2017). Further, as discussed throughout this volume, peers also play a central role in shaping adolescent substance use and other risk behaviors (also see Henneberger et al., 2021; Hoeben et al., 2016; Rulison et al., 2019). Most early research portrayed parents and peers as competing sources of influence, but there has been a growing recognition that in addition to their independent contributions, parents and peers jointly shape adolescent's lives (Brown & Bakken, 2011; Kandel, 1996; Ladd & Parke, 2021). For example, parents can shape who their children choose as friends and whether their children are susceptible to influence from these friends. In this chapter, we review research that explores how parents and peers interact to shape substance use during adolescence. We recognize that there are multiple adults who may serve as primary caregivers, including biological parents, adoptive parents, stepparents, foster parents, grandparents, or other guardians. For simplicity, we use the term *parents* throughout the chapter to refer collectively to all such core caregivers.

Kelly L. Rulison, Avery Chahl, and Evelien M. Hoeben, *The role of parenting in shaping the friendship context of adolescent substance use*. In: *Teen Friendship Networks, Development, and Risky Behavior*. Edited by: Mark E. Feinberg and D. Wayne Osgood, Oxford University Press. © Mark E. Feinberg and D. Wayne Osgood 2024.
DOI: 10.1093/oso/9780197602317.003.0008

In the following sections, we briefly review the existing literature about the link between parents and peers. Based on this review, we argue that there are at least three important ways through which parents shape the peer context of adolescent substance use: First, parents can directly shape their child's peer networks by influencing who adolescents select as friends and how much (unsupervised) time they spend with these friends. Second, parents can shape how susceptible their child is to influence from these friends. Third, parents can influence the behavior of their children's friends, much like neighbors or other adults in tight-knit communities can provide support as well as intervene if they observe adolescents engaging in unacceptable behavior (i.e., "It takes a village to raise a child"). After reviewing this literature, we discuss the findings from three empirical studies that tested research questions about how parents and peers interact to shape substance use. Specifically, these studies tested the extent to which parenting practices shape friendship selection and influence (Study 1) and the extent to which adolescents are shaped by the parenting practices of their *friends'* parents (Studies 2 and 3). These studies capitalized on the special strengths of the PROSPER (Promoting School-community-university Partnerships to Enhance Resilience) Peers data set as it is one of the few data sets that includes longitudinal measures of both parenting and friendship networks. Finally, we conclude the chapter with a brief discussion of future research questions that should be addressed and implications of this work for parents, prevention program developers, and policymakers.

HOW PARENTING SHAPES THE PEER CONTEXT OF ADOLESCENT SUBSTANCE USE

Parents shape who adolescents select as friends

As noted in Chapters 1 and 5, friendship selection is critical for shaping later substance use: adolescents who become friends with drug-using peers are in danger of being influenced by their friends' prodrug use attitudes and behaviors (Osgood et al., 2013). Therefore, one way that parents can steer their children away from substance use is by shaping who their children select as friends. Parental influence on friendship selection can be direct, such as when parents control the pool of available peers. Parents control this pool, for example, by deciding where to live, by limiting the amount of unsupervised time that adolescents get to spend with their peers, or by explicitly encouraging or discouraging certain friendships. Parental influence on friendship selection can also be indirect, such as when parents shape how adolescents interact with their friends or when parents shape their child's attitudes and behaviors, which in turn affects who their child selects as friends. We describe each of these processes in more detail below.

At the broadest level, many parents directly control the pool of potential friends by deciding where to live and which school the adolescent will attend (Kandel, 1996; Ladd & Parke, 2021; Mounts, 2000). For example, adolescents who live in neighborhoods with higher "collective efficacy" (i.e., close-knit neighborhoods where neighbors can be trusted and are likely to intervene if they observe children causing trouble; Sampson et al., 1997), and adolescents who live in more advantaged neighborhoods are less likely to be friends with deviant peers (Haynie et al., 2006; Tompsett et al., 2016). In addition, adolescents whose parents chose to live in their current neighborhood because it had good schools are less likely to have deviant friends and more likely to have prosocial friends (Knoester et al., 2006).

Of course, not all parents have equal opportunities to choose where they live, as many families are bound to certain locations due to income, employment, or existing social ties. There are other ways, however, in which all parents can directly control the pool of available peers. For example, parents can regulate their children's leisure activities, monitor their children's daily activities (Kerr & Stattin, 2000; Stattin & Kerr, 2000), and limit the amount of time that adolescents spend hanging out with peers in unsupervised, unstructured settings (Janssen et al., 2014). These unstructured settings not only provide opportunities for substance use to occur (Hoeben et al., 2016; Osgood et al., 1996), but also increase the chance that adolescents will meet substance-using peers (Felson, 2003; Hoeben & Weerman, 2016). Further, adolescents who spend less time in unstructured socializing are more likely to select friends from school or from other organized activity settings (e.g., team sports, performing arts). These friendships are more likely to be with well-adjusted peers (Eccles et al., 2003), whereas friendships formed in nonschool settings are more likely to be with substance-using or otherwise deviant peers (Dishion et al., 1995).

Another way that parents can directly control friendship selection is through "peer management" or "friendship facilitation" (Ladd & Parke, 2021; Mounts, 2000). For example, parents can forbid adolescents from spending time with specific friends who they consider to be bad influences, encourage adolescents to engage in activities with friends they consider to be positive influences, and share their opinions about their child's friends (Mounts, 2000). Although some regulation efforts, such as open conversation, can foster high-quality friendships (Mounts, 2004; Tu et al., 2017; Vernberg et al., 1993), prohibiting friendships can also have unintended effects. For example, adolescents who feel overcontrolled may seek out or maintain friendships with deviant peers, possibly as a way to rebel (Goldstein et al., 2005; Keijsers et al., 2012; Mounts, 2000; Tilton-Weaver et al., 2013).

Parents can also indirectly shape their children's friendships by affecting how adolescents interact with friends. The parent-child relationship lays the foundation for emotional and psychological development (e.g., emotional security, autonomy, cooperation), which then facilitates or constrains the types of relationships adolescents can form and maintain. Parents also affect adolescents' attitudes about what relationships should look like. Together, these factors can influence how adolescents establish and maintain friendships. For example, adolescents are more likely to form friendships with deviant peers if their parents are hostile or overprotective or if their parents use harsh discipline or withdrawal of affection to establish compliance (Simons et al., 2007; Soenens et al., 2009). By contrast, adolescents are less likely to form friendships with deviant peers if their parents are affectionate and use nonpunitive, compliance-gaining techniques (Deković et al., 2004; Soenens et al., 2009; Van Ryzin et al., 2012). Further, children who develop a secure attachment with their caregivers exhibit more social competence in their other relationships (Groh et al., 2014, 2017), which might make it easier for them to maintain friendships with prosocial peers.

Finally, parents can shape who adolescents select as friends by influencing their children's own attitudes and behavior (e.g., Rulison et al., 2016). As noted in Chapters 1 and 5, most people choose friends who are similar to themselves (also see McPherson et al., 2001). Indeed, adolescents often select friends whose substance use attitudes and behaviors match their own (Henneberger et al., 2021; Ivaniushina & Titkova, 2021; Ragan, 2014, 2016). Therefore, by engaging in parental practices that reduce substance use, parents make it less likely that their children will select—and in turn be influenced by—substance-using friends. Although a full review of how parents directly steer their children away from substance use is outside the scope of this chapter, briefly, parents can discourage substance use by monitoring adolescents' activities and whereabouts, by avoiding substance use themselves, by communicating disapproval of substance use, and by building strong, open, affectionate, noncontrolling relationships with their adolescent (see reviews by Lac Crano, 2009; Trucco, 2020; Yap et al., 2017). Parents can also promote adolescents' internalization of antisubstance use values by explaining why rules are necessary, by discussing how the adolescents' behaviors may affect others or affect their own future, and by using consistent and appropriate discipline (Grusec & Goodnow, 1994; Robichaud et al., 2020; Vansteenkiste et al., 2014).

Few studies have directly tested whether parenting practices influence friendship selection by shaping adolescents' own behaviors, but those that did have generally found support for this idea (e.g., Brown et al., 1993; Dishion, 1990). For example, positive parenting practices, such as acceptance, knowledge, consistent discipline, and cohesion, are linked to lower adolescent aggression, which in turn is linked to decreased association with deviant peers (Cashwell & Vacc, 1996). These links are similar for both European American and Latino adolescents (Padilla-Walker et al., 2011). Similarly, parental substance use is linked to adolescent substance use, which in turn increases the likelihood that adolescents have friends who smoke or drink (Engels et al., 1999).

Parents shape adolescents' susceptibility to peer influence

In addition to shaping friendship selection, there are multiple ways that parents can affect adolescents' susceptibility to influence from these friends. First, adolescents whose parents discourage substance use may develop strong moral objections to substance use. As a result, these adolescents may be less easily persuaded by their peers to use drugs (Gerstner & Oberwittler, 2018; Thomas & McCuddy, 2020; Wikstrom et al., 2012). Second, parental monitoring limits the amount of unsupervised time that adolescents spend with their peers (Janssen et al., 2014) and thus may also reduce opportunities for adolescents to be influenced by their peers. Third, adolescents whose parents encourage them to be self-sufficient and express themselves (i.e., "autonomy granting"; Silk et al., 2003) may think and act more independently in their relationship with peers, thereby reducing their susceptibility to peer influence. (Parents can nurture such autonomous development, for example, by including the adolescent in family decisions, acknowledging the adolescent's unique perspective, allowing the adolescent to make own decisions about activities, and encouraging the adolescent to voice their opinion even when different from that of the parents; Silk et al., 2003.) Research demonstrated that parental autonomy granting is indeed related to increased autonomy in peer relationships (Allen et al., 2012; Oudekerk et al., 2015). Fourth, parents can provide suggestions to adolescents about how to handle issues with their peers, thereby increasing adolescents' assertiveness in their interactions with peers (Mounts, 2011). Finally, adolescents who have stronger relationships with their parents may be less likely to engage in behaviors, such as substance use, that their parents might condemn, regardless of what their friends do (Hirschi, 1969; Stattin & Kerr, 2000). For example, one study found that adolescents who had more supportive maternal relationships were less influenced by their peers' substance use (Allen et al., 2012), suggesting that adolescents who have stronger relationships with their parents may be more concerned about gaining approval from their parents than they are about gaining approval from their peers.

Influence from friends' parents

Thus far, we have focused on how parents shape the peer context for their own children, in terms of both whom adolescents select as friends and the extent to which adolescents are influenced by these friends. Yet, as the saying "It takes a village to raise a child" indicates, adolescents are often influenced by the broader community. For example, adolescents often form connections to adults outside of their own family, including teachers, neighbors, and family friends, each of whom can invest in the adolescent, encourage norms about positive behaviors, and share information (i.e., "bridging social capital"; Dufur et al., 2019; Putnam, 2000). These adults also have a role in monitoring adolescents' activities and intervening in unwanted behavior, thereby steering adolescents away from substance use and delinquency (Sampson & Groves, 1989; Shaw & McKay, 1969; Simons & Burt, 2011).

Building on this idea, an often overlooked way that parents can affect adolescent substance use is by shaping the behavior of their children's friends. When parents know the parents of their children's friends ("intergenerational closure"; Coleman, 1990), they can reinforce shared values and exchange information. Our team has argued, however, that parents do not necessarily need to interact, or even know each other, in order to influence their children's friends (Ragan et al., 2014). Instead, there are multiple processes through which adolescents can be influenced by their friends' parents. We outline three of these processes below.

Social learning by observing friends interact with their parents. To start, adolescents may be directly influenced by the parenting practices (e.g., consistent discipline) used by their friends' parents. Most adolescents (>90%) report knowing at least some of their friends' parents (Fletcher et al., 1995), suggesting that adolescents likely interact at least occasionally with their friends' parents. These interactions allow adolescents to observe interactions between their friends and their friends' parents. Importantly, adolescents learn behavior by watching others, such as observing what behaviors are rewarded or punished (Bandura, 1971; Burgess & Akers, 1966; Crick & Dodge, 1994; Sutherland, 1947). Although most work emphasizes how adolescents learn by observing their friends or parents, they could also learn by observing how friends' parents respond to friends' behavior (Ragan et al., 2014; Simons & Burt, 2011). Adolescents who observe their friends repeatedly getting away with inappropriate behaviors may decide that such behaviors are inconsequential. By contrast, adolescents who observe their friends' parents consistently and firmly punishing inappropriate behaviors may decide that these behaviors are undesirable. Further, by observing interactions between their friends and friends' parents, adolescents might refine their perceptions of what relationships should look like. For example, adolescents often apply communication patterns that they develop at home to their interactions with peers (Black, 2002; Herrera & Dunn, 1997). It is plausible that adolescents would similarly imitate communication patterns they have observed between their friends and friends' parents, affecting adolescents' ability to maintain friendships with prosocial peers as well as their susceptibility to influence from deviant peers.

Parental monitoring by friends' parents: it takes a village. Adolescents also may be directly influenced by the monitoring activities of their friend's parents. Support for this idea comes from studies that have linked community- and school-level characteristics with adolescent outcomes. At the community level, higher rates of "collective efficacy"—the ability and willingness of adults to exert social control in their community—are strongly linked with lower rates of adolescent delinquency, crime, and violence (Maimon & Browning, 2010; Pratt & Cullen, 2005; Simons & Burt, 2011). It has been theorized that this community-level supervision is facilitated by stable connections among adults, mutual trust, and shared expectations (Sampson et al., 1997) because adults may be more willing to step in when they believe that other community members would approve of such intervention (Sampson, 2012; Warner & Sampson, 2017). Further, low collective efficacy can weaken the effects of positive parenting practices, as adolescents who report low collective efficacy in the neighborhood are more likely to be delinquent and to have deviant peers, even if their parents engage in positive parenting practices (Simons et al., 2005). At the school level, one study demonstrated that in schools with higher rates of parental knowledge, adolescents reported less unstructured socializing, which in turn was linked with lower rates of delinquency (Osgood & Anderson, 2004). This effect suggests that it matters what other parents in the community are doing: parents' supervision likely extend to their child's peers when their child spends time with these peers. Alternatively, if parents do not supervise their child, they may enable their child's peers to spend more unsupervised time in unstructured activities.

Parents can raise adolescents who positively influence their friends. Adolescents do not necessarily need to interact with their friends' parents in order to be influenced by them; instead, there could be an indirect effect of friends' parents on an adolescent's substance use. As noted previously, parents play a critical role in shaping adolescents' behaviors (Lac & Crano, 2009; Steinberg, 2001; Trucco, 2020; Yap et al., 2017), and adolescents, in turn, play a critical role in shaping their friends' behaviors (Henneberger et al., 2021; Hoeben et al., 2016; Rulison et al., 2019; Trucco, 2020). Therefore, when many of an adolescent's friends experience positive parenting practices, these friends will be less likely to use substances, meaning that the adolescent will have fewer friends who can influence them toward substance use. Support for this idea comes from one of the few studies that has directly looked at the effect of friends' parents on adolescents' substance use (Fletcher et al., 1995). In that study, friends' substance use fully explained the link between network authoritativeness (defined as the number of friends whose parents were responsive, engaged in monitoring, and used noncoercive discipline) and adolescent's substance use.

In sum, the parenting practices that friends experience may be either directly linked to adolescent substance use or they may be indirectly linked to adolescent substance use by first shaping friends' substance use. Further, parenting practices experienced by friends may also amplify or cancel the effects of the parenting practices that adolescents experience at home (Fletcher et al., 1995). For example, an *amplification effect* would be evident if adolescents who already experience positive parenting practices at home might benefit most when their friends' also experience positive parenting practices at home. Alternatively, a countermanding effect would be evident if adolescents who experience negative parenting practices at home might benefit most by exposure to positive parenting practices from their friends' parents.

EMPIRICAL FINDINGS FROM THE PROSPER PEERS PROJECT

In the previous sections, we hypothesized that there are at least three key ways through which parents might affect adolescents' peer context and thereby their likelihood of using drugs. Testing these hypotheses requires a data set that includes measures of both parent and peer relationships. Such data sets are scarce, particularly those that measure both of these relationships over time. The PROSPER Peers data are therefore exceptionally suitable to test how parents and peers interact to shape adolescent substance use. In the following sections, we illustrate the usefulness of these data by summarizing the methods and key results of three studies. Table 8.1 provides an overview and comparison of all three studies. Briefly, the first study (Hoeben et al., 2021) tested the extent to which parenting practices shaped friendship selection and influence. The second and third studies

Table 8.1 SUMMARY OF THREE PROSPER PEERS STUDIES THAT TESTED HOW PARENTS AND PEERS INTERACT TO SHAPE SUBSTANCE USE

Study	Specific research questions	Measures	Key findings
To what extent do parents shape friendship selection and influence with respect to substance use?			
Hoeben et al., 2021	1. Do adolescents select friends who experience similar parenting practices as they do (i.e., homophily with respect to parenting practices)? 2. Do parenting practices shape whether adolescents select alcohol-using peers as friends? 3. Do parenting practices shape whether adolescents are influenced by their friends' alcohol use?	IV = Adolescent's own parental knowledge, parental discipline, and unsupervised time spent with friends DV = Past month alcohol use (0 = no use, 1 = 1 time, 2 = 2+ times)	1. Adolescents select friends who experience similar parenting practices. 2. Adolescents who reported consistent parental discipline and adolescents who spent less unsupervised time with friends were less likely to befriend alcohol-using peers. 3. Adolescents who reported consistent parental discipline and better parental knowledge were more likely to be influenced by their friends' level of alcohol use.
To what extent do *friends'* parents shape adolescent substance use?			
Cleveland et al., 2012	1. Do collective parenting practices within an adolescent's friendship group predict the adolescent's own substance use? 2. Do collective parenting practices within an adolescent's friendship group amplify or cancel the effects of adolescents' own reports of parenting practices? 3. To what extent does friends' substance use explain the link between friends' parenting practices and adolescent's substance use?	IV = Average (a) parental knowledge, (b) inconsistent discipline, and (c) inductive reasoning reported by members of an adolescent's friendship group DV = Past month alcohol use, drunkenness, cigarette use, and marijuana use (0 = no use, 1 = any use)	1. Friendship groups' higher average parental knowledge and lower average inconsistent discipline predicted lower substance use. 2. Better parental knowledge and discipline in the friendship group primarily benefited adolescents with more positive parenting practices (i.e., amplification effect). 3. Friends' substance use fully explained the link between friends' parenting practices and both alcohol use and drunkenness, but only partially explained the link between friends' parenting practices and both cigarette and marijuana use.

(*continued*)

Table 8.1 CONTINUED

Study	Specific research questions	Measures	Key findings
Ragan et al., 2014	1. Are there direct effects of friends' parenting practices on adolescent's alcohol use? 2. Can friends' alcohol use explain the link between friends' parenting practices and adolescent's alcohol use?	IV = Average (a) parental knowledge and (b) inconsistent discipline reported by friends DV = Past month alcohol use (0 = no use, 1 = 1 time, 2 = 2+ times)	1. Friends' higher average parental knowledge and lower average inconsistent discipline predicted lower alcohol use. 2. Friends' alcohol use partially explained the link between friends' parenting practices and alcohol use.

IV = independent variable and DV = dependent variable.

(Cleveland et al., 2012; Ragan et al., 2014) tested the extent to which friends' parents shaped adolescents' substance use.

Study 1: To what extent do parents shape friendship selection and influence?

In a study by Hoeben and colleagues (2021), our team tested whether three parenting practices—parental knowledge, parental discipline, and unsupervised time with friends—led some adolescents to avoid friendships with alcohol-using peers and whether these same parenting practices protected adolescents from being influenced by their friends' alcohol use. Building on past research, our team hypothesized that adolescents who reported more consistent discipline from their parents, adolescents who reported more parental knowledge, and adolescents who spent less unsupervised time with their friends would be less likely to befriend alcohol-using peers and that they would be less susceptible to influence from these friends. Although it was not the central focus of the study, the team also tested whether adolescents selected friends who were more similar to themselves with respect to parenting behaviors.

Sample. This study used data from the middle six waves of PROSPER Peers, when adolescents were in 6th to 11th grade; data from the first wave was dropped because it was the only wave that occurred during the fall semester, and data from the final wave was dropped as participation rates in 12th grade were lower than at the other waves. A total of 46 networks were included in the analysis. (These analyses excluded one district [two networks] because a fire created a chaotic pattern of school transitions that could not be easily modeled within our analytic approach, one network that was missing a wave of data, and five networks that did not achieve acceptable convergence for one or more of our models.) The final analytic sample was 12,335 adolescents who completed one or more surveys during these six waves.

Measures. This study used three measures to capture parenting practices: *parental knowledge* (i.e., adolescent reports about how much their parents know what they are doing and who they are with); *consistent discipline* (e.g., "When my parents ask me to do something and I don't do it right away, they give up"; "When I do something wrong, my parents lose their temper and yell at me," recoded so that higher scores indicated more consistent, less harsh discipline); and *unsupervised time with friends* (maximum amount of time spent with any friend "just hanging around outside of school without adults around"). This study also used adolescents' reports about how often they drank alcohol in the past month; their responses were recoded so that 0 = no alcohol use, 1 = used alcohol once in the past month, and 2 = used alcohol two or more times in the past month.

Analytic plan. To test the research questions, the team used RSiena to estimate separate models for each of the parenting practices. Each model included a "parenting ego by alcohol alter" interaction term to test whether adolescents who reported better parenting practices (e.g., more parental knowledge) were less likely to select alcohol-using friends. Each model also included a "parenting ego by average friends' alcohol use" interaction term to test whether adolescents who reported better parenting practices were less likely to be influenced by their friends' alcohol use. As with other RSiena models used within PROSPER Peers (see Chapter 3), the network models used in this study controlled for structural parameters (e.g., out-degree, reciprocity, transitive triplets), along with alter, ego, and selection effects for gender, race, and alcohol use. The behavioral models controlled for gender, race/ethnicity, and living with both biological parents. In addition, all models controlled for the ego, alter, and selection effects due to parenting practices and the effect of parenting practices on alcohol use. The team estimated a separate model for each network and then aggregated the results using a three-level, hierarchal, linear meta-analysis, with network parameters nested within grade cohorts (Level 2), which were nested within school districts (Level 3).

Results and interpretation. In general, the results suggested that parenting practices shaped who adolescents selected as friends. First, as hypothesized, adolescents who reported more consistent parental discipline and adolescents who spent less unsupervised time with friends were less likely to select alcohol-using peers as friends (see Figures 8.1A and 8.1B). Contrary to expectations, however, parental knowledge did not affect the likelihood of selecting alcohol-using peers as friends. Second, there was consistent evidence that adolescents were drawn to peers who experienced similar parenting practices: adolescents were significantly more likely to select friends who reported similar parental knowledge ($OR = 1.10$), parental discipline ($OR = 1.14$), and time spent with friends ($OR = 1.12$) than they were to select friends who differed on these characteristics. Finally, all three parenting practices shaped alcohol use directly: Those who reported experiencing more consistent discipline and greater parental knowledge

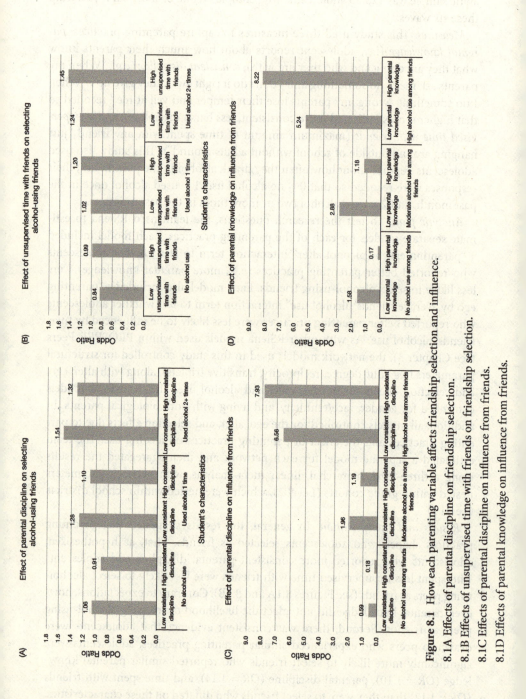

Figure 8.1 How each parenting variable affects friendship selection and influence.
8.1A Effects of parental discipline on friendship selection.
8.1B Effects of unsupervised time with friends on friendship selection.
8.1C Effects of parental discipline on influence from friends.
8.1D Effects of parental knowledge on influence from friends.

were less likely to use alcohol, whereas those who spent more unsupervised time with peers were more likely to use alcohol. Because adolescents selected friends who reported similar levels of alcohol use (or nonuse), these results suggest that by engaging in behaviors that directly shape alcohol use, parents can also indirectly affect who their child selects as friends. For example, adolescents whose parents had better knowledge of their whereabouts were less likely to use alcohol, which in turn meant they were less likely to befriend alcohol-using peers. Thus, the study offers support for an indirect effect of parenting on friend selection through shaping adolescents' own substance use.

Not only did the examined parenting practices shape who adolescents selected as friends, but also shaped extent to which adolescents were influenced by these friends. The "parental discipline ego by friends' alcohol use" and "parental knowledge ego by friends' alcohol use" interaction terms were significantly linked to adolescent's alcohol use. Plots of these interactions (see Figures 8.1C and 8.1D) indicated that the direction of these effects was opposite of what our team had hypothesized: adolescents who experienced more consistent discipline and those who reported more parental knowledge were *more* (instead of less) likely to be influenced by their friends' level of alcohol use. At first glance, these results seem to suggest that more positive parenting practices may be counterproductive, as adolescents who reported more consistent discipline and those who reported higher parental knowledge became more likely to use alcohol when they had many alcohol-using friends. At the same time, however, this greater susceptibility to peer influence was actually *protective* for adolescents whose friends did not drink or drank very little: among these adolescents, those who experienced more positive parenting practices were less likely to drink, as their non-drinking or moderately drinking friends influenced them away from alcohol use.

Taken together, these results suggest that parenting practices shape both peer selection and peer influence processes. Positive parenting practices reduce the likelihood that adolescents will befriend alcohol-using peers. For example, among adolescents who experienced high consistent discipline, only 6.6% (sixth grade) to 16.0% (11th grade) had friends with a high average level of alcohol use. At the same time, such practices can increase susceptibility to peer influence once friendships are formed. Whether this increased susceptibility is beneficial or harmful depends on the characteristics of the friends. Specifically, it seems that parents who use consistent discipline and who ensure that adolescents do not spend much unsupervised time with friends can limit the adolescent's exposure to risky peer contexts by making it less likely for them to befriend alcohol-using peers. In turn, consistent discipline and parental knowledge interact with friends' characteristics such that adolescents with few or no alcohol-using friends are then influenced *away* from alcohol use by these friends. By contrast, adolescents who do select many alcohol-using friends are at increased risk of alcohol use when their parents exert consistent discipline and have greater knowledge about their activities. Notably, this increased risk was substantially weaker than the protective effect of greater susceptibility to positive peer influence among adolescents with few to no alcohol-using friends. Further, very few adolescents fell in the category of both experiencing positive parenting practices and having friends with high average levels of alcohol use: under 2.5% for consistent discipline across waves and under 3.3% for parental knowledge. Still, future studies should explore why positive parenting practices may be counterproductive for adolescents who select alcohol-using peers as friends and identify ways to counteract this pull toward higher alcohol use.

Study 2

The nature of the PROSPER Peers data, particularly the availability of close to complete network information, also allowed our team to explore the extent to which friends' parents shaped adolescent substance use. In Study 2 (Cleveland et al., 2012), our team tested whether the collective parenting practices among members of an adolescent's friendship group in ninth grade predicted the adolescent's own substance use in 10th grade. In Study 3 (Ragan et al., 2014), our team extended this work by testing whether the collective parenting practices among all of an adolescent's friends predicted the adolescent's own alcohol use from sixth to ninth grade.

In the first of these two studies, our team examined three specific research questions about the extent to which 10th graders were influenced by the collective parenting practices within their friendship group assessed a year earlier (Cleveland et al., 2012). First, we tested whether these collective parenting practices predicted the adolescent's own substance use a year later, over and above the effect that the adolescent's own parents had on their substance use. We hypothesized that more positive parenting practices within the adolescent's friendship group would be linked to lower rates of substance use. Second, we tested whether the collective parenting practices within an adolescent's friendship group interacted with their own parents' behaviors to shape substance use: In other words, do more positive parenting practices experienced by members of an adolescent's friendship group mostly benefit adolescents who already experience positive parenting practices at home (i.e., an amplification effect) or can they protect adolescents from substance use even if their own parents engage in negative parenting practices (i.e., a countermanding effect)? Finally, we tested the extent to which friends' substance use explained the link between collective parenting practices within the friendship group and adolescent's substance use (i.e., whether friends' parents had a direct effect on adolescent substance use or whether the effect was indirect, driven by friends' parents shaping friends' behaviors).

Sample. This study used data from Waves 5 and 6 of PROSPER Peers, when adolescents were in 9th and 10th grade. A total of 10,359 adolescents completed surveys in ninth grade. Given that the focus was on how friendship *groups* shaped substance use, we excluded 426 adolescents who were isolates (i.e., had no friends) and 352 adolescents who were liaisons (i.e., belonged to more than one group) from the analyses. In addition, we excluded adolescents who were in groups with more than 40 members, as the meaning of a "group" is likely different within such large groups. The final analytic sample was 7,439 adolescents who were in a friendship group in 9th grade and provided data in 10th grade.

Measures. This study used a variant of Moody's (2001) CROWDS algorithm to identify distinct friendship groups that prioritized friendship ties within groups over friendship ties between groups (see also Chapter 4 and Kreager et al., 2011). The study also used three adolescent-reported measures about parenting practices: *parental knowledge, inconsistent discipline,* and *inductive reasoning* (e.g., "My parents give me reasons for their decisions"). Finally, the study included adolescent-reported measures about the extent to which they drank alcohol, got drunk, smoked any cigarettes, and smoked marijuana in the past month. Each measure was dichotomized so that 0 = no use and 1 = any use.

Analytic plan. This study used three-level hierarchical linear models to account for the nesting of 7,439 adolescents (Level 1) within 897 friendship groups (Level 2), which were nested within 54 school cohorts (Level 3). Our team estimated a separate model for each substance use outcome. The key predictor variables in each model were the three measures of friends' collective parenting practices, computed as the average parenting practices reported by members of the friendship group (e.g., average parental knowledge reported by everyone in the friendship group). Each model also controlled for the adolescent's own report of each parenting practice, the adolescent's gender, and their ninth-grade substance use at Level 1 and treatment assignment at Level 3. Initially, the models included interactions between the parenting measures and both gender and treatment, but the final models excluded these interactions because they were not significant. We estimated a second series of models to test whether friends' substance use could explain the relationship between collective parenting among friends and adolescent's substance use (i.e., whether friends' parenting practices had an indirect effect on adolescents' substance use through their friends' substance use). In these models, we added friends' ninth-grade substance use as an additional Level 2 predictor variable.

Results and interpretation. As hypothesized, the first series of models demonstrated that the average level of parental knowledge among an adolescent's friendship group predicted lower use across all four drugs ($OR = 0.38$ for marijuana use to $OR = 0.60$ for alcohol use); these effects occurred even after controlling for the effect of adolescent's own reported parental knowledge on their substance use, which was also significant. In addition, the average level of inconsistent discipline among an adolescent's friendship group predicted higher alcohol use ($OR = 1.31$), cigarette use ($OR = 1.83$), and marijuana use ($OR = 1.86$). Contrary to expectation, however, neither average inductive reasoning experienced within the friendship group nor the adolescent's own experienced inductive reasoning predicted any of the substance use outcomes. Cross-level interactions between an adolescent's own reported parenting practices and friendship groups' parenting practices indicated support for an amplification effect but not for a countermanding effect. Specifically, the findings indicated that alcohol use and marijuana use were higher if *either* adolescents or their friendship group reported low parental knowledge. For example, as shown in Figure 8.2A, adolescents were more likely to use alcohol

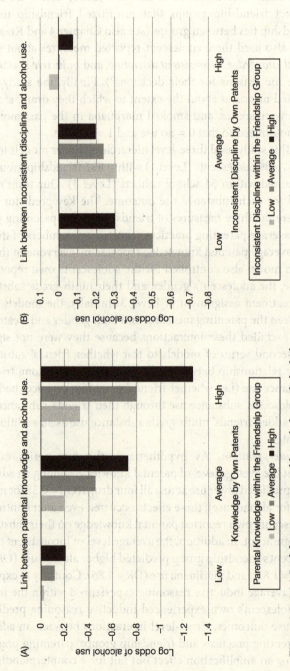

Figure 8.2 8.2A Link between parental knowledge and alcohol use. 8.2B Link between inconsistent discipline and alcohol use.

if they themselves reported low parental knowledge (i.e., the three bars on the left had the highest log odds of alcohol use) or if their friendship group reported low parental knowledge (i.e., light gray bars). In other words, better parental knowledge within the friendship group, while having a small protective effect against substance use, was insufficient to overcome the negative effect of limited knowledge of adolescents' own parents. Similarly, alcohol use was higher if *either* the adolescent or their friendship group reported more inconsistent discipline (Figure 8.2B). These results suggest an amplification effect in which more positive parenting practices among the adolescent's friendship group mostly benefited adolescents who already experienced positive parenting practices at home.

The second series of models demonstrated that much of the effect of friendship group parenting practices on alcohol use and drunkenness could be explained by friends' substance use. Specifically, after controlling for friends' substance use, neither friendship groups' parental knowledge nor their inconsistent discipline significantly predicted adolescents' alcohol use or drunkenness. By contrast, the effects of friendship groups' average levels of parental knowledge and inconsistent discipline still had significant direct effects on cigarette and marijuana use, even though friends' substance use reduced the effects of parenting practices on these substance use behaviors by 14%–40%.

Taken together, the findings from this study indicated that friends' parents matter: the average parenting behaviors within an adolescent's friendship group predicted changes in substance use from 9th to 10th grade. The pattern of results suggests that much of the effect of friends' parents may occur by shaping friends' substance use, although friends' reported parental knowledge and inconsistent discipline appeared to also independently shape adolescents' substance use, over and above the effect that these parenting practices had on their friends' substance use. Importantly, problematic parenting practices either in the adolescent's own family or among their friends' parents can increase the risk of alcohol use and, to a lesser extent, marijuana use; it did not appear that positive parenting at one level fully compensated for the risk of poor parenting practices at the other level. That is, both individual and friendship group parenting practices shaped adolescent substance use. Further, it appeared that positive parenting practices within the friendship group had a larger benefit for adolescents who already experienced more positive parenting practices at home (i.e., an amplification effect).

Study 3

In Study 3 (Ragan et al., 2014), our team extended the findings from the Cleveland et al. (2012) study in several ways. First, this study used data from all friends that adolescents reported, rather than just friendships in the adolescent's bounded friendship group. This approach allowed us to test influence from *all* friends rather than just influence from friendship group members. This approach also allowed us to include adolescents who were not in friendship groups (i.e., isolates), those who bridged multiple friendship groups (i.e., liaisons), and those who were members of extremely large groups; all of these adolescents had been excluded from the previous study. Second, this study used a different analytic approach, which controlled for structural network effects and friendship selection processes that had not been addressed before. Third, this study focused on changes from 6th to 9th grade, whereas the earlier study only focused on changes between 9th and 10th grade. Importantly, these changes allowed us to test whether the stability of our findings persisted across different definitions of the peer group (i.e., friendship group vs. dyadic friendships) and across a longer developmental period.

Sample. This study used data from the first five waves of PROSPER Peers, when adolescents were in sixth–ninth grade. Any adolescent who completed a survey at least once during these waves was included in the analyses, and adolescents were included as part of the network for any wave in which they were enrolled in the school. Over 12,000 adolescents from 48 networks were included in the analysis, with approximately 8,600 adolescents providing data at each wave.

Measures. Collective parenting among an adolescent's friends was measured as the average *parental knowledge* and average *inconsistent discipline* reported by the adolescent's friends. This study also used adolescent's reports about how often in the past month they drank alcohol, recoded so that 0 = no alcohol use, 1 = used alcohol once in the past month, and 2 = used alcohol two or more times in the past month.

Analytic plan. This study used SIENA to test the research questions. Our team estimated two models for each of the parenting behaviors. Model 1 included collective parenting practices as the key predictor of an adolescent's alcohol use. Model 2 then added the average alcohol use among an adolescent's friends to determine the extent to which the link between friends' parenting practices and adolescent's alcohol use could be attributed to friends' alcohol use. Our team first estimated these models separately for each parenting practice, then estimated models that included both parenting practices in the same model. As with other SIENA models used within PROSPER Peers, the network models used here controlled for structural parameters (e.g., out-degree, reciprocity, transitive triplets), along with alter, ego, and selection effects for gender, race, and alcohol use. The behavioral side of the models controlled for gender, race, living with both biological parents, school adjustment and bonding, and risk and sensation seeking. Each model also controlled for the ego, alter, and selection effects for each parenting practice and the effect of the corresponding parenting practice on substance use. We estimated separate models for each of the 48 school/grade networks and then aggregated the results using a three-level, hierarchal, linear meta-analysis, with network parameters nested within grade cohorts (Level 2), which were nested within school districts (Level 3).

Results and interpretation. The results provided evidence of both direct and indirect effects of friends' parenting practices on adolescent alcohol use. Specifically, both collective parental knowledge experienced among friends and collective parental discipline experienced among friends predicted adolescent's own alcohol use, even after controlling for the effect of the parenting practices of each adolescent's own parents on their substance use. Specifically, adolescents whose friends reported better parental knowledge (i.e., their parents knew where they and who they spent time with were) were less likely to drink, as were adolescents whose friends reported that their parents used more consistent discipline. Unlike the previous study (Cleveland et al., 2012), these effects were only partially reduced, and not eliminated, when friends' average alcohol use was added to the model. In other words, friends' alcohol use only partially explained the relationship between the parenting experienced by friends and adolescent's own alcohol use. The differences in results between these two studies likely reflects the greater power within Study 3, which used more waves of data, although it could also reflect differences between friendship groups and dyadic friendships.

When both parenting practices were included together in the model, friends' parental knowledge remained a strong predictor of adolescent's alcohol use, even after controlling for friends' alcohol use. The effect for friends' parental discipline, however, was reduced considerably and only marginally significant in the model without friends' alcohol use. Further, the effect of friends' parental discipline on adolescents' alcohol use was no longer statistically significant after friends' alcohol use was added to the model.

In sum, these results provided support for several of the proposed mechanisms through which friends' parents shape alcohol use. First, the direct effect of collective parental knowledge on adolescent's alcohol use suggested that friends' parents may limit opportunities for drinking to occur; by knowing where their child is, and perhaps by limiting how much unsupervised time their child can spend with peers, friends' parents may make it more difficult for adolescents to find opportunities to drink. Second, there was evidence that at least some of the effect of friends' parents on adolescent's alcohol use can be explained by the link between friends' parenting practices and friends' alcohol use. In other words, positive parenting practices can reduce friends' alcohol use, which in turn means that there are fewer friends within the peer network who can influence an adolescent toward alcohol use. Notably, there was less support of direct influence from adolescents observing how their friends' parents interact with their friends, at least in terms of parental discipline, as this effect was limited after controlling for the parental knowledge experienced among friends. Importantly, all of these effects occurred even after controlling for adolescent's tendency to select peers who are similar to themselves with respect to a range of demographic and behavioral characteristics. Therefore, the effect of friends' parents was established over and above any effects the parents had on who their child selected as friends.

CONCLUSION

Parents and peers are two of the most important social contexts in adolescents' lives, yet their effect on adolescent behavior is often examined in isolation. It is becoming increasingly clear, however, that the influence of these groups on adolescent behavior is not independent: parents and peers exert unique as well as joint influences on adolescents' development (Allen et al., 2012; Brown & Bakken, 2011; Collins et al., 2000; Kandel, 1996; Ladd & Parke, 2021; Tilton-Weaver et al., 2013).

Our work with the PROSPER Peers data provided consistent support for the argument that influences from parents and peers intersect to shape adolescent substance use. Enabled by the rare combination of longitudinal parenting measures and longitudinal friendship network data, our team demonstrated that parents shape not only who adolescents choose to befriend but also the extent to which adolescents are influenced by the friends that they choose (Hoeben et al., 2021). In addition, because we had close to complete network data, our team was able to demonstrate that friends link adolescents to the influence of adults outside of their own immediate family; these findings were consistent irrespective of whether the focus was on friendship groups (Cleveland et al., 2012) or on all friendships (Ragan et al., 2014). Another notable strength of our work is that it included a measure of consistent discipline. By contrast, much of the existing work on how parents and peers jointly influence substance use has focused on parental monitoring or knowledge (e.g., Becerra et al., 2014; Giannotta et al., 2011; McAdams et al., 2014; Pesola et al., 2015; Schofield et al., 2015), but our findings demonstrated that other parenting practices that are known to shape adolescent substance use may also be important in shaping the peer context. These findings are also consistent with emerging literature suggesting that factors such as parents' substance use behaviors can predict adolescents' own substance use behaviors (Mercken et al., 2013; Wang et al., 2015).

Future research

The three studies described here helped to clarify how parents and peers work together to shape adolescent substance use. Going forward, however, more research is needed to extend the current findings. First, in our literature review as well as in the three empirical studies that we described, we focused on parents and friends, but other family members (e.g., siblings) and other types of peer relationships (e.g., romantic partners) also play important roles in adolescents' lives (Ardelt & Day, 2002; Brechwald & Prinstein, 2011; Rogers et al., 2021). Therefore, future work should explore how these different family members and peer groups interact to jointly influence adolescent substance use. Similarly, most adolescents who participated in PROSPER were white adolescents living in lower to middle class rural communities. Although past studies have used diverse samples to test research questions about the parent-peer linkages, studies rarely compare results across contexts within the same study. Future work should explore how the parent and peer context interact across different social classes, cultural groups, and neighborhood contexts (Brown & Bakken, 2011), as all of these contexts shape how much autonomy parents can appropriately grant to adolescents (Hill et al., 2007).

Second, future studies should explore how interactions between parents and peers change across adolescence. Just as the strength of peer influence varies across age (Blakemore & Mills, 2014; see also Chapter 5), so might the effects of parenting practices on the peer context. For example, monitoring by adolescents' own parents appears to play a stronger role in influencing behavior during early adolescence compared to later adolescence (Cleveland et al., 2008; Fagan et al., 2011; Mak et al., 2020).

Third, following the adage "it takes a village," future work should continue to explore the extent to which school-wide and community-wide parenting shape adolescent substance use. This work should also explore which processes can explain these links, such as norm internalization (Bandura, 1971; Crick & Dodge, 1994); views of relationships (Simons & Burt, 2011); shaping leisure activities (Osgood & Anderson, 2004); or amplification effects (Simons et al., 2005).

Fourth, in our studies, we focused exclusively on how parenting can shape the peer context; yet, some have argued that the peer context could also influence parenting behaviors and the parent-child relationship (e.g., Kandel, 1996). For example, one study found evidence of bidirectional longitudinal effects between parental knowledge and amount of time spent with peers (Reitz et al., 2007). Another study found that adolescents who reported experiencing peer victimization were less likely to report positive support from their parents 1 year later (Wright, 2016). Further research is needed to clarify when and how friendships with deviant peers affect parenting practices and the parent-child relationship.

Finally, future work should clarify the meaning of different parenting measures to understand why they are linked with adolescent substance use. For example, Stattin and Kerr (2000; Kerr & Stattin, 2000) argued that measures of "parental monitoring" were better described as parental knowledge, which can result from both active parental monitoring and children's spontaneous disclosure of information. In other words, not only might parents' monitoring behaviors shape substance use, but also adolescents who tend to disclose information about their whereabouts to parents may be less likely to use substances. Similarly, the amount of unsupervised time that adolescents spend with peers may result from not only parents successfully implementing rules to monitor their children, but also adolescents' willingness to cooperate with such rules (Forgatch & DeGarmo, 1999; McCann et al., 2019). Importantly, adolescents' willingness to cooperate likely depends on their relationship with their parents, as well as their desire to spend time with peers away from supervision, which might be stronger if they engage in activities such as substance use that they wish to hide from their parents. Future research should attempt to disentangle the extent to which "parenting" measures capture parenting behavior alone versus a combination of parenting behavior and adolescents' own characteristics.

Implications

Parents. One implication from our work is that even though youth begin spending more time with their peers during adolescence, parents continue to matter. Indeed, parents continue to shape attitudes and behavior even as adolescents enter college (e.g., Rulison et al., 2016). In addition to directly affecting their children's behavior, parents can shape adolescent substance use by influencing the peer context. For example, parents can shape who their children befriend by choosing where to live and where to send their children to school, by encouraging their children to avoid certain friends, and by shaping their child's characteristics, which in turn can affect who the adolescent selects as friends. Parents also affect the extent to which their children are influenced by their friends' substance use. In sum, results from past research as well as from our own work suggest that parents should develop an affectionate, open, and supportive relationship with their adolescent, provide autonomy while also monitoring their adolescent, and use consistent discipline. By engaging in these positive parenting practices, parents can guide adolescents toward befriending prosocial peers, who can in turn help steer adolescents away from substance use and other risk behaviors.

Program developers and researchers. Another implication from our work is that family-based interventions should continue to focus on parenting practices, such as teaching parents to provide "love and limits," as is done by the Strengthening Families Program for Parents and Youth 10-14 (see Chapter 2; also see Molgaard et al., 1987, 1997). A second implication is that when evaluating the impact of intervention programs, prevention scientists should evaluate not only the direct effect of parenting practices on an adolescents' behavior, but also whether these parenting practices shape the peer context and whether they shape *friends'* behaviors (see Chapter 11). Further work that clarifies how parenting practices shape the peer context could help researchers trace how existing interventions lead to changes in substance use and how such effects could be magnified.

REFERENCES

Allen, J. P., Chango, J., Szwedo, D., Schad, M., & Marston, E. (2012). Predictors of susceptibility to peer influence regarding substance use in adolescence. *Child Development*, 83, 337–350. https://doi.org/10.1111/j.1467-8624.2011.01682.x

Ardelt, M., & Day, L. (2002). Parents, siblings, and peers: Close social relationships and adolescent deviance. *Journal of Early Adolescence*, 22(3), 310–349. https://doi.org/10.1177/02731602022003004

Bandura, A. (1971). *Social learning theory*. General Learning Corporation.

Becerra, D., Castillo, J. T., Ayón, C., & Blanchard, K. N. (2014). The moderating role of parental monitoring on the influence of peer pro-drug norms on alcohol and cigarette use among adolescents in Mexico. *Journal of Child & Adolescent Substance Abuse*, 23(5), 297–306. https://doi.org/10.1080/1067828X.2013.869138

Black, K. A. (2002). Associations between adolescent-mother and adolescent-best friend interactions. *Adolescence*, 37(146), 235–253.

Blakemore, S.-J., & Mills, K. L. (2014). Is adolescence a sensitive period for sociocultural processing? *Annual Review of Psychology*, 65, 187–207. https://doi.org/10.1146/annurev-psych-010213-115202

Brechwald, W. A., & Prinstein, M. J. (2011). Beyond homophily: A decade of advances in understanding peer influence processes. *Journal of Research on Adolescence*, 21, 166–179. https://doi.org/10.1111/j.1532-7795.2010.00721.x

Brown, B. B., & Bakken, J. P. (2011). Parenting and peer relationships: Reinvigorating research on family–peer linkages in adolescence. *Journal of Research on Adolescence*, *21*(1), 153–165. https://doi.org/10.1111/j.1532-7795.2010.00720.x

Brown, B. B., Mounts, N., Lamborn, S. D., & Steinberg, L. (1993). Parenting practices and peer group affiliation in adolescence. *Child Development*, *64*, 467–482. https://doi.org/10.1111/j.1467-8624.1993.tb02922.x

Burgess, R. L., & Akers, R. L. (1966). A differential association-reinforcement theory of criminal behavior. *Social Problems*, *14*(2), 128–147.

Cashwell, C. S., & Vacc, N. A. (1996). Family functioning and risk behaviors: Influences on adolescent delinquency. *School Counselor*, *44*(2), 105–114.

Cleveland, M. J., Feinberg, M. E., Bontempo, D. E., & Greenberg, M. T. (2008). The role of risk and protective factors in substance use across adolescence. *Journal of Adolescent Health*, *43*(2), 157–164. https://doi.org/10.1016/j.jadohealth.2008.01.015

Cleveland, M. J., Feinberg, M. E., Osgood, D. W., & Moody, J. (2012). Do peers' parents matter? A new link between positive parenting and adolescent substance use. *Journal of Studies on Alcohol and Drugs*, *73*, 423–433.

Coleman, J. S. (1990). *Foundations of social theory*. Harvard University Press.

Collins, W. A., Maccoby, E. E., Steinberg, L., Hetherington, E. M., & Bornstein, M. H. (2000). Contemporary research on parenting. The case for nature and nurture. *American Psychologist*, *55*(2), 218–232.

Crick, N. R., & Dodge, K. A. (1994). A review and reformation of social information-processing mechanisms in children's social adjustment. *Psychological Bulletin*, *115*(1), 74–114.

Deković, M., Wissink, I. B., & Marie Meijer, A. (2004). The role of family and peer relations in adolescent antisocial behaviour: Comparison of four ethnic groups. *Journal of Adolescence*, *27*(5), 497–514. https://doi.org/10.1016/j.adolescence.2004.06.010

Dishion, T. J. (1990). The family ecology of boys' peer relations in middle childhood. *Child Development*, *61*(3), 874–892. https://doi.org/10.1111/j.1467-8624.1990.tb02829.x

Dishion, T. J., Andrews, D. W., & Crosby, L. (1995). Antisocial boys and their friends in early adolescence: Relationship characteristics, quality, and interactional process. *Child Development*, *66*(1), 139–151. https://doi.org/10.1111/j.1467-8624.1995.tb00861.x

Dufur, M. J., Thorpe, J. D., Barton, H. S., Hoffmann, J. P., & Parcel, T. L. (2019). Can social capital protect adolescents from delinquent behavior, antisocial attitudes, and mental health problems? *Archives of Psychology*, *3*(6).

Eccles, J. S., Barber, B. L., Stone, M., & Hunt, J. (2003). Extracurricular activities and adolescent development. *Journal of Social Issues*, *59*(4), 865–889. https://doi.org/10.1046/j.0022-4537.2003.00095.x

Engels, R. C. M. E., Knibbe, R. A., Vries, H. D., Drop, M. J., & Breukelen, G. J. P. v. (1999). Influences of parental and best friends' smoking and drinking on adolescent use: A longitudinal study. *Journal of Applied Social Psychology*, *29*(2), 337–361. https://doi.org/10.1111/j.1559-1816.1999.tb01390.x

Fagan, A. A., Lee Van Horn, M., Antaramian, S., & Hawkins, J. D. (2011). How do families matter? Age and gender differences in family influences on delinquency and drug use. *Youth Violence and Juvenile Justice*, *9*(2), 150–170. https://doi.org/10.1177/1541204010377748

Felson, M. (2003). The process of co-offending. In M. Smith & D. Cornish (Eds.), *Crime prevention studies: Theory for practice in situational crime prevention* (Vol. 16, pp. 149–167). Criminal Justice Press.

Fletcher, A. C., Darling, N. E., Steinberg, L., & Dornbusch, S. (1995). The company they keep: Relation of adolescents' adjustment and behavior to their friends' perceptions of authoritative parenting in the social network. *Developmental Psychology, 31*(2), 300–310. https://doi.org/10.1037/0012-1649.31.2.300

Forgatch, M. S., & DeGarmo, D. (1999). Two faces of Janus: Cohesion and conflict. In M. Cox & J. Brooks-Gunn (Eds.), *Conflict and closeness: The formation, functioning, and stability of families* (pp. 167–184). Erlbaum.

Gerstner, D., & Oberwittler, D. (2018). Who's hanging out and what's happening? A look at the interplay between unstructured socializing, crime propensity and delinquent peers using social network data. *European Journal of Criminology, 15*(1), 111–129. https://doi.org/10.1177/1477370817732194

Giannotta, F., Ortega, E., & Ciairano, S. (2011). A two-year follow-up investigation of parenting and peer influences on tobacco use onset among Italian early adolescents. *European Journal of Developmental Psychology, 8*(5), 573–586. https://doi.org/10.1080/17405629.2011.579408

Goldstein, S. E., Davis-Kean, P. E., & Eccles, J. S. (2005). Parents, peers, and problem behavior: A longitudinal investigation of the impact of relationship perceptions and characteristics on the development of adolescent problem behavior. *Developmental Psychology, 41*(2), 401–413. https://doi.org/10.1037/0012-1649.41.2.401

Groh, A. M., Fearon, R. P., Bakermans-Kranenburg, M. J., van Ijzendoorn, M. H., Steele, R. D., & Roisman, G. I. (2014). The significance of attachment security for children's social competence with peers: A meta-analytic study. *Attachment & Human Development, 16*(2), 103–136. https://doi.org/10.1080/14616734.2014.883636

Groh, A. M., Fearon, R. M. P., Ijzendoorn, M. H. v., Bakermans-Kranenburg, M. J., & Roisman, G. I. (2017). Attachment in the early life course: Meta-analytic evidence for its role in socioemotional development. *Child Development Perspectives, 11*(1), 70–76. https://doi.org/10.1111/cdep.12213

Grusec, J. E., & Goodnow, J. J. (1994). Impact of parental discipline methods on the child's internalization of values: A reconceptualization of current points of view. *Developmental Psychology, 30*(1), 4–19. https://doi.org/10.1037/0012-1649.30.1.4

Hawkins, J. D., Catalano, R. F., & Miller, J. Y. (1992). Risk and protective factors for alcohol and other drug problems in adolescence and early adulthood: Implications for substance abuse prevention. *Psychological Bulletin, 112*(1), 64–105. https://doi.org/10.1037/0033-2909.112.1.64

Haynie, D. L., Silver, E., & Teasdale, B. (2006). Neighborhood characteristics, peer networks, and adolescent violence. *Journal of Quantitative Criminology, 22*(2), 147–169. https://doi.org/10.1007/s10940-006-9006-y

Henneberger, A. K., Mushonga, D. R., & Preston, A. M. (2021). Peer influence and adolescent substance use: A systematic review of dynamic social network research. *Adolescent Research Review, 6*(1), 57–73. https://doi.org/10.1007/s40894-019-00130-0

Herrera, C., & Dunn, J. (1997). Early experiences with family conflict: Implications for arguments with a close friend. *Developmental Psychology, 33*(5), 869–881. https://doi.org/10.1037//0012-1649.33.5.869

Hill, N. E., Bromell, L., Tyson, D. F., & Flint, R. (2007). Developmental commentary: Ecological perspectives on parental influences during adolescence. *Journal of*

Clinical Child and Adolescent Psychology, 36(3), 367–377. https://doi.org/10.1080/15374410701444322

Hirschi, T. (1969). *Causes of delinquency.* University of California Press.

Hoeben, E. M., Meldrum, R. C., Walker, D. A., & Young, J. T. N. (2016). The role of peer delinquency and unstructured socializing in explaining delinquency and substance use: A state-of-the-art review. *Journal of Criminal Justice, 47,* 108–122.

Hoeben, E. M., Rulison, K. L., Ragan, D. T., & Feinberg, M. E. (2021). Moderators of friend selection and influence in relation to adolescent alcohol use. *Prevention Science, 22*(5), 567–578. https://doi.org/10.1007/s11121-021-01208-9

Hoeben, E. M., & Weerman, F. M. (2016). Why is involvement in unstructured socializing related to adolescent delinquency? *Criminology, 54*(2), 242–281.

Hoeve, M., Dubas, J. S., Eichelsheim, V. I., van der Laan, P. H., Smeenk, W., & Gerris, J. R. M. (2009). The relationship between parenting and delinquency: A meta-analysis. *Journal of Abnormal Child Psychology, 37*(6), 749–775. https://doi.org/10.1007/s10802-009-9310-8

Ivaniushina, V., & Titkova, V. (2021). Peer influence in adolescent drinking behavior: A meta-analysis of stochastic actor-based modeling studies. *PLoS One, 16*(4), e0250169. https://doi.org/10.1371/journal.pone.0250169

Janssen, H. J., Deković, M., & Bruinsma, G. J. N. (2014). Parenting and time adolescents spend in criminogenic settings: A between- and within-person analysis. *British Journal of Criminology, 54*(4), 551–567. https://doi.org/10.1093/bjc/azu032

Kandel, D. B. (1996). The parental and peer contexts of adolescent deviance: An algebra of interpersonal influences. *Journal of Drug Issues, 26*(2), 289–315.

Keijsers, L., Branje, S., Hawk, S. T., Schwartz, S. J., Frijns, T., Koot, H. M., van Lier, P., & Meeus, W. (2012). Forbidden friends as forbidden fruit: Parental supervision of friendships, contact with deviant peers, and adolescent delinquency. *Child Development, 83*(2), 651–666. https://doi.org/10.1111/j.1467-8624.2011.01701.x

Kerr, M., & Stattin, H. (2000). What parents know, how they know it, and several forms of adolescent adjustment: Further support for a reinterpretation of monitoring. *Developmental Psychology, 36,* 366–380. https://doi.org/10.1037/0012-1649.36.3.366

Knoester, C., Haynie, D. L., & Stephens, C. M. (2006). Parenting practices and adolescents' friendship networks. *Journal of Marriage and Family, 68*(5), 1247–1260. https://doi.org/10.1111/j.1741-3737.2006.00326.x

Kreager, D. A., Rulison, K. L., & Moody, J. (2011). Delinquency and the structure of adolescent peer groups. *Criminology, 49,* 95–127. https://doi.org/10.1111/j.1745-9125.2010.00219.x

Lac, A., & Crano, W. D. (2009). Monitoring matters: Meta-analytic review reveals the reliable linkage of parental monitoring with adolescent marijuana use. *Perspectives on Psychological Science, 4*(6), 578–586. https://doi.org/10.1111/j.1745-6924.2009.01166.x

Ladd, G. W., & Parke, R. D. (2021). Themes and theories revisited: Perspectives on processes in family–peer relationships. *Children, 8*(6), 507. https://doi.org/10.3390/children8060507

Maimon, D., & Browning, C. R. (2010). Unstructured socializing, collective efficacy, and violent behavior among urban youth. *Criminology, 48*(2), 443–474. https://doi.org/10.1111/j.1745-9125.2010.00192.x

Mak, H. W., Russell, M. A., Lanza, S. T., Feinberg, M. E., & Fosco, G. M. (2020). Age-varying associations of parental knowledge and antisocial peer behavior with adolescent substance use. *Developmental Psychology, 56*(2), 298–311. https://doi.org/10.1037/dev0000866

McAdams, T. A., Salekin, R. T., Marti, C. N., Lester, W. S., & Barker, E. D. (2014). Co-occurrence of antisocial behavior and substance use: Testing for sex differences in the impact of older male friends, low parental knowledge and friends' delinquency. *Journal of Adolescence, 37*(3), 247–256. https://doi.org/10.1016/j.adolescence.2014.01.001

McCann, M., Jordan, J.-A., Higgins, K., & Moore, L. (2019). Longitudinal social network analysis of peer, family, and school contextual influences on adolescent drinking frequency. *Journal of Adolescent Health, 65*(3), 350–358. https://doi.org/10.1016/j.jadohealth.2019.03.004

McPherson, M., Smith-Lovin, L., & Cook, J. M. (2001). Birds of a feather: Homophily in social networks. *Annual Review of Sociology, 27*, 415–444.

Mercken, L., Sleddens, E. F. C., de Vries, H., & Steglich, C. E. G. (2013). Choosing adolescent smokers as friends: The role of parenting and parental smoking. *Journal of Adolescence, 36*(2), 383–392. https://doi.org/https://doi.org/10.1016/j.adolescence.2012.12.004

Molgaard, V., Kumpfer, K., & Fleming, E. (1987). *Strengthening Families Program.* Iowa State University Research Foundation.

Molgaard, V. M., Kumpfer, K. L., & Fleming, E. (1997). *The Strengthening Families Program for Parents and Youth 10-14: A video-based curriculum.* Institute for Social and Behavioral Research.

Moody, J. (2001). Peer influence groups: Identifying dense clusters in large networks. *Social Networks, 23*(4), 261–283. https://doi.org/10.1016/s0378-8733(01)00042-9

Mounts, N. S. (2000). Parental management of adolescent peer relationships: What are its effects on friend selection? In K. A. Kerns, J. M. Contreras, & A. M. Neal-Barnett (Eds.), *Family and peers: Linking two social worlds* (pp. 169–193). Praeger Publishers/Greenwood Publishing Group.

Mounts, N. S. (2004). Adolescents' perceptions of parental management of peer relationships in an ethnically diverse sample. *Journal of Adolescent Research, 19*(4), 446–467. https://doi.org/10.1177/0743558403258854

Mounts, N. S. (2011). Parental management of peer relationships and early adolescents' social skills. *Journal of Youth and Adolescence, 40*(4), 416–427. https://doi.org/10.1007/s10964-010-9547-0

Osgood, D. W., & Anderson, A. L. (2004). Unstructured socializing and rates of delinquency. *Criminology, 42*(3), 519–550. https://doi.org/https://doi.org/10.1111/j.1745-9125.2004.tb00528.x

Osgood, D. W., Ragan, D. T., Wallace, L., Gest, S. D., Feinberg, M. E., & Moody, J. (2013). Peers and the emergence of alcohol use: Influence and selection processes in adolescent friendship networks. *Journal of Research on Adolescence, 23*, 500–512. https://doi.org/10.1111/jora.12059

Osgood, D. W., Wilson, J. K., O'Malley, P. M., Bachman, J. G., & Johnston, L. D. (1996). Routine activities and individual deviant behavior. *American Sociological Review, 61*, 635–655. https://doi.org/10.2307/2096397

Oudekerk, B. A., Allen, J. P., Hessel, E. T., & Molloy, L. E. (2015). The cascading development of autonomy and relatedness from adolescence to adulthood. *Child Development, 86*(2), 472–485. https://doi.org/10.1111/cdev.12313

Padilla-Walker, L. M., Bean, R. A., & Hsieh, A. L. (2011). The role of parenting and personal characteristics on deviant peer association among European American and Latino adolescents. *Children and Youth Services Review*, 33(10), 2034–2042. https://doi.org/10.1016/j.childyouth.2011.05.034

Pesola, F., Shelton, K. H., Heron, J., Munafo, M., Hickman, M., & van den Bree, M. B. (2015). The developmental relationship between depressive symptoms in adolescence and harmful drinking in emerging adulthood: The role of peers and parents. *Journal of Youth and Adolescence*, 44(9), 1752–1766. https://doi.org/10.1007/s10964-015-0295-z

Pinquart, M. (2017). Associations of parenting dimensions and styles with externalizing problems of children and adolescents: An updated meta-analysis. *Developmental Psychology*, 53(5), 873–932. https://doi.org/10.1037/dev0000295

Pratt, T. C., & Cullen, F. T. (2005). Assessing macro-level predictors and theories of crime: A meta-analysis. *Crime and Justice*, 32, 373–450. https://doi.org/10.1086/655357

Putnam, R. D. (2000). *Bowling alone: The collapse and revival of American community*. Simon and Schuster.

Ragan, D. T. (2014). Revisiting "what they think": Adolescent drinking and the importance of peer beliefs. *Criminology*, 52(3), 488–513. https://doi.org/10.1111/1745-9125.12044

Ragan, D. T. (2016). Peer beliefs and smoking in adolescence: A longitudinal social network analysis. *The American Journal of Drug and Alcohol Abuse*, 42(2), 222–230. https://doi.org/10.3109/00952990.2015.1119157

Ragan, D. T., Osgood, D. W., & Feinberg, M. E. (2014). Friends as a bridge to parental influence: Implications for adolescent alcohol use. *Social Forces*, 92, 1061–1085. https://doi.org/10.1093/sf/sot117

Reitz, E., Prinzie, P., Deković, M., & Buist, K. L. (2007). The role of peer contacts in the relationship between parental knowledge and adolescents' externalizing behaviors: A latent growth curve modeling approach. *Journal of Youth and Adolescence*, 36(5), 623–634. https://doi.org/10.1007/s10964-006-9150-6

Robichaud, J.-M., Roy, M., Ranger, F., & Mageau, G. A. (2020). The impact of environmental threats on controlling parenting and children's motivation. *Journal of Family Psychology*, 34(7), 804–813. https://doi.org/10.1037/fam0000657

Rogers, C. R., Lee, T.-H., Fry, C. M., & Telzer, E. H. (2021). Where you lead, I will follow: Exploring sibling similarity in brain and behavior during risky decision making. *Journal of Research on Adolescence*, 31(1), 34–51. https://doi.org/10.1111/jora.12581

Rulison, K. L., Patrick, M. E., & Maggs, J. (2019). Linking peer relationships to substance use across adolescence. In S. Brown & R. A. Zucker (Eds.), *The Oxford handbook of substance use* (pp. 389–420). Oxford University Press.

Rulison, K. L., Wahesh, E., Wyrick, D. L., & DeJong, W. (2016). Parental influence on drinking behaviors at the transition to college: The mediating role of perceived friends' approval of high-risk drinking. *Journal of Studies on Alcohol and Drugs*, 77(4), 638–648. https://doi.org/10.15288/jsad.2016.77.638

Sampson, R. J. (2012). *Great American city: Chicago and the enduring neighborhood effect*. University of Chicago Press.

Sampson, R. J., & Groves, W. B. (1989). Community structure and crime: Testing social-disorganization theory. *American Journal of Sociology*, 94(4), 774–802. https://doi.org/10.1086/229068

Sampson, R. J., Raudenbush, S. W., & Earls, F. (1997). Neighborhoods and violent crime: A multilevel study of collective efficacy. *Science*, *277*(5328), 918.

Schofield, T. J., Conger, R. D., & Robins, R. W. (2015). Early adolescent substance use in Mexican origin families: Peer selection, peer influence, and parental monitoring. *Drug and Alcohol Dependence*, *157*, 129–135. https://doi.org/10.1016/j.drugalcdep.2015.10.020

Shaw, C. R., & McKay, H. D. (1969). *Juvenile delinquency and urban areas*. University of Chicago Press.

Silk, J. S., Morris, A. S., Kanaya, T., & Steinberg, L. (2003). Psychological control and autonomy granting: Opposite ends of a continuum or distinct constructs? *Journal of Research on Adolescence*, *13*(1), 113–128. https://doi.org/10.1111/1532-7795.1301004

Simons, R. L., & Burt, C. H. (2011). Learning to be bad: Adverse social conditions, social schemas, and crime. *Criminology*, *49*(2), 553–598. https://doi.org/10.1111/j.1745-9125.2011.00231.x

Simons, R. L., Simons, L. G., Burt, C. H., Brody, G. H., & Cutrona, C. (2005). Collective efficacy, authoritative parenting and delinquency: A longitudinal test of a model integrating community- and family-level processes. *Criminology*, *43*(4), 989–1029. https://doi.org/10.1111/j.1745-9125.2005.00031.x

Simons, R. L., Simons, L. G., Chen, Y.-F., Brody, G. H., & Lin, K.-H. (2007). Identifying the psychological factors that mediate the association between parenting practices and delinquency. *Criminology*, *45*(3), 481–517. https://doi.org/10.1111/j.1745-9125.2007.00086.x

Soenens, B., Vansteenkiste, M., & Niemiec, C. P. (2009). Should parental prohibition of adolescents' peer relationships be prohibited? *Personal Relationships*, *16*(4), 507–530. https://doi.org/10.1111/j.1475-6811.2009.01237.x

Stattin, H., & Kerr, M. (2000). Parental monitoring: A reinterpretation. *Child Development*, *71*(4), 1072–1085. https://doi.org/10.1111/1467-8624.00210

Steinberg, L. (2001). We know some things: Parent-adolescent relationships in retrospect and prospect. *Journal of Research on Adolescence*, *11*(1), 1–19. https://doi.org/10.1111/1532-7795.00001

Sutherland, E. H. (1947). *Principles of criminology* (4th ed.). Lippincott.

Thomas, K. J., & McCuddy, T. (2020). Affinity, affiliation, and guilt: Examining between- and within-person variability in delinquent peer influence. *Justice Quarterly*, *37*(4), 715–738. https://doi.org/10.1080/07418825.2019.1634752

Tilton-Weaver, L. C., Burk, W. J., Kerr, M., & Stattin, H. (2013). Can parental monitoring and peer management reduce the selection or influence of delinquent peers? Testing the question using a dynamic social network approach. *Developmental Psychology*, *49*(11), 2057–2070. https://doi.org/10.1037/a0031854

Tompsett, C. J., Veits, G. M., & Amrhein, K. E. (2016). Peer delinquency and where adolescents spend time with peers: Mediation and moderation of home neighborhood effects on self-reported delinquency. *Journal of Community Psychology*, *44*(2), 263–270. https://doi.org/10.1002/jcop.21759

Trucco, E. M. (2020). A review of psychosocial factors linked to adolescent substance use. *Pharmacology, Biochemistry, and Behavior*, *196*, 172969. https://doi.org/10.1016/j.pbb.2020.172969

Tu, K. M., Gregson, K. D., Erath, S. A., & Pettit, G. S. (2017). Custom-fit parenting: How low- and well-accepted young adolescents benefit from peer-related parenting.

Parenting, Science and Practice, 17(3), 157–176. https://doi.org/10.1080/15295 192.2017.1332298

Vansteenkiste, M., Soenens, B., Van Petegem, S., & Duriez, B. (2014). Longitudinal associations between adolescent perceived degree and style of parental prohibition and internalization and defiance. *Developmental Psychology, 50*(1), 229–236. https://doi.org/10.1037/a0032972

Van Ryzin, M. J., Fosco, G. M., & Dishion, T. J. (2012). Family and peer predictors of substance use from early adolescence to early adulthood: An 11-year prospective analysis. *Addictive Behaviors, 37*(12), 1314–1324. https://doi.org/10.1016/j.addbeh.2012.06.020

Vernberg, E. M., Beery, S. H., Ewell, K. K., & Absender, D. A. (1993). Parents' use of friendship facilitation strategies and the formation of friendships in early adolescence: A prospective study. *Journal of Family Psychology, 7*(3), 356–369. https://doi.org/10.1037/0893-3200.7.3.356

Wang, C., Hipp, J. R., Butts, C. T., Jose, R., & Lakon, C. M. (2015). Alcohol use among adolescent youth: The role of friendship networks and family factors in multiple school studies. *PloS One, 10*(3), e0119965. https://doi.org/https://doi.org/10.1371/journal.pone.0119965

Warner, B. D., & Sampson, R. J. (2017). Social disorganization, collective efficacy, and macro-level theories of social control. In F. T. Cullen, P. Wilcox, R. J. Sampson, & B. D. Dooley (Eds.), *Challenging criminological theory: The legacy of Ruth Rosner Kornhauser* (pp. 215–236). Transaction Publishers.

Warr, M. (1993). Parents, peers, and delinquency. *Social Forces, 72*(1), 247–264. https://doi.org/10.2307/2580168

Wikstrom, P.-O. H., Oberwittler, D., Treiber, K., & Hardie, B. (2012). *Breaking rules: The social and situational dynamics of young people's urban crime.* Oxford University Press.

Wright, M. F. (2016). Cybervictimization and substance use among adolescents: The moderation of perceived social support. *Journal of Social Work Practice in the Addictions, 16*(1–2), 93–112. https://doi.org/10.1080/1533256X.2016.1143371

Yap, M. B. H., Cheong, T. W. K., Zaravinos-Tsakos, F., Lubman, D. I., & Jorm, A. F. (2017). Modifiable parenting factors associated with adolescent alcohol misuse: A systematic review and meta-analysis of longitudinal studies. *Addiction, 112*(7), 1142–1162. https://doi.org/10.1111/add.13785

9

Dating, sexuality, and adolescent friendship networks

NAYAN G. RAMIREZ, ROSE WESCHE, AND DEREK A. KREAGER ■

INTRODUCTION

Although prior research has made significant progress in understanding how friends matter for adolescent delinquency, friendships are not the only influential relationships for adolescent social development. Across the teen years, romantic relationships become increasingly common, committed, and emotionally intimate, providing another potentially important conduit for peer influence (Connolly & McIsaac 2011; Meier & Allen 2009) parallel to the role of parents explored in Chapter 8. The emergence of romantic and sexual relationships is a defining feature of adolescence (Collins et al., 2009; Giordano, 2003). National U.S. estimates suggest that dating prevalence triples from 25% to over 70% between ages 12 and 18, and that over half of 18-year-olds report having experienced sexual intercourse (Carver et al., 2003). The rapid onset and increasing emotional and sexual intimacy of romantic relationships, particularly as they unfold in preexisting friendship networks, make them critical for understanding adolescent development.

According to developmental task theory (Roismen et al., 2004), romantic relationships are emergent adolescent developmental tasks that transition to salient ones during young adulthood. As such, individuals are likely to explore romantic and sexual identities, roles, and behaviors during adolescence but continue to fall back on existing friendships and parental relationships for personal and social support. Additionally, even though heartbreak in adolescence is new and likely painful, the consequences of romantic relationships for internalizing symptoms and overall satisfaction are expected to be greater in young adulthood than during adolescence (Collibee & Furman, 2015). This theory then predicts that adolescent romance is likely to be more exploratory, transitory, and experimental compared to more durable same-sex friendships, which often begin early in primary school. (Although contemporary scholarship recognizes the nonbinary and fluid nature of gender and sexuality, we use language associated with binary biological sex categories [e.g., "same-sex", "opposite-sex", "boys," and "girls"] due to the way that gender was operationalized in the PROSPER [Promoting School-community-university Partnerships to Enhance Resilience] study.) Developmental task theory is also consistent with stage theories of social development that connect adolescent friendship and dating by suggesting that friendships in primarily unisexual peer groups influence the transition to dating and plant the seeds for emerging mixed-sex peer groups typical of midadolescence (Brown, 1999; Dunphy, 1963).

Although theoretical attention to the connections between adolescent romantic relationships and friendships has been long standing, data limitations have prevented researchers from conducting empirical studies that situate romantic relationships within adolescent social structures (Brown et al., 1999). To adequately understand the social and contextual dynamics of adolescent dating and friendship, one needs information on both types of relationships among all individuals in a bounded setting, such as school. Additionally, longitudinal network data of multiple schools would increase causal inference and the generalizability of results. The National Longitudinal Study of Adolescent to Adult Health (Add Health) met several of these criteria and was foundational for network science (e.g., Harris et al., 2009), but even this study was limited because it only collected longitudinal network data in a small subset of schools. In this chapter, we overview a portfolio of studies examining adolescent dating and friendship using more recent and expansive longitudinal data from the PROSPER Peers study (described in the introductory chapters of this volume).

In addition to infrequent attention to the social network dynamics of friendships and romantic relationships, most existing research on adolescent friendships and sexuality has focused on the experiences of heterosexual adolescents. Sexual minority adolescents face additional stressors that may influence their friendships, creating differences from the friendship networks of heterosexual youth. For example, sexual minority adolescents have the additional burden of integrating their sexual orientation as part of their personal identity (Erikson, 1959, 1980), a process that can alter connections with peers (D'Augelli & Hart, 1987; Mathy et al., 2004). Moreover, sexual minorities often must manage their visibility within school to ensure that they do not disclose their sexual orientation to anyone who may put them in danger (Lasser & Tharinger, 2003). As a result of these challenges associated with identity management and homophobia, sexual minority adolescents may face social isolation and peer victimization (D'Augelli & Hart, 1987; Martin-Storey et al., 2015; Mathy et al., 2004; Hatzenbuehler et al., 2012, 2013).

In this chapter, we explore three interconnected research questions related to adolescent friendships and sexuality. First, we examine how adolescent friendships affect the formation of romantic relationships. Second, we assess how adolescent friendships and romantic relationships are related to health behaviors, including sexual health and substance use. Last, we present new findings using PROSPER

Peers data examining differences in the characteristics of sexual minority youth's adolescent friendships compared with those of their heterosexual peers.

BACKGROUND

Peer network data and understanding romance, sexual behaviors, and health

Involvement in romantic relationships typically emerges in adolescence, with 16 as the median age of the first dating relationship and 17 as the median age of first saying, "I love you," and first sexual intercourse (Carver et al., 2003; Regan et al., 2004). As adolescents age, their social lives become increasingly structured around romantic relationships, relying less on friendship groups as predominant sources of social interaction (Brown, 1999). These transitions within romantic relationships are embedded within larger social networks, with common features as well as distinctions from other peer relationships. For example, although friendships and romantic relationships both serve the social purposes of identity development and socialization, romantic relationships are marked by distinctive emotional intensity, affection, and exclusivity that distinguish them from other peer relationships (Brown, 1999; Furman & Collins, 2009). Romantic relationships are also the primary context of sexual exploration; most adolescents' sexual experiences occur within romantic relationships (Gibbs, 2013; Manning et al., 2005). Simultaneously, many adolescents also initiate sexual activity in nonromantic contexts. By young adulthood, the majority of individuals have had a casual sexual experience (e.g., Kuperberg & Padgett, 2016), highlighting the diversity of adolescents' sexual experiences.

Understanding adolescent romantic and sexual relationships is key to understanding adolescent health. Because of their unique characteristics, romantic and sexual relationships have implications for health and development, including emotional health, substance use, and sexual health. The distinctive emotional intensity of romantic relationships facilitates both emotional growth and emotional pain, with some studies finding involvement in romantic relationships associated with worse emotional health (Davila, 2008; Furman & Collibee, 2014; Whitton et al., 2018). Relationship dissolution also explains links between dating and poor mental health, with breakups among the strongest predictors of a first depressive episode in adolescence (Monroe et al., 1999). Additionally, involvement in casual sexual relationships may affect emotional health, although findings vary as to whether such an association is positive or negative (Wesche et al., 2021). For substance use, adolescents in romantic relationships are more likely to use substances compared to their peers who are not romantically involved (Furman et al., 2009; Rouvés & Poulin, 2016), although this finding may be limited to adolescents in serious romantic relationships (Beckmeyer, 2015). Finally, involvement in romantic and sexual relationships brings possibilities of pregnancy and sexually transmitted infections (STIs).

Although prior studies found clear associations between adolescent romantic relationships, sexual behaviors, and health, the mechanisms and causal directions underlying these associations are less well understood, requiring additional data along with the application of more sophisticated methods. For example, as with findings of friendship homophily, between-partner health similarities may result from both selection and influence processes. Accordingly, dyadic homophily in romantic relationships can exist prior to the romantic relationship, suggesting a selection process based on partner preferences or resulting from partners becoming more similar as they get to know one another and exert influence on each other over time. Isolating selection and influence processes between romantic partners is statistically challenging. Comparable to studying influence between friends (see Chapters 1 and 3), it is best accomplished by collecting longitudinal data from both partners (i.e., dyadic data) or from individuals as they enter and exit multiple partnerships over time. Such data can then be analyzed with models that account for relational and temporal dependence, including actor-partner interdependent models or fixed-effects models of within-person change (Vasilenko et al., 2015).

PROSPER is unique in permitting the disentanglement of romantic partner selection and influence processes by collecting data on adolescent relationships over extended periods of time and within the same participants. Additionally, a random subset of almost 1,000 PROSPER participants were surveyed in their homes each year and asked more sensitive questions regarding sexual development and sexual health behaviors. PROSPER also followed an overlapping subsample of approximately 2,000 participants at age 19 as they left high school and entered young adulthood. Together, the various PROSPER samples and surveys permit longitudinal analyses of the associations between adolescent-period romantic relationships and friendships with sexual and health risk behaviors over time.

Other underinvestigated areas are the peer contexts in which adolescent romantic and sexual relationships are embedded and that help to shape health-related attitudes and behaviors. Friendships provide the pool of potential partners; simultaneously, romantic partnerships can restructure friendship networks to permit additional routes of social influence (Kreager & Haynie, 2011). Understanding these structural dynamics, as well as their implications for changing health-related behaviors, requires longitudinal data on friendship ties, romantic/sexual dyads, and behaviors over time. Again, PROSPER fulfills these requirements with its friendship and romantic nominations collected between 6th and 12th grades in 27 school communities. Network analysis of these data then allows us to disentangle friendship and partner associations with individual health outcomes.

Sexual identity and peer networks

Finally, the intersections between sexual development, friendship networks, and health may vary substantially between sexual minority and heterosexual adolescents. The peer networks of sexual minority youth create opportunities for investigating research questions related to social integration and potential risks facing this population. Limited research has examined the peer networks of sexual minority youth, leaving uncertain how sexual orientation affects the full scope of sexual minority youth's social integration in schools.

Addressing this gap is important because adolescent friendships serve as conduits for learning social and emotional skills (Hartup & Stevens, 1999) and provide opportunities to gain social status in school (Coleman, 1961). However, sexual minority youth generally tend to characterize their friendships as more fragile, expressing greater concern about losing their friends compared with other youth (Diamond & Lucas, 2004; Diamond & Savin-Williams, 2003). A possible explanation for these findings may lie in sexual minorities' violation of typical gendered behavior. Behavior that does not adhere to typical gendered expectations is often met with taunting or bullying (Birkett et al., 2009), placing sexual minorities at higher risk of being discriminated against or explicitly victimized for their nonnormative sexuality (Pascoe, 2007).

During adolescence, all youth explore and develop their identities (Erikson, 1959, 1980), yet sexual minority youth have the added task of consolidating their nonnormative sexual orientation as part of their personal identity. This added dimension of a nonnormative sexual orientation can potentially affect sexual minority youth's peer relationships in various ways, leading to social isolation or differences in the composition of friendship networks. For example, sexual minority youth may feel they need to hide their sexual orientation (Lasser & Tharinger, 2003), leading them to withdraw from peer groups through social isolation. Sexual minority youth may also face social rejection due to stigma (Hatzenbuehler et al., 2013; Kiekens et al., 2020; Meyer, 1995, 2003). Alternatively, sexual minority youth may have different friendship networks based on the type of youth that may be more likely to befriend them (Ueno, 2010). For example, sexual minority boys may be more likely to have female friends compared with heterosexual boys due to greater female acceptance of sexual minority youth. Yet, prior studies focusing on this topic have had limitations such as the use of small, convenience samples (e.g., Diamond & Lucas, 2004) or Add Health data on adolescents being limited to two waves during youth's high school years (e.g., Ueno, 2010).

Social integration of sexual minority youth has important research and policy implications. Past research suggested that stigma is a driving force in creating population health inequities due to the compounded stress, leading to disparities throughout the life course (Hatzenbuehler et al., 2013). Indeed, sexual minorities in general tend to be at greater risk of victimization, mental health problems, substance use, delinquency, and other health risk behaviors compared to their peers (e.g., Birkett et al., 2009; Bontempo & D'Augelli, 2002; Himmelstein & Bruckner, 2011; Kiekens et al., 2021; Marshal et al., 2008). These elevated risks and exposures make adolescence a stressful developmental period for sexual minority youth (Meyer, 1995, 2003). By leveraging the strengths of PROSPER, including from the subsample of PROSPER participants completing questionnaires during young adulthood, we can assess differences between sexual minority participants and their heterosexual peers to address our third research question and present novel findings in this chapter.

PROSPER FINDINGS

Adolescent friendships and romantic relationship formation

We first used PROSPER data to explore the friendship network origins of adolescent romantic relationships. As adolescent romantic and sexual relationships primarily occur between opposite-sex partners, developmental scholars have focused attention on the gendered contexts of adolescent friendships to understand the origins of heterosexual dating and sexual relationships. Dunphy (1963) was among the first to connect adolescent friendships and dating. In a qualitative longitudinal analysis of Australian peer groups, he observed that unisexual early adolescent friendship groups typically transition to heterosexual crowds as upper status group members begin dating each other. By the end of adolescence, crowds themselves begin disintegrating and are replaced by loosely associated groups of heterosexual couples. Subsequent scholars elaborated Dunphy's (1963) stage model with quantitative study designs. In particular, Connolly and colleagues (Connolly et al., 2000, 2004) used survey data of adolescents to document that (1) consistent with Dunphy's model, dating adolescents tended to have larger peer networks composed of more opposite-sex friends than do nondating adolescents and (2) adolescents' affiliations with mixed-gender friendship groups typically precede future dyadic romantic relationships.

The finding that mixed-sex friendships precede adolescent dating suggests a merger of same-sex peer groups in early adolescence (see also Molloy et al., 2014, for a PROSPER example) but leaves unanswered the question of whether specific opposite-sex friendships *transition* to romantic relationships. In other words, are opposite-sex friends likely to become romantically involved, or are they more likely to remain in the "friend zone"? Connolly et al. (2004) speculated that exposure to mixed-gender peer settings provides opportunities to date friends, but the authors lacked the relational (e.g., social network) information to empirically test this hypothesis.

Kreager, Molloy, et al. (2016) leveraged PROSPER's longitudinal friendship and dating data to assess if adolescent dating partners begin with a period of friendship. Starting in the eighth grade, participants in 27 of PROSPER's Iowa and Pennsylvania rural communities were asked to nominate their "current or most recent boyfriend or girlfriend, if you had any within the last year," in addition to the friendship nominations of previous grades. The authors then focused on daters at the ninth grade and correlated these with eighth-grade friendship covariates. Of the 4,326 total dating nominations from ninth-grade PROSPER participants, 1,161 were matched to another PROSPER participant and comprised the focal sample.

Prior to examining the prior year friendship status of ninth-grade couples, the authors replicated findings from Connolly et al. (2004) that adolescent daters are likely to belong to mixed-sex friendship groups. Relying on self-reported friendship nominations, Kreager, Molloy, et al. (2016) found that ninth-grade daters were significantly more likely than ninth-grade nondaters to nominate at least one opposite-sex friendship and be a member of a mixed-sex friendship group (identified through the methods described in Chapter 3). Daters were also found to be from similar (high) status and central positions within eighth-grade friendship groups. Together, these findings support prior results in that mixed-sex peer group membership tends to precede opposite-sex romantic involvement and, consistent with Dunphy's (1963) earlier results, high-status boys and girls tend to date one another. However, these results do not test whether boys and girls who are friends are likely to transition to dating or if high-status boys and girls are likely to be in the same peer groups prior to dating. Answering these questions requires further analysis using the network data available in PROSPER.

To answer these questions, the Kreager, Molloy, et al. (2016) examined if opposite-sex adolescent dyads who began dating between the eighth- and ninth-grade surveys reported each other as a friend in the eighth grade. They found that in only 8% of ninth-grade couples, at least one partner previously reported the other as a friend. Moreover, the dyads in this category (i.e., friends who transitioned to dating) represented only 2% of all opposite-sex friendship dyads in the eighth grade. In other words, 98% of eighth-grade opposite-sex friendships *did not* result in a dating relationship (and 25% of those friendships remained stable between the waves). These descriptive statistics suggest that is very *unlikely* that early adolescent opposite-sex friendships transition to dating 1 year later. In subsequent analyses, the authors also found that dating couples tended to not be very close to one another in the prior year's friendship network. This suggests that dating connects individuals from quite different positions in a school's peer network. These results, combined with results related to daters' popularity and mixed-sex friendship membership, suggest that daters connect to one another based on similar social positions (i.e., structural equivalence) rather than through direct friendship or social proximity. Such findings have important implications for the way that opposite-sex dating relationships rewire friendship groups in the early adolescent years. Similar to Dunphy's (1963) original formulation, Kreager, Molloy, et al.'s (2016) findings suggest that popular adolescents reach across peer groups to date similarly situated opposite-sex peers and thus create structural bridges and further-integrated friendship groups.

Exploring adolescent sexual double standards

In the same year that Kreager, Molloy, et al. (2016) published their study, Kreager, Staff, et al. (2016) used PROSPER data to invert the friendship-romance association and examine how peer networks changed with the onset of adolescent romantic and sexual involvement. Drawing on literature of the sexual double standard (Bordini & Sperb, 2013; Reiss, 1956), Kreager, Staff, et al. (2016) tested if within-person changes in adolescents' self-reported romantic and sexual behaviors corresponded with changes in peer acceptance (i.e., received peer friendship nominations) and if this association varied by adolescent gender. This study was an extension of Kreager and Staff's (2009) cross-sectional analysis of the association between sexual partners and peer acceptance using network data collected in the Add Health. In that prior study, and consistent with a sexual double standard, the authors found that adolescent boys tended to receive more peer friendship nominations as the number of their self-reported sexual partners increased, whereas the opposite pattern was observed for girls. Although suggestive, that study was limited by its cross-sectional data, which permitted only between-person analyses and was therefore vulnerable to spuriousness due to omitted time-stable variables or reversed causal ordering between peer nominations and reported sexual partnerships.

PROSPER's longitudinal friendship networks and self-reported romantic and sexual behaviors allowed Kreager, Staff, et al. (2016) to examine a potential adolescent sexual double standard more rigorously. Specifically, the authors operationalized sexual behavior with a time-varying "had sex in past year" measure collected from over 800 sixth- through ninth-grade PROSPER participants in the more detailed "in-home" survey. Estimating multivariate fixed-effects models that account for unobserved heterogeneity on stable characteristics, the authors then examined how the "had sex" measure correlated with between-wave changes in peer acceptance, the latter operationalized as the total number of friendship nominations received from peers. Consistent with the sexual double standard, Kreager, Staff, et al. (2016) found that, net of other time-varying covariates and age trends, adolescent girls were significantly likely to *lose* friendship nominations in years that they had sex, whereas boys were significantly likely to *gain* friendship nominations in years that they had sex. These findings provide strong evidence for a continued sexual double standard during adolescence.

In the same study, Kreager, Staff, et al. (2016) moved beyond traditional measures of sexual behavior (i.e., sexual intercourse) to examine the friendship correlates of "making out," a measure of "light" sexual contact. They found that, net of "had sex," adolescent girls who "made out" significantly increased their received friendship nominations, and the opposite pattern occurred for boys. This reversed double standard suggests that there are social benefits for adolescents who conform to traditional gender scripts, such that girls are rewarded by peers for displaying romantic behavior without sex and boys are socially rewarded for sex, regardless of the romantic contexts. The persistence of these sexual double standards continues to confine individual sexual development and increase pressure on girls to gatekeep sexual behaviors and boys to disregard girls' sexual feelings and preferences.

Friendships, romantic relationships, and adolescent health risk behaviors

A strong correlation between peer behavior and adolescent delinquency is one of the most long-standing findings in criminology. Drawing on classic theoretical perspectives, such as Sutherland's (1947) theory of differential association and Akers's (2017; Akers et al., 1979; Burgess & Akers, 1966) social learning theory, early criminologists found strong positive associations between self-reported delinquency and perceived friends' delinquency (Pratt et al., 2010; Warr 2002). As elaborated in Chapter 1, to overcome potential projection bias, subsequent scholars used peer-reported social network data (Haynie 2001) and continued to document a significant association between individuals' delinquency and the average delinquency of friends. More recently, network scholars have disentangled the direction of this correlation using longitudinal network data and, on average, found evidence for both peer selection and peer influence processes (Jose et al., 2016; McMillan et al., 2018; Weerman, 2011).

Given the gendered nature of delinquency, where girls tend to report significantly less delinquency than do boys, participation in a romantic relationship can create an opposing force to same-sex peer influence (McCarthy et al., 2004). Some prior research has examined the delinquency and romantic partner association (Giordano et al., 2010; Haynie et al., 2005; McCarthy & Casey, 2008; Rebellon & Manasse, 2004), but these studies tended to have data limitations or ignore the broader peer context of adolescence. One study that did examine the potential connection between dating, friendship networks, and delinquent behavior was conducted by Kreager and Haynie (2011). These authors used romantic partner and friendship nomination data collected in Add Health to estimate the independent estimates of partner, friendship network, and friends-of-partner friendship network on individual drinking behavior in the next year. They found that, consistent with a hypothesis that romantic partners bridge adolescent peer networks, both romantic partner drinking and friends-of-partner drinking had large independent correlations with future drinking behavior.

Using PROSPER's longitudinal dating and friendship data, Kreager et al. (2013) replicated the earlier Add Health findings for drinking behavior. Specifically, they examined the friendship and partner behaviors of 744 ninth-grade couples and found that friends-of-partners' prior drinking and drunkenness were significantly correlated with daters' subsequent drinking behaviors, and this effect was larger than that of romantic partners and the daters' own friends, again supporting the network bridging hypothesis. Interestingly, the reverse was found for smoking behaviors, such that daters' partners' and friends' prior smoking was predictive of individual smoking, while friends-of-partners' smoking was uncorrelated with the same outcome. Kreager et al. (2013) interpreted these findings as suggesting that dating partners (and their friends) were likely to be more similar on their smoking than drinking behaviors, and this homophily removed bridging opportunities from friends of partners. This study thus provided both an important replication in a more recent sample and pointed to potentially consequential variation across behavior.

Because PROSPER contains sociometric data from adolescents, their in-grade friends, and their in-grade romantic partners, Wesche, Kreager, and Lefkowitz (2019) added attitudes and unstructured socializing to understanding the roles of friends, romantic partners, and partners' friends in explaining individuals' alcohol use. In contrast to differential association and social learning theories, social ecological theories propose that individuals adopt behaviors that their environments support (Hawley, 1950; Osgood et al., 1996). Regarding alcohol use, environments with many opportunities for unstructured socializing create opportunities for adolescents to drink. These theories have been frequently applied to understand how friends influence alcohol use (e.g., Cheadle et al., 2015; Hoeben et al., 2016; Sun & Longazel, 2008), but it was less clear the extent to which these mechanisms may be similar or different for romantic partners or partners' friends. Understanding the roles of these peer relationships could enable the expansion of peer-focused prevention programming.

The authors conducted multilevel models examining within-person variation in frequency of drunkenness as a function of peers' alcohol-related behaviors and attitudes. Friends', romantic partners', and partners' friends' frequency of drunkenness were predictors aligning with differential association theory and social learning theory. Similar to the findings in Chapter 5 which examined how both peers' beliefs and behavior matters, peers' alcohol-related attitudes were predictors aligning with differential association theory. Unstructured socializing with friends, unstructured socializing with romantic partners, and romantic partners' unstructured socializing with friends were predictors aligning with social ecological theories of peer influence. Age interactions with each of these predictors assessed how the associations changed as adolescents aged. Separate analyses were conducted for male and female adolescents to avoid concerns about interdependence between boyfriends' and girlfriends' data. Analyses focused on data collection waves corresponding to eighth through twelfth grade, which is when romantic relationships were measured.

Through these analyses, it was apparent how complementary theories of social influence applied to multiple peer relationships. The results indicated that the mechanisms of social influence on adolescents' alcohol use may differ across social relationships. Consistent with Kreager et al. (2011, 2013), friends' and partners' friends' frequency of drunkenness predicted changes in adolescents' own frequency of drunkenness, such that adolescents were drunk more frequently when their friends and partners' friends were drunk more frequently. In contrast, romantic partners' attitudes predicted adolescents' frequency of drunkenness. Adolescents were drunk more frequently when their romantic partners had more positive attitudes toward alcohol.

Results for unstructured socializing indicated that the link between unstructured socializing and alcohol use was stronger for older adolescents and differed according to adolescents' gender. Unstructured socializing with friends was not associated with changes in adolescents' frequency of drunkenness in eighth grade, but it predicted increased frequency of drunkenness later in adolescence. In addition, changes in girls' romantic partners' unstructured socializing with friends increasingly predicted changes in girls' frequency of drunkenness over time.

Stated simply, what friends and partners' friends did mattered more for individuals' drunkenness than what friends and partners' friends thought. However, what romantic partners thought mattered more than what they did. Although heterosexual adolescents may not view their romantic partners as models of alcohol use (possibly because of gendered standards for drinking behavior), they may find it important to adhere to partners' alcohol-related attitudes in order to maintain their partners' approval.

This research broadened theoretical understanding of peer influences on health behavior by identifying how mechanisms of peer influence on adolescent alcohol use may differ across peer relationships. Social learning and social ecological influences on drinking appear to be stronger for friendships and relationships with romantic partners' friends, compared to romantic relationships. However, differential association, with its focus on attitude transference, may be a particularly important process for explaining changes in adolescents' alcohol use within their romantic relationships.

Prevention scientists have used many strategies to intervene on adolescent alcohol use, some of which rely on peer relationships to diffuse healthy attitudes and behaviors related to drinking (e.g., Tebes et al., 2007; Valente et al., 2004). The results of the present research suggest that these prevention efforts should include romantic relationships, although different prevention strategies may be needed to address romantic partners' influence compared to other peer influences on alcohol use.

Adolescent peer acceptance and young adult sexual health

In the above section, the structure of PROSPER data allowed theoretical advancement by addressing how friendships intersected with and diverged from romantic relationships in their associations with alcohol use. In the next example, Wesche, Kreager, Feinberg, and Lefkowitz (2019) used PROSPER data to examine intersections between friendships and romance/sex in a different way. The authors measured associations of peer acceptance in adolescence with sexual behaviors and sexual health outcomes at age 19 by leveraging the follow-up subsample data. This research demonstrated the broad reach of friendships into romantic and sexual relationships, again with implications for health. The ability to understand how friendships potentially influence health into young adulthood is possible because of PROSPER's longitudinal design, continuing to follow participants beyond their high school years.

Friendships and romantic/sexual relationships are closely linked. Previously in this chapter, we discussed Kreager, Molloy, et al.'s (2016) work demonstrating that romantic relationships may act as bridges with consequences for friendships. In addition to romantic/sexual relationships influencing friendships, friendships may influence romantic/sexual relationships. Well-liked adolescents have a broader pool of potential sexual partners, which creates more opportunities for engaging in sexual behavior. Sexual behavior in adolescence also symbolizes maturity and social status, which may lead adolescents who are well liked or who place importance on being well liked to engage in sexual behavior (Cooper et al., 1998; Hawke & Rieger, 2013; Prinstein et al., 2003).

Because of the role of friends in determining adolescents' sexual opportunities, peer acceptance may have consequences for adolescents' sexual health into young adulthood. Sexual health outcomes established in adolescence, such as some STIs, may last throughout the life span. In addition, sexual practices established during adolescence, such as condom use or engaging in casual sex, may become behavioral patterns that last into young adulthood. Understanding how adolescent peer acceptance is associated with adolescent and young adult sexual health outcomes will help establish how best to approach peer relationships to efforts to promote sexual health.

Wesche, Kreager, Feinberg, and Lefkowitz (2019) operationalized peer acceptance using incoming friendship nominations (in-degree) standardized within school and wave and averaged across Waves 1-7 of the study. They calculated network centrality by Bonacich's (1987) index, again standardized within school and wave and averaged across measurement occasions. Sexual health outcomes included early sexual intercourse (before age 16) as well as several outcomes measured at Wave 9 of the study (approximately age 19): lifetime sexual intercourse, lifetime STI diagnosis, number of sexual partners in the past year, whether participants had casual sex in the past year, and condom use at last sexual intercourse. Regression analyses with standard errors clustered by school tested associations between peer acceptance and sexual outcomes. Different regression strategies were used for dichotomous outcomes (logistic regression) and count outcomes (negative binomial regression). Gender interactions were included for each measure of peer acceptance.

Boys and girls who were more accepted by their peers were more likely to initiate sex by age 16. Peer acceptance was also associated with an increased likelihood of having had sex by age 19 but was protective against having had an STI by age 19. For boys, peer acceptance was linked with a greater number of past year sexual partners at age 19. Peer acceptance was not associated with past year casual sex, condom use at last intercourse, or girls' number of past year sexual partners at age 19. Together, these findings suggest that, despite its association with early sexual initiation, peer acceptance in adolescence is generally associated with a healthy trajectory of sexual development by young adulthood.

These findings highlight the reach of friendships in determining sexual health. By its association with lifetime sexual intercourse by age 16 and age 19, it appears that peer acceptance may create opportunities for engaging in sexual behavior in adolescence. Therefore, we see the importance of friends in possibly influencing sexual relationships. In addition, there is some evidence that this influence extends into young adulthood, given the associations of adolescent peer acceptance with STI diagnoses and boys' number of sexual partners. Interestingly, this influence is not inherently toward greater risk behaviors. Peer acceptance was associated with a lower probability of STI diagnosis, suggesting that well-liked individuals may take appropriate precautions while engaging in sexual behavior or may have low-risk sexual partners.

We also see limits of adolescent peer relationships in determining sexual health. By young adulthood, peer acceptance was not associated with condom use, casual sex, or girls' number of sexual partners in the past year. As adolescents age and sexual behavior becomes more normative, engaging in sexual behavior may become less of a marker of social status. Therefore, peer relationships may become less important determinants of sexual behavior.

Original research: The friendships of sexual minority adolescents

Differences in peer relationships by sexual minority status may explain why sexual minority youth are at greater risk for internalizing (Button, 2015; Russell, 2003) and externalizing behaviors (Conover-Williams, 2014; Himmelstein & Bruckner, 2011). The potential importance of social integration for the self-esteem and mental health of sexual minority youth is evident in the results of the few studies on the topic (e.g., Diamond & Lucas, 2004; Diamond & Savin-Williams, 2003; Martin-Storey et al., 2012). Most of the work conducted on sexual minorities has involved community samples in urban areas or nationally representative studies (e.g., Add Health). However, the experiences of sexual minority youth differ substantially depending on their social environment (Martin-Storey et al., 2015). For example, the difficulties experienced by sexual minorities during adolescence are amplified in rural settings, where they are more likely to face a heterosexist environment and limited social support (D'Augelli & Hart, 1987; Mathy et al., 2004). These additional difficulties likely affect how well integrated sexual minorities are in their schools and who composes their friendship networks.

One of the unique aspects of the PROSPER data set is that the adolescent participants all grew up in rural communities. This feature has important implications for the experiences of sexual minority youth in these communities. For example, the risk of experiencing stigma or being victimized exists regardless of where sexual minorities live, but it is often greater in rural settings (Cohn & Hastings, 2010; D'Augelli & Hart, 1987; Poon & Saewyc, 2009). Unlike urban centers, systems of social support to help sexual minorities cope with the stress resulting from stigmatization are less likely to exist in rural settings (Willging et al., 2006; Yarbrough, 2004). In rural communities, sexual minorities are more likely to become socially isolated because of this lack of access to resources and fewer opportunities to be a part of supportive peer groups, especially ones consisting of other sexual minorities (Swank et al., 2012; Yarbrough, 2004).

In addition, compared with their heterosexual peers, sexual minorities are more likely to have higher rates of not conforming to typical gender roles (Bailey & Zucker, 2005; D'Augelli et al., 2006), placing them at risk for rejection and victimization from their peers. Because of the high social value placed on masculinity, boys experience a large amount of pressure, especially during early adolescence, to conform to a masculine sex role (Galambos et al., Petersen 1990; Massad, 1981). This demand burdens gender-atypical sexual minority adolescents whose feelings and behavior may not meet expected gendered behavior. Conversely, research also suggests that girls do not show a comparable dramatic rise in adherence to femininity during the same time (Galambos et al., 1990). This difference likely exists because feminine attributes are not as highly valued in patriarchal societies, lessening the need for strict adherence to specific feminine standards. Because most adolescent friendships are unisexual, this dynamic sets up the possibility that sexual minority boys may be less socially integrated compared with not only sexual majority youth but also sexual minority girls.

Examining patterns of mixed-sex friendships is important because of their role in reducing social anxiety. Past research examining the role of mixed-sex friendships found that having a best friend of the opposite sex led to lower social anxiety among sexual minority individuals (Baiocco et al., 2014). These types of friendships appear to be important because individuals in these cross-orientation friendships do not compete for the romantic affection of the same individuals (Muraco, 2012; Baiocco et al., 2014). These friendships also have the potential to expose or protect youth from certain risky behaviors through social learning processes (Burgess & Akers, 1966). For example, criminological research has shown that boys are much more likely to engage in delinquency compared to girls (Kruttschnitt, 2013; Steffensmeier & Allan, 1996), and thus having a greater proportion of female friends, especially for adolescent boys, may serve as a protective mechanism from engaging in delinquent behavior (Faris & Felmlee, 2011). Individuals with predominantly female friendship groups may simply have fewer opportunities to learn delinquent behavior.

Strained peer relationships during early adolescence could potentially lead to low social integration through high school and as a source of continued strain into adulthood (Martin-Storey et al., 2015). Conversely, if some sexual minority adolescents can form friendships with prosocial friends, this may protect them from exposure to risky behaviors or beliefs (Haynie, 2002). Examining measures related to social integration, including centrality, network embeddedness, and social isolation, is important in understanding whether sexual minority youth are simply less connected to their schools' social world compared to their peers. Compositional differences in the networks of sexual minorities could help explain their levels of involvement in externalizing and internalizing behaviors, such as sex composition, as discussed in the previous section.

Another important aspect of peer relationships that influences involvement in different behaviors is friendship quality. Two measures of friendship quality are included in the analyses: reciprocity and time spent with friends. Reciprocity is an important network measure because mutual friendships tend to be more significant for adolescents, especially as influential ties. In addition to the influences of reciprocal friendships, nonmutual friendships may cause adverse effects among youth, including depression and lower self-esteem (Bukowski et al., 1994; Rivera et al., 2010). Examining differences in time spent with friends is important in understanding how friends may expose youth to certain types of behaviors. During adolescence, time spent with friends greatly increases in comparison with time spent with family or parents (Crosnoe, 2000; Larson & Richards, 1991). Unstructured socializing with friends outside of school has the potential to provide youth opportunities for risky behaviors, such as substance use or delinquency (Osgood & Anderson, 2004; Osgood et al., 1996).

Assessing which aspects of sexual minorities' friendship networks are different and how they affect behavior can help us better understand how to serve sexual minority youth to improve their social integration, increase their resilience, and prevent maladaptive behaviors. Specifically, this research question assesses difference in network characteristics (degree, centrality, density, closure); the composition of the friendship networks of sexual minorities (proportion of same-gender friends); and relationship quality with these friends (time spent with friends, reciprocity).

In addition, to address possible peer mechanisms related to strain and stress theories, we examined patterns of reciprocity by comparing whether sexual minority adolescents' friends were equally likely to name them as friends, compared with their heterosexual peers. Although PROSPER does not include explicit measures of peer rejection, we examined friendship stability from wave to wave to see whether sexual minorities had higher friendship turnover across adolescence. Social isolation may also be more likely to occur in strained individuals compared to their peers.

For our research on sexual minority youth in PROSPER, our analytic sample included individuals who provided a response to the sexual identity question during at least one of the follow-up waves at ages 19 and 21. A key issue when assessing issues related to sexual minorities is how best to identify the subpopulation. In the past, adolescence researchers have cautioned that adolescents may be more likely to misreport certain types of responses in self-report surveys, especially during adolescence (Durso & Gates, 2013; Fan et al., 2006; Robinson & Espelage, 2011). For example, after the first two waves of Add Health, Udry and Chantala (2005) found that 83% of adolescent boys who reported same-sex attraction did not report being attracted to the same sex at Wave II. Savin-Williams and Joyner (2014) suggested using retrospective indicators of sexual orientation (collected during young adult years) as an appropriate means to examine the role of sexual orientation among youth who are more prone to misreporting, especially during adolescence. Moreover, various studies (Hu et al., 2015; Robinson-Cimpian, 2014) also found that same-sex attraction tended to stabilize as youth aged into adulthood, lending further support for the use of a retrospective measure of sexual orientation as more meaningful than current reports during adolescence.

As part of the follow-up (i.e., after high school) PROSPER surveys, respondents were asked to self-identify their sexual orientation as either heterosexual (attracted to people of the opposite sex), homosexual (attracted to people of the same sex), or bisexual (attracted to people of both sexes). If individuals selected a homosexual or bisexual identity during at least one of the waves, they were identified as sexual minority. This operationalization also included individuals who identified consistently as "not sure" or "don't know" during both follow-up waves or individuals who identified as sexual minority at one wave and "not sure," "don't know," or "refused" at the other wave. These restrictions led to a total analytic sample of 1,852 individuals with 119 (6.4%) sexual minority adolescents and 1,733 (93.6%) heterosexual adolescents.

The analytic strategy to examine the role of sexual minority status on adolescent friendship network characteristics employed three-level hierarchical linear models (HLMs). Grade cohorts within school districts served as the Level 3 unit of analysis, individuals were the Level 2 units, and wave served as the Level 1 unit. Models estimated the within-sex difference such that each estimate reflected the difference between a sexual minority individual and a nonminority individual of the same sex. Time was interacted with the within-sex differences to reflect the change per wave in the size of the difference between sexual minority individuals and nonminority individuals. Finally, wave was group-mean centered so that "main effect" within-sex difference results reflected average differences across the time period (from sixth through twelfth grade). This modeling strategy allowed the interaction coefficient to be interpreted as the change in slope of the within-sex difference for boys and girls across the waves of the study. Wald tests were also calculated across all models to compare whether the within-sex difference estimates varied significantly between the sexes.

Table 9.1 presents results from models that explored the relationship between adolescents' sexual minority status and friendship network characteristics. Across the models, estimates provided clear evidence that sexual minority adolescents, regardless of their sex, were less socially integrated in school compared with their heterosexual peers. Looking first at the centrality coefficients, sexual minorities, in general, were less central within their same-grade school network relative to their same-sex peers. Sexual minority boys and girls received fewer friendship nominations (i.e., in-degree) compared to their heterosexual peers, whereas only sexual minority girls made fewer friendship nominations compared to heterosexual girls. Sexual minorities, regardless of sex, were also less central based on their Bonacich and closeness centrality scores compared with their heterosexual peers. The results of both analyses suggested that sexual minorities were not connected with other highly connected individuals and thus were generally found in the peripheries of their schools' social networks.

Sexual minorities also had fewer transitive ties compared with their heterosexual peers. This finding suggested that sexual minorities were not part of tight-knit groups and were more likely to be friends with individuals who were not connected with one another. Transitivity is important in social networks because social balance in individuals' relationships alleviates possible stress, or negative cognitive states among individuals when one's friends are not friends with each other (Felmlee & Faris, 2013). Having fewer transitive ties reinforces the fragility of sexual minorities' friendships during adolescence.

The results also indicated differences in one aspect of the friendship characteristics of sexual minority boys, but not girls, compared to their heterosexual peers. Sexual minority boys have dramatically fewer friendships with members of the same sex, as demonstrated in Figure 9.1. Sexual minority boys started off middle school (i.e., sixth grade) with fewer friends of the same sex compared with heterosexual boys at approximately 1.5 friends versus 2.3, respectively, and by the end of high school sexual minority boys only had about 0.2 male friends versus 1.8. This pattern was distinct from all other subgroups; even sexual minority girls retained

Table 9.1 DIFFERENCES IN NETWORK OUTCOMES BY SEXUAL MINORITY STATUS AND SEX

Network outcomes	Sexual minority boys compared with heterosexual boys				Sexual minority girls compared with heterosexual girls				Significant sex difference?
	No controls		Add controls		No controls		Add controls		
	Coef.	RSE	Coef.	RSE	Coef.	RSE	Coef.	RSE	
Centrality									
In-degree	−0.312 *	0.131	−0.301 *	0.132	−0.249 ***	0.061	−0.190 **	0.055	Yes ***
Out-degree	−0.142 *	0.057	−0.134	0.056	−0.193 ***	0.051	−0.162 **	0.049	Yes **
Bonacich centrality	−0.247 ***	0.060	−0.234 ***	0.061	−0.272 ***	0.051	−0.190 ***	0.046	Yes ***
Closeness centrality, all ties	−0.018 *	0.008	−0.018 *	0.007	−0.025 ***	0.006	−0.019 **	0.006	Yes ***
Betweenness centrality, undirected	0.000	0.002	0.000	0.002	−0.002	0.002	−0.002	0.002	No
Embeddedness									
Ego network density	−0.050	0.050	0.038	0.055	−0.006	0.027	0.004	0.026	No
Transitivity of sent ties	−0.071 **	0.021	−0.066 **	0.024	0.038 **	0.015	−0.025 †	0.014	Yes *
Isolation									
Isolated, incoming ties	0.498 **	0.189	0.546 **	0.193	0.358 ***	0.081	0.274 **	0.083	Yes ***
Isolated, outgoing ties	0.103	0.125	0.092	0.127	0.312 *	0.132	0.218	0.133	No
Isolated, all ties	0.342	0.403	0.277	0.384	1.533 ***	0.193	1.333 ***	0.183	Yes ***
Friendship characteristics									
Number of same-sex friends, all ties	−1.365 ***	0.175	−1.328 ***	0.174	−0.061	0.114	−0.070	0.117	Yes ***
Number of reciprocated ties	−0.250 *	0.118	−0.231 †	0.126	−0.078	0.086	−0.044	0.086	No
Time spent with friends	−0.297 *	0.135	−0.273 *	0.131	−0.067	0.093	−0.118	0.090	No

Notes: Controls included white, two-parent household, grades, family relations, school bonding, risk and sensation seeking, and free- and reduced lunch. All controls are grand-mean centered. Coef. = coefficient; RSE = robust standard error.
*** $p < 0.001$, ** $p < 0.01$, * $p < 0.05$, † $p < 0.10$.

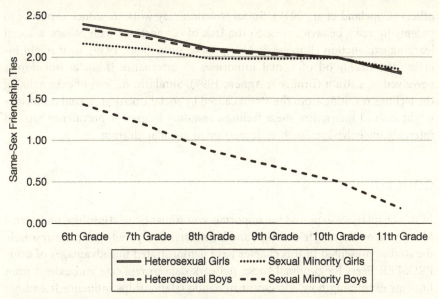

Figure 9.1 Number of same-sex friendship ties across time by sexual minority status and sex.

a similar number of same-sex friends compared with heterosexual girls. This sets up the possibility that sexual minority boys are particularly protected from exposure to risky behaviors, such as delinquency or substance use, given their greater number of female friendships (Faris & Felmlee, 2011; Kruttschnitt, 2013).

In addition to the number of same-sex friends, sexual minority boys had a lower number of reciprocated ties and spent less time with their friends compared with heterosexual boys. Lower rates of reciprocity and less time spent with friends suggested that even when sexual minority boys could make friends, these friendships were more fragile than heterosexual boys' friendships. Theories related to unstructured socializing (Osgood & Anderson, 2004) suggest that time spent with friends is key in assessing exposure to peers' attitudes and behaviors. If sexual minority boys are spending less time with their friends, this may even further explain their low levels of involvement in externalizing behaviors. However, if sexual minority boys have more fragile peer relationships, past research suggested that this may increase their susceptibility to issues related to internalizing behaviors (Hartup & Stevens, 1999).

Last, sexual minorities appeared particularly susceptible to social isolation, in particular sexual minority girls, compared with their heterosexual counterparts. Sexual minority boys and girls were both more likely to be isolated based on incoming ties (i.e., not being named as a friend by anyone else), while sexual minority girls were also more likely to be socially isolated based on both incoming and outgoing ties (i.e., not naming any friends either). For sexual minority boys, the lack of significantly greater social isolation based on outgoing ties suggested that they were not necessarily withdrawn but were more likely to be avoided by others (Copeland et al., 2017). Social isolation may work to reduce exposure to potentially risky behaviors due to the lack of connections with others, a social learning explanation (Burgess & Akers, 1966; Sutherland, 1939), or it might increase the likelihood of sexual minorities to externalize if social isolation is perceived as a strain (Broidy & Agnew, 1997). Similarly, instead of externalizing the feelings resulting from the strain caused by social isolation, sexual minorities might instead internalize these feelings, resulting in greater prevalence rates of internalizing behaviors, such as depression or suicidal ideation.

CONCLUSION

In this chapter, we explored the importance of romantic relationships and sexual identity on adolescent friendships and behaviors. Compared with prior research, the studies presented in this chapter have demonstrated the advantages of using PROSPER Peers longitudinal social network data to replicate and extend prior findings examining how adolescent romantic relationships influence friendship formation and health risk behaviors. In addition, we presented novel findings examining how sexual minority youth differed in their adolescent friendships compared with their heterosexual peers.

Our first research question addressed the association between adolescent friendship and romantic relationship formation. Kreager, Molloy, et al. (2016) found evidence that adolescent romantic partners were more likely to belong to mixed-sex groups before dating compared with adolescents who did not date. Additionally, adolescents who dated were likely to have similarly high social status and to be more central in their friendship networks. However, we did not find evidence that being friends in the year prior led to the formation of an opposite-sex romantic relationship for most youth. Instead, similar social positioning in a friendship network appears to be more important in romantic relationship formation than social proximity or direct friendship. In addition to examining the role of prior relationships, Kreager, Staff, et al. (2016) also assessed whether friendship networks changed with the onset of romantic and sexual involvement. Confirming the persistence of a sexual double standard, heterosexual adolescent girls were more likely to lose friends after engaging in sex compared with heterosexual adolescent boys, who gained friends in years that they had sex. Conversely, making out led to increased friendships for heterosexual girls but not for heterosexual boys. Together, these results pointed to the importance of network position and status for romantic relationship formation and how adolescents continued to conform to traditional gender scripts when it came to sexual intercourse.

Second, we examined how adolescent friendships and romantic relationships were associated with substance use and sexual health among heterosexual adolescents. Kreager et al. (2013) found that prior drinking and drunkenness among romantic partners' friends were significantly related with daters' drinking behavior. However, behavior of the friends of romantic partners and of the daters themselves were not found to be significant predictors. Yet, the reverse pattern was found for smoking behavior; daters' partners and friends were found to be predictive of smoking but not romantic partners' friends. Wesche, Kreager, and Lefkowitz (2019) extended prior work by examining whether attitudes toward substance use and unstructured socializing patterns influenced individuals' alcohol use. The authors found that an individual's friends' and their partner's friends' frequency of drunkenness predicted an adolescent's own alcohol use. Additionally, romantic partners' attitudes toward alcohol use were predictive of an individual's frequency of drunkenness, and unstructured socializing was a stronger predictor of alcohol use during late adolescence but not during eighth grade. We also examined how adolescent friendships and romantic relationships affected sexual health during adolescence. Wesche, Kreager, Feinberg, and Lefkowitz (2019) found that more popular boys and girls were more likely to have had sex by age 16 or age 19. Moreover, greater peer acceptance during adolescence was found to be protective against having had an STI but was not associated with casual sex or condom use. Results from this research question demonstrated the interconnected roles of friendships and romantic relationships in contributing to adolescents' health. Romantic partners played an important role in exposing adolescents to substance use, and sexual health behaviors were linked to adolescent peer acceptance.

Our final research question examined differences in the adolescent friendships of sexual minority boys and girls compared with their heterosexual peers. Overall, sexual minority boys and girls were less likely to be socially integrated compared with heterosexual youth. Sexual minority youth were less central in their friendship networks, were less likely to have transitive friendship ties, and were more likely to be socially isolated. In addition, sexual minority boys had far fewer friends of the same sex, and this difference grew markedly with age. Further, on average they had fewer reciprocated ties and spent less time with their friends compared with heterosexual boys. These findings suggested that sexual minority youth's friendships were more likely to be fragile, placing sexual minorities at particular risk for low levels of social integration across adolescence.

The interconnectedness of friendships and romantic relationships has implications for prevention and intervention. If program developers want to intervene on peer relationships to promote adolescent health, we must understand how diverse social relationships can enhance or undermine the effects of interventions. For example, when sexual risk is rewarded with greater social status, friendships can dampen the effects of interventions to promote safer sex with romantic partners, such as those interventions that teach behavioral skills for negotiating condom use. Alternatively, addressing condom use norms within entire peer groups may enhance the effects of such interventions (see Chapter 11 regarding diffusion of PROSPER's substance use prevention effects). Interventions have adopted this strategy by utilizing peer facilitators to address safer sex norms, albeit with mixed effectiveness (Abdi & Simbar, 2013; Tolli, 2012).

The persistence of a sexual double standard suggests that norms of "appropriate" sexual and romantic behavior continue to be present in secondary schools. This evidence of a sexual double standard among adolescents contrasts to research assessing such behavior among undergraduates, which tends to find a single standard or weaker norms, at least when examining attitudes. Evidence of peer enforcement of a double standard has implications for not only policing heterosexual behavior, but also sexual minority youth. Similar to PROSPER's effects on the centrality of substance users (see Chapter 11), policies should also seek to reduce the popularity associated with boys' sexual relationships and destigmatize girls' sexual behavior.

As with other research on peer relationships and health discussed in this chapter, Wesche, Kreager, Feinberg, and Lefkowitz's (2019) research demonstrated the utility of including peer relationships in health promotion efforts. As they do for alcohol use, peers play a role in organizing sexual behavior in adolescence. Therefore, it is important for prevention scientists to consider how to leverage peer relationships to promote sexual health. Because well-liked adolescents are more likely to engage in sexual behaviors but may not be at high risk of poor sexual health outcomes, they may be good candidates for peer leader roles in sexual health promotion efforts, serving as sources of information and referral to services (Chandra-Mouli et al., 2015).

In addition, schools can help increase sexual minority youth's social integration in a variety of ways. First, schools can include or increase the amount of class content related to lesbian, gay, bisexual, transgendered, and queer (or questioning; LGBTQ) information. By incorporating issues related to sexual minority youth into curricula, sexual minority youth may feel like they belong more in school. Moreover, heterosexual youth in schools would increase their understanding of issues related to sexual minorities, which would improve the school climate by making it more tolerant (Snapp et al., 2015a, 2015b). In particular, health classes often completely ignore issues related to LGBTQ sexual health, increasing the likelihood of sexual minorities engaging in health risk behaviors due to a lack of knowledge. These policy changes can potentially change local norms and expectations, which down the road can lead to wider adoption of such policies. Research has demonstrated that curricula that are inclusive of sexual minorities issues lead to greater feelings of belonging and safety as well as reduced victimization (Snapp et al., 2015b). Last, intervention programs, such as PROSPER, could tailor their programs to address issues relevant to sexual minority youth to promote positive youth development and decreased involvement in health risk behaviors. Moreover, interventions that include programming for parents of sexual minority youth would also serve to improve sexual minority youth's home lives as well. Schools should continue to seek opportunities to improve marginalized students' feelings of belonging and support at school to increase sexual minority youth's social integration and overall well-being.

As we have demonstrated in this chapter, adolescent friendships, romantic relationships, and sexuality are inextricably linked. They influence each other, and peer relationships influence overall adolescent well-being. To promote health among adolescents, researchers and practitioners must account for the broad peer context in which adolescents live. PROSPER has enriched our view of what these embedded social contexts look like and has opened the field for future exploration of peers' influence on health, romance, and sexuality. Future research should further incorporate important features of contemporary adolescent social life and sexuality, such as social media, gender fluidity, and online pornography, among other factors.

REFERENCES

Abdi, F., & Simbar, M. (2013). The peer education approach in adolescents—Narrative review article. *Iranian Journal of Public Health*, 42(11), 1200.

Akers, R. (2017). *Social learning and social structure: A general theory of crime and deviance*. Routledge.

Akers, R. L., Krohn, M. D., Lanza-Kaduce, L., & Radosevich, M. (1979). Social learning and deviant behavior: A specific test of a general theory. *American Sociological Review*, 44(4), 636–655. https://doi.org/10.2307/2094592

Bailey, J. M., & Zucker, K. J. (1995). Childhood sex-typed behavior and sexual orientation: A conceptual analysis and quantitative review. *Developmental Psychology; Washington*, 31(1), 43.

Baiocco, R., Santamaria, F., Lonigro, A., Ioverno, S., Baumgartner, E., & Laghi, F. (2014). Beyond similarities: Cross-gender and cross-orientation best friendship in a sample of sexual minority and heterosexual young adults. *Sex Roles*, 70(3–4), 110–121. https://doi.org/10.1007/s11199-014-0343-2.

Beckmeyer, J. J. (2015). Comparing the associations between three types of adolescents' romantic involvement and their engagement in substance use. *Journal of Adolescence*, 42, 140–147.

Birkett, M., Espelage, D. L., & Koenig, B. (2009). LGB and questioning students in schools: The moderating effects of homophobic bullying and school climate on negative outcomes. *Journal of Youth and Adolescence*, 38(7), 989–1000. https://doi.org/10.1007/s10964-008-9389-1

Bonacich, P. (1987). Power and centrality: A family of measures. *American Journal of Sociology*, 92(5), 1170–1182.

Bontempo, D. E., & D'Augelli, A. R. (2002). Effects of at-school victimization and sexual orientation on lesbian, gay, or bisexual youths' health risk behavior. *Journal of Adolescent Health*, 30(5), 364–374. https://doi.org/10.1016/S1054-139Xno.0100415-3

Bordini, G., & Sperb, T. (2013). Sexual double standard: A review of the literature between 2001 and 2010. *Sexuality & Culture*, 17, 686–704. https://doi.org/10.1007/s12119-012-9163-0

Broidy, L., & Agnew, R. (1997). Gender and crime: A general strain theory perspective. *Journal of Research in Crime and Delinquency*, 34(3), 275–306. https://doi.org/10.1177/0022427897034003001

Brown, B. B. (1999). "You're going out with who?": Peer group influences on adolescent romantic relationships. In W. Furman, B. B. Brown, & C. Feiring (Eds.), *The development of romantic relationships in adolescence* (pp. 291–329). Cambridge Studies in Social and Emotional Development. Cambridge University Press. https://doi.org/10.1017/CBO9781316182185.013

Brown, B. B., Feiring, C., & Furman, W. (1999). Missing the love boat: Why researchers have shied away from adolescent romance. In W. Furman, B. B. Brown, & C. Feiring

(Eds.), *The development of romantic relationships in adolescence* (pp. 1-16). Cambridge University Press. https://doi.org/10.1017/CBO9781316182185.002

Bruinsma, G. (2014). Differential association theory. In G. Bruinsma & D. Weisburd (Eds.), *Encyclopedia of criminology and criminal justice* (pp. 1065-1075). Springer. https://doi.org/10.1007/978-1-4614-5690-2_691

Bukowski, W. M., Hoza, B., & Boivin, M. (1994). Measuring friendship quality during pre- and early adolescence: The development and psychometric properties of the friendship qualities scale. *Journal of Social and Personal Relationships*, *11*(3), 471-484. https://doi.org/10.1177/0265407594113011

Burgess, R. L., & Akers, R. L. (1966). A differential association-reinforcement theory of criminal behavior. *Social Problems*, *14*(2), 128-147.

Button, D. M. (2015). A general strain approach comparing the effects of victimization, social support, and perceived self-efficacy on LGBQ and heterosexual youth suicidality. *Criminal Justice Studies*, *28*(4), 484-502. https://doi.org/10.1080/1478601X.2015.1081850

Carver, K., Joyner, K., & Udry, J. R. (2003). National estimates of adolescent romantic relationships. In P. Florsheim (Ed.), *Adolescent romantic relations and sexual behavior: Theory, research, and practical implications* (pp. 23-56). Lawrence Erlbaum Associates Publishers.

Chandra-Mouli, V., Lane, C., & Wong, S. (2015). What does not work in adolescent sexual and reproductive health: A review of evidence on interventions commonly accepted as best practices. *Global Health: Science and Practice*, *3*(3), 333-340. https://doi.org/10.9745/GHSP-D-15-00126

Cheadle, J. E., Walsemann, K. M., & Goosby, B. J. (2015). Teen alcohol use and social networks: The contributions of friend influence and friendship selection. *Journal of Alcoholism and Drug Dependence*, *3*(5), 224. https://doi.org/10.4172/2329-6488.1000224

Cohn, T. J., & Hastings, S. L. (2010). Resilience among rural lesbian youth. *Journal of Lesbian Studies*, *14*(1), 71-79. https://doi.org/10.1080/10894160903060325

Coleman, J. S. (1961). *The adolescent society: The social life of the teenager and its impact on education*. Free Press of Glencoe.

Collibee, C., & Furman, W. (2015). Quality counts: Developmental shifts in associations between romantic relationship qualities and psychosocial adjustment. *Child Development*, *86*(5), 1639-1652. https://doi.org/10.1111/cdev.12403

Collins, W. A., Welsh, D. P., & Furman, W. (2009). Adolescent romantic relationships. *Annual Review of Psychology*, *60*(1), 631-652. https://doi.org/10.1146/annurev.psych.60.110707.163459

Connolly, J., Craig, W., Goldberg, A., & Pepler, D. (2004). Mixed-gender groups, dating, and romantic relationships in early adolescence. *Journal of Research on Adolescence*, *14*(2), 185-207. https://doi.org/10.1111/j.1532-7795.2004.01402003.x

Connolly, J., Furman, W., & Konarski, K. (2000). The role of peers in the emergence of heterosexual romantic relationships in adolescence. *Child Development*, *71*(5), 1395-1408.

Conover-Williams, M. (2014). The queer delinquent: Impacts of risk and protective factors on sexual minority juvenile offending in the U.S. In D. Peterson & R. V. Panfil (Eds.), *Handbook of LGBT communities, crime, and justice* (pp. 449-472). Springer New York. http://dx.doi.org/10.1007/978-1-4614-9188-0_21

Cooper, M. L., Shapiro, C. M., & Powers, A. M. (1998). Motivations for sex and risky sexual behavior among adolescents and young adults: A functional perspective. *Journal of Personality and Social Psychology, 75*(6), 1528–1558. https://doi.org/10.1037/0022-3514.75.6.1528

Copeland, M., Bartlett, B., & Fisher, J. C. (2017). Dynamic associations of network isolation and smoking behavior. *Network Science, 5*(3), 257–277. https://doi.org/10.1017/nws.2017.9

Crosnoe, R. (2000). Friendships in childhood and adolescence: The life course and new directions. *Social Psychology Quarterly, 63*(4), 377–391. https://doi.org/10.2307/2695847

D'Augelli, A. R., Grossman, A. R., & Starks, M. T. (2006). Childhood gender atypicality, victimization, and PTSD among lesbian, gay, and bisexual youth. *Journal of Interpersonal Violence, 21*(11), 1462–1482. https://doi.org/10.1177/0886260506293482

D'Augelli, A. R., & Hart, M. M. (1987). Gay women, men, and families in rural settings: Toward the development of helping communities. *American Journal of Community Psychology, 15*(1), 79–93. https://doi.org/10.1007/BF00919759

Davila, J. (2008). Depressive symptoms and adolescent romance: Theory, research, and implications. *Child Development Perspectives, 2*(1), 26–31.

Diamond, L. M., & Lucas, S. (2004). Sexual-minority and heterosexual youths' peer relationships: Experiences, expectations, and implications for well-being. *Journal of Research on Adolescence, 14*(3), 313–340. https://doi.org/10.1111/j.1532-7795.2004.00077.x

Diamond, L. M., & Savin-Williams, R. C. (2003). The intimate relationships of sexual-minority youths. In G. R. Adams and M. D. Berzonsky (Eds.), *Blackwell handbook of adolescence* (pp. 393–412). Blackwell Handbooks of Developmental Psychology. Blackwell Publishing.

Dunphy, D. C. (1963). The social structure of urban adolescent peer groups. *Sociometry, 26*(2), 230–246. https://doi.org/10.2307/2785909

Durso, L. E., & Gates, G. J. (2013). Best practices: Collecting and analyzing data on sexual minorities. In A. K. Baumle (Ed.), *International handbook on the demography of sexuality* (pp. 21–42). Springer Netherlands. http://link.springer.com/chapter/10.1007/978-94-007-5512-3_3

Erikson, E. H. (1959). Identity and the life cycle: Selected papers. *Psychological Issues, 1*, 1–171.

Erikson, E. H. (1980). *Identity and the life cycle.* Norton & Company.

Fan, X., Miller, B. C., Park, K.-E., Winward, B. W., Christensen, M., Grotevant, H. D., & Tai, R. H. (2006). An exploratory study about inaccuracy and invalidity in adolescent self-report surveys. *Field Methods, 18*(3), 223–244. https://doi.org/10.1177/1525822X06289161

Faris, R., & Felmlee, D. (2011). Status struggles network centrality and gender segregation in same- and cross-gender aggression. *American Sociological Review, 76*(1), 48–73. https://doi.org/10.1177/0003122410396196

Furman, W., & Collibee, C. (2014). A matter of timing: Developmental theories of romantic involvement and psychosocial adjustment. *Development and Psychopathology, 26*(4), 1149–1160.

Furman, W., & Collins, W. A. (2009). Adolescent romantic relationships and experiences. In K. H. Rubin, W. M. Bukowski, & B. Laursen (Eds.), *Handbook of peer interactions, relationships, and groups* (pp. 341-360). The Guilford Press.

Furman, W., Low, S., & Ho, M. J. (2009). Romantic experience and psychosocial adjustment in middle adolescence. *Journal of Clinical Child & Adolescent Psychology*, 38(1), 75-90.

Galambos, N. L., Almeida, D. M., & Petersen, A. C. (1990). Masculinity, femininity, and sex role attitudes in early adolescence: Exploring gender intensification. *Child Development*, 61(6), 1905-1914.

Gibbs, L. (2013). Gender, relationship type and contraceptive use at first intercourse. *Contraception*, 87(6), 806-812.

Giordano, P. C. (2003). Relationships in adolescence. *Annual Review of Sociology*, 29(1), 257-281. https://doi.org/10.1146/annurev.soc.29.010202.100047

Giordano, P. C., Lonardo, R. A., Manning, W. D., & Longmore, M. A. (2010). Adolescent romance and delinquency: A further exploration of hirschi's "cold and brittle" relationships hypothesis. *Criminology: An Interdisciplinary Journal*, 48(4), 919-946. https://doi.org/10.1111/j.1745-9125.2010.00208.x

Harris, K. M., Halpern, C. T., Whitsel, E., Hussey, J., Tabor, J., Entzel, P., & Udry, J. R. (2009). The national longitudinal study of adolescent to adult health: Research design [WWW document]. *URL*: http://www.cpc.unc.edu/projects/addhealth/design.

Hartup, W. W., & Stevens, N. (1999). Friendships and adaptation across the life span. *Current Directions in Psychological Science*, 8(3), 76-79. https://doi.org/10.1111/1467-8721.00018

Hatzenbuehler, M. L., McLaughlin, M. A., & Xuan, Z. (2012). Social networks and risk for depressive symptoms in a national sample of sexual minority youth. *Social Science & Medicine*, 75(7), 1184-1191. https://doi.org/10.1016/j.socscimed.2012.05.030

Hatzenbuehler, M. L., Phelan, J. C., & Link, B. G. (2013). Stigma as a fundamental cause of population health inequalities. *American Journal of Public Health*, 103(5), 813-821. https://doi.org/10.2105/AJPH.2012.301069

Hawke, S., & Rieger, E. (2013). Popularity, likeability, and risk-taking in middle adolescence. *Health*, 5(6), 41-52. https://doi.org/10.4236/health.2013.56A3007

Hawley, H. A. (1950). *Human ecology: A theory of community structure*. New York: The Ronald Press Company.

Haynie, D. L. (2001). Delinquent peers revisited: Does network structure matter? *American Journal of Sociology*, 106(4), 1013-1057. https://doi.org/10.1086/320298

Haynie, D. L. (2002). Friendship networks and delinquency: The relative nature of peer delinquency. *Journal of Quantitative Criminology*, 18(2), 99-134. https://doi.org/10.1023/A:1015227414929

Haynie, D. L., Giordano, P. C., Manning, W. D., & Longmore, M. A. (2005). Adolescent romantic relationships and delinquency involvement. *Criminology*, 43(1), 177-210. https://doi.org/10.1111/j.0011-1348.2005.00006.x

Himmelstein, K. E. W., & Brückner, H. (2011). Criminal-justice and school sanctions against nonheterosexual youth: A national longitudinal study. *Pediatrics*, 127(1), 49-57. https://doi.org/10.1542/peds.2009-2306

Hoeben, E. M., Meldrum, R. C., Walker, D., & Young, J. T. N. (2016). The role of peer delinquency and unstructured socializing in explaining delinquency and substance use: A state-of-the-art review. *Journal of Criminal Justice*, 47, 108-122. https://doi.org/10.1016/j.jcrimjus.2016.08.001

Hu, Y., Xu, Y., & Tornello, S. L. (2015). Stability of self-reported same-sex and both-sex attraction from adolescence to young adulthood. *Archives of Sexual Behavior, 45*(3), 1–9. https://doi.org/10.1007/s10508-015-0541-1

Jose, R., Hipp, J. R., Butts, C. T., Wang, C., & Lakon, C. M. (2016). Network structure, influence, selection, and adolescent delinquent behavior: Unpacking a dynamic process. *Criminal Justice and Behavior, 43*(2), 264–284. https://doi.org/10.1177/0093854815605524

Kiekens, W., la Roi, C., Bos, H. M. W., Kretschmer, T., van Bergen, D. D., & Veenstra, R. (2020). Explaining health disparities between heterosexual and LGB adolescents by integrating the minority stress and psychological mediation frameworks: Findings from the TRAILS study. *Journal of Youth and Adolescence, 49*(9), 1767–1782. https://doi.org/10.1007/s10964-020-01206-0

Kiekens, W. J., la Roi, C., & Dijkstra, J. K. (2021). Sexual identity disparities in mental health among U.K. adults, U.S. adults, and U.S. adolescents: Examining heterogeneity by race/ethnicity. *Psychology of Sexual Orientation and Gender Diversity, 8*(4), 407–419. https://doi.org/10.1037/sgd0000432

Kreager, D. A., & Haynie, D. L. (2011). Dangerous liaisons? Dating and drinking diffusion in adolescent peer networks. *American Sociological Review, 76*(5), 737–763. https://doi.org/10.1177/0003122411416934

Kreager, D. A., Haynie, D. L., & Hopfer, S. (2013). Dating and substance use in adolescent peer networks: A replication and extension. *Addiction, 108*(3), 638–647. https://doi.org/10.1111/j.1360-0443.2012.04095.x

Kreager, D. A., & Staff, J. (2009). The sexual double standard and adolescent peer acceptance. *Social Psychology Quarterly, 72*(2), 143–164. https://doi.org/10.1177/019027250907200205

Kreager, D. A., Molloy, L. E., Moody, J., & Feinberg, M. E. (2016). Friends first? The peer network origins of adolescent dating. *Journal of Research on Adolescence, 26*(2), 257–269. https://doi.org/10.1111/jora.12189

Kreager, D. A., Staff, J., Gauthier, R., Lefkowitz, E. S., & Feinberg, M. E. (2016). The double standard at sexual debut: Gender, sexual behavior and adolescent peer acceptance. *Sex Roles, 75*(7), 377–392. https://doi.org/10.1007/s11199-016-0618-x

Kruttschnitt, C. (2013). Gender and crime. *Annual Review of Sociology, 39*(1), 291–308. https://doi.org/10.1146/annurev-soc-071312-145605

Kuperberg, A., & Padgett, J. E. (2016). The role of culture in explaining college students' selection into hookups, dates, and long-term romantic relationships. *Journal of Social and Personal Relationships, 33*(8), 1070–1096.

Larson, R., & Richards, M. H. (1991). Daily companionship in late childhood and early adolescence: Changing developmental contexts. *Child Development, 62*(2), 284–300. https://doi.org/10.1111/j.1467-8624.1991.tb01531.x

Lasser, J., & Tharinger, D. (2003). Visibility management in school and beyond: A qualitative study of gay, lesbian, bisexual youth. *Journal of Adolescence, 26*(2), 233–244. https://doi.org/10.1016/S0140-1971no. 0200132-X

Manning, W. D., Longmore, M. A., & Giordano, P. C. (2005). Adolescents' involvement in non-romantic sexual activity. *Social Science Research, 34*(2), 384–407.

Marshal, M. P., Friedman, M. S., Stall, R., King, K. M., Miles, J., Gold, M. A., Bukstein, O. G., & Morse, J. Q. (2008). Sexual orientation and adolescent substance use: A Meta-analysis and methodological review. *Addiction, 103*(4), 546–556. https://doi.org/10.1111/j.1360-0443.2008.02149.x

Martin-Storey, A., Cheadle, J. E., Skalamera, J., & Crosnoe, R. (2015). Exploring the social integration of sexual minority youth across high school contexts. *Child Development*, 86(3), 965-975. https://doi.org/10.1111/cdev.12352

Massad, C. M. (1981). Sex role identity and adjustment during adolescence. *Child Development*, 52(4), 1290-1298.

Mathy, R. M., Carol, H. M., & Schillace, M. (2004). The impact of community size on lesbian and bisexual women's psychosexual development. *Journal of Psychology & Human Sexuality*, 15(2-3), 47-71. https://doi.org/10.1300/J056v15n02_04

McCarthy, B., & Casey, T. (2008). Love, sex, and crime: Adolescent romantic relationships and offending. *American Sociological Review*, 73(6), 944-969. https://doi.org/10.1177/000312240807300604

McCarthy, B., Felmlee, D., & Hagan, J. (2004). Girl friends are better: Gender, friends, and crime among school and street youth. *Criminology*, 42(4), 805-836. https://doi.org/10.1111/j.1745-9125.2004.tb00537.x

McMillan, C., Felmlee, D., & Osgood, D. W. (2018). Peer influence, friend selection, and gender: How network processes shape adolescent smoking, drinking, and delinquency. *Social Networks*, 55, 86-96. https://doi.org/10.1016/j.socnet.2018.05.008

Meier, A., & Allen, G. (2009). Romantic relationships from adolescence to young adulthood: Evidence from the National Longitudinal Study of Adolescent Health. *The Sociological Quarterly*, 50(2), 308-335. https://doi.org/10.1111/j.1533-8525.2009.01142.x

Meyer, I. H. (1995). Minority stress and mental health in gay men. *Journal of Health and Social Behavior*, 36(1), 38-56. https://doi.org/10.2307/2137286

Meyer, I. H. (2003). Prejudice, social stress, and mental health in lesbian, gay, and bisexual populations: Conceptual issues and research evidence. *Psychological Bulletin*, 129(5), 674-697. https://doi.org/10.1037/0033-2909.129.5.674

Molloy, L. E., Gest, S. D., Feinberg, M. E., & Osgood, D. W. (2014). Emergence of mixed-sex friendship groups during adolescence: Developmental associations with substance use and delinquency. *Developmental Psychology*, 50(11), 2449.

Monroe, S. M., Rohde, P., Seeley, J. R., & Lewinsohn, P. M. (1999). Life events and depression in adolescence: Relationship loss as a prospective risk factor for first onset of major depressive disorder. *Journal of Abnormal Psychology*, 108(4), 606-614.

Muraco, A. (2012). *Odd couples: Friendships at the intersection of gender and sexual orientation*. Duke University Press.

Osgood, D. W., & Anderson, A. L. (2004). Unstructured socializing and rates of delinquency. *Criminology*, 42(3), 519-550. https://doi.org/10.1111/j.1745-9125.2004.tb00528.x

Osgood, D. W., Wilson, J. K., O'Malley, P. M., Bachman, J. G., & Johnston, L. D. (1996). Routine activities and individual deviant behavior. *American Sociological Review*, 61(4), 635-655.

Pascoe, C. J. (2007). *Dude, you're a fag: Masculinity and sexuality in high school*. University of California Press.

Poon, C. S., & Saewyc, E. M. (2009). Out yonder: Sexual-minority adolescents in rural communities in British Columbia. *American Journal of Public Health*, 99(1), 118-124. https://doi.org/10.2105/AJPH.2007.122945

Pratt, T. C., Cullen, F. T., Sellers, C. S., Winfree, L. T., Madensen, T. D., Daigle, L. E., Fearn, N. E., & Gau, J. M. (2010). The empirical status of social learning theory: A meta-analysis. *Justice Quarterly*, 27(6), 765-802. https://doi.org/10.1080/07418820903379610

Prinstein, M. J., Meade, C. S., & Cohen, G. L. (2003). Adolescent oral sex, peer popularity, and perceptions of best friends' sexual behavior. *Journal of Pediatric Psychology, 28*(4), 243–249. https://doi.org/10.1093/jpepsy/jsg012

Rebellon, C. J., & Manasse, M. (2004). Do "Bad Boys" really get the girls? Delinquency as a cause and consequence of dating behavior among adolescents. *Justice Quarterly, 21*(2), 355–389. https://doi.org/10.1080/07418820400095841

Regan, P. C., Durvasula, R., Howell, L., Ureño, O., & Rea, M. (2004). Gender, ethnicity, and the developmental timing of first sexual and romantic experiences. *Social Behavior and Personality: An International Journal, 32*(7), 667–676.

Reiss, I. L. (1956). The double standard in premarital sexual intercourse: A neglected concept. *Social Forces, 34*(3), 224–230. https://doi.org/10.2307/2574041

Rivera, M. T., Soderstrom, S. B., & Uzzi, B. (2010). Dynamics of dyads in social networks: Assortative, relational, and proximity mechanisms. *Annual Review of Sociology, 36*(1), 91–115. https://doi.org/10.1146/annurev.soc.34.040507.134743

Robinson, J. P., & Espelage, D. L. (2011). Inequities in educational and psychological outcomes between LGBTQ and straight students in middle and high school. *Educational Researcher, 40*(7), 315–330. https://doi.org/10.3102/0013189X11422112

Robinson-Cimpian, J. P. (2014). Inaccurate estimation of disparities due to mischievous responders several suggestions to assess conclusions. *Educational Researcher, 43*(4), 171–185. https://doi.org/10.3102/0013189X14534297

Roisman, G. I., Masten, A. S., Coatsworth, J. D., & Tellegen, A. (2004). Salient and emerging developmental tasks in the transition to adulthood. *Child Development, 75*(1), 123–133. https://doi.org/10.1111/j.1467-8624.2004.00658.x

Rouvés, V., & Poulin, F. (2016). Romantic involvement and alcohol use in middle and late adolescence. *International Journal of Adolescence and Youth, 21*(1), 104–118.

Russell, S. T. (2003). Sexual minority youth and suicide risk. *American Behavioral Scientist, 46*(9), 1241–57. https://doi.org/10.1177/0002764202250667

Savin-Williams, R. C., & Joyner, K. (2014). The politicization of gay youth health: Response to Li, Katz-Wise, and Calzo (2014). *Archives of Sexual Behavior, 43*(6), 1027–1030. https://doi.org/10.1007/s10508-014-0359-2

Snapp, S. D., Hoenig, J. M., Fields, A., & Russell, S. T. (2015a). Messy, Butch, and Queer LGBTQ Youth and the School-to-Prison Pipeline. *Journal of Adolescent Research, 30*(1), 57–82. https://doi.org/10.1177/0743558414557625

Snapp, S. D., McGuire, J. K., Sinclair, K. O., Gabrion, K., & Russell, S. T. (2015b). LGBTQ-inclusive curricula: Why supportive curricula matter. *Sex Education, 15*(6), 580–596. https://doi.org/10.1080/14681811.2015.1042573

Steffensmeier, D., & Allan, E. (1996). Gender and crime: Toward a gendered theory of female offending. *Annual Review of Sociology, 22*(1), 459–487. https://doi.org/10.1146/annurev.soc.22.1.459

Sun, I. Y., & Longazel, J. G. (2008). College students' alcohol-related problems: A test of competing theories. *Journal of Criminal Justice, 36*(6), 554–562.

Sutherland, E. H. (1939). Differential association. In Edwin Sutherland (Ed.), *Principles of criminology* (pp. 4–7). Rowman & Littlefield.

Sutherland, E. H. (1947). *Principles of criminology* (4th ed.). Lippincott.

Swank, E., Frost, D. M., & Fahs, B. (2012). Rural location and exposure to minority stress among sexual minorities in the United States. *Psychology & Sexuality, 3*(3), 226–243. https://doi.org/10.1080/19419899.2012.700026

Tebes, J. K., Feinn, B., Vanderploeg, J. J., Chinman, M. J., Shepard, J., Brabham, T., Genovese, M., & Connell, C. (2007). Impact of a positive youth development program in urban after-school settings on the prevention of adolescent substance use. *Journal of Adolescent Health, 41*(3), 239–247. https://doi.org/10.1016/j.jadohealth.2007.02.016

Tolli, M. V. (2012). Effectiveness of peer education interventions for HIV prevention, adolescent pregnancy prevention and sexual health promotion for young people: A systematic review of European studies. *Health Education Research, 27*(5), 904–913.

Udry, R. J., & Chantala, K. (2005). Risk factors differ according to same-sex and opposite-sex interest. *Journal of Biosocial Science, 37*(04), 481–497. https://doi.org/10.1017/S0021932004006765

Ueno, K. (2010). Patterns of cross-orientation friendships in high schools. *Social Science Research, 39*(3), 444–458. https://doi.org/10.1016/j.ssresearch.2009.10.001

Valente, T. W., Gallaher, P., & Mouttapa, M. (2004). Using social networks to understand and prevent substance use: A transdisciplinary perspective. *Substance Use & Misuse, 39*(10–12), 1685–1712. https://doi.org/10.1081/ja-200033210

Vasilenko, S. A., Kreager, D. A., & Lefkowitz, E. S. (2015). Gender, contraceptive attitudes, and condom use in adolescent romantic relationships: A dyadic approach. *Journal of Research on Adolescence, 25*(1), 51–62. https://doi.org/10.1111/jora.12091

Warr, M. (2002). *Companions in crime: The social aspects of criminal conduct.* Cambridge University Press.

Weerman, F. M. (2011). Delinquent peers in context: A longitudinal network analysis of selection and influence effects. *Criminology, 49*(1), 253–286. https://doi.org/10.1111/j.1745-9125.2010.00223.x

Wesche, R., Claxton, S. E., & Waterman, E. A. (2021). Emotional outcomes of casual sexual relationships and experiences: A systematic review. *The Journal of Sex Research, 58*(8), 1069–1084. https://doi.org/10.1080/00224499.2020.1821163

Wesche, R., Kreager, D. A., Feinberg, M. E., & Lefkowitz, E. S. (2019). Peer acceptance and sexual behaviors from adolescence to young adulthood. *Journal of Youth and Adolescence, 48*(5), 996–1008. https://doi.org/10.1007/s10964-019-00991-7

Wesche, R., Kreager, D. A., & Lefkowitz, E. S. (2019). Sources of social influence on adolescents' alcohol use. *Journal of Research on Adolescence, 29*(4), 984–1000. https://doi.org/10.1111/jora.12439

Whitton, S. W., Dyar, C., Newcomb, M. E., & Mustanski, M. (2018). Romantic involvement: A protective factor for psychological health in racially-diverse young sexual minorities. *Journal of Abnormal Psychology, 127*(3), 265.

Willging, C. E., Salvador, M., & Kano, M. (2006). Brief reports: Unequal treatment: Mental health care for sexual and gender minority groups in a rural state. *Psychiatric Services, 57*(6), 867–870. https://doi.org/10.1176/ps.2006.57.6.867

Yarbrough, D. G. (2004). Gay adolescents in rural areas. *Journal of Human Behavior in the Social Environment, 8*(2–3), 129–144. https://doi.org/10.1300/J137v08n02_08

10

Variation in network processes across community and school district contexts

CASSIE MCMILLAN, DANIEL T. RAGAN, AND ALANA COLINDRES ■

INTRODUCTION

Relationships with peers are embedded within different levels of social organization (e.g., classroom, schools) and across varied social environments (e.g., neighborhoods, communities). This chapter addresses whether, and how, features of the school district and larger community play a role in shaping peer network dynamics. Research on social networks includes a healthy tradition of studying the interplay between social *structure*—including the immediate settings and larger societal factors that both constrain available choices and provide opportunities—and individual *agency*, or the ability for persons to make choices and implement goals (Giddens, 1979; Sewell, 1992). Theories of community influence emphasize the role that the larger social environment plays in shaping adolescent behavior, particularly risky behaviors (Sampson et al., 2002; Shaw & McKay, 1942). However, it remains unclear whether peer network structures or processes that guide the formation of risky behaviors differ across communities. If there is community-level variability in such processes, these phenomena may mediate the influence of broader community social factors (e.g., disorganization) on adolescent substance use. By understanding how network-related processes operate as a link between community context and individual outcomes, we can better address the needs of at-risk youth.

A rich body of research has investigated both how adolescents select friends and the consequences of such friendships (see Chapter 1). For instance, adolescents

Cassie McMillan, Daniel T. Ragan, and Alana Colindres, *Variation in network processes across community and school district contexts*. In: *Teen Friendship Networks, Development, and Risky Behavior*. Edited by: Mark E. Feinberg and D. Wayne Osgood, Oxford University Press. © Mark E. Feinberg and D. Wayne Osgood 2024. DOI: 10.1093/oso/9780197602317.003.0010 tend to become friends with others who share attributes similar to themselves (Goodreau et al., 2009; McPherson et al., 2001). Those who engage in risky behaviors tend to be named as a friend more than others (Haynie, 2001; Moody et al., 2011). And, once a friendship is established, youth change their beliefs and behaviors to be more similar to their friends (Kandel, 1978; Osgood et al., 2013, 2015). It remains unclear, however, whether these network processes are relatively universal and, if not, how and why they vary across different settings. An absence of variability in these processes would point to the possibility that some elements of adolescent social and behavioral development are relatively universal, at least within the particular sociocultural context under study (i.e., predominantly white, rural, and semirural communities in the United States). Alternatively, the strength of some network processes may differ across school and community contexts. Variation in network processes, and the identification of school and community factors associated with these differences, may provide insight into the particular ways that adolescent friendship networks unfold across different settings and affect risky behaviors and health. Such an understanding would present opportunities to tailor intervention programs to specific communities to enhance program effectiveness.

In the current chapter, we address two questions related to peer relationships, risky behavior, and the larger social environment. First, we ask whether peer influence and peer selection mechanisms vary across the different adolescent peer networks studied in the PROSPER (Promoting School-community-university Partnerships to Enhance Resilience) Peers project. Specifically, we focus on how these peer network processes operate with relation to three risky behaviors: delinquency, alcohol use, and smoking tobacco. Next, we examine how the broader community and school district context shapes peer processes across our sample of friendship networks. Here, we explore whether features of the community and school district shape processes of friendship selection and influence. The innovative research presented in this chapter provides insights into the links between the broader social context and the processes linking adolescent friendships and problem behaviors. Finally, we point to areas where future research in this area may prove fruitful.

BACKGROUND

Neighborhood context, schools, and adolescent problem behavior

A key theme across social-ecological theories of behavior is that neighborhood and community characteristics have the ability to impact individual behaviors, development, and well-being. Much of the empirical research related to neighborhood effects has its roots in the Chicago school of sociology (Park & Burgess, 1925; Shaw & McKay, 1942). Shaw and McKay (1942), for example, argued that the structural conditions of a neighborhood—concentrated poverty, racial and ethnic heterogeneity, and high levels of residential mobility—were indicators of social disorganization, which undermines residents' collective ability to solve problems and pursue goals. In neighborhoods with lower levels of social disorganization, community members are more able to effectively raise children with the cooperation of neighbors, who provide additional informal social control over youth. Socially disorganized neighborhoods, however, lack the ability to do so. Subsequent work, such as that by Bursik and Grasmick (1993), expanded on these ideas by placing increased emphasis on the importance of relational networks among residents. According to this approach, markers of social disorganization disrupt the ability to establish and maintain various types of relational ties that protect neighborhoods from delinquency and crime. Thus, interpersonal relationships play a prominent role in the social-ecological literature linking community characteristics to deviant behavior, as social disorganization inhibits the cooperation needed for successful community supervision of adolescent groups. A substantial portion of research related to neighborhood-level research has subsequently focused on problem- and health-related behaviors (Sampson et al., 2002), and the underlying theory provides a useful guide for thinking about connections between the social network processes and the broader social structure.

The importance of the broader community and interpersonal networks to adolescent behavior has also been identified by those who study youth development and friendships. Indeed, a number of prominent theoretical perspectives explicitly recognize how close friends interact within broader communities. Bronfenbrenner's (1977) ecological framework for studying human development, for example, highlights how the interactions between individuals and their environments change over time. Bronfenbrenner advanced the argument that different levels of the environment are both *nested* and *interconnected*. More specifically, peer groups and schools are meso-level components that may interact with macro-level systems in which they are embedded, such as neighborhoods and communities. Several of the key themes of Bronfenbrenner's framework are echoed by other scholars. Brown (2004), for example, contended that interactions between adolescent peers occur at multiple levels. This begins at the level of the dyad, or pair of individuals, and scales up to "crowds" that bring together large numbers of young people up to the level of a school, for example. In addition to the observation that close friendship networks are embedded in larger, less personal networks, Brown also noted that these the larger networks may exert influence over interpersonal relationships, and "the peer system itself is embedded within other social contexts, such as the school or neighborhood" (p. 367).

Current research supports the position that the broader community context can impact adolescents' individual-level participation in different types of problem behaviors. For instance, young people's involvement with substance use and delinquency tends to vary according to whether they live in metropolitan versus rural areas, although findings in this area are mixed. On the one hand, previous work found higher rates of adolescent alcohol and marijuana use among those residing in rural communities, as opposed to those living in urban areas, largely due to variations in community stability (Lo et al., 2013). Youth living in micropolitan areas, or communities with populations of less than 50,000 residents, have greater rates of heavy drinking than those from areas with larger populations (Martino et al., 2008). On the other hand, other research found that youth living in small towns tend to report less frequent drinking when compared to their peers in metropolitan areas (Slutske et al., 2016).

There is also some evidence that youth living in communities defined by higher levels of socioeconomic instability and fewer economic resources are at a higher risk of participating in certain problem behaviors. Chilenski (2011) found that community-level economic risk does not significantly increase adolescents' odds of participating in delinquent behaviors in the PROSPER sample. However, there is also evidence that adolescents with many schoolmates in economically precarious situations are at higher risk of engaging in criminal behaviors and reporting favorable views toward substance use (Chilenski & Greenberg, 2009). Furthermore, community-level racial and ethnic diversity may help explain why we observe community variation adolescent problem behavior. One study found neighborhoods with higher populations of Black residents had relatively lower levels of cigarette use among Black youth, while living in a predominantly white neighborhood was associated with higher levels of cigarette usage by both Black and white youth (Xue et al., 2007).

In addition to the role that neighborhood context plays in shaping the daily lives of adolescents and problem behaviors, the school is recognized as an especially important social institution during this point of the life course. Social ties to peers and friends become more salient than bonds to parents during adolescence, and schools represent a primary context for such peer relationships (Umberson et al., 2010). Coleman's (1961) seminal study of adolescent social life, for example, found that the organization of school structures plays a crucial role in shaping students' lives both within and outside of the classroom. For example, by providing a diversity of extracurricular activities and fostering the development of supportive bonds among students, teachers, and parents, schools can encourage the development of social capital and improve adolescent well-being (Crosnoe, 2011). When school districts do not provide such opportunities and support, this can increase individuals' risks of adverse outcomes, including delinquency and substance use (Crosnoe, 2011).

In line with these perspectives, empirical work found that several characteristics of schools and school districts are associated with adolescents' participation in problem behaviors. For example, students' engagement in risky behavior tends to vary with the size of a school's student body and the average number of students per class (Leung & Ferris, 2008). Students who attend larger schools, particularly those with a wide age range of pupils, are more likely to report involvement with delinquency (Gottfredson et al., 2005). Relatedly, Hoffmann and Xu (2002) found that youth tend to engage in less delinquent behavior when enrolled in schools with larger ratios of teachers per student. The authors suspected that the smaller class sizes that result from high student-teacher ratios facilitate student monitoring, which can curtail problem behavior participation.

Prior research also found that normative, structural transitions, such as the change from middle to high school, can impact individual-level involvement in different problem behaviors. After experiencing these normative transitions, adolescents tend to report lower academic grades and fewer within-school friendships when compared to peers who did not change schools during the same period (Felmlee et al., 2018; Temkin et al., 2018). Yet, perhaps surprisingly, this change in school context is simultaneously associated with less participation in various delinquent behaviors, such as getting into physical fights, stealing, and gang involvement (Carson et al., 2017; Freelin et al., 2023). Thus, while school transitions can be challenging for young people to navigate, they may also offer a chance to start anew and sever previous ties to antisocial peers who negatively influence delinquency (Carson et al., 2017).

Finally, young people who attend schools characterized by healthy social climates (i.e., positive student-teacher relationships) and high levels of morale are less likely to participate in risky behaviors than peers who attend school in less supportive environments. For example, students are suspended at lower rates when they attend school districts defined by high levels of teacher support and encouragement to excel academically (Gregory et al., 2012). Young people also report less engagement in problem behaviors when they perceive higher levels of within-school safety (Hoffmann & Xu, 2002) and more prosocial classroom environments (Lo et al., 2010).

Implications for peer influence and friend selection

Given that peer network processes shape adolescents' risky problem behaviors, a large body of work considers how peer influence and various friend selection mechanisms inform adolescent delinquency, drinking, and smoking. Yet despite this body of research, researchers have yet to reach a consensus on the degree to which peer networks shape and are shaped by adolescent problem behaviors (Veenstra et al., 2013). For example, some researchers argue that peer influence plays a primary role in explaining risky behavior homophily (e.g., Weerman, 2011), while others show that the effect of peer influence is minimal after accounting for friend selection processes (e.g., Knecht et al., 2010). Furthermore, our own line of research finds evidence that adolescents both select friends according to their engagement in problem behaviors and are influenced by the participation levels of these peers (e.g., Osgood et al., 2013, Osgood et al., 2015).

Our purpose in drawing attention to these disparate results is to highlight that the evidence supporting the existence of peer influence and selection mechanisms in the extent literature is inconsistent. We believe that there are two possible reasons why previous studies reached varying conclusions regarding the peer processes that inform youth problem behaviors. First, there may be substantively meaningful differences in the school- and community-based contexts that define the various samples considered by previous work (McMillan & Felmlee, 2020). Although some researchers have begun collecting rich, sociocentric network data from a diversity of communities both within and outside the United States, most individual studies focus on a single network (e.g., Schaefer et al., 2012) or a sample of networks drawn from relatively homogeneous populations (e.g., Knecht et al., 2010; Poulin et al., 2011). Thus, the seemingly contradictory findings across previous work could be due to true variations in peer influence and selection mechanisms across different community and school environments.

On the other hand, methodological idiosyncrasies may mislead researchers when they interpret their findings, resulting in studies that lead to contradictory conclusions. In addition to an increase in sociocentric data, the past decades have witnessed advances in computationally intensive methodologies for analyzing complex network data sets, including stochastic actor-oriented models (SAOMs). These statistical techniques enable scholars to disentangle the effects of peer influence and friend selection with a level of methodological rigor that is rarely attainable when applying conventional techniques (Steglich et al., 2010). However, recent work found that estimates of network processes derived from SAOMs may be imprecise—that is, the point estimates are accompanied by large standard errors—particularly when the size of the network is small or even moderate (Ragan et al., 2022). As a result, estimates of network processes drawn from a sample of networks are likely to vary, and it is often difficult to determine whether observed variation reflects genuine differences across types of neighborhoods and schools or random variability due to a lack precision across statistical models.

Although few studies consider whether peer influence and friend selection vary across different school- and community-level contexts (for an exception, see McFarland et al., 2014), we argue that there is value in examining such differences. Understanding whether the processes linking peer networks and risky behavior are relatively universal and, if not, how and why they vary across different settings has the potential to inform school-based prevention programs and improve adolescents' well-being. For instance, McMillan and Schaefer's (2021) simulation-based study found that network-based intervention programs hold great potential to reduce population-wide levels of underage drinking in some school environments. However, these same intervention designs can lead to negligible reductions or even increase the average drinking level of a student body in other school districts. Given these implications for intervention effectiveness, our chapter aims to answer the following research questions:

1. Do peer network processes related to delinquency, drinking, and tobacco use vary across community-cohort combinations in the PROSPER study?
2. How do characteristics of the community and school district shape peer network processes that relate to problem behavior?

METHODS

To evaluate whether the connection between peer networks and risky behavior varies across contexts, we analyzed five waves of friendship network data, from the fall of sixth-grade year to the spring of ninth grade. We consider 51 friendship networks—one for each district-cohort combination.

Measures

Our measure of *delinquency* considers respondents' answers to 12 questions about past-year participation in different types of delinquent activities. Survey questions asked students how often they got into physical fights, vandalized property, stole, and participated in other delinquent acts during the past 12 months. We used variety scoring to create a count of the number of delinquent activities in which each student participated, resulting in a measure ranging from 0 to 12. To improve the convergence of our models, we recoded this skewed measure into four ordinal categories ranging from *no past year delinquency* to *participation in four or more delinquent behaviors* (following McMillan et al., 2018; Osgood et al., 2015). Measures of individual *tobacco smoking* and *alcohol drinking* behaviors were constructed from students' responses to two questions that asked how often they "smoked any cigarettes" or "had beer, wine, wine coolers, or hard liquor" during the past month. The individual-level measures for both drinking and smoking were recoded into three ordered categories: *no past month participation, once in the past month,* and *more than once in the past month* (following Osgood et al., 2013; Ragan, 2020).

We evaluated whether neighborhood- and school-level factors moderated estimates of four peer processes—peer influence, similarity in friend selection, receiving ties, and sending ties—for each of the three problem behaviors. For each school-grade cohort network in our study, we estimated three SAOMs, one for each problem behavior. These analyses relied on the same estimates as those from the baseline models presented by Osgood et al. (2015) and McMillan et al. (2018). We point readers to the original publications for additional information on the model specification and goodness-of-fit diagnostics.

For each problem behavior, we extracted estimates of peer influence, friend similarity, and the association between the behavior and sending/receiving friendship nominations by considering the coefficients of specific SAOM effects. Peer influence was captured by considering the coefficients of effects commonly used in the SAOM literature for each problem behavior. More specifically, we used the coefficient values of the *average similarity* effect to address our first research question and those of the *average alter* effect to address our second question. Larger coefficients values for both measures suggest that adolescents were more likely to change their rates of problem behavior to become more similar to their friends' rates as the relationship developed over time. To measure friend similarity, we considered each network's coefficient for the *problem behavior similarity* effect. Larger values of this coefficient suggest that respondents tended to seek out friendships with peers who participated in the behavior at similar rates as themselves prior to the relationship's inception. To evaluate whether receiving more friendship ties is associated with increased risky behavior participation, we considered the coefficient for each grade-cohort's *problem behavior alter* network effect. The coefficient for this effect is positive when adolescents who participated in the risky behavior tended to receive more friendship ties. Finally, we considered the coefficient of the *problem behavior ego* effect, which evaluates whether adolescents who report more problem behaviors were more likely to send friendship nominations to their peers.

Variation across school-cohort networks

Rather than present estimates of SAOM parameters for each set of network-specific models, we instead aggregated these estimates with "variance-known" multilevel models to address our first research question. These three-level models employ the SAOM estimates as outcomes at Level 1, and the squared standard errors of these estimates (also from the SAOMs) serve as their known variances. Random effects for the grade-cohort (Level 2) and community (Level 3) helped to correct for the nonindependent clustering of data in the PROSPER study design. Estimating variance-known multilevel models is a useful approach for aggregating results from models that are estimated independently across a number of networks. This procedure is essentially a meta-analysis, where the observed SAOM estimates are weighted inversely to their corresponding standard errors (i.e., the estimates with smaller standard errors contribute more toward the aggregate estimate).

While the average estimates produced by this approach are often of the most interest, these models also provide information that is needed to answer our first research question about the variability of network processes. Computing a simple variance or standard deviation across the network-specific SAOM estimates is inadequate for that purpose because it includes the error variance inherent in all of them, as well as the genuine variation in the processes across networks. Our three-level model provides relevant estimates of the latent or true variation at both the grade-cohort level and the community level, above and beyond the known error variance (captured by the network-specific standard errors). We obtained the total latent variance by adding together the variance estimates from these two levels, and we then took the square root of the resulting sum to estimate the standard deviation for the latent or true variation of the process across the networks. Joint likelihood ratio chi-square tests of the variance components indicate whether the total variation across the two levels is statistically significant at conventional alpha levels.

Community and school district factors

To address our second research question about the role that community- and school-district factors play in explaining variations in network processes related to problem behaviors, we included a variety of controls in our multilevel models. First, we included three community-level covariates to test whether the links between networks and risky behaviors varied according to community-level characteristics. To evaluate whether peer processes related to risky behaviors varied according to the rurality of adolescents' communities, we included the *percentage of the population living in rural areas*. This measure equals the percentage of the total population who lived in areas designated as rural in the county where each school district was located (i.e., neighborhoods with less than 2,500 residents). Additionally, we include the *percentage of households living below the poverty line* and the *percentage of racial/ethnic minorities* who lived in each school district's county to test for community-level variations in risky behavior peer processes. Data used to construct all three community-level variables are from American Community Survey (ACS) data collected at the year that the first cohort began the study (2002).

We also included three independent variables that were based on school-level factors in our multilevel models. We began by including an independent variable that indicated the *total number of school transitions* that students in each school district experienced from sixth through ninth grade. Here, we defined transitions as normative, structural changes from a lower level school to a higher level school (e.g., the transition from elementary to middle school). The districts in our sample experienced up to two transitions during our study. These normative, structural transitions occurred between sixth and seventh grade and/or eighth and ninth grade. We also included a network-level measure of *average school bonding* to assess how school climate shaped peer processes for the three problem behaviors. To construct this measure, we averaged individual-level responses to eight survey questions about a school's climate for each network across all five waves considered in the current study. Responses were coded such that higher values indicated greater levels of school bonding and adjustment. Finally, we included a measure of each grade-cohort's *average size* to evaluate whether peer processes varied according to school size. This measure equals the mean number of actors in each network across all five waves of the study.

We included three network-level control variables that could be associated with variations in peer processes and problem behavior participation. We included binary indicators for the *state* where each school district was located (1 = *Pennsylvania*) and the *cohort* represented in each network (1 = *Cohort 1*). Additionally, we controlled for the *average level of participation* for each problem behavior (delinquency, drinking, or smoking). We calculated this measure by taking the mean value of the individual-level participation scores for each grade-cohort of students at each wave.

RESULTS

Variation across networks

To address our first research question, selected results are presented in Table 10.1 (additional results are available in Osgood et al., 2015, and discussed in Chapter 5). The first three columns list the minimum values, maximum values, and standard

Table 10.1 VARIABILITY OF NETWORK SELECTION AND INFLUENCE PROCESSES

	Observed SAOM estimates			Variance-known results			
	Min	Max	Std. Dev.	Estimated Mean	Latent Std. Dev.	95% range Lower	95% range Upper
Alter selection parameters							
Delinquency	−0.031	0.102	0.030	0.029	0.007	0.015	0.043
Alcohol use	−0.364	0.340	0.125	0.082	0.014	0.055	0.109
Smoking	−0.274	0.385	0.143	0.112	0.043	0.028	0.196
Ego selection parameters							
Delinquency	−0.180	0.160	0.070	−0.015	0.049 ***	−0.111	0.081
Alcohol use	−0.373	0.251	0.147	−0.039	0.077 ***	−0.190	0.112
Smoking	−0.440	0.892	0.247	−0.007	0.131 ***	−0.264	0.250
Similarity selection parameters							
Delinquency	−0.085	0.535	0.152	0.220	0.093 **	0.038	0.402
Alcohol use	−1.048	1.074	0.361	0.289	0.011	0.267	0.311
Smoking	−0.292	1.296	0.365	0.439	0.096	0.251	0.627
Friends' behavioral influence parameters							
Delinquency	−0.899	3.117	0.714	1.108	0.018	1.073	1.143
Alcohol use	−1.328	4.086	0.936	1.278	0.017	1.245	1.311
Smoking	0.359	15.866	2.480	2.023	0.030	1.964	2.082

Note. ***$p < 0.001$. **$p < 0.01$. *$p < 0.05$.

deviations for the observed estimates from SAOM models. Notably, most estimates of peer processes are defined by a large range of variation, which carries important implications for the substantive meaning of these coefficients. For example, there is at least one grade-cohort network in our sample where drinking alcohol was associated with receiving fewer friendship ties (minimum alcohol use alter coefficient = −0.364), while drinkers tended to receive more nominations in other networks (maximum alcohol use alter coefficient = 0.340). The remaining columns present results derived from the variance-known multilevel models and contain the aggregate (weighted) estimate of the mean. Although not the focus of this chapter, the magnitude of this estimate provides necessary context for understanding the variability of the estimate. The next column contains the estimated latent standard deviation of that mean, reflecting variation beyond the separate estimates' standard errors. This column also reports the corresponding significance test for the estimates of variability at the grade-cohort and community levels. The final columns present the range within which 95% of the networks' true parameter values are predicted to fall.

It is also useful to contrast the estimated latent standard deviation from the variance-known multilevel models and the corresponding range derived from it to the standard deviation of the observed (raw) coefficients. For each parameter, the latent standard deviation was considerably smaller than the observed standard deviation, and the predicted range of estimates was notably smaller than the observed range. The latent standard deviation of the ego selection parameter for each problem behavior was statistically significant (*delinquency*: estimated SD = 0.049, $p < 0.001$; *alcohol use*: estimated SD = 0.077, $p < 0.001$; *smoking*: estimated SD = 0.131, $p < 0.001$). The only other latent standard deviation that achieved statistical significance is the similarity selection parameter for delinquency (estimated SD = 0.093, $p < 0.01$). Overall, these results suggest that most peer processes related to delinquency, drinking, and smoking tended to be consistent across our sample of school contexts.

The significant variability in the association between risky behavior participation and sending friendship nominations is particularly interesting. The estimated mean for each behavior is near zero (ranging from −0.039 to −0.007), while the estimates of the latent standard deviations suggest a much wider range of variation. Meanwhile, estimates for youth to select friends with similar levels of delinquency indicate that the tendency for individuals to gain friends with similar levels of reported delinquency is fairly weak (although still positive) in some networks, but substantial in others.

For the parameter estimates of other processes—those for the alter selection parameters, the peer influence parameters, and the similarity selection parameters for alcohol use and smoking—the estimated latent standard deviation fails to achieve statistical significance at conventional alpha levels. Thus, for most of the parameters it appears that the variability of the observed estimates across the networks is most likely due to the imprecision of the estimates rather than true population differences.

Variation by community- and school-level factors

To address our second research question, we estimated additional multilevel models that assess whether the link between peer networks and problem behavior varied according to community- and school-level factors. We present our results in Table 10.2. We found that certain community-level factors were associated with variations in some peer processes related to smoking. The tendency to select friends who smoke at levels similar to ones' own was significantly greater in largely rural (*proportion rural*: $b = 0.009$, *SE (standard error)* = 0.004, $p < 0.05$) and predominantly white communities (*proportion racial minority*: $b = -0.048$, $SE = 0.021$, $p < 0.05$). In other words, adolescents were more likely to befriend peers with similar smoking behaviors as their own in communities that were more rural and less racially diverse. We did not find any significant associations between any of the community-level measures and peer processes related to delinquency or drinking alcohol.

Additionally, we found some evidence that school-level factors shaped the relationship between peer networks and problem behaviors. Students who attended school districts defined by a greater number of compulsory transitions were

Table 10.2 COEFFICIENTS FOR COMMUNITY- AND SCHOOL-LEVEL VARIATION IN NETWORK SELECTION AND INFLUENCE PROCESSES

	Influence	Similarity	Ego	Alter
Delinquency				
Community-level factors				
Proportion rural	0.001	0.001	−0.000	−0.000
	(0.002)	(0.002)	(0.001)	(0.000)
Proportion below poverty line	0.017	−0.022	−0.002	0.002
	(0.015)	(0.014)	(0.004)	(0.004)
Proportion racial minority	−0.003	−0.010	−0.001	0.003
	(0.009)	(0.010)	(0.003)	(0.002)
School-level factors				
Number of transitions	−0.173 *	0.094	0.001	−0.013
	(0.068)	(0.071)	(0.020)	(0.019)
Average school bonding	−0.270	0.274	−0.084	−0.061
	(0.459)	(0.466)	(0.134)	(0.123)
Average network size (100s)	0.029	0.101	0.033 *	−0.012
	(0.053)	(0.052)	(0.015)	(0.014)
Intercept	2.372	−0.445	0.362	0.551
	(2.245)	(2.407)	(0.658)	(0.604)
Drinking				
Community-level factors				
Proportion rural	−0.003	0.002	−0.000	−0.001
	(0.004)	(0.002)	(0.001)	(0.002)
Proportion below poverty line	0.018	0.003	−0.004	0.017
	(0.037)	(0.020)	(0.009)	(0.014)
Proportion racial minority	−0.022	−0.013	−0.007	−0.005
	(0.024)	(0.070)	(0.006)	(0.010)
School-level factors				
Number of transitions	0.037	0.028	−0.006	−0.028
	(0.156)	(0.094)	(0.046)	(0.060)
Average school bonding	−0.310	0.704	−0.014	−0.537
	(1.027)	(0.517)	(0.284)	(0.365)
Average network size (100s)	0.108	0.078	0.093 **	0.014
	(0.169)	(0.089)	(0.033)	(0.062)
Intercept	1.917	−2.299	−0.001	2.154
	(4.078)	(2.071)	(1.373)	(1.460)
Smoking				
Community-level factors				
Proportion rural	−0.002	0.009 *	0.001	0.001
	(0.007)	(0.004)	(0.002)	(0.002)
Proportion below poverty line	0.064	0.053	−0.007	−0.001
	(0.085)	(0.037)	(0.014)	(0.016)
Proportion racial minority	−0.003	−0.048 *	−0.016	−0.016
	(0.037)	(0.021)	(0.011)	(0.009)
School-level factors				
Number of transitions	−0.323	−0.185	0.008	−0.058
	(0.327)	(0.123)	(0.076)	(0.056)

Table 10.2 CONTINUED

	Influence	Similarity	Ego	Alter
Average school bonding	−2.149	0.337	0.145	0.027
	(1.244)	(0.595)	(0.380)	(0.247)
Average network size (100s)	−0.132	−0.071	0.081	0.025
	(0.246)	(0.125)	(0.055)	(0.050)
Intercept	9.045	−0.216	−1.091	0.435
	(4.916)	(2.333)	(2.059)	(0.966)

Notes. All models include controls for cohort, state, and the average level of the behavior of interest across the five waves of the study. Standard errors are in parentheticals.

**$p < 0.01$, *$p < 0.05$.

expected to be less influenced by their friends' delinquent behaviors ($b = -0.173$, $SE = 0.068$, $p < 0.05$). For each additional normative transition in a school system, youth were more likely to be shaped by the delinquent behaviors of their friends. Additionally, in schools with larger student bodies, adolescents who participated in delinquency and drank alcohol tended to send more friendship nominations than peers who abstained from these problem behaviors ($b = 0.033$, $SE = 0.0154$, $p < 0.05$ and $b = 0.093$, $SE = 0.033$, $p < 0.01$, respectively). In other words, delinquency and drinking increased the number of friendship nominations a student made in large schools, but this was less of the case in small schools. No other school-level factors were significantly associated with variations across the three peer processes related to delinquency, drinking, and smoking.

DISCUSSION

Research on adolescent problem behaviors finds conflicting evidence about the connection between peer network processes and youth delinquency and substance use. In the current chapter, we consider whether these inconsistencies are the result of substantively meaningful differences in school and community contexts or due to methodological artifacts. By leveraging the more than 50 longitudinal networks from the PROSPER study across five waves of data, we considered several network processes that inform adolescent delinquency, drinking, and smoking. With some notable exceptions, we found that these processes did not significantly vary across PROSPER community contexts.

In general, we found that much of the between-network variation was likely the result of statistical noise rather than true variations across networks. However, our results also suggested that the relationship between peer networks and problem behavior occasionally varied across the networks in our sample. Most notably, we uncovered significant true variability across peer networks in the tendency for adolescents involved with delinquency, drinking, and smoking to send more (or less) ties than peers who abstained from these behaviors. For instance, in some networks, increasing one's frequency of smoking was associated with sending as much as 23% fewer ties, while in other communities, tobacco use could increase the number of friends and adolescent nominated by up to 28%. At the same time, estimates of peer influence, selection of friends based on shared behavior, and attracting friendship nominations based on risky behavior participation were almost the same across peer networks. This finding suggests that peer network processes shape adolescents' delinquency, drinking, and smoking in a similar manner.

In the second set of results, we found certain school- and community-level factors moderated the relationship between peer networks and problem behavior. Adolescents who attended school in districts defined by a greater number of normative school transitions tended to be less influenced by the delinquency of their peers, for example. Since previous work found that school transitions can lead to a decline in school-based friendships (e.g., Felmlee et al., 2018, Temkin et al., 2018), we suspect that students who make these normative transitions may be more apt to look outside of their school-based networks when forming intimate, trustworthy relationships. With more close friends outside of school, and thus more options for friendship activities, youth in districts defined by multiple transitions may be less inclined to adopt the delinquent behaviors of their within-school connections.

Additionally, we found that in schools with large student bodies, students tended to send more friendship ties as their level of participation in delinquency and drinking increased. In smaller schools, adolescents who engaged in these problem behaviors did not send more friendship nominations than their peers who abstained from these activities. In schools with large student bodies, the high number of friendship nominations sent by delinquent students and alcohol users increased the odds that any student would be tied to a deviant peer. This will result in greater numbers of students who are at risk of being influenced by their friends' problematic behaviors and may help explain why larger schools are characterized by higher levels of delinquent behavior (e.g., Gottfredson et al., 2005).

Finally, we found that networks in communities defined by either high levels of rurality or low degrees of racial diversity demonstrated more friend selection on shared smoking behavior. Previous work found that adolescents tended to befriend classmates with whom they shared similar demographic characteristics and behaviors (Kreager et al., 2011; McPherson et al., 2001), and that these tendencies toward similarity varied across networks (McFarland et al., 2014; Moody, 2001). Perhaps in the absence of substantial racial diversity on which similarity-based friendships can develop, young people are more likely to seek out friends who participate in similar risky behaviors as their own.

While our chapter sheds new light on possible reasons why peer processes related to risky behavior can vary across networks, there are important limitations to note. First, the networks in our sample were all drawn from small-to-medium, fairly racially homogeneous communities in Pennsylvania and Iowa. Future work should apply the analytical approach discussed here to study adolescent networks across a more diverse range of schools and communities. Additionally, the current project assumes that the links between peer network processes and problem behavior remain consistent across all waves of the study. However, recent work found that the strength of peer influence and friend selection tended to vary over the course of adolescence (Ragan, 2020). Future research should consider whether school- and community-related factors play a role in informing these differences over time.

Despite these limitations, we believe our findings carry the potential to inform school-based prevention and intervention campaigns. By and large, network phenomena and adolescent problem behavior remained consistent across networks embedded in varying community and school contexts. This uniformity suggests that when intervention programs rely on network processes, they are apt to see the same levels of success when applied to different groups of young people. In addition to carrying implications for prevention campaigns, we believe these findings highlight the value of collecting large-scale network data sets that collect relational data from numerous boundary-defined populations. Previous work that analyzed the 51 longitudinal networks from the PROSPER study demonstrated the value of using techniques from multilevel modeling to calculate precise estimates of network processes (e.g., McMillan et al., 2018; Osgood et al., 2015; Ragan, 2020). Larger network data sets will enhance our ability to understand when school- and community-level differences shape adolescent outcomes.

REFERENCES

Bronfenbrenner, U. (1977). Toward an experimental ecology of human development. *American Psychologist, 32*(7), 513–531.

Brown, B. B. (2004). Adolescents' relationships with peers. In R. M. Lerner & L. Steinberg (Eds.), *Handbook of adolescent psychology* (pp. 363–394). John Wiley & Sons Inc.

Bursik, R. J., Jr., & Grasmick, H. G. (1993). Economic deprivation and neighborhood crime rates, 1960–1980. *Law & Society Review, 27*, 263.

Carson, D. C., Melde, C., Wiley, S. A., & Esbensen, F. A. (2017). School transitions as a turning point for gang status. *Journal of Crime and Justice, 40*(4), 396–416.

Chilenski, S. M. (2011). From the macro to the micro: A geographic examination of the community context and early adolescent problem behaviors. *American Journal of Community Psychology, 48*, 352–364.

Chilenski, S. M., & Greenberg, M. T. (2009). The importance of the community context in the epidemiology of early adolescent substance use and delinquency in a rural sample. *American Journal of Community Psychology, 44*, 287–301.

Coleman, J. S. (1961). *The adolescent society*. Free Press of Glencoe.

Crosnoe, R. (2011). *Fitting in, standing out: Navigating the social challenges of high school to get an education*. Cambridge University Press.

Felmlee, D., McMillan, C., Inara Rodis, P., & Osgood, D. W. (2018). Falling behind: Lingering costs of the high school transition for youth friendships and grades. *Sociology of Education, 91*(2), 159–182.

Freelin, B. N., McMillan, C., Felmlee, D., & Osgood, D. W. (2023). Changing contexts: A quasi-experiment examining adolescent delinquency and the transition to high school. *Criminology, 61*(1), 40–73.

Giddens, A. (1979). *Central problems in social theory: Action, structure and contradiction in social analysis.* University of California Press.

Goodreau, S. M., Kitts, J. A., & Morris, M. (2009). Birds of a feather, or friend of a friend? Using exponential random graph models to investigate adolescent social networks. *Demography, 46*(1), 103–125.

Gregory, A., Cornell, D., & Fan, X. (2012). Teacher safety and authoritative school climate in high schools. *American Journal of Education, 118*(4), 401–425.

Gottfredson, G. D., Gottfredson, D. C., Payne, A. A., & Gottfredson, N. C. (2005). School climate predictors of school disorder: Results from a national study of delinquency prevention in schools. *Journal of Research in Crime and Delinquency, 42*(4), 412–444.

Haynie, D. L. (2001). Delinquent peers revisited: Does network structure matter? *American Journal of Sociology, 106*(4), 1013–1057.

Hoffmann, J. P., & Xu, J. (2002). School activities, community service, and delinquency. *Crime & Delinquency, 48*(4), 568–591.

Kandel, D. B. (1978). Homophily, selection, and socialization in adolescent friendships. *American Journal of Sociology, 84*(2), 427–436.

Knecht, A., Snijders, T. A., Baerveldt, C., Steglich, C. E., & Raub, W. (2010). Friendship and delinquency: Selection and influence processes in early adolescence. *Social Development, 19*(3), 494–514.

Kreager, D. A., Rulison, K., & Moody, J. (2011). Delinquency and the structure of adolescent peer groups. *Criminology, 49*(1), 95–127.

Leung, A., & Ferris, J. S. (2008). School size and youth violence. *Journal of Economic Behavior & Organization, 65*(2), 318–333.

Lo, C. C., Kim, Y. S., Allen, T. M., Allen, A. N., Minugh, P. A., & Lomuto, N. (2010). The impact of school environment and grade level on student delinquency: A multilevel modeling approach. *Crime & Delinquency, 57*(4), 622–657.

Lo, C. C., Weber, J., & Cheng, T. (2013). Urban–rural differentials: A spatial analysis of Alabama students' recent alcohol use and marijuana use. *The American Journal of Addictions, 22*(3), 188–196.

Martino, S. C., Ellickson, P. L., & McCaffrey, D. F. (2008). Developmental trajectories of substance use from early to late adolescence: A comparison of rural and urban youth. *Journal of Studies on Alcohol and Drugs, 69*(3), 430–440.

McFarland, D. A., Moody, J., Diehl, D., Smith, J. A., & Thomas, R. J. (2014). Network ecology and adolescent social structure. *American Sociological Review, 79*(6), 1088–1121.

McMillan, C., & Felmlee, D. (2020). Beyond dyads and triads: A comparison of tetrads in twenty social networks. *Social Psychology Quarterly, 83*(4), 383–404.

McMillan, C., Felmlee, D., & Osgood, D. W. (2018). Peer influence, friend selection, and gender: How network processes shape adolescent smoking, drinking, and delinquency. *Social Networks, 55*, 86–96.

McMillan, C., & Schaefer, D. R. (2021). Comparing targeting strategies for network-based adolescent drinking interventions: A simulation approach. *Social Science & Medicine, 282*, 114136.

McPherson, M., Smith-Lovin, L., & Cook, J. M. (2001). Birds of a feather: Homophily in social networks. *Annual Review of Sociology, 27*(1), 415–444.

Moody, J. (2001). Race, school integration, and friendship segregation in America. *American Journal of Sociology, 107*(3), 679-716.

Moody, J., Brynildsen, W. D., Osgood, D. W., Feinberg, M. E., & Gest, S. (2011). Popularity trajectories and substance use in early adolescence. *Social Networks, 33*(2), 101-112.

Osgood, D. W., Feinberg, M. E., & Ragan, D. T. (2015). Social networks and the diffusion of adolescent problem behavior: Reliable estimates of selection and influence from sixth through ninth grades. *Prevention Science, 16*(6), 832-843.

Osgood, D. W., Ragan, D. T., Wallace, L., Gest, S. D., Feinberg, M. E., & Moody, J. (2013). Peers and the emergence of alcohol use: Influence and selection processes in adolescent friendship networks. *Journal of Research on Adolescence, 23*(3), 500-512.

Park, R. E., & Burgess, E. W. (1925). *The city*. Chicago University Press.

Poulin, F., Kiesner, J., Pedersen, S., & Dishion, T. J. (2011). A short-term longitudinal analysis of friendship selection on early adolescent substance use. *Journal of Adolescence, 34*(2), 249-256.

Ragan, D. T. (2020). Similarity between deviant peers: Developmental trends in influence and selection. *Criminology, 58*(2), 336-369.

Ragan, D. T., Osgood, D. W., Ramirez, N. G., Moody, J., & Gest, S. D. (2022). A comparison of peer influence estimates from SIENA stochastic actor-based models and from conventional regression approaches. *Sociological Methods & Research, 51*(1), 357-395.

Sampson, R. J., Morenoff, J. D., & Gannon-Rowley, T. (2002). Assessing "neighborhood effects": Social processes and new directions in research. *Annual Review of Sociology, 28*(1), 443-478.

Schaefer, D. R., Haas, S. A., & Bishop, N. J. (2012). A dynamic model of US adolescents' smoking and friendship networks. *American Journal of Public Health, 102*(6), e12-e18.

Sewell, W. H. (1992). A theory of structure: Duality, agency, and transformation. *American Journal of Sociology, 98*(1), 1-29.

Shaw, C. R., & McKay, H. D. (1942). *Juvenile delinquency and urban areas*. University of Chicago Press.

Slutske, W. S., Deutsch, A. R., & Piasecki, T. M. (2016). Neighborhood contextual factors, alcohol use, and alcohol problems in the United States: Evidence from a nationally representative study of young adults. *Alcoholism: Clinical & Experimental Research, 40*(5), 1010-1019.

Steglich, C., Snijders, T. A., & Pearson, M. (2010). Dynamic networks and behavior: Separating selection from influence. *Sociological Methodology, 40*(1), 329-393.

Temkin, D., Gest, S. D., Osgood, D. W., Feinberg, M., & Moody, J. (2018). Social network implications of normative school transitions in non-urban school districts. *Youth & Society, 50*(4), 462-484.

Umberson, D., Crosnoe, R., & Reczek, C. (2010). Social relationships and health behavior across the life course. *Annual Review of Sociology, 36*, 139-157.

Veenstra, R., Dijkstra, J. K., Steglich, C., & Van Zalk, M. H. (2013). Network-behavior dynamics. *Journal of Research on Adolescence, 23*(3), 399-412.

Weerman, F. M. (2011). Delinquent peers in context: A longitudinal network analysis of selection and influence effects. *Criminology, 49*(1), 253-286.

Xue, Y., Zimmerman, M. A., & Caldwell, C. H. (2007). Neighborhood residence and cigarette smoking among urban youths: The protective role of prosocial activities. *Journal of Public Health, 97*(10), 1865-1872.

11

Peer networks and the diffusion of intervention outcomes

KELLY L. RULISON AND MARK E. FEINBERG ■

INTRODUCTION

As noted throughout this volume, peer networks strongly influence adolescents' health risk behaviors. Despite this clear link, most interventions focus on changing individuals rather than addressing network influences or using the peer network to change behavior (Hunter et al., 2019; Valente et al., 2015; Valente & Pitts, 2017). Further, most program evaluations only measure the attitudes and behaviors of intervention participants. These individual-focused evaluations likely underestimate the true effect of the intervention by failing to measure how interventions shape—and are shaped by—peer networks. For example, school-based interventions may alter school-based friendship networks by facilitating relationships or by reducing the ability of antisocial peers to influence their friends (Gest et al., 2011). At the same time, peer networks can shape intervention effects by accelerating or deterring behavior change and by promoting or hindering diffusion of intervention outcomes beyond the original intervention participants. Using this information, prevention scientists can even develop and implement interventions that use peer networks to facilitate more positive outcomes (Shelton et al., 2019; Valente, 2012; Valente et al., 2015). In this chapter, we argue that the link between interventions and peer networks goes both ways: interventions can change dynamics within the peer network; at the same time, peer networks can also shape intervention outcomes.

In what follows, we briefly review the existing literature about the bidirectional link between interventions and peer networks. We then discuss the findings from four studies that used data from the PROSPER (Promoting School-community-university Partnerships to Enhance Resilience) Peers project, one of the only existing

Kelly L. Rulison and Mark E. Feinberg, *Peer networks and the diffusion of intervention outcomes*. In: *Teen Friendship Networks, Development, and Risky Behavior*. Edited by: Mark E. Feinberg and D. Wayne Osgood, Oxford University Press. © Mark E. Feinberg and D. Wayne Osgood 2024. DOI: 10.1093/oso/9780197602317.003.0011 data sets that includes longitudinal peer network measures within the context of an intervention evaluation. Study 1 tested the extent to which PROSPER shaped the friendship network. Studies 2 and 3 tested how friendship networks shaped the diffusion of intervention outcomes from the family-based intervention implemented as part of PROSPER. Study 4 used simulations informed by PROSPER's network data to estimate the likely effects of different network-based strategies for identifying intervention participants. We then conclude the chapter with a brief discussion of future research questions that still need to be addressed and the implications of this work for prevention scientists, program facilitators, and school staff.

INTERVENTIONS CAN INFLUENCE PEER NETWORKS

Interventions are often delivered in group settings. For example, most substance use interventions for adolescents are delivered in classroom settings (e.g., All Stars, Project Alert) or to groups of adolescents and parents (e.g., Strengthening Families for Parents and Youth 10-14). In many cases, it is more cost-effective and efficient to implement group-based interventions than it is to implement individual-focused interventions. In other cases, an explicit goal of the intervention is to create connections and improve social support among participants (e.g., Alcoholics Anonymous). Regardless of the motivation, these group-based interventions necessarily involve networks among participants, yet program evaluations rarely measure when or how peer networks change in response to these interventions (Gesell et al., 2013; Molloy Elreda et al., 2016). As our team has argued elsewhere (Gest et al., 2011), however, interventions can change relationships and behavioral dynamics within the peer network. We describe each of these outcomes in more detail below.

First, interventions can change how peer networks are structured, such as facilitating new or better relationships among network members. For example, some school-based interventions use classroom meetings to improve relationships among students (Battistich et al., 2000). Other interventions reorganize the school into smaller subunits to facilitate closer relationships among students and between students and teachers (Felner et al., 1993). Still other interventions use cooperative learning activities to facilitate new friendships among students as a way to integrate socially isolated children into the network (e.g., Stevens & Slavin, 1995). Typically, most evaluations do not measure whether these intervention strategies actually change the structure of the network. One exception is a pilot study of a community-based parenting intervention, which demonstrated that the density of ties in both advice and discussion networks doubled between Week 4 and Week 12 of the intervention (Gesell et al., 2013).

Second, interventions can change behavioral dynamics within the peer network. For example, interventions can change who is selected as a friend, either directly by encouraging adolescents to choose prosocial friends (e.g., Botvin & Griffin, 2004; Ellickson et al., 2003; Hansen & Dusenbury, 2004; Hansen et al., 2007) or indirectly by teaching parents to use parental monitoring and discourage friendships with antisocial peers (e.g., Molgaard et al., 1997; R. Spoth et al., 2004). If these interventions are successful, fewer students will choose antisocial adolescents as friends, and as a result, antisocial adolescents will become less central within the networks and therefore less likely to negatively influence their peers. Similarly, even without explicitly addressing friendship processes, interventions may change who is viewed as popular by changing norms or changing the prevalence of behaviors within the network. In addition, interventions may either unintentionally change whether people select friends who are similar to themselves (e.g., DeLay et al., 2016) or intentionally encourage relationships between antisocial and prosocial peers (Hektner et al., 2003; Mikami et al., 2005; Prinz et al., 1994). Finally, interventions may change peer influence processes by changing the strength of peer influence, by changing who is influential, and by changing susceptibility to influence. For example, some substance use interventions teach participants how to resist negative peer influence as a way to make students less susceptible to peer influence (e.g., Hansen et al., 2007).

PEER NETWORKS CAN SHAPE INTERVENTION EFFECTS

Peer networks are integral to every aspect of behavior change: people learn about, experiment with, and ultimately decide whether to adopt or reject new behaviors within the context of their peer networks (Rogers, 2003; Valente & Pitts, 2017). Therefore, is it not surprising that peer networks can influence whether or not an intervention is effective. For example, peer networks can either support or undermine the effectiveness of an intervention, and they can facilitate or hinder the diffusion of intervention outcomes from those who participated in an intervention to those who did not. In addition, program developers can use information about the peer network to identify who should be included in an intervention. We explore each of these possibilities in more detail below.

Peer networks can support or undermine intervention effectiveness. As noted above, many interventions occur in groups. Peer networks among participants within these group-based interventions can support the intervention's effectiveness. For example, Molloy Elreda and colleagues (2016) evaluated parent and adolescent groups within a mindfulness-based adaptation of the Strengthening Families Program. They found that participants who were more connected to their group also viewed sessions as more valuable and reported more self-efficacy. In addition, within-group connections predicted better outcomes for both mothers and adolescents. Similarly, in their evaluation of a 12-week workplace intervention, Hunter and colleagues (2015) used sensors to determine who spent time together; they found that participants who engaged in physical activity with others maintained higher activity levels throughout the intervention compared to those who participated alone.

At the same time, however, peer networks can undermine an intervention's effectiveness. For example, aggregating at-risk adolescents into intervention groups often has *harmful* effects on a range of outcomes, including smoking and delinquency (Dishion & Dodge, 2005; Dishion et al., 1999; Dishion & Tipsord, 2011; McCord, 2003; Poulin et al., 2001). These unanticipated results can be explained by interactions among deviant group members, in which group members modeled and reinforced each other's deviant attitudes and behaviors (e.g., laughing in response to rule-breaking talk), a process known as "deviancy training" (Dishion et al., 2001).

An individual's existing peer network can also influence intervention outcomes (Valente & Pitts, 2017), including whether behavior change is maintained over time (Kwasnicka et al., 2016). Perceived social norms are powerful influences on attitudes and behavior (Berkowitz, 2004; Mrug & McCay, 2013; Neighbors et al., 2007; Wu et al., 2015). As a result, intervention participants who believe their peer group would not support the attitudes and behaviors promoted by an intervention may not adopt these attitudes and behaviors or they may revert back to their old behaviors after the intervention ends. For example, adolescents whose friends use drugs may be unlikely to change their attitudes and behaviors in response to an intervention. Few studies have tested these possibilities. One exception is a study by Valente, Ritt-Olsen, et al. (2007), which found that a network-based adaptation of the Towards No Drug Use school-based intervention was only effective for participants whose friends did not use drugs. Participants whose friends used drugs actually *increased* their substance use after participating in the intervention.

Peer networks can facilitate or hinder the diffusion of intervention outcomes. Peer networks can also influence the overall impact of the intervention by facilitating (or hindering) the diffusion of intervention outcomes. According to diffusion of innovations theory (Rogers, 2003; Valente, 1995, 2010), after a new practice is introduced to a population, it can spread or "diffuse" through peer networks, much like contagious diseases spread from person to person. This theory emphasizes the central role that contextual and social influences play in shaping behavior rather than the cognitive factors that are often the focus of individual-level theories (Valente & Pitts, 2017). Building on diffusion theory, some interventions identify and train opinion leaders to promote the diffusion of specific attitudes or behaviors (e.g., Campbell et al., 2008; Kelly et al., 1997; Starkey et al., 2009; Valente & Pumpuang, 2007; Wyman et al., 2010, 2021). These interventions capitalize on the potential influence that high-status, well-connected individuals have on their peers (Cohen & Prinstein, 2006).

Notably, intervention outcomes can diffuse even when diffusion was not part of the program model. Because adolescents are embedded within peer networks, once an intervention changes a participant's attitudes and behavior, these attitudes and behaviors can diffuse from that participant to others around them. Indeed, diffusion can occur any time an intervention is targeted to only a subset of a population or any time only a subset of the population participates in an intervention. For example, participation rates in universal family-based interventions rarely exceed 30% (Heinrichs et al., 2005; R. Spoth & Redmond, 2000) Thus, in the absence of diffusion, most of the targeted population will not be reached by the intervention. When these interventions are targeted to students at the same school, however, diffusion may allow nonparticipants to benefit from the program. Consistent with this idea, an evaluation of the Iowa Strengthening Families Program (ISFP) found that 4 years after the intervention was implemented, substance use was lower among all students at intervention schools, including those whose families did not participate in ISFP (R. L. Spoth et al., 2001). Diffusion can also occur outside of the originally targeted population, such as diffusion from students who participated in a school-based intervention to their parents and siblings (White et al., 2020).

Diffusion is not a universal process, however, and even when it does occur, it can be slow (Rogers, 2003; Valente, 2010). Many factors can affect the rate at which diffusion occurs, including the characteristics of the innovation or practice (e.g., whether it is viewed as advantageous; Rogers, 2003) and characteristics of the network itself. For example, both network-level characteristics (e.g., how clustered the network is; how interconnected people within the network are) and individual-level characteristics (e.g., whether or not intervention participants are popular) can affect whether and how fast diffusion occurs (Centola, 2010; Rulison, Feinberg, et al., 2015; Rulison, Gest, & Osgood, 2015; Valente & Vega Yon, 2020).

Information about peer networks can be used to design interventions. Given that peer networks can shape intervention success (or failure), prevention scientists have started considering peer networks as they design and implement interventions. These network interventions use information about peer networks to facilitate social influence, accelerate behavior change, and/or promote the diffusion of intervention outcomes (Valente, 2012).

There are four types of network interventions (Hunter et al., 2019; Valente, 2012). *Individual interventions* use network information about individuals, such as how many friendship nominations they receive, to select intervention participants, or alternatively, to decide who should deliver the intervention. These interventions include those that identify potentially influential opinion leaders to deliver intervention content (see above). *Segmentation interventions* recruit people to participate in the intervention with their friends (e.g., Harper et al., 2014; Kim et al., 2015; Minnis et al., 2014; Shaya et al., 2014). These interventions recognize that because groups often have their own norms, it may be more effective to change group norms rather than individual norms. By changing group norms, this strategy also helps to prevent existing peer networks from undermining the intervention effects after an intervention ends. *Induction interventions* take advantage of existing ties within the peer network to help diffuse information or behaviors (e.g., Cobb et al., 2016; Latkin et al., 1996; Valente, Ritt-Olson, et al., 2007). For example, word-of-mouth interventions rely on existing peer network connections to spread information or "go viral." *Alteration interventions* attempt to change the network in some way, creating new or ending existing relationships (e.g., Graham et al., 2017; Litt et al., 2009). For example, Alcoholics Anonymous encourages participants to become friends with other nondrinkers, who can provide support and help them maintain their sobriety, potentially replacing relationships with other drinkers. Some school-based interventions place students into groups to work together as a way to facilitate new friendships. Alteration interventions can also attempt to end negative relationships.

EMPIRICAL FINDINGS FROM THE PROSPER PEERS PROJECT

In the previous sections, we argued that the interventions and peer network shape each other. The PROSPER Peers project is exceptionally well suited for testing this assertion, as it is one of the few studies that measured friendship networks over time within the context of an intervention trial (see Chapter 1). Further, the PROSPER Peers project followed over 10,000 adolescents with a reasonably large sample of networks, allowing our team to test both network-level and individual-level effects. In the following sections, we illustrate the usefulness of these data by summarizing the methods and key results of four studies. Briefly, the first study (Osgood et al., 2013) tested whether the PROSPER interventions as a whole influenced behavioral dynamics within friendship networks. The second and third studies (Rulison, Feinberg, et al., 2015; Rulison, Gest, & Osgood, 2015) tested whether friendship networks influenced intervention outcomes by facilitating the diffusion of intervention outcomes from adolescents who participated in a family-based intervention to those who did not. The final study (McMillan & Schaefer, 2021) used simulations based on the PROSPER friendship network data to estimate the likely effectiveness of different strategies for selecting intervention participants.

Study 1: To what extent do interventions shape the peer network?

Our team's first empirical study of interventions and friendship networks (Osgood et al., 2013) tested whether prosocial adolescents in intervention communities became more central members of their networks compared to adolescents who engaged in problem behavior. Our team expected that the intervention would likely lead to more prosocial norms within schools that implemented PROSPER. As such, adolescents whose attitudes and behavior matched these prosocial norms would receive more friendship nominations and have better connections to other students, and thus be in a better position to influence their peers (i.e., higher "influence potential"). The central hypothesis for this study was that PROSPER would increase the influence potential of prosocial adolescents compared to their antisocial peers. Specifically, we expected measures of network centrality to be negatively related to problem behavior within networks randomly assigned to the intervention condition compared to networks in control schools.

Sample. This study used network-level posttest data from Waves 2–5 of PROSPER Peers, when students were in sixth through ninth grade. These analyses included two consecutive cohorts of students in 26 of the PROSPER communities (omitting the community that did not permit collection of the friendship network data and its paired community in the random assignment process). Some of the communities had more than one middle school, and the team excluded eight small networks (<25 students) due to insufficient data for a meaningful analysis. Therefore, the final sample for this analysis was 256 school-cohort-wave combinations.

Measures. This study included four measures of problem behavior: (1) past month substance use, (2) substance use attitudes, (3) delinquency, and (4) a composite measure of problem behavior (i.e., standardized versions of the other three measures averaged together). This study also included six individual measures of network centrality: (1) degree centrality, (2) closeness centrality, (3) reach centrality, (4) betweenness centrality, (5) Bonacich centrality, and (6) information centrality, along with a composite centrality index (i.e., standardized versions of the other centrality measures averaged together). The team used undirected ties (i.e., a tie existed between two students if either student named the other one) to compute Bonacich centrality and information centrality and used both incoming ties (i.e., nominations received) and undirected ties for all other measures. More information about centrality measures is provided in Chapter 3.

Analytic approach. To test the central hypothesis, the team first computed network-level outcomes for the 256 school-cohort-wave combination by regressing each of the four problem behavior measures onto one of the 12 centrality measures and saving the bivariate regression coefficient for that network. These outcome variables captured the extent to which problem behavior was linked to centrality; a negative value indicated that antisocial students were less central members of that network. The team then used these 48 network-level outcomes (i.e., regression coefficients for 4 problem behavior measures times 12 network centrality measures) as dependent variables in a four-level multilevel model, with school-cohort-wave (Level 1) nested within schools (Level 2) nested within school districts (Level 3) nested within pairs of random assignment (Level 4) and estimated these models in the MLwiN software program.

Results and interpretation. Before conducting the primary analyses, the team first explored whether there were any baseline differences between intervention and control networks. At baseline, the relationship between problem behavior and centrality was the same in intervention and control networks: Out of the 48 baseline effects that were tested, only one was significant, and this effect was opposite the hypothesized direction. Specifically, there was a *positive* effect of the intervention on the link between the undirected Bonacich centrality measure and substance use (B = 0.110, p = 0.048), indicating that at baseline, adolescents who reported substance use were *more* popular in the intervention networks compared to the control networks. The overall lack of baseline differences suggested that randomization was effective. By contrast, posttest analyses indicated that within intervention networks, adolescents who engaged in problem behavior generally became less central members of their networks compared to their peers. As shown in Figure 11.1, the results were in the hypothesized direction for 47 out of 48 outcome variables. The results were statistically significant at $p < 0.05$ (black bars) in 26 cases (including between the composite measures of problem behavior and centrality) and marginally significant at $p < 0.10$ (dark gray bars) in another four cases.

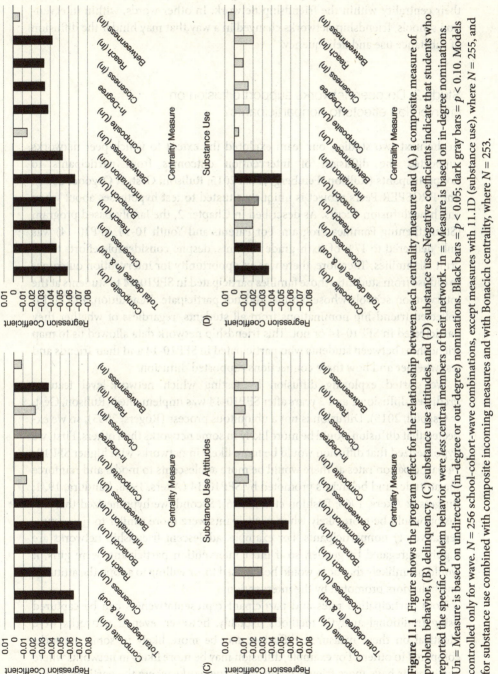

Figure 11.1 Figure shows the program effect for the relationship between each centrality measure and (A) a composite measure of problem behavior, (B) delinquency, (C) substance use attitudes, and (D) substance use. Negative coefficients indicate that students who reported the specific problem behavior were *less* central members of their network. In = Measure is based on in-degree nominations. Un = Measure is based on undirected (in-degree or out-degree) nominations. Black bars = $p < 0.05$; dark gray bars = $p < 0.10$. Models controlled only for wave. N = 256 school-cohort-wave combinations, except measures with 11.1D (substance use), where N = 255, and for substance use combined with composite incoming measures and with Bonacich centrality, where N = 253.

Overall, these results supported our argument that interventions can change peer networks. In this case, PROSPER appeared to reduce the influence potential of adolescents who engaged in a range of problem behaviors, by lowering their centrality within the friendship network. In other words, within intervention schools, friendship networks changed in a way that may hinder the diffusion of substance use and delinquency.

Study 2: Do peer networks support diffusion on intervention effects to nonparticipants?

In the next two studies, our team explored the extent to which peer networks supported the diffusion of intervention outcomes from participants to nonparticipants (Rulison, Feinberg, et al., 2015; Rulison, Gest, & Osgood, 2015). The PROSPER Peers project is uniquely situated to test hypotheses about when and how diffusion occurs. As described in Chapter 2, the family-based program (Strengthening Families Program: For Parents and Youth 10-14, SFP10-14) was only delivered to 17% of sixth-grade students, despite considerable efforts to recruit all families. Therefore, there was an opportunity for intervention outcomes to diffuse from students whose families participated in SFP10-14 to students at the intervention schools whose families did not participate. In addition, PROSPER collected friendship nominations from all students, regardless of whether they participated in SFP10-14 or not. This friendship network data allowed us to map friendships between students who participated in SFP10-14 and their friends and test whether and how these connections supported diffusion.

We started exploring diffusion by testing which network-level features predicted diffusion 1 and 2 years after SFP10-14 was implemented (Rulison, Gest, & Osgood, 2015). Diffusion is not a ubiquitous process (Rogers, 2003), so we expected that diffusion would be more likely in some networks than others. First, we hypothesized that diffusion would be more likely in networks with higher SFP10-14 participation rates as there would be more adolescents to model and reinforce the attitudes and behaviors promoted by SFP10-14 (Akers, 1998; Bandura, 1971; Burgess & Akers, 1966; Dishion et al., 1996). Second, we hypothesized that diffusion would be more likely when participants were more similar to (i.e., representative of) nonparticipants. For example, adolescent friendship networks are highly segregated by gender, so if most intervention participants were girls, it would be unlikely that boys would be exposed to, or willing to adopt, the attitudes and behaviors promoted by the intervention.

Both participation rates and participant representativeness can be captured using traditional analytic methods. Notably, however, even if networks were identical on these measures, diffusion may be more likely in some networks compared to others. For example, diffusion may be more likely in networks where participants have more friends compared to networks where the participants are unpopular. Therefore, we also expected that features of the network itself would affect diffusion. Specifically, we hypothesized that diffusion would be more likely in socially integrated networks, where adolescents were highly connected to each other. We also hypothesized that diffusion would be more likely in networks where intervention participants were popular and spread throughout the network, rather than just friends with each other, making it easier for them to connect to, and influence, nonparticipants. These network-level features cannot be captured with traditional analytic methods. Instead, social network analytic methods are needed.

Sample. Data for this study were from Waves 1–4 (i.e., pretest, posttest, 1- and 2-year follow-ups). Given the focus of the hypotheses on how network features shape diffusion, we conducted all analyses at the network level using data from 42 networks at the intervention schools. There were two cohorts in each school; in school districts with multiple middle/junior high schools, we treated each school as a separate network. We also excluded one network because it did not collect any friendship nominations and four networks because they had 0 or 1 SFP participant(s), and thus no diffusion was likely to occur. These 42 networks included 5,784 students ($M = 11.8$ years; 49.6% female at baseline).

Measures. Network-level features of diffusion potential were measured at pretest (fall sixth grade) and posttest (spring sixth grade) because, as we noted above, interventions can shape peer networks, and it is unknown whether initial network features, or network features after the intervention occurs, are more likely to shape diffusion. We tested two traditional, nonnetwork measures of diffusion potential: (1) SFP10-14 participation rate and (2) representativeness with respect to behavioral and demographic characteristics, measured as the similarity between participants and nonparticipants. We also tested 10 social network analytic measures of diffusion potential, which captured different aspects of social integration and where intervention participants were located within the network.

Diffusion was defined as the difference in substance use scores between participants and nonparticipants in each network. Specifically, we computed the Cohen's *d* for substance use between participants and nonparticipants and multiplied the absolute value of these scores by -1 so that higher scores indicated more similarity between participants and nonparticipants (i.e., more diffusion within that network). We measured diffusion at the 1- and 2-year follow-up (i.e., spring of seventh and eighth grade); because diffusion is a slow process that unfolds over time, we expected that evidence of diffusion might not arise until several years after an intervention occurred.

Analytic approach. We used partial correlations to test the relationship between each of the network-level measures and diffusion scores. We conducted four sets of analyses: (1) We computed the partial correlation between each network-level measure at *pretest* and diffusion scores at *1-year follow-up*. These analyses controlled for network size and survey participation rate at the 1-year follow-up, the diffusion score at pretest to control for initial similarity between participants and nonparticipants, and SFP10–14 participation rate at pretest. We then repeated these analyses for (2) each network-level measure at *posttest* and diffusion scores at the *1-year follow-up*, (3) each network-level measure at *pretest* and diffusion scores at the *2-year follow-up*, and (4) each network-level measure at posttest and diffusion scores at the *2-year follow-up*. Each analysis controlled for network size and survey participation rate at the 1- or 2-year follow-up and the diffusion score and SFP10-14 participation rate at pretest or posttest.

Results and interpretation: Traditional nonnetwork measures. As expected, there was a positive relationship between SFP10-14 participation rate and diffusion scores at the 2-year follow-up (see Figure 11.2). In other words, diffusion appeared to be more likely when there were more students to model and reinforce the attitudes and behaviors promoted by SFP10-14. These results are consistent with the idea that diffusion accelerates once a "tipping point" or "critical mass" of adopters is reached (Rogers, 2003; Valente, 1995). By contrast, representativeness was unrelated diffusion. We had expected that when potential adopters (i.e., nonparticipants) were more similar to, or representative of, adopters (i.e., participants), they would be more likely to be influenced by these peers, yet the only demographic or behavioral characteristics positively linked to diffusion scores was representativeness in terms of grades.

Social network analytic measures: Social integration measures. Diffusion was more likely in highly interconnected, less cliquish (i.e., less clustered), and less hierarchical networks (see Figure 11.3). Specifically, there was a positive relationship between diffusion and structural cohesion (defined as mean number of "node-independent paths"; see Moody & White, 2003), a negative relationship between diffusion and both measures of clustering (i.e., Freeman's segregation index; Freeman, 1978, and the transitivity ratio; Wasserman & Faust, 1994), and a negative relationship between diffusion and in-degree centralization (a measure of hierarchy within the network). Taken together, these results suggest that diffusion was more likely when students had more opportunities to interact, model, and reinforce each other's attitudes and behaviors (Valente et al., 2004), either by being more connected to each other or by having fewer students acting as gatekeepers at the top of a hierarchy.

Social network analytic measures: Location of SFP participants. Diffusion was also more likely in networks where a higher proportion of nonparticipants were within two steps of an intervention participant, defined as being either friends with an SFP10-14 participant or having friends who were friends with a participant. These results might explain why SFP10-14 participation rate was linked to diffusion: When more students participated, nonparticipants might have been more likely to come into contact with, and thus be influenced by, participants. Contrary to expectation, however, diffusion was no more likely to occur when participants had higher status in the network compared to their peers, measured using Cohen's *d* to quantify differences between participants' and nonparticipants' average in-degree centrality (number of friendship nominations received) and differences in their average betweenness centrality (the extent to which a student connects otherwise disconnected students). These results were inconsistent with research showing that opinion leaders can successfully diffuse intervention messages (e.g., Campbell et al., 2008; Kelly et al., 1997; Starkey et al., 2009; Valente & Pumpuang, 2007; Wyman et al., 2010, 2021). One possible explanation for this surprising finding is that this study did not consider whether the participants

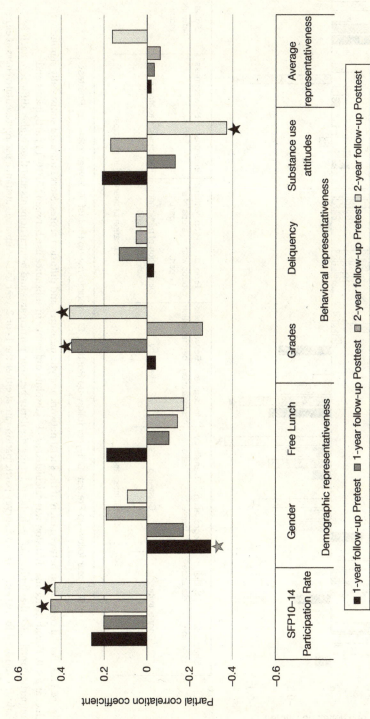

Figure 11.2 Partial correlation between each of the traditional analytic measures and substance use diffusion. Substance use diffusion was calculated as -1* |absolute difference in substance use between SFP10-14 participants and nonparticipants|, such that higher scores indicated more similarity between participants and nonparticipants and thus higher diffusion. Each analysis controlled for network size and survey participation rate at either the 1- or 2-year follow-up and substance use representativeness at either pretest or posttest. Each analysis except for SFP10-14 participation rate also controlled for SFP10-14 participation rate. Black stars indicate a statistically significant effect at $p < 0.05$, and gray stars indicate a trend at $p < 0.10$.

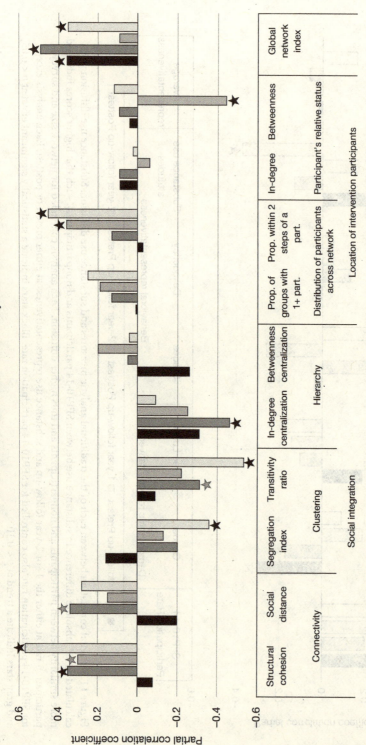

Figure 11.3 Partial correlation between each of the social network analytic measures and diffusion scores. Stars indicate a statistically significant effect at $p < 0.05$. Substance use diffusion was calculated as -1* |absolute difference in substance use between SFP10-14 participants and nonparticipants|, such that higher scores indicated more similarity between participants and nonparticipants and thus higher diffusion. Each analysis controlled for network size and survey participation rate at either the 1- or 2-year follow-up and substance use representativeness at either pretest or posttest. Each analysis except for SFP10-14 participation rate also controlled for SFP10-14 participation rate. Black stars indicate a statistically significant effect at $p < 0.05$, and gray stars indicate a trend at $p < 0.10$.

actually adopted the attitudes and behaviors promoted by SFP10-14. Given that high-status individuals are often invested in the status quo that helped them obtain their status (Valente, 2012), some higher status participants may have been less likely to change in response to SFP10-14, thus limiting diffusion in these networks.

In sum, network-based measures of diffusion potential were better predictors of diffusion than traditional nonnetwork measures. Although SFP10-14 participation rate predicted diffusion at the 2-year follow-up, grade representativeness was the only representativeness measure linked to diffusion. Further, a composite measure, which averaged across all five representativeness measures, was unrelated to diffusion. By contrast, several social integration measures, one of the location measures, and a global network index (which averaged across all network-based measures) predicted diffusion over and above the effect of SFP10-14 participation rate and representativeness. Therefore, multiple network-level features, which cannot be captured with traditional analytic methods, shaped how likely it is for diffusion to occur. Taken together, these results underscore the importance of clarifying how friendship networks can promote diffusion as a way to maximize the impact of future interventions.

Study 3: Did nonparticipants with more SFP-attending friends report lower rates of use?

Building on these network-level findings about diffusion, our team next wanted to determine whether there was evidence of diffusion at the individual level, and if so, what mechanisms could explain how diffusion occurred. Therefore, we explored two questions in a subsequent study (Rulison, Feinberg, et al., 2015): (1) Did nonparticipants who had more SFP-attending friends report lower rates of substance use? (2) If so, what mechanisms explained the link between this *indirect exposure* to SFP10-14v and nonparticipants' substance use?

To identify potential mechanisms, or *mediators*, that might explain this link, we first considered how SFP10-14 affected participants. Past studies have found that SFP improves parental discipline and family relationships, reduces the amount of unstructured time that participants spend time hanging out with peers without adults around, and reduces participants' positive attitudes toward substance use (Molgaard & Spoth, 2001; Redmond et al., 1999). These outcomes, in turn, led to lower rates of substance use among participants. Therefore, we expected that nonparticipants who had more SFP-attending friends would have more *friends* who (1) experienced positive parental discipline, (2) had better family relationships, (3) spent less unstructured time with friends, and (4) had more negative attitudes toward substance use. These friends would then be less likely to engage in substance use. As a result, nonparticipants with many SFP-attending friends would have more negative attitudes toward substance use and subsequently would be less likely to engage in substance use.

Sample. Data for this study were from Waves 2–5 (i.e., postintervention waves), when students were in sixth–ninth grade. The analytic sample included 5,449 students who (1) attended intervention schools, (2) did not participate in SFP10-14, (3) provided friendship nominations at least once, and (4) had friends who also completed the survey at least once.

Measures. This study tested two outcome variables: past month drunkenness and past month cigarette use (0 = no use, 1 = any past month use). For our descriptive analyses, we defined indirect exposure to the intervention as the total number of SFP-attending friends. For our inferential analyses, we defined indirect exposure as the average proportion of SFP-attending friends across the current wave and each previous postintervention wave. This measure captured cumulative exposure to SFP, rather than just exposure at the current moment in time. To test our proposed mediators, we also included measures of (1) friends' parental discipline, (2) friends' parent-youth relationships, (3) amount of time nonparticipants spent hanging out with their friends without adults around (i.e., unstructured socializing), (4) friends' substance use attitudes, (5) friends' substance use, and (6) nonparticipants' own antisubstance use attitudes.

Analytic approach. To descriptively test the link between total number of SFP-attending friends and nonparticipants' substance use, we computed separate chi-square analyses at each wave. Then, to test the link between cumulative indirect exposure and nonparticipants' substance use at that wave, we conducted multilevel analyses with time (Level 1) nested within students (Level 2), nested within school cohorts (Level 3). These analyses controlled for gender, race, network size (natural log), wave, receiving free or reduced-price lunch, frequency of church attendance, family discipline, and parent-youth relationships. We then added each hypothesized mediator of diffusion separately to calculate how much the association between indirect exposure and substance use decreased when that mediator was added to the model; greater reductions indicated that the proposed mediator did a better job at explaining the link between indirect exposure and nonparticipants' substance use.

Results and interpretation. Our descriptive analyses provided initial evidence of diffusion. Total number of SFP-attending friends was unrelated to drunkenness and cigarette use at baseline (before SFP10-14 was implemented) and at immediate posttest (before effects from SFP10-14 had time to diffuse). At each of the following waves, however, adolescents who had more SFP-attending friends reported lower rates of past month drunkenness and past month cigarette use. Our multilevel analyses also provided evidence of diffusion: adolescents who had a higher cumulative proportion of SFP-attending friends had lower rates of past month drunkenness (adjusted odds ratio = 0.57) and past month cigarette use (adjusted odds ratio = 0.49). Taken together, these results suggest that effects from SFP10-14 spread from participants to nonparticipants.

Unstructured socializing was the strongest mediator of the link between indirect exposure and substance use; adding it to the model reduced the link between indirect exposure and substance use by 37% for drunkenness and by 24% for cigarette use. In other words, nonparticipants who had a higher proportion of SFP-attending friends spent less unstructured time with their friends, and this in turn was linked to lower rates of substance use. This finding is consistent with past research that has found a strong link between unstructured socializing and deviant behaviors such as substance use and delinquency (Haynie & Osgood, 2005; Hoeben et al., 2016; Light et al., 2013; Osgood & Anderson, 2004; Osgood et al., 1996). It is also consistent with past research demonstrating that friends' parents matter (see Chapter 8). For example, when friends' parents participated in SFP10-14, they may have improved their parental monitoring and as a result spent more time supervising their own child and, by extension, their child's friends.

Friends' substance use attitudes were also a strong mediator of the link between indirect exposure and substance use; adding it to the model reduced the link between indirect exposure and substance use by 31% for drunkenness and by 24% for cigarette use. Overall, the pattern of results suggested that SFP10-14 reduced participants' positive attitudes toward substance use, and participants then conveyed these attitudes to their friends who did not participate. These nonparticipants then became less likely to use cigarettes or get drunk.

By contrast, neither friends' parent-youth relationship quality nor friends' parental discipline consistency were significant mediators. Although both of these measures of parenting practices were individually linked to nonparticipants' substance use, their link with nonparticipants' substance use disappeared after we controlled for nonparticipants' unstructured socializing. In other words, parenting practices might facilitate diffusion, but only through affecting how much time adolescents spent engaging in unstructured socializing. There was also limited evidence of mediation through friends' actual substance use. Although adding friends' substance use to the model reduced the link between indirect exposure and nonparticipants' substance use by 8%–11%, the influence of friends' substance use on nonparticipants' outcomes was fully accounted for when we included the other mediators in the model.

In sum, the results from this study indicated that diffusion can occur by cumulative indirect exposure to the intervention through friendship networks: Adolescents who did not attend SFP, but whose friends did attend, were less likely to engage in substance use compared to their classmates. Further, our results suggest that SFP10-14 diffused to nonparticipants by reducing their opportunities for substance use (i.e., reducing unstructured, unsupervised socializing) and by changing participants' substance use attitudes.

Study 4: How can information about peer networks be used to design interventions?

A fourth study by our team used simulations to estimate the likely effectiveness of different network-based strategies for selecting intervention participants (McMillan & Schaefer, 2021). As noted above, *individual interventions* select participants based on network characteristics, such as identifying who is more central in the network. Because they focus on well-connected individuals, the goal of these types of interventions is to increase diffusion of intervention outcomes to nonparticipants. These interventions can also simultaneously reduce diffusion of risky behaviors: because popular adolescents often engage in substance use and other problem behaviors (e.g., Kreager et al., 2011; Mayeux et al., 2008; Moody et al., 2011; Valente et al., 2005), enlisting them and changing their attitudes and behavior may limit the spread of problem behaviors by reducing the extent to which popular adolescents engage in these behaviors. Therefore, our team expected that interventions using individual strategies to select participants would be effective for both participants and nonparticipants. By contrast, *segmentation interventions* select groups of friends to participate in the intervention together. The goal of these interventions is to improve outcomes for participants by enrolling their friends who can provide positive reinforcement and help buffer negative influence from other peers. Therefore, our team expected that interventions using segmentation strategies would be highly effective for participants by helping them to sustain intervention outcomes over time.

Sample. The simulations in this study were based on data from Waves 5–7, when adolescents were in ninth through eleventh grade. This study included data from 28 networks (14 control schools districts times 2 cohorts); only control schools were included so that the effects of the simulated intervention strategies would not be influenced by effects from the PROSPER interventions. The final simulations used data from 4,819 students who were in the control schools at all three waves to reduce any biases due to students moving in and out of a school.

Measures. This study evaluated six different selection strategies. In the first strategy, a random sample of adolescents was selected to participate in the intervention. This random-targeting strategy served as a control to evaluate the remaining five network-based strategies (described in Table 11.1). The second and third strategies used individual-based targeting to select the most well-connected adolescents in the network. Specifically, these strategies selected adolescents who received the most friendship nominations (i.e., high in-degree centrality) and adolescents who connected distinct parts of the network (i.e., high betweenness centrality). The remaining three strategies used segmentation-based targeting by initially selecting a random set of participants and then including one, three, or all of their friends to also participate in the intervention. In these three strategies, if a selected adolescent did not name any friends, they still could participate, just without any friends. To determine the effect of "dosage," defined as the percentage of the network who participated in the intervention, the exact number of targeted participants was based on selecting 10%, 20%, or 30% of the total number of adolescents in the network. In all, our team tested 18 different conditions (6 targeting strategies times 3 dosages).

Once participants were identified, they were subjected to the simulated intervention. To simulate an intervention that is immediately successful for all participants, our team set the initial drinking level for all participants to zero in ninth grade. Because interventions often try to improve adolescents' ability to resist negative peer influence, the simulations treated participants as if they had been "inoculated" from influence: whether and how much they drank after ninth grade was shaped only by individual-level factors, rather than peer influence. They could, however, influence their friends. Because inoculation effects may fade

Table 11.1 DESCRIPTION AND SUMMARY OF KEY RESULTS FOR EACH OF THE NETWORK-BASED SELECTION STRATEGIES

Strategy	Selected adolescents	Summary of significant results[a]
Individual-based strategies		
In-degree	Adolescents who received the most friendship nominations	• *Full sample:* Average drinking 0.020–0.024 lower for all 3 dosages • *Participants:* Average drinking 0.023–0.028 lower for all 3 dosages • *Nonparticipants:* Average drinking 0.018–0.020 lower for all 3 dosages o Greater reductions when peer influence is stronger
Betweenness	Adolescents who form bridges to different parts of the network (i.e., high betweenness centrality)	• *Full sample:* Average drinking 0.01 lower at 30% dosage • *Participants:* Average drinking 0.034–0.043 lower for all 3 dosages o Greater reductions when peer influence is stronger • *Nonparticipants:* No overall reduction in drinking at any dosage o Greater reductions when peer influence is stronger
Segmentation strategies		
Bring 1 friend	Random sample of adolescents & 1 of their friends (randomly selected from all friends)	• *Participants:* Average drinking lower by 0.005 at 10% dosage • *Nonparticipants:* Reduction in drinking only when controls included o Greater reductions when peer influence is stronger
Bring 3 friends	Random sample of adolescents & up to 3 of their friends (randomly selected from all friends)	• *Participants:* Average drinking 0.010–0.013 lower at 10% & 20% dosages o Greater reductions when peer influence is stronger • *Nonparticipants:* Reduction in drinking only when controls included o Greater reductions when peer influence is stronger
Bring all friends	Random sample of adolescents & all of the friends they named	• *Participants:* Average drinking 0.012–0.019 lower for all 3 dosages o Greater reductions when peer influence is stronger • *Nonparticipants:* Average drinking 0.003–0.005 *higher* for 10%–20% dosages

Note. Drinking popularity did not affect intervention effectiveness for either participants or nonparticipants for any strategy.

[a]Results indicate the difference between the average drinking level in a specific condition (e.g., using the indegree strategy at 10% dosage) and the average drinking level in the random condition; when ranges are provided, they indicate the range of differences across different dosages; all reported results were significant at $p < 0.05$. See Table 1 in McMillan and Shaefer et al 2021 for the actual average drinking levels in each condition.

over time, the simulations selected a random sample of participants at each wave to lose the protective benefits of inoculation, after which they could be influenced by their friends in addition to individual factors. The simulations assumed that all participants lost the benefits of inoculation by the end of the 2 years.

This study evaluated the effectiveness of each strategy by determining the prevalence of drinking within the simulated network at the end of 11th grade, which was 2 years after the intervention was implemented. Our team calculated prevalence using adolescents' reports of how often they drank alcohol in the past month, recoded so that 0 = no use, 1 = used alcohol once in the past month, and 2 = used alcohol more than once in the past month.

Analytic approach. Following similar studies (e.g., Adams & Schaefer, 2016; Schaefer et al., 2013), this study used the simulation capabilities within RSiena to simulate how each of the different conditions affected the prevalence of alcohol use within each network. The simulation process is described in more detail in the original publication (McMillan & Schaefer, 2021). Briefly, this process involved three steps. First, the team used RSiena to estimate model parameters for each network, using the standard terms that our team has included in other PROSPER analyses (e.g., alter, ego, and selection effects for gender, race, and drinking; average drinking similarity among friends; see Chapter 3). Second, using these parameters, the team conducted 1,000 simulation runs for each condition in each network, then recorded the prevalence of drinking at the end of each simulation (i.e., 2 years after the intervention was implemented), first for the full sample and then separately for participants and nonparticipants. Finally, the team used *t* tests to compare prevalence of drinking for each dosage of the five network-based selection strategies to the corresponding dosage in the random selection strategy. In addition, the team used three-level multilevel models with selection strategy (Level 1), nested within dosage level (Level 2), nested within network (Level 3) to test whether there were cross-level interactions between selection strategy and either peer influence or drinker popularity. These models controlled for multiple factors that might affect intervention effectiveness, including average initial drinking level among selected students at Level 1 and average initial drinking level within the network and network characteristics at Level 3.

Results and interpretation. Table 11.1 summarizes the results for each selection strategy compared to the random strategy. As expected, the individual-based strategies reduced drinking for participants and, to a lesser extent, nonparticipants. Specifically, both individual-based strategies reduced drinking among participants at all three dosages, with betweenness leading to the largest overall reduction in drinking among participants across all conditions. By contrast, in-degree was the only strategy that had an overall effect on drinking among nonparticipants, and the effect was particularly strong in networks with more peer influence. Betweenness also reduced drinking among nonparticipants, albeit to a lesser extent, in networks with more peer influence.

The segmentation strategies generally reduced drinking for participants, with the "bring-all-friends" strategy reducing drinking the most compared to the random condition. These results supported the idea that having friends participate in the intervention can help buffer the effects of the intervention wearing off over time. Notably, the segmentation strategies did not work well for nonparticipants. The "bring-1-friend" and "bring-3-friends" strategies only worked in networks where peer influence was stronger, and the "bring-all-friends" strategy actually *increased* drinking among nonparticipants at the 10% and 20% dosage levels.

Taken together, the results indicated that most strategies were effective for participants, but only the in-degree strategy (and to a lesser extent the betweenness strategy) also promoted diffusion of intervention outcomes to nonparticipants. These results likely reflected that, by definition, high in-degree adolescents had a lot of friends, so they were in a good position to influence others. Adolescents high in betweenness did not necessarily have many connections even though they connected distinct parts of the network, which explains why this strategy was not as effective unless peer influence was strong. In addition, randomly selected students who participated with their friends were not necessarily in a strong position to influence others. Further, as larger groups of friends were included in the intervention, a growing number of adolescents were not connected to participants and thus were unaffected by the intervention. In other words, bringing in adolescents and their friends limited the connections between participants and non-participants, reducing opportunities for diffusion to occur.

CONCLUSION

In conclusion, our literature review and the results from our studies demonstrated that interventions can both shape and be shaped by peer networks. Importantly, neither the school-based nor family-based interventions implemented within the PROSPER trial were "network interventions": they did not explicitly use peer networks or information about peer networks as part of their design. Even so, we found that the PROSPER interventions shaped peer networks by elevating the status of prosocial adolescents (Osgood et al., 2013). We also found that peer networks facilitated the diffusion of intervention outcomes from adolescents who participated in the family-based intervention to those who did not (Rulison, Feinberg, et al., 2015; Rulison, Gest, & Osgood, 2015). These results are consistent with findings from other studies, which demonstrated that peer networks can shape intervention outcomes, even when the peer networks are "hidden" (i.e., unobserved) or when network effects are unintended (DeLay et al., 2016; Dishion et al., 1999; Hunter et al., 2015). Finally, we found that using different strategies to select intervention participants can affect the extent to which intervention effects diffuse to nonparticipants (McMillan & Schaefer, 2021).

Future research

The four studies described here demonstrated that school-based interventions and friendship networks shaped each other. Going forward, however, more research is needed to extend our findings. First, more studies should explore when and how existing peer networks influence intervention outcomes. Intervention participants do not exist in a vacuum: peer networks can either encourage or discourage participants from adopting and sustaining positive health behaviors (Dishion & Tipsord, 2011; Valente & Pitts, 2017). Just as we demonstrated that intervention participants can shape their friend's outcomes (Rulison, Feinberg, et al., 2015), participant's friends can shape how the participant responds to an intervention. In other words, higher risk peer networks may undermine program effectiveness and sustainability. For example, popular adolescents and adolescents whose friends engage in problem behavior may be less likely to change their attitudes and behaviors if they view these changes as counter to peer norms (Kwasnicka et al., 2016; Valente, 2012).

Second, we identified several mediators of diffusion (Rulison, Feinberg, et al., 2015), but more work is needed to identify *how* peer networks shape intervention outcomes (Valente & Pitts, 2017). For example, future studies should clarify how peer networks facilitate (or hinder) change within the intervention itself, shape the diffusion of intervention outcomes, and support the maintenance of behavioral change. Peers can influence each other's substance use and delinquency in multiple ways (e.g., direct peer pressure, modeling, normative regulation, providing access—opportunity; Rulison et al., 2019), and it is likely that different processes are linked to different aspects of behavior change and in diffusing intervention outcomes to different people (e.g., older vs. younger siblings; Rulison, 2020). Given that interventions can be expensive to implement, simulation studies should be utilized to explore the effects that different interventions may have. As McMillan and Schaefer (2021) demonstrated, using simulations informed by actual network data can be an efficient way to compare approaches.

Third, our studies focused on the link between interventions and school-based friendship networks, but more work is needed to explore the link between interventions and other types of social networks. For example, adolescents often have friends outside of school (Kerr et al., 2007), and having close out-of-school friends is a risk factor for antisocial behavior (Kiesner et al., 2004). These out-of-school friends may undermine the effects of school-based interventions, suggesting that it may be beneficial to use segmentation-based strategies to include these friends in the intervention or to use other strategies (e.g., alteration interventions) to encourage adolescents to form new relationships that will support their behavior changes. In addition, intervention effects can diffuse to family members. For example, one study demonstrated that effects from a school-based smoking prevention program diffused to fathers and siblings (White et al., 2020). Conversely, family-based interventions may shape peer networks (e.g., teaching parents to monitor their children), which can affect who adolescents select as friends (see Chapter 8). Other social networks that could facilitate behavior change and support diffusion are social networks among community organizations (Valente, Chou, & Pentz, 2007) and connections between students and trusted adults at their school (Pickering et al., 2018; Wyman et al., 2019).

Implications

An important takeaway from this work is that prevention scientists, program facilitators, and school staff who ignore peer networks when designing, implementing, and evaluating interventions often do so at their own peril. Any group- or setting-level interventions can create ties or facilitate interactions among participants even if these interactions are unintended. For example, as researchers discovered, in some cases interactions among participants can undermine the intervention effectiveness to the point of *harming* participants (Dishion & Dodge, 2005; Dishion et al., 1999, 2001; Dishion & Tipsord, 2011; McCord, 2003; Poulin et al., 2001). At the same time, however, interactions among intervention participants can improve intervention effectiveness by providing social support and promoting acceptance (Hunter et al., 2015; Molloy Elreda et al., 2016). Below, we highlight several implications of our findings for designing, implementing, and evaluating interventions.

Implications for intervention design. There is growing evidence that network interventions are effective (Hunter et al., 2019), suggesting that program developers should carefully consider how to address the peer networks when designing interventions. Indeed, interventions that use peer networks to facilitate and support behavior change are more likely to be effective than interventions that ignore peer networks (Valente et al., 2015). As reviewed previously in this chapter and discussed elsewhere (Hunter et al., 2019; Shelton et al., 2019; Valente, 2012, 2015), there are many different strategies that can be used, depending on the intervention goals. Program developers should also consider how peer networks could facilitate the diffusion of intervention outcomes to increase the reach and sustainability of the intervention. For example, interventions can train peer opinion leaders to spread intervention messages, attempt to change peer network characteristics to facilitate diffusion, or include content that might facilitate diffusion, such as targeting unstructured socializing with peers. Another benefit of using network interventions is that they may be ideal for reaching, retaining, and changing behavior among hard-to-reach populations, such as people who inject drugs (Hunter et al., 2019).

Implications for intervention implementation. It is also important for program facilitators to consider how peer networks can facilitate or hinder intervention effects when they implement an intervention. For example, facilitators should be trained in behavior management practices and how to provide adequate supervision to reduce the likelihood of peer contagion and deviancy training within intervention groups (Dishion & Tipsord, 2011; Dodge et al., 2006). In addition, Gesell and colleagues (Gesell et al., 2013) developed the Social Network Diagnostic Tool, which identifies ties within a group or setting and then uses these ties to provide specific recommendations to facilitators regarding how to build more or better connections among group members. For example, facilitators can pair isolated members with highly central members, use a "talking stick" to ensure everyone has the opportunity to participate, and ensure that members who already know each other are not allowed to form subgroups. This tool could be adapted to use within classroom settings to help teachers identify strategies for building cohesion and preventing social isolation among their students.

Implications for intervention evaluation. In addition to addressing peer networks within interventions, evaluation studies should include measures of peer networks to obtain valid estimates of program outcomes (Valente & Pitts, 2017), to better determine how many people were reached by the intervention, and to identify potential mechanisms that might facilitate or hinder behavior change within the intervention. Peer network measures could include friendship measures (as we obtained in PROSPER), measures of other social relationships likely to be affected by the intervention (e.g., family relationships; see White et al., 2020), or measures of social processes within the intervention group (Molloy Elreda et al., 2016). Importantly, prevention scientists should include these measures, even when an intervention is not network based by design. For example, our studies using data from PROSPER demonstrated that peer network measures can capture intervention outcomes (e.g., how PROSPER affected the social status of prosocial students) and help us better understand how peer networks shape intervention effects.

Although prevention scientists typically view the spread of intervention effects from participants to nonparticipants in a randomized trial as "contamination," promoting such diffusion will likely enhance intervention outcomes and increase the likelihood that intervention effects will be sustained. As noted by one of the early diffusion researchers: "It is as unthinkable to study diffusion without some knowledge of the social structures in which potential adopters are located as it is to study blood circulation without adequate knowledge of veins and arteries" (Katz, 1961, as cited in Rogers, 2003, p. 25). Therefore, going forward prevention scientists should pay careful attention to the bidirectional link between peer networks and interventions.

REFERENCES

Adams, J., & Schaefer, D. R. (2016). How initial prevalence moderates network-based smoking change: Estimating contextual effects with stochastic actor-based models. *Journal of Health and Social Behavior, 57*(1), 22–38. https://doi.org/10.1177/0022146515627848

Akers, R. L. (1998). *Social learning and social structure: A general theory of crime and deviance.* Northeastern University Press.

Bandura, A. (1971). *Social learning theory.* General Learning Corporation.

Battistich, V. A., Schaps, E., Watson, M., Solomon, D., & Lewis, C. (2000). Effects of the Child Development Project on students' drug use and other problem behaviors. *Journal of Primary Prevention, 21*(1), 75–99.

Berkowitz, A. D. (2004). An overview of the social norms approach. In L. C. Lederman & L. P. Stewar (Eds.), *Changing the culture of college drinking* (pp. 193–214). Hampton Press.

Botvin, G. J., & Griffin, K. W. (2004). Life Skills Training: Empirical findings and future directions. *Journal of Primary Prevention, 25*(2), 211–232.

Burgess, R. L., & Akers, R. L. (1966). A differential association-reinforcement theory of criminal behavior. *Social Problems, 14*(2), 128–147.

Campbell, R., Starkey, F., Holliday, J., Audrey, S., Bloor, M., Parry-Langdon, N., Hughes, R., & Moore, L. (2008). An informal school-based peer-led intervention for smoking prevention in adolescence (ASSIST): A cluster randomised trial. *The Lancet, 371,* 1595–1602. https://doi.org/10.1016/s0140-6736(08)60692-3

Centola, D. (2010). The spread of behavior in an online social network experiment. *Science, 329*(5996), 1194–1197. https://doi.org/10.1126/science.1185231

Cobb, N. K., Jacobs, M. A., Wileyto, P., Valente, T., & Graham, A. L. (2016). Diffusion of an evidence-based smoking cessation intervention through Facebook: A randomized controlled trial. *American Journal of Public Health, 106*(6), 1130–1135. https://doi.org/10.2105/AJPH.2016.303106

Cohen, G. L., & Prinstein, M. J. (2006). Peer contagion of aggression and health risk behavior among adolescent males: An experimental investigation of effects on public conduct and private attitudes. *Child Development, 77*(4), 967–983.

DeLay, D., Ha, T., Van Ryzin, M., Winter, C., & Dishion, T. J. (2016). Changing friend selection in middle school: A social network analysis of a randomized intervention study designed to prevent adolescent problem behavior. *Prevention Science: The Official Journal of the Society for Prevention Research, 17*(3), 285–294. https://doi.org/10.1007/s11121-015-0605-4

Dishion, T. J., & Dodge, K. A. (2005). Peer contagion in interventions for children and adolescents: Moving towards an understanding of the ecology and dynamics of change. *Journal of Abnormal Child Psychology, 33*(3), 395–400.

Dishion, T. J., McCord, J., & Poulin, F. (1999). When interventions harm: Peer groups and problem behavior. *American Psychologist, 54*(9), 755–764. https://doi.org/10.1037//0003-066x.54.9.755

Dishion, T. J., Poulin, F., & Burraston, B. (2001). Peer group dynamics associated with iatrogenic effects in group interventions with high-risk young adolescents. *New Directions for Child and Adolescent Development, 91,* 79–92.

Dishion, T. J., Spracklen, K. M., Andrews, D. W., & Patterson, G. R. (1996). Deviancy training in male adolescents friendships. *Behavior Therapy, 27,* 373–390. https://doi.org/10.1016/S0005-7894(96)80023-2

Dishion, T. J., & Tipsord, J. M. (2011). Peer contagion in child and adolescent social and emotional development. *Annual Review of Psychology, 62,* 189–214.

Dodge, K. A., Dishion, T. J., & Lansford, J. E. (2006). *Deviant peer influences in programs for youth problems and solutions.* Guilford Press.

Ellickson, P. L., McCaffrey, D. F., Ghosh-Dastidar, B., & Longshore, D. L. (2003). New inroads in preventing adolescent drug use: Results from a large-scale trial of Project ALERT in middle schools. *American Journal of Public Health, 93,* 1830–1836. https://doi.org/10.2105/AJPH.93.11.1830

Felner, R. D., Brand, S., Adan, A. M., Mulhall, P. F., Flowers, N., Sartain, B., & DuBois, D. L. (1993). Restructuring the ecology of the school as an approach to prevention during school transitions: Longitudinal follow-ups and extensions of the School Transitional Environment Project (STEP). *Prevention in Human Services, 10*(2), 103–136.

Freeman, L. C. (1978). Segregation in social networks. *Sociological Methods and Research*, 6, 411–429. https://doi.org/10.1177/004912417800600401

Gesell, S. B., Barkin, S. L., & Valente, T. W. (2013). Social network diagnostics: A tool for monitoring group interventions. *Implementation Science*, 8(1), 116. https://doi.org/10.1186/1748-5908-8-116

Gest, S. D., Osgood, D. W., Feinberg, M. E., Bierman, K. L., & Moody, J. (2011). Strengthening prevention program theories and evaluations: Contributions from social network analysis. *Prevention Science*, 12(4), 349–360. https://doi.org/10.1007/s11121-011-0229-2

Graham, A. L., Papandonatos, G. D., Cha, S., Erar, B., Amato, M. S., Cobb, N. K., Niaura, R. S., & Abrams, D. B. (2017). Improving adherence to smoking cessation treatment: Intervention effects in a web-based randomized trial. *Nicotine & Tobacco Research*, 19(3), 324–332. https://doi.org/10.1093/ntr/ntw282

Hansen, W. B., & Dusenbury, L. (2004). All Stars Plus: A competence and motivation enhancement approach to prevention. *Health Education*, 104(6), 371–381. https://doi.org/10.1108/09654280410564141

Hansen, W. B., Dusenbury, L., Bishop, D., & Derzon, J. H. (2007). Substance abuse prevention program content: Systematizing the classification of what programs target for change. *Health Education Research*, 22(3), 351–360. https://doi.org/10.1093/her/cyl091

Harper, G. W., Dolcini, M. M., Benhorin, S., Watson, S. E., & Boyer, C. B. (2014). The benefits of a friendship-based HIV/STI prevention intervention for African American youth. *Youth and Society*, 46(5), 591–622. https://doi.org/10.1177/0044118X12444210

Haynie, D. L., & Osgood, D. W. (2005). Reconsidering peers and delinquency: How do peers matter? *Social Forces*, 84(2), 1109–1130. https://doi.org/10.1353/sof.2006.0018

Heinrichs, N., Bertram, H., Kuschel, A., & Hahlweg, K. (2005). Parent recruitment and retention in a universal prevention program for child behavior and emotional problems: Barriers to research and program participation. *Prevention Science*, 6, 275–286. https://doi.org/10.1007/s11121-005-0006-1

Hektner, J. M., August, G. J., & Realmuto, G. M. (2003). Effects of pairing aggressive and nonaggressive children in strategic peer affiliation. *Journal of Abnormal Child Psychology*, 31(4), 399–412. https://doi.org/10.1023/a:1023891502049

Hoeben, E. M., Meldrum, R. C., Walker, D. A., & Young, J. T. N. (2016). The role of peer delinquency and unstructured socializing in explaining delinquency and substance use: A state-of-the-art review. *Journal of Criminal Justice*, 47, 108–122.

Hunter, R. F., de la Haye, K., Murray, J. M., Badham, J., Valente, T. W., Clarke, M., & Kee, F. (2019). Social network interventions for health behaviours and outcomes: A systematic review and meta-analysis. *PLoS medicine*, 16(9), e1002890. https://doi.org/10.1371/journal.pmed.1002890

Hunter, R. F., McAneney, H., Davis, M., Tully, M. A., Valente, T. W., & Kee, F. (2015). "Hidden" social networks in behavior change interventions. *American Journal of Public Health*, 105(3), 513–516. https://doi.org/10.2105/AJPH.2014.302399

Kelly, J. A., Murphy, D. A., Sikkema, K. J., McAuliffe, T. L., Roffman, R. A., Solomon, L. J., Winett, R. A., & Kalichman, S. C. (1997). Randomized, controlled, community-level HIV-prevention intervention for sexual-risk behaviour among homosexual men in US cities. *The Lancet*, 350, 1500–1505. https://doi.org/10.1016/s0140-6736(97)07439-4

Kerr, M., Stattin, H. k., & Kiesner, J. (2007). Peers and problem behavior: Have we missed something? In R. C. M. E. Engels, M. Kerr, & H. k. Stattin (Eds.), *Friends, lovers, and groups: Key relationships in adolescence* (pp. 125–153). Wiley.

Kiesner, J., Kerr, M., & Stattin, H. (2004). "Very important persons" in adolescence: Going beyond in-school, single friendships in the study of peer homophily. *Journal of Adolescence, 27*, 545–560. https://doi.org/10.1016/j.adolescence.2004.06.007

Kim, D. A., Hwong, A. R., Stafford, D., Hughes, D. A., O'Malley, A. J., Fowler, J. H., & Christakis, N. A. (2015). A randomised controlled trial of social network targeting to maximise population behaviour change. *Lancet, 386*(9989), 145–153. https://doi.org/10.1016/S0140-6736(15)60095-2

Kreager, D. A., Rulison, K. L., & Moody, J. (2011). Delinquency and the structure of adolescent peer groups. *Criminology, 49*, 95–127. https://doi.org/10.1111/j.1745-9125.2010.00219.x

Kwasnicka, D., Dombrowski, S. U., White, M., & Sniehotta, F. (2016). Theoretical explanations for maintenance of behaviour change: A systematic review of behaviour theories. *Health Psychology Review, 10*(3), 277–296. https://doi.org/10.1080/17437199.2016.1151372

Latkin, C. A., Mandell, W., Vlahov, D., Oziemkowska, M., & Celentano, D. D. (1996). The long-term outcome of a personal network-oriented HIV prevention intervention for injection drug users: The SAFE study. *American Journal of Community Psychology, 24*(3), 341–364. https://doi.org/10.1007/bf02512026

Light, J. M., Greenan, C. C., Rusby, J. C., Nies, K. M., & Snijders, T. A. B. (2013). Onset to first alcohol use in early adolescence: A network diffusion model. *Journal of Research on Adolescence, 23*, 487–499. https://doi.org/10.1111/jora.12064

Litt, M. D., Kadden, R. M., Kabela-Cormier, E., & Petry, N. M. (2009). Changing network support for drinking: Network Support Project two-year follow-up. *Journal of consulting and clinical psychology, 77*(2), 229–242. https://doi.org/10.1037/a0015252

Mayeux, L., Sandstrom, M. J., & Cillessen, A. H. N. (2008). Is being popular a risky proposition? *Journal of Research on Adolescence, 18*(1), 49–74. https://doi.org/10.1111/j.1532-7795.2008.00550.x

McCord, J. (2003). Cures that harm: Unanticipated outcomes of crime prevention programs. *The Annals of the American Academy of Political and Social Science, 587*(1), 16–30. https://doi.org/10.1177/0002716202250781

McMillan, C., & Schaefer, D. R. (2021). Comparing targeting strategies for network-based adolescent drinking interventions: A simulation approach. *Social Science & Medicine (1982), 282*, 114136. https://doi.org/10.1016/j.socscimed.2021.114136

Mikami, A. Y., Boucher, M. A., & Humphreys, K. (2005). Prevention of peer rejection through a classroom-level intervention in middle school. *The Journal of Primary Prevention, 26*(1), 5–23.

Minnis, A. M., vanDommelen-Gonzalez, E., Luecke, E., Dow, W., Bautista-Arredondo, S., & Padian, N. S. (2014). Yo Puedo—A conditional cash transfer and life skills intervention to promote adolescent sexual health: Results of a randomized feasibility study in San Francisco. *The Journal of Adolescent Health: Official Publication of the Society for Adolescent Medicine, 55*(1), 85–92. https://doi.org/10.1016/j.jadohealth.2013.12.007

Molgaard, V. M., Kumpfer, K. L., & Fleming, E. (1997). *The Strengthening Families Program for Parents and Youth 10–14: A video-based curriculum.* Institute for Social and Behavioral Research.

Molgaard, V., & Spoth, R. (2001). The Strengthening Families Program for young adolescents: Overview and outcomes. *Residential Treatment for Children & Youth, 18*, 15–29. https://doi.org/10.1300/J007v18n03_03

Molloy Elreda, L., Coatsworth, J. D., Gest, S. D., Ram, N., & Bamberger, K. (2016). Understanding process in group-based intervention delivery: Social network analysis and intra-entity variability methods as windows into the "black box." *Prevention Science, 17*(8), 925–936. https://doi.org/10.1007/s11121-016-0699-3

Moody, J., Brynildsen, W. D., Osgood, D. W., Feinberg, M. E., & Gest, S. D. (2011). Popularity trajectories and substance use in early adolescence. *Social Networks, 33*, 101–112. https://doi.org/10.1016/j.socnet.2010.10.001

Moody, J., & White, D. R. (2003). Structural cohesion and embeddedness: A hierarchical concept of social groups. *American Sociological Review, 68*, 103–127.

Mrug, S., & McCay, R. (2013). Parental and peer disapproval of alcohol use and its relationship to adolescent drinking: Age, gender, and racial differences. *Psychology of Addictive Behaviors, 27*, 604–614. https://doi.org/10.1037/a0031064

Neighbors, C., Lee, C. M., Lewis, M. A., Fossos, N., & Larimer, M. E. (2007). Are social norms the best predictor of outcomes among heavy-drinking college students? *Journal of Studies on Alcohol and Drugs, 68*, 556–565.

Osgood, D. W., & Anderson, A. L. (2004). Unstructured socializing and rates of delinquency. *Criminology, 42*(3), 519–550. https://doi.org/https://doi.org/10.1111/j.1745-9125.2004.tb00528.x

Osgood, D. W., Feinberg, M. E., Gest, S. D., Moody, J., Ragan, D. T., Spoth, R., Greensberg, M., & Redmond, C. (2013). Effects of PROSPER on the influence potential of prosocial versus antisocial youth in adolescent friendship networks. *Journal of Adolescent Health, 53*, 174–179. https://doi.org/10.1016/j.jadohealth.2013.02.013

Osgood, D. W., Wilson, J. K., O'Malley, P. M., Bachman, J. G., & Johnston, L. D. (1996). Routine activities and individual deviant behavior. *American Sociological Review, 61*, 635–655. https://doi.org/10.2307/2096397

Pickering, T. A., Wyman, P. A., Schmeelk-Cone, K., Hartley, C., Valente, T. W., Pisani, A. R.,Rulison, K. L., Hendricks Brown, C., &LoMurray, M. (2018). Diffusion of a peer-led suicide preventive intervention through school-based student peer and adult networks. *Frontiers in Psychiatry, 9*. https://doi.org/10.3389/fpsyt.2018.00598

Poulin, F., Dishion, T. J., & Burraston, B. (2001). 3-Year iatrogenic effects associated with aggregating high-risk adolescents in cognitive-behavioral preventive interventions. *Applied Developmental Science, 5*(4), 214–224. https://doi.org/10.1207/s1532480xads0504_03

Prinz, R. J., Blechman, E. A., & Dumas, J. E. (1994). An evaluation of peer coping-skills training for childhood aggression. *Journal of Clinical Child Psychology, 23*(2), 193–203. https://doi.org/10.1207/s15374424jccp2302_8

Redmond, C., Spoth, R., Shin, C., & Lepper, H. S. (1999). Modeling long-term parent outcomes of two universal family-focused preventive interventions: One-year follow-up results. *Journal of Consulting and Clinical Psychology, 67*, 975–984. https://doi.org/10.1037/0022-006x.67.6.975

Rogers, E. M. (2003). *Diffusion of innovations*. Free Press.

Rulison, K. L. (2020). Commentary on White et al. (2019): Future directions in studying the diffusion of intervention effects. *Addiction, 115*(5), 992–993. https://doi.org/10.1111/add.14977

Rulison, K. L., Feinberg, M., Gest, S. D., & Osgood, D. W. (2015). Diffusion of intervention effects: The impact of a family-based substance use prevention program on friends of participants. *Journal of Adolescent Health*, *57*, 433–440. https://doi.org/10.1016/j.jadohealth.2015.06.007

Rulison, K. L., Gest, S. D., & Osgood, D. W. (2015). Adolescent peer networks and the potential for the diffusion of intervention effects. *Prevention Science*, *16*, 133–144. https://doi.org/10.1007/s11121-014-0465-3

Rulison, K. L., Patrick, M. E., & Maggs, J. (2019). Linking peer relationships to substance use across adolescence. In S. Brown & R. A. Zucker (Eds.), *The Oxford handbook of substance use* (pp. 389–420). Oxford University Press.

Schaefer, D. R., Adams, J., & Haas, S. A. (2013). Social networks and smoking: Exploring the effects of peer influence and smoker popularity through simulations. *Health Education & Behavior: The Official Publication of the Society for Public Health Education*, *40*(1 Suppl.), 24S–32S. https://doi.org/10.1177/1090198113493091

Shaya, F. T., Chirikov, V. V., Howard, D., Foster, C., Costas, J., Snitker, S., Frimpter, J., & Kucharski, K. (2014). Effect of social networks intervention in type 2 diabetes: A partial randomised study. *Journal of Epidemiology and Community Health*, *68*(4), 326–332. https://doi.org/10.1136/jech-2013-203274

Shelton, R. C., Lee, M., Brotzman, L. E., Crookes, D. M., Jandorf, L., Erwin, D., & Gage-Bouchard, E. A. (2019). Use of social network analysis in the development, dissemination, implementation, and sustainability of health behavior interventions for adults: A systematic review. *Social Science & Medicine (1982)*, *220*, 81–101. https://doi.org/10.1016/j.socscimed.2018.10.013

Spoth, R., Redmond, C., Shin, C., & Azevedo, K. (2004). Brief family intervention effects on adolescent substance initiation: School-level growth curve analyses 6 years following baseline. *Journal of Consulting and Clinical Psychology*, *72*(3), 535–542. https://doi.org/10.1037/0022-006x.72.3.535

Spoth, R., & Redmond, C. (2000). Research on family engagement in preventive interventions: Toward improved use of scientific findings in primary prevention practice. *Journal of Primary Prevention*, *21*, 267–284. https://doi.org/10.1023/a:1007039421026

Spoth, R. L., Redmond, C., & Shin, C. (2001). Randomized trial of brief family interventions for general populations: Adolescent substance use outcomes 4 years following baseline. *Journal of Consulting and Clinical Psychology*, *69*, 627–642. https://doi.org/10.1037/0022-006x.69.4.627

Starkey, F., Audrey, S., Holliday, J., Moore, L., & Campbell, R. (2009). Identifying influential young people to undertake effective peer-led health promotion: the example of A Stop Smoking In Schools Trial (ASSIST). *Health Education Research*, *24*(6), 977–988. https://doi.org/10.1093/her/cyp045

Stevens, R. J., & Slavin, R. E. (1995). The cooperative elementary school: Effects on students' achievement, attitudes, and social-relations. *American Educational Research Journal*, *32*(2), 321–351. https://doi.org/10.2307/1163434

Valente, T. W. (1995). *Network models of the diffusion of innovations*. Hampton Press.

Valente, T. W. (2010). *Social networks and health: Models, methods, and applications*. Oxford University Press.

Valente, T. W. (2012). Network interventions. *Science*, *337*(6090), 49–53. https://doi.org/10.1126/science.1217330

Valente, T. W., Chou, C. P., & Pentz, M. A. (2007). Community coalitions as a system: Effects of network change on adoption of evidence-based substance abuse prevention. *American Journal of Public Health*, 97(5), 880–886. https://doi.org/10.2105/AJPH.2005.063644

Valente, T. W., Gallaher, P., & Mouttapa, M. (2004). Using social networks to understand and prevent substance use: A transdisciplinary perspective. *Substance Use & Misuse*, 39, 10–12. https://doi.org/10.1081/ja-200033210

Valente, T. W., Palinkas, L. A., Czaja, S., Chu, K.-H., & Brown, C. H. (2015). Social network analysis for program implementation. *PLoS One*, 10(6), e0131712. https://doi.org/10.1371/journal.pone.0131712

Valente, T. W., & Pitts, S. R. (2017). An appraisal of social network theory and analysis as applied to public health: Challenges and opportunities. *Annual Review of Public Health*, 38(1), 103–118. https://doi.org/10.1146/annurev-publhealth-031816-044528

Valente, T. W., & Pumpuang, P. (2007). Identifying opinion leaders to promote behavior change. *Health Education & Behavior*, 34(6), 881–896.

Valente, T. W., Ritt-Olson, A., Stacy, A., Unger, J. B., Okamoto, J., & Sussman, S. (2007). Peer acceleration: Effects of a social network tailored substance abuse prevention program among high-risk adolescents. *Addiction*, 102(11), 1804–1815.

Valente, T. W., Unger, J. B., & Johnson, C. A. (2005). Do popular students smoke? The association between popularity and smoking among middle school students. *Journal of Adolescent Health*, 37(4), 323–329. https://doi.org/10.1016/j.jadohealth.2004.10.016

Valente, T. W., & Vega Yon, G. G. (2020). Diffusion/contagion processes on social networks. *Health Education & Behavior: The Official Publication of the Society for Public Health Education*, 47(2), 235–248. https://doi.org/10.1177/1090198120901497

Wasserman, S., & Faust, K. (1994). *Social network analysis: Methods and applications*. Cambridge University Press.

White, J., Holliday, J., Daniel, R., Campbell, R., & Moore, L. (2020). Diffusion of effects of the ASSIST school-based smoking prevention intervention to non-participating family members: A secondary analysis of a randomized controlled trial. *Addiction (Abingdon, England)*, 115(5), 986–991. https://doi.org/10.1111/add.14862

Wu, L.-T., Swartz, M. S., Brady, K. T., & Hoyle, R. H. (2015). Perceived cannabis use norms and cannabis use among adolescents in the United States. *Journal of Psychiatric Research*, 64, 79–87. https://doi.org/10.1016/j.jpsychires.2015.02.022

Wyman, P. A., Brown, C. H., LoMurray, M., Schmeelk-Cone, K., Petrova, M., Yu, Q., Walsh, E., Tu, X., & Wang, W. (2010). An outcome evaluation of the Sources of Strength suicide prevention program delivered by adolescent peer leaders in high schools. *American Journal of Public Health*, 100, 1653–1661. https://doi.org/10.2105/AJPH.2009.190025

Wyman, P. A., Pickering, T. A., Pisani, A. R., Rulison, K., Schmeelk-Cone, K., Hartley, C., Gould, M., Caine, E. D., Hendricks Brown, C., & Valente, T. W. (2019). Peer-adult network structure and suicide attempts in 38 high schools: Implications for network-informed suicide prevention. *Journal of Child Psychology and Psychiatry*, 60(10), 1065–1075. https://doi.org/https://doi.org/10.1111/jcpp.13102

Wyman, P. A., Rulison, K., Pisani, A. R., Alvaro, E. M., Crano, W. D., Schmeelk-Cone, K., Elliot, C., K., Wortzel, J., Pickering, T. A., & Espelage, D. L. (2021). Above the influence of vaping: Peer leader influence and diffusion of a network-informed preventive intervention. *Addictive Behaviors*, 113, 106693. https://doi.org/10.1016/j.addbeh.2020.106693

12

Genetic susceptibility to peers

GABRIEL L. SCHLOMER, AMANDA M. GRIFFIN,
H. HARRINGTON CLEVELAND, AND DAVID J. VANDENBERGH ∎

INTRODUCTION

Adolescence reflects a significant transition period when youth are gradually granted greater autonomy over their own behavior. During this transition, youth increasingly spend less time with their family and more time outside the home, particularly with peers (Larson et al., 1996). As described in the introductory chapters, adolescents and their friends can be remarkably similar to one another due to two complimentary processes that result from peer relationships. First, adolescents tend to befriend others who are already similar to them. This process, termed *selection*, contributes to adolescent-peer similarity. Second, adolescents and their friends mutually influence each other over time, via socialization, leading them to become even more similar (Brechwald & Prinstein, 2011). During early- to mid-adolescence, opportunities for both peer selection and peer socialization (Larson et al., 1996) are greater than during childhood (Lam et al., 2014) as adolescents increase the amount of time spent with peers and decrease time spent with parents (Nelson et al., 2005).

From a developmental perspective, at no other point in the life course do peers have a greater influence than they do during adolescence, and peers influence a broad range of developmental outcomes. Affiliating with prosocial peers is associated with reduced violence and substance use during adolescence (Prinstein et al.; Spoth et al., 1996). Conversely, affiliating with delinquent peers is associated with adolescents' increased risk of alcohol use and delinquency (Dishion et al., 1996; Fisher et al., 2007). However, peer influence on behavior is not uniform across adolescents, and some adolescents are more easily influenced by their peers than others. Developmental research has identified individual characteristics (e.g., self-esteem, depression, sensation seeking, impulsivity) and environmental factors (e.g., parent characteristics) associated with the strength of both

Gabriel L. Schlomer, Amanda M. Griffin, H. Harrington Cleveland, and David J. Vandenbergh, *Genetic susceptibility to peers*. In: *Teen Friendship Networks, Development, and Risky Behavior*. Edited by: Mark E. Feinberg and D. Wayne Osgood, Oxford University Press. © Mark E. Feinberg and D. Wayne Osgood 2024. DOI: 10.1093/oso/9780197602317.003.0012 peer selection and socialization (e.g., Donohew et al., 1999; Laible, 2007). In the last 20 years, this body of research has been furthered by demonstrating genetic and environmental underpinnings of peer selection and socialization (Brendgen, 2012). Specifically, whom adolescents select to befriend and how sensitive they are to peer influence appears to be, in part, genetically influenced.

In this chapter, we discuss a series of studies from the genetic extension of PROSPER (Promoting School-community-university Partnerships to Enhance Resilience)—referred to as gPROSPER—that tests hypotheses about individual differences in adolescent susceptibility to peer influences. DNA-derived genotypes collected as part of gPROSPER were used to determine if specific genetic variants could modify the impact of peer influences on adolescent development as well as the possible role of genes in who adolescents choose to befriend. Among the described studies, two also utilized friendship-network data from the PROSPER Peers project, which are ideal for testing the sensitivity hypothesis in genetic research. Before discussing these studies, we provide contextual background by first briefly reviewing prior twin-based research on the genetics of adolescent-peer relationships and how these studies relate to the relatively newer DNA-based inquiries. Following this overview, we introduce differential susceptibility theory, which was the guiding theoretical framework of the gPROSPER studies. After describing the peer-focused gPROSPER studies and how they build on each other, we finish with some general conclusions as well as implications for policy and practice.

BEHAVIORAL AND MOLECULAR GENETIC APPROACHES TO STUDYING ADOLESCENT-PEER RELATIONS

Identifying genetic influences on peer relationships began with behavioral genetic approaches for estimating variance in behaviors or traits explained by genetic and environmental influences. Behavioral genetics approaches take advantage of naturally occurring variation in genetic relatedness among family members to disentangle genetic from environmental influences. Twin designs, the most common behavioral genetic approach, estimate genetic, shared environmental, and nonshared environmental influences by comparing the similarity of monozygotic twins (who share 100% of their genes) and dizygotic twins (who share 50% of their genes, on average). Shared environmental influences are nongenetic influences that account for similarities between twins, such as common parenting experiences or shared neighborhood influences. Nonshared environmental influences account for nongenetic within-family differences—they are environmental causes of differences between twins. Nonshared environments might include differences in victimization or differences in peer relationships. Behavioral genetic approaches have advanced the literature on peer relationships by demonstrating both genetic and environmental influences on peer relationships (e.g., Cleveland et al., 2005), which were historically assumed to be exclusively environmental phenomena. For example, estimates of genetic influence (also called heritability) on affiliating with peers characterized as college oriented or popular range from 0% to 72%, depending on the reporter, age of the child, and type of study (Iervolino et al., 2002). Findings for genetic influences on affiliating with peers characterized as delinquent are more consistent with heritability estimates, ranging from 20% to 42% (for review, see Brendgen, 2012). Behavioral genetic evidence is consistent with the idea that genetic variability influences the kinds of friends that individuals select. Similarly, individual differences in the degree to which adolescents' own behaviors are influenced by their peers might also depend on adolescents' genetic factors.

The insights from behavioral genetics studies of heritability in peer relationships have been augmented by research using a molecular genetic approach. Genetic research in human development, and psychology more broadly, has undergone rapid advances due to decreasing costs of collecting and processing DNA. Complementing behavioral genetic estimates of heritability, molecular genetic research is focused on showing how measured genetic variability (i.e., genotypes) influences behaviors and offers a unique opportunity to investigate the direct effect of genes on peer relationships. Specifically, researchers have the ability to investigate individual differences in genotypes as precursors to processes that underlie peer selection and variation in susceptibility to peers. Genetic variation is a particularly robust marker of individual differences because the DNA sequence does not change in response to environmental experiences (unlike epigenetic states, which can be impacted by environmental exposures). To date, however, a limited number of studies have examined the molecular genetics of peer relationships.

Behavioral and molecular genetic approaches have their own strengths and limitations (Harden, 2021), and both can be used to investigate gene–environment correlations (rGE) and gene–environment interactions (GxE). Gene–environment correlation (rGE) is the concept that environments, rather than being randomly distributed across genotypes, can covary with genetic differences due to genetics' influences impacting the environments to which individuals are exposed. There are three types of rGE: passive, active, and evocative. *Passive rGE* occurs when genes and environments are correlated because parents and children share genes and parents provide the rearing environment, which is correlated with the child's genes (and the parents'). For example, the correlation between hostile parenting and adolescent aggression may reflect, at least in part, genes shared between parents and children that are related to hostile parenting in the parent and aggression in the children. What would otherwise appear to be an environmentally directed correlation between hostile parenting and child aggression can be partly due to shared genes, which impact environments provided by parents and are passed down from parents to children. *Evocative rGE* refers to environmental responses that are evoked by a child's genes, or genetically influenced characteristics. For example, a child's genetically influenced behaviors may evoke behaviors from peers. *Active rGE* is when individuals select an environment based on their genes (or genetically influenced characteristics). For example, more prosocial adolescents may choose to affiliate with more prosocial peers (and be chosen by prosocial peers) based on genetically influenced characteristics related to prosocial behavior (e.g., friendliness, agreeableness). As adolescents are better able than children to select and shape their environments in ways that correlated with their genes due to increased autonomy, there are—in principle—greater opportunities for active and evocative rGE during adolescence (e.g., Scarr & McCartney, 1983). In contrast, circumstances promoting passive rGE may peak in strength during childhood.

Much of the behavioral genetic research on peer relationships has focused on genetic correlations, and there is strong evidence of evocative rGE in adolescent-peer relationships (Burt, 2008, 2009). Although the majority of research has focused on negative aspects of peer relationships, demonstrating that genetically influenced negative behaviors toward peers evoke negative behaviors in return, there is also evidence that children's genetically influenced prosocial behavior toward peers evokes similar positive behaviors in return (Burt, 2008).

Complimenting behavioral genetic research on rGE in peer relationships, molecular genetic studies tend to focus on GxE and identifying genetic variation that affects susceptibility to peer influence. The gPROSPER studies on peer susceptibility primarily use this approach. GxE research examines whether the relationship between two variables differs as a function of a third variable, known as a moderator variable. This process can be conceptualized in two equivalent ways: (1) how the effect of genes on developmental outcomes is modified by environments; and (2) how the effect of environments on developmental outcomes is modified by genes. Whether the former or latter conceptualization is used largely depends on the theoretical orientation, hypothesis tested, and genes and environments examined. Molecular genetic GxE research has largely used candidate genes to test gene-by-peer interactions. Candidate GxE studies constitute research wherein a single or few specific genetic variants are examined in relation to a phenotype (i.e., characteristics of the individual) and/or its interaction with a measured environment. In this approach, researchers focus on genetic variants that have a known impact on biological functioning relative to the outcome or environmental influence under study.

Taking a molecular genetic approach to understanding individual differences in environmental susceptibility allows researchers to frame questions about vulnerability or susceptibility to peers in terms of biology (Griffin et al., 2015). When using genetic variants that have well-articulated biological functions, questions can be asked about the specific neurobiological pathways to help understand why some adolescents are more susceptible to peer influence. Likewise, research can begin to determine what biological factors, linked to genetic variability, are associated with resistance to negative peer influences. Identifying the biological bases of vulnerability or susceptibility would set the groundwork for understanding other, well-studied endophenotypic (e.g., emotion regulation) and physical/behavioral (e.g., temperament) sources of individual variability in susceptibility to environmental influence. Ultimately, this work may lead to more precise preventive intervention approaches by identifying the drivers of individual differences in environmental response, including susceptibility to peers, and possible intervention strategies that target peer relations. In addition, research on the genetic and biological basis of differences in environmental sensitivity might inform targeting prevention (August & Gewirtz, 2019) by identifying those individuals who are most likely to benefit from a positive environmental influence, such as a prevention program. Similarly, identifying those adolescents who may be more resistant to the positive effects of intervention programming could lead the field to develop alternative strategies and/or implement stronger interventions for those individuals.

DIFFERENTIAL SUSCEPTIBILITY THEORY

Models of environmental susceptibility have undergone a revolution of sorts over the past decade. Early theorizing about individual differences in environmental susceptibility, including susceptibility to peers, largely took an approach using multiple risk factors (Ellis et al., 2011). Environmental susceptibility was conceptualized as vulnerability, and research focused on determining what environmental conditions (environmental risk factors) might act as triggers to exacerbate individual propensities for a specific outcome (individual risk). Individual risks or vulnerabilities such as genetic risk for alcoholism, for example, might surface or be exacerbated when exposed to peers who misuse substances. Similarly, an adolescent with a genetic propensity tending toward impulsivity might manifest disruptive, aggressive, and/or antisocial behavior if exposed to peers exhibiting high levels of delinquent and aggressive behavior. It is important to highlight that within this model, often termed diathesis stress, whether or not an outcome occurs is due to a combination of individual and environmental risk. That is, what matters is both the degree of individual risk/vulnerability and the strength of the adverse (negative) environment. Antisocial behaviors may never develop, even at high individual risk (e.g., impulsivity), if there is no exposure to external risk (e.g., peers with conduct problems). Conversely, poor outcomes among individuals at low genetic risk may still occur when the environment is sufficiently adverse.

Recognizing that the risk for negative outcomes is a function of the degree of individual risks and adverse environments also points out a unique aspect of the diathesis stress framework: it is inherently negatively focused (see Figure 12.1). By definition, individual risks are conceptualized as increasing the chances of a poor outcome, which are provoked by adverse environments. In contrast to the exclusive focus on negative outcomes, differential susceptibility theory (Ellis et al., 2011) reconceptualizes individual risk/vulnerability factors as sensitivity or susceptibility factors. The central tenet of differential susceptibility theory is that those same individual characteristics that would otherwise increase risk for poor outcomes in adverse environments may actually benefit an individual—leading to more positive outcomes—when they are exposed to more positive circumstances (Figure 12.1). Factors that might dispose adolescents to greater antisocial behavior when exposed to antisocial peers, for example, could also lead to greater prosociality when exposed to more prosocial peers. For example, greater sensitivity to social rewards could dispose an adolescent toward prosocial or antisocial behavior, depending on the levels of these behaviors within their peer network.

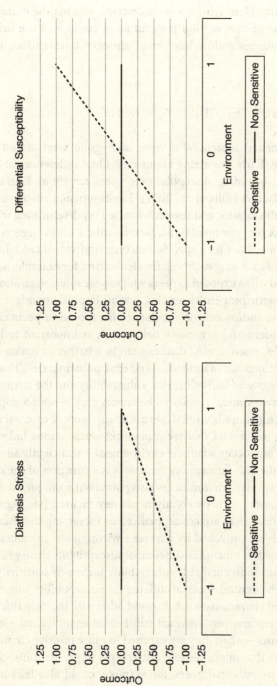

Note. Sensitivity according to diathesis stress includes only the negative sides. Differential susceptibility includes the full range of positive and negative for both outcome and environment.

Figure 12.1 Interaction forms for diathesis stress and differential susceptibility.

Thus, factors conceptualized as risk/vulnerability under diathesis stress are theoretically related to both poor *and* beneficial outcomes under differential susceptibility theory, depending on the environmental exposure (Bakermans-Kranenburg & Van Ijzendoorn, 2015).

Differential susceptibility theory and related models of individual differences in environmental response provide a guiding foundation for understanding why some adolescents are more influenced by peers than others. Many studies that examine the molecular genetic basis of individual differences in susceptibility to peers have used differential susceptibility theory as their theoretical framework. Differential susceptibility theory is inherently about how risk factors interact (i.e., moderate): the effects of environmental factors depend on individual susceptibility or, as the corollary, the effect of individual "risks" depends on environmental contexts.

Gene-by-environment interaction research is also inherently transactional: Genes modify environment-phenotype associations and/or environments moderate gene-phenotype associations. Note, however, that there are many forms of statistical interactions, and not all such interactions between measured genes and environments necessarily indicate differential susceptibility. Differential susceptibility theory stipulates that the effect of an individual sensitivity factor is altered by both negative and positive aspects of the environment; accordingly, a differential susceptibility interaction should show a "crossover pattern" wherein one slope is significantly different from zero (sensitive group), and the other slope is not (not sensitive group; see Figure 12.1).

TESTING GENETIC SUSCEPTIBILITY TO PEERS IN THE PROSPER PROJECT

The PROSPER data have several advantages for testing molecular genetic GxE, many of which address the limitations of previous research. First is PROSPER's large sample size. In total, the PROSPER project includes data on over $N = 9,000$ at each wave, and among these, DNA data are available for over $N = 2,000$. Longitudinal data are also a strength given the possibility of within-person analyses, which are statistically more powerful than cross-sectional, between-person methods. In addition, PROSPER data include several high-quality measures of adolescent and peer constructs, which can further increase power by better capturing true construct variability (as opposed to error). A unique measurement aspect of the PROSPER data with regard to studying peer influence is the longitudinal friendship nomination data. As reviewed in Chapter 1, adolescent reports of their peers' behavior may reflect adolescents' own attitudes and behaviors rather than serving as an independent assessment of their peers. Measuring peer behaviors via peers own self-reports better separates the true environmental influence of peers from adolescents' own behavior. Measures that better capture actual environmental influences, when available, are ideal for testing GxE and differential susceptibility hypotheses. Along these lines, including the PROSPER randomized intervention as part of the analysis further strengthens tests of GxE. Randomization eliminates the possibility of systematic selection into specific experimental environments (i.e., intervention vs. control groups). With randomization, it is implausible that genes are correlated with the environmental exposure (through passive or active rGE), ruling out alternative explanations for GxE.

DNA for gPROSPER was first collected from a subset ($n = 537$) of PROSPER adolescents who completed both in-school assessments and in-home interviews at Wave 5 (approximately age 15). At a later survey collection during young adulthood (approximately age 20), DNA was collected from an additional $n = 1,495$ PROSPER youth who earlier had participated only in the in-school assessments. At both assessments, DNA was collected via buccal swab. In total, the gPROSPER sample consists of $N = 2,032$ participants—the largest adolescent data set that contains both DNA information and a randomized preventive intervention.

Genetic assays. gPROSPER participants' DNA has been genotyped on a selected set of variable number of tandem repeats (VNTRs; e.g., *DRD4, 5-HTTLPR*) as well as on over 250 single-nucleotide polymorphisms (SNPs) specifically selected for their known or potential role in substance use phenotypes. VNTRs were genotyped using a modified phenol-chloroform technique (Freeman et al., 2003) to purify the DNA, and then individual polymerase chain reaction (PCR) and/or a multiplex PCR technique (Haberstick et al., 2014). SNPs were genotyped using a custom TaqMan SNP genotyping assay from Applied Biosystems (Life Technologies, Carlsbad, CA). In addition, participants in the initial DNA data collection ($n = 537$) were also genotyped using the Affymetrix (Santa Clara, CA) Axiom™ Genome-Wide Exome Array, which includes genotypes on 318,000 SNPs from human exons, approximately 41,000 of which have a minor allele frequency of less than 0.05. To ensure genotyping accuracy, a number of quality control steps have been implemented, such as comparisons between genotyped and self-reported sex and tests of Hardy-Weinberg equilibrium. Last, in molecular genetic studies, GxE associations could be spurious if the frequency of genetic variants differs across populations with distinguishable genetic ancestry backgrounds. Termed population stratification (Freedman et al., 2004), observed associations may actually be due to the cross-population differences in the frequency of the variant (and the outcome) and not due to the variant itself. The risk for spurious findings due to population stratification can be reduced by controlling for DNA-derived indices of genetic ancestry, which are included across all gPROSPER studies (see Cleveland et al., 2015).

Does susceptibility to peers differ according to different genotypes?

Dopamine receptor D4 (DRD4). The gPROSPER data were used to address the overarching research question of whether susceptibility to peers differs across different genotypes. Our initial work in this area focused on the dopamine receptor D4 variant (*DRD4*). Variation in *DRD4* has been linked to dopamine activation in areas of the brain related to reward salience and reward magnitude, such as greater sensitivity to environmental rewards (e.g., gambling; Glazer et al., 2020). More specifically, the *DRD4* gene contains a VNTR in the third exon (Van Tol et al., 1992) that ranges between 2 and 11 repeats with the 4 and 7 repeat alleles the most common. *DRD4* variation is often coded in terms of the presence or absence of the 7-repeat allele (i.e., 7+ vs. 7-) given its relation to suppressed D4 receptor expression (Schoots & Van Tol, 2003).

Importantly, two experimental studies found that *DRD4* moderated the impact of social experiences (Creswell et al., 2012; Larsen et al., 2010). Creswell et al. (2012) found that individuals who possessed a specific *DRD4* genotype and who consumed alcohol in a group context reported greater perceived social bonding. A similar experimental study found that the same genetic variant was associated with an increased sensitivity to alcohol-related cues, such as being in the presence of a same-age individual who drank heavily, which resulted in increased alcohol consumption (Larsen et al., 2010). Given these findings that suggest links between genetic variation in peer influence, our research group sought to evaluate whether molecular genetic variation is related to individual differences in susceptibly to peers during adolescence, specifically regarding externalizing behavior problems, including alcohol use, aggression, and delinquency.

Drawing on these *DRD4* experimental findings, and guided by differential susceptibility theory, we used the gPROSPER data to examine the longitudinal hypothesis that antisocial peer pressure in seventh grade, operationalized as attempts to persuade adolescents into antisocial behaviors (self-reported by the target adolescent), would be related to adolescent lifetime alcohol use measured at 12th grade. We further hypothesized that antisocial peer pressure would show a stronger effect on alcohol use at 12th grade among *DRD4* 7+ adolescents compared to 7- adolescents. Results were consistent with the genomic hypothesis: Adolescents who carried at least one copy of the *DRD4* 7-repeat allele (7+) were prone to significantly higher alcohol use by 12th grade in the context of high levels of antisocial peer pressure compared to similar youth who did not carry the 7-repeat allele (Griffin et al., 2015). Among 7- adolescents, no association was found. This crossover interaction (see Figure 12.1) was consistent with differential susceptibility theory and suggests greater susceptibility to antisocial peers within one group (7+) and relative insensitivity in the other (7-). Further, *DRD4* variation and peer antisocial behavior were uncorrelated, making *r*GE an unlikely alternative explanation for the observed GxE.

These findings (Griffin et al., 2015) not only indicated that the alcohol use of adolescents with the 7-repeat allele may be more sensitive to peer pressure but they also suggested a mechanism for this individual difference. Adolescents who carry the *DRD4* 7-repeat allele may have a heightened sense of social reward from joining their peers in antisocial behaviors and may feel stronger social connections with their peers as a result. As a test of differential susceptibility theory, however, the study was limited in that it only examined the negative side of the susceptibility equation. Absence of antisocial peer pressure does not necessarily mean exposure to prosocial peers. This limitation was addressed in a subsequent study

(Griffin et al., 2014), which investigated the interaction between *DRD4* and positive peer relationships on past month and lifetime alcohol use by the 12th grade. Positive peer relationships were operationalized using adolescents' self-reports. Items consisted of how "cool" (i.e., 1 = not cool, 2 = OK, 3 = cool) they thought their friends would think they were if they took part in school activities, school sports, worked hard to get good grades, and similar items. While positive peer relationships were associated with reduced alcohol use, there was a lack of an effect of *DRD4*, and the associations between positive peer relations and adolescent alcohol use did not differ between *DRD4* 7+ and 7- adolescents. Notably, one possible reason for these null results may be due to the outcomes used. Differential susceptibility theory indicates that sensitive individuals may benefit more from more positive environments and be harmed more by negative ones. Strict adherence to the theory would suggest that positive environmental exposures would most strongly be associated with a positive outcome, such as adolescents' prosocial behaviors. While sensitivity to positive peer influences *could* result in reduced alcohol use, stronger effects might be expected for positive outcomes.

Oxytocin receptor gene (OXTR). The research on *DRD4*, substance use, and peers suggests that one reason for variation in susceptibility to peers might be heightened perceived rewards of joining peers in antisocial behavior. This pathway is likely not the only mechanism that gives rise to variation in peer influence, given research that shows multiple different phenotypes are related to peer sensitivity. For example, social processes such as affiliation (Andari et al., 2010) and interpersonal trust (Kosfeld et al., 2005) are regulated, in part, by the oxytocin system. Oxytocin is a neuromodulator involved in the regulation of social behavior and cognition (Donaldson & Young, 2008). Genetic variability related to oxytocin (oxytocin receptor gene; *OXTR*) has been linked to numerous social processes relevant for peer selection and socialization during adolescence, such as pair bonding (Walum et al., 2012).

Given research implicating *OXTR* variation as important for these social processes, variation in susceptibility to peer influence might also be related to *OXTR*. Our research group tested this hypothesis using the gPROSPER data (Cleveland et al., 2018). As previously discussed, affiliation with substance-using peers is partly heritable (Cleveland et al., 2005), so it is possible that *OXTR* variation could be linked to peer selection based on substance use. In addition, because peer relationships, such as reducing exposure and influence of substance-using peers, are among the targets of the PROSPER-delivered interventions (see Chapters 2 and 11), Cleveland et al. (2018) tested the hypothesis that intervention participation would moderate the association between *OXTR* variation and affiliation with substance-using peers. If *OXTR* is related to greater affiliation with substance-using peers, an indicator of peer selection based on *OXTR*, it is possible that the PROSPER-delivered interventions could mitigate this selection effect via reduced peer exposure and influence. Stemming from this line of thinking, we hypothesized that adolescents high on *OXTR* sensitivity who are in the control group may affiliate with substance-using friends, while those in the intervention group may not, or at least less so.

A notable advance in this study over our previous research (Griffin et al., 2014, 2015) is that we were able to utilize PROSPER's friendship nomination data to measure affiliation with substance-using peers. Peer substance use during ninth grade was based on the nominated peers' own reports of their substance use in the past month, including how often they drank any alcohol, drank enough alcohol to become intoxicated, smoked cigarettes, and used marijuana.

In addition, multiple SNPs were used to characterize *OXTR* variation. In our prior studies, we relied on individual variants associated with specific genes; however, any single genetic variant is expected to show only a small association with a phenotype (Dick et al., 2015), and the field has moved progressively toward using genomic aggregates in place of single variants. The practice of aggregating relies on the tenet that greater genomic prediction can be obtained by adding together the small effects of many individual variants. There are several advantages to this approach, including, for example, larger gene-phenotype associations, which may result in more reliable GxE tests (see Dick et al., 2015). Drawing from previous research on *OXTR*, five SNPs within *OXTR* that were not strongly correlated with one another (i.e., nonredundant) were selected to form an additive, overall genetic score for *OXTR*. An additional strength of this approach is that sensitivity, operationalized here by *OXTR* variation, is measured in a more continuous manner, in contrast to single-gene studies, which rely on only dichotomous measures of a gene variant (e.g., DRD4 7+ vs. 7-). Although individual differences in sensitivity are often described in terms of categories (i.e., sensitive vs. not sensitive), differential susceptibility theory posits that sensitivity is graded, where some individuals are more versus less sensitive (Ellis et al., 2011). Operationalizing genetic sensitivity in a continuous manner is more theoretically consistent than dichotomous characterizations.

Results of our study showed that adolescents in the intervention had friends who used fewer substances, and that adolescents with higher *OXTR* sensitivity had friends who used more substances. This latter finding is consistent with the hypothesis that *OXTR* will be related to peer selection based on substance use. In addition to these main effects, a two-way interaction between the *OXTR* score and the intervention was found, although not in the predicted pattern. Specifically, we hypothesized that high *OXTR* sensitivity would be related to higher peer substance use within the control group, and that no association would be found in the intervention group. Support for this hypothesis would indicate that the intervention might reduce the link between higher *OXTR* sensitivity and affiliation with friends who use more substances. However, our study unexpectedly showed that the association was specific to the intervention: lower *OXTR* sensitivity was related to lower peer substance use, and no effect was found within the control group (a diathesis stress pattern; see Figure 12.1). Interestingly, this result suggests that the intervention may facilitate low *OXTR* risk adolescents in choosing peers low in substance use. Additional analyses showed that peer substance use was considerably associated with adolescent's own alcohol use across combinations of *OXTR* variability and intervention condition. Taken together, the finding that the PROSPER-delivered interventions impacted the association between *OXTR* and affiliation with substance-using peers was consistent with the interventions' intended impact on exposure to substance-using peers and suggests additional intervention targets may be related to *OXTR*, such as peer attachment, trust, and bonding.

Genetic index of sensitivity. These three gPROSPER studies, as well as studies by others (e.g., Trucco et al., 2017) demonstrated the principle that individual differences in susceptibility to peers are associated with individual genes. However, there is a debate about the reliability of GxE findings using candidate genes (see Dick et al., 2015; Schlomer et al., 2015). As a result, molecular genetic GxE research increasingly relies on aggregates of variants from numerous genes in place of single-candidate genes (Neale et al., 2021). In the *OXTR* study, we used multiple SNPs from *OXTR* to form an overall aggregate; however, we still only captured variation from a single gene. To move our work further in the direction of creating multigene aggregates, our research group built on our previous *DRD4*-based studies by testing the hypothesis that a genetic index comprising three genetic variants previously implicated in research on susceptibility to peer influence would moderate the impact of peer conduct problem behaviors (stealing, truancy, vandalism) on adolescent conduct problem behaviors (Schlomer et al., 2021).

The genetic index consisted of *DRD4*, *5-HTTLPR* (*serotonin transporter-linked polymorphic region*), and *GABRA2* (*GABA receptor alpha 2*). The *5-HTTLPR* site has been the subject of intense research over a number of years regarding its potential role in susceptibility to environmental factors (Tielbeek et al., 2016), including association with susceptibility to peer influence (Stenseng et al., 2018). *5-HTTLPR* is a variable number of tandem repeats within the *SLC6A4* (*serotonin transporter*) gene's promoter and is typically characterized in terms of long and short versions. Functional magnetic resonance imaging (fMRI) research suggests that individuals who have the *5-HTTLPR* short variant may be more neurologically susceptible to peers via greater amygdala reactivity in the presence of stress (Hariri et al., 2002). Research on *GABRA2* has shown that adolescents with more sensitivity-associated alleles who affiliate with delinquent peers have high externalizing behavior problems (Villafuerte et al., 2014) and lower externalizing behavior problems among those who affiliate with more prosocial peers (Trucco et al., 2017). Similar to *5-HTTLPR*, fMRI research suggests *GABRA2* variation is associated with differences in neural response to emotional stimuli (Trucco et al., 2018), implicating variation in *GABRA2* as a possible indicator of environmental sensitivity, including sensitivity to peers.

The genetic index was scored such that *DRD4* 7+, *5-HTTLPR* short allele, and the T allele of the rs279845 SNP within *GABRA2* were coded as sensitive. Using this three-gene genetic index, we analyzed growth in adolescents' self-reported conduct problem behaviors and growth in their friends' conduct problem behaviors. In this study, we used latent growth curve modeling to test whether adolescent and friend conduct problem behaviors changed in similar ways during adolescence. In addition, we tested the hypothesis that change in adolescent and friend conduct problem behaviors would be more strongly correlated among adolescents who were more genetically sensitive (Schlomer et al., 2021).

Results showed this was indeed the case. The change in peer conduct problem behaviors was correlated with change in adolescent conduct problem behaviors over time regardless of genetic sensitivity (both tended to increase together during adolescence). However, this association was strongest among adolescents with the maximum number of sensitivity alleles from the genetic index and weakest among those with the fewest. These results suggest that the influence of peer behavior problems was highest among adolescents who were the most genetically sensitive, as measured via our three-variant genetic index. Although we presume, based on the friend-nomination-based measure of peer behavior problems, that the peer associations found here reflect peer influence on adolescent behavior problems, it is also possible that these associations reflect bidirectional processes in that adolescents also influence their friends' behavior problems. The fact that we detected sensitivity to peers based on adolescent genotype suggests, in accordance with differential susceptibility theory, that at least a portion of this association is indeed peer influence.

CONCLUSION

Behavioral genetic studies of heritability indicate that peer selection and influence are subject to both environmental and genetic regulation. The results of four studies using gPROSPER data on the molecular genetics of peer influence indicated that specific genetic variants can help explain these processes. Griffin et al. (2015) found that *DRD4* moderated the association between antisocial peer pressure and adolescent alcohol use such that more susceptible adolescents demonstrated higher alcohol use when exposed to antisocial peers than similarly exposed adolescents who were less susceptible. In a follow-up study, however, Griffin et al. (2014) did not find that *DRD4* moderated the association between positive peer relationships and adolescent alcohol use. This null association may be the result of examining the association between positive peer relations and alcohol use rather than a more prosocial outcome, as might be suggested by differential susceptibility theory. Responding to calls for studies to expand beyond examining single variants, Cleveland et al. (2018) found that a multi-SNP *OXTR* score and the PROSPER-delivered interventions influenced peer selection. Specifically, the PROSPER-delivered interventions were found to have a protective effect on substance-using peer selection among adolescents who were low on the *OXTR* score. Finally, building on prior *DRD4* research and using a genetic index approach, Schlomer et al. (2021) found that adolescent and peer conduct problems covaried over time. Importantly, the association was strongest among adolescents who were highest in genetic sensitivity—based on *DRD4*, *5-HTTLPR*, and *GABRA2* variation—and weakest among those lowest in sensitivity, a pattern consistent with differential susceptibility theory (see Figure 12.1). Although the environment and outcome examined did not encompass the full range of positive and negative outcomes, follow-up tests indicated the interaction pattern conformed to the expected sensitivity pattern, and not diathesis stress.

When considered together, this set of studies builds on behavior genetic research by providing preliminary evidence that genetic variation, using measured genotypes, influences peer selection and influence processes. Some caution is warranted, however, since these findings need to be replicated. Replication issues represent a major hurdle for many candidate gene studies (e.g., Dick et al., 2015) and may be particularly troublesome for studies with unique data characteristics. The PROSPER project includes rich longitudinal data, a randomly assigned substance use preventive intervention component, and peer information based on nomination data (see Chapters 1 and 2). Finding studies with samples of similar populations (e.g., age, race, and demographics), measures, and other features relevant for replication that also have an adequate sample size is challenging. However, the gPROSPER data have been used to successfully corroborate research findings from a different study (see Brody et al., 2009; Schlomer et al., 2017), providing some confidence that these peer studies could be replicated as well.

In addition to replicating these studies, future research on the molecular genetics of susceptibility to peers should move toward a fuller integration of genetic aggregates, especially polygenic scores (PGSs), in place of candidate gene approaches. Genomic research in the social and behavioral sciences has methodologically advanced toward using PGSs, which are based on the results of genome-wide association studies. PGSs typically comprise hundreds to thousands (or more) individual genetic variants aggregated into an overall score. By aggregating many genes, each of which will only have small phenotypic association, PGSs show much larger associations than any individual candidate gene. In addition, genomic aggregates of this magnitude reflect the biological reality that complex phenotypes, like substance use and conduct problems, are related to many more than one or a few genes. Although our research group took steps in this direction by creating genetic aggregates based on multiple variants and genes, this approach does not reach the power obtained by aggregating across thousands. PGS creation requires genotyping on hundreds of thousands of genetic variants. The genomic density in gPROSPER currently consists of a few hundred variants specifically selected for their biological role in substance use and other targets of the gPROSPER interventions. Although a relatively new approach, PGSs have promise for advancing our understanding of how genes and peers influence development and marks the logical next step for the gPROSPER project.

Finally, future research should carefully consider developmental changes in susceptibility to peers and how associations between genetic variability and behavioral outcomes might change over time. The age of adolescent participants may matter for detecting genetic moderation of peer effects since the strength of peer influence wanes as children progress across adolescence (Lam et al., 2014; see also Chapter 5 of this volume). As the relationship between adolescents and their peers changes, so may genetic associations with susceptibility to peers. Longitudinal methods that are sensitive to these changes will be needed to adequately evaluate change in *r*GE and GxE across adolescence. One promising method is time-varying effects modeling (TVEM; Tan et al., 2012). Although not focused on peers, two TVEM studies using gPROSPER data have tested gene-by-intervention interactions on adolescent alcohol use (Russell et al., 2018) and delinquency (Schlomer et al., 2019) over time. Together, these studies demonstrated that GxE effects can be sensitive to developmental timing and that genetic interactions with peer environments may be similarly sensitive.

Implications for policy and practice

Taking a molecular genetic approach to peer relationship research provides a basis for identifying the biological underpinnings of peer selection, influence, and individual differences in susceptibility to peers. The biology of peer relations can provide insights for multiple points of possible intervention, beginning just downstream of genetic variation, ending at behavioral outcomes, and potentially including all of the processes in between. Nonetheless, practical applications of molecular genetic findings to peer-based interventions (as well as other interventions) is currently premature (Musci & Schlomer, 2017). There may be unintended consequences of, for example, assigning adolescents to different interventions (or no intervention) based on their DNA. Using genotype information to place children into programs may have detrimental effects, such as stigmatization, which could outweigh the positive effects of intervention participation. In addition, there remain many unanswered questions with regard to individual differences in sensitivity. The genetics of sensitivity are not fully understood, and it is unclear if differences in environmental sensitivity are domain specific (i.e., sensitivity to only one aspect of the environment) or domain general (i.e., sensitivity to all environment aspects; Belsky et al., 2021). These outstanding issues will need to be addressed before genetic information can be safely used in developing and targeting interventions.

REFERENCES

Andari, E., Duhamel, J. R., Zalla, T., Herbrecht, E., Leboyer, M., & Sirigu, A. (2010). Promoting social behavior with oxytocin in high-functioning autism spectrum disorders. *Proceedings of the National Academy of Sciences of the United States of America, 107*(9), 4389–4394. https://doi.org/10.1073/pnas.0910249107

August, G. J., & Gewirtz, A. (2019). Moving toward a precision-based, personalized framework for prevention science: Introduction to the special issue. *Prevention Science, 20*(1), 1–9. https://doi.org/10.1007/s11121-018-0955-9

Bakermans-Kranenburg, M. J., & Van Ijzendoorn, M. H. (2015). The hidden efficacy of interventions: Gene × environment experiments from a differential susceptibility perspective. *Annual Review of Psychology, 66*, 381–409. https://doi.org/10.1146/annurev-psych-010814-015407

Belsky, J., Zhang, X., & Sayler, K. (2021). Differential susceptibility 2.0: Are the same children affected by different experiences and exposures? *Development and Psychopathology, 34*(3), 1025–1033. https://doi.org/10.1017/S0954579420002205

Brechwald, W. A., & Prinstein, M. J. (2011). Beyond homophily: A decade of advances in understanding peer influence processes. *Journal of Research on Adolescence, 21*(1), 166–179. https://doi.org/10.1111/j.1532-7795.2010.00721.x

Brendgen, M. (2012). Genetics and peer relations: A review. *Journal of Research on Adolescence, 22*(3), 419–437. https://doi.org/10.1111/j.1532-7795.2012.00798.x

Brody, G. H., Beach, S. R. H., Philibert, R. A., Chen, Y.-F., & Murry, V. M. (2009). Prevention effects moderate the association of *5-HTTLPR* and youth risk behavior initiation: Gene × environment hypotheses tested via a randomized prevention design. *Child Development, 80*(3), 645–661. https://doi.org/10.1111/j.1467-8624.2009.01288.x

Burt, S. A. (2008). Genes and popularity: Evidence of an evocative gene-environment correlation. *Psychological Science, 19*(2), 112–113. https://doi.org/10.1111/j.1467-9280.2008.02055.x

Burt, S. A. (2009). A mechanistic explanation of popularity: Genes, rule breaking, and evocative gene-environment correlations. *Journal of Personality and Social Psychology, 97*(1), 57–57. https://doi.org/10.1037/a0016431

Cleveland, H. H., Griffin, A. M., Wolf, P. S. A., Wiebe, R. P., Schlomer, G. L., Feinberg, M. E., Greenberg, M. T., Spoth, R. L., Redmond, C., & Vandenbergh, D. J. (2018). Transactions between substance use intervention, the oxytocin receptor (*OXTR*) gene, and peer substance use predicting youth alcohol use. *Prevention Science, 19*(1), 15–26. https://doi.org/10.1007/s11121-017-0749-5

Cleveland, H. H., Wiebe, R. P., & Rowe, D. C. (2005). Sources of exposure to smoking and drinking friends among adolescents: A behavioral-genetic evaluation. *The Journal of Genetic Psychology, 166*(2), 153–169. https://doi.org/10.15288/jsa.2003.64.182

Creswell, K. G., Sayette, M. A., Manuck, S. B., Ferrell, R. E., Hill, S. Y., & Dimoff, J. D. (2012). *DRD4* polymorphism moderates the effect of alcohol consumption on social bonding. *PLoS One, 7*(2), e28914–e28914. https://doi.org/10.1371/journal.pone.0028914

Dick, D. M., Agrawal, A., Keller, M. C., Adkins, A., Aliev, F., Monroe, S., Hewitt, J. K., Kendler, K. S., & Sher, K. J. (2015). Candidate gene-environment interaction research: Reflections and recommendations. *Perspectives on Psychological Science, 10*(1), 37–59. https://doi.org/10.1177/1745691614556682

Dishion, T. J., Spracklen, K. M., Andrews, D. W., & Patterson, G. R. (1996). Deviancy training in male adolescent friendships. *Behavior Therapy, 27*(3), 373–390. https://doi.org/10.1016/S0005-7894(96)80023-2

Donaldson, Z. R., & Young, L. J. (2008). Oxytocin, vasopressin, and the neurogenetics of sociality. *Science, 322*(5903), 900–904. https://doi.org/10.1126/science.1158668

Donohew, L., Clayton, R. R., Skinner, W. F., & Colon, S. (1999). Peer networks and sensation seeking: Some implications for primary socialization theory. *Substance Use & Misuse, 34*(7), 1013–1023. https://doi.org/10.3109/10826089909039393

Ellis, B. J., Boyce, W. T., Belsky, J., Bakermans-Kranenburg, M. J., & van Ijzendoorn, M. H. (2011). Differential susceptibility to the environment: An evolutionary-neurodevelopmental theory. *Development and Psychopathology, 23*(01), 7–28. https://doi.org/10.1017/S0954579410000611

Fisher, L. B., Miles, I. W., Austin, S. B., Camargo, C. A., & Colditz, G. A. (2007). Predictors of initiation of alcohol use among US adolescents: Findings from a prospective cohort study. *Archives of Pediatrics & Adolescent Medicine, 161*(10), 959–966. https://doi.org/10.1001/archpedi.161.10.959

Freedman, M. L., Reich, D., Penney, K. L., McDonald, G. J., Mignault, A. A., Patterson, N., Gabriel, S. B., Topol, E. J., Smoller, J. W., Pato, C. N., Pato, M. T., Petryshen, T. L., Kolonel, L. N., Lasnder, E. S., Sklar, P., Henderson, B., Hirschhorn, J. N., & Altshuler, D. (2004). Assessing the impact of population stratification on genetic association studies. *Nature Genetics*, *36*(4), 388–393. https://doi.org/10.1038/ng1333

Freeman, B., Smith, N., Curtis, C., Huckett, L., Mill, J., & Craig, I. W. (2003). DNA from buccal swabs recruited by mail: Evaluation of storage effects on long-term stability and suitability for multiplex polymerase chain reaction genotyping. *Behavior Genetics*, *33*(1), 67–72. https://doi.org/10.1023/A:1021055617738

Glazer, J., King, A., Yoon, C., Liberzon, I., & Kitayama, S. (2020). DRD4 polymorphisms modulate reward positivity and P3a in a gambling task: Exploring a genetic basis for cultural learning. *Psychophysiology*, *57*(10), 1–14. https://doi.org/10.1111/psyp.13623

Griffin, A. M., Cleveland, H. H., Schlomer, G. L., Vandenbergh, D. J., & Feinberg, M. E. (2015). Differential susceptibility: The genetic moderation of peer pressure on alcohol use. *Journal of Youth and Adolescence*, *44*(10), 1841–1853. https://doi.org/10.1007/s10964-015-0344-7

Griffin, A. M., Schlomer, G. L., Cleveland, H. H., & Vandenbergh, D. J. (2014). *Differential susceptibility to effects of peer pressure and positive friend support on alcohol expectation during adolescence*. Society for Research on Adolescence (SRA). Austin, TX.

Haberstick, B. C., Smolen, A., Stetler, G. L., Tabor, J. W., Roy, T., Casey, R., Pardo, A., Roy, F., Ryals, L. A., Hewitt, C., Whitsel, E. A., Halpern, C. T., Killeya-Jones, L. A., Lessem, J. M., Hewitt, J. K., & Hewitt, J. K. (2014). Simple sequence repeats in the National Longitudinal Study of Adolescent Health: An ethnically diverse resource for genetic analysis of health and behavior. *Behavior*, *44*(5), 487–497. https://doi.org/10.1007/s10519-014-9662-x

Harden, K. P. (2021). "Reports of my death were greatly exaggerated": Behavior genetics in the postgenomic era. *Annual Review of Psychology*, *72*, 37–60. https://doi.org/10.1146/annurev-psych-052220-103822

Hariri, A. R., Mattay, V. S., Tessitore, A., Kolachana, B., Fera, F., Goldman, D., . . . Weinberger, D. R. (2002). Serotonin transporter genetic variation and the response of the human amygdala. *Science*, *297*(5580), 400–403. https://doi.org/10.1126/science.1071829

Iervolino, A. C., Pike, A., Manke, B., Reiss, D., Hetherington, E. M., & Plomin, R. (2002). Genetic and environmental influences in adolescent peer socialization: Evidence from two genetically sensitive designs. *Child Development*, *73*(1), 162–174. https://doi.org/10.1111/1467-8624.00398

Kosfeld, M., Heinrichs, M., Zak, P. J., Fischbacher, U., & Fehr, E. (2005). Oxytocin increases trust in humans. *Nature*, *435*(7042), 673–676. https://doi.org/10.1038/nature03701

Laible, D. (2007). Attachment with parents and peers in late adolescence: Links with emotional competence and social behavior. *Personality and Individual Differences*, *43*(5), 1185–1197. https://doi.org/10.1016/j.paid.2007.03.010

Lam, C. B., McHale, S. M., & Crouter, A. C. (2014). Time with peers from middle childhood to late adolescence: Developmental course and adjustment correlates. *Child Development*, *85*(4), 1677–1693. https://doi.org/10.1111/cdev.12235

Larsen, H., van der Zwaluw, C. S., Overbeek, G., Granic, I., Franke, B., & Engels, R. C. M. E. (2010). A variable-number-of-tandem-repeats polymorphism in the dopamine

D4 receptor gene affects social adaptation of alcohol use: Investigation of a gene-environment interaction. *Psychological Science, 21*(8), 1064–1068. https://doi.org/10.1177/0956797610376654

Larson, R. W., Richards, M. H., Moneta, G., Holmbeck, G., & Duckett, E. (1996). Changes in adolescents' daily interactions with their families from ages 10 to 18: Disengagement and transformation. *Developmental Psychology, 32*(4), 744–754. https://doi.org/10.1037/0012-1649.32.4.744

Musci, R. J., & Schlomer, G. L. (2017). The implications of genetics for prevention and intervention programming. *Prevention Science, 19*, 1–5. https://doi.org/10.1007/s11121-017-0837-6

Neale, Z. E., Kuo, S. I. C., & Dick, D. M. (2021). A systematic review of gene-by-intervention studies of alcohol and other substance use. *Development and Psychopathology, 33*(4), 1410–1427. https://doi.org/10.1017/S0954579420000590

Nelson, E. E., Leibenluft, E., McClure, E. B., & Pine, D. S. (2005). The social re-orientation of adolescence: A neuroscience perspective on the process and its relation to psychopathology. *Psychological Medicine, 35*(2), 163–174. https://doi.org/10.1017/S0033291704003915

Prinstein, M. J., Boergers, J., & Spirito, A. (2001). Adolescents' and their friends' health-risk behavior: Factors that alter or add to peer influence. *Journal of Pediatric Psychology, 26*(5), 287–298. https://doi.org/10.1093/jpepsy/26.5.287

Russell, M. A., Schlomer, G. L., Cleveland, H. H., Feinberg, M. E., Greenberg, M. T., Spoth, R. L., Redmond, C., & Vandenbergh, D. J. (2018). PROSPER intervention effects on adolescents' alcohol misuse vary by *GABRA2* genotype and age. *Prevention Science, 19*(1), 27–37. https://doi.org/10.1007/s11121-017-0751-y

Scarr, S., & McCartney, K. (1983). How people make their own environments: A theory of genotype → environment effects. *Child Development, 54*(2), 424–435. https://doi.org/10.2307/1129703

Schlomer, G. L., Cleveland, H. H., Deutsch, A. R., Vandenbergh, D. J., Feinberg, M. E., Greenberg, M. T., Spoth, R. L., & Redmond, C. (2019). Developmental change in adolescent delinquency: Modeling time-varying effects of a preventative intervention and *GABRA2* halpotype linked to alcohol use. *Journal of Youth and Adolescence, 48*(1), 71–85. https://doi.org/10.1007/s10964-018-0929-z

Schlomer, G. L., Cleveland, H. H., Feinberg, M. E., Murray, J. L., & Vandenbergh, D. J. (2021). Longitudinal links between adolescent and peer conduct problems and moderation by a sensitivity genetic index. *Journal of Research on Adolescence, 31*(1), 189–203. https://doi.org/10.1111/jora.12592

Schlomer, G. L., Cleveland, H. H., Feinberg, M. E., Wolf, P. S. A., Greenberg, M. T., Spoth, R. L., Redmond, C., Tricou, E. P., & Vandenbergh, D. J. (2017). Extending previous cGxI findings on *5-HTTLPR*'s moderation of intervention effects on adolescent substance misuse initiation. *Child Development, 88*(6), 2001–2012. https://doi.org/10.1111/cdev.12666

Schlomer, G. L., Cleveland, H. H., Vandenbergh, D. J., Fosco, G. M., & Feinberg, M. E. (2015). Looking forward in candidate gene research: Concerns and suggestions. *Journal of Marriage and Family, 77*(2), 351–354. https://doi.org/10.1111/jomf.12165

Schoots, O., & Van Tol, H. H. M. (2003). The human dopamine D4 receptor repeat sequences modulate expression. *The Pharmacogenomics Journal, 3*(6), 343–348. https://doi.org/10.1038/sj.tpj.6500208

Spoth, R., Redmond, C., Hockaday, C., & Yoo, S. (1996). Protective factors and young adolescent tendency to abstain from alcohol use: A model using two waves of intervention study data. *American Journal of Community*, *24*(6), 749–770.

Stenseng, F., Li, Z., Belsky, J., Hygen, B. W., Skalicka, V., Guzey, I. C., & Wichstrøm, L. (2018). Peer problems and hyperactivity–impulsivity among Norwegian and American children: The role of *5-HTTLPR*. *Child Development*, *89*(2), 509–524. https://doi.org/10.1111/cdev.12766

Tan, X., Shiyko, M. P., Li, R., Li, Y., & Dierker, L. (2012). A time-varying effect model for intensive longitudinal data. *Psychological Methods*, *17*(1), 61–77. https://doi.org/10.1037/a0025814

Tielbeek, J. J., Karlsson Linnér, R., Beers, K., Posthuma, D., Popma, A., & Polderman, T. J. C. (2016). Meta-analysis of the serotonin transporter promoter variant (*5-HTTLPR*) in relation to adverse environment and antisocial behavior. *American Journal of Medical Genetics, Part B: Neuropsychiatric Genetics*, *171*(5), 748–760. https://doi.org/10.1002/ajmg.b.32442

Trucco, E. M., Cope, L. M., Burmeister, M., Zucker, R. A., & Heitzeg, M. M. (2018). Pathways to youth behavior: The role of genetic, neural, and behavioral markers. *Journal of Research on Adolescence*, *28*(1), 26–39. https://doi.org/10.1111/jora.12341

Trucco, E. M., Villafuerte, S., Burmeister, M., & Zucker, R. A. (2017). Beyond risk: Prospective effects of GABA receptor subunit alpha-2 (*GABRA2*) × positive peer involvement on adolescent behavior. *Development and Psychopathology*, *29*(3), 711–724. https://doi.org/10.1017/S0954579416000419

Van Tol, H. H. M., Wu, C. M., Guan, H. C., Ohara, K., Bunzow, J. R., Civelli, O., Kennedy, J., Seeman, P., Niznik, H. B., & Jovanovic, V. (1992). Multiple dopamine D4 receptor variants in the human population. *Nature*, *358*(6382), 149–152. https://doi.org/10.1038/358149a0

Villafuerte, S., Trucco, E. M., Heitzeg, M. M., Burmeister, M., & Zucker, R. A. (2014). Genetic variation in *GABRA2* moderates peer influence on externalizing behavior in adolescents. *Brain and Behavior*, *4*(6), 833–840. https://doi.org/10.1002/brb3.291

Walum, H., Lichtenstein, P., Neiderhiser, J. M., Reiss, D., Ganiban, J. M. J., Spotts, E. L., ... Westberg, L. (2012). Variation in the oxytocin receptor gene (*OXTR*) is associated with pair-bonding and social behavior. *Biological Psychiatry*, *71*(5), 419–426. https://doi.org/10.1016/j.biopsych.2011.09.002

SECTION III

Conclusions

13

Future directions for research on networks and adolescent health

THOMAS W. VALENTE ■

INTRODUCTION

The PROSPER (Promoting School-community-university Partnerships to Enhance Resilience) Peer project has been a "tour de force" exposition of the creativity and rigorousness of a group of dedicated scientists investigating a critical public health issue, namely, the role of peers in adolescent development. This chapter attempts to provide observations on how PROSPER's results suggest new directions for research on the role of adolescent networks on health and other behaviors. Indeed, one of the main contributions of PROSPER has been the ability to analyze a broad range of health behaviors rather than focusing on a limited set of behaviors, usually necessitated by the stricture of research funding. For example, many studies may be funded to address adolescent tobacco use (and today vaping or e-cigarette behavior) and thus do not have the luxury of including measures of delinquency; internalizing behaviors (i.e., depression, anxiety); sexual risk taking; and so on. PROSPER seems almost unique in its focus on many different adolescent health behaviors.

There are four areas of future directions informed by PROSPER contributions I would like to address: (1) network measurement, (2) network interventions, (3) moderation and mediation, and (4) analytic progress. Each of these domains has seen tremendous progress in the past few decades of research on peer influences on adolescent behavior (Valente et al., 2012). The PROSPER work and contributions have implications for each of these areas going forward. These developments have provided a springboard for even more significant research

Thomas W. Valente, *Future directions for research on networks and adolescent health*. In: *Teen Friendship Networks, Development, and Risky Behavior*. Edited by: Mark E. Feinberg and D. Wayne Osgood, Oxford University Press.
© Mark E. Feinberg and D. Wayne Osgood 2024. DOI: 10.1093/oso/9780197602317.003.0013

on this topic, enabling greater specificity of peer influences and more confident conclusions.

NETWORK MEASUREMENT

Many researchers often claim "network data are difficult and expensive to collect." In my estimation, nothing could be further from the truth. The PROSPER study shows that network data are quite easy to collect. The researchers merely added a page to the survey inviting students to write the names of their best friends. This is easy enough, and adolescents know who their friends are. The network cost for PROSPER arose because those handwritten names had to be entered into a database and then matched to rosters. Had PROSPER included some resources for network data collection in the beginning, more efficient, accurate, and valid methods for data collection could have been used.

For example, a year before PROSPER's initial data collection, we included an unfunded extension of an existing funded tobacco prevention study designed to test a culturally tailored prevention program. I had recently relocated from Johns Hopkins University to the University of Southern California and was eager to launch a new trajectory in my career with new colleagues. Thus, I persuaded my colleagues to include an opinion leader implementation substudy within the broader study, necessitating unfunded network data collection. We obtained rosters of every class and invited students to write the names of other students in the class "who would make for good leaders in a class project" and "who are their closest friends." Beside each name, students entered the roster ID for each fellow student. I could then enter these numbers into Excel, run my computer algorithm written in GAUSS, a platform for mathematical computing, and provide the identities of the peer opinion leaders and group assignments to the research team and teachers within days.

The PROSPER team was genius enough in anticipating the importance of peer friendship networks as both influences on behaviors (in the many ways they demonstrate in this volume and their many publications) and mediators and moderators of intervention effects. The PROSPER study was very large, thus providing a large and rich data set with the power to investigate many theories and hypotheses regarding peer influences. Our study was small and restricted nominations to within classroom (we randomized network implementation condition by classroom) and involved approximately 2,000 middle school students, thus making the roster method more feasible but the data less rich.

Friendship network data collection is now easier, quicker, and more efficient than ever. Most adolescent data are being collected on computers, phones, and other electronic devices. Consequently, researchers can preload student rosters and invite adolescents to enter the first few letters of their friends' names; the autoloaded options then appear, making the selection of friends (and other relations) easy to do. To be sure, there is still some post–data collection matching necessary and some instances that are more complicated as adolescents share the same first name. (Ideally, formative work would identify these cases in advance and input the names along with how they are known in the school, e.g., "Maddy B" and "Maddy K.") In our current study, we ask the friendship network question this way:

> Name up to seven (7) of your closest friends in your grade at school in the spaces below. Enter your friend's first and last real name, not their nickname. For example, if you call your friend "Tony" but his real name is "Anthony Smith" enter "Anthony Smith." As you enter the first few letters of their first name, possible choices will automatically appear on the screen. Please select the friend you want to name. If no name matches, just enter the name you wish to enter.

Fortunately, the PROSPER team selected the right name generator: friendship. Comparison of the rate of peer effects (peer influence in this case) estimated between different name generators has been conducted and showed that adolescents were more likely to be influenced by their friends than other relations, such as who do you "admire," "think is successful," "think is popular," or "desire a romantic relationship with" (Valente et al., 2013). So, the PROSPER team's choice of friendship as the relation, the "name generator," was propitious.

It may be the end of an era for adolescent researchers to be able to study peer and social effects on adolescent behaviors within a closed context such as a school. Social media has increased the ability of adolescents to reach beyond their school boundaries to connect with others with similar interests and to be influenced by companies using social media to promote their products (Vassey et al., 2022). The good news is that the strongest influences on adolescents are likely to be from their friends in real life (IRL) with whom they are also connected on social media. Nonetheless, incorporating measures of adolescent social media and online activity will need to be considered in future studies.

In sum, I think social network data collection is getting both easier and more challenging. It is easier due to the salience of social networks and friendships among youth who will all have social media accounts, and easier because the technology to gather this information is more adaptable and fluid. It is more challenging because peer boundaries are more fluid as adolescents make friendships via social media to a more geographically dispersed set of peers, and relations may more frequently span schools or school districts.

NETWORK INTERVENTIONS

The future contains great opportunities for advancing the field of adolescent health as well as the science of using network data to design interventions. By creating network intervention experiments, we can advance the field of adolescent health by enabling researchers to understand more fully how peer social networks influence health and other behaviors. Network experiments provide ideal laboratories for understanding how to design effective interventions. The PROSPER team has further shown that school- and community-based interventions can diffuse through social networks (Rulison & Feinberg, Chapter 11, this volume, Valente & Vega Yon, 2020) and provide data for simulating intervention choices (McMillan & Schaefer, 2021).

The field of network interventions has continued to grow and demonstrate significant effects. Most behavior change programs include some component of a network intervention without explicitly being labeled as such. For example, (social) media campaigns often create messages and materials they hope will "go viral." The communications are specifically designed so that they can be easily shared by being reposted on twitter, Instagram, or Snapchat. For example, when purchasing tickets on StubHub one can select a button to post on one's media feed.

"Network interventions are purposeful efforts to use social networks or social network data to generate social influence, accelerate behavior change, improve performance, and/or achieve desirable outcomes among individuals, communities, organizations, or populations" (Valente, 2012, p. 49). Given the importance of school-based adolescent friendships, incorporating peers into intervention development seems critically important. There is an extensive, varied, and ever-expanding list of network intervention possibilities. Many of these are supremely appropriate for school-based adolescent health behavior change efforts.

For example, our study referenced above used network data to identify opinion leaders and match them to their nearest peers defined on sociometric distance (Valente & Davis, 1999). That is, leaders highest on in-degree centrality were selected, and those who nominated them were assigned to them as a group. If a person was not directly connected to a leader, he or she was assigned to one they were two steps removed from, then three, and so on. This condition was compared to (a) teacher-identified leaders and groups and (b) leaders identified via highest in-degree, but group members were assigned randomly. Results revealed the network matching method for leaders and group members was the most effective at improving antitobacco attitudes and reducing susceptibility to smoking (Valente et al., 2003, 2007).

Other studies have identified peer opinion leaders and trained them to promote behavior change throughout the school. For example, the A Stop Smoking in Schools Trial (ASSIST) trial in the United Kingdom was successful at identifying peer opinion leaders through friendship networks and engaging them to promote antitobacco and smoking prevention behaviors (Starkey et al., 2009). A high school–based sexual violence intervention recruited peer opinion leaders via friendship networks to participate in out-of-school camps and clubs to increase awareness of sexual violence and promote proactive bystander behaviors (Waterman et al., 2022). Recent studies have used friendship networks to combat the rise of vaping and e-cigarette use (Chu et al., 2021) as well as for suicide prevention (Wyman et al., 2021). The peer opinion leader model is clearly appropriate and seems effective for adolescent health promotion efforts. Given that adolescents are perhaps hyperaware of the social structure in schools, having opinion leaders endorse health promotion efforts, whether purposively or not, may be a prerequisite to achieving positive intervention outcomes.

Other intervention strategies and tactics are also worth exploring. For example, identifying bridging individuals that can ameliorate conflicts between subgroups and gangs could be important to investigate. Adolescent networks are often composed of relatively well-defined cliques and groupings. Intervention approaches that incorporate this structure may be quite effective. This is done sometimes by addressing teams and clubs individually; however, including network information may provide more accurate boundary conditions on those groups. Network alteration strategies are likely difficult to implement because adolescents form friendships and affinities for many individual, familial, and cultural reasons that can be difficult to adjust. Nonetheless, the movie *The Breakfast Club* provided a vivid and entertaining example of how people from different groups/identities have been surprised by their commonalities, resulting in positive social outcomes.

Another consideration, somewhat akin to the point made above, is which network to use to design the intervention. In our network matching study, we choose to use the "peer leader" network to identify leaders and groups because this is the network generator term used for decades to recruit student peer leaders to participate in intervention development and deployment. These studies were not network-based interventions other than this initial step, as the network data were then discarded. Subsequent research has shown that friendship seems to be the most salient relationship for adolescents, and thus interventions using the friendship network are likely to be the most effective. A study is waiting to be conducted, however, to demonstrate whether this is true.

One of the signature highlights of the PROSPER study is its acknowledgment of the many different health promotion challenges faced in adolescent health. Some teens struggle with obesity and physical activity (PA), others with mental health, substance abuse, sexual identity, sociality, and more. Consequently, no one intervention will be appropriate for everyone, and successful school-based intervention needs to take a holistic perspective by understanding the networks and the distribution of health challenges within them. For example, many athletes are likely to be connected to one another and do not need obesity or PA intervention but likely would benefit from alcohol prevention programs; conversely, some other students may benefit from a PA intervention. Indeed, one may argue that standards of practice for school-based adolescent health interventions would require adolescent input in design, deployment, and execution, and in any large system, multiple and varied approaches may be necessary.

MEDIATION AND MODERATION

Network data can improve intervention program evaluations by enabling us to study network-based moderation and mediation. Moderation occurs when a program is effective for some individuals with certain characteristics but not others.

For example, a sex education program may be more effective for girls than boys. Mediation occurs when an intervention changes a particular characteristic (risk or protective factor), and those changes are associated with changes in the outcome of interest. For example, suppose an intervention was designed to portray tobacco use as uncool, and the program depressed tobacco use uptake only for those students who increased their perception that smoking was not cool. (The ads created showing animals with cigarettes in their mouths was designed to do that.) Perceptions of smoking coolness is the mediator that the program changed, leading to reduced smoking uptake.

Network moderation and mediation occur when network variables are used as the moderator/mediator. There are some exciting examples of this: We found that a reproductive health media campaign accelerated contraceptive adoption for women with few existing contraceptive users in their friendship network compared to those with a majority of contraceptive users in their network (Valente, 1996; Valente & Saba, 1998). This network variable (percentage contraceptive users in one's friendship network) acted as a moderator. One can imagine that e-cigarette prevention/cessation programs are likely to be less effective for adolescents whose friends in the majority are users.

Moderation and mediation could occur on several network variables at the individual, dyadic, and network levels of analyses (Moody & Osgood, Chapter 3, this volume). Moderation can occur for many of the individual network measures we routinely calculate, such as centrality, bridging, density, constraint, homophily, and more. In each case, we may find the intervention is differentially effective for those who are high versus low on each of these metrics. For example, we may find that improving school attachment is more effective for students high on popularity as the school represents a safe and supportive social environment, but less so for those on the periphery.

Network mediation occurs when an intervention changes a network metric, and that network change induces behavior change for the adolescent. Again, we can hypothesize network mediation regarding many individual measures, such as centrality, bridging, density, homophily, and more. An intervention designed to promote school attachment may be effective for those students who become more popular in the school. Or, a school-based sexual violence program may be effective for those who increase the number of friends they report in the school.

Network moderation and mediation at the dyadic level necessitate testing whether interventions are effective for those who have certain ties (e.g., moderation based on having cross-gender ones) or those who create such bonds (e.g., mediation via initiating cross-gender ties). At the network level, measures such as centralization, density, and fragmentation all may exhibit moderating or mediating effects when conducting the evaluation. Given the importance of adolescent social relationships and their dynamics in shaping youth attitudes and behaviors, it is quite likely there are strong moderating and mediating influences on program outcomes.

To take this contribution another step forward, we can consider the interaction of peer networks at the individual and network levels with the effect of health

Table 13.1 POTENTIAL INTERACTIONS BETWEEN NETWORK- AND INDIVIDUAL-LEVEL METRICS

	Individual level		
	Degree	Centrality	Bridging
Network level			
Density	High-degree individuals are more prominent in sparse networks than in dense ones		
Centralization		Centrality is more consequential in centralized networks	
Fragmentation			Bridging is of greater signficance in fragmented networks

promotion interventions. Table 13.1 shows three common individual measures and three network-level ones in cells that highlight the micro-macro nature of social networks. In the Cell corresponding to Centralization and Centrality, we cross individual centrality measures with level of network centralization, which reveals that being central in a centralized network is much more important/consequential than being central in a decentralized one. For intervention moderation/mediation, this suggests that school-based interventions may have differential impacts based on the interaction of individual and network-level indicators. For example, the intervention was effective for central adolescents in centralized networks, but less so in decentralized ones.

ANALYTIC PROGRESS

As the chapters in this book attest, there are multiple analytic strategies available to understand social networks, which is both an opportunity and a challenge. These approaches can be categorized in increasing levels of complexity: analysis of individual measures (centrality), inclusion of alter characteristics (homophily), inclusion of alter behaviors (exposure to peer smoking), regression-type models, multilevel models, exponential random graph models (ERGMs), and stochastic actor-oriented models (SAOMs) as implemented in RSIENA. More than any other set of studies, the PROSPER team has contributed to this wide array of analytic approaches.

There are several PROSPER studies demonstrating the utility of individual network measures for understanding adolescent dynamics. For example, Moody et al. (2011) showed that there is variability in who is popular (friendship in-degree), which is consistent with many network studies. They also showed that popularity is associated with substance abuse both cross-sectionally and dynamically, such that "popularity level is associated with high use, but the trend matters. Those with *either* strongly increasing or decreasing popularity (as well as those with highly variable but non-trending popularity) are more likely to use substances" (p. 110). This intriguing result is interpreted in part not by peer influence effects of being popular, but by needs of individuals to shore up social status and how substance abuse may confer status to the individual.

Compositional studies have been numerous using PROSPER data. For example, Siennick and others (2016) studied whether internalizing symptoms would be associated with greater exposure to influence of peers on individual substance use. The study showed that exposure effects persist regardless of individual internalizing symptoms. More complex longitudinal models, such as those by Hoeben and colleagues (2021), demonstrated how these data can be used to estimate rates of peer selection and influence and moreover showed how these can be moderated by other factors, in this case parental monitoring. For me, one of the most significant papers from the PROSPER team was published by Ragan and colleagues in which they compared traditional regression-like estimates of peer influence to those obtained from SIENA.

The Ragan et al. (2022) study is critical for several reasons: (1) It has been assumed that, due to the nonindependence of observations, estimates from exposure models overestimate peer influence; (2) many researchers have become convinced that one must perform SIENA estimates in all social network research; and (3) sometimes SIENA models do not work. By showing that regression models do not overstate peer influence, researchers do not necessarily have to estimate SIENA models with their data. There are many instances in which SIENA is an incredibly valuable tool, and it enables the testing of many complex network processes. But it is not the only tool. Further, in many studies there will be missing and incomplete data, and regression models can be quite robust to missing data.

Going forward, this result means that researchers daunted, overwhelmed, and unable to use SIENA for their longitudinal data need not despair. Indeed, it opens up research terrain to investigate many other dimensions of network influences and cross-level (individual, dyadic, network) models to be tested. This can be particularly useful for situations in which SIENA models do not converge. For example, we recently estimated SIENA models on a two-wave longitudinal sample of friendship networks and e-cigarette use. When we included terms for both influence and selection, the models would not converge. The Ragan et al. (2022) study enables us to say with confidence that the influence and selection effects we estimate with the regression models are not overly biased.

CONCLUSIONS

There have been hundreds of studies investigating the association and influence of social networks on a wide variety of adolescent health behaviors; many studies examined the effects of school-based interventions, sometimes accompanied by network data; and there have been a handful of school-based, network-informed interventions. PROSPER Peers has undoubtedly been one of, if not the most, influential studies to investigate peer network effects on adolescent behavior. This volume and the many other PROSPER network study references will be required reading for the next decade as researchers attempt to understand how friendship, and other networks, influence adolescent behavior.

In this chapter, I discussed four areas in which I see future development in network study and intervention related to adolescent health: (1) measurement; (2) intervention; (3) moderation/mediation; and (4) analytic strategies. The measurement issue is one of the more intriguing ones as a lack of funding for network research has often resulted in studies in which data collection is launched on a substantive topic such as substance use, obesity, or delinquency, and a single network question is added on at the end, as in PROSPER. And yet, the addition of this one question yielded an unparalleled richness of data. Studies that embrace networks more fully can contribute even more. New computational tools now make network data collection easier than ever.

There is a robust body of evidence emerging that network interventions can be quite effective (Flodgren et al., 2011; Hunter et al., 2019; Valente, 2012). Network interventions, and techniques for network implementation (Valente et al., 2015), are likely most effective for adolescents given the heightened importance of peer relations during this stage of development. Moreover, given the well-defined boundary and well-established institutional norms regarding schooling, the school provides an ideal laboratory for testing network interventions.

Network data also provide a valuable addition to standard evaluation methods. Network-based moderation and mediation were introduced as a means to test for how individual, dyadic, and network-level characteristics affect whether an intervention is effective for various individuals. The social context within which an intervention is delivered and received will likely have a profound effect on how it is interpreted.

Finally, I turned attention to network analytic strategies and observed how the PROSPER team had employed many different approaches, from the calculation of simple network metrics such as centrality to complex stochastic-oriented models as estimated in SIENA. The contributions are manifold and extensive, yet for me the demonstration that regression-type models do not overestimate peer influence stands out as a shining contribution as it enables researchers to collect and analyze a network even when they cannot (due to convergence issues) or will not (due to training barriers) use RSIENA.

Future research in these areas can extend the impressive list of PROSPER findings and expand both the reach and impact of our efforts on improving health and understanding the social contextual conditions to maximize them. Unfortunately, there is no shortage of challenges adolescents face as they navigate the treacherous journey from childhood to adulthood, and measuring social networks to understand those challenges and using network methods to support adolescents' health and development is now more critical than ever.

ACKNOWLEDGMENT

Support for the writing of this chapter was provided by grant #R01-DA051843 from the National Institute on Drug Abuse, the National Institutes of Health (NIH).

REFERENCES

Chu, K. H., Sidani, J., Matheny, S., Rothenberger, S. D., Miller, E., Valente, T., & Robertson, L. (2021). Implementation of a cluster randomized controlled trial: Identifying student peer leaders to lead E-cigarette interventions. *Addictive Behaviors, 114*, 106726.

Flodgren, G., Parmelli, E., Doumit, G., Gattellari, M., O'Brien, M. A., Grimshaw, J., & Eccles, M. P. (2011). Local opinion leaders: Effects on professional practice and health care outcomes. *Cochrane Database of Systematic Reviews*, CD000125.

Hoeben, E. M., Rulison, K. L., Ragan, D. T., & Feinberg, M. E. (2021). Moderators of friend selection and influence in relation to adolescent alcohol use. *Prevention Science, 22*, 567–578.

Hunter, R. F., de la Haye, K., Murray, J. M., Badham, J., Valente, T. W., Clarke, M., & Kee, F. (2019). Social network interventions for health behaviours and outcomes: A systematic review and meta-analysis. *PloS Medicine, 16*(9), e1002890. https://doi.org/10.1371/journal.pmed.1002890

McMillan, C., & Schaefer, D. R. (2021). Comparing targeting strategies for network-based adolescent drinking interventions: A simulation approach. *Social Science & Medicine, 282*:114136.

Moody, J., Brynildsen, W. D., Osgood, D. W., & Feinberg, M. E. (2011). Popularity trajectories and substance use in early adolescence. *Social Networks, 33*, 101–112.

Ragan, D. T., Osgood, D. W., Ramirez, N. G., Moody J., & Gest, S. (2022). A comparison of peer influence estimates from SIENA stochastic actor–based models and from conventional regression approaches. *Sociological Methods & Research, 51*, 357–395.

Siennick, S. E., Widdowson, A. O., Woessner, M., & Feinberg, M. E. (2016). Internalizing symptoms, peer substance use, and substance use initiation. *Journal of Research on Adolescence, 26*, 645–657.

Starkey, F., Audrey, S., Holliday, J., Moore, L., & Campbell, R. (2009). Identifying influential young people to undertake effective peer-led health promotion: The example of A Stop Smoking in Schools Trial (ASSIST). *Health Behavior Research, 24*, 977–988.

Valente, T. W. (2012). Network interventions. *Science, 337*, 49–53.

Valente, T. W. (1996). Social network thresholds in the diffusion of innovations. *Social Networks, 18*, 69–89.

Valente, T. W., & Davis, R. L. (1999). Accelerating the diffusion of innovations using opinion leaders. *The Annals of the American Academy of the Political and Social Sciences*, 566, 55–67.

Valente, T. W., Fujimoto, K., Soto, D., Meeker, D., & Unger, J. B. (2013). Variations in network boundary and type: A study of adolescent peer influences. *Social Networks*, 35, 309–316.

Valente, T. W., Fujimoto, K., Soto, D., Ritt-Olson, A., & Unger, J. (2012). A comparison of peer influence measures as predictors of smoking among predominately Hispanic/Latino high school adolescents. *Journal of Adolescent Health*, 52, 358–364.

Valente, T. W., Hoffman, B. R., Ritt-Olson, A., Lichtman, K., & Johnson, C. A. (2003). The effects of a social network method for group assignment strategies on peer led tobacco prevention programs in schools. *American Journal of Public Health*, 93, 1837–1843.

Valente, T. W., Palinkas, L. A., Czaja, S., Chu, K. H., & Brown, C. H. (2015). Social network analysis for program implementation. *PloS One*, 10(6), e0131712.

Valente, T. W., Ritt-Olson, A., Unger, J., Stacy, A., Okamoto, J., & Sussman, S. (2007). Peer acceleration: Effects of a network tailored substance abuse prevention program among high risk adolescents. *Addiction*, 102, 1804–1815. PMID: 17784893.

Valente, T. W., & Saba, W. (1998). Mass media and interpersonal influence in a reproductive health communication campaign in Bolivia. *Communication Research*, 25, 96–124.

Valente, T. W., Unger, J., Ritt-Olson, A., Cen, S. Y., & Johnson, A. C. (2020). The interaction of curriculum and implementation method on 1 year smoking outcomes. *Health Education Research: Theory & Practice*, 21, 315–324.

Valente, T. W., & Vega Yon, G. Y. (2020). Diffusion/contagion processes on social networks. *Health Education & Behavior*, 47, 235–248.

Vassey, J., Valente, T. W., Baker, J., Stanton, C., Li, D., Laestadius, L., I., Cruz, T. B., & Unger, J. B. (2022). E-cigarette brands and social media influencers on instagram: A social network analysis. *Tobacco Control*. doi:10.1136/tobaccocontrol-2021-057053

Waterman, E. A., Edwards, K. M., Keyes, A. B., Zulfiqar, H., Banyard, V. L., & Valente, T. W. (2022). The stability of youth popular opinion leaders selected over time using social network analysis. *American Journal of Community Psychology*, 70, 202–210. http://doi.org//10.1002/ajcp.1295

Wyman, P. A., Rulison, K., Pisani, A. R., Alvaro, E. M., Crano, W. D., Schmeelk-Cone, K., Chelsea Keller Elliot, C. K., Joshua Wortzel, J., Pickering, T. A., & Espelage, D. L. (2021). Above the influence of vaping: Peer leader influence and diffusion of a network-informed preventive intervention. *Addictive Behaviors*, 113, 106693. doi:10.1016/j.addbeh.2020.106693

14

The growth of longitudinal social network analysis

A review of the key data sets and topics in research on child and adolescent development

RENÉ VEENSTRA, TERESA BERTOGNA, AND
LYDIA LANINGA-WIJNEN ■

INTRODUCTION

The PROSPER (PROmoting School-community-university Partnerships to Enhance Resilience) Peers project has been impressive in many ways: researchers on this project were among the very first to examine peer networks in adolescence, in an incredibly large sample, across a wide time span. The use of friendship networks allowed PROSPER researchers to expand on previous work by considering interdependencies in networks, to test hypotheses related to selection and influence in the context of substance use and mental health problems. The friendship nominations also enabled PROSPER researchers to use aggregated network constructs, such as individuals' status in a group, and to examine how these related to young people's development. The other chapters in this book show the depth and breadth of topics that could be addressed using this high-quality data set, such as how the intervention can change dynamics within peer networks (see Chapter 11) or how family relationships can influence dynamics in peer relations and behavior (see Chapter 8). PROSPER Peers has been very informative for both research and practice and undoubtedly will continue to be so in the future.

In order to fully understand the scientific contribution of PROSPER Peers, it is important to evaluate and compare it with other social network data sets. This chapter evaluates the growth of social network studies on children and adolescents and highlights the characteristics of these data sets as well as avenues for further research.

René Veenstra, Teresa Bertogna, and Lydia Laninga-Wijnen, *The growth of longitudinal social network analysis*.
In: *Teen Friendship Networks, Development, and Risky Behavior*. Edited by: Mark E. Feinberg and D. Wayne Osgood,
Oxford University Press. © Mark E. Feinberg and D. Wayne Osgood 2024. DOI: 10.1093/oso/9780197602317.003.0014

Currently, large numbers of researchers worldwide examine social networks of children and adolescents. In questionnaires, they list all classmates, students in the same grade, or schoolmates, asking: "Who are your best friends?", "Who do you dislike?", "Who bullies you?", or "Who helps you?" Students may sometimes nominate as many peers as they wish; other times, the number of nominations is limited.

Social network researchers have investigated similarity in friendship networks. Similarity between friends was established as far back as classical antiquity (see McPherson et al., 2001). Resemblance is an important basis for the survival of friendships. Similarity in characteristics, attitudes, or behaviors means that friends understand each other more quickly, have common interests to talk about, know better where they stand with each other, and have more trust in each other (Laursen & Veenstra, 2021). As a result, such relationships are more stable and valuable. Moreover, looking more alike makes young people more confident and strengthens them in developing their identity (Hallinan, 1980). Similarity in behavior can result from two processes: selection (birds of a feather flock together) and influence (one rotten apple spoils the barrel).

These two processes can be distinguished using longitudinal social network analysis in the R package SIENA (Simulation Investigation for Empirical Network Analyses; Ripley et al., 2022; Snijders et al., 2010; Steglich et al., 2010). Since 2006, approximately 220 SIENA articles on children and adolescents have been published (see Figure 14.1). The introduction to stochastic actor-based models was published in 2010 (Snijders et al., 2010), a handbook chapter was published in 2012 (Veenstra & Steglich, 2012), and longitudinal social network analysis became mainstream after the publication of a special issue of the *Journal of Research on Adolescence* containing 15 empirical articles (Veenstra et al., 2013). Since that period, about 15 to 20 new SIENA articles have appeared per year.

MOST FREQUENTLY USED SOCIAL NETWORK DATA SETS

Figure 14.2 contains the 15 most frequently used social network data sets. The National Longitudinal Study of Adolescent Health (*Add Health*) is the most used adolescent network data set in the world. Friendships were measured twice, in 1995 and 1996. Add Health included 16 schools in the United States, where efforts were made to collect complete network data on all students attending seventh to 12th grades. Two schools were large (Jefferson High, a mostly white, Midwest school with 1,000 students, and Sunshine High, an ethnically diverse school in a Western metropolitan area with 2,100 students); the other 14 were much smaller (rural schools with fewer than 300 students). Longitudinal social network studies using Add Health focused on friendship processes related to the following behavioral outcomes: academic achievement (e.g., Duxbury & Haynie, 2020); alcohol use (e.g., Cheadle et al., 2013); body mass index (e.g., Simpkins et al., 2013); delinquency (e.g., Haynie et al., 2014); depression (e.g., Cheadle & Goosby, 2012);

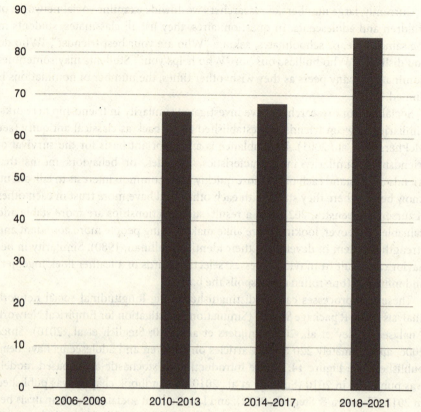

Figure 14.1 The number of longitudinal social network papers per 4-year period.

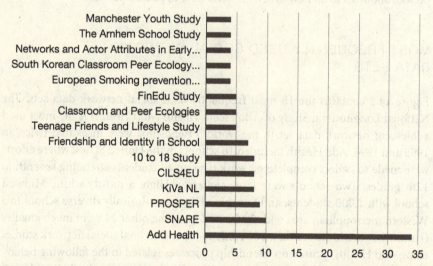

Figure 14.2 The number of longitudinal social network papers for the most used data sets.

marijuana use (de la Haye et al., 2013); physical activity (Simpkins et al., 2013); religious attitudes and behaviors (Adams et al., 2020; Cheadle & Schwadel, 2012); screen time use (Shoham et al., 2012); sexual debut (Trinh et al., 2019); smoking (e.g., Haas & Schaefer, 2014); sports participation (Shoham et al., 2012); violence (e.g., Haynie et al., 2014); and weight control (Simone et al., 2018).

SNARE (Social Network Analysis of Risk behavior in Early adolescence) is a Dutch adolescent peer network data set. SNARE contains two seventh-grade cohorts and one eighth-grade cohort, with about 1,800 students from two schools: one in the middle and one in the north of the Netherlands (Dijkstra et al., 2015). Data collection for the first cohorts started during 2011–2012 and for the second cohort during the following school year. Data collection occurred in October, December, and March for 2 to 4 years, resulting in at least six waves (and running up to 12 waves) of data for each cohort. Longitudinal social network studies using SNARE focused on friendship processes related to academic achievement (Gremmen et al., 2017, 2019; Laninga-Wijnen, Gremmen, et al., 2019); aggression (Laninga-Wijnen et al., 2017, 2020); externalizing behavior (Franken, Moffitt, et al., 2016; Franken, Prinstein, et al., 2016; Franken et al., 2017); helping (Van Rijsewijk et al., 2016, 2020); music genre preference (Franken et al., 2017); and prosocial behavior (Laninga-Wijnen et al., 2020). Additional data collection for SNARE took place in 2015–2016, referred to as *SNARE Genetics*. About 1,000 seventh to ninth graders in an additional secondary school answered almost the exact same social network questions as students in the other two SNARE schools, and half of them provided saliva to allow researchers to retrieve genetic information. Thus, in total, SNARE consists of networks from three schools and about 2,800 students (Laninga-Wijnen, Harakeh, et al., 2019).

PROSPER (PROmoting school-community-university Partnerships to Enhance Resilience) is the second U.S. adolescent peer network data set. PROSPER contains two sixth-grade cohorts, with more than 14,000 students from 28 (semi)rural communities in Iowa and Pennsylvania. Data collection for the first cohort started during 2002–2003 and for the second cohort 1 year later. Data collection occurred in the fall and spring in the sixth grade and then every spring through the 12th grade, resulting in eight waves of data for each cohort (see Chapter 1). Longitudinal social network studies using PROSPER focused on friendship selection and influence related to alcohol use (Hoeben et al., 2021; McMillan et al., 2018; Osgood et al., 2013, 2015; Ragan, 2014; Ragan et al., 2014); arrests (Jacobsen et al., 2022); delinquency (McMillan et al., 2018; Osgood et al., 2015); parental knowledge and parental discipline (Ragan et al., 2014); self-control (Ragan, Osgood, & Kreager, 2022); and smoking (McMillan et al., 2018; Osgood et al., 2015; Ragan, 2016).

KiVa (the Finnish word for "nice" and an acronym for "against bullying") is a data set collected as part of the evaluation of the KiVa antibullying intervention in the Netherlands (Huitsing et al., 2020). KiVa NL contains cohorts of third, fourth, fifth, and sixth graders: about 10,000 students from 98 schools in total. Data collection started in 2012 with a preassessment in Grades 2–5 and was followed up in October and May for 2 years, resulting in five waves of data for each cohort. Longitudinal social network studies using KiVa NL focused on the codevelopment of, on the one hand, bullying and victimization, and, on the other hand, antipathies (Kisfalusi et al., 2022); defending (Hooijsma et al., 2021; Huitsing et al., 2014); friendships (Hooijsma et al., 2020; Rambaran, Dijkstra, & Veenstra, 2020); and perceived popularity (Van der Ploeg et al., 2020). Two other network studies on victim-bully relationships examined the impact of single-grade and multigrade classrooms (Rambaran et al., 2019) and school and classroom stability (Rambaran, van Duijn, et al., 2020).

CILS4EU (Children of Immigrants Longitudinal Survey in four European Countries) is a data set collected in four countries: Germany, the Netherlands, Sweden, and the United Kingdom. The participants were eighth and ninth graders, with about 5,000 students per country. The first wave was collected in 2010–2011 and the second a year later. Six longitudinal social network studies using CILS4EU used only the German data and focused on academic achievement (Lorenz, Boda, & Salikutluk, 2021); academic self-concept (Jansen et al., 2022); antischool behavior (Lorenz, Boda, & Salikutluk, 2021); educational expectations (Kretschmer & Roth, 2021; Lorenz et al., 2020; Lorenz, Salikutluk, et al., 2021); school effort (Lorenz, Boda, & Salikutluk, 2021); and Muslim religiosity (Leszczensky & Kretschmer, 2022). Two CILS4EU studies used only the Swedish data and focused on antischool behavior (Geven et al., 2017) and STEM (science, technology, engineering, and mathematics) preference (Raabe et al., 2019).

The *10 to 18 Study* was a cohort-sequential study in a small Swedish town (with a population of about 26,000). The initial data collection took place during the 2001–2002 school year, with annual follow-ups. Five waves of data were collected among 2,000 respondents. At each wave, more than 90% of all young people in the community in Grades 4 through 12 responded (roughly ages 10–18). Longitudinal social network studies using the 10 to 18 Study focused on alcohol use (Burk et al., 2012; DeLay et al., 2022); delinquency (Burk et al., 2008, 2007; Kerr et al., 2012; Tilton-Weaver et al., 2013); depression (Van Zalk et al., 2010); psychopathic traits (Kerr et al., 2012); school involvement (Burk et al., 2008); and social anxiety (Van Zalk & Kerr, 2011).

Friendship and Identity in School focused on the formation of interethnic friendships and ethnic identifications. Three waves of data were collected in May 2013 ($N = 1,668$ students), February 2014 ($N = 1,862$ students), and November 2014 ($N = 1,889$). A total of 1,249 students took part in all three waves. Researchers using this data set focused on friendship processes related to academic achievement (Kretschmer et al., 2018; Stark et al., 2017); ethnic self-identification (Jugert et al., 2018); ethnic-racial identity development (Jugert et al., 2020; Leszczensky & Pink, 2019); and Christian and Muslim religiosity (Leszczensky & Pink, 2017, 2020).

The other eight data sets (with at least four published social network studies) in Table 14.1 are discussed briefly, with a focus on the behavioral outcomes examined. Using data from the *Teenage Friends and Lifestyle Study*, researchers examined the following outcomes: alcohol use (Pearson et al., 2006; Steglich et al., 2010); marijuana use (Pearson et al., 2006); music genre preference (Lomi

Table 14.1 Characteristics of the most used social network data sets

Data set	Country	Setting	Sample size	M age at baseline	Time of collection	Waves (interval)
Manchester Youth Study	United States	G	480	11–12	1998–2000	3 (12 m)
The Arnhem School Study	The Netherlands	C	1,082	12–13	2008–2009	3 (3 m)
Networks and Actor Attributes in Early Adolescence	The Netherlands	C	3,171	12	2003–2004	4 (3 m)
South Korean Classroom Peer Ecology and Adolescent Development	South Korea	C	736	11–12	2014–2015	2 (5 m)
European Smoking prevention Framework Approach	Denmark, Finland, The Netherlands, Portugal, Spain, United Kingdom	G	7,704	13	1998–2001	4 (12 m)
FinEdu Study	Finland	G	1,419	16–17	2005–2006	2 (12 m)
Classroom and Peer Ecologies	United States	C	901	11–12	2011–2012	2 (6 m)
Teenage Friends and Lifestyle Study	Scotland	S	129	13	1995–1997	3 (12 m)
Friendship and Identity in School	Germany	C	1,249	13	2013–2014	3 (9 m)
10 to 18 Study	Sweden	T	2,000	13–14	2001–2005	5 (12 m)
CILS4EU	Germany, The Netherlands, Sweden, United Kingdom	C	5,000 per country	15	2011–2012	2 (12 m)
KiVa NL	The Netherlands	C; S	10,000	10	2012–2014	5 (6 m)
PROSPER	United States	S	14,000	11–12	2002–2009	8 (12 m)
SNARE	The Netherlands	C; G	2,843	13	2011–2016	6+ (4 m)
Add Health	United States	G	3,500	16	1995–1996	2 (12 m)

Note. m = months. Setting: C = class; G = grade; S = school; T = town.

& Stadtfeld, 2014; Steglich et al., 2006); pocket money (Block, 2018); and smoking (Pearson et al., 2006; Steglich et al., 2010). The *Classroom and Peer Ecologies* project focused on friendship processes related to academic adjustment (Laninga-Wijnen et al., 2018; Shin & Ryan, 2014a, 2014b); disruptive classroom behavior (Shin & Ryan, 2017); and teacher-reported prosocial and aggressive behavior (Shin et al., 2019). The *FinEdu Study* focused on alcohol use (Kiuru et al., 2010); depression (Kiuru et al., 2012); interest in academic subjects (Chow et al., 2018); school engagement (Wang et al., 2018); and smoking (DeLay et al., 2013; Kiuru et al., 2010). The *European Smoking prevention Framework Approach* (ESFA) study was used to investigate friendship dynamics related to smoking behavior in six European countries (Mercken et al., 2009), in Finland and Britain specifically (Mercken et al., 2010a, 2010b). Moreover, friendship processes related to alcohol use were examined among Finnish adolescents (Mercken et al., 2012). The only non-Western data set, stemming from the *South Korean Classroom Peer Ecology and Adolescent Development* project, was used to examine friendship selection and influence related to academic behavior (Shin, 2022b), bullying and victimization (Shin, 2022a), help-seeking tendencies (Shin, 2018), and physical aggression, prosocial behavior, perceived popularity, and social preference (Shin, 2017). Data from the project *Networks and Actor Attributes in Early Adolescence* were used to examine friendship selection and influence related to alcohol use (Knecht et al., 2011); behavioral problems at school (Geven et al., 2013); delinquency (Knecht et al., 2010); and teacher-reported study effort, such as being attentive in class and doing homework (Steglich & Knecht, 2014). The *Arnhem School Study* was used to examine intergroup attitudes (Zingora et al., 2020); music genre preference (Stark & Flache, 2012); negative outgroup attitudes (Stark, 2015); risk attitudes (Rambaran et al., 2013; Stark & Flache, 2012); and school attitudes (Stark & Flache, 2012). The *Manchester Youth Study* was used to examine antipathies (Rambaran et al., 2015); perceived popularity (Dijkstra et al., 2013); physical and relational victimization (Sentse et al., 2013); and weapon carrying (Dijkstra et al., 2012).

A COMPARISON OF SOCIAL NETWORK STUDIES

Sample size

With 14,000 respondents, PROSPER is the social network data set with the largest sample size. Another large data set, the Finnish KiVa study, with 9,000 respondents, has only been used once for longitudinal social network analysis (Sentse et al., 2014). Some studies had a large initial sample size, such as KiVa NL or CILS4EU. So far, the KiVa NL studies have been restricted to about 3,250 students in the control schools (see Rambaran, Dijkstra, et al., 2020), whereas the CILS4EU papers were restricted to about 2,500 adolescents in moderately stable classrooms in Germany or Sweden. Some Add Health researchers focused only on Jefferson and Sunshine High (for an exemplary study, see Haynie et al., 2014), whereas others also included the smaller high schools (see Cheadle et al., 2013).

The other social network studies presented in Table 14.1 had samples of between 736 and 7,704 students, with the exception of two old social network studies, the Manchester Youth Study and the Teenage Friends and Lifestyle Study, with 480 and 129 respondents respectively.

Number of Waves

Most studies had two or three waves of data, whereas PROSPER, SNARE, KiVa NL, and the 10 to 18 Study had five or more waves. Most studies had one wave annually or two waves within one academic year, whereas both the Arnhem School Study and SNARE had three assessments within a year.

A relatively new approach is to examine social network information on a more frequent (e.g., daily) basis. A recent social network study combined a time-based online diary with an event-based smartphone survey. The aim of the time-based online diary (Van Zalk et al., 2020) was to collect repeated measures of friendships and self-reported extraversion. The aim of the smartphone survey, four waves in 15 weeks, was to obtain information on real-life interactions and examine interaction quality (a rating on a 7-point scale, from positive to negative) and sociable behavior (a rating on a 7-point scale, from sociable to reclusive). They found that freshmen who were more similar in extraversion enjoyed their interactions more, which increased the odds that they would befriend each other, suggesting that interaction quality may be the social glue that facilitates friendships between freshmen similar in extraversion (Van Zalk et al., 2020). Other researchers collected a daily pain logbook and a daily interaction diary among 17 participants in a 3-week hiking expedition in Greenland (Block et al., 2018). They found that friends influenced each other's mood, whereby there was stronger influence for negative than for positive mood (Block & Burnett Heyes, 2022). Another network study, with biweekly assessments, provided evidence that changes in delinquency were related to situational changes in unstructured socializing, alcohol use, and marijuana use (Weerman et al., 2018).

Time Window

Figure 14.3 shows the time window of the most used social network studies. The youngest students were third graders in KiVa NL. The oldest students were 12th graders in the 10 to 18 Study, PROSPER, and Add Health. The time window between 10 and 18 is dominant in longitudinal social network research. There was substantial heterogeneity in the length of time windows, with some studies following the same students for 8 years (PROSPER) and others following students for half a year (e.g., Classroom and Peer Ecologies).

Few longitudinal social network studies have considered early childhood. A Finnish study followed 1,000 children from Grades 1 to 4 and examined whether children selected friends based on their levels of reading fluency and comprehension as well as whether children were influenced by their friends' reading skills (Kiuru et al., 2017). Selection occurred based on reading fluency rather than reading comprehension, but peer influence occurred for both reading

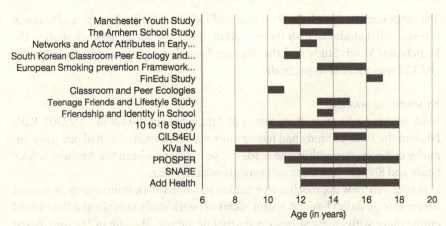

Figure 14.3 The time window of the most used social network data sets.

fluency and comprehension. This peer influence was stronger for children with high reading fluency and a high self-concept of reading ability. A U.S. study on 3- and 4-year-old children examined whether selection and influence processes among preschoolers were related to positive affect, negative affect, and effortful control (Neal et al., 2017). Both the temperament trait and social network data were based on observations. The results indicated that preschoolers selected each other on positive affect only, whereas peer influence occurred for positive affect and effortful control.

There are also several social network studies on (emerging) adults. An exemplary data set in young adulthood is the Swiss StudentLife Study (Vörös et al., 2021), which focused on topics such as the effects of social integration on the academic achievement of undergraduate students (Stadtfeld et al., 2019) and the short- and long-term effects of meeting opportunities on friendship networks (Boda et al., 2020). Another study examined peer selection and influence for marijuana use in an entire cohort of first-year college students (Barnett et al., 2022). The findings provided evidence that students were more likely to select others with similar marijuana use, and students with friends who frequently used marijuana increased their marijuana use. Another study demonstrated that freshmen chose friends who were as extraverted as they were and became more like their friends in their own extraversion (Van Zalk et al., 2020). Last, one study among young adults demonstrated the importance of considering differences in relationship strengths for influence and selection processes (Elmer et al., 2017). Respondents were asked to evaluate the quality of their relationship with every other participant on an 8-point scale. Strong ties were with peers who were perceived as high-ranking friends, close friends, or family members. Weak ties were acquaintances and low- or medium-ranking friends. Influence and selection processes regarding emotional well-being were stronger for strong ties. Young adults selected strong-tied friends based on emotional well-being and were influenced by their strong-tied rather than their weak-tied friends' emotional well-being.

NETWORK QUESTIONS

Most studies contained only data on friendships. Add Health asked respondents to nominate up to five male and up to five female best friends; FinEdu, ESFA, CILS4EU, the Teenage Friends and Lifestyle Study, PROSPER, and the Friendship and Identity in School Study used a maximum of 3, 5, again 5, 6, 7, and 10 nominations, respectively. Friendships in the 10 to 18 Study were measured by asking students to identify up to three friends, defined as people they talked with, hung out with, and did things with. These three friendship nominations were usually combined with the nominations for two other network questions, in which students were asked to name students they spent time with in school (up to 10 nominations) or out of school (up to 10 nominations). SNARE, KiVa NL, the South Korean Peer Ecology and Adolescent Development Study, the Arnhem School Study, and the Manchester Youth Study used unlimited friendship nominations. SNARE, KIVa NL, the South Korean Peer Ecology and Adolescent Development Study, the Classroom and Peer Ecologies project, and the Manchester Youth Study also contained unlimited antipathy nominations (who dislikes whom) as well as perceived status nominations (e.g., who perceives whom as popular, who likes whom). CILS4EU limited the number of popularity nominations to five.

KiVa NL and SNARE also contain other dyadic relationships. KiVa NL contains various dyadic questions on bullying, victimization, and defending. SNARE has information on positive relationships, such as helping (who helps whom) and trusting (who shares secrets with whom), negative relationships, such as bullying (who is victimized by whom) and gossiping (who spreads rumors about whom), and preferential attachment (who likes to hang out with whom, but is not associated yet). A SNARE paper on helping relationships showed that students can also be surrounded by peers who are not necessarily their friends, but who are willing to help them (Van Rijsewijk et al., 2016). Popular students supported other popular peers emotionally, instrumentally, or practically, but refrained from helping nonpopular peers. Other helping relationships were formed based on dissimilarities: higher-achieving students helped the lower academic achievers. Related to this, another study examined the codevelopment of academic partnerships (who studies with whom) and friendships (Palacios et al., 2019). This study demonstrated that adolescents in high-ability classrooms, but not in low-ability classrooms, chose high-achieving peers as academic partners and avoided peers engaged in school misconduct as academic partners. Furthermore, in both high- and low-ability classrooms, academic relationships led to friendship relationships and vice versa. Unlimited nominations for who studies (does their homework) with whom were also collected in CILS4EU (Jansen et al., 2022).

UNIQUE POSSIBILITIES IN SOCIAL NETWORK RESEARCH

The default in social network studies is to examine selection and influence processes. Peer selection is based on similarity in delinquency, alcohol use, and smoking (Gallupe et al., 2019; Henneberger et al., 2021; Ivaniushina & Titkova, 2021), but is less likely for internalizing symptoms and aggression (Neal & Veenstra, 2021; Sijtsema & Lindenberg, 2018). Peer influence occurs more for internalizing problems, victimization, delinquency, alcohol use, and indirect aggression than for smoking or direct aggression (Gallupe et al., 2019; Henneberger et al., 2021; Ivaniushina & Titkova, 2021; Neal & Veenstra, 2021; Sijtsema & Lindenberg, 2018). The following sections discuss other possibilities that social network analysis offers.

Types of influence

Convergence versus contagion. Some types of influence may be convergence processes, such as mutual encouragement, deviancy training, and corumination, and others may be contagion processes, such as imitation and peer pressure (Laninga-Wijnen & Veenstra, 2023; Veenstra & Laninga-Wijnen, 2022). Convergence refers to a process in which friends' average behavior affects one's behavior both upward and downward (an *average similarity* effect in RSiena). Contagion refers to a process in which students with friends with relatively high levels of behaviors increase in these behaviors (an *average alter* effect in RSiena). An exemplary peer network study modeled two types of influence effects on depression to better understand the type of peer influence (Kiuru et al., 2012). The findings provided evidence for convergence rather than contagion because influence processes led to both increases and decreases in adolescent depression.

Initiation versus continuation. Social network analyses also enable researchers to distinguish the influence of friends on the initiation versus the cessation of a behavior. A network diffusion model allows comparison of the influence of friends on the onset versus the continuation of behaviors. Some researchers have applied this model to examine how peers contribute to the onset of substance use: adolescents were particularly influenced by their friends in the *onset* of substance use, which can be defined as the transition from no experience with drinking alcohol to having a first full drink (Light et al., 2013), or as having a first heavy drinking episode (Light et al., 2019), but also as starting to use marijuana (de la Haye et al., 2013) or starting to smoke (de la Haye et al., 2019). The network diffusion models point to social processes whereby exposure to friends who use substances provides information about socially attractive events like parties with popular peers as well as a social context in which peers model and approve of such behavior. In that way, exposure creates a normative context in which substances are easily available, which may influence adolescents' substance use expectations and hence facilitate the initiation of substance use. These exposure effects involve a unilateral transmission of a behavior from adolescents who engage in it to peers who do not. Another example of an exposure effect is that social networks affect whether young people reach the milestone of having sex (Trinh et al., 2019). The findings suggested that having friends who have already had sex increases the odds of adolescents' own sexual debut.

Cross-behavior influence. Research has demonstrated that cross-behavior influence also plays a role in behavioral change. For instance, friends' depressive symptoms and friends' impulsivity predicted an increase in adolescents' nonsuicidal self-injury behaviors (Giletta et al., 2013). Another study found that adolescents with relatively more aggressive friends were likely to decrease in prosocial behavior, whereas adolescents with relatively few aggressive friends were more likely to increase in prosocial behavior (Laninga-Wijnen et al., 2020).

Bundles of behaviors. Besides cross-behavior influence, adolescents may be influenced by their friends in *bundles* of behavior. Through "interpreted abstraction" processes, individuals may consider certain behaviors to belong together and to jointly form a lifestyle. For example, adolescents who engage in risky sexual behavior are also more likely to engage in substance use or direct aggression (Zweig et al., 2002), and engaging in this bundle of behaviors may be seen as a lifestyle. Thus, rather than adopting a specific behavior from friends, adolescents may adopt an entire bundle of behaviors or a lifestyle from others. An exemplary study identified three lifestyles: a mostly healthy, a discordant, and a mostly unhealthy lifestyle (Adams et al., 2022). The healthy group had high rates of nonsmokers, nondrinkers, individuals who had not had sex, and individuals who always wore a seatbelt. The unhealthy group showed high rates of substance use, did not use a condom when they last had sex, and had lower levels of physical activity. The patterns in the discordant group diverged between the schools. Overall, adolescents not only primarily selected each other as friends based on these lifestyles but also influenced their peers' lifestyles (Adams et al., 2022).

Being more susceptible or influential. Moderating effects of individual characteristics in the influence of friends have been tested in some social network studies. Boys were more susceptible to influence by delinquent friends (Burk et al., 2007), whereas girls were more susceptible to influence by depressed friends (Van Zalk et al., 2010). Impulsive youth were more susceptible to influence by alcohol-drinking friends (Rabaglietti et al., 2012), but not to influence by delinquent friends (Franken, Moffitt, et al., 2016). Adolescents with high levels of hostile attribution bias (Molano et al., 2013) or low self-esteem (Van Zalk, 2015) were more inclined to adopt their friends' antisocial and violent behavior. Youth with psychopathic traits as well as high-status youth were less susceptible to the influence of friends' delinquency (Kerr et al., 2012). Adolescents with high levels of social acceptance were less susceptible to influence on antischool behavior (Geven et al., 2013), whereas adolescents with low levels of social acceptance were more susceptible to influence on alcohol misuse (DeLay et al., 2022). Peers with high levels of social acceptance may be especially influential (Zingora et al., 2020). A novel network procedure allows researchers to assess who is more susceptible to influence and who is more influential (DeLay et al., 2022); the procedure uses an *individual susceptibility model* (to test whether peer influence differed as a function of an attribute of the recipient of influence), a *peer influence model* (to test whether peer influence differed as a function of an attribute of the agent of influence), and a *dyadic difference model* (to test whether peer influence or susceptibility to influence differed as a function of the absolute difference in an attribute between the recipient and the agent of influence).

Types of complexity

The impact of social norms. It is likely that adolescents balance the costs and the benefits of certain behaviors before displaying them, and in particular benefits in terms of peer status and approval may be attractive to adolescents (LaFontana & Cillessen, 2010). Social norms are thought to define which behaviors may be approved of and seen as normative among peers (Chang, 2004). Therefore, adolescents may be more likely to select friends and be influenced by their friends on the basis of these normative behaviors. Accordingly, one prior study found that when adolescents perceived bullying norms to be positive, bullying behaviors were more likely to be used as a friendship selection criterion, and adolescents who scored high in bullying others had a greater tendency to select high-bullying peers as friends (Shin, 2022a). In addition, as adolescents perceived higher bullying norms, friendship influence on bullying and victimization was magnified. When they anticipate positive consequences of bullying, bullies seemed to be more likely to adopt the bullying behavior of their high-bullying friends and engage in bullying even more frequently. Furthermore, when adolescents perceived that their classmates condoned bullying, they seemed to be less likely to act on their empathy and intervene on behalf of or defend the victims because of their increased concerns about being potential future targets of bullies. Accordingly, when young people perceived bullying norms as positive, victimization experiences were more severe and friendship influence on victimization was stronger (Shin, 2022a). Whereas this prior study examined individuals' perceptions of peer norms, other research focused on peer norms *as context* for peer selection and influence processes. These studies examined whether friendship selection and influence processes varied across classrooms depending on descriptive norms (average behaviors in classroom) versus popularity norms (the within-classroom correlation between popularity and a behavior). It was found that the norms of popular peers (popularity norms) rather than the norms of all peers (descriptive norms) enhanced peer influence on risk attitudes (Rambaran et al., 2013), aggression (Laninga-Wijnen et al., 2017), and academic adjustment (Laninga-Wijnen et al., 2018). Popular peers may be more visible and central than other peers and more powerful in providing vicarious reinforcement or sanctioning deviation, and adolescents themselves may proactively try to fulfill their increasing desire for popularity or to avoid unpopularity (Laninga-Wijnen, 2020).

Complementarity and distinctiveness. The focus of social network studies has been to explain similarities among friends. Indeed, being similar is an important basis for friendship, but being different from each other and complementing each other can be beneficial within friendships as well (Urberg et al., 1998). For instance, young people who strongly strive for status were more likely to befriend submissive rather than dominant peers, as this reduced conflict and enabled them to achieve their own goal for dominance (Dryer & Horowitz, 1997; Ojanen et al., 2013). Moreover, adolescents may attach value to developing a unique identity and therefore may aim to develop in somewhat different ways from their friends (Brewer, 1991). Some studies have demonstrated a decreasing return to multiple similarity (Block & Grund, 2014; Leszczensky & Pink, 2020). Their findings indicated that the effects of similarity on various dimensions were positive, but that the interaction of selection similarity effects was negative. These decreasing returns for similarity on many dimensions suggest that individuals seek social contact with others who are similar in some, but not in all, ways and allow heterogeneous groups to form. Another study (Block, 2018) demonstrated that having one joint forum for interaction increased the opportunities for friendship formation, but that every additional social situation was less important.

The impact of other actors. Some social network researchers have incorporated parental characteristics in their models (see also Chapter 8). The findings suggested that adolescents may select friends with similar levels of parental control (McCann et al., 2019) or parental knowledge and parental discipline (Ragan et al., 2014). Parental influence may also interact with peer influence: parental monitoring diminished adolescents' selection of delinquent friends (Tilton-Weaver et al., 2013), but only when adolescents did not feel overcontrolled. Parents who communicated disapproval had unintended effects on adolescents who were initially *not* delinquent: they became more susceptible to the influence of delinquent friends (Tilton-Weaver et al., 2013). Regarding alcohol use, it was found that those who reported consistent parental discipline, better parental knowledge, and fewer positive social expectations were more strongly influenced by their friends' level of alcohol use (Hoeben et al., 2021).

Friendship networks also connect adolescents to influence from a broader group of adults beyond their own families (Ragan et al., 2014). Parents' knowledge about the whereabouts of their children had a unique influence on the alcohol use of not only their own children, but also the friends of their children.

In an exemplary study, the influence of "actors at distance two" was examined (Cheadle et al., 2013). Influence on alcohol consumption also took place in networks of indirect relationships, so-called weak ties. Adolescents were affected by not only by their own friends but also the friends of their friends (Cheadle et al., 2013). In certain social settings, such as bars or parties, indirect contacts were likely to form norms and opportunities affecting alcohol use. Influence processes can thus occur in settings in which adolescents know each other only superficially (see Chapter 5).

Coevolving networks. The codevelopment of various relationships can be examined using multiplex social network analysis. Two studies examined the codevelopment of, on the one hand, victim-bully relationships and, on the other hand, victim-defender relationships (Huitsing et al., 2014) or friendships (Rambaran, Dijkstra, et al., 2020). Those longitudinal studies took as a starting point the similarity between victims (with victims being victimized by the same bully being positively associated through defending or friendship) and similarity between bullies (with bullies targeting the same victim being positively associated through defending or friendship). The question posed in these studies was whether selection or influence led to similarity in network positions between victims and bullies. Victims selected other victims as defenders to seek support against the same bullies, but defenders of victims ran the risk that the bullies would retaliate and that they would become victimized themselves (Huitsing et al., 2014). Bullies selected other bullies as friends to collectively target the same victims (Rambaran, Dijkstra, et al., 2020). Being friends with a bully was also contagious: friends assisted bullies first, but later also bullied the victims themselves (Rambaran, Dijkstra, et al., 2020). Another study documented that friendships between bullies were more likely among same-sex than cross-sex bullies (Hooijsma et al., 2020).

Research on antipathies also found evidence for influence effects, suggesting that, over time, friends have a tendency to agree about whom to dislike (Berger & Dijkstra, 2013; Pál et al., 2016; Rambaran et al., 2015). Another study found that disliked children were likely to bully others over time, to be victimized by those who previously disliked them, and to be victimized by other schoolmates as well (Kisfalusi et al., 2022). Victims were likely to be more disliked by their bullies over time and to dislike their own bullies over time. Over and above these dyadic effects, victims did not become more disliked by children other than their own bullies, whereas bullies became more disliked by other children.

Another interesting area is the examination of the coevolution of friendships and romantic relationships (see Chapter 9): partner choices were less likely to grow out of previous direct or indirect friendships than to stem from having similar levels of prominence or status in the network.

CONCLUSION

The field of social network studies has expanded in recent decades. This chapter described the 15 data sets that have been the most central in research on social networks, including the PROSPER Peers data set. PROSPER is the social network data set with the largest sample size and follows adolescents for many years, which allows the examination of longer term development. Other network data sets are distinctive in other ways, for instance because they have unlimited nominations or network questions other than friendships or because they focus on age spans that generally have been overlooked.

The most used data sets predominantly stem from American and European—and mostly white—samples. Yet, prior work has detected cross-cultural variation in peer processes and development (e.g., Choukas-Bradley et al., 2015; see also Chapter 10); therefore, future researchers are encouraged to collect data among more diverse samples of adolescents. In addition, researchers have predominantly investigated networks of friendships, whereas considering the influence of other peers or types of networks is crucial to truly understand the size of peer influence during childhood and adolescence. The most frequently investigated time window is between 10 and 18 years of age, a developmental period in which peers are increasingly essential (Laursen & Veenstra, 2021). Yet, the importance of peers in childhood and adulthood should not be overlooked and needs more exploration.

Most studies included in this review were based on data collected at least a decade ago, and the data set that has been used most frequently was collected prior to 2000. It is important to highlight this given the rapidly changing landscape of adolescent peer interactions. Several new data collections have taken place since the onset of COVID-19 (e.g., PRIMS—a project on the transition from PRIMary to Secondary education—in the Netherlands, Zwier et al., 2023; CHALLENGE—a project on the characteristics and conditions of youth who remain victimized or continue bullying others despite targeted interventions— in Finland, Salmivalli, 2023), and these have the potential to render important insights into the role of peers in young people's adjustment during these times. The increase in social media connectivity has also transformed peer interactions and redefined network boundaries and influence (Nesi et al., 2018). The apps that students use enable them to fully track the whereabouts of peers they know at any time (e.g., Snapmap). This not only may enhance connectedness among adolescents, but also may cause young people to feel excluded; for instance, if they see that two of their peers are meeting while they have not been invited. Applying social network analyses to investigate such processes will provide a breakthrough in the literature.

Another characteristic of the "new generation" of adolescents (compared with the generation of 10 years ago) is that they seem to have become healthier. In the past decade, adolescents tend to smoke less, drink less alcohol (De Looze et al., 2015; Kraus et al., 2018), and postpone their age of sexual debut (Havaei et al., 2019). Social network studies may provide insights into the underlying explanatory mechanisms for these patterns and enable researchers to detect the "risks" of this new generation of adolescents (i.e., with regard to cosmetic surgery; De Vries et al., 2014; Saiphoo & Vahedi, 2019).

Ways to further improve SIENA models are needed (e.g., regarding its robustness; Edmonds & Meyer, 2013). As noted in Chapter 4, a large share of social network studies have yielded potentially imprecise results, with confidence intervals ranging from very small or negative to very large or positive (Gallupe et al., 2019). It was also found that findings based on conventional regression analyses, as long as appropriate controls are included, may not suffer from an inherent upward bias and should not be automatically discounted simply because they were not produced by SIENA (Ragan, Osgood, Ramirez, et al., 2022). Another study created an actor-based model to evaluate the estimation of selection and influence effects by SIENA, and they found that even though *influence estimates* were consistently robust to variation in SIENA specification, *selection estimates* were highly sensitive to misspecification in case of simple assumptions (Daza & Kreuger, 2021). It is, therefore, important that critical comparisons between SIENA and conventional regressions be performed on other big data sets as well, and it is highly useful to replicate social network studies using conventional regression studies and vice versa. Notably, SIENA remains exceptionally suitable for estimating alternative and complex forms of influence that are difficult to estimate using conventional regression, such as the relative impact of asymmetrical versus reciprocal ties, cross-behavior processes, various susceptibility models, different types of influence, and the strength of influence in increases versus decreases in behavior. Thus, social network studies have the advantage of allowing examination of the different types of influence and complexity of social networks, as described in this chapter.

Another direction for future research is to explore the conditions under which friendship selection and influence may, or may not, occur. The role of genetics in social networks, for instance, is an underexplored area of research (see Chapter 12). Following differential susceptibility theory (Belsky & Pluess, 2009), genetic factors may both increase the risk for poor outcomes in adverse contexts and increase positive outcomes in beneficial contexts. Future work is encouraged to examine whether adolescents may be attracted to friends with similar phenotypes, or whether certain phenotypes could make adolescents particularly susceptible to friendship influence. Furthermore, in SIENA, the average similarity among adolescents and their friends is calculated, without considering whether the similarity may vary as a function of the strength of the friendship. However, it is plausible that adolescents are similar to some—potentially their closest—friends, but not to others (Elmer et al., 2017).

Not only individual or dyadic factors may increase susceptibility to peer processes, but also contextual factors, such as peer norms. An important question is how norms can best be conceptualized (Veenstra & Lodder, 2022). Several social network studies have analyzed norms as an individual's perception of what is prevalent or what is approved (e.g., Shin, 2022a). Although valuable, assessing norms in this way entails the risk of projection bias. Other work has assessed peer norms by aggregating outgoing peer nominations on behaviors or by correlating peer-nominated popularity with peer-nominated behavior within classrooms (e.g., Laninga-Wijnen et al., 2017). Nevertheless, it remains to be investigated whether these measures of norms are ideal and capture the consensus of young people on what behaviors are appropriate or expected in a particular setting.

This chapter has summarized the state of the art in social network studies. The PROSPER data set and other large-scale data sets have contributed greatly to the social network literature, and many interesting and innovative directions for future studies have been formulated. The ongoing refinement of social network methods, their application, and critical evaluation will undoubtedly give a boost to numerous innovative studies on topics that matter for the new generation of adolescents.

REFERENCES

Adams, J., Lawrence, E., Goode, J., Schaefer, D. R., & Mollborn, S. (2022). Peer network processes in adolescents' health lifestyles. *Journal of Health and Social Behavior*, 63, 125–141.

Adams, J., Schaefer, D. R., & Vest Ettekal, A. (2020). Crafting mosaics: Person-centered religious influence and selection in adolescent friendships. *Journal for the Scientific Study of Religion, 59*, 39–61.

Barnett, N. P., DiGuiseppi, G. T., Tesdahl, E. A., & Meisel, M. K. (2022). Peer selection and influence for marijuana use in a complete network of first-year college students. *Addictive Behaviors, 124*, 107087.

Belsky, J., & Pluess, M. (2009). Beyond diathesis stress: Differential susceptibility to environmental influences. *Psychological Bulletin, 135*, 885–908.

Berger, C., & Dijkstra, J. K. (2013). Competition, envy, or snobbism? How popularity and friendships shape antipathy networks of adolescents. *Journal of Research on Adolescence, 23*, 586–595.

Block, P. (2018). Network evolution and social situations. *Sociological Science, 5*, 402–431.

Block, P., & Burnett Heyes, S. (2022). Sharing the load: Contagion and tolerance of mood in social networks. *Emotion, 22*, 1193–1207.

Block, P., & Grund, T. (2014). Multidimensional homophily in friendship networks. *Network Science, 2*, 189–212.

Block, P., Heathcote, L. C., & Burnett Heyes, S. (2018). Social interaction and pain: An arctic expedition. *Social Science and Medicine, 196*, 47–55.

Boda, Z., Elmer, T., Vörös, A., & Stadtfeld, C. (2020). Short-term and long-term effects of a social network intervention on friendships among university students. *Scientific Reports, 10*, 2889.

Brewer, M. B. (1991). The social self: On being the same and different at the same time. *Personality and Social Psychology Bulletin, 17*, 475–482.

Burk, W. J., Kerr, M., & Stattin, H. (2008). The co-evolution of early adolescent friendship networks, school involvement, and delinquent behaviors. *Revue Francaise de Sociologie, 49*, 499–522.

Burk, W. J., Steglich, C. E. G., & Snijders, T. A. B. (2007). Beyond dyadic interdependence: Actor-oriented models for co-evolving social networks and individual behaviors. *International Journal of Behavioral Development, 31*, 397–404.

Burk, W. J., Van der Vorst, H., Kerr, M., & Stattin, H. (2012). Alcohol use and friendship dynamics: Selection and socialization in early-, middle-, and late-adolescent peer networks. *Journal of Studies on Alcohol and Drugs, 73*, 89–98.

Chang, L. (2004). The role of classroom norms in contextualizing the relations of children's social behavior to peer acceptance. *Developmental Psychology, 40*, 691–702.

Cheadle, J. E., & Goosby, B. J. (2012). The small-school friendship dynamics of adolescent depressive symptoms. *Society and Mental Health, 2*, 99–119.

Cheadle, J. E., & Schwadel, P. (2012). The "friendship dynamics of religion," or the "religious dynamics of friendship"? A social network analysis of adolescents who attend small schools. *Social Science Research, 41*, 1198–1212.

Cheadle, J. E., Stevens, M., Williams, D. T., & Goosby, B. J. (2013). The differential contributions of teen drinking homophily to new and existing friendships: An empirical assessment of assortative and proximity selection mechanisms. *Social Science Research, 42*, 1297–1310.

Choukas-Bradley, S., Giletta, M., Cohen, G. L., & Prinstein, M. J. (2015). Peer influence, peer status, and prosocial behavior: An experimental investigation of peer socialization of adolescents' intentions to volunteer. *Journal of Youth and Adolescence, 44*, 2197–2210.

Chow, A., Kiuru, N., Parker, P. D., Eccles, J. S., & Salmela-Aro, K. (2018). Development of friendship and task values in a new school: Friend selection for the arts and physical education but socialization for academic subjects. *Journal of Youth and Adolescence, 47*, 1966–1977.

Daza, S., & Kreuger, L. K. (2021). Agent-based models for assessing complex statistical models: An example evaluating selection and social influence estimates from SIENA. *Sociological Methods and Research, 50*, 1725–1762.

de la Haye, K., Green, H. D., Kennedy, D. P., Pollard, M. S., & Tucker, J. S. (2013). Selection and influence mechanisms associated with marijuana initiation and use in adolescent friendship networks. *Journal of Research on Adolescence, 23*, 474–486.

de la Haye, K., Shin, H., Vega Yon, G. G., & Valente, T. W. (2019). Smoking diffusion through networks of diverse, urban American adolescents over the high school period. *Journal of Health and Social Behavior, 60*, 362–376.

DeLay, D., Burk, W. J., & Laursen, B. (2022). Assessing peer influence and susceptibility to peer influence using individual and dyadic moderators in a social network context: The case of adolescent alcohol misuse. *International Journal of Behavioral Development, 46*, 208–221.

DeLay, D., Laursen, B., Kiuru, N., Salmela-Aro, K., & Nurmi, J. E. (2013). Selecting and retaining friends on the basis of cigarette smoking similarity. *Journal of Research on Adolescence, 23*, 464–473.

De Looze, M., Raaijmakers, Q., Ter Bogt, T., Bendtsen, P., Farhat, T., Ferreira, M., Godeau, E., Kuntsche, E., Molcho, M., Pförtner, T. K., Simons-Morton, B., Vieno, A., Vollebergh, W., & Pickett, W. (2015). Decreases in adolescent weekly alcohol use in Europe and North America: Evidence from 28 countries from 2002 to 2010. *European Journal of Public Health, 25*, 69–72.

De Vries, D. A., Peter, J., Nikken, P., & De Graaf, H. (2014). The effect of social network site use on appearance investment and desire for cosmetic surgery among adolescent boys and girls. *Sex Roles, 71*, 283–295.

Dijkstra, J. K., Cillessen, A. H. N., & Borch, C. (2013). Popularity and adolescent friendship networks: Selection and influence dynamics. *Developmental Psychology, 49*, 1242–1252.

Dijkstra, J. K., Gest, S. D., Lindenberg, S., Veenstra, R., & Cillessen, A. H. N. (2012). Testing three explanations of the emergence of weapon carrying in peer context: The roles of aggression, victimization, and the social network. *Journal of Adolescent Health, 50*, 371–376.

Dijkstra, J. K., Kretschmer, T., Pattiselanno, K., Franken, A., Harakeh, Z., Vollebergh, W. A. M., & Veenstra, R. (2015). Explaining adolescents' delinquency and substance use: A test of the maturity gap. *Journal of Research on Crime and Delinquency, 52*, 747–767.

Dryer, D. C., & Horowitz, L. M. (1997). When do opposites attract? Interpersonal complementarity versus similarity. *Journal of Personality and Social Psychology, 72*, 592–603.

Duxbury, S. W., & Haynie, D. L. (2020). School suspension and social selection: Labeling, network change, and adolescent, academic achievement. *Social Science Research, 85*, 102365.

Edmonds, B., & Meyer, R. (2013). *Simulating social complexity: A handbook*. Springer.

Elmer, T., Boda, Z., & Stadtfeld, C. (2017). The co-evolution of emotional well-being with weak and strong friendship ties. *Network Science, 5*, 278–307.

Franken, A., Keijsers, L., Dijkstra, J. K., & ter Bogt, T. (2017). Music preferences, friendship, and externalizing behavior in early adolescence: A SIENA examination of the music marker theory using the SNARE study. *Journal of Youth and Adolescence, 46,* 1839–1850.

Franken, A., Moffitt, T. E., Steglich, C. E. G., Dijkstra, J. K., Harakeh, Z., & Vollebergh, W. A. M. (2016). The role of self-control and early adolescents' friendships in the development of externalizing behavior: The SNARE study. *Journal of Youth and Adolescence, 45,* 1800–1811.

Franken, A., Prinstein, M. J., Dijkstra, J. K., Steglich, C. E. G., Harakeh, Z., & Vollebergh, W. A. M. (2016). Early adolescent friendship selection based on externalizing behavior: The moderating role of pubertal development. The SNARE study. *Journal of Abnormal Child Psychology, 44,* 1647–1657.

Gallupe, O., McLevey, J., & Brown, S. (2019). Selection and influence: A meta-analysis of the association between peer and personal offending. *Journal of Quantitative Criminology, 35,* 1–23.

Geven, S., Jonsson, J. O., & van Tubergen, F. (2017). Gender differences in resistance to schooling: The role of dynamic peer-influence and selection processes. *Journal of Youth and Adolescence, 46,* 2421–2445.

Geven, S., Weesie, J., & Van Tubergen, F. (2013). The influence of friends on adolescents' behavior problems at school: The role of ego, alter and dyadic characteristics. *Social Networks, 35,* 583–592.

Giletta, M., Burk, W. J., Scholte, R. H. J., Engels, R. C. M. E., & Prinstein, M. J. (2013). Direct and indirect peer socialization of adolescent nonsuicidal self-injury. *Journal of Research on Adolescence, 23,* 450–463.

Gremmen, M. C., Berger, C., Ryan, A. M., Steglich, C. E. G., Veenstra, R., & Dijkstra, J. K. (2019). Adolescents' friendships, academic achievement, and risk behaviors: Same-behavior and cross-behavior selection and influence processes. *Child Development, 90,* e192–e211.

Gremmen, M. C., Dijkstra, J. K., Steglich, C. E. G., & Veenstra, R. (2017). First selection, then influence: Developmental differences in friendship dynamics regarding academic achievement. *Developmental Psychology, 53,* 1356–1370.

Haas, S. A., & Schaefer, D. R. (2014). With a little help from my friends? Asymmetrical social influence on adolescent smoking initiation and cessation. *Journal of Health and Social Behavior, 55,* 126–143.

Hallinan, M. T. (1980). Patterns of cliquing among youth. In H. C. Foot, A. J. Chapman, & J. R. Smith (Eds.), *Friendship and social relations in children* (pp. 321–342). Wiley.

Havaei, F., Doull, M., & Saewyc, E. (2019). A trend analysis of sexual health behaviours of a national sample of Canadian adolescents using HBSC data from 2002-2014. *Canadian Journal of Human Sexuality, 28,* 17–25.

Haynie, D. L., Doogan, N. J., & Soller, B. (2014). Gender, friendship networks, and delinquency: A dynamic network approach. *Criminology, 52,* 688–722.

Henneberger, A. K., Mushonga, D. R., & Preston, A. M. (2021). Peer influence and adolescent substance use: A systematic review of dynamic social network research. *Adolescent Research Review, 6,* 57–73.

Hoeben, E. M., Rulison, K. L., Ragan, D. T., & Feinberg, M. E. (2021). Moderators of friend selection and influence in relation to adolescent alcohol use. *Prevention Science, 22,* 567–578.

Hooijsma, M., Huitsing, G., Kisfalusi, D., Dijkstra, J. K., Flache, A., & Veenstra, R. (2020). Multidimensional similarity in multiplex networks: Friendships between same- and cross-gender bullies and same- and cross-gender victims. *Network Science, 8*, 79–96.

Hooijsma, M., Kisfalusi, D., Huitsing, G., Kornelis Dijkstra, J., Flache, A., & Veenstra, R. (2021). Crossing ethnic boundaries? A social network investigation of defending relationships in schools. *Group Processes and Intergroup Relations, 24*, 1391–1408.

Huitsing, G., Lodder, G. M. A., Browne, W. J., Oldenburg, B., van der Ploeg, R., & Veenstra, R. (2020). A large-scale replication of the effectiveness of the KiVa antibullying program: A randomized controlled trial in the Netherlands. *Prevention Science, 21*, 627–638.

Huitsing, G., Snijders, T. A. B., Van Duijn, M. A. J., & Veenstra, R. (2014). Victims, bullies, and their defenders: A longitudinal study of the coevolution of positive and negative networks. *Development and Psychopathology, 26*, 645–659.

Ivaniushina, V., & Titkova, V. (2021). Peer influence in adolescent drinking behavior: A meta-analysis of stochastic actor-based modeling studies. *PloS One, 16*, e0250169.

Jacobsen, W. C., Ragan, D. T., Yang, M., Nadel, E. L., & Feinberg, M. E. (2022). Arrested friendships? Justice involvement and interpersonal exclusion among rural youth. *Journal of Research in Crime and Delinquency, 59*, 365–409.

Jansen, M., Boda, Z., & Lorenz, G. (2022). Social comparison effects on academic self-concepts: Which peers matter most? *Developmental Psychology, 58*, 1541–1556.

Jugert, P., Leszczensky, L., & Pink, S. (2018). The effects of ethnic minority adolescents' ethnic self-identification on friendship selection. *Journal of Research on Adolescence, 28*, 379–395.

Jugert, P., Leszczensky, L., & Pink, S. (2020). Differential influence of same- and cross-ethnic friends on ethnic-racial identity development in early adolescence. *Child Development, 91*, 949–963.

Kerr, M., Van Zalk, M. H. W., & Stattin, H. H. (2012). Psychopathic traits moderate peer influence on adolescent delinquency. *Journal of Child Psychology and Psychiatry, 53*, 826–835.

Kisfalusi, D., Hooijsma, M., Huitsing, G., & Veenstra, R. (2022). How dislike and bullying co-develop: A longitudinal study of negative relationships. *Social Development, 31*, 797–810.

Kiuru, N., Burk, W. J., Laursen, B., Nurmi, J. E., & Salmela-Aro, K. (2012). Is depression contagious? A test of alternative peer socialization mechanisms of depressive symptoms in adolescent peer networks. *Journal of Adolescent Health, 50*, 250–255.

Kiuru, N., Burk, W. J., Laursen, B., Salmela-Aro, K., & Nurmi, J. E. (2010). Pressure to drink but not to smoke: Disentangling selection and socialization in adolescent peer networks and peer groups. *Journal of Adolescence, 33*, 801–812.

Kiuru, N., DeLay, D., Laursen, B., Burk, W. J., Lerkkanen, M. K., Poikkeus, A. M., & Nurmi, J. E. (2017). Peer selection and influence on children's reading skills in early primary grades: A social network approach. *Reading and Writing, 30*, 1473–1500.

Knecht, A. B., Burk, W. J., Weesie, J., & Steglich, C. E. G. (2011). Friendship and alcohol use in early adolescence: A multilevel social network approach. *Journal of Research on Adolescence, 21*, 475–487.

Knecht, A. B., Snijders, T. A. B., Baerveldt, C., Steglich, C. E. G., & Raub, W. (2010). Friendship and delinquency: Selection and influence processes in early adolescence. *Social Development, 19*, 494–514.

Kraus, L., Seitz, N. N., Piontek, D., Molinaro, S., Siciliano, V., Guttormsson, U., ... Hibell, B. (2018). "Are the Times A-Changin"? Trends in adolescent substance use in Europe. *Addiction, 113*, 1317–1332.

Kretschmer, D., Leszczensky, L., & Pink, S. (2018). Selection and influence processes in academic achievement: More pronounced for girls? *Social Networks, 52*, 251–260.

Kretschmer, D., & Roth, T. (2021). Why do friends have similar educational expectations? Separating influence and selection effects. *European Sociological Review, 37*, 201–217.

LaFontana, K. M., & Cillessen, A. H. N. (2010). Developmental changes in the priority of perceived status in childhood and adolescence. *Social Development, 19*, 130–147.

Laninga-Wijnen, L. (2020). They get the power! Consequences and antecedents of aggressive, prosocial and academic popularity norms in adolescents' classrooms. [Doctoral dissertation, Urecht University.]

Laninga-Wijnen, L., Gremmen, M. C., Dijkstra, J. K., Veenstra, R., Vollebergh, W. A. M., & Harakeh, Z. (2019). The role of academic status norms in friendship selection and influence processes related to academic achievement. *Developmental Psychology, 55*, 337–350.

Laninga-Wijnen, L., Harakeh, Z., Garandeau, C. F., Dijkstra, J. K., Veenstra, R., & Vollebergh, W. A. M. (2019). Classroom popularity hierarchy predicts prosocial and aggressive popularity norms across the school year. *Child Development, 90*, e637–e653.

Laninga-Wijnen, L., Harakeh, Z., Steglich, C. E. G., Dijkstra, J. K., Veenstra, R., & Vollebergh, W. (2017). The norms of popular peers moderate friendship dynamics of adolescent aggression. *Child Development, 88*, 1265–1283.

Laninga-Wijnen, L., Ryan, A. M., Harakeh, Z., Shin, H., & Vollebergh, W. A. M. (2018). The moderating role of popular peers' achievement goals in 5th-and 6th-graders' achievement-related friendships: A social network analysis. *Journal of Educational Psychology, 110*, 289–307.

Laninga-Wijnen, L., Steglich, C. E. G., Harakeh, Z., Vollebergh, W., Veenstra, R., & Dijkstra, J. K. J. K. (2020). The role of prosocial and aggressive popularity norm combinations in prosocial and aggressive friendship processes. *Journal of Youth and Adolescence, 49*, 645–663.

Laninga-Wijnen, L., & Veenstra, R. (2023). Peer similarity in adolescent social networks: Types of selection and influence, and factors contributing to openness to peer influence. In B. Halpern-Felsher (Ed.), *The encyclopedia of child and adolescent health*. Elsevier, doi:10.1016/B978-0-12-818872-9.00047-9.

Laursen, B., & Veenstra, R. (2021). Toward understanding the functions of peer influence: A summary and synthesis of recent empirical research. *Journal of Research on Adolescence, 31*, 889–907.

Leszczensky, L., & Kretschmer, D. (2022). Religious friendship preferences of Muslim and non-Muslim students in German schools: Bright boundaries everywhere or contingent on the proportion of Muslim classmates? *Social Networks, 68*, 60–69.

Leszczensky, L., & Pink, S. (2017). Intra-and inter-group friendship choices of Christian, Muslim, and non-religious youth in Germany. *European Sociological Review, 33*, 72–83.

Leszczensky, L., & Pink, S. (2019). What drives ethnic homophily? A relational approach on how ethnic identification moderates preferences for same-ethnic friends. *American Sociological Review, 84*, 394–419.

Leszczensky, L., & Pink, S. (2020). Are birds of a feather praying together? Assessing friends' influence on Muslim youths' religiosity in Germany. *Social Psychology Quarterly, 83*, 251–271.

Light, J. M., Greenan, C. C., Rusby, J. C., Nies, K. M., & Snijders, T. A. B. (2013). Onset to first alcohol use in early adolescence: A network diffusion model. *Journal of Research on Adolescence, 23*, 487–499.

Light, J. M., Mills, K. L., Rusby, J. C., & Westling, E. (2019). Friend selection and influence effects for first heavy drinking episode in adolescence. *Journal of Studies on Alcohol and Drugs, 80*, 349–357.

Lomi, A., & Stadtfeld, C. (2014). Social networks and social settings: Developing a coevolutionary view. *KZfSS Kölner Zeitschrift Für Soziologie Und Sozialpsychologie, 66*, 395–415.

Lorenz, G., Boda, Z., & Salikutluk, Z. (2021). Oppositional culture revisited. Friendship dynamics and the creation of social capital among Turkish minority adolescents in Germany. *Journal of Ethnic and Migration Studies, 47*, 3986–4005.

Lorenz, G., Boda, Z., Salikutluk, Z., & Jansen, M. (2020). Social influence or selection? Peer effects on the development of adolescents' educational expectations in Germany development of adolescents' educational expectations in. *British Journal of Sociology of Education, 41*, 643–669.

Lorenz, G., Salikutluk, Z., Boda, Z., Jansen, M., & Hewstone, M. (2021). The link between social and structural integration: Co- and interethnic friendship selection and social influence within adolescent social networks. *Sociological Science, 8*, 371–396.

McCann, M., Jordan, J. A., Higgins, K., & Moore, L. (2019). Longitudinal social network analysis of peer, family, and school contextual influences on adolescent drinking frequency. *Journal of Adolescent Health, 65*, 350–358.

McMillan, C., Felmlee, D., & Osgood, D. W. (2018). Peer influence, friend selection, and gender: How network processes shape adolescent smoking, drinking, and delinquency. *Social Networks, 55*, 86–96.

McPherson, M., Smith-Lovin, L., & Cook, J. M. (2001). Birds of a feather: Homophily in social networks. *Annual Review of Sociology, 27*, 415–444.

Mercken, L., Snijders, T. A. B., Steglich, C. E. G., & de Vries, H. (2009). Dynamics of adolescent friendship networks and smoking behavior: Social network analyses in six European countries. *Social Science & Medicine, 69*, 1506–1514.

Mercken, L., Snijders, T. A. B., Steglich, C. E. G., Vartiainen, E., & De Vries, H. (2010a). Dynamics of adolescent friendship networks and smoking behavior. *Social Networks, 32*, 72–81.

Mercken, L., Snijders, T. A. B., Steglich, C. E. G., Vartiainen, E., & De Vries, H. (2010b). Smoking-based selection and influence in gender-segregated friendship networks: A social network analysis of adolescent smoking. *Addiction, 105*, 1280–1289.

Mercken, L., Steglich, C., Knibbe, R., & De Vries, H. (2012). Dynamics of friendship networks and alcohol use in early and mid-adolescence. *Journal of Studies on Alcohol and Drugs, 73*, 99–110.

Molano, A., Jones, S. M., Brown, J. L., & Aber, J. L. (2013). Selection and socialization of aggressive and prosocial behavior: The moderating role of social-cognitive processes. *Journal of Research on Adolescence, 23*, 424–436.

Neal, J. W., Durbin, C. E., Gornik, A. E., & Lo, S. L. (2017). Codevelopment of preschoolers' temperament traits and social play networks over an entire school year. *Journal of Personality and Social Psychology, 113*, 627–640.

Neal, J. W., & Veenstra, R. (2021). Network selection and influence effects on children's and adolescents' internalizing behaviors and peer victimization: A systematic review. *Developmental Review, 59*, 100944.

Nesi, J., Choukas-Bradley, S., & Prinstein, M. J. (2018). Transformation of adolescent peer relations in the social media context: Part 1—A theoretical framework and application to dyadic peer relationships. *Clinical Child and Family Psychology Review, 21*, 267–294.

Ojanen, T., Sijtsema, J. J., & Rambaran, A. J. (2013). Social goals and adolescent friendships: Social selection, deselection, and influence. *Journal of Research on Adolescence, 23*, 550–562.

Osgood, D. W., Feinberg, M. E., & Ragan, D. T. (2015). Social networks and the diffusion of adolescent problem behavior: Reliable estimates of selection and influence from sixth through ninth grades. *Prevention Science, 16*, 832–843.

Osgood, D. W., Ragan, D. T., Wallace, L., Gest, S. D., Feinberg, M. E., & Moody, J. (2013). Peers and the emergence of alcohol use: Influence and selection processes in adolescent friendship networks. *Journal of Research on Adolescence, 23*, 500–512.

Pál, J., Stadtfeld, C., Grow, A., & Takács, K. (2016). Status perceptions matter: Understanding disliking among adolescents. *Journal of Research on Adolescence, 26*, 805–818.

Palacios, D., Dijkstra, J. K., Villalobos, C., Treviño, E., Berger, C., Huisman, M., & Veenstra, R. (2019). Classroom ability composition and the role of academic performance and school misconduct in the formation of academic and friendship networks. *Journal of School Psychology, 74*, 58–73.

Pearson, M., Steglich, C. E. G., & Snijders, T. (2006). Homophily and assimilation among sport-active adolescent substance users. *Connections, 27*, 47–63.

Raabe, I. J., Boda, Z., & Stadtfeld, C. (2019). The social pipeline: How friend influence and peer exposure widen the STEM gender gap. *Sociology of Education, 92*, 105–123.

Rabaglietti, E., Burk, W. J., & Giletta, M. (2012). Regulatory self-efficacy as a moderator of peer socialization relating to Italian adolescents' alcohol intoxication. *Social Development, 21*, 522–536.

Ragan, D. T. (2014). Revisiting "What they think": Adolescent drinking and the importance of peer beliefs. *Criminology, 52*, 488–513.

Ragan, D. T. (2016). Peer beliefs and smoking in adolescence: A longitudinal social network analysis. *American Journal of Drug and Alcohol Abuse, 42*, 222–230.

Ragan, D. T., Osgood, D. W., & Kreager, D. A. (2022). Impulsivity, peers, and delinquency: A dynamic social network approach. *Journal of Quantitative Criminology*. https://doi.org/10.1007/s10940-022-09547-8

Ragan, D. T., Osgood, D. W., Ramirez, N. G., Moody, J., & Gest, S. D. (2022). A comparison of peer influence estimates from SIENA stochastic actor-based models and from conventional regression approaches. *Sociological Methods and Research, 51*, 357–395.

Ragan, D. T., Osgood, D. W., & Feinberg, M. E. (2014). Friends as a bridge to parental influence: Implications for adolescent alcohol use. *Social Forces, 92*, 1061–1085.

Rambaran, A. J., Dijkstra, J. K., Munniksma, A., & Cillessen, A. H. N. (2015). The development of adolescents' friendships and antipathies: A longitudinal multivariate network test of balance theory. *Social Networks, 43*, 162–176.

Rambaran, A. J., Dijkstra, J. K., & Stark, T. H. (2013). Status-based influence processes: The role of norm salience in contagion of adolescent risk attitudes. *Journal of Research on Adolescence, 23*, 574–585.

Rambaran, A. J., Dijkstra, J. K., & Veenstra, R. (2020). Bullying as a group process in childhood: A longitudinal social network analysis. *Child Development, 91*, 1336–1352.

Rambaran, A. J., van Duijn, M. A. J., Dijkstra, J. K., & Veenstra, R. (2020). Stability and change in student classroom composition and its impact on peer victimization. *Journal of Educational Psychology, 112*, 1677–1691.

Rambaran, A. J., Van Duijn, M. A. J., Dijkstra, J. K., & Veenstra, R. (2019). Peer victimization in single-grade and multigrade classrooms. *Aggressive Behavior, 45*, 561–570.

Ripley, R. M., Snijders, T. A. B., Boda, Z., Vörös, A., & Preciado, P. (2022). *Manual for RSiena*. University of Oxford/University of Groningen.

Saiphoo, A., & Vahedi, Z. (2019). A meta-analytic review of the relationship between social media use and body image disturbance. *Computers in Human Behavior, 101*, 259–275.

Salmivalli, C. (2023). Focus on targeted interventions addressing bullying: What explains their success or failure? *European Journal of Developmental Psychology*, doi:10.1080/17405629.2022.2156857.

Sentse, M., Dijkstra, J. K., Salmivalli, C., & Cillessen, A. H. N. (2013). The dynamics of friendships and victimization in adolescence: A longitudinal social network perspective. *Aggressive Behavior, 39*, 229–238.

Sentse, M., Kiuru, N., Veenstra, R., & Salmivalli, C. (2014). A social network approach to the interplay between adolescents' bullying and likeability over time. *Journal of Youth and Adolescence, 43*, 1409–1420.

Shin, H. (2017). Friendship dynamics of adolescent aggression, prosocial behavior, and social status: The moderating role of gender. *Journal of Youth and Adolescence, 46*, 2305–2320.

Shin, H. (2018). The role of friends in help-seeking tendencies during early adolescence: Do classroom goal structures moderate selection and influence of friends? *Contemporary Educational Psychology, 53*, 135–145.

Shin, H. (2022a). The role of perceived bullying norms in friendship dynamics: An examination of friendship selection and influence on bullying and victimization. *International Journal of Behavioral Development, 46*, 432–442.

Shin, H. (2022b). Social contagion of academic behavior: Comparing social networks of close friends and admired peers. *PloS One, 17*, e0265385.

Shin, H., & Ryan, A. M. (2014a). Early adolescent friendships and academic adjustment: Examining selection and influence processes with longitudinal social network analysis. *Developmental Psychology, 50*, 2462–2472.

Shin, H., & Ryan, A. M. (2014b). Friendship networks and achievement goals: An examination of selection and influence processes and variations by gender. *Journal of Youth and Adolescence, 43*, 1453–1464.

Shin, H., & Ryan, A. M. (2017). Friend influence on early adolescent disruptive behavior in the classroom: Teacher emotional support matters. *Developmental Psychology, 53*, 114–125.

Shin, H., Ryan, A. M., & North, E. (2019). Friendship processes around prosocial and aggressive behaviors: The role of teacher–student relatedness and differences between elementary-school and middle-school classrooms. *Merrill-Palmer Quarterly, 65*, 232–263.

Shoham, D. A., Tong, L., Lamberson, P. J., Auchincloss, A. H., Zhang, J., Dugas, L., . . . Luke, A. (2012). An actor-based model of social network influence on adolescent body size, screen time, and playing sports. *PLoS One, 7*, e39795.

Sijtsema, J. J., & Lindenberg, S. M. (2018). Peer influence in the development of adolescent antisocial behavior: Advances from dynamic social network studies. *Developmental Review, 50*, 140–154.

Simone, M., Long, E., & Lockhart, G. (2018). The dynamic relationship between unhealthy weight control and adolescent friendships: A social network approach. *Journal of Youth and Adolescence, 47*, 1373–1384.

Simpkins, S. D., Schaefer, D. R., Price, C. D., & Vest, A. E. (2013). Adolescent friendships, BMI, and physical activity: Untangling selection and influence through longitudinal social network analysis. *Journal of Research on Adolescence, 23*, 537–549.

Snijders, T. A. B., Van de Bunt, G. G., & Steglich, C. E. G. (2010). Introduction to stochastic actor-based models for network dynamics. *Social Networks, 32*, 44–60.

Stadtfeld, C., Vörös, A., Elmer, T., Boda, Z., & Raabe, I. J. (2019). Integration in emerging social networks explains academic failure and success. *Proceedings of the National Academy of Sciences of the United States of America, 116*, 792–797.

Stark, T. H. (2015). Understanding the selection bias: Social network processes and the effect of prejudice on the avoidance of outgroup friends. *Social Psychology Quarterly, 78*, 127–150.

Stark, T. H., & Flache, A. (2012). The double edge of common interest: Ethnic segregation as an unintended byproduct of opinion homophily. *Sociology of Education, 85*, 179–199.

Stark, T. H., Leszczensky, L., & Pink, S. (2017). Are there differences in ethnic majority and minority adolescents' friendships preferences and social influence with regard to their academic achievement? *Zeitschrift Fur Erziehungswissenschaft, 20*, 475–498.

Steglich, C. E. G., & Knecht, A. B. (2014). Studious by association? Effects of teacher's attunement to students' peer relations. *Zeitschrift Fur Erziehungswissenschaft, 17*, 153–170.

Steglich, C. E. G., Snijders, T. A. B., & Pearson, M. (2010). Dynamic networks and behavior: Separating selection from influence. *Sociological Methodology, 41*, 329–393.

Steglich, C. E. G., Snijders, T. A. B., & West, P. (2006). Applying SIENA: An illustrative analysis of the coevolution of adolescents' friendship networks, taste in music, and alcohol consumption. *Methodology, 2*, 48–56.

Tilton-Weaver, L. C., Burk, W. J., Kerr, M., & Stattin, H. (2013). Can parental monitoring and peer management reduce the selection or influence of delinquent peers? Testing the question using a dynamic social network approach. *Developmental Psychology, 49*, 2057–2070.

Trinh, S. L., Lee, J., Halpern, C. T., & Moody, J. (2019). Our buddies, ourselves: The role of sexual homophily in adolescent friendship networks. *Child Development, 90*, e132–e147.

Urberg, K. A., Değirmencioğlu, S. M., & Tolson, J. M. (1998). Adolescent friendship selection and termination: The role of similarity. *Journal of Social and Personal Relationships, 15*, 703–710.

Van der Ploeg, R., Steglich, C. E. G., & Veenstra, R. (2020). The way bullying works: How new ties facilitate the mutual reinforcement of status and bullying in elementary schools. *Social Networks, 60*, 71–82.

Van Rijsewijk, L. G. M., Dijkstra, J. K., Pattiselanno, K., Steglich, C. E. G., & Veenstra, R. (2016). Who helps whom? Investigating the development of adolescent prosocial relationships. *Developmental Psychology, 52*, 894–908.

Van Rijsewijk, L. G. M., Snijders, T. A. B., Dijkstra, J. K., Steglich, C. E. G., & Veenstra, R. (2020). The interplay between adolescents' friendships and the exchange of help: A longitudinal multiplex social network study. *Journal of Research on Adolescence, 30*, 63–77.

Van Zalk, M. H. W. (2015). Violent peer influence: The roles of self-esteem and psychopathic traits. *Development and Psychopathology, 27*, 1077–1088.

Van Zalk, M. H. W., & Kerr, M. (2011). Socialization of social anxiety in adolescent crowds. *Journal of Abnormal Child Psychology, 39*, 1239–1249.

Van Zalk, M. H. W., Kerr, M., Branje, S. J. T., Stattin, H., & Meeus, W. H. J. J. (2010). It takes three: Selection, influence, and de-selection processes of depression in adolescent friendship networks. *Developmental Psychology, 46*, 927–938.

Van Zalk, M. H. W., Nestler, S., Geukes, K., Hutteman, R., & Back, M. D. (2020). The codevelopment of extraversion and friendships: Bonding and behavioral interaction mechanisms in friendship networks. *Journal of Personality and Social Psychology, 118*, 1269–1290.

Veenstra, R., Dijkstra, J. K., Steglich, C. E. G., & Van Zalk, M. H. W. (2013). Network-behavior dynamics. *Journal of Research on Adolescence, 23*, 399–412.

Veenstra, R., & Laninga-Wijnen, L. (2022). Peer network studies and interventions in adolescence. *Current Opinion in Psychology, 44*, 157–163.

Veenstra, R., & Lodder, G. M. A. (2022). On the microfoundations of the link between classroom social norms and behavioral development. *International Journal of Behavioral Development, 46*, 453–460.

Veenstra, R., & Steglich, C. E. G. (2012). Actor-based model for network and behavior dynamics: A tool to examine selection and influence processes. In B. Laursen, T. D. Little, & N. A. Card (Eds.), *Handbook of developmental research methods* (pp. 598–618). Guilford.

Vörös, A., Boda, Z., Elmer, T., Mepham, K., Hoffman, M., Raabe, I. J., . . . Stadtfeld, C. (2021). The Swiss StudentLife Study: Investigating the emergence of an undergraduate community through dynamic, multidimensional social network data. *Social Networks, 65*, 71–84.

Wang, M. T., Kiuru, N., Degol, J. L., & Salmela-Aro, K. (2018). Friends, academic achievement, and school engagement during adolescence: A social network approach to peer influence and selection effects. *Learning and Instruction, 58*, 148–160.

Weerman, F. M., Wilcox, P., & Sullivan, C. J. (2018). The short-term dynamics of peers and delinquent behavior: An analysis of bi-weekly changes within a high school student network. *Journal of Quantitative Criminology, 34*, 431–463.

Zingora, T., Stark, T. H., & Flache, A. (2020). Who is most influential? Adolescents' intergroup attitudes and peer influence within a social network. *Group Processes and Intergroup Relations, 23*, 684–709.

Zweig, J. M., Phillips, S. D., & Lindberg, L. D. (2002). Predicting adolescent profiles of risk: Looking beyond demographics. *Journal of Adolescent Health, 31*, 343–353.

Zwier, D., Lorijn, S. J., Van den Brink, E., Bol, T., Geven, S., Van de Werfhorst, H. G., Engels, M. C., & Veenstra, R. (2023). *PRIMS, Data collection report and codebook, version 1.0*, DataverseNL, https://doi.org/10.34894/U6XDT0.

15

Social capital and adolescent development

Concluding thoughts

MARK E. FEINBERG

INTRODUCTION

The PROSPER (PROmoting School-community-university Partnerships to Enhance Resilience) project focused on prevention of substance use through community-school-university partnerships. Through the leadership of Dick Spoth and Mark Greenberg and support of the National Institute on Drug Abuse (NIDA), the project followed over 11,000 sixth graders in 28 school districts beyond middle school, into high school and then young adulthood. The project included a detailed investigation of almost 1,000 families from sixth through ninth grades via home visits, including observations of family interactions and extensive data collection about the communities and schools through key informant interviews with principals and PROSPER prevention team members. Additional National Institutes of Health (NIH) support allowed a team to collect genetic data. By adding additional questions about peer friendships into the original student surveys and then gaining support from W. T. Grant and NIDA, we have been able to add an additional layer of longitudinal peer network data that allowed us to ask questions about substance use and problem behavior across the full period of adolescence. In what became a rich, multilayer data set, the PROSPER peer network researchers were able to ask myriad questions about adolescent substance use that incorporated levels of analysis including genes, attitudes and behaviors, mental health, school performance, dyadic friendships and group relations, parenting, and features of schools and communities such as prevention programming.

Given such a large sandbox, there is no single statement or rubric with which one can summarize the insights from this research project. We have developed no single grand theory. As described in the introduction, our grant-funded work was motivated by the central theme of exploring peer influence and selection on risky behaviors, but our published work expanded beyond that theme in numerous directions. In this expansive investigation, I believe we have held true to the insights of Moreno, touched on in Chapter 3, who developed sociometry in the setting of psychodrama and therapy to help quantify intuitions about the central importance of social relationships in individual mental health and behavior. In this concluding chapter, I offer an idiosyncratic summary of key insights that have struck me over the past 20 years of this work.

I organize my concluding comments around the general notion of social capital, which has been an underlying perspective of my own approach, throughout my career, whether in work on families, peers, or communities. Although there is no single grand theory, I do want to offer an underlying perspective. In my first independent research study, my undergraduate ethnographic study of three small block neighborhoods in East Boston, Massachusetts, I studied the racist attitudes and behaviors expressed by the white ethnic working class, long-time residents toward the Vietnamese and Cambodian refugees who were settling in the neighborhood. In an analysis that ranged from the micro-organization of neighborly relations to the community-wide impacts and impingements of the nearby airport and local power structures, including the residents' involvement in the Vietnamese war and resulting political and social attitudes about the American dream, I found an overarching principle: Social relationships and behaviors are two sides of a single coin. Social relations channel and organize attitudes; behaviors emerge from this constellation of attitudes and relationships and reciprocally affect relationships. I would later find in researching racism in Europe that every form of racism is unique, with unique themes and beliefs and racist practices. However, I continued to find that each form of racism is rooted in a history of actual social relations on the one hand and race-related cultural, sociopolitical beliefs on the other.

This perspective about the intertwined nature of relationships and beliefs/attitudes that lead to particular actions and behaviors underlies much social network research. In our case in the PROSPER project, we were interested in how adolescent friendships channeled the development and spread of substance use attitudes and behaviors, and how such attitudes and behaviors influenced the friendships that were formed and maintained. In our broad (and ongoing) investigation, I found myself intrigued by repeated findings that related to the ways that the quantity or qualities of friendships were related to sociodemographic characteristics. Here, I want to speculate about the role of friendships in adolescence as social capital and how such friendship social capital may be part of the dynamics by which inequality, deprivation, and stigma are produced and possibly reproduced across generations.

First, however, I want to acknowledge the leadership of Wayne Osgood in developing and sustaining the social capital of our enterprise. After I convened a small group of Penn State scholars to discuss the potential for leveraging the peer network questions that principal investigators Dick Spoth, Mark Greenberg, and Karen Bierman agreed to include in the PROSPER data collection, Wayne agreed to take the baton and lead the development of grant proposals and oversee a growing team of experts, colleagues, and students in coding and analyzing the data over the next 15 years. Working with Wayne has been one of the most rewarding experiences of my career. He is a brilliant methodologist who can see the trees (and branches, stems, and leaves as well) but never loses sight of the forest and simultaneously is a wise and well-informed social theorist. I was often struck by his writing, which has a quality very much needed in academia through which he conveys the most complicated ideas in ways that are clear and easily apprehended. And ever more notably, he has led our team with grace, always kindly, and encouraging to all, capable of offering even critical feedback in ways that are honest but not off-putting. I have learned a great deal from and am grateful for the opportunity to have worked closely with him.

SOCIAL CAPITAL AND FRIENDSHIPS

Before reviewing the findings in our PROSPER peer network research that relate to social capital in adolescent development, I discuss several interrelated ideas about social capital in terms of knowledge, friendships, and mobility. It has been common for social theorists and political activists to acknowledge that knowledge conveys power. But knowledge is power only as it is applied in particular social structures and contexts for certain purposes, as Daniel Bell (1973) taught us. Neither knowledge nor technology by themselves lead to any particular technological implementation or social class relations. Social relationships and goals facilitate and channel action, and in doing so they serve as a form of capital—that is, social capital.

From a related perspective, friendships serve as social capital for individuals. Recent research based on a database of over 20 billion friendships on Facebook reveals that living in a community with a high rate of friendships across socioeconomic (SES) strata is one of the strongest identifiable influences on upward mobility among lower income individuals (Chetty et al., 2022). We typically refer to our American system as a meritocracy based on talent, intelligence, and skills. However, research demonstrates that people skills (i.e., relational capacities) are actually a strong influence on academic achievement and success. Although the adage that "it's who you know, not what you know" is often taken cynically to indicate that cronyism trumps individual merit; it is also true that simply being a nice person and having a range of friendships is a key ingredient for success in life. Data from the Fast Track project have shown that kindergarten teacher ratings about whether a child is nice predicts educational attainment, employment, imprisonment, and use of welfare supports 20 years later (Jones, Greenberg, & Crowley, 2015). Of course, in this type of research, scholars don't use the term "nice" (or the word my grandparents used, "mensch"). Rather, the common term for nice in the literature is "social-emotional competence." Social-emotional competence is measured by teacher or parent items that assess a child's ability to make friends, share, and get along with others—personality dimensions that comprise common decency and make one, in effect, a nice person.

The reason that niceness matters is that social relationships are a key factor in achieving academic and work success. Friends provide positive role models, encouragement, and advice. Friends can tell you what the homework was that you forget to write down, cue you to prepare for a test, tell you how to sign up for standardized tests, start you thinking about going to college, and help shape positive life goals. Friends can also connect one to job opportunities, whether an afterschool part-time job or later a career-advancing opportunity. On the other hand, friends can distract you from schoolwork; convey negative, undermining attitudes; or tempt you into risky behaviors that lead to punitive consequences and unsuccessful trajectories. In *Learning to Labour*, Paul Willis (1978) showed in detail how friends in a British underclass context created and reinforced an oppositional subculture that provides support and self-esteem to each other, but results in failure to succeed in school and career.

Social capital can be conceptualized in different ways. The approach taken by Chetty et al. (2022) in examining predictors of social mobility was to focus on "bridging social capital," that is, connections to higher income peers. They found that the proportion of friendships in a community across SES strata are highly predictive of overall social mobility. However, other forms of social capital—cohesive, dense personal networks of friends and civic engagement—were not closely related to upward mobility. However, these forms of social capital have been linked with other outcomes. Cohesive friendship groups are linked with health, for example, in other research.

Against this background, it was of interest in our PROSPER work when we noticed dimensions of social capital in specific dyadic, group, and network-wide relations and dynamics of adolescent friendships. In much of this research, we did not explicitly consider the life trajectory implications of cohesive friendships, diversity of friendship pairings versus homophily, and so forth. But from a social capital perspective, our findings take on new importance in illuminating how certain groups and individuals flourish or not, how inequality is reproduced, and how certain events and decisions lead to future trajectories. I summarize some of the findings here in order to bring them together for consideration, and then I make recommendations about future research and the potential for new forms of supportive intervention for children and adolescents.

SOCIAL CAPITAL IN PROSPER PEERS

Financial status. We found that low-income youth—as measured by free or reduced-lunch status—had relatively fewer friendship connections than nonpoor youth. Given the potential for friendships to provide both emotional support and instrumental assistance in academic and occupational success, lower levels of friendships among less well-off youth may be an avenue through which deprivation is reproduced across generations.

Race and gender. Corresponding to both popular ideas about gender differences and other research, in general, girls received more friendship nominations than boys, and girls had more reciprocal friendships than boys. Thus, adolescent girls lived more socially embedded lives than boys. However, we also found that the same social experiences may have very different meanings—at least different social consequences—for youth, depending on gender. For example, we found a gendered double standard that may make girls more vulnerable to a downside of social relations: rejection. Girls who had sex were more likely to experience a decrease in number of friends, while boys who had sex were more likely to see an increase in friendship nominations. Thus, sexual debut in adolescence may have opposite social capital implications—and thus life trajectory implications—for boys and girls.

We found a similar difference in social consequences for arrest or suspension across white and nonwhite youth. First, nonwhite youth (in our majority white schools) had fewer friendships on average than white youth. Then, exacerbating that difference, we found that arrest or suspension was linked to greater declines in friendships for nonwhite youth than white youth. In this case, the findings suggest a complicated dynamic involved in the social reproduction of inequality. Experiencing arrest or suspension—which occurs more frequently for nonwhite than white youth in society generally—had more negative impacts on nonwhite adolescents' social integration, social capital, and, presumably, future life success.

Mental health. Depression has long been understood to be reflected in reduced motivation for and ability to sustain social relations. Indeed, we found that at the group level, overall levels of depressive symptoms among members of a friendship group were related to relatively lower levels of connection and integration of the group. Thus, the social experiences of those with mental health problems may further reinforce and exacerbate tendencies toward isolation. In addition to the opportunities and influences friends provide in terms of schooling and jobs, as mentioned above, we also found that friends connect adolescents to friends' parents. Thus, the lower levels of cohesive friendships found for youth with mental health problems also reduce the likelihood of contact with potentially supportive adults. Further, we found that depressive symptoms may create an increased vulnerability toward substance use though an enhanced motivation to use substances to be "cool." Adolescent substance use that is initiated in the hopes of gaining greater social status and more friends can unfortunately take on a life of its own, as substance use alters brain chemistry, leading to craving and dependence.

Alcohol. The role of alcohol in socializing became quite clear in our research. Although underage alcohol use is illegal and linked to other risky behaviors and poor outcomes, alcohol use is also associated with positive features. In society, when not abused, alcohol use is associated with socializing. Alcohol is frequently enjoyed in social situations with coworkers and can be seen as a potent force facilitating greater social connection, enjoyment, social integration with consequences for friendship formation, and emotional and instrumental support. Similarly, despite its illegal status and risks during adolescence, we found that alcohol use appears linked to socializing and social integration among adolescents.

Preventive intervention. As PROSPER was designed as an experimental study of a prevention program, we were able to observe the ways that participation in the family component of the intervention—with an uptake of less than 20% of student's families—affected participating youth and their friends. Kelly Rulison's graduate thesis examined these diffusion pathways and found that the effects of the family intervention did diffuse to nonparticipating friends in a dose-response manner. Thus, friendships, we found, not only linked an individual to other peers (e.g., dating someone from a different part of the school network linked one to the influence of the romantic partner's friends) and other adults (e.g., the parents of friends), but also the health-promoting effects of organized school and community programs. Typically, prevention and intervention researchers are loathe to see diffusion as this can represent "contamination" of our research designs—the influence of an intervention on control condition individuals via contact with intervention condition individuals. In PROSPER, randomization at the community level removed our concern with contamination processes, and instead we were very happy to see Kelly's results indicating that, despite low levels of participation, programs can have wider effects on youth via diffusion processes. In terms of social capital, this leads to the idea that one can benefit from the positive, health-promoting experiences of friends, and thus the exposures of friends to such programs form a kind of shared social capital.

Genetic factors. Apart from the social dynamics discussed above, there is also a question of why certain individuals are capable of upward mobility, greater mental health and well-being, and ability to enjoy more integrated friendship circles than other individuals. Almost all behaviors and outcomes, from personality to parenting quality to health conditions, have been found to be influenced by both genes and environmental experiences—often in complex ways. Here, I mention some of the genetic findings from our PROSPER work, not to dismiss the complexities of development or ignore environmental influences, but as an illustration of some of the ways that individual characteristics influence individual trajectories. Genes have the advantage of being relatively discrete units of information, in contrast to environments (e.g., parent or sibling relations), which are complex, changing, multilayer phenomenon that we try to capture through snapshots with measures like questionnaires or observations.

Although considerable research has explored the ways that certain genes are related to substance use, our work helped expand the smaller body of research on how genes intersect with social dynamics around risky behaviors and substance use. For example, we found that an index of three genetic factors related to three different neurotransmitter systems was related to the similarity of an adolescent and their friends' level of conduct problems. These three factors have been linked to various kinds of sensitivity to social relations, and the finding may suggest that such genetic factors provide a cumulative sensitivity to peer influence. Such a sensitivity can be beneficial for youth when a friend exhibits prosocial behaviors, but can also lead to poor outcomes when a friend exhibits antisocial or risky behaviors and attitudes.

In research on single genes, we found that the effects of the PROSPER substance use prevention programs differed based on the oxytocin genetic variant: The intervention condition youth with the variant associated with lower oxytocin sensitivity showed relatively less affiliation (i.e., compared with similar control condition youth) with substance-using youth. In other words, it appeared that the intervention was able to have a greater impact on youth (i.e., encouraging them to have more distance from peers with more substance use) whose genetic factors were associated with a lower sensitivity to oxytocin and thus lower sensitivity to social affiliation in general. As oxytocin is related to social connection, bonding, and affiliation, the implication is that the intervention had more difficulty encouraging youth with greater social sensitivities to distance from substance-using peers. Although we are far from comfortable with the idea of utilizing genes to assign youth to particular programs in the prevention field, one implication is that youth with greater social sensitivities may require more intensive intervention, or a slightly different intervention strategy, to avoid affiliating with substance-using peers.

CONCLUSION

An investigation of social capital processes in adolescent peer networks may represent an important new way forward in research and intervention around healthy development. A focus on enhancing social-emotional competencies from early childhood on, facilitating healthy social relationships, would provide considerable support for many youth during the difficult years of adolescence. Such efforts may also help counter the reproduction of inequality that takes place through a complex of economic, social, and academic/school processes. Programs facilitating social-emotional competence exist, but more policies (e.g., countering tracking and sorting in schools and communities) and programs can be developed, tested, and, most importantly, funded and implemented.

The large number of authors and coauthors of the chapters of this volume have contributed to the social-capital findings summarized above and of course to many other findings described throughout the volume. The social capital of our peer network research team was seeded by the original PROSPER investigators, nurtured by funding from Penn State, W.T. Grant, and NIDA, and cultivated over 15 years under the leadership of Wayne Osgood. I trust that the social and intellectual capital of this research network will continue to expand as we find new ways to advance knowledge of adolescent development, leading ultimately to better and stronger ways to promote the health and well-being of adolescents and communities.

REFERENCES

Bell, D. (1973). *The coming of post-industrial society: A venture in social forecasting.* Basic Books.

Chetty, R., Jackson, M. O., Kuchler, T., Stroebel, J., Hendren, N., Fluegge, R. B., Gong, S., Gonzalez, F., Grondin, A., Jacob, M., Johnston, D., Koenen, M., Laguna-Muggenburg,

E., Mudekereza, F., Rutter, T., Thor, N., Townsend, W., Zhang, R., Bailey, M., . . . Wernerfelt, N. (2022). Social capital I: Measurement and associations with economic mobility. *Nature*, *608*, 108–121. https://doi.org/10.1038/s41586-022-04996-4

Jones, D. E., Greenberg, M., & Crowley, M. (2015). Early social-emotional functioning and public health: The relationship between kindergarten social competence and future wellness. *American Journal of Public Health*, *105*(11):2283–2290. https://doi.org/10.2105/AJPH.2015.302630.

Willis, P. (1978). *Learning to labour*. Ashgate Publishing Limited.

APPENDIX

PART 1: PUBLICATIONS OF THE PROSPER PEERS PROJECT

As of July 2022

2010
Moody, J., Feinberg, M. E., Osgood, D. W., & Gest, S. D. (2010). Mining the network: Peers and adolescent health. *Journal of Adolescent Health*, 47, 324–326. https://doi.org/10.1016/j.jadohealth.2010.07.027

2011
Gest, S. D., Osgood, D. W., Feinberg, M. E., Bierman, K. L., & Moody, J. (2011). Strengthening prevention program theories and evaluations: Contributions from social network analysis. *Prevention Science*, 12(4), 349–360. https://doi.org/10.1007%2Fs11121-011-0229-2

Kreager, D. A., Rulison, K. L., & Moody, J. (2011). Delinquency and the structure of adolescent peer groups. *Criminology*, 49(1), 61–94. https://doi.org/10.1111/j.1745-9125.2010.00219.x

Moody, J., Brynildsen, W. D., Osgood, D. W., & Feinberg, M. E. (2011). Popularity trajectories and substance use in early adolescence. *Social Networks*, 33(2), 101–112. https://doi.org/10.1016/j.socnet.2010.10.001

2012
Cleveland, M. J., Feinberg, M. E., Osgood, D. W., & Moody, J. (2012). Do peers' parents matter? A new link between positive parenting and adolescent substance use. *Journal of Studies on Alcohol and Drugs*, 73, 423–433. https://doi.org/10.15288/jsad.2012.73.423

Kreager, D. A., Haynie, D. L., & Hopfer, S. (2013). Dating and substance use in adolescent peer networks: A replication and extension. *Addiction*, 108, 638–647. https://doi.org/10.1111/j.1360-0443.2012.04095.x

Siennick, S. E., & Osgood, D. W. (2012). Hanging out with which friends? Friendship-level predictors of unstructured and unsupervised socializing in adolescence. *Journal of Research on Adolescence, 22*(4), 646–661. https://doi.org/10.1111/j.1532-7795.2012.00812.x

2013

Osgood, D. W., Feinberg, M. E., Gest, S. D., Moody, J., Ragan, D. T., Spoth, R., Greenberg, M., & Redmond, C. (2013). Effects of PROSPER on the influence potential of prosocial versus antisocial youth in adolescent friendship networks. *Journal of Adolescent Health, 53*, 174–179. https://doi.org/10.1016/j.jadohealth.2013.02.013

Osgood, D. W., Ragan, D. T., Wallace, L., Gest, S. D., Feinberg, M. E., & Moody, J. (2013). Peers and the emergence of alcohol use: Influence and selection processes in adolescent friendship networks. *Journal of Research on Adolescence, 23*(3), 500–512. https://doi.org/10.1111/jora.12059

Smith, J. A., & Moody, J. (2013). Structural effects of network sampling coverage I: Nodes missing at random. *Social Networks, 35*, 652–668. https://doi.org/10.1016/j.socnet.2013.09.003

2014

Molloy, L. E., Gest, S. D., Feinberg, M. E., & Osgood, D. W. (2014). Emergence of mixed-sex friendship groups during adolescence: Developmental associations with substance use and delinquency. *Developmental Psychology, 50*(11), 2449–2461. https://doi.org/10.1037/a0037856

Osgood, D. W., Feinberg, M. E., Wallace, L. N., & Moody, J. (2014). Friendship group position and substance use. *Addictive Behaviors, 39*, 923–933. https://doi.org/10.1016/j.addbeh.2013.12.009

Ragan, D. T. (2014). Revisiting "what they think": Adolescent drinking and the importance of peer beliefs. *Criminology, 52*(3), 488–513. https://doi.org/10.1111/1745-9125.12044

Ragan, D. T., Osgood, D. W., & Feinberg, M. E. (2014). Bridge to parental influence: Implications for adolescent alcohol use. *Social Forces, 92*(3), 1061–1085. https://doi.org/10.1093/sf/sot117

Rulison, K. L., Gest, S. D., & Osgood, D. W. (2015). Adolescent peer networks and the potential for the diffusion of intervention effects. *Prevention Science, 16*, 133–144. https://doi.org/10.1007/s11121-014-0465-3

Rulison, K. L., Kreager, D. A., & Osgood, D. W. (2014). Delinquency and peer acceptance in adolescence: A within-person test of Moffitt's hypotheses. *Developmental Psychology, 50*(11), 2437–2448. https://doi.org/10.1037/a0037966

2015

Osgood, D. W., Feinberg, M. E., & Ragan, D. T. (2015). Social networks and the diffusion of adolescent problem behavior: Reliable estimates of selection and influence from 6th through 9th grade. *Prevention Science, 16*(6), 832–843. https://doi.org/10.1007/s11121-015-0558-7

Rulison, K., Feinberg, M., Gest, S. D., & Osgood, D. W. (2015). Diffusion of intervention effects: The impact of a family-based substance use prevention program on friends of participants. *Journal of Adolescent Health*, 57(4), 433–440. https://doi.org/10.1016/j.jadohealth.2015.06.007

Siennick, S. E., Widdowson, A. O., Woessner, M., & Feinberg, M. E. (2016). Internalizing symptoms, peer substance use, and substance use initiation. *Journal of Research on Adolescence*, 26(4), 645–657. https://doi.org/10.1111/jora.12215

2016

Kreager, D. A., Molloy, L. E., Moody, J., & Feinberg, M. (2016). Friends first? The peer network origins of adolescent dating. *Journal for Research on Adolescence*, 26(2), 257–269. https://doi.org/10.1111/jora.12189

Kreager, D. A., Ragan, D. T., Nguyen, H., & Staff, J. (2016). When onset meets desistance: Cognitive transformation and adolescent marijuana experimentation. *Journal of Developmental and Life Course Criminology*, 2(2), 135–161. https://doi.org/10.1007/s40865-016-0032-7

Kreager, D. A., Staff, J., Gauthier, R., Lefkowitz, E. S., & Feinberg, M. E. (2016). The double standard at sexual debut: Gender, sexual behavior and early adolescent peer acceptance. *Sex Roles*, 75, 377–392. https://doi.org/10.1007/s11199-016-0618-x

Ragan, D. T. (2016). Peer beliefs and smoking in adolescence: A longitudinal social network analysis. *American Journal of Drug and Alcohol Abuse*, 42(2), 222–230. https://doi.org/10.3109/00952990.2015.1119157

2017

Copeland, M., Bartlett, B., & Fisher, J. C. (2017). Dynamic associations of network isolation and smoking behavior. *Network Science*, 5(3), 257–277. https://doi.org/10.1017/nws.2017.9

Siennick, S. E., Widdowson, A. O., & Ragan, D. T. (2017). New students' peer integration and exposure to deviant peers: Spurious effects of school moves? *Journal of Early Adolescence*, 37(9), 1254–1279. https://doi.org/10.1177/0272431616659563

Siennick, S. E., Widdowson, A. O., Woessner, M., Feinberg, M. E., & Spoth R. (2017). Risk factors for substance misuse and adolescents' symptoms of depression. *Journal of Adolescent Health*, 60(1), 50–56. https://doi.org/10.1016/j.jadohealth.2016.08.010

Wesche, R., Lefkowitz, E. S., Kreager, D. A., & Siennick, S. E. (2017). Early sexual initiation and mental health: A fleeting association or enduring change? *Journal of Research on Adolescence*, 27(3), 611–627. https://doi.org/10.1111/jora.12303

2018

Cleveland, H. H., Griffin, A. M., Wolf, P. S. A., Wiebe, R. P., Schlomer, G. L., Feinberg, M. E., Greenberg, M. T., Spoth, R. L., Redmond, C., & Vandenbergh,

D. J. (2018). Transactions between substance use intervention, the oxytocin receptor (OXTR) gene, and peer substance use predicting youth alcohol use. *Prevention Science, 19*(1), 15–26. https://doi.org/10.1007/s11121-017-0749-5

Copeland, M., Fisher, J. C., Moody, J., & Feinberg, M. E. (2018). Different kinds of lonely: Dimensions of isolation and substance use in adolescence. *Journal of Youth and Adolescence, 47*(8), 1755–1770. https://doi.org/10.1007/s10964-018-0860-3

Felmlee, D., McMillan, C., Rodis, P., & Osgood, D. W. (2018). Falling behind: Lingering costs of the high school transition for youth friendships and GPA. *Sociology of Education, 91*(2), 158–182. https://doi.org/10.1177/0038040718762136

Felmlee, D. H., McMillan, C., Rodis, P. I., & Osgood, D. W. (2018). The evolution of youth friendship networks from 6th to 12th grade: School transitions, popularity and centrality. In D. F. Alwin, D. H. Felmlee, & D. A. Kreager (Eds.), *Social networks and the life course: Integrating the development of human lives and social relational networks* (pp. 161–184). Springer.

Fisher, J. C. (2018). Exit, cohesion, and consensus: social psychological moderators of consensus among adolescent peer groups. *Social Currents, 5*(1), 49–66. https://doi.org/10.1177/2329496517704859

McMillan, C., Felmlee, D., & Osgood, D. W. (2018). Peer influence, friend selection, and gender: How network processes shape adolescent smoking, drinking, and delinquency. *Social Networks, 55*, 86–96. https://doi.org/10.1016/j.socnet.2018.05.008

Rulison, K. L., Gest, S. D., Feinberg, M., & Osgood, D. W. (2018). Impact of school-based prevention programs on friendship networks and the diffusion of substance use and delinquency. In D. F. Alwin, D. H. Felmlee, & D. A. Kreager (Eds.), *Social networks and the life course: Integrating the development of human lives and social relational networks* (pp. 453–475). Springer.

Temkin, D. A., Gest, S. D., Osgood, D. W., Feinberg, M. E., & Moody, J. (2018). Social network implications of normative school transitions in non-urban school districts. *Youth and Society, 50*(4), 462–484. https://doi.org/10.1177/0044118X15607164

2019

Copeland, M., Siennick, S. E., Feinberg, M. E., Moody, J., & Ragan, D. T. (2019). Social ties cut both ways: Self-harm and adolescent peer networks. *Journal of Youth and Adolescence, 48*, 1506–1518. https://doi.org/10.1007/s10964-019-01011-4

Fisher, J. C. (2019). Social space diffusion: Applications of a latent space model to diffusion with uncertain ties. *Sociological Methodology, 49*(1), 258–294. https://doi.org/10.1177/0081175018820075

Wesche, R., Kreager, D. A., Feinberg, M. E., & Lefkowitz, E. S. (2019). Peer acceptance and sexual behaviors from adolescence to young adulthood. *Journal of Youth and Adolescence, 48*, 996–1008. https://doi.org/10.1007/s10964-019-00991-7

Wesche, R., Kreager, D. A., & Lefkowitz, E. S. (2019). Sources of social influence on adolescents' alcohol use. *Journal of Research on Adolescence, 29*(4), 984–1000. https://doi.org/10.1111/jora.12439

2020

Hoeben, E. M., Osgood, D. W., Siennick, S. E., & Weerman, F. M. (2020). Hanging out with the wrong crowd? The role of unstructured socializing in adolescents' specialization in delinquency and substance use. *Journal of Quantitative Criminology, 37*, 141–177. https://doi.org/10.1007/s10940-019-09447-4

Jacobsen, W. (2020). School punishment and interpersonal exclusion: Rejection, withdrawal, and separation from friends. *Criminology, 58*(1), 35–69. https://doi.org/10.1111/1745-9125.12227

Ragan, D. T. (2020). Similarity between deviant peers: Developmental trends in influence and selection. *Criminology, 58*(2), 336–359. https://doi.org/10.1111/1745-9125.12238

Siennick, S., & Picon, M. (2020). Adolescent internalizing symptoms and the "tightknittedness" of friendship groups. *Journal of Research on Adolescence, 30*(S2), 391–402. https://doi.org/10.1111/jora.12484

Siennick, S. E., Widdowson, A. O., & Feinberg, M. E. (2020). Youth with co-occurring delinquency and depressive symptoms: Do they have better or worse delinquent outcomes? *Journal of Youth and Adolescence, 49*, 1260–1276. https://doi.org/10.1007/s10964-020-01213-1

Widdowson, A. O., Ranson, J. W. A., Siennick, S. E., Rulison, K. L., & Osgood, D. W. (2020). Exposure to persistently delinquent peers and substance use onset: A test of Moffitt's social mimicry hypothesis. *Crime & Delinquency, 66*(3), 420–445. https://doi.org/10.1177/0011128719869190

2021

Copeland, M. (2021). The long shadow of peers: Adolescent networks and young adult mental health. *Social Sciences, 10*(6), 231–243. https://doi.org/10.3390/socsci10060231

Hoeben, E. M., Rulison, K. L., Ragan, D. T., & Feinberg, M. E. (2021). Moderators of friend selection and influence in relation to adolescent alcohol use. *Prevention Science, 22*, 567–578. https://doi.org/10.1007/s11121-021-01208-9

McMillan, C., & D. R. Schaefer. (2021). Comparing targeting strategies for network-based adolescent drinking interventions: A simulation approach. *Social Science & Medicine, 282*, 114136. https://doi.org/10.1016/j.socscimed.2021.114136

2022

Jacobsen, W. C., Ragan, D. T., Yang, M., Nadel, E. L., & Feinberg, M. E. (2022). Arrested friendships? Justice involvement and interpersonal exclusion among rural youth. *Journal of Research in Crime and Delinquency, 59*(3), 365–409. https://doi.org/10.1177/00224278211048942

LoBraico, E. J., Fosco, G. M., Fang, S., Spoth, R. L., Redmond, C., & Feinberg, M. E. (2022). Collateral benefits of evidence-based substance use prevention programming during middle-school on young adult romantic relationship functioning. *Prevention Science, 23*, 618–629. https://doi.org/10.1007/s11121-021-01332-6

McMillan, C. (2022). Worth the weight: Conceptualizing and measuring strong versus weak tie homophily. *Social Networks, 68*, 139–147. https://doi.org/10.1016/j.socnet.2021.06.003

Osgood, D. W., Ragan, D. T., Dole, J. L., & Kreager, D. A. (2022). Similarity of friends versus nonfriends in adolescence: Developmental patterns and ecological influences. *Developmental Psychology, 58*(7), 1386–1401. https://doi.org/10.1037/dev0001359

Ragan, D. T., Osgood, D. W., & Kreager, D. A. (2022). Impulsivity, peers, and delinquency: A dynamic social network approach. *Journal of Quantitative Criminology.* https://doi.org/10.1007/s10940-022-09547-8

Ragan, D. T., Osgood, D. W., Ramirez, N., Moody, J., & Gest, S. D. (2022). A comparison of peer influence estimates from SIENA stochastic actor-based models and from conventional regression approaches. *Sociological Methods and Research, 51*(1), 357–395. https://doi.org/10.1177/0049124119852369

2023

Freelin, B. N., McMillan, C., Felmlee, D., & Osgood, D. W. (2023). Changing contexts: A quasi-experiment examining adolescent delinquency and the transition to high school. *Criminology, 61*(1), 40–73.

Tinney, E. (2023). Investigating the "STICKINESS" of stigma following a friend's police contact. *Criminology, 61*(2), 354–383.

Appendix

PART 2: PROSPER PEERS PROJECT PERSONNEL

Personnel were affiliated with Pennsylvania State University (PSU) unless otherwise noted.

Planning and proposal phase investigators

Wayne Osgood, Principal Investigator
Mark Feinberg, Co-Principal Investigator
Karen Bierman
Scott Gest
James Moody, Ohio State University

Phase 1 investigators

Wayne Osgood, Principal Investigator
Mark Feinberg, Co-Principal Investigator
Scott Gest
Derek Kreager
James Moody, Ohio State University and Duke University

Phase 2 investigators

Lead team
Wayne Osgood, Principal Investigator
Mark Feinberg, Co-Principal Investigator
Scott Gest
Derek Kreager
James Moody, Duke University
Sonja Siennick, Florida State University

Additional investigators
Diane Felmlee
Eva Lefkowitz
Daniel Ragan, University of New Mexico
Kelly Rulison, University of North Carolina Greenborough and PSU
David Schaefer, Arizona State University and University of California, Irvine

Graduate assistants

A large share of graduate assistants continued their involvement in PROSPER Peers after completing their degrees and taking permanent positions.

Pennsylvania State University
Doug Baals
Evelien Hoeben (visiting from the Netherlands Institute for the Study of
    Crime and Law Enforcement and the Vrije Universiteit Amsterdam)
Alyssa Howard-Tripp
Wade Jacobsen
Cassie McMillan
Lauren Molloy Elreda
Daniel Ragan
Nayan Ramirez
Kelly Rulison
Sonja Siennick
Deborah Temkin
Liann Tucker
Lacey Wallace
Rose Wesche
April Woolnough

Duke University
Wendy Brynildsen
Molly Copeland
Jake Fisher
Robin Gautier
Jaemin Lee

Florida State University
Mayra Picon
Alex Widdowson
Mathew Woessner

University of North Carolina, Greensboro
Kelly Massengale

University of New Mexico
Jenna Dole

University of Maryland
Erin Tinney

Postdoctoral researchers

Michael Cleveland
Angela Henneberger
Suellen Hopfer

INDEX

For the benefit of digital users, indexed terms that span two pages (e.g., 52–53) may, on occasion, appear on only one of those pages

Tables and figures are indicated by *t* and *f* following the page number

abstraction, interpreted, 337
academic partnerships, 335
actors at distance two, 339
Add Health. *See* National Longitudinal Study of Adolescent to Adult Health
adjacency matrix, 70*f*, 70–71
adolescent development, 25–26
    research review, 326–52
    social capital and, 353–60
adolescent health, 220–22, 341
    challenges, 319
    future directions for research, 315–25
    mental health, 173–75, 183–84
    risk behaviors, 225–28
    sexual health, 228–30, 236–37
adolescents. *See also* youth
    alcohol use, 114
    arrests of, 149–53, 156*f*, 156–60, 163–66
    at-risk, 266–67
    behavior of, 103–7
    cigarette smoking, 114
    competencies, 51
    disconnected kids, 75
    friendships, 3–33, 113–45, 191–93, 223–24, 230–36 (*see also* friends and friendships)
    marijuana use, 52, 53*f*, 114
    mental health of, 173–75, 183–84
    networks, 103–7
    new generation, 341
    parents of, 57, 191–94, 196
    peer acceptance, 228–30
    peer groups, 3–33
    peer relations, 294–97
    peers, 8–9, 173–75

    problem behavior, 51–54, 53*f*, 248–51
    PROSPER youth, 146, 147*f*
    risky behavior, 8, 9–10
    romantic relationships, 223–24
    sexual double standards, 224–25
    sexual minority, 219, 221–22, 230–36
    subcultures, 130
    substance use, 51–54, 53*f*, 113–45, 122*f*, 190–217
    susceptibility to peer influence, 193–94
    who positively influence their friends, 196
Adolescent Transitions Program (ATP), 48
adults, other, 339
Alcoholics Anonymous, 265, 268
alcohol use
    adolescent, 114
    choosing friends who drink, 124
    community-level variation, 257–59, 258*t*
    drinking behavior, 226
    emergence of, 123–24
    friends and, 133*f*–37*f*, 136
    friendship groups and, 128*f*, 129, 132, 133*f*, 134
    friendship nominations and, 159
    friendship selection and, 122*f*, 122–23, 124
    measures of drinking, 253
    parental knowledge and, 203–5, 204*f*, 207
    peer influence and, 122*f*, 122–24
    related behaviors and attitudes, 227
    risk factors for drinking, 123–24
    school-level variation, 257–59, 258*t*
    social capital and, 357
    social influence on, 227–28
    variation across networks, 255–57, 256*t*

All Stars, 48–49, 265
alteration interventions, 268
alter effects, 336
alter selection, 18f, 20f, 20–21
    community-level variation, 257–59, 258t
    across networks, 255–57, 256t
    positive, 20f, 20
    school-level variation, 257–59, 258t
analysis. *See also* network analysis
    levels of, 71–72
    longitudinal, 322
    progress, 321–22
antipathy, 335, 340
appropriate behavior, 237–38
archetypes, 69
Arnhem School Study, 328f, 330–33, 331t, 334f, 335
arrests
    of adolescents, 149–53, 156f, 156–60, 163–66
    and friendship ties, 150–52, 154–56, 157–60, 158t, 161t, 162f, 163–65
    prevalence of, 156f, 156–57, 163
    among PROSPER youth, 152–53, 162f, 163–64
    unofficial, 150, 165–66
assessment
    follow-up, 44f, 51–52
    high school, 45, 46t
    in-home, 43
    in-school survey, 44f
    intervention process, 45
    key constructs, measures, and indicators, 45, 46t
    post-high school, 45, 46t
    school, 43
assessment samples, 43–45
A Stop Smoking in Schools Trial (ASSIST), 318–19
ATP (Adolescent Transitions Program), 48
at-risk adolescents, 266–67
attitudes
    alcohol-related, 227
    social network variables and, 104–7, 105f
    substance use, 279
autonomy granting, 193–94

behavior. *See also* problem behavior
    adolescent, 103–7
    alcohol-related, 227
    appropriate, 237–38
    bundles of, 337
    cross-behavior influence, 337
    discrete choice model for, 79–80
    friends', 11–12
    initiation vs continuation of, 336
    measurement of, 11–12
    network models for, 70–83
    peer influence, 335–36
    PROSPER findings, 51–54, 53f
    PROSPER youth, 88–109
    risky, 104–7, 111–311
    romantic relationships and, 236–39
    sensation-seeking, 159
    sexual behaviors, 220–22, 228
    sexual identity and, 236–39
    social network variables and, 104–7, 105f
    substance misuse, 51–55, 53f
    types of influence, 336–38
behavioral genetics
    approaches to studying adolescent-peer relations, 294–97
    of heritability, 305
benchmarking systems, 49–50
betweenness centrality, 74–75
bias, attribution, 337–38
Bierman, Karen, 4, 6, 354–55
binary relations, 71
bisexuality, 232
Black youth, 148, 149, 151–52, 250
block models, 75
Bonacich power centrality, 74, 184, 185
The Breakfast Club, 319
bridging, 320–21, 321t
bridging individuals, 319
bullying, 335
bundles of behaviors, 337

Cambodian refugees, 354
capital, social
    and adolescent development, 353–60
    bridging, 194, 356
    and friendships, 355–56

Index

genetic factors, 358–59
  in PROSPER peers, 356–59
caregivers. *See* parents and parenting
casual sexual relationships, 220
centrality, 321
  betweenness, 74–75
  closeness, 74–75
  individual-level, 320–21, 321*t*
  power, 74–75, 184, 185
  problem behavior and, 270, 271*f*
centrality scores, 74, 75
centralization, 75
CES (Cooperative Extension System), 34, 36–37
CHALLENGE project, 341
change, 25–26
child development research, 326–52
Children of Immigrants Longitudinal Survey in four European Countries (CILS4EU), 328*f*, 330, 331*t*, 332–33, 334*f*, 335
cigarette smoking
  adolescent, 114
  among Black youth, 250
  community-level variation, 257–59, 258*t*
  European Smoking prevention Framework Approach (ESFA) study, 328*f*, 330–32, 331*t*, 335
  friends and, 133*f*, 136
  friendship groups and, 128*f*, 129, 132–34, 133*f*
  friendship selection and, 122*f*, 122–23
  interventions against, 318–19
  measures of, 253
  peer influence and, 122*f*, 122–23
  school-level variation, 257–59, 258*t*
  A Stop Smoking in Schools Trial (ASSIST), 318–19
  variation across networks, 255–57, 256*t*
  among white youth, 250
CILS4EU (Children of Immigrants Longitudinal Survey in four European Countries), 328*f*, 330, 331*t*, 332–33, 334*f*, 335
Classroom and Peer Ecologies data set, 328*f*, 330–32, 331*t*, 334*f*
clients, 38–39

cliques, 71–72, 319
closeness centrality, 74–75
coding, 93–94
coevolving networks, 339–40
cohesive groups, 71–72, 76–77
Coleman, James, 67–68
collective efficacy, 191–92, 195–96
collective parenting, 202–5
community(-ies), 254–55
  identification methods, 71–72
  peer network processes, 247–63, 256*t*, 258*t*
  racial and ethnic diversity, 250
competencies, adolescent, 51
complementarity, 338–39
completion rates, 89–91, 90*f*, 91*f*
complexity, 338–40
composition measures, 73
conduct problems, 54, 297
conflict resolution, 319
connections, 67–70, 126
contagion, 336
contamination, 286
continuation, 336
continuum-of-intervention approach, 57
contraceptive use, 320
convergence vs contagion, 336
coolness, 357
Cooperative Extension System (CES), 34, 36–37
cost-effectiveness, 56
cost-efficiency, 56
costs, day-of-implementation, 56
COVID-19, 68
criminal justice contact
  and friendship ties, 146–70
  methods of analysis, 154–56
  national trends, 146, 147*f*
  racial differences, 148
criminal justice system, 148
cronyism, 355–56
crossover effects, 56
crowds, 71–72, 249
cultural stereotypes, 164

data, nonindependent, 69–70
data collection, 43, 44*f*, 316–17

data sets most frequently used, 327–32,
    328f, 340–41
  characteristics, 331t
  sample sizes, 332–33
  time windows, 333–34, 334f
data structure, 70f, 70–71
dating, 218–46
day-of-implementation costs, 56
delinquency
  centrality and, 270, 271f
  community-level variation, 257–59, 258t
  friendship groups and, 132, 134
  friendship nominations and, 159
  measurement of, 104, 253
  prevalence of, 104–5, 106f
  school-level variation, 257–59, 258t
  variation across networks, 255–57, 256t
delinquent groups, 132
delinquent peers, 293–94
delinquent subculture, 130
demographics, 89–91
depression, 171–89
  analytical strategy, 180
  friends' average, 179–80
  new analyses, 178–79
  peer network position and, 181–83, 182t, 183t
  PROSPER Peers research on, 176–78
  social networks and, 183–84
  study measures, 179–80, 180t
  study methods, 179–80
  study results, 181–83
descriptive norms, 338
development, 25–26, 111–311
developmental change
  intervention-related pathways of, 40f, 40–41
  model for pathways of, 40f, 40–41
  in peer influence and friendship selection, 137–39, 139f
  in similarity of friends, 135–37
diathesis stress, 297–99, 298f
differential association theory, 9, 225–26
differential susceptibility theory, 297–99, 298f
diffusion of intervention outcomes, 286
  definition, 273
  mediators, 277, 284

peer networks and, 267–68, 272–77, 275f, 276f, 283
directed networks, 71
discipline
  consistent, 199, 201–2
  inconsistent, 203, 206
  parental, 207
disconnected kids, 75
discrete choice model
  for behavior, 79–80
  for network links, 78–79
distinctiveness, 338–39
dizygotic twins, 294–95
dopamine receptor D4 *(DRD4)*, 300–2, 305
double standards, sexual, 224–25, 237–38
DRD4 (dopamine receptor D4), 300–2, 305
drinking alcohol. *See* alcohol use
drug use. *See* substance use
dyadic difference model, 337–38

early adolescence
  Networks and Actor Attributes in Early Adolescence project, 328f, 330–32, 331t, 334f
  SNARE (Social Network Analysis of Risk behavior in Early adolescence), 4–5, 331t, 333, 334f, 335
  SNARE Genetics, 329
EBIs. *See* evidence-based interventions (EBIs)
e-cigarette use, 318–19
economic outcomes, 56
education systems, 38–40
ego networks, 71
ego selection, 18f, 20f, 20–21
  community-level variation, 257–59, 258t
  negative, 20f, 20
  across networks, 255–57, 256t
  school-level variation, 257–59, 258t
emerging adults
  problem behavior outcomes, 54–55
  samples, 43, 44f
  social network studies, 334
environmental risk factors, 297
epigenetics, 295
ERGMs (exponential random graph models), 321

ESFA (European Smoking prevention Framework Approach) study, 328*f*, 330–32, 331*t*, 335
ethnic diversity, 250
ethnic minorities, 254–55
European Smoking prevention Framework Approach (ESFA) study, 328*f*, 330–32, 331*t*, 334*f*
evidence-based interventions (EBIs), 34. *See also specific interventions*
  delivery systems, 36–37
  diffusion based in education systems, 38–40
  family-focused programs, 36, 48
  knowledge gaps, 37–38
  need for, 36
  partnership-based pathways across developmental phases, 40*f*, 40–41
  PROSPER program menu, 48–49
  school-based programs, 48–49
  sustained quality implementation, 50–51
  underutilized delivery infrastructures, 36–37
  youth-focused, 36
exponential random graph models (ERGMs), 321
external resource agents, 38–39

Facebook, 355–56
family-focused interventions, 48
  delivery systems, 36–37
  Iowa Strengthening Families Program (ISFP), 267–68
  need for, 36
  Strengthening Families Program: For Parents and Youth 10–14 (SFP 10–14), 48, 265, 272
family functioning, 51
Fast Track, 355–56
Feinberg, Mark, 4, 6
financial status, 356
FinEdu Study, 328*f*, 330–32, 331*t*, 334*f*, 335
follow-up assessment, 44*f*, 51–52
Freeman, Linton, 67–68
free or reduced-price lunch (FRL), 89, 91, 95
  delinquency and, 104–5, 106*f*
  group membership and, 100, 102*f*

friends and friendships. *See also* peers; social networks; teen friendship networks
  adolescent health risk behaviors and, 225–28
  adolescents who positively influence their friends, 196
  alcohol use and, 123–24, 133*f*, 136
  arrests and, 150–52, 154–56, 157–60, 158*t*, 161*t*, 162*f*, 163–64
  behavior of, 11–12, 255–57, 256*t*
  coevolution of, 340
  complementarity of, 338–39
  criminal justice contact and, 146–70
  depression in, 179–80
  developmental change in, 135–39, 139*f*
  distinctiveness of, 338–39
  facilitation of, 192
  formation of, 223–24
  of friends, 339
  group membership, 100–2, 101*f*–2*f*
  health risk behaviors and, 225–28
  homophily, 68–69, 99*f*, 99–100, 100*f*
  in-degree, 322
  influence from friends' parents, 194–96
  influence from what they think or what they do, 124–26
  measures of, 286
  methods of analysis, 154–56
  mixed-sex, 223, 224, 231
  nomination questions, 91–92
  number of nominations, 95–97, 96*f*
  number of ties, 94–97, 95*f*
  observing, 195
  opposite-sex, 223–24
  parents and, 197*t*, 198–202, 200*f*
  parents of friends, 194–96, 197*t*, 202–5, 207, 279
  positive influence on, 196
  PROSPER coding, 93–94
  PROSPER study findings, 59
  PROSPER youth, 108, 152–53
  quality of, 231–32
  reciprocity, 97, 98*f*
  risky behavior and, 105–7, 107*f*, 225–28
  romantic relationships and, 236–39
  same-sex, 233–35, 235*f*

friends and friendships (*cont.*)
   selection, 10–13, 18*f*, 18–22, 19*f*, 20*f*, 77–81, 120–23, 137–39, 191–93, 197*t*, 198–202, 200*f*, 251–52, 255–59, 256*t*, 258*t*, 293
   selection for substance use, 118–26, 122*f*
   self-harm in, 179–80
   sexual health and, 228–30
   sexual identity and, 236–39
   of sexual minority adolescents, 230–36, 237
   similarity of, 135–37
   social capital and, 355–56
   stability of ties, 97–99, 98*f*
   strength of, 120–23
   substance use and, 113–45, 137*f*, 190–217
   substance use attitudes, 279
   teen, 3–33, 113–45, 191–93, 223–24, 230–36
   time spent with, 231–32
   unsupervised time with, 199
Friendship and Identity in School study, 328*f*, 330, 331*t*, 334*f*, 335
friendship groups
   delinquent, 132
   position of, 127–29, 128*f*
   stability of, 131
   structural cohesion, 131
   structure of, 129–39, 133*f*
   substance use and, 126–34, 128*f*, 133*f*
FRL. *See* free or reduced-price lunch
functional magnetic resonance imaging (fMRI), 304
future directions
   for PROSPER, 57–59
   for research, 58, 208–9, 210, 283–84, 306–7, 315–25, 341–42

GABA receptor alpha 2 (*GABRA2*), 304, 305
gender-atypical sexual minority adolescents, 230–31
gender differences
   in adolescent substance use, 116, 117*f*
   in effects of arrest, 151–52, 155–56, 160, 161*t*, 162*f*, 164–65
   in prevalence of arrests, 163
   in social capital, 357
gene–environment correlations (*r*GE), 295–96
   active, 295–96
   evocative, 295–96
   passive, 295–96
gene–environment interactions (GxE), 295–96
gene-moderated effects, 56–57
generalized status, 74–75
genetic index of sensitivity, 304–5
genetic influence(s), 294–95
genetic studies
   of adolescent-peer relations, 294–97
   behavioral approaches, 294–97
   molecular approaches, 294–97, 307
   SNARE Genetics, 329
   of social capital, 358–59
genetic susceptibility, 293–311
genomic research, 306
genotypes, 295, 300–5, 307
Gest, Scott, 6
gossiping, 335
gPROSPER, 294, 296, 299–305, 306
Greenberg, Mark, 4, 353, 354–55
groups
   cohesive, 76–77
   friendship, 126–34
   membership in, 100–2, 101*f*–2*f*
   in networks, 23–24, 76–77
   substance use and, 126–34
Guiding Good Choices (formerly called Preparing for the Drug Free Years), 48

Harvard University, 67–68
health, 220–22, 341
   public, 58–59
   sexual, 228–30, 236–37
health behavior, 228
health challenges, 319
health promotion, 318–19, 320–21, 321*t*
health risk behaviors, 225–28
helping relationships, 335
heritability, 294–95, 305
heterosexuality, 232
high school assessment, 45, 46*t*

Hispanic youth, 148
home assessment samples, 43
homework, 335
homophily, 68–69, 99f, 99–100, 100f, 321
   change across adolescence, 135–36
   developmental change in, 138, 139f
homosexuality, 232
horizontal linkage, 39
hostile attribution bias, 337–38
5-HTTLPR (serotonin transporter-linked polymorphic region), C12P27, C12P30

identity, sexual, 221–22, 236–39
illicit drug use, 55
implementation quality, 50
impulsivity, 297
in-degree, 20–21, 72–73, 94–97
indices, 72–77
individual interventions, 268, 279–80, 281t, 282
individual positions, 22–23
individual susceptibility model, 337–38
induction interventions, 268
inductive reasoning, 203
influence
   adolescents who positively influence their friends, 196
   developmental change in, 137–39, 139f
   estimates of, 341–42
   individual characteristics of, 337–38
   measures of, 253–54
   network processes and, 251–52
   paths of, 14–15, 15f
   peer, 10–13, 14–17, 15f, 16f, 120–23, 122f, 137–39, 139f, 193–94, 201–2, 251–52, 335–36
   processes of, 201–2
   selection and, 10–13, 68–69, 201–2, 257–59, 258t
   susceptibility to, 337–38
   types of, 336–38
   varieties of, 15–17, 16f
influence potential, 269
in-home assessment samples, 43
initiation vs continuation, 336
innovation, 38–39

in-school survey assessment, 44f
INSNA (International Network for Social Network Analysis), 67–68
intergenerational closure, 194
internal capacity agents, 38–39
International Network for Social Network Analysis (INSNA), 67–68
interpreted abstraction, 337
intervention(s). *See also* evidence-based interventions (EBIs)
   alteration, 268
   for at-risk adolescents, 266–67
   continuum-of-intervention approach, 57
   design, 268, 279–83, 285
   and developmental change, 40f, 40–41
   diffusion of outcomes, 267–68, 272–77, 275f, 276f, 283, 286
   effectiveness of, 266–67
   evaluation of, 286
   family-focused, 36–37, 48
   future directions for research, 284
   implementation, 285–86
   individual, 268, 279–80, 281t, 282
   induction, 268
   mediators of outcomes, 277
   network, 283, 317–19
   network-based selection of participants for, 280–83, 281t
   partnership-based, 40f, 40–41, 45–49, 47f
   and peer networks, 265–86, 275f, 276f
   preventive, 358
   school-based, 268, 283–84, 320–21
   segmentation, 268, 279–80, 281t, 282–83
   selection of participants for, 280–83, 281t
   simulated, 280–82
   and social networks, 284
intervention groups, 266–67
intervention process assessment samples, 45
Iowa Strengthening Families Program (ISFP), 267–68

Journal of Research on Adolescence, 327

KiVa, 329–30, 332–33
KiVa NL, 328f, 329–30, 331t, 332–34, 334f, 335
knowledge gaps, 37–38
Kreager, Derek, 7–8

labeling theory, 9
language, 166, 218–19
leaders and leadership
  identification of, 318–20
  opinion leaders, 318–19
  peer leader networks, 319
leading crowds, 75
learning, social, 195
learning opportunities, 49
liaisons, 127, 128f, 129
LifeSkills Training, 48–49
local teams, 34–35, 47f, 47, 49–50
longitudinal analysis, 322
  data sets most frequently used, 327–32, 328f, 331t
  growth of, 326–52, 328f
low-income youth, 356

magnetic resonance imaging, functional (fMRI), 304
Manchester Youth Study, 328f, 330–33, 331t, 334f, 335
marijuana use
  adolescent, 52, 53f, 114
  emerging adulthood, 54
  friends and, 136, 137f
  friendship groups and, 128f, 129, 133f, 134
  friendship nominations and, 159
  PROSPER youth, 118f, 118
mediation, 319–21
mediators of diffusion, 277, 284
mental distress, 178
mental health
  of adolescents, 173–75, 183–84
  network position characteristics associated with distress, 178
  peers and, 173–75
  PROSPER youth, 175–79
  social capital and, 357
  social networks and, 174–75, 183–84

micropolitan areas, 249–50
Middle School and High School Diversity Project (UCLA), 4–5, 6
mixed-sex friendships, 223, 224, 231
moderation, 319–21
moderator variables, 296
molecular genetics, 294–97, 307
monitoring
  by friends' parents, 195–96
  parental, 195–96
monozygotic twins, 294–95
Moody, Jim, 6
moral approval, 125
morale, 251
multilevel models, 81–83

narcotic misuse, 52, 53f
National Institute on Drug Abuse (NIDA), 4, 7, 353
National Institutes of Health (NIH), 353
National Longitudinal Study of Adolescent to Adult Health (Add Health), 6, 219, 327–29
  characteristics, 331t
  longitudinal studies with, 327–29, 328f
  network questions, 335
  sample size, 332–33
  time window, 333–34, 334f
national trends, 146, 147f
negative ego selection, 20f, 20
neighborhoods
  adolescent problem behavior, 248–51
  collective efficacy, 191–92
nerds, 69
Netherlands Institute for the Study of Crime and Law Enforcement (NSCR), 4–5
network analysis. See also social network analysis
  basic methods, 70f, 70–83
  block models, 75
  connections vs positions, 67–70
  data structure, 70f, 70–71
  indices, 72–77
  levels of, 71–72
  models for youth behavior, 66–67
  multilevel models, 81–83

Index

progress, 321–22
summary, 83
network diffusion models, 336
network equivalence, 75
network interventions, 283. *See also* intervention(s)
   design, 268
   types, 268
networks. *See* peer networks; social networks; teen friendship networks
Networks and Actor Attributes in Early Adolescence project, 328*f*, 330–32, 331*t*, 334*f*
new generation adolescents, 341
niceness, 355–56
nonindependent data, 69–70

Ohio State University, 6
ongoing spin-off studies, 56–57
opinion leaders, 318–19
opposite-sex friendships, 223–24
Osgood, Wayne, 354–55
out-degree, 20–21, 72–73, 94–97
oxytocin receptor gene *(OXTR)*, 302–4, 305, 358–59

parental discipline, 207
parental knowledge, 199, 203–5, 204*f*, 206, 207
parental monitoring, 209
parents and parenting
   of adolescents, 57, 191–94
   of adolescents who positively influence their friends, 196
   collective, 202–5
   community-wide, 209
   empirical findings, 196–207, 197*t*
   of friends, 194–96, 197*t*, 202–5, 207, 279
   friendship facilitation by, 192
   friendship selection and, 191–93, 197*t*, 198–202, 200*f*
   future research, 208–9
   influence of, 339
   as mediators, 279
   monitoring by, 195–96
   peer management by, 192
   positive practices, 201–2
   role of, 190–217
   and substance use, 190–217, 197*t*
   and susceptibility to peer influence, 193–94
   and who adolescents select as friends, 191–93
partnership-based interventions
   across developmental phases, 40*f*, 40–41
   PROSPER system model and implementation, 45–49
   PROSPER system structure, 45–48, 47*f*
party culture, 130, 134
peer cluster theory, 9
peer groups, 3–33
peer influence model, 337–38
peer leader networks, 319
peer networks. *See also* social networks; teen friendship networks
   diffusion of intervention outcomes through, 267–68
   genetic approaches to study of, 294–97
   interventions and, 265–86, 275*f*, 276*f*
   measures of, 286
   mental health and, 174
   peer influence and, 251–52
   position in, 179, 181–83, 182*t*, 183*t*
   problem behavior and, 253–54, 255–61, 256*t*, 258*t*
   process variations, 247–63, 256*t*, 258*t*
   PROSPER data, 221
   PROSPER samples, 89–91
   school-cohort, 254
   selection of intervention participants based on, 280–83, 281*t*
   self-harm and, 185
   sexual identity and, 221–22
   of sexual minority youth, 221–22
peer opinion leaders, 318–19
peers. *See also* friends and friendships
   acceptance by, 228–30
   in adolescence, 8–9, 173–75, 193–94
   adolescents' susceptibility to peer influence, 193–94
   and alcohol use, 123–24
   Classroom and Peer Ecologies data set, 328*f*, 330–32, 331*t*, 334*f*
   conceptual framework, 10–26

peers (*cont.*)
  delinquent, 293–94
  developmental change in influence of, 137–39, 139*f*
  and friendship selection, 10–13, 118–26
  future research, 208–9
  genetic susceptibility to, 293–311
  and health behavior, 228
  influence of, 10–13, 201–2, 335–36
  management of, 192
  measures of influence, 253–54
  and mental health, 173–75
  network perspective on, 13–18
  network processes and influence of, 251–52
  parents and, 201–2, 208–9
  paths of influence, 14–15, 15*f*
  processes of influence, 201–2
  prosocial, 293–94
  PROSPER Peers research on, 15–17, 16*f*
  research on, 115–16
  and risky behavior, 9–10
  and sexual health, 228–30
  SIENA analysis of, 77–81
  South Korean Classroom Peer Ecology and Adolescent Development project, 328*f*, 330–32, 331*t*, 334*f*, 335
  strength of influence, 120–23, 122*f*
  and substance use, 113–45, 122*f*, 191–96, 197*t*
  susceptibility to, 300–5
  types of influence, 15–18, 16*f*, 336–38
Penn State University, 6, 7–8
perceived status, 335
person-centered language, 166
polygenic scores (PGSs), 306
popularity, 102–3, 184, 185, 322
popularity mobility, 102–3
popularity norms, 338
position(s), 74–75
  characteristics associated with mental distress, 178
  connections vs, 67–70, 126
  new analyses, 178–79
positive alter selection, 20*f*, 20
positive influence, 196
positive parenting practices, 201–2

positive relationships, 335
positive social expectations, 125
post–high school assessment, 45, 46*t*
poverty, 254–55, 257–59, 258*t*
power or status, 74–75
Preparing for the Drug Free Years (now called Guiding Good Choices), 48
prevention coordinator/TA providers, 49
prevention coordinator/TA provider teams, 47*f*, 47
preventive intervention, 358
PRIMS (PRIMary to Secondary education) project, 341
problem behavior
  adolescent, 51–54, 53*f*, 248–51
  and centrality, 270, 271*f*
  community-level variation, 257–59, 258*t*
  conduct problems, 54
  emerging adulthood, 54–55
  interventions for (*see* intervention[s])
  measures of, 253–54, 270, 278
  neighborhood context and, 248–51
  peer networks and, 253–54, 255–61, 256*t*, 258*t*
  school-level variation, 257–59, 258*t*
  schools and, 248–51
  similarity network effects, 253–54
  variation across networks, 255–57, 256*t*
problem behavior theory, 9
program development, 210
program implementation
  challenges and solutions, 49–50
  level of quality, 50
  supports for, 49
  sustained, 50–51
programs. *See* intervention(s)
Project Alert, 48–49, 265
prosocial peers, 293–94
PROSPER (Promoting School-community-university Partnerships to Enhance Resilience) Peers project, 3, 4–8, 113, 315, 326, 329, 354
  analytic progress, 321–22
  challenges and solutions, 49–50
  coding of friendship nominations, 93–94
  combined with screening-referral, 57

conceptual framework, 10–26, 22f
conceptual underpinnings, 38–41
core components, 45
crossover effects, 56
data set, 230, 331t, 353
day-of-implementation costs, 56
demographic characteristics, 89–91
design, 358
distal outcomes, 51–56
economic outcomes, 56
empirical findings, 196–207, 197t, 269–83
evidence-based menu, 48–49
findings, 50–57, 58–59, 88–109, 122f, 122–23, 128–29, 131–34, 136–37, 196–207, 197t, 223–36, 269–83, 358–59
focus, 353
friendship network data, 91–94
friendship network structure, 94–103
friendship nomination questions, 91–92
funding, 4, 7
future directions, 57–59
genetic extension (gPROSPER), 294, 296, 299–305, 306
genetic findings, 358–59
goals, 10, 35
groundwork, 42
hypotheses, 42
intervention outcome model, 40f, 40–41
key constructs and measures, 45, 46t
local teams, 34–35, 47f, 47
longitudinal studies with, 328f
mental health and networks, 175–79
methodological advantages, 119–20
network questions, 335
number of waves, 333
ongoing studies, 56–57
overview, 34–35
partnership-based delivery system, 45–49, 47f
peer network data, 221
personnel, 366–68
phases, 41–42
prevention coordinator/TA provider teams, 47f, 47
proximal outcomes, 51

publications, 361–66
research design, 5–6
research on depressive symptoms and self-harm, 176–78
research on genetic susceptibility to peers, 299–305
research on peer influence, 15–17
sample sizes, 89–91, 332–33
with screening, brief intervention, and referral to treatment (SBIRT) components, 57
significance and gaps addressed, 35–38
social capital, 356–59
spin-off studies, 56–57
state management teams, 47f, 47–48
study samples, 42–45
summary, 57–59
supports, 49
survey completion rates, 89–91, 90f, 91f
team, 6–8
time window, 333–34, 334f
trial design, 41–45
versions of networks, 19f, 19–20
youth social networks and behavior findings, 88–109
public health, 58–59
public schools, 36–37

quality
  friendship, 231–32
  level of, 50
  sustained implementation, 50–51

racial differences
  community-level diversity, 250
  in effects of arrest, 151–52, 155–56, 160, 161t, 164–65
  in prevalence of arrests, 163
  in social capital, 357
racial minorities, 254–55, 257–59, 258t
racism, 354
reciprocity, 231–32
  in PROSPER students' friendships, 97, 98f
  within-group, 131
recruitment, 50
Redmond, Cleve, 4

reference group theory, 9
refugees, 354
regular equivalence, 75
rejection, 146–48, 150–51
relationships, P2. *See also* friends and friendships
reproductive health campaigns, 320
research. *See also specific studies*
    future directions, 58, 208–9, 210, 283–84, 306–7, 315–25, 341–42
    genetic, 294–97
    genomic, 306
    key data sets and topics, 326–52
    on peer influence, 15–17, 16*f*
    on peers and substance use, 115–16
    PROSPER Peers, 15–17, 16*f*
    review, 326–52
    social network, 335–38
    unique possibilities, 335–38
resistance skills, 10
resource systems, 38–39
risky behavior, 111–311
    in adolescence, 8, 9–10
    and friendships, 105–7, 107*f*
    health risk behaviors, 225–28
    interventions for (*see* intervention[s])
    peers and, 9–10
    rationale for study of, 8–10
    school characteristics and, 251
    SNARE (Social Network Analysis of Risk behavior in Early adolescence), 4–5, 331*t*, 333, 334*f*, 335
    SNARE Genetics, 329
    social network variables and, 104–7, 107*f*
romance, 220–22
romantic behavior, appropriate, 237–38
romantic relationships, 218–19, 220–21, 236–39
    and adolescent health risk behaviors, 225–28
    coevolution of, 340
    formation of, 223–24
rSIENA program, 7–8, 321
Rulison, Kelly, 7–8
rural youth
    arrests, 150, 151–52, 163

criminal justice contact, 148, 149–50
need for family- and youth-focused EBIs, 36
peer networks and problem behavior, 257–59, 258*t*
population, 254–55
PROSPER data set, 230
sexual minority, 230

same-sex friendships, 233–35, 235*f*. *See also* friends and friendships
SAOMs (stochastic actor-oriented models), 252, 321, 327
school-based programs, 48–49, 268, 283–84, 320–21
school bonding, 255, 257–59, 258*t*
school districts, 254–55
    adolescent problem behavior, 250
    peer network processes, 247–63, 256*t*, 258*t*
    selection of, 42–43
    student suspensions, 251
School Project (NSCR), 4–5
schools
    adolescent problem behavior, 248–51
    adolescent risky behavior, 251
    assessment samples from, 43
    morale, 251
    peer networks and problem behavior, 257–61, 258*t*
    social networks, 66
    student suspensions, 153, 251
    student-teacher relationships, 251
school transitions, 255, 257–59, 258*t*
screening, brief intervention, and referral to treatment (SBIRT), 57
screening-referral, PROSPER plus, 57
second-generation effects, 57
segmentation interventions, 268, 279–80, 281*t*, 282–83
selection, friendship, 12–13, 18–22, 19*f*, 77–81, 251–52, 293
    alter, 18*f*, 20*f*, 20–21, 255–59, 256*t*, 258*t*
    developmental change in, 137–39, 139*f*
    ego, 18*f*, 20*f*, 20–21, 255–59, 256*t*, 258*t*
    estimates of, 341–42
    vs influence, 68–69

Index

and parents, 191–93, 197t, 198–202, 200f
and peers, 10–13, 118–26, 137–39
SIENA analysis of, 77–81
for similarity, 18f, 18–20
structural, 21–22
for substance use, 118–26, 122f
types of, 18f, 18
self-esteem, 337–38
self-harm, 171–89
analytical strategy, 180
of friends, 179–80
new analyses, 178–79
peer network position and, 181–83, 182t, 183t
PROSPER Peers research on, 176–78
social networks and, 183–84, 185
study measures, 179–80, 180t
study methods, 179–80
study results, 181–83
self-medication, 127
sensation-seeking behavior, 159
serotonin transporter (SLC6A4), 304
serotonin transporter-linked polymorphic region (5-HTTLPR), 304, 305
sex education programs, 319–20
sexual behavior(s), 220–22, 228
appropriate, 237–38
casual relationships, 220
sexual double standards, 224–25, 237–38
sexual health, 228–30, 236–37
sexual identity, 221–22, 236–39
sexuality, 218–46
sexually transmitted infections (STIs), 220
sexual minority adolescents and youth, 219, 222
friendships, 230–36, 234t, 235f, 237
gender-atypical, 230–31
peer networks, 221–22
in rural settings, 230
social integration, 222
sexual relationships, 220
sexual violence intervention, 318–19
SFP 10-14 (Strengthening Families Program: For Parents and Youth 10–14), 48, 265, 272
SIENA. See Simulation Investigation for Empirical Network Analysis

Siennick, Sonja, 7–8
similarity effects, 336
similarity selection, 18f, 18–20, 257–59, 258t
Simulation Investigation for Empirical Network Analysis (SIENA), 116, 322, 327, 342
analysis of friendship selection and peer influence processes with, 77–81
lessons learned, 80–81
with longitudinal data, 322
mathematical forms, 78–80
rSIENA, 7–8, 321
ways to improve, 341–42
SLC6A4 (serotonin transporter), 304
smartphone surveys, 333
smoking. See cigarette smoking
Snapmap, 341
SNARE (Social Network Analysis of Risk behavior in Early adolescence), 4–5
characteristics, 331t
longitudinal studies with, 328f
network questions, 335
number of waves, 333
time window, 334f
SNARE Genetics, 329
social capital
and adolescent development, 353–60
bridging, 194, 356
and friendships, 355–56
genetic factors, 358–59
in PROSPER peers, 356–59
social control theory, 127
social disorganization theory, 9
social-emotional competence, 355–56
social expectations, positive, 125
social integration
measures of, 274
of sexual minority youth, 222
social isolation, 75, 235–36
socialization
to cultural stereotypes, 164
unstructured socializing, 16f, 17–18, 103, 104f, 107f, 278–79
social learning, 195
social learning theory, 9

social network analysis, 67–68, 122. *See also specific studies by name*
    basic, 70*f*, 70–83
    block models, 75
    comparison of studies, 332–35
    composition measures, 73
    data sets most frequently used, 327–32, 328*f*, 331*t*, 340–41
    discrete choice model, 78–79
    in-degree, 20–21, 72–73, 94–97
    longitudinal, 326–52, 328*f*
    measures for, 72–75, 274–77, 276*f*
    network questions, 335
    number of waves, 333
    out-degree, 20–21, 72–73, 94–97
    positional metrics, 74–75
    progress, 321–22
    research possibilities, 335–38
    sample sizes, 332–33
    strategies available, 321
    strong vs weak components, 73–74
    studies of emerging adults, 334
    time windows, 333–34, 334*f*
    volume measures, 72–73
Social Network Analysis of Risk behavior in Early adolescence (SNARE). *See* SNARE (Social Network Analysis of Risk behavior in Early adolescence)
social networks. *See also* peer networks; teen friendship networks
    adolescent, 103–7
    characteristics of, 104–7, 105*f*
    coevolving, 339–40
    cohesive groups in, 76–77
    components of, 73–74
    composition of, 73
    conceptual framework, 10–26
    connections vs positions, 67–70
    depression and, 171–89
    development and change, 25–26
    directed, 71
    example, 13–15, 14*f*, 15*f*
    future directions for research, 284
    groups in, 23–24
    importance of, 68
    individuals' positions in, 22–23
    interventions and, 284
    mental health and, 174–79, 183–84
    methods, 66–87
    paths of influence, 14–15, 15*f*
    peer influence, 13–18
    positions in, 74–75, 178–79
    PROSPER youth, 19*f*, 19–20, 88–109, 175–79
    self-harm and, 171–89
    structure of, 174–75
    and substance use, 113–45
    theory of, 67–70
social norms, 338
Social Science Research Institute (SSRI), 6, 7
socioeconomic status (SES), 89, 91, 95
sociograms, 70*f*, 70–71
sociology, 248–49
sociometry, 67–68
South Korean Classroom Peer Ecology and Adolescent Development project, 328*f*, 330–32, 331*t*, 334*f*, 335
spin-off studies, 56–57
Spoth, Dick, 4, 353, 354–55
stability of friendship ties, 97–99, 98*f*
Stanford University, 67–68
state management teams, 47*f*, 47–48
statistical complications, 69–70
status, 74–75
    generalized, 74–75
    perceived, 335
stereotypes
    of arrested youth, 146–48, 150–51
    cultural, 164
    socialization to, 164
stigma, 146–48, 166
STIs (sexually transmitted infections), 220
stochastic actor-oriented models (SAOMs), 252, 321, 327
strain theory, 9, 127
Strengthening Families Program: For Parents and Youth 10–14 (SFP 10–14), 48, 265, 272
stress, diathesis, 297–99, 298*f*
structural equivalence, 75
structural selection, 21–22
students
    higher-risk participants, 43
    suspensions, 153, 251
    -teacher relationships, 251
subcultures, 130

Index

substance use
  adolescent, 51–54, 53f, 113–45, 122f, 190–217
  attitudes toward, 279
  and centrality, 270, 271f
  change across adolescence, 135–39
  diffusion through peer networks, 274, 275f
  emerging adulthood, 54–55
  friends and, 136, 137f, 236–37
  friendship context of, 190–217
  friendship groups and, 126–34, 128f
  friendship selection for, 118–26
  gender differences, 116
  onset of, 336
  parenting and, 190–217, 197t
  peer context of, 113–45, 122f, 191–96, 197t
  PROSPER youth, 116–18, 118f
  rates of, 116–18, 117f, 118f
  research on, 115–16
  resistance to, 10
  as self-medication, 127
  social networks and, 113–45
  teen friendships and, 113–45
suicide prevention interventions, 318–19
survey completion rates, 89–91, 90f, 91f
susceptibility, 337–38
suspension from school, 153, 251
sustained quality implementation, 50–51
Sutherland's differential association theory, 9
Swiss StudentLife Study, 334
symbolic interaction theory, 9

talking sticks, 285–86
technical assistance (TA), 34–35, 37, 49
  prevention coordinator/TA provider, 49
  prevention coordinator/TA provider teams, 47f, 47
Teenage Friends and Lifestyle Study, 328f, 330–33, 331t, 334f, 335
teen friendship networks. See also peer networks; social networks
  analysis of (see social network analysis)
  coevolving, 339–40
  data collection, 316–17
  dating and, 218–46
  future directions for research, 283–84, 315–25
  individual measures, 322
  interventions, 317–19
  measurement of, 316–17, 322
  mediation and moderation of, 319–21, 321t
  PROSPER data, 91–94
  PROSPER structure, 94–103
  rationale for study of, 8–10
  school-based interventions and, 283–84
  sexuality and, 218–46
  of sexual minority adolescents, 233, 234t
teens. See adolescents
10 to 18 Study, 330
  characteristics, 331t
  longitudinal studies with, 328f
  network questions, 335
  number of waves, 333
  time window, 333–34, 334f
time, unsupervised, 199
time-based online diary studies, 333
time spent with friends, 231–32
time windows, 333–34, 334f
tobacco smoking. See cigarette smoking
Towards No Drug Use intervention, 267
Tracking Adolescents' Individual Lives Survey (TRAILS), 4–5
training and learning opportunities, 49
transitivity, within-group, 131
trusting, 335
twins, 294–95

United States
  adolescence, 8
  criminal justice involvement, 146, 147f
  University of California Irvine, 67–68
  University of California–Los Angeles (UCLA), 4–5, 6
  University of Chicago, 67–68
  University of Groningen, Netherlands
    SNARE (Social Network Analyses of Risk behavior in Early adolescence), 4–5, 331t, 333, 334f, 335
    SNARE Genetics, 329
    Tracking Adolescents' Individual Lives Survey (TRAILS), 4–5

unstructured socializing, 16f, 17–18, 103, 104f
   measurement of, 107f
   as mediator, 278–79

vaping, 318–19
vertical linkage, 39
Vietnamese refugees, 354
volume measures, 72–73

W. T. Grant Foundation, 4, 7, 353
Wellman, Barry, 67–68
White, Harrison, 67–68
white youth, 148, 149, 151–52, 250
withdrawal, 146–48, 150–51

young adults
   follow-up assessment, 44f
   sexual health, 228–30
   social network studies on, 334
youth. *See also* adolescents
   low-income, 356
   sexual minority, 221, 222
   social capital, 356
youth behavior. *See also* behavior
   network models for, 70–83
   PROSPER youth, 88–109
   socialization to cultural stereotypes, 164
youth-focused interventions, 36–37. *See also* intervention(s)
   need for, 36